Limited Classical Reprint Library

OBADIAH

AND

HABAKKUK

EDWARD MARBURY

Klock & Klock Christian Publishers
2527 GIRARD AVE. N.
MINNEAPOLIS, MINNESOTA 55411

Originally published in separate volumes
London, 1649-1650
Reprinted in single volume by Nisbet, London, 1865

Copy from the library of
Central Baptist Theological Seminary
Minneapolis, Minnesota

Printed by Klock & Klock in the U.S.A.
1979 Reprint

FOREWORD

Edward Marbury was a minister in London in the 17th century. He served the congregations of St. James, Garlickhithe in London and of St. Peter's, Paul's Wharf. His commentaries on Obadiah and Habakkuk were written late in life (1649-1650). He died about the year 1655.

Spurgeon says of Marbury: "His spirituality of mind prevents his learning becoming dull. He says in the preface, 'all my desire is to do all the good I can,' and he writes in that spirit!" Spurgeon says of Marbury's commentary on Habakkuk: "Here Marbury holds the field among the old English authors, and he does so worthily. There is about him a vigorous, earnest freshness which makes his pages glow.

Marbury's commentaries are written after the manner of the 16th century scholar, copiously illustrated, for the most part from the Old Testament. Occasionally he will level a point against the papists whom he despised. His works are not so much critical, textual commentaries as they are homiletical series. As a result they contain extensive homiletical outlining and applications for pulpit use.

Marbury was familiar with the Latin and Greek languages, often qouting or phrasing something in Latin. Normally however, this is immediately translated into English.

This old English work has illustrative and homiletical value to the 20th century student of the Word of God. He will also find that Marbury brings together useful materials and unusual relevant quotations otherwise wholly distant and unavailable.

Dr. Bernard E. Northrup
Director of Graduate Studies
Central Baptist Seminary
Minneapolis, Minnesota

OBADIAH

VER. 1. *The vision of Obadiah.* This short prophecy calleth to my remembrance the words of David concerning God: Ps. xviii. 26, ' With the pure thou wilt shew thyself pure, and with the froward thou wilt shew thyself froward.' Ver. 27, ' For thou wilt save the afflicted people ; but wilt bring down high looks.'

For in the former part of this prophecy God thundereth with the terrors of his judgments ; in the latter part we hear the whisper and still voice of his mercy.

Two things set consideration a-work at first :

1. The title, which sheweth (1.) Whose ; (2.) What.

2. The prophecy itself.

(1.) Whose, Obadiah. Whether this were the proper name of a man, or a notation only, to express the calling of him that wrote this prophecy, we may doubt ; for *Abad, servus,* a *servant ;* and *Jah, dominus, a lord,* may denote this prophet in his function, a servant of the Lord ; and so are all the ministers of the word, in a special service, concerning the building up of the house of God.

That which Lyranus saith to be the judgment of most ecclesiastical writers, that this was the same Obadiah that was steward of king Ahab's house, 1 Kings xviii. 4, and hid the prophets in the cave, and fed them with bread and water, and was contemporary with Elias; that, how great authors soever it hath, is so clearly confuted in the words of this prophecy, that we resolve against it.

For the prophecy, it mentioneth the taking of Jerusalem was eight hundred years after Ahab.

It is likely that it was the proper name of the prophet; and Dorotheus thinketh him the same that lived in Ahab's time, which cannot be, as I have shewed.

It must suffice us that we know this prophecy to have been ever received in the canon of the church.

Melito, in his epistle to Onesimus, Euseb. iv. 25, naming the books of canonical Scripture, doth name one book of the twelve prophets, whereof this is one. And I never read the authority of this prophecy doubted of in any age of the church: he was one of those 'holy men who wrote and spake as they were moved by the Holy Ghost,' 2 Peter ii.

The maid that came to the door when Peter knocked, Acts xii. 14, knew him by his voice; and surely the majesty and weight that is in the canonical Scriptures doth declare them to be the voice of God, which wanteth in all the apocryphal assumements, as a reader diligently exercised in the Scriptures may easily discern.

These holy writings, addressed to the perpetual light of the church, are spare in their inscriptions.

Who wrote the books of Joshua, Judges, Ruth, Samuel, Kings, Chronicles, Esther?

They are written, they are ours, the wisdom of God is seen in them, the grace of God is confirmed by them, the church of God ever received them, the Spirit of God testifieth of them, and God in all ages hath been glorified by them.

The church of Rome doth attribute to the church a power of authorising books of Scripture, and maketh the church's authority the warrant for the authorising thereof.

St Augustine alloweth the church the reputation of a witness, but not the power of authority herein; for he saith,* *Platonis, Aristotelis, Ciceronis libros unde*

* Contra Faust. xxxiii. 6.

noverint homines, quod ipsorum sint, nisi temporum sibi succedentium contestatione continua? Therefore, that these books were the canon of Scripture, the testimony of all ages in their successions doth maintain; but this testimony doth not give them authority, but witnesseth the authority given them by the Spirit of God.

We find that even the authority of holy Scriptures hath been denied by heretics.

Sadducæi nullas Scripturas recipiebant, nisi quinque libros Mosis. Simon prophetas minimè curandos dixit, quia a mundi fabricatoribus angelis prophetias acceperunt. (Iren. i. 20). *Saturninus totum vetus test. repudiabat. Ptolemaitæ libros Mosis.* (Epiph. Hær. xxxiii.) *Nicolaitæ et Gnostici, librum Psalmorum. Anabapt. Cant. Salomonis: Et lib. Job. Porphyrius scripsit volumen Cont. lib. Danielis.*

The New Testament hath had many enemies. The children of darkness have ever made war against light.

We are better taught; and seeing the Holy Ghost hath not satisfied us from whence this our prophet came, but hath only given us his name, and his prophecy, this contenteth us. The vessel was but of earth which brought us this treasure; and if we have lost the vessel and kept the treasure;—

The messenger was a man like us; the message was the Lord's. If the messenger be gone, and the message do yet remain, the matter is not great.

Let us glorify God for his saints, whom God hath used as instruments of our good, and praise him for all his prophets, and holy men by whom these heavenly oracles were received from him, and communicated to the church.

The son of Sirach, Ecclus. iv. Let us now commend the famous men in the old time, by whom the Lord hath gotten great glory; let the people speak of their wisdom, and the congregation of their praise. Of this there is a double use:

1. That we that do *legere*, read, may learn *legere, sanctorum vitas*, to live the lives of saints, and do the church of God all the good service we can.

2. That God may be honoured *in sanctis*, in the

saints, as St Jerome saith : *Honoramus servos, ut honor servorum redundet ad Dominum.* This is the honour of God, and this is the praise of the prophet Obadiah ; whosoever he was, he liveth in this prophecy, to preach the will of God to you here present, and to let you know both the justice of God against the enemies of his church, and his mercy to his own beloved people.

For, as the apostle doth say of Abel's faith, Heb. xi. 4, ' And by it he being dead yet speaketh,' so may we say of all this and all other penmen of holy Scripture, that by these works of theirs, though they be dead, yet they do now speak in the church of God.

Abel spake two ways ; for there was,

1. *Vox sanguinis,* a voice of blood, which cried for judgment,' Gen. iv. 10 ; and,

2. *Vox fidei,* a voice of faith, which is example for imitation, Heb. xi. 4.

Thus all ecclesiastical writers do speak ; and we in our studies do confer with dead men, and take light from them.

That is the reason that the elect of God do not arise to their full reward before the resurrection of all flesh, because their works do follow them in order as they are done, and their light goeth not out by night; death doth not quench their candle.

Thus the ancient fathers of the church have left living monuments of their holy learning, and we come after them, and enter upon their labours.

They are unthankful and spiteful that despise their names, and refuse their testimonies which they have given to the truth, and blemish their memory, as if they were unworthy to be named in our sermons, or, to their judgments, to be held in any estimation.

It is the only way for a man gloriously to outlive himself, to be the instrument of doing good to the church of God when he is gone hence, and is no more seen. ' Blessed is that servant whom his Master, when he cometh, shall find so doing.'

2. What ?   The vision.

Some have confounded these two terms, *vision* and *prophecy,* as both expressing the same act of prophetical vocation.

I find three of these titles used together: 1 Chron.
xxix. 29, 'Now the acts of David the king, first and
last, behold, they are written in the book of Samuel
the seer, and in the book of Nathan the prophet, and
in the book of Gad the seer;' where, though our English translation do use the same word for Samuel and
Gad, calling them both *seers*, the Hebrew distinguisheth them; and a learned professor of divinity* doth
read, *in verbis Samuelis inspicientis*, the inspector;
Nathan prophetæ, the prophet; *Gad videntis*, the
seer.

I do not take these to be three distinct offices, but
three parts of the same office; for,

1. Such must be *videntes*, seers; God must open
their eyes, that they may see what the will of God is.

Balaam being to prophesy at the request of Balak
against Israel, beginneth thus, Num. xxiv. 3, 'Balaam
the son of Beor hath said, the man whose eyes are open
hath said: he hath said, which heard the words of
God, which saw the vision of the Almighty, who had
his eyes shut, but now open.'

Therefore they must be *videntes*, seers; for if the
blind do lead the blind, you know where to find them
both.

2. Such must be *inspicientes*, inspectors; and that
both in regard of the suggestion that it be no human
phantasy, no Satanical illusion, but a divine and
spiritual revelation.

As also in regard of the thing suggested, that they
may rightly inform themselves in the will of God, and
so far as God revealeth it ἐν τῇ βουλῇ τοῦ θελήματος
αὐτοῦ, that they may boldly say and maintain, Sic
dicit Dominus, Thus saith the Lord.

3. Thus prepared, they may be *prophets*, that is, the
publishers of this will of God to them to whom they be
sent.

So that vision and inspection belong to preparation,
prophecy to execution of that office; from whence,
docemur, we are taught,

Doct. 1. The faithful minister of the word of God
must receive his information and instruction from the

* Dr Hump. Decor. Interpret. lib. iii.

Spirit of God before he preach or prophesy.

We are ambassadors and messengers from God, and the warrant of our calling is our mission. The apostle saith, 'How shall he preach except he be sent?' for mission importeth fit instructions in the errand.

God hath laid blame upon them that run unsent; 'and no man putteth himself' in that employment 'but he that was sent, as was Aaron.'

The Son of God himself was sent; and when he came to do the will of him that sent him, he saith, *Lex tua scripta est in corde meo*. He professeth to Nicodemus, John iii. 11, 'Verily, verily, I say unto thee, we speak that we know, and testify that we have seen;' and the Baptist saith, John i. 34, 'I saw and bare record.' Christ giveth this account to his Father in his holy prayer: John xvii. 8, 'I have given them the word which thou gavest me.' For so St Peter admonisheth: 1 Peter iv. 11, 'If any man speak, let him speak as the oracles of God; if any man minister, let him do it as of the ability which God giveth: that God in all things may be glorified.' If any man build upon this foundation of Jesus Christ either timber, hay, or stubble, the fire of God's Spirit will soon consume it. If we build gold or silver, this fire will try and refine it.

Surely this vision was not *oculare*, but *mentale*, a divine revelation of the will of God. The eye is the most noble of the senses, and the most sure of the object, therefore he in the comedy saith,

> Oculatus testis unus pluris est faciendus quàm
> auriti decem.

St John, 'That which we have seen with our eyes, that declare we unto you.'

The understanding is the eye of the soul, and that seeth much more perfectly than the eye of the body; for as the poet saith,

> Fallunt nos oculi vagique sensus,
> Ut turris prope quæ quadrata surgit
> Detritis procul angulis rotetur.

The distance of the object, and the debility of the organ, can make the sight of the eye fallible; but *intellectus rectus*, a right understanding, taketh sight from the Spirit of God, which searcheth all things, *etiam arcana Dei*, even the hidden things of God.

Therefore the apostle, desiring to fit Timothy for this holy calling, admonisheth him of his duty, and saith, 2 Tim. ii. 7, 'Consider what I say, and the Lord give thee understanding in all things!'

But false prophets had their visions, and did boast of their revelations, and came as boldly amongst the people with *Sic dicit Dominus*, Thus saith the Lord, as any true prophet of the Lord did.

Satan will so transform himself into an angel of light, 2 Cor. xi. 14, that you cannot know him from one of God's holy angels easily; and he will carry the metamorphosis so cunningly, ' that if it were possible, he would deceive the very elect of God.' Simon Magus called himself 'the great power of God.' Celsus inscribeth his oration for paganism *Vera Oratio*, a true oration. Manichæus calleth himself *Manichæus apostolus Jesu Christi*, the apostle of Jesus Christ; and saith, *Hæc sunt salubria verba de fonte perenni*. Chrysostom saith that the Macedonian heretics did say, *Nos recta fide incedimus*. St Augustine, *Nullus error se audet extollere ad congregandas sibi turbas imperitorum, qui non Christiani nominis velamenta conquirat*.* Faustus saith, *Salus quam Christus promisit, apud me est; ego dabo*.

Therefore, that the hearers may be able to distinguish *inter verum et verisimile*, that which is true and truth-like; and as the apostle biddeth, to 'try the spirits whether they be of God or no;' that we may beware of false prophets, and know them from such as receive their instructions for their message from God, observe these notes of difference:

1. Lawful calling. We read of no true prophet but he had a mission; as before. Christ took not this honour upon him to be the great angel of the covenant, but was sent by his Father, Heb. v. 5.

---

* Cont. Fau. lib. xiii. cap. 14.

But false prophets run, and are not sent; God sendeth none such on his errands into his church.

But this is not so easily discovered, because none do make more show of lawful calling than the false prophets do, Jer. xiv. 14.

2. The application of the prophecy is a clearer sign; for the apostle saith, 1 Cor. xiv. 3, 'He that prophesieth, speaketh to men [to] edification, exhortation, comfort.'

This edification is building up of the church of God. False prophets seek the pulling down of God's church, and the diverting of men from all good ways. They seek to hinder the course of the gospel, and to discourage the hearts of them that fear God.

Here a false prophet may have a true prophecy tending to the good of the church, and the prophecy is to be received and the prophet refused, as Caiaphas prophesied, John xi. 50, *Expedit ut unus moriatur*, it is meet one die ; and Balaam prophesied truly, yet was he a false prophet.

3. By observing the aim and end of these prophets ; for such as prophesy aright do say with Christ, *Non quæro gloriam meam*, 'I seek not my own glory ;' but false prophets seek either filthy gain, or they seek their own vain glory. The apostle saith, Rom. xvi. 18, 'They seek not, they serve not, the Lord, but their own bellies.'

4. God himself giveth this note of difference in the event of their prophecies : Deut. xviii. 22, 'When a prophet speaketh in the name of the Lord, if the thing follow not nor come to pass, that is the thing which the Lord hath not spoken, but the prophet hath spoken it presumptuously.'

And the name of a *vision*, given to prophecy, doth declare the certainty of the event, for it is a thing so revealed to the prophet as if he saw it with his eye.

5. The persons of the prophets and their carriage doth detect them ; for if they be men sanctified and fitted with eminent graces for that service, the graces of God do testify of them, for God doth send none but with all fit preparations for the execution of so great an office.

2. This title of vision doth give us assurance of all that followeth in this prophecy, for God revealed it, and the prophet saw it.

Therefore, so many of you as desire to receive any good from the interpretation of this prophecy, remember that it is a vision, and therefore bring your eyes with you to this place, not the eyes of your body only, but the spiritual eyes of your understanding, and pray with David, *Ut videam mirabilia tua*, ' Lord, open thou mine eyes that I may see thy wonders.' Christ, in opening the eyes of the blind who had lost their sight, and in giving sight to them that were born blind, did declare himself so to be more than man, that his enemies could not tell how to deny his Godhead.

He worketh a greater wonder every day in his spiritual illuminations of men's understandings, by which the ignorant and simple do learn knowledge, and poor men receive the gospel, and, as the apostle saith, grace ' rich in faith,' and are declared heirs of that kingdom which he hath promised to them that love him, James ii. 5.

Ver. 1. *Thus saith the Lord concerning Edom.*
The prophecy followeth. This hath two parts :
1. Against Edom, ver 1 to 16.
2. For the Israel of God, ver. 17 to the end.

The title of the first part is my text, ' Thus saith the Lord concerning Edom.' Consider here,
1. The subject of the prophecy, ' Edom.'
2. The author of it, *Dicit Dominus*, ' Thus saith the Lord.'

1. Of the subject, ' Edom.'

Isaac had two sons by Rebekah, Esau and Jacob. Esau was called Edom. The reason of that name is thus given : Jacob had made red pottage, and when Esau came home from the field hungry and faint, he said to his brother Jacob, ' Feed me, I pray thee, with that red pottage, for I am faint,' Gen. xxv. ; therefore was his name called Edom, because he so affected that red colour, being himself also red and very hairy.

This name doth maintain the memory of a quarrel, for he bought that red pottage dear enough, with the sale of his birthright.

Esau and Jacob are a figure of the church of God and the synagogue of Satan, for they strove in the womb of their mother, so that Rebekah wondered at it, saying, ' If it be so, why am I thus ?' ver. 12.

The blessing, howsoever usurped by Esau, belongeth to Jacob; and when Jacob hath his right, Esau is angry.

From this natural antipathy between these two brethren, and the grudge that the elder should serve the younger ;

From the sentence of this difference, which was, ' I have loved Jacob, and have hated Esau :' there was ever mutual war and hatred between Israel and Edom in their succeeding posterities, for the posterity of Esau did increase both in number and wealth, and grew both many and strong.

Thus doth the world gather riches and strength, and armeth itself against the church of God, and therefore the church is called militant.

Concerning Edom is this part of the prophecy, declaring both God's quarrel against them and his judgment threatened.

We may take notice here of one point by the way: Edom is a mighty people, a strong and rich nation, able to molest the Lord's Israel, that God from heaven undertaketh the quarrel of his church.

Do you not see that they whom God hates may have riches, and honour, and strength, and may increase, and grow into multitudes. How cometh it then to pass that so many in the world do measure the love and favour of God by these outward things, as one flattered his prince,

> O nimium dilecte, deo tibi militat æther ?

What though their oxen be strong to labour ; what though their sheep bring forth thousands, and though they have the fruits of the womb, of the herb, and purchase lands *donec non sit locus*, till there be no room ; what though they have power and high places : all this had Edom, whom God hated ; and doth not our Saviour make it an hard thing for the rich to enter into the kingdom of heaven?

Outward things are the gifts of God, and he doth not value them at so high a rate as we do. He doth not care if his enemies have them.

His own Son, when he took upon him our flesh, had none of them more than for necessity; and his apostle persuadeth us, if we have food and raiment, to be therewith content.

For there be snares in these outward things, and if God give not a blessing with them, they be the rods of God to scourge the sons of men, and great impediments to godly life.

There is an holy use may be made of them, but they are not our happiness, seeing they whom God hateth may have them in a greater abundance than those whom God loveth best.

2. The author of the prophecy, 'Thus saith the Lord.'

This is the assurance of the truth of all that followeth in this prophecy, and it is the ground of our faith to believe what is here revealed; it is no passionate motion in the heart and affections of the prophet against Edom, but it is the word of the Lord.

These be the bounds that are set to the prophets and holy ministers of the Lord; we may go no further than the word of the Lord. Christ himself saith often, 'The word which thou gavest me, I gave them."

And Balaam did his office and calling right when he told the king of Moab, Num. xxii. 38, &c., 'Lo, I am come unto thee: have I any power to say anything? the word that God putteth in my mouth, that shall I speak.' ' Must I not take heed to speak what the Lord hath put in my mouth?' ' All that the Lord speaketh, that must I do.' 'And Balaam said unto Balak, Spake I not to thy messengers, saying, If Balak would give me his house full of silver and gold, I cannot go beyond the commandment of the Lord, to do either good or bad of mine own mind; but what the Lord saith, that will I speak.'

When God designed Jeremiah to the office of a prophet, who did fear to undertake that great employment,

God said to him, Jer. xvii., 'Say not I am a child: for thou shalt go to all that I shall send thee, and whatsoever I command thee shalt thou speak.'

When our Saviour sent forth his disciples, he so limited them: Mat. xxviii. 20, 'Teach them to observe all things whatsoever I have commanded you.'

And accordingly St Paul doth profess, 1 Cor. xv. 3, 'First of all I delivered unto you that which I also received.'

Thus doth the apostle again profess, being accused of the Jews, Acts xxvi. 22, 'I obtained help of God, and continue unto this day, witnessing unto small and great, saying no other things than those which the prophets and Moses did say should come.'

1. This limitation we find in the titles of our office, for we are the Lord's workmen, and we must do his work, not our own; the Lord's builders, he provideth the materials, we work not by great but by day-work.

We are the Lord's messengers and ambassadors; we may not digress from our instructions; the messenger of the Lord must speak the Lord's message.

2. This is necessary in respect of those to whom we are sent for the settling of their faith; so the apostle hath declared it: 1 Cor. ii. 4, 'And my speech and my preaching was not in the enticing words of man's wisdom, but in the demonstration of the Spirit and power, that your faith should not stand in the wisdom of men, but in the power of God. But we speak the wisdom of God in a mystery.'

There is nothing that giveth faith firm footing but the word of God. That is the Lord's fan which purgeth away the chaff and trash from the good corn. That is the bread of our Father's house; words of men's brains be the husks that the prodigal gathered up in his famine. That is the two-edged sword that divideth between the bone and the marrow; that is the medicine that searcheth the sores and diseases of the inward man. Human wisdom put into the best words is but as a wooden dagger; it may dry beat, it will never kill the body of sin; it is an unguent, it corrodeth not.

3. Great is the danger of those that shall speak anything but the word of God to God's people, or shall conceal anything of that which is given them to speak.

So God saith to Jeremiah, chap. i. 17, 'Thou therefore truss up thy loins, arise, and speak unto them all that I command thee: be not afraid of their faces, lest I destroy thee before them.'

And to Ezekiel, chap. iii. 18, 'If thou sound not the trumpet, nor give warning to the wicked man of his wicked way, his blood will I require at thy hand.'

This is not our own trumpet, but the Lord's; ours giveth an uncertain sound, the Lord's trumpet awaketh men to the battle.

From hence both the minister and the people have their lessons.

1. The minister. We are taught to exercise ourselves in the holy studies of the word of God, that we may be able to divide the word of God aright, that we may wisely understand the word of God, to be able to minister the word of God in due season.

The ignorant and unlearned man is no fit man for this employment; to such saith God, Hosea iv. 6, 'Because thou hast refused knowledge, I will also refuse thee: thou shalt be no priest to me.'

For why should any dare to intrude himself into this great service to teach others in the word, seeing himself untaught? for, Mal. ii. 31, 'The priest's lips should preserve knowledge, and the people must seek the law at their mouth.' Doth any man send a lame man of his errand, or put his message into the mouth of a dumb man? We are the Lord's messengers. Doth any man set an unskilful man to build, that knoweth not how to use his tools? We are the Lord's builders. Doth any man set an unexperienced man to take charge of his sheep? We are the Lord's shepherds of his flock.

Jeroboam took the right way to destroy true religion, and to set up idolatry: 1 Kings xiii. 33, 34, 'He made of the lowest of the people priests of the high places: whosoever would, he consecrated him, and he became one of the priests of the high places. And this thing became sin to the house of Jeroboam, even to cut it off and to destroy it from off the face of the earth.'

Surely such ministers, though they have the outward calling of the church, yet do they want the inward calling of God; and being darkness, they possess the place of light, and they are blind leaders of the blind, as Christ calleth them.

Two sorts of ministers are here excluded.

(1.) Those that know not what the Lord saith, and therefore use the holy calling of the ministry but as a means for their maintenance, without care or conscience of feeding the flock of Christ, and woe is to them because they preach not the gospel; they usurp the wool and milk of the flock, and have no right to the inheritance of God, that is, the tithes of the people.

(2.) Those who know not, understand not the word of the Lord, yet, trusting to their own natural parts, do boldly step up and usurp the chair of Moses, and are *imperitorum magistri*, teachers of the unlearned, before they have been *peritorum discipuli*, scholars of the learned. And these are the more dangerous of the two; better an unpreaching minister that readeth the word of God distinctly, than an ignorant preacher that presumeth *ex puris naturalibus*, from his pure naturals to deal with those things which are too high and deep for him.

2. Ministers are taught their great duty of faithfulness, of which the apostle saith, 1 Cor. iv. 2, 'Moreover, it is required of stewards that a man be found faithful.'

He must say, *Thus saith the Lord*. That is, he must say,

1. *Quod dicit Dominus*, what the Lord saith is the truth.

2. *Omne quod dicit*, all that, all the truth.

3. *Quomodo dicit*, in the same manner, *Thus*.

1. For we may not go from our instructions to speak of ourselves anything, but we must first receive from the Lord, and then we must speak that. It was

Nathan's error, when David did open to him his purpose for building of the Lord's house, that before he had understood the will of God therein, he encouraged him, saying, ' Do all that is in thy heart ;' and therefore he was sent again to him to unsay it.

2. Neither may we suppress anything of that which is put into our mouths. The apostle saith, Acts iv. 20, ' We cannot but speak those things which we have seen and heard.' And Saint Paul saith to the elders of Ephesus, Acts xx. 26, 27, ' I take you to record this day, that I am pure from the blood of all men ; for I have concealed nothing, but have revealed to you all the counsel of God.'

For surely, as God told Ezekiel, it is as much as our salvation is worth to leave any part of God's revealed will in Scripture untaught.

3. Neither may we change the manner of God's speakings ; for there is a form of doctrine delivered to us, and there is a form of words ; we must not only say *this*, but *thus* saith the Lord.

For so Saint Peter admonisheth : 1 Pet. iv. 11, ' If any man speak, let him speak as the oracles of God.' Not mingling human fancies with divine doctrines ; not mingling words of human wisdom with holy exhortations ; not mingling our own spirit of contradiction with our confutations of the adversary ; not mingling any of our own spirit of bitterness and passions with our just reprehensions of sin, drawing against Satan and sin no other sword but ' the sword of the Spirit, which is the word of God.' Thus shall we be ' unto God the sweet savour of Christ in them that are saved,' 2 Cor. ii. 13.

We shall meet with many discouragements in this our office, and we shall lose a great deal of labour ; but so did our Master, it is his complaint, though never any were so sufficient for this service as he was.

1. For his calling : Isa. xlix. 4, ' The Lord hath called me from the womb ; from the bowels of my mother hath he made mention of my name.'

2. For his fitting to that calling : ver. 2, ' He hath made my mouth like a sharp sword ; in the shadow of his hand hath he hid me, and made me a polished

shaft.' Yet he complaineth: ver. 4, 'Then I said, I have laboured in vain; I have spent my strength for nought, and in vain.' Yet his comfort was: 'Yet surely my judgment is with the Lord, and my work (or my reward) with my God.'

Object. Here some think that the limitation of us to *Thus saith the Lord*, doth so restrain the minister of the word to the word of God, that it is not lawful to mention the names either of the ancient fathers of the church, or of any heathen writers in our sermons.

A point touched somewhat to the quick by a great and learned divine even upon this text in print.

To which my moderate and just answer is,

1. That as there is *authoritas Scripturæ*, the authority of Scripture, which is the ground of faith, so there must be *testimonium ecclesiæ*, the witness of the church, as Vincent. Lyrinensis well adviseth,* *Quia Scripturam sacram non uno eodemque sensu universi acceperunt.*

And in this case, not having *antiquitatem ministrantem*, universal consent, and we are put to it to search out what the most learned and most sincere divines in all ages have taught concerning this point; and here there is a necessity of consulting and declaring the constant judgment of the church for the testimony to the truth.

2. In all points of doctrine, it giveth a great assurance to our hearers of our faithfulness, if we declare ourselves to be such as feed our hearers with the same bread of life which our fathers before us did break to their children.

3. Whereas it is surmised that these citations of fathers be but a pride of our feeding,† and a vain boast of our learning, it were more charitable to think,

1. That our humility is such, that we are not ashamed to profess by whom we learn anything.

2. That we have so unworthy an opinion of our own judgments, that we choose rather to apply the learned judgments of those that have gone before us than our own.

* Chap. ii.   † Qu. 'reading'?—ED.

And who can deny but that our preaching out of them is with the warrant of our text? *Sic dicit Dominus*, Thus saith the Lord, if the Lord spake by them to his church?

For the use of heathen writers, I only say, with St Augustine, *Omnis scientia in genere bonorum est, in arundine sterili potest uva pendere.* Truth is the language of God, and if ignorant men, wicked men, devils, do speak truth, we may quote and write them; and we may say truly, *Sic dicit Dominus*, Thus saith the Lord.

The prophecy of wicked Balaam, and of Caiaphas, was the word of the Lord; and the confession of devils testifying of Christ is a good confession; there is no wrong done to the word. *Qui non est contra me, mecum est*, he that is not against me is with me.

2. The hearer's lesson. You are all taught to receive this wholesome doctrine which the minister preacheth from the mouth of the Lord. 'It is not you that speak,' saith Christ; 'he that hath ears to hear must hear,' *quod Spiritus dicit*, 'what the Spirit speaketh.'

When we tell the house of Jacob of their sins, this is the word of the Lord.

When we say unto you, going in an evil way, as Lot to the Sodomites, 'Do not so wickedly,' do not say, *Durus est hic sermo*, he railed to-day against swearing, or against drunkenness, &c. I will tell you how you shall receive both comfort and great profit by our ministry; and 'the word is given to profit withal.'

'Do not my words do good to him that walketh uprightly? 'Micah ii. 7. *Recto judicio : rectis moribus.*

I will give you a fair example.

Israel said to Moses, Deut. v. 27, 28, 'Go thou now near, and hear all that the Lord our God shall say; and speak thou unto us all that the Lord our God shall speak unto thee, and we will hear it, and do it.' God took it well, and said to Moses, 'I have heard the voice of this people: they have well said all that they have spoken.'

We must tell you that the word of the Lord, which he sendeth forth in our ministry, shall not return to him empty, it shall finish the thing for which it was sent.

Therefore take you heed how you hear, and consider what we say; hide the word that we preach in your hearts, that you sin not against God.

If we do our duty, he that heareth us and receiveth us receiveth Jesus Christ that sent us, and in these earthen vessels rich treasures are brought unto him.

He that refuseth us and our ministry refuseth him that sent us; and the word of the Lord which we bring to them will prove a rod [of] correction to chastise them; and although they feel not the pain presently, it will be owing to them till affliction or death assault them, and then they will remember the word of the Lord with much horror.

Ver. 1. *We have heard a rumour from the Lord, and an ambassador is sent among the heathen, Arise ye, and let us arise against her in battle.*

We are now come to the prophecy itself, which holdeth to the end of the sixteenth verse. The parts whereof are four.

    1. The judgment intended against Edom, vers. 1, 2.
    2. All the hopes of Edom despaired, ver. 3-9.
    3. The cause provoking God to this severe process against them, ver. 10-14.
    4. God's revenge upon them, vers. 15, 16.
    1. In the judgment intended, observe,
    (1.) The discovery thereof.
    (2.) The effect of it.
    (1.) In the discovery, observe,
    [1.] By whom it was discovered.
    [2.] How, two ways: *first*, by a rumour of the Lord; *secondly*, by ambassadors.

[1.] To whom this threatened judgment was discovered, we have heard. We, that is, the prophets of the Lord; for although Obadiah writ this present prophecy, yet was not this judgment only revealed to him, but to many more of the holy prophets; for so

saith the prophet Amos, chap. iii. 7, 'Surely the Lord
will do nothing, but he revealeth his secret to his servants
the prophets,' not unto one only, but to more. And
so fully was this revealed to Jeremiah, that he doth
prophesy even in the same words against Edom, but
under the name of Bozrah, which was the name of a
principal city in Edom, as appeareth Gen. xxxvi. 33.
The words of the prophecy are these, Jer. xlix. 13,
'I have sworn by myself, saith the Lord, that Bozrah
shall become a desolation, a reproach, a waste, and a
curse, and all the cities thereof shall be perpetual
wastes.' 'I have heard a rumour from the Lord, an
ambassador is sent to the heathen, saying, Gather ye
together and come against her,' &c. The margins of
the Bibles refer you to that place: Deut. xxiii. 7,
'The Lord gave great charge to Israel concerning
Edom, Thou shalt not abhor an Edomite, for he is
thy brother.'

Yet because the Edomite was ever an enemy to
Israel, God revealed his judgment against them to
many of his prophets.

Balaam foretold their subjection to Israel: Num.
xxiv. 18, 19, 'And Edom shall be a possession, Seir
also shall be a possession for his enemies; and Israel
shall do valiantly. Out of Jacob shall he come that
shall have dominion, and shall destroy him that remaineth of that city.'

The psalmist prayeth for their punishment: Ps.
cxxxvii. 7, 'Remember, O Lord, the children of
Edom,'

It had not been lawful for the prophet to have provoked the justice of God against Edom, unless God
had revealed his purpose of judgment intended against
them to him. For David's imprecations be all prophecies. 'The burden of Dumah (that is, of Idumea).
He calleth unto me out of Seir, Watchman, what was
in the night?' &c., Isa. xxi. 11. 'The sword of the
Lord is filled with blood; it is made fat with fatness,
&c. For the Lord hath a sacrifice in Bozrah, and a
great slaughter in the land of Idumea,' Isa. xxxiv. 6.
'Rejoice and be glad, O daughter of Edom, that
dwellest in the land of Uz: the cup also shall pass

through unto thee; thou shalt be drunken, and shalt make thyself naked,' Lam. iv.

As to the young man, Rejoice, O young man, Ironice *q. d.*, make thee merry whilst thou mayest, for thou art like to have sorrow and care enough. Amos also foretold as much, chap. i. 11, ' Thus saith the Lord, For three transgressions, and for four, I will not turn away the punishment thereof; because he did pursue his brother with the sword, and did cast off all pity, and did tear perpetually, and kept his wrath for ever.' Which causes are after in this prophecy alleged. 'But I will send fire upon Teman, which shall devour the palaces of Bozrah.' Ezek. xxv. 12, ' Thus saith the Lord God, Because that Edom hath dealt against the house of Judah by taking vengeance, and hath revenged himself upon them; I will also stretch out my hand upon Edom, and I will cut off man and beast from it; and I will make it desolate from Teman; and they of Dedan shall fall by the sword. And I will lay my vengeance upon Edom by the hand of my people Israel: and they shall do in Edom according to mine anger, and according to my fury; and they shall know my vengeance, saith the Lord.' Chap. xxxv. 2, ' Son of man, set thy face against mount Seir, and prophesy against it, and say unto it, Thus saith the Lord God, Behold, O mount Seir, I am against thee, and I will stretch out my hand against thee, and I will make thee most desolate,' &c.

I may say now as the messengers sent to bring Micaiah to king Ahab said, 1 Kings xxii. 13, but in a contrary, Behold, the words of the prophets declare evil unto Edom with one mouth.

And now you see what reason this prophet hath to say, ' We have heard,' for God hath revealed this threatened judgment to his servants the prophets, and with one mouth they declare it. From whence we are taught,

Doct. 1. That the decrees of God's judgment upon the wicked are constant and unchangeable.

1. For God is without variableness and shadow of alteration. Hos. xiii. 14, 'The word is gone out of my mouth, it shall not return empty, but it shall finish the thing for which it is sent; repentance is hid from mine eyes.' 'God is not as man, that he should repent; he hath sworn in his wrath they shall not enter into his rest.' And, 'The Lord hath sworn, and will not repent.'

2. From the nature of the wicked, against whom he threateneth judgment, for they have hearts that cannot repent, and therefore they heap up wrath against the day of wrath. God's hatred doth deprive them of all the means of grace, and none can be effectual in them or to them; and he hath said, 'I have hated Esau.'

Sin is folly, sinners are fools. 'Bray a fool in a mortar, yet will not his foolishness depart from him.' Therefore they are under the rods and scorpions of wrath, and cannot avoid the same.

3. From the faithfulness of his prophets; for the prophets of the Lord, that threaten these judgments from his mouth, shall not be found liars; seeing their prophecies are no self-given notions, but inspirations of his Spirit, which is the Spirit of truth.

You know how Jonah was troubled to be a messenger of judgment to Nineveh, when he was persuaded that God would shew them mercy, and so his prophecy fall to the ground. He could rather have looked on to see the utter destruction of Nineveh, than that his prophecy should be found unperformed; therefore he went another way at first, and would not come to Nineveh, and when he had prophesied he went out of the city, and there expected the event of his prophecy, and was angry that it succeeded not.

Quer. We find that in that example God changed, and repented him of the evil which he had threatened against Nineveh; how then do we say, that the judgments of God against the wicked be unreversible? Jonah iii. 10, 'And God saw their works, that they turned from their evil way; and God repented of the evil that he had said he would do unto them, and he did it not.'

Sol. To this we answer, that God's repentance was no change of his mind, or any alteration of his counsel or decree, but a deferring of the execution of his judgment.

The change was in Nineveh, and the repentance was in them. They humbled themselves before God, and they both did the works of mortification, and they also believed God, chap. iii. 5. This was not a justifying faith, which is *credere in Deum*, to believe in God, but an historical, which is *credere Deo*, to believe God.

And God would have his church see, that if Ahab humble himself and go in sackcloth, if Nineveh give over evil works and repent them of their sins, he will turn from the fierceness of his wrath, all to encourage repentance. But Jonah was a true prophet of God's judgment; their repentance was not *pænitentia non pænitenda*, a repentance not to be repented of, for they resumed their evil ways; and Nahum doth renew the threatenings of Jonah, and declareth the Lord's judgments against Nineveh. For the repentance of the wicked is but for a season, and as it is temporary so it removeth judgment for a time; but they returning to their sins, he returneth also to the execution of his intended punishment. So Ahab was forborne for a time upon his humiliation, but he escaped not the hand of judgment; for God cannot lie. His prophets speak sure words, as the apostle saith, 2 Pet. i. 19, 'We have a more sure word of prophecy, to which you do well if you take heed, as to a light,' &c.

Quer. When Abraham had heard the decree of God against the transgressing cities, did not he know that God's decrees of judgment were immutable? How then did he solicit God for the reversing of the same? Did he well in so doing?

Sol. Abraham's plea doth clear this point; for upon the first notice from God of his intended judgment, he pleadeth for Sodom, Gen. xviii. 23, not to turn away the wrath from the ungodly there, but he saith, 'Wilt thou also destroy the righteous with the wicked?' &c. The care of Abraham was for the place and for the persons of the righteous; he doth not solicit God for the wicked there.

Again, to pray for the ungodly and wicked, to divert judgment from them, when God hath revealed his displeasure against them, is not unlawful.

1. Because Christian charity 'hopeth all things, believeth all things.'

2. Because many of God's judgments are temporal, and his anger against the sons of men continueth not long; so that we may hope that either God may divert the evil, or mitigate the same, or give patience to bear it, or sanctify the chastisement, *ad dignam emendationem,* for their amendment, for only the Lord knoweth who are his.

When Saul was rejected, and Samuel was the messenger of that heavy judgment, yet 'Samuel did not cease mourning for Saul until the day of his death,' 1 Sam. xv. 35.

That is the most effectual manner of praying, even that which the Holy Ghost useth in us, with sighs and groans, *Plus fletu quam afflatu.* Thus when Abraham saw Ishmael cast out for a scorner and persecutor of Isaac, yet he prayed, 'Oh that Ishmael might live in thy sight.' And God said, 'I have heard thee also concerning him,' somewhat is obtained. Therefore let us still be praying for all men, especially seeing God doth not make us of his counsel so far as to declare to us whom he accepteth, and whom he rejecteth.

From this lesson of the certainty of the judgments of God upon the wicked; certain, whether we consider the nature of God, without change, or the weakness of man, without any possibility of resisting, or the nature of the reprobate, without any ability of repenting, we are taught,

1. To rest in the decree of God. Let us know that he cannot deny himself; and therefore though wrath go not out from the Lord presently, and although his judgment is delayed, yet let us resolve that upon the wicked he will rain snares, and he will break the impenitent with rods of iron.

He was an hundred and twenty years preaching to the old world, and they repented not, so long was he ere he would pluck his hand out of his bosom; yet at last he smote the world with a great slaughter, and drowned all but eight persons.

Two errors do grow in us, if we do not wisely weigh this doctrine.

1. An error in judgment.

'These things hast thou done, and I kept silence: thou thoughtest that I was altogether such a one as thyself,' Ps. x. 21. As Augustine, *Deum quia non pateris ultorem, vis habere participem, quia malefacta tua placent tibi, tu putas etiam ea placere mihi.*

2. An error in manners.

'Because sentence against an evil work is not executed speedily, therefore the heart of the sons of men is fully set in them to do evil,' Eccles. viii. 11.

For, indeed, what maketh men to walk so unconscionably on earth, blaspheming the sacred name of the highest Majesty, polluting his holy Sabbaths, making their belly, their penny, their pleasure their god, but this corrupt opinion of God's either not seeing, or not caring, or pardoning of sins, the presuming on his mercy; not knowing this, that the judgments of God, howsoever deferred, will surely light where they are threatened.

Therefore let every man, in hearing and reading of the word of God, observe his own sins, how they are threatened; and let him know that he hath no way nor means but by his serious repentance to escape that judgment.

1. Let us take heed of dallying with the almighty God, for be not deceived, God is not mocked; they that think to find him when they list, know not that there is a time when he will be found, and they that neglect that time do lose their season of him.

2. But especially let men take heed of abusing his patience, and making that a motive to and a strength of sin: for *læsa patientia fit furor*, patience abused turns to fury; when men sin against the mercy of God, they spill the medicine that should heal them, they cut the bough that they stood on; for it is that which keepeth our heads above water and standeth in the gap.

3. To conclude, let men take heed of falling so far from God, as to make a covenant with death, and an agreement with hell, that is, to make peace with Satan; for this bed, the prophet saith, is too short, and this covering is too narrow to cover us.

We are taught here not to repine at the present prosperity of the wicked.

This hath much disquieted very godly persons. David confesseth it to have unrested him, and his foot had almost slipped, Ps. lxxiii.

It made some wise men among the heathen doubt, *an sit providentia,* whether there be a providence; and no human wisdom can maintain providence, because, *bonis malefit,* good men suffer.

There is a parting of the Red Sea, and then it will appear who be Israelites, and who be Egyptians. What if it last prosperous all their life long? At the parting of the soul and body, Lazarus and the rich man shall feel a change; therefore grudge not the wicked their pleasures of sin for a season.

[2.] By what means this intelligence of the judgment against Edom was given. The means are two:

First, By a rumour from the Lord.

Secondly, By the ambassadors sent from the heathen.

First, The rumour from the Lord.

Jeremiah useth the same word, chap. xlix. 14, the interlin.* *Auditum audivimus a cum domino.* His meaning is, as before is expressed, that God hath put this prophecy in the mouth of many of his prophets, so that it is not a particular instinct by revelation to some one, but a rumour, that is, a general opening of the same, filling the mouths of many, which declareth the consent of the prophets in this prophecy.

Doct. It advanceth the message of God amongst men, when the Lord's trumpet doth *dare sonum certum,* give a certain sound, when they all agree together as one man in the ministry thereof.

The messenger that came from Micaiah to bring him to the two kings, Jehoshaphat and Ahab, 1 Kings

---

* That is, an interlineal Latin version.—ED.

xxii. 13, thought he had used a great argument to persuade Micaiah to prophesy good success to that intended expedition against Ramoth-Gilead, saying, 'Behold now, the words of the prophets declare good unto the king with one mouth: let thy word, I pray thee, be like the word of one of them,' &c. These false prophets all joined together to flatter that expedition. God revealeth the secret hereof by Micaiah: there was an evil spirit offered his service to God, saying, 'I will go forth, and I will be a lying spirit in the mouth of all his prophets. And God said, Thou shalt persuade him, and prevail also.'

The prophets and ministers of God do consent in their message; and Satan, that studieth the ruin of the church, doth his best to make his false prophets agree all in a tale, to make the fairer show of truth, that he may deceive many.

It is one of the great objections of the papists against our religion, that it cannot be the truth of God, because we ministers do not agree in the preaching thereof.

To whom we answer, that the church of England in all points, both of religion and discipline, is as a city which is at unity within itself: if some particular persons in the ministry leave the way of the church, and go in their own way, that is no fault of the church, but the schism of private men.

Such as they are discovered, so are they restrained and separated from the rest: to room then* *Parcius ista viris tamen objicienda memento*, personal oppositions do not fasten imputation upon any entire church of God.

And we say to the Roman church, *Novimus et qui te*, &c. For we have good evidence even from their own writings, that the church of Rome hath in later times dissented from those tenets which in former times it hath maintained, not in matters of light moment, but in the main points of Christian religion.

1. For the books of canonical Scripture, the learned of former times did refuse all those books which we

---

* Apparently a misprint.—ED.

call Apocryphal, as well as we; yet the Council of Trent hath since placed them in the canon, and given them equal authority with the canonical Scriptures.

2. For the sufficiency, their own best learned have heretofore acknowledged the same as much as we.

3. The vulgar translation hath been by their learned refused, the original preserved.

4. For the conception of the Virgin Mary without sin, it is not yet determined in the church, but contradictories are allowed.

5. The distinction of mortal and venial sins.

6. The doctrines of merit, of supererogation, of the seven sacraments, of transubstantiation, of purgatory, of praying to saints, worshipping of images, indulgences, pope's supremacy, all refused.

Therefore let them no longer charge us with differences; our church doth maintain one truth in all these things with the former church of Rome, against this that now is.

Therefore let us observe the settled doctrine of the church in which we live, and receive that, against the perverse oppositions of all schismatical coiners of new doctrines, and that is the safest way for us to walk in, for this *rumor Domini* is no rumour of the Lord.

Doct. 2. Because it is *auditus a Domino*, heard from the Lord; whence we are taught to distinguish between the rumours which we hear from men, and those rumours which we hear from the Lord. Let us judge them by the word of God, and let us learn of the church, the spouse of Christ, who best discerneth these spiritual things, because they are deposited with it, and the Spirit of God is with it, and abideth with it for ever.

How holy Scriptures must be interpreted.

Let every man put his own particular fancies and humours to silence, and as the apostle saith, 'let us receive with meekness the word of God, and let it be graffed in us.'

For the word of the Lord endureth for ever, that is, like him that gave it, without variableness; there is in it no shadow of change. It was David's rest, *Audiam quid loquatur Deus*, I will hear what the Lord speaketh.

And that we may hear this rumour of the Lord profitably, 'the word is given to profit withal,' let me shew you who they be that receive the word of God profitably; these, namely, who,

1. Receive it in their understanding.
2. In their judgment.

1. In their understanding, knowing what the Lord speaketh in his word, for the word is the revelation of the good will of God.

To this is necessary,

(1.) A preparation to this understanding.
(2.) An use of the means.

(1.) For the preparation of our understanding, two things are necessary, as Saint Paul speaketh.

[1.] 'Be not conformed to this world,' Rom. xii. 2. This world is our enemy; we must shake off all acquaintance with it: it is the serpent's fair fruit, wherewith he tempteth us; he setteth the eye and the heart a-lusting, and filleth us with the pride of life.

Christ first separated his disciples from the world, then he fitteth them to his service.

They deceive themselves that think they may embrace true religion and the world too, following the vanities of fashion, and surfeiting in the pleasures of life: for godliness and vanity cannot dwell together; and the god of this world blindeth the eye of the understanding, that they which love the world cannot love God, and the secrets of the Lord are revealed to none but such as love and fear God.

[2.] 'Be ye transformed by the renewing of the mind:' that is, be ye new creatures, casting off the old man which is corrupt; for this new wine must be put in new casks.

We must sing a new song, *Canticum novum, novus homo*, a new man; none else can sing it. Therefore David desired *cor novum*, a new heart; and *spiritum rectum*, a right spirit. It is the only new fashion, as in many of ours, to renew the old fashion, the image of God stamped in us in our creation, which is decayed, and repaired anew by the image of the new Adam who came to restore us.

(2.) A use of the means, which are,

[1.] Delight in reading of the word; give attendance to reading, 1 Tim. iv. 15. What though thou understandest not what thou readest? No more did the eunuch: but God sent Philip to him; he was in the way of illumination.

Idle and wanton books take up too much of our time from the reading of God's book. *Rumor populi*, a rumour of the people takes us from reading this *rumor Domini*, this rumour of the Lord. Yet these things are written for our use, and only these things make the man of God wise to salvation.

[2.] Meditation, for that helpeth the understanding, and layeth up what we read in the memory, that we may know where to have it again when we have need of it. It is said of Mary, Luke ii. 51, that ' she kept all these sayings in her heart.'

The wise son of Sirach saith well,* 'The inner parts of a fool are like a broken vessel, and he will hold no knowledge as long as he liveth.' Truly the cause of all our sins and frailties is want of meditation in the word, want of keeping it in our heart. We see in ourselves, how we are affected here in hearing of the word of God; if we did meditate on it, we should have the same affections still.

[3.] Hear the word preached, for this is God's ordinance for the saving of souls. Ezra had a pulpit of wood made him; he stood up, he read the law, and gave the sense, and all the people wept when they heard the wonderful things of the law, Nehem. viii.

But it is said, all the people were attentive, both men and women, yet he preached not by the glass, but from morning till midday. And Paul preached from evening till midnight, for ' it pleaseth God by the foolishness of preaching to save those that believe.' Be swift to hear.

[4.] Meditation is necessary also after hearing the word in the public ministry; for the minister speaking to a mixed auditory, if he divideth the word aright, he hath a portion for every hearer, milk for some, stronger

* Ecclus. xxi. 14.

meat for others ; some have need of information in things unknown, some of comfort, some of resolution in doubts, some of confutation of errors, some of chiding, some have need to have their dullness spurred, others their deadness quickened, others their weakness strengthened, others their young and hopeful beginnings encouraged, others their zeals inflamed.

[5.] Conference is another good means to increase our knowledge, for one man's memory may help another's, so one man's understanding may be more clear than another's. For as we are many members of one body, so have we many graces bestowed upon us to make us useful and helpful one to another.

Conference one with another, especially with our minister, doth call to mind that which might else have slipped away from us ; and the very purpose of conference doth add a desire to learn by the word, that we may rather teach than be taught.

2. We must receive the word of God in our judgment.

This is the wisdom that teacheth us to make use of it ; for knowledge is not for itself, but for use. We shall know whether we have wisely heard the word by two things :

(1.) By the increase of our faith.

(2.) By our new obedience.

(1.) By the increase of our faith. For faith cometh from the saving hearing of God's word. The word is not the power of God to salvation, but only where it begetteth faith. The word never profiteth where it is not mixed with faith in them that hear it, Heb. iv. 2. So soon as Satan shook the faith of Eve, and made her doubt of the word of God, the word had lost the power of God in her to preserve her.

(2.) By our obedience. Many boast of their knowledge ; the apostle saith, ' He that doth think he knoweth anything,' that is, proud of his knowledge, and loveth his knowledge for itself, ' knoweth nothing yet as he ought to know.' For in religion he knoweth no more than he practiseth. What is it for a man to get a clear and good glass, and to behold his face in it, and to forget presently what his form is ? Such are the knowers of the word, as Saint James saith, that are not doers of the same. And what profit is it to us to know our master's will, and not to do it, but the gain of many stripes ?

Doct. 3. Here is a great judgment threatened. The prophet's intelligence is *rumor Domini*, a rumour of the Lord.

There is great cause of fear when God doth give out what his judgments shall be, and how he will punish, for his word is like the sword of Saul, 2 Sam. i. 12. It never returned empty from the blood of the slain.

We have no particular prophecies that do point out our nation, as this and many more did point out Edom for judgment, but yet we must not neglect the voice of God; for as faith layeth hold on the general promises of God to his church, and applieth particular examples in Scripture to the building of us up in comfort, so fear layeth hold on the general threatenings of God's judgments, and applieth them to the begetting and increasing of terror. So that when you shall hereafter see what sins Edom committed, we shall perceive how those sins provoked God's anger, and how severely God threatened them, you may say, *Auditum audivi a Domino,* We have heard a rumour from the Lord: that if the land we live in, or we that live in this land, be guilty of these sins, we have no *quietus est,* no discharge against these plagues; for these two go together, ' Come out of her, my people, that you be not partakers of her sins, and receive not of her plagues.' The drunkard may see in Noah and Lot, who sinned but once that way, how God did punish that sin. Miriam's sin resisting Moses. The adulterer may see in David, that God spareth not his own beloved children, he maketh their sins smart upon them. But the examples of his judgments upon the reprobates are full of terror; Cain, and Saul, and Judas, Korah and his company. This is *rumor Domini.* The Scripture dealeth plainly with us to tell the church these things, *ne veniant in locum tormenti,* that they come not into the place of torment.

Doct. 4. To comfort the hearts of such whose consciences are tender, and who do join, with care and fear, revenge upon themselves, and all to destroy the body of sin.

Many of these do too much discomfort and deject themselves about giving themselves over, as if they were vessels of wrath, or doomed to destruction. Satan useth fiery darts to such, and by all means tempteth such to despair; he saith unto them, *Non est tibi salus in Deo tuo*, there is no safety for thee in thy God. Therefore to such I say, Take heed, and examine well the suggestion, hearken diligently, *si rumor sit a Domino*, if it be a rumour from the Lord.

Satan laboureth most against our faith, for that is the victory by which we overcome the world. Christ told Peter, 'Satan hath desired to winnow thee.' He knew which way he bent his strength. *Oravi ne deficeret fides tua*, 'I have prayed that thy faith fail not,' Luke xxii. 32.

Our own fear is another great enemy to our peace, for when we do consider ourselves, and how weak our faith is, we do presently apply to ourselves all the judgments of God.

Yet this is *rumor a Domino*, a rumour from the Lord.

The Lord hath delight in this broken heart, he will repair and build up the branches thereof; the ground that is thus broken up is fittest for the immortal seed of his word, and of his grace to be sown in it, to bear fruit.

What a woful case was David in, when his foot had almost slipped, when he feared that God would no more be entreated, and hearkened to the rumour of his conscience, till God, who is greater than the conscience, refreshed him with his sweet consolations.

And saint Paul hearkening to the rumour of his conscience, crieth out, 'O wretched man that I am, who shall deliver me?' &c. But the sweet and comfortable voice of joy is heard in the tabernacles of the righteous, as there, 'Thanks be unto God through our Lord Jesus,' &c. Therefore as he saith, 'When you hear of wars, and rumours of wars, be not afraid;' that is, fear not servilely nor despairingly, 'for the end is not yet.'

Ver. 1. *An ambassador is sent amongst the heathen: Arise ye, and let us arise against her in battle.*

2. Means of the intelligence, 'an ambassador is sent amongst the heathen.' This is *rumor populi*, a rumour of the people, for commonly rumour of war doth go before war, seeing the preparation of war cannot be concealed.

Concerning this ambassador, the learned expositors of this prophecy are not well agreed.

Some think he is some prophet of the Lord sent to stir up a war between Edom and other nations.

Others, that one nation doth by ambassadors stir up another against Edom.

The LXX read ἢ ἀγγέλους εἰς ἔθνη ἀπέστειλεν,* whereupon some understand that God sent his angel to provoke this war.

The point material is agreed on by all, that God hath an hand in this judgment, and he useth the nations for a rod to scourge Edom.

This rumour of war is *terror Domini*, the terror of the Lord; and it stirreth up and awaketh those that are in danger to look to themselves: which doth shew that this judgment threatened against Edom shall not surprise them suddenly; they have warning to stand upon their guard, and to arm themselves against invasion.

This is therefore declared, as I conceive, to shew the careless security of Edom, that would take no warning, for that is expressed in the prophecy of Isaiah in the burden of Dumah, contempt and scorn of their warning: for 'he calleth unto me out of Seir, Watchman, what was in the night? watchman, what was in the night?' as deriding the prophet, who had foretold their night of calamity, which should put out their candle, and leave them darkling; for if the voice of the prophets will not move them, how will they take it when they shall hear the nations sending ambassadors one to another to confederate against them?

---

* This is probably from some other Greek version. That of the LXX is καὶ περιοχὴν εἰς τὰ ἔθνη ἐξαπέστειλεν.—ED.

But the wicked are despisers, they will take no warning.

The old world made a scorn of Noah's preaching and building, and thereby vexing his righteous soul, even to the day that the flood came and swept them all away. They of Sodom, even the sons-in-law of Lot, when he warned them of the wrath to come, did despise the warning.

Yet God, to make their judgment more heavy when it cometh, and to make their scorn more inexcusable, threateneth them with the rumour first, before he smiteth them.

The pride and vanity of these times, the drunkenness and profaneness, the contentions, and all the clamorous and loud-voiced sins which overgrow into excess; they do all arise from the contempt of the word of God, and from a negligence in observing the course of God's justice in the punishing of these sins, and from a scornful undervaluing of those ambassadors whom God doth send into the world to reconcile the world to himself.

The apostle saith, 'We as ambassadors from God do beseech you.' But the ministers of God's word have very harsh welcome in the world, for the profane despise them all, and will not hear their message; the precise will hear but some of them, they despise others; they that be for Paul will not hear Apollos; and they that be for Peter will hear neither Paul, nor Apollos, nor Jesus Christ himself.

But consider, ambassadors are not sent but upon serious occasions. This is such, to awake and stir us up against our common enemies, the flesh, the world, and the devil, and to tell us of our great danger, for we shall not fight against flesh and blood only, but against powers and principalities. If we despise the noise of this rumour, these enemies may take us at advantage.

Edom would take no warning; no more will they whom God hath delivered over to the guidance of their own lusts.

2. The effect of the message and rumour, being the judgment itself: 'Arise ye, and let us arise against

her in battle.' When I compare these words with those of Balaam's prophecy,—Num. xxiv. 18, 'Edom shall be a possession, Seir also shall be a possession for his enemies; and Israel shall do valiantly. Out of Jacob shall he come that shall have dominion, and shall destroy him that remaineth of that city,'—I find here from whence the ambassador cometh, even from the house of Jacob: 'And Israel shall stir up the heathen against Edom, and Israel shall have dominion over them.' This appeareth in Ezekiel's prophecy: Ezek. xxv. 14, 'And I will lay my vengeance upon Edom, by the hand of my people Israel; and they shall do in Edom according to my anger, and according to my fury, and they shall know my vengeance, saith the Lord God.'

So the people of God shall stir up the heathen nations against Edom.

From whence we do learn these lessons:

1. That all wars are ordered by God.
2. That God punisheth one evil man by the hand of another, and so one evil nation.
3. That war is one of God's punishments, by which he chasteneth men for sin.
4. That the people of God may lawfully make war.

Doct. 1. All wars are ordered by God.

It is the word of the Lord that these nations shall come together in war against Edom: Prov. xxi. 31, 'The horse is prepared for the day of battle; but the victory is of the Lord.' Ps. cxliv. 1, 'He teacheth my hands to fight, and my fingers to battle.' Melchizedec saith to Abraham, after his victory in the rescue of Lot, Gen. xiv. 20, 'Blessed be the most high God, which hath delivered thine enemies into thy hand.' When Israel prevailed against Benjamin for abusing the Levite's concubine, Judges xx. 35, it is said, 'The Lord smote Benjamin before Israel.' Gideon's cry was, Judges vii. 20, 'The sword of the Lord and of Gideon.'

The reason hereof is in sight.

1. By the general providence of God, who ruleth all things and all persons; for 'He abaseth himself to behold things in heaven and in earth,' Ps. cxiii. 6.

2. By the particular interest that God hath in wars, for he is called *Dominus exercituum*, the Lord of hosts. The uses follow.

Use 1. In all wars, to have respect unto the cause, not to put ourselves into an unjust quarrel; let the cause be God's, and we may promise ourselves to have God on our side. The wise man saith, Prov. xx. 18, 'By counsel, wars must be enterprised;' Prov. xxiv. 6, 'By wise counsel thou shalt make thy war prosperous.' If Jehoshaphat join with Ahab against Ramoth in Gilead, he shall speed accordingly. The sword of the Lord first, then of Gideon.

Use 2. The cause being good and warrantable, we must not trust to our strength, neither must we neglect the means, presuming on the defence of God.

1. Not trust our own strength; for some trust in chariots, and some in horses, as Benhadad did in the multitude of his men, so great, that the land against which he fought was not enough to give every one of them an handful. But David saith, Ps. xxxiii. 17, 'A king is not saved by the multitude of an host, neither is the mighty man delivered by much strength: an horse is a vain help.'

2. It is another extreme to cast all upon God, and not to use the means: first, the sword of the Lord, and then with it the sword of Gideon.

Use 3. This serveth to take off all fear from our hearts when we fight the Lord's battles. It was a cheerful speech of Joab, encouraging the people when he had divided his army, part against the Syrians and part against Ammon, 2 Sam. x. 12, 'Be of good courage, and let us play the men, for our people, and for the cities of our God; and the Lord do that which seemeth him good.' It was David's resolution, Ps. iii. 6, 'I will not be afraid of ten thousand of the people that should beset me round about: Arise, O Lord, save me, my God: for thou smitest all mine enemies upon the cheek bone.'

Use 4. This teacheth us our duty, before the war, in the war, and after the war.

1. Before the war, and in the war, to join prayers with our preparations and our attempts; for God

declared, in the wars of Israel with Amalek, that Moses praying on the hill with Aaron and Hur, and Joshua fighting below in the valley, were both of them the forces of God, Exod. xvii. And that prayers were the better fighting; for when Moses ceased praying, Amalek prevailed.

2. After the war, we are taught to whom to attribute the victory and good success of the war; that is, to give the glory thereof to the Lord, and so say with David, 'The right hand of the Lord hath done valiantly; the right hand of the Lord bringeth mighty things to pass.' So the daughter of Jephthah, Judges xi. 36, came out with timbrels to meet her father, and confessed to her father, 'The Lord hath taken vengeance for thee of thine enemies, even of the children of Ammon.'

Yet may we not herein smother the well-deserving prowess and valour of valiant commanders and soldiers, but give them their due honour; so even the women meet Saul returning from the slaughter of the Philistines, and they answered one another in their song, saying, 'Saul hath killed his thousands, and David his ten thousands,' 1 Sam. xviii. 7.

Doct. 2. Whereas Israel saith to the heathen, 'Arise ye, and let us arise,' making use of the power and strength of the heathen against Edom, we are taught, that God doth use one evil man and one evil nation to punish another. The Lord did smite the Moabites by the Ammonites, and took from them some part of their land. Chedorlaomer maketh war against other kings, and taketh away their substance. The Midianites were their own conquerors: Judges vii. 22, 'The Lord set every one's sword against his fellow throughout all the host.'

The children of Israel did call the heathen here to them; they joined in one war against Edom, as if at this day princes of the popish religion should join themselves with a protestant prince, to maintain him in his kingdom against the emperor, the pope's eldest son.

Is not this setting Egyptians against Egyptians, and defending the church by the enemies of the church?

The reason why God doth this, is not for want of other strength, for he is Lord of hosts; but to declare him to be King and Lord over all; he doth whatsoever he will in heaven and in earth, and in the sea, and all deeps. What doth more declare his absolute sovereignty than his power to whip and scourge the enemies of his church by one another of them, which is to make Satan cast out Satan? This sheweth that Satan's kingdom is subordinate to the kingdom of God; there is but one kingdom of which it may be truly said, *Et imperiis ejus non est finis,* 'There is no end of his kingdom.' Christ shall one day make this good, when he shall have put down all his enemies; for then he shall deliver up the kingdom to God. In the mean time, the subjects of Satan's kingdom are the vassals of God, and Satan himself shall be and is at his command, to be the rod of God for execution of his wrath where he pleaseth.

2. God useth to punish the wicked, to declare to the church that there can be no true love but where there is love of the truth; only true religion doth unite the hearts of men, and all that embrace not that want the bond of peace. They may cry a confederacy, and give one another the right hand of fellowship for a time; but if God be not the knot of their union, all other respects will come short of settling a constant concurrency. We see this clearly in the vicissitudes of confederacies and wars amongst the enemies of true religion; temporal respects make their leagues, temporal respects do again dissolve them.

The uses of this point.

Use 1. This doth serve to reform our judgments, and to settle our hearts in our great vexation; for did not the foot of David almost slip when he saw the prosperity of the ungodly, and compared it with the main and great troubles of the church? For seeing God doth make this use of them, to be his sword, marvel not that he keepeth his sword by his side, that he keepeth it in his sheath, that he keepeth it bright. And David saith, Ps. xvii. 13, ' Deliver my soul from the wicked, which is thy sword.' That is one cause why God rewardeth the wicked with some temporal favours, because he maketh use of them to punish his enemies. This is fully expressed: for thus saith the Lord to the prophet, Ezek. xxix. 18, 19, 'Son of man, Nebuchadnezzar king of Babel caused his army to serve a great service against Tyrus. Every head was made bald, and every shoulder was peeled, yet had he no wages, nor the army for Tyrus that served against it: therefore thus saith the Lord God, Behold, I will give the land of Egypt into the hand of Nebuchadnezzar king of Babylon, and he shall take her multitudes, and take her spoils, and take her prey, and it shall be the wages for his army.'

This may satisfy us, that we grieve not at the prosperous estate of the wicked, for God hath use of them, and he will not let them serve him for nothing.

The elect of God have fairer hopes; let them stay their stomach, and let them wait the Lord's leisure.

Use 2. We may see in this example in my text, and in many more, that God maketh use of the wicked in the behalf of his church, and therefore we must not give the glory of God's justice to the means, but to God.

The wicked know not what they do when they fight the battles of the Lord; yet God doth put such metal into them that they do most valiantly perform his will. A full example hereof is, Jer. xxxvii. 8, ' The word of the Lord to Zedekiah king of Judah, by his prophet Jeremiah : The Chaldeans shall come again, and fight against this city, and take it, and burn it with fire. Thus saith the Lord, Deceive not yourselves, saying, The Chaldeans shall depart from us, for they shall not depart. For though ye had smitten the whole army of the Chaldeans that fight against you, and there remained but wounded men amongst them, yet should they rise up, every man in his tent, and burn the city with fire.'

This must needs be the hand of the Lord, and therefore the glory must be given to God only. The means are weak, but the Lord is strong; he alone must be exalted, and all the glory of victory must be ascribed to him.

The church may use the help of the heathen and of idolaters in the Lord's battles, for they are the sword of the Lord, as you have heard.

Use 3. We are taught that though Israel and the heathen do come together, though the godly do use the help of the wicked to execute the will of God upon God's enemies, yet they must be very careful not to join with them in their wickedness and idolatry. We may use the help of papists for the maintenance of the Lord's cause, but we must take heed that we fall not into the sin of Israel : Ps. cvi. 35, ' They were mingled with the heathen, and learned their wickedness, and served their idols, which were their ruin.' Let us not make the covenant with them that Ruth the Moabitess made with Naomi, Ruth i. 16, ' Thy people shall be my people, and thy God my God.'

3. The third doctrine.

War is one of the punishments wherewith God doth punish his enemies : Lev. xxvi. 25, ' And I will bring a sword upon you, that shall avenge the quarrel of my covenant.' It is one of the four sore judgments, as God himself doth call it, Ezek. xiv. 21, and it is first named ; used to cut off man and beast.

When Israel was, by the favour of God, put into possession of the promised land, they sinned against God in contempt of religion, in idolatry, theft, and whoredom, for which God punished them with war ; for the Amorites, Philistines, Midianites, Moabites, Canaanites, and Ammonites fought against them, and opposed them three years, as appeareth in the book of Judges.

The misery of war is great, as Moses doth express it : Deut. xxviii. 50, 51, ' They shall not regard the person of the old, nor have compassion of the young, they shall eat the fruit of thy cattle, they shall consume the profit of thy land, they shall besiege thee within thy walls, they shall drive thee to eat thy children, the fruit of thy body, during the siege, and straitness wherewith they shall compass thee in thy cities.' God hath a quiver ; it is full of arrows ; this is one of them, Ezek. v. 16, 17.

The reason hereof is because they that make no conscience of their duty to God, nor of obedience to his word, have put themselves out of God's protection, and he is become their enemy. The protection of God is the fence of the vine; if that hedge be once broken up, not only the foxes will come in and devour the grapes, but the wild boar will also come in and root it up.

2. They that make no conscience of charity to their brethren, in the just judgments of God are delivered into the hands of men, and as one saith, *Nullum animal morosius*, so *Nullum animal ferocius*. Oh, saith David, 'Let me not fall into the hand of man.'

Let men fall softly and easily when they fall into thy hands, so shalt thou fall gently into their hands, for God is love, and the merciful man shall not want mercy.

But, as in the natural body, sometimes it is wholesome to open a vein and let out blood; so it is in the body politic; the sword must sometimes draw blood, to purge the body of noxious and offensive humours. And wheresoever this punishment lighteth as medicinal, it amendeth many faults; where it lighteth as a judgment of indignation, it cutteth off evil doers from the face of the earth.

The uses of this doctrine follow.

Use 1. Let us consider the lamentable estate of those that profess the same faith with us, who have no other outward means of safety to preserve their liberty and rights but by the sword, against whom great and mighty princes do say one to another, 'Arise ye, and let us arise against them in battle.'

You know who is at this time thus endangered, even some of the branches of that vine under which we sit. The forward, free, and cheerful offerings of your hands have testified your good affections to that rightful cause; let lifting up of your hands secure that free opening of them, that is, let your prayers fight for them, and give God no rest till he hath settled peace in these walls, and prosperity within these palaces. Surely they shall prosper that love it; for our brethren and companions' sake, the worshippers of the same God, the professors of the same faith with us, let us wish them now prosperity ; for the house of God's sake, which they seek to enlarge and advance, let us seek and study to do them good.

Use 2. Let us thankfully consider our own peace. We are *filii pacis*, children of peace, born and brought up in times of peace : the prophecy of Zechariah is fulfilled in our land, chap. viii. 4. We have old men and women dwelling in our towns, even men with staves in their hands for very age, and the streets of our cities and towns full of boys and girls playing in the streets thereof. And that promise of God to the obedient, Lev. xxvi. 6, is performed in us, ' I will send peace in the land, and ye shall sleep, and none shall make you afraid ; and the sword shall not go through your land.'

The happy days of the long reign of Queen Elizabeth, of everlasting memory, the mother of our peace, were crowned with peace, and she left a legacy of peace in the commonwealth in her succession. Our Solomon, her heir, hath maintained peace under his happy government, both at home and abroad. What nation is there now under heaven which saith, Arise ye, and let us arise against England in battle ? We may say, ' This is the Lord's doing,' and we must give him the glory of it ; for, as David saith, Ps. xlvi. 9, ' He maketh wars to cease, he breaketh the bow, and cutteth the spear in sunder, and burneth the chariots in the fire.'

The use. ' Be still, and know that I am God ; I will be exalted in the earth.'

Use 3. Seeing we have outward peace from foreign enemies, and none riseth up against us in battle, we must be tender of maintaining peace one with another: ' Take heed ye bite not one another, lest ye be devoured one of another.' Better it were we had wars abroad than that we should fight one with another of us at home by uncivil contentions, by fraudulent and cunning underminings, by slanderous and lying calumniations, or by any other uncharitable means of molestation to breed unjust wars amongst ourselves. For by this cursed crossness we do provoke God to draw his sword against us.

Use 4. Seeing God hath delivered us from the calamity of war, and given us the blessing of peace, let us know that this is the fittest time for semination of the gospel of peace ; this is the seed-time for the word of God. In such a time was Christ born, in the peaceable reign of Augustus Cæsar. Then were swords turned into scythes, and spears into ploughshares, and so the noise of our redemption, and the sound of the gospel, went over all the world.

We see that those years of peace have made learning and arts flourish in our land ; and for the light of religion, it never shined clearer than now, and the light thereof still increaseth. Let us know that now God hath so fenced in his vine in our land, and bestowed such cost on it, he looketh that it should bring forth grapes ; not fair and spreading branches only, not large and green leaves, not shows and semblances, and seemings of godliness, but grapes ; not *labruscas*, not sour grapes, but *fructus dignos pœnitentia*, fruits worthy of repentance. These be the best presents we can make to God, the best ensigns of our peace. Otherwise the calamities of peace will fall on us worse than those of war, idleness, wantonness, fulness of bread, drunkenness, and all the worms of prosperity which will destroy our vine.

Doct. 4. Because Jeremiah saith, *Arise ye*, stirring up others to battle, and addeth, *we will arise*, I conclude,—

That it is lawful for the children of God to make war.

For a defensive war nature provideth, for that is no more but *se tueri*, to defend himself. But this is an offensive war against Edom, their enemy, and this is lawful.

The land of promise, though given so many years before to the sons of Shem, in the line of Jacob, yet was possessed by the sons of Ham, of whose son Canaan took name, and Israel came into the possession of that land by the sword. They had God's own warrant for it : Deut. vii. 2, ' When the Lord bringeth thee into the land whither thou goest to possess it, and shall root out many nations before thee, then thou shalt smite them, thou shalt utterly destroy them,' &c.

Yea, he doth not only allow of a just war, but David saith, Ps. xviii. 34, 'He teacheth my hands to fight.' Moses, from God, saith to Israel, Num. xxv. 17, 'Vex the Midianites, and smite them.'

1. Because, as I taught before, war is one of the judgments of God, one of the arrows of his quiver, one of his rods wherewith he doth chasten the wicked, therefore the faithful may and must arise when they are called forth into battle. In such a case it was said, Jer. xlviii. 10, 'Cursed is he that doeth the work of the Lord negligently;' Judges v. 23, 'Curse ye Meroz, curse ye Meroz, saith the angel of the Lord; curse ye the inhabitants thereof bitterly, because they came not to the help of the Lord, to the help of the Lord against the mighty.'

There it is called helping the Lord, because men be the hands of execution in these lawful wars, by whom God doth punish his enemies, and because God is holpen in those that are by just means maintained.

2. Because an offensive war is revenge of injuries, and God hath said, 'Vengeance is mine,' so that the Lord is called 'Lord of hosts;' and just wars are called 'the battles of the Lord.' They that fight in such wars, God covereth their heads in the day of battle.

The wars of Israel against Amalek were offensive; they were the Lord's vengeance against Amalek for smiting the hindermost and weakest of them in their passage to the promised land. This war against Edom was such, as it followeth God's revenge upon Edom for their cruelty towards Israel.

3. We find that when the Israelites* came to John Baptist and asked, 'What shall we do?' he did not bid them leave the profession of arms, but only said to them, Luke iii. 13, 'Do violence to no man, accuse no man falsely, and be content with your wages.' Wherein he required of them fair wars without injury to any; for none but unjust violence is there forbidden.

* Qu. 'soldiers'?—Ed.

And we shall find in the catalogue of the faithful, Heb. xi. 32, 33, Gideon, Barak, Samson, Jephthah, David, ' which through faith subdued kingdoms,' &c.

The uses follow.

Seeing the faithful may make lawful wars;

Use 1. We are taught to satisfy our conscience, before we undertake any war, that it is lawful and just, for else we cannot either promise ourselves good success, or solicit God for his aid.

(1.) It is a lawful war to preserve our right against them that invade it, as was ours in '88 against the Spaniard, then our enemy, who prepared himself for the invasion of this kingdom.

(2.) The judges of Israel did redeem Israel from their oppressors that had invaded them, and redeemed their own right. So Abraham made a just war against those that had wronged the king of Sodom, and took Lot prisoner.

(3.) To chasten and destroy the common enemies of intercourse and trade between nation and nation; such is the sea-war intended against the pirates and sea-thieves, that hinder the trade of nations by their piracies; wasps and drones that rob the hives of painful bees.

(4.) To defend confederate nations from the oppression of their enemy; for so Joshua will not suffer the Ammonite to vex and wrong the Gibeonites, because the oath of God is between them.

Thus, for the common peace, it is lawful for Christians to confederate with Turks and infidels, for protestants to make leagues of peace and civil society with papists, catholics with heretics. And when the league goeth no further than the just defence of them in their rights, we may borrow and lend help each to other; for the common love of humanity teacheth us to do as we would be done to; and the apostle biddeth, Rom. xii. 19, ' as much as in us, to have peace with all men.'

But to assist infidels and heretics in their unjust wars, it is utterly unlawful; so Jehoshaphat joined with Ahab against Ramoth in Gilead, and the prophet of the Lord reproved him for it: 2 Chron. xix. 2, ' And

Jehu the son of Hanani the seer went out to meet him, and said to king Jehoshaphat, Wouldst thou help the wicked, and love them that hate the Lord? Therefore, for this thing is the wrath of the Lord upon thee.'

If the league between the godly and ungodly nations have these bonds, 1, to assure one another against injury from each other; 2, to defend each other's rights, without prejudice of religion; 3, to maintain commerce between them; I see no cause why it may not be lawful for Christians and infidels to confederate.

1. For defence against injury of others. If the ox of an infidel, or his ass, should fall into a pit, ought I not to shew him mercy in his beast, and to save him if I can? Shall I do this to his beast, and shall I not do it to him? If thieves would rob him, shall I pass by and see him rifled, and shall I not give him aid? What duty one man oweth to another, that doth one nation owe to another; this is preservation of justice, *suum cuique*.

2. For binding ourselves not to do infidels any hurt unjustly. It is the law of God; we must not only abstain from robbing them, but we must preserve their right; we may not take away from them their lives, their wives, their goods, or anything of theirs; we may promise interchangeably to do them no wrong.

3. For commerce. Some of our late divines* affirm it unlawful to sell to infidels, or heretics, any commodity which they may abuse to any idolatrous use. For example, to sell to the papists wax, because they make candles thereof, which they do use in their false worship of God; so frankincense, cloth, &c.; this is made a breach of the second commandment. But this rule is too strict and unwarrantable; for what providence can prevent abuse of all the commodities that any land affordeth? We sell wheat, of which they may make their wafer-gods; we exchange gold with

* Perk. Arm. Aur. in 2 Præcept.—[This is scarcely a fair statement of the doctrine of Perkins. He does not forbid the selling of articles which *may* be used for idolatrous purposes; but of those which the seller *knows* to be bought for such purposes. What he says is forbidden, is 'Societas contractûs, quâ quis sciens, spe lucri et mercedis, idololatris ea vendat, quæ idolis sciat subvenire.'—Ed.]

some of them, they may gild their images with it. Some of them send us in wine, which is much abused to drunkenness; and silks of all sorts, which is abused to pride, &c. This is *nimia sapientia, nimia justitia,* to be over-wise, over-just.

Use 2. Seeing the godly and faithful may lawfully make just wars, we are taught to exercise arms, and to study military discipline, and to value the worthy soldier as a necessary member of the commonwealth, and to give him all good encouragement.

That peace which rusteth the armour, and despiseth the soldier, and disuseth arms, is dangerous; it weakeneth the hands and hearts of men of action, it disableth the commonwealth, it provoketh the adversary to assault, and putteth all into hazard.

As John biddeth the soldiers to be content with their pay, so he alloweth them a pay, and imposeth the charge of their maintenance upon the commonwealth.

Let not daring and worthy spirits complain, as Themistocles did, that they are like to the platanes; in a storm, men fly under them for shelter; in fair weather, *vellicant*, pluck off their leaves.

Use 3. We are taught, when just occasions of war arise, to gather courage, as being helpers to our God in his battles.

When Hezekiah saw that Sennacherib was come to fight against Jerusalem, he said to his commanders and soldiers, 'Be strong and courageous, fear not, nor be afraid, for the king of Ashur, neither for all the multitude that is with him: for there is more with us than with him. With him is an arm of flesh, but with us is the Lord our God, for to help us, and to fight our battles,' 2 Chron. xxxii. 7. So Nehemiah encouraged the people against Tobiah and Sanballat, when they came to hinder the building of the walls of Jerusalem : 'Be not afraid of them, remember the great Lord, and the fearful, and fight for your brethren, your sons and your daughters, your wives and your houses.' There be that have said, that true religion doth make men cowards, and destroyeth fortitude and true valour. It is not so.

1. Because true religion doth settle the conscience in the goodness of the cause, which the heathen did not respect.

2. True religion casteth us upon the protection of almighty God, which also the heathen regarded not, but trusted to them that were no gods.

Therefore, let us say to our soldiers in the wars of God, as we read it said by the officers to the people by the commandment of Moses, Deut. xx. 8, ' What man is there that is fearful and faint-hearted ? Let him go and return to his house, lest his brethren's heart do faint, as his heart fainteth.' For it was a base and unkingly answer that Ahab sent Benhadad, who said, ' Thy silver and thy gold is mine, thy women and thy children are mine.' He answered, ' My lord king, according to thy saying, I am thine, and all that I have.' They that put their trust in the Lord do not fear what man can do unto them.

Use 4. Seeing wars are lawful, we conclude that it is lawful also to use all witty means of circumvention to ensnare the enemy ; those are called stratagems of war.

So Joshua may lie in wait, and come against Ai on the back side of the city, Josh. viii. 2. So Abraham may divide his company, and smite the enemy in the night, when he attempteth the rescue of Lot, Gen. xiv. 15. So the Israelites may use advice to draw the men of Gibeah out of their city, and so take advantage against them unawares, Judges xx. 29.

Use 5. Seeing just wars may be undertaken by the servants of God, let them prepare themselves as God's servants to them.

Deut. xxiii. 9, ' When thou goest out with an host against thine enemy, then keep thyself from every wicked thing. The Lord thy God walketh in the midst of the camp to deliver thee, and to give thee thine enemies before thee ; therefore let thine host be holy, that he see no filthy thing in thee, and turn away from thee.'

Amongst the heathen, it was wont to be said that the camp was the school of virtue ; much more ought it to be so amongst Christians, for there is a terror of death, and we know that immediately after death cometh judgment. How ought men to sanctify themselves, and to repent them of their sins, and to purge their hearts from all wickedness, that serve under almighty God in his battles! God hath threatened: Lev. xxvi. 14, 17, 'If you will not obey me, nor do all these commandments, I will set my face against you, and ye shall fall before your enemies; and they that hate you shall reign over you, and ye shall fly when none pursueth you.' Surely such are of the forlorn hope that come not to serve the living God; therefore the strongest army is of them that are religious, and make conscience of doing any wicked thing to displease God.

Use 6. Seeing it is lawful to make just wars, there must be a willing yielding to the charge thereof; moneys are the sinews of war, Rom. xiii., 'and for this cause pay we tribute.' 'Give unto Cæsar that that is Cæsar's.' God hath given our lawful princes an interest in our goods for the common good, and the apostle allegeth this cause of tribute and subsidy to our princes. 'For they are God's ministers appointed for this very thing,' that is, to execute wrath upon them that do evil, and to defend their own right.

Use 7. This reproveth those that sensually and securely play and sleep out their time, without care of their own safety, till the enemies come on them and make them a prey. This was the ruin of Laish: Judges xviii. 7, 'The children of Dan sent five men who came to Laish, and behold, the people that were therein dwelt careless, after the manner of the Zidonians, quiet and secure.' This gave encouragement to the children of Dan to assault them.

Use 8. This doctrine of the lawfulness of just wars doth seem to confute the Manichees and Marcionites of old times, and the Anabaptists and those of the 'family of love' in later days, who have maintained it unlawful for Christians to make any either offensive or defensive war, or so much as to wear a weapon.

Obj. 1. Christ saith, Mat. v. 39, 'Resist not evil; if one smite thee on one cheek, turn the other: if one sue thee for thy coat, give him thy cloak.'

Sol. 1. This must not be literally understood, for Christ himself, who gave this precept, did not so; he was smitten in the high priest's hall, and he turned not the other cheek, but reproved him that smote him, saying, John xviii. 22, 23, 'If I have spoken evil, bear witness of the evil; but if well, why smitest thou me?'

This, then, is spoken by our Saviour to forbid private revenge, that no man should be the judge of his own wrong, but should bear it with patience.

It is St Augustine's answer, *Obedientia ista non in ostentatione corporis est, sed in preparatione cordis.* And he saith, *Non maxillam tantum obtulit, sed totum corpus dedit figendum cruci.* And he addeth, *Quanto melius et respondit vere placatus, et ad perferenda graviora paratus est.* He could have withdrawn his cheek from the smiter, but he would fulfil the prophecy: Lam. iii. 30, 'He giveth his cheek to him that smiteth him; he is filled with reproaches.'

Private revenge Christ forbiddeth us. Christ did not take it against his adversary that smote him; he reproved it in Peter; he amended the maim that he made, and healed his smiter. But war is a public revenge, and the magistrate beareth the sword to that purpose, ' to execute revenge upon evil doers.' Vengeance is God's, and where he committeth the trust of execution thereof, as he doth to the magistrate, there it is lawful.

This cleareth many other like objections, as that, *Qui gladio ferit, gladio peribit,* he that smiteth with the sword shall perish by the sword; we must recompense to no man evil for evil. For all this is meant of our revenge, but the revenge of the magistrate is the vengeance of God, because he is God's minister.

Obj. 2. The prophet Isaiah foretold, chap. ii. 4, that in the time of the gospel, ' They shall beat their swords into ploughshares, and their spears into pruning-hooks; nation shall not lift up sword against nation, neither shall they learn war any more.'

Sol. These words bear three interpretations.

1. That this was a sign of the coming of the Mes-

siah into the world. He was born in a time of cessation from wars, when the Roman monarchy had leisure to levy a taxation by the poll. So when David had rest, then he thought of numbering his people.

2. That this was fulfilled in the spiritual peace and unity of the church, collected now out of all nations of the world, Jew and Gentile made one.

3. That this is the proper effect of the gospel, where it was embraced faithfully, to make peace.

Under the name of Edom, we may understand all the enemies of the truth of God and Christian religion: such as are schismatics and heretics, who, understanding not the mystery of godliness and peace, do set their wits against the church, to corrupt the truth therein deposited and professed, or to disturb the quiet professors thereof.

1. *Heretics.* These are our brethren by outward profession, calling themselves Christians; but they see that we have gotten the birthright and the blessing from them, and therefore they hate us, and are comforted against us to destroy us.

The church is God's Israel, the children of the promise, *filii regni, filii thalami, filii lucis,* children of the kingdom, of the bridechamber, and of the light.

The ambassadors that are sent to stir up to war against those, be the ministers of the word of God; for to this purpose we are sent forth, to confirm the brethren against those, to reconcile these to God. And we are commanded to arise against these in battle. The war, and so the weapons with which we fight against these are not carnal, but spiritual; the clear light of the gospel, which is the power of God to salvation to them that believe, and the truth of God which is strong, and prevaileth against them that believe not.

It is time for us to join together as one man in battle against these:

Especially the papists, whose religion is ambition, whose piety is worldly policy, whose zeal is combustion, whose faith is fury, who hide the word of light in the darkness of an unknown tongue, to keep the people ignorant, that they may not know God's right hand from his left, to emplunge them in the flames of their imagined purgatory, that they may be well paid to release them thence.

They mingle the sacrament of baptism with their own inventions, which they make equivalent in virtue to the power of God's ordinance.

They mangle the sacrament of the Lord's supper, by robbing the people of one half thereof, taking the cup from them.

They disable the sacrifice of Christ's sufficient satisfaction for sin, by addition of human merits, of erogation, and supererogation.

They weaken the sole intercession of Christ, by intrusion of more mediators, angels, the mother of our Lord, and saints.

They shorten the free and full grace of God, which Christ himself from heaven told Paul was sufficient, by their lying doctrine of free will.

They flatter and abet some by their doctrine of indulgences, which attributeth to the pope power of pardoning sins past and to come.

They dishonour the holy, sufficient word of God, by equibalancing with the same human traditions and false legends.

They destroy true and saving faith, by their false doctrine of implicit faith, teaching that [it] is enough to believe as the church believeth, not declaring what the church believeth, and upon what ground their faith is built.

They maintain flat idolatry, by teaching the worshipping of images, and praying to saints.

And for the power which they give to the pope against God in dispensing with the breach of his covenants, in coining new articles of faith, in defining the interpretation of Scripture, in usurping authority over temporal princes, to enthrone and to dethrone at pleasure, to arm their natural subjects against them; to animate incendiaries, to abet treasons, to blow up states.

All these things, and many more, call upon us to take arms and join our strengths against this Edom, this red, and hairy, and bloody enemy, whose mercies are cruel.

The best weapon against this kingdom of darkness is the light of truth; the more we carry this light about us, the more will the ignorant amongst them know how they are abused and misled. For our war is spiritual, not against their persons, but against their heresies.

2. *Schismatics.* These also call us brethren, but they break the unity and uniformity of the church.

All the children of peace must arise against these in battle. This also is a spiritual war, and the sword of the Spirit must be drawn and used against these, to cut them off, as St Paul wisheth, ' I would they were cut off that trouble you ;' or if the word of God cannot prevail with them, to convert them to peace, the discipline of the church, which St Paul calleth his rod, must be used against them, to cut them off from our congregations. The apostle calleth them leaven, and saith, that 'a little leaven soureth the whole lump.' So do schismatics; for a few of them do corrupt many, and divert them from the congregations whereof they are members, and distaste the established ministry to them, and set them in opposition to authority, and at last tempt them to separation.

Mr Perkins, upon the article of the holy catholic church, doth learnedly handle this point.

First, saith he, they object that our assemblies are full of grievous blots and enormities.

He answereth, the defects must be either, 1, in doctrine; or, 2, in manners.

1. Defects in doctrine. (1.) Either errors *præter fundamentum*, besides the foundation. (2.) Or *contra fundamentum*, against the foundation.

He maintaineth that our Church of England doth teach no doctrine *against* the foundation of Christian religion.

2. For corruption in manners he declareth, that it cannot make a church no church, but an imperfect church; therefore Christ commandeth to hear them which preach well and live ill, as the scribes and pharisees which sit in Moses's chair.

Again, he findeth it objected that the church of England doth hold Christ in word, but denieth him in deed.

Answer: Denial of Christ is either in judgment or in fact.

To deny Christ in judgment, which obstinacy is against the foundation, and maketh a Christian no Christian.

To deny Christ in fact only, sheweth us to be weak and imperfect in our profession of the gospel; and the best of God's servants cannot keep out of this rank, because it is impossible for them that carry a body of sin, who do the evil that they would not, to hold conformity of life and conversation with their knowledge and good desires.

And truly the authors or the actors of schism do shew much uncharitableness in their separation from our church, for the apostle's rule is, 2 Cor. vi. 14, 'Be not unequally yoked with infidels; what concord hath Christ with Belial? what agreement hath the temple of God with idols? Wherefore come out from among them, and separate yourselves, saith the Lord.'

And do they judge their brethren to be infidels, the sons of Belial, idolaters, that they do separate from us? Again, the same apostle saith, 2 Tim. vi. 3, 'If any man teach otherwise, and consent not to the wholesome words of our Lord Jesus Christ, and to the doctrine which is according to godliness, from such separate yourselves.' Can any lay this to the charge of our church, that we offend in this kind? It is true that nothing is more easy than to accuse, but men and devils cannot prove this against our church.

The church of the Jews, in the times immediately after Christ's ascension, was the church of God, neither did Christ forsake that church in his time, nor the apostles after him. Acts xii. 9, 'But when certain men hardened and disobeyed, speaking evil of the ways of God,' Saint Paul departed from them, and separated from them, and separated the disciples of Ephesus. From certain schismatics he separated, but not from the church.

Therefore arise against such in battle, detect them to public authority, seek their amendment; or if that cannot be compassed, prosecute the ridding them out of the church; for those Edomites do not love the welfare of our Jerusalem, and they will not know those things which belong to peace : ' The way of peace they have not known.'

Under the name and title of Edom we may understand the whole kingdom of Satan ; and Israel, the church of God, stirred up by the ambassadors, the ministers of God, to arise against it in battle.

For this is our life called a warfare, because we fight against Satan, the professed enemy of the church, and against all his forces ; both his outward forces in the world, and his inward forces, *corpus peccati*, the body of sin.

The holy apostle Saint Paul, knowing the danger of the elect, doth not only awake us to fight, and giveth us his own example, ' So fighting, not as one that beateth the air,' but he prescribeth to us a fit armour, and teacheth us how to put it on, that we may be able to defend ourselves, and to resist Satan, Eph. vi. 19, &c.

This is no power of our own, but our strength in the Lord, and in the power of his might.

3. To come nearer home. As God told Rebekah when Jacob and Esau were yet in her womb there striving, There be two nations in thy womb ; so Saint Paul will tell you that there is in every regenerate man two opposite forces, the flesh and the spirit, and these strive. The spirit hath God put into us to rule; 'the flesh rebelleth against the spirit.' ' Therefore to will is present with us, but we are not able to do the good that we would ; ' yea, he confesseth that he cannot do the good that he would, and that he doeth the evil that he would not. The Spirit of God is God's ambassador, calling upon our spirits to arise against the flesh in battle ; and that is the true use of all doctrines of mortification, and of godly life, to strengthen the spirit against the flesh, to weaken the power of the body of sin. And for this Saint Paul did bring his body in subjection ; for such is the nature of this fight, that the more we resist our natural and sensual desires, the more we advance the force of our spirits against our flesh.

And it is a most glorious conquest for any servant of God to overcome himself.

Ver. 2. *Behold, I have made thee small among the heathen: thou art greatly despised.*

2. The effect of this judgment.

(1.) From God, 'I have made thee small,' &c.

(2.) From God and man, 'Thou art greatly despised.'

(1.) From God. Three circumstances aggravate the judgment.

[1.] Edom is made small.

[2.] Made small among the nations.

[3.] I have done it.

(2.) From God and man. Two circumstances.

[1.] Thou art despised.

[2.] Thou art despised greatly.

Before I handle these parts, two things offer themselves to consideration, which make easy way unto the understanding of the prophecy.

1. The preface to this prophecy, *Behold*.

2. The phrase thereof.

1. The preface. *Behold*.

Whereby he openeth the eyes of the Idumeans, to look into their future state. It is a word much used in holy Scripture, and ever maketh way to some worthy and considerable matter. Here the Lord would have the Idumeans take notice of the judgment and wrath to come; not that they should repent them of their sins and turn to God, for God hated them, and set his face against them, and they had hearts that they could not repent; but hence we learn,

Doct. It is God's manner to give warning of his judgments, even to those who will not take warning, that they may be without excuse; and Ezekiel must prophesy to those that will not receive him: chap. ii. 7, 'And thou shalt speak my words unto them, whether they will hear, or whether they will forbear, for they are most rebellious.' He giveth a reason before: 'Yet they shall know that there hath been a prophet amongst them.'

Use. God will have the ungodly know that he hath tendered to them the means of escape from his judgments by the ministry of his word, that they may have nothing to plead for themselves in the day of judgment, that they may see and perceive and confess that their perdition cometh from themselves.

From whence we conclude, that to the reprobate all the means of grace are altogether ineffectual to salvation. The light that is in them is darkness; their knowledge swelleth them, their faith is presumption, their fear is despair, their joy is carnal, their hope temporal: Tit. i. 15, 'Their mind and conscience is defiled, abominable, and disobedient, and to every good work reprobate.'

Of this justice of God against the reprobate I can give no other account than that which the apostle doth yield: Rom. ix. 18, 'He hath compassion on whom he will, and whom he will he hardeneth.' Or if we would hear the same from the Son of God himself: Mat. xiii. 11, 'To them it is not given'; and, chap. xi. 26, 'Even so, O Father, because thy good pleasure was such.'

So he saith *Behold* to them whose eyes in his justice he hath shut; and he saith *Hear* to such whose ears in justice he hath stopped; and he giveth warning of his judgments to them whom he hateth, as in my text.

'O Lord, how unsearchable are thy judgments, and thy ways past finding out!'

Use. Therefore let them use their eyes that can see, and let them hear that can hear, and let them take notice of the judgment and wrath to come.

The elect of God shall find many impediments, and shall feel a great reluctation of the flesh against the spirit; let not such be faint-hearted, but let them so fight, not as they that beat the air, and let them so run that they may obtain.

2. The phrase of this prophecy of judgment is, 'I have made thee small, thou art greatly despised;' for God saith that is done already which yet is not executed.

But consider the ground laid in the beginning, 'Thus saith the Lord.'

The Lord, to whom all time is present, and whose decrees give present resolution of all things, though he suspend the execution thereof.

But it was not long before this commination was fulfilled upon Edom: 'I hated Esau, and laid his mountains and his heritage waste for the dragons of the wilderness. Whereas Edom saith, We are impoverished, but we will return and build the desolate places. Thus saith the Lord of hosts, They shall build, but I will throw down; and they shall call them the border of wickedness, and the people against whom God shall have indignation for ever.'

Concerning the fulfilling of this prophecy, it was long ere it was perfectly accomplished; for this was the work of sundry nations, to effect the judgment here denounced. For first they were wasted by the Chaldeans, and carried into captivity; yet it is clear that they returned many of them back again: then was it fulfilled that is spoken before: 'An ambassador is sent amongst the heathen, Arise ye,' for first the heathen arise. Then in the time of the Maccabees* Judas fought against the children of Esau in Idumea, at Arabatine, because they besieged Israel, and he gave them a great overthrow, and abated their courage and took their spoils. And again, after this, the Idumeans having gotten into their hands the most commodious holds, &c.: 'Then they that were with Maccabeus made supplication, and besought God that he would be their helper, and so they run with violence upon the strongholds of the Idumeans; and assaulting them strongly, they won the holds, and kept off all that fought upon the wall, and killed no fewer than twenty thousand.'† There was an escape then of nine thousand, who had taken a strong castle; these many of them by corruption of money made an escape, which cost the blood of more than twenty thousand; and so was fulfilled that other part of this prophecy, 'We also will arise against her in battle.'

Yet did not the Idumeans sink, for they recovered strength, and did vex the city Jerusalem,‡ and came

* 1 Mac. v. 3.
† 2 Mac. x. 15, 16.
‡ Josephus de Bello Jud. lib. iv. c. vi.

against it with a great army, being by letters, and by a set oration of one called Jesus, entreated first to help their brethren the Jews, then to lay down arms, and not to fight against them. They brake into Jerusalem in the night with fury of war, and he saith,* *Templum redundavit sanguine. Octo millia et quingentos mortuos dies invenit; duodecim millia nobilium periere ab Idumæa trucidata,* after the destruction of Jerusalem† and the dispersion of the Jews that remained of that cruel massacre, wherein the conqueror left no cruelty undone. He saith,‡ *Horum furoris æmuli etiam Idumæi fuere: illi enim sceleratissimi peremptis pontificibus, ne qua pars conservaretur pietatis in Deum, totum quod ex civitatis facie supererat abscidere.*

Thus the Jews that remained after all these bloody wars were dispersed, and do yet continue in dispersion, but with promise of being recalled before the end of the world; but the Edomites are now perished from the face of the earth; no mention of their names is left in the world, no promise of their restitution; so that this prophecy is at last fulfilled, and hath been many years accomplished. So long was it before the performance hereof, and judgment began at God's house, yet in the end it was executed in their final ruin upon the earth.

This text calleth all this done, for no length of time could evacuate the truth of God herein; which teacheth us to look assuredly for all these things which God hath said shall come to pass, especially the fall of antichrist, the calling of the Jews, the resurrection of the dead, the last judgment, and everlasting life.

Let us come now to the parts of this text.

1. The effects of this judgment from God.

(1.) Edom must be made small.

Edom or Esau, though he lost the first blessing after he had sold his birthright, yet he obtained a blessing of his father: Gen. xxvii. 39, 40, 'Behold, thy dwelling shall be the fatness of the earth, and of the dew of heaven from above; and by thy sword thou shalt live, and shalt serve thy brother; and it shall

---

* Cap. vii.   † Lib. v. c. i.   ‡ Lib. vii. c. **xxviii.**

come to pass, when thou shalt have the dominion, that thou shalt break his yoke from off thy neck.' This blessing was a prophecy of the greatness of Edom, whose increase was such that Moses doth rehearse that he was fain to depart from his brother Jacob, and dwell in Seir: Gen. xxxvi. 7, 'For their riches were more than that they could dwell together; and the land wherein they were strangers could not bear them because of their cattle.' Verse 31, 'They had many dukes and kings of Edom, before there reigned any king over the children of Israel.' So that in greatness they outstripped Jacob. This greatness continued seven hundred years after the prophecy of Isaac till Daniel's * time. 2 Sam. viii. 15, 'And he put garrisons in Edom: throughout all Edom put he garrisons; and all they of Edom became David's servants.' There God made them small.

Again, 2 Kings xiv. 7, 'Amaziah, king of Judah, prevailed against them: he slew of Edom in the valley of salt ten thousand, and took Selah by war.' This made them small.

They suffered many changes, yet this is noted of them, that,

1. They were grown often very great, yet still God made them small.

2. That they were great before Jacob, and continued so after Jacob's posterity were gone into dispersion.

3. That now their memory is so extinguished on earth, that their posterity is not known.

Let no man measure the favours of God by the access of his possession, by the territories of his dominion, by the multitude of his men, by the force of his strength. God gave all these things to Esau, whom he hated.

Rather let men fortunate and prosperous in their ways, who have the desires of their hearts satisfied, and whose hearts be anointed with butter, suspect that God hath set them in slippery places, *Vivunt inter laqueos.* Let them know that their fulness doth come of God's open hand, *aperit et implet;* and let them know that the Lord giveth, and the Lord taketh away,

* Qu. ' David's '?—ED.

and therefore let them take out Saint Paul's lessons: 'I have learned how to abound, and how to want.'

We are not to seek in our own times of examples of smallness turned into greatness, and of greatness again made small.

It is a judgment that David complained of: 'Thou hast lifted me up, and cast me down.' How much more peace have they in their bosoms, that were ever small, than they who have risen above others, are stooped beneath themselves, and laid so low that the foot of pride treadeth on them. Down, stout heart, there is no perpetuity in things temporal. Great Edom is made small; rough and boisterous Edom, that carries all by strong hand, is made meek and tame.

(2.) Made small amongst the heathen.

These were numbered among the heathen, and amongst them they were great. They separated from the church of God, like the sons of sober and religious parents that turn gallants and roarers; and amongst these they shine a while. Amongst these Edom was made small.

Abraham had an Ishmael that was cast out among the heathen.

Isaac had an Esau that put himself in amongst them; all the sons of Jacob were patriarchs, great fathers of the church.

Esau, where he rose to glory and greatness, there he sunk into smallness; the eyes that saw him in his shining saw him eclipsed.

(3.) God hath done this; there be few that look so high when they are down, but they do rather complain of evil fortune, or of some great wrong done to them here below, failing of means, desertion of friends, or injustice in superiors. The heathen look to second causes, and to natural agents; they consider not that it is God who lifteth up and casteth down. But God taketh it upon himself, and would have Edom know that this is *dextra Jehovæ*, the right hand of the Lord. Others look high at first, and upon every degree of downfall do charge God with hard measure, and murmur at his uneven hand, as if he had not done them right, which, as Job saith, is to 'charge God foolishly.'

But let men take it how they will, God is the author of the rising and falling of the sons of men, of their growth and withering. Can God hate, and his hatred sit idle and look on? As his love is operative, so is his hatred. Such is his love, that all things work together for the best to them whom he hath called. Saint Augustine addeth, *etiam peccata,* even their sins; another, *etiam adversa,* their adversary;* and such is his hatred, that all things work contrary, to the ruin, of them whom he hateth; *etiam prosperitas,* even their prosperity, for 'the prosperity of fools doth destroy them.'

2. This judgment is aggravated by two circumstances from God and man:

(1.) Thou art despised.

(2.) Greatly despised.

(1.) Despised.

The children of Edom had two great temptations to swell them, that is, riches and power; these they insolently abused to oppression of their neighbours. God, who 'poureth contempt upon princes,' covered them with contempt. This is the severest vengeance that pride feareth. Edom, that was highest, and bore rule over the nations, and lived by the sword, is now made small. After this fall followeth contempt.

God hath said it, 'They that despise me shall be despised.'

(2.) Despised greatly.

Pride will have a fall; it never falleth lower here on earth than when it falleth into great contempt.

1. Of God, that he turneth away from them, or setteth his face against them.

2. Of man, and that,

(1.) When the prophets of the Lord do set their faces against them, as in this case, Ezek. xxxv. 2, 'Son of man, set thy face against mount Seir, and prophesy against it.' It is no small matter to have the messengers of God against us, which do carry his sure word of prophecy; for they speak from the mouth of the Lord, and where they denounce the judgment of God against impenitent sinners, 'Whosoever's sins they retain, they are retained.'

* Qu. 'adversity'?—ED.

(2.) When the Lord hath expressed his hatred, and pronounced his judgment, the church of God despiseth their power, and derideth their malice, saying, 'Thou, O God, seest it; for thou beholdest ungodliness and wrong, to take the matter into thy hand.'

3. This maketh it a great and full contempt, when they that served them shall be lords over them, and their sword can no longer help them; so is Edom despised among the heathen. This is great contempt, to have the contempt of God and man. You see their punishment.

These points of doctrine do follow by just consequence.

1. That God's enemies, though for a time they prosper and thrive in the world, yet they shall by little be at last consumed.

The whole course of holy story runneth very clear this way: Cain, a runagate, and, many learned do think, after killed by Lamech; Ishmael, every man's sword against him; Pharaoh, drowned in the Red Sea, Exod. xiv. 28; Sennacherib, slain by his own sons, 2 Kings xx. 37; Haman, hanged on his own gallows, Esther iv. 9, which the poet calls *arte perire suâ;* Nebuchadnezzar turned beast, Dan. iv. 30; the Jews have Christ's blood on them and their children; Herod, eaten with worms, Acts xii. 23; Judas went to his own place.

But in the execution of judgment, God doth not all at once always.

Moses telleth Israel, Deut. vii. 21, 'God will root out these nations before thee by little and little: thou must not consume them at once.'

As Amos prophesieth, chap. iv. 9, blasting and mildew, then the palmer-worm, then the pestilence, then the sword, and at last as Sodom and Gomorrah. So he destroyed Egypt with ten plagues, one succeeding another. He doth not empty his quiver all at once; so here are two points considerable.

1. He doth destroy them.
2. Not all at once, but by little and little.
1. The reason why he doth destroy them: 2 Thess.

i. 6, 7, 'It is a righteous thing with God to render tribulation to them that trouble you.'

2. 'When he maketh inquisition for blood, he remembereth the complaint of the poor. His mercy endureth for ever,' Ps. cxxxvi. 13.

3. The enemies of the church are God's enemies. *Exurgat Deus et dissipentur inimici sui,* 'Let God arise, and let his enemies be scattered.' 'Out of the mouth of babes and sucklings hast thou ordained strength, because of thine enemies, that thou mayest still the enemy and avenger.'

The use. 1. It teacheth us to exercise our patience in all afflictions, as Christ saith, 'Fear not them that can kill the body,' &c. 'Patience bringeth forth experience, and experience hope,' Rom. v. 3. 'Here is the patience of the saints,' Rev. xiv. 12.

Use 2. It stoppeth any course of revenge that we may think upon; that is God's title.

'O Lord God the avenger, O God the avenger, shew thyself clearly,' Ps. xciv. 1. 'Dearly beloved, avenge not yourselves,' Rom. xii. 19.

Use 3. It ministereth matter of joy to the church, and of thanksgiving to God, when the ungodly fall. The feast of *Purim* was kept with joy for the fall of Haman and the delivery of the church, Esther ix. 17. There is great joy at the fall of Babylon.

Use 4. This ministereth matter of terror to the ungodly, to hear that the Lord Jesus cometh with thousands of his angels. He will render vengeance unto them with flaming fire, and punish them with everlasting perdition from the presence of the Lord, and from the glory of his power, Rev. xix., 2 Thes. i. 6–8. Isa. viii. 9, 10, 'Gather together on heaps, O ye people, and ye shall be broken in pieces; hearken, all ye of far countries, gird yourselves, and ye shall be broken in pieces; take counsel together, yet shall it be brought to nought; pronounce a decree, yet shall it not stand; for God is with us.' Judges v. 31, 'So let all thine enemies perish, O Lord; but they that love him shall be as the sun when he riseth in his might.'

2. But this is not done all at once; God doth judge the wicked by little and little ofttimes. The reason is,

(1.) In respect of the wicked themselves, that they might finish their unrighteousness: 'Suffer ye the tares to grow till the harvest.' When the harvest is yellow, then he putteth in the sickle; and tarrieth, as David saith, till their abominable wickedness be found worthy to be punished.

(2.) In respect of his church, that he may exercise the patience of his saints. Prov. xxiv. 10, 'If thou faint in the day of adversity, thy strength is small.' Therefore God said he would not cast out before Israel any of the nations that Joshua left, 'that through them he might prove Israel, whether they will keep the way of the Lord to walk therein or not,' Judges ii. 20.

(3.) In respect of himself, for the glory of his justice; for his justice is not speedily executed upon them that do evil. All the world shall see that God hath awaited the repentance of the wicked, and given them time for it; and because they will not repent, 'he doth whet his sword, and he prepareth instruments of death.'

Use. This teacheth us to tarry the Lord's leisure. The sons of thunder were too quick with Christ, to offer to pray to God for fire from heaven to consume the Samaritans. This is our common fault when any one offendeth us, that we straight fall to cursing, wishing the pox and the plague, the vengeance and curse of God upon them. If our fury had the managing of God's vengeance, who should live? Take heed of provoking the patience of God: that justice that thou dost awake by thy curses, owes thee a punishment for thy impatience and uncharitableness.

2. We are taught that the reward of pride is fall and contempt. So David saith, 'Thou wilt bring down high looks:' no sooner doth God make the great ones of the world small, but they are greatly despised.

It needs no proof, where examples of great falls do fall so thick as they have done on this side the Alps within these few years. Never ran the stream and current of suitors more strong to rising, and growing, and grown greatness, than it ran away from the fall thereof, and sought another channel. And they that flattered these in their spring, and tendered them service, and made them their gods in their fair weather, in their fall of leaf forsake them, and then humble petitions turn to scornful libels.

I may say of our times truly, as Hecuba,*

> Non unquam tulit
> Documenta fors majora, quam fragili loco starent superbi.

Thus men lay by the walls the ladders that they climb by, and like those people of whom Boemus writeth, they bless the rising, but curse the setting sun. Every man seeks the face of the ruler; so again, low hedges are trodden on.

This is the language of this prophecy, and Edom is one example hereof. This point is thoroughly pressed afterwards. Therefore 'let him that thinketh he standeth, take heed lest he fall.'

There is a natural evil eye, which beholdeth the prosperity of rising men with much envy; that eye is glad of the fall of great ones; observe the text, how soon it follows, ' I have made thee small; thou art greatly despised.' So soon doth contempt follow after a fall.

Let Edom be Satan, and let God bind him in chains, and give us faith to resist and overcome him; how do we despise him and scorn him disarmed! Let the world be Edom, and let God declare the vanity and casualty that is in all these things that Satan tempteth men withal, and we shall see the servants of God will despise it, and use it as though they used it not. Let a man's own corruptions be the Edom, the lusts of the flesh that fight against the soul, that make a man forget his piety to God, his charity to his brother; but let God by his word reveal to us the body of sin, and by his law humble us under the mighty hand of God: we shall despise and contemn the desires of our heart, and we shall say, ' I will go and return to my first love, for then I was better than now.'

This making small is ruin to the ungodly; it is medicine to the just; the narrow gate that leadeth to

---

* Sen. Troas.

life is easily entered by them whom God hath made small in their own eyes and estimation of themselves.

Christ made himself of no reputation, not only *ad sacrificium*, to a sacrifice, but *ad exemplum*, to an example, that we might walk as he walked.

Small threads will pass through a needle's eye, great cables are too big. God resisteth the proud. A small womb containeth us; a small tomb burieth us; and never doth the favour of God shine more on us, or the attending service of angels more minister unto us, than when the world despiseth our low growth, and our contentment with our daily bread. There is much difference between those that be *humiles*, humble, and those that be *humiliati*, humbled; and between those that be *humiliati ad vindictam*, humbled to punishment, and those that be *humiliati ad medicinam*, humbled to medicine.

This prophecy is full for it, that ' God resisteth the proud,' and pride shall have a fall; and after the fall followeth contempt.

And what reward have they of all those things? ' The pride of thy heart hath deceived thee, thou that dwellest in the clefts of the rock, whose habitation is high, that saith in his heart, Who shall bring me down to the ground? Though thou exalt thyself as an eagle, and though thou set thy nest among the stars, thence will I bring thee down, saith the Lord.'

2. Now he foretelleth how all the hopes of the children of Edom are dispersed.

1. They had hope in their own pride, ver. 3.
2. In the safety of their situation, ver. 3–6.
3. In the strength and assurance of their confederates, ver. 7.
4. In the wisdom, ver. 8.
5. In the strength, of their own men, ver. 9.

For the first, ' The pride of thy heart hath deceived thee.' Thou didst think better of thyself than there was cause. Self-opinion is the bane of all virtue; for by it men become their own flatterers, and build castles in the air. It is *tumor cordis*, the swelling of the heart; this is of the world, and one of that cursed trinity which undoes the world, 'the lust of the flesh, the lust of the eye, and the pride of life,' 1 John ii. 16.

The cunning serpent breathed this poison in our first parents; for when Eve heard him say, *Similes eritis Deo*, you shall be like unto God, she soon ate of the forbidden fruit, and gave of the same to Adam. Pride swelleth the heart, that it is not capable of grace; it filleth it full of itself, and leaveth no room for Christ in that inn. Therefore one saith to a proud man, *Deus præsto est largiri sapientiam, sed tu non habes ubi eam recipias.* Pride is contrary to humility, for humility is not only virtue, but *vas virtutum*, the receptacle of virtue. 'God giveth grace to the humble;' but pride, like the woman that had filled all her vessels with oil, and at last *vas defuit*, there wanted a vessel, it so filleth the heart with the oil of self-flattery, that there is no room left, no vessel to receive any grace. It filleth the firkins up to the brim. Whatsoever good parts are in a man or woman, pride spoils all, and turns them into vice, as one long ago truly and facetely rhymed,

> Si tibi gratia, si sapientia, formaque detur,
> Inquinat omnia sola superbia, si comitetur:

This is esteemed the queen of vices, 'Woe to the crown of pride,' Isa. lxxxii. 1. It is one of the late repentances of the damned, beholding the happiness of the just, and feeling the misery of their damnation. What hath our pride profited us? or what good hath riches with our vaunting brought us?*

Satan is called a prince ruling in the air, the god of this world, and that leviathan who is a king over all the children of pride. This vice opposeth God, and transgresseth and trespasseth the majesty of God; it began to all the other sins, it infected glorious angels, and turned them into devils.

One observeth that pride is no recusant; it will come to church. A man that lives in the light of religion, and hath any moral goodness in him, will lay down his covetousness, gluttony, luxury, idleness,

* Wisd. v.

envy, anger, for service time ; but the proud person
will bring pride to church along with him : ' Two men
went up to the temple to pray, one a proud pharisee.'
Pride mingleth itself with our best actions, and
claimeth share with God in many of our good works.
It also filleth us with contempt of our neighbour,
' not as that publican,' *non ut alii*, not as other men.
Edom lived by his sword, and awed men with his
power, and this did fill his heart with pride.

Riches unsanctified make men proud ; so Jack becomes a gentleman, and mechanicals find some false
pedigrees to enable them, or purchase places of eminency, to put them before their betters. Power unsanctified makes men boisterous, and heavy to the
poor.

Learning unsanctified, and the very knowledge of
religion, doth breed pride; and that maketh contention,
for pride is the root of schism and heresy.

This turns faith into presumption in some professors
of religion, but it turneth it into contention in others;
in others into separation ; in the profane, it breedeth
contempt of God and of his word.

Wisdom, knowledge, honour, riches, power with
humility, no pride to corrupt them, they are the ornaments of life, and the faculties of virtue, and the factors of grace, and the fear of God. It is a good saying of Hugo de Sancto Victore, *Superbia mihi Deum
aufert, invidia proximum, ira meipsum;* pride depriveth me of God, envy of my neighbour, anger of
myself.

Behold his soul, which is lifted or puffed up in him,
is not upright in him ; ' but the just shall live by
faith,' Hab. ii. 4.

Pride in the wicked taketh room and place of faith ;
for as faith in the elect doth lay hold on all the gracious promises of God which do concern this life and
a better, so pride in the wicked maketh them believe
that they are worthy of all favours of the time, and of
all temporal graces ; therefore the prophet setteth
them in opposition. Therefore God beginneth to tax
this people of their pride, teaching us that pride is
abominable to God. Here we are compassed with a

cloud of witnesses : it was pride that cast down the angels, that deceived Eve, that made Cain a murderer, Lamech a boaster, Nimrod a hunter, Ishmael a scorner, Edom an oppressor, &c. And the pharisee, that could put off the aspersion of other sins, extortion, injustice, adultery, he could not add pride ; of this every one hath a share. Diogenes wanted not his part, as Plato taxed him most justly, for it is so insinuating a vice as that they which labour most to express humility cannot but take some pride, even in that.

This pride of Edom deceived Edom. Faith buildeth upon a rock ; no storm can shake it ; it is fortified by the prayer of Christ: ' I have prayed that thy faith may not fail.' Pride buildeth on sand ; the foundation is false ; every wash and wave that beats on it shakes it and ruins it.

There is no creature that comes into the world more naked and more disarmed than man doth, yet none so proud, and therefore none so promising to itself as man is ; for as one saith, *Colligit de vite spinas, pro uvis tribulos*, for out of the good blessings of God he maketh matter of self-opinion and false glory.

This is a monstrous birth, *ex bono malum*. *Lumen quod in te est tenebræ sunt :* when thou thinkest thyself more happy than others, and goest in this transport far, at last thou seest that thou hast been thine own impostor.

It is a good saying of Saint Gregory, that he that boasteth, and is proud of any of God's gifts, *se interficit medicamine*, the medicine that should heal kills him. That which all this while supported the glory of Edom, which was Edom's pride, proves Edom's ruin ; it hath deceived him.

The doctrines of the church of Rome do maintain this pride of the heart, therefore they are deceitful; for,

1. They say we have free will to do good.

2. They teach that a man in this life may fulfil the whole law of God.

3. They teach that a man may be justified before God by the merit of his works.

4. That a man may overdo the law, and do works of supererogation, which may increase the treasure

of the church, and may help out them that come short in good works, by mending their store.

All these doctrines seem to maintain the pride of the heart, and to give flesh wherein to rejoice, against which we oppose the doctrines of humility.

5. That the sacraments do confer grace *ex opere operato*, and therefore whosoever is made partaker of them hath the grace whereof they be seals.

First, So in baptism; they affirm that original sin is quite done away, so that infants baptized are certainly saved; and such as depart the world without baptism are separated from the sight of God.

Whosoever receiveth their sacrament of the altar doth verily, and really, and carnally feed on the same body of Jesus Christ that was born of the Virgin Mary, and suffered death upon the cross.

Secondly, Neither do they only attribute this virtue to the sacraments which Christ ordained in his church, but unto those five which they have since added and equibalanced with the holy ordinances of God.

(1.) For their sacrament of penance. They hold that the grace of baptism may be finally lost; and so, to recover man again from that downfall, they have devised this sacrament. This is Trent divinity, Sess. xiv. cap. 1. *Si in regeneratis omnibus gratitudo erga Deum esset, ut justitiam in baptismo ipsius gratia et beneficio susceptam tuerentur, non fuisset opus aliud sacramentum instituere.* But because this serves not, penance doth come in; for how else should they bring in their auricular confession, by which they dive into men's hearts, and their imposed power, by which they dive into men's purses, for satisfaction? And this concludes with *Ego te absolvo*, I absolve thee; which doth wash them as clean from all sins past, as if they had never sinned.

(2.) For the sacrament of marriage. They do that but a little honour, save only in belying it to be a sacrament, and pronouncing *anathema* to all that do deny it to be a sacrament ordained by God himself in paradise.

First, But neither do they make it the means to convey any spiritual grace, which is the chief use of a sacrament, but only make it a bare sign of the conjunction between Christ and his church.

Secondly, Neither do they leave it at large for all persons, but curse those that allow it to priests.

Thirdly, Neither do they honour the state of matrimony with equal honour to virginity, but pronounce *anathema* to them that prefer it before virginity.

(3.) For the sacrament of orders; they make the priest some amends, for therein he hath a sacrament which the lay partake not in. To this they attribute the power of absolution, the power of binding, the power of turning bread into the body of Christ, the power of conferring grace.

(4.) For confirmation. That is another help to baptism, to relieve the imperfection of Christ's ordinance, *novam gratiam tribuit.*

(5.) For extreme unction. As the sacrament of baptism is *sacramentum introeuntium*, the sacrament of entrance, so this is *sacramentum exeuntium*, of going out. This makes *expeditiorem ad cœlum viam*, a quick way to heaven, and is to be administered *in articulo mortis*, the point of death, and it carries the soul to heaven directly.

May we not behold the pride of the church of Rome in all these, how they have taken to their own hands the keys of David? They open, and no man shutteth; they shut, and no man openeth. It is in the power of the priest to give, it is in the power of the people to take salvation, and I do not see any great need of Jesus Christ in these doctrines; neither can I find that they have left him any absolute, but only given him a dependent, power over them, that he cannot save without them. Surely all this pride deceiveth them that put trust therein, for,

1. Against free will we oppose 1 Cor. xv. 12, 'In Adam we all die, in Christ made alive;' and that this stretcheth to a corporal, spiritual, and eternal death, hear the same apostle: Eph. ii. 2, 'We are by nature children of wrath.' Saint Paul was a vessel of election, he had the Spirit of God, he received the office

of his apostleship immediately from God, yet he saith: Rom. vii. 15, 'The good that I would do, I do not; the evil that I would not do, I do.' Whence is then this free will?

2. Against the fulfilling of the law of God in this life: Eccles. vii. 20, 'There is not a just man upon earth, who doeth good and sinneth not;' and James iii. 2, 'He that breaketh the least of the commandments is guilty of all;' that is, he is found a transgressor, *legis*, of the law; but *in multis offendimus omnes*, in many things we all offend, *justus cadit septies*, Prov. xxiv. 16.

3. Against merit of works Christ saith, Luke xvii. 7, &c., 'They that have done all that is commanded, have done but their duty;' *servi inutiles*, unprofitable servants.

And what proportion is there, *finiti ad infinitum*, of the finite to the infinite? The works of men be finite, the glory of God is infinite: Isa. lxiv. 6, 'All our righteousness is like defiled cloths.'

4. Against supererogation, that pride deceiveth them, for there is nothing to be done in obedience, or in love to God, which is not commanded in his law, that requireth all the soul, and all the mind, and all the strength of both these. He that can find anything more to do, and can do it, may supererogate.

5. Concerning their sacraments, they dishonour baptism, and make it of no account, when they teach that the grace of baptism may be lost, and devise three sacraments to help it, confirmation to strengthen it, penance to renew it, extreme unction to perfect it.

We acknowledge God powerful in his own ordinance; we hold that the grace given to the elect in baptism is sealed and imprinted an indelible character.

Confirmation is no more but a watering of the plants which the ordinance of God hath graffed. Penance is no more but a stirring up of the grace given in baptism; extreme unction is of no necessity, it was a temporal practice in those times when the gift of healing was in the church, instead whereof we have prayers both in private and in public congregations. The grace of baptism we hold sufficient for the whole life to sanctify it, and in the elect of God it is not, it cannot be, lost.

The true sacrament of confirmation is the Lord's supper, for that representeth to us the body that was broken for us, and the blood that cleanseth us from all our sins. That is often repeated, to call us to repentance, and to strengthen our faith. If we flatter ourselves that the act of receiving doth sanctify us, that is a deceiving of our own hearts; for 'the flesh profiteth nothing, it is the Spirit that quickeneth.' We know that it may be eaten to condemnation; if there were carnal presence of Christ, none could eat of it but he must be joined so with Christ as he could not perish.

Lastly, for the sacrament of orders, they deceive themselves in the pride of their hearts, thinking that God hath given them the kingdom of grace and of glory, to bestow where they will. We are the ministers of God, sent forth as God's ambassadors, to carry his pardon to such as are penitent. The pardon doth set forth who are capable of it; we are the ministers of God, to make tender of the means of grace to such as are capable of them. We cannot make a man capable either of grace or salvation, yet none can have either but by our ministry, except God will shew his prerogative and say, *Ecce ego creabo rem novam in terra*, 'Behold I create a new thing upon earth.'

Humility deals truly with us; for if I be humble, I am content with that I have, and think it more than I deserve. I do not envy either greater graces in others, or higher places, for I know mine own wickedness, and 'my sins are ever before me;' and therefore I think it happy with me, and acknowledge it a great mercy that I am not consumed. I do not glory in mine own knowledge, but with Agur the son of Jakeh, Prov. xxx. 2, 3, I say and confess, ' Surely I am more brutish than any man, and have not the understanding of a man: I have neither learned wisdom, nor have the knowledge of the holy.' I do not glory in mine own righteousness, but looking to my heart within, and into my ways without, I say with Saint Paul, 'Of sinners I am chief.'

An humble man hath this advantage of a proud man, for he cannot fall; his estate may grow both higher and fuller, but his heart keepeth one point of elevation, and is fixed at that; he never graspeth for wind to hold it; he hunteth not after opinion; he doth not flatter himself with vain hopes. Well may an humble man suffer from others, but he will keep so good a watch upon his own heart, that that shall never deceive him by any information of self-wisdom.

But I commend a virtue that but half keeps a living man in the earth, saith the gallant. True, but as the root is deep embosomed in the earth, which makes a tree bear a storm the better.

But this keepeth men from putting forth themselves where they may exercise their other virtues. Ay, but it joyeth all well affected, that church and commonwealth aboundeth so in choice that there is no need of me. And those whom pride putteth forth have an evil edition.

2. Their next confidence was in the situation of their dwelling, resembled to an eagle's building her nest in the clefts of a rock on high; so there meets to make up their confidence, strength and height of dwelling.

That is their confidence, and that is dispersed in the fourth verse, 'Thence will I bring thee down, saith the Lord.'

This opinion of the strength of an impregnable habitation hath deceived many. After David had reigned seven years in Hebron, 2 Sam. v. 6, 'The king and his men went to Jerusalem to the Jebusites, the inhabitants of the land, which spake unto David, saying, Except thou take away the blind and the lame, thou shalt not come in hither, thinking David cannot come hither.'

The Hebrews have made a figurative construction of these words, namely, that the Jebusites did preserve two images, the one of Isaac, who was blind, the other of Jacob, who was lame; these two, Isaac and Jacob, made a covenant with Abimelech, in which league they comprehended the Jebusites; therefore the league must be broken which was made with Isaac and Jacob if they did come thither to remove the Jebusites. But this is vain and fabulous. The true meaning is, that the Jebusites did think their hold so strong that so long as there were any men therein (though blind and lame), they would be able to defend the place against David. But that hope was despaired, for, ver. 9, 'David dwelt in that fort, and called it the city of David,' &c.

The like example we have of Babylon. Hear her in her ruff and in the pride of her heart: Isa. xiv. 13, 'Thou hast said in thy heart, I will ascend into heaven, I will exalt my throne among the stars of God : I will sit also upon the mount of the congregation, in the sides of the north : I will ascend above the heights of the clouds : I will be like the Most High.' Which pride of heart smarteth in them, for it followeth, 'Yet thou shalt be brought down to hell, to the sides of the pit.'

I deny not but this is literally to be understood of Babylon; but it troubleth me that any learned man of our days* should charge so many great judgments as have applied this to the fall of the angels with unskilful application thereof. I know the learnedst and gravest judgments have gone that way, as far as we have anything written of the fall of angels ; and men of yesterday do not well to impute unskilfulness to such expert scribes. But in the posthumous writings of great learned men, the publisher may shuffle in some of his own bran amongst their wheat.

For understand this either literally of Babylon, or allegorically of the angels that fell, either of them thought their dwellings impregnable, and therefore safe.

Jerusalem, called the joy of the whole earth, was compassed so with mountains, that the prophet, to express the safety of the church, resembleth it to Jerusalem : Ps. cxxv. 2, 'As the mountains are about Jerusalem, so is the Lord round about his people,' &c. 'They that trust in the Lord shall be as mount Sion.' Yet we know how it was destroyed.

David was gone far that way in presuming upon the safety of his person and state: *Dixi, Nunquam movebor*,

* Dr Rainolds on Obad.

'I said I shall not be removed; thou, Lord, of thy goodness hast made my mountain so strong.'

All which examples and all experience meeteth in one point of doctrine, that it is a vain confidence to trust in the strength of our state and dwelling on earth. A full proof of this truth we find in the example of the Philistines' garrison, 1 Sam. xiv. 4, for 'Between the passages by which Jonathan fought to go over to the Philistines' garrisons, there was a sharp rock on the one side, and a sharp rock on the other side. Yet Jonathan climbed up on his hands and on his feet, and his armour-bearer after him, and they fell before Jonathan,' &c.

The reason of this is given by God himself: 'I will bring thee down, saith the Lord.' The Lord taketh on him to bring down high looks, and whosoever be the instrument and means of their overthrow, it is the Lord's doing.

In this very example in my text, God claimeth the glory of Edom's ruin; for the prophet asketh who it is that cometh from Edom, and why his garments be red? Isa. lxiii. 1. It is answered, 'I have trod the wine-press alone, there was not one with me.' Which prophecy looketh two ways, both to the destruction of Edom in the letter, which God assumeth to himself as his own work, and specially to the kingdom of Satan, which Christ in the blood of his passion did alone conquer.

We had a fair example hereof in '88; the invincible armada of Spain, then our enemy, now our reconciled friend, came forth in the strength of ships, and ordnance, and men, and promised themselves the conquest of this land. They said, 'We will rejoice and divide Shechem, and mete out the valley of Succoth.' God gave us victory, and declared that no strength prevaileth against the Lord.

Therefore let no man trust in the strength of his dwelling; we have an island encompassed and moated about with the sea, walled in with sands, and rocks, and shelves, which maketh the passage to us full of dangers, and is a great security to our land, yet have the Romans, the Danes, and the Normans conquered this land. Therefore our trust is not in the strength of our dwellings, but God is our rock. On the cliffs of this rock we dwell safe; so that faith, and not presumption, do build our nest. To him if we address our prayers, to him if we give the sacrifices of praise, if to him we perform the duties of obedience, who can harm us? God of his goodness hath made our mountain so strong, that we need not fear what man can do against us.

The trust of Edom was vain, and the vanity thereof is described in the miserable waste that was made therein.

Ver. 5, 6, *If thieves come to thee, if robbers by night (how art thou cut off!), would they not have stolen till they had enough? If the grape-gatherers come to thee, would they not leave thee some grapes? How are the things of Esau searched out! how are his hid things sought up!*

The words do express the full ruin of Edom, for all his strong habitation.

Thieves that rob an house by night do not carry away all, and they that gather grapes nearly, the law requires to leave some clusters for the poor, the fatherless, and the widow, Lev. xix. 10.

But in the sacking of Edom there should be a carrying away of all in sight, and a curious search for all hidden things; there should be nothing left. Neither men nor goods should be concealed, but the eye of search should find them out all. There should neither be a satiety in their enemies nor a compassion, neither fulness nor pity should exempt any from spoil. That maketh the prophet so pathetical, that he interposeth this admiration, How art thou cut off!

In the prophecy of Jeremiah, chap. xlix. 10, it is added for an interpretation of this text, 'I have made Esau bare, I have uncovered his secret places, and he shall not be able to hide himself: his seed is spoiled, and his brethren, and his neighbours, and he is not.'

This is not to be understood so as if the nation and name of Edom should cease for ever upon this vastation, but for a time; for they were again to build, and were again to pluck down, as Malachi prophesied. But in the end there should be nothing left of Edom, his very name should be forgotten upon earth, even as it is at this day; for who can say, This is the seed of Esau?

From hence, 1, we are taught that where God cometh to the spoil there is no secret and close receptacle, either for the persons or for the wealth and treasures of men, but he will search it out and lay it open. Their bellies be full of hid treasure; those bellies will he rip up, and into those secret parts shall his search penetrate; nothing shall be safe from it. As in the fury of the wars of the Jews, we read that some of the Jews, having no other means left to preserve something to relieve their wants, swallowed certain pieces of gold, to keep them from the hand of the enemy, which coming to the ears of the Roman soldiers, they ripped up many of the Jews' bellies to seek for gold.

Edom dwelt in mount Seir amongst the rocks, and many of their dwellings were in rooms hewed out of the hard stone, yet all their secret cabins were searched and spoiled.

Ishbosheth is not safe on his bed, nor Ehud in his parlour. 'Whither shall I fly from his presence?' saith David.

God himself hath spoken to this purpose: Amos ix. 1–4, 'I will slay the last of them with the sword: he that flieth shall not fly away; and he that escapeth of them shall not be delivered. Though they dig into hell, thence shall my hand take them; though they climb up to heaven, thence shall my hand bring them down: and though they hide themselves in the top of Carmel, I will search and take them out thence; and though they may be hid from my sight in the bottom of the sea, or go into captivity, thence will I command the sword, and it shall slay them: and I will set mine eyes upon them for evil, and not for good.'

Those searchers of Edom be of God's sending, and they are his privy search; he will bring to light things hidden in darkness.

Use. Trust not to the secret treasures of ungodliness, not to the goods thou hast laid up for many years to come; there is nothing so secret but shall be laid open. God's search is not like Laban's; he searched all the places but where Rachel sat, but God leaveth no place unsought. If the secret store escape, *fures perfodiunt et furantur*, yet there is *tinea et ærugo*, the moth and the rust; and if nothing else, *tempus edax rerum*, time, the consumer of all things. For so saith the wise man, 'There is a time to gather, and a time to scatter.'

Let us not be too much in love with these things that we possess here. We know that when our Augustus Cæsar began his reign here over us, all neighbouring and remote nations offered him peace, and he accepted it, and turned all our swords into sighs.* I need not speak figuratively. Much armour was turned into utensils for domestical uses, and then there was no noise abroad of hostility. Even then, in the peaceful time of the church and commonwealth, the religion of Rome stirred up certain searchers, that digged into the bowels of the earth, and their hunger after protestant blood brake through strong walls, and there heaped up such instruments of massacre as would have searched our hidden things. Those thieves would never have had enough, those grape-gatherers would have left never a cluster to relieve the poor church; they would have rooted up vine and all, and have laid the vineyard of the Lord of hosts desert and waste. These were papists, the ministers of hell; this was religion, falsely so called, the zeal of furies. Such thieves lurk in many several corners of the land, such grape-gatherers hide themselves under the shade of our vine. Let all that love the peace of Jerusalem take heed of them; our houses, closets, nay, our cellars, are not safe from them; they will seek out our hidden things if they can take advantage against

* Qu. 'scythes'?—ED.

us. Against this Edom let us bend our forces, and the idolatry, and superstition, and ignorance, and imposture of that religion let us search out and detect.

It is his majesty's express command, that in every parish the sworn men do search for recusants, that forsake all our churches, and for our own malcontent professors, that love any church better than their own. He would separate the clean from the vile, and the peaceable from the factious, Edom from Israel; for we hold nothing in safety, we can hide nothing out of sight, so long as those searchers and underminers be abroad; the peace and honour and safety of the church is their prey they hunt after.

2. We are taught what a fearful thing it is to fall into the hands of the living God; when he plucketh his hand out of his bosom, he smiteth home, as he saith, 'Affliction shall not arise a second time;' he calleth himself in his law 'a jealous God,' his jealousy burns like fire.

He can give Edom high and strong mountains for his habitation; he can give him the fat of the earth, and the dew of heaven, and let him multiply on the earth exceedingly; he can forbear him in his wickedness and cruelty for a long time. But when he cometh to execute judgment, his right hand will find out all his enemies, he will not leave a place or corner unsearched, but he 'will cut off head and tail, branch and root, in one day, for his hand is not shortened, but is stretched out still.'

Why, then, doth the pride of our hearts deceive us, flattering us that all shall be well with us, though we walk in the lusts of our own hearts; though pride disguise us in our clothing, though gluttony fill us up to the throats, though drunkenness stagger us, and our oaths and blasphemies fly up as high as heaven. Hath God forgotten to be righteous, and is his judgment-seat turned all to mercy, that we dare him with our crying sins, and awake his vengeance with our abominable impieties? Can we sin the sins of Edom, and not smart with their punishment? He hath a curious and searching eye, he hath looked upon our works, he hath set our sins before him, our secret sins in the sight of his countenance.

First, his eye searcheth out the sins of men, then his right hand searcheth out all his enemies; 'If he be angry, yea, but a little, blessed are all they that put their trust in him.' 'They shall say one to another, Come and see what desolations he hath made in the earth;' and, as it is in my text, 'How are they cut off!' but 'peace shall be upon Israel.'

3. Out of the manner of speech and phrase of this prophecy against Edom, I observe the use that all ages of the church must make of the examples of God's judgments upon other persons and nations before us, recorded in Scripture, or in story registered, for the benefit of after times. For,

(1.) He interposeth this clause of admiration, 'How art thou cut off!' as declaring an admirable judgment to be executed upon them, enough to strike all that see it or hear of it with fear.

(2.) By a comparison of dissimilitudes he sheweth that thieves and vine-robbers shall be merciful men in comparison of them that shall fight the Lord's battles against Edom. For they shall leave somewhat behind them, these wasting depopulators of Edom shall leave nothing.

(3.) He saith not categorically and positively, 'The things of Esau are searched out, his hid things are sought up;' but in a more pathetical language of amplification, by way of question, 'How are the things of Esau searched out!' and resuming the matter, but with addition and amplification, 'How are his hid things sought up!'

Which questions do put it upon us to take the judgment of God upon Edom into a serious consideration.

It is a question amongst great learned divines of former ages, which was the greatest miracle that ever Christ wrought whilst he lived upon earth?

St Jerome answereth, Some think the raising of Lazarus; others the giving sight to the blind; others the voice that was heard at his baptism; others his transfiguration; but he, for his own judgment, he thinks that the whipping of men that bought and sold in the temple, twice by him performed, was the greatest of all his miracles. For that a man so weak in his own person, so despised of men, so opposed by the merchants of the temple, should play *Rex* in the temple, and should there execute judgment, and subdue the hearts of so many men, who thought they did well, and had some colour to defend what they did, and that they should without resistance suffer the lash, and abandon the place;—

St Origen doth admire this miracle of his justice, as declaring him to be God, as David saith. God is known by executing judgment, *quo domantur hominum ingenia*, whereby the wits of men are subdued.

Therefore, when the judgments of God are preached, let men fear. The doctrines of Paul were soft and gentle, when he spake of righteousness and temperance; but when he spake of the judgment to come, Felix trembled; but it is probably thought that that last doctrine of judgment to come put him into that quaking and shaking fit, and made the earth to quake within him.

Therefore the prophet David, having shewed what search God maketh for sin, addeth, Ps. l. 22, 'Now consider this, you that forget God, lest I tear you in pieces, and there be none to deliver.'

His judgments are over all the earth; it is a meditation for the Sabbath,* it is proper for the day. And David saith, Ps. xcii. 4, 'Thou hast made me glad through thy work.' (One of his works is of judgment.) 'When the wicked spring as grass, and when all the workers of iniquity flourish, it is that they shall be destroyed for ever.' 'For lo, thine enemies, O Lord, lo, thine enemies shall perish; all the workers of iniquity shall be scattered.'

This is matter of comfort for the church of God; it is joy in the tabernacles of the righteous; for they say the right hand of the Lord bringeth mighty things to pass.

It serveth also to mingle some trembling with their joy, and some fear with their faith, to keep it from overgrowing to presumption; therefore the elect of God, upon consideration of the severe judgments of

* That is, it occurs in Ps. xcii. the title of which is, 'A Psalm or Song for the Sabbath-day.'—ED.

God, do feel in themselves a renewed fear of the majesty of God, which humbleth them, as Habakkuk confesseth: chap. iii. 16, 'When I heard, my belly trembled; my lips quivered at the voice: rottenness entered into my bones, and I trembled in myself, that I might rest in the day of trouble.' This is the sweet fruit of that consideration, for it prepareth rest for the souls of them that fear the Lord.

Therefore let fortune's and time's delicate minions, the daughters of ease and plenty, which study nothing but trim and bravery, and waste the precious moments of time, which should be spent in the contrite repentance of their sins, in the curious dress of their bodies; let them read the judgment of God upon the daughters of Sion, Isa. iii. 16. See how fine they were, and how God threateneth them with the scab, with discovery of their nakedness, with stink, with baldness, with divesting, with sackcloth.

Let the drunkards of our time hear what God threatened Ephraim: Isa. xxviii. 3, 'The crown of pride, the drunkards of Ephraim shall be trod under foot.'

Let the schismatical resisters of authority, which despise Moses their king and Aaron their priest, Num. xii. 1, and think much to be subject to the ordinances which are set down, remember Miriam the sister of Moses, who, resisting Moses, was punished with a leprosy, and though Aaron besought God for her, could not be healed till she had been shut out of the camp seven days.

Read and study holy Scriptures; whatsoever is there written is for our learning. Our God is the same, and his years fail not; he hath the same eye that once he had to find out sinners; he hath the same hatred that once he had to sin; he hath the same justice that once he had to censure it, and the same right hand to execute his wrath.

All Scriptures will tell you that he doth it severely, his sword is sharp and his arm is strong. 'O Lord, be merciful to me a sinner.'

Ver. 7. *All the men of thy confederacy have brought thee even to the border: the men that were at peace with thee have deceived thee, and prevailed against thee; they that eat thy bread have laid a wound under thee, there is no understanding in him.*

The third confidence of Edom disappointed.
This point is rhetorically amplified,
1. In the persons in whom Edom trusted.
2. In the failing of them.
1. The persons are called,

(1.) Men of their confederacy, such as had entered into league with them, saying, Your friends shall be our friends, your enemies shall be our enemies, we will engage our strength mutually with you, we will seek our good in the common good of both; as in the Proverbs, one purse, one army.

(2.) The men that were at peace with her, that had promised them love from themselves, and all offices of humanity.

(3.) They that eat thy bread; such as did communicate with them in the necessities of life, as Judas did with Christ, *commensales convivæ*, table guests.

2. Their failing is also amplified.

(1.) They have brought thee even to the border; that is, whilst Edom trusted to their help, they came forth of their strongholds to meet with their enemies in the borders of their territories, who but for their trust in them might have been more safe in their own fortresses. For, trusting to their help, whom they found perfidious, they left their habitations and strong castles empty, to keep the enemy from coming upon their borders; whilst their false friends expose them to invasion, and their gates to direption, in their absence. *Relinquentes et prodentes.*

Thus they gave their enemies advantage against them, to keep them from returning again into their strongholds.

(2.) They have deceived thee, and prevailed against thee. For they that were trusted as friends to Edom, betrayed them to their enemies, and fought against them and prevailed.

(3.) They have laid a wound under thee; that is, they have secretly conveyed under thee an instrument to wound thee; therefore others read *posuerunt insidias subter te*, declaring how cunningly their false friends had concealed their malice, and how dangerously they had laid their plot for the overthrow of Edom, so near as under them, even to blow them up: like our powder traitors, for they laid wounds under the Parliament House, instruments and means to wound and to destroy all.

And therefore he concludes of Edom, 'there is no understanding in him;' that is, Edom was blinded and befooled with this vain confidence, to trust in the perfidious friendship of their false friends.

From this place these doctrines arise:

1. It was Edom's sin against the first commandment to put confidence in man, and therefore God punisheth them by those whom they trusted. From whence ariseth this doctrine,

That God punisheth one sin by another; the sin of injury and oppression of Israel by the sin of false confidence in men.

2. Consider against whom Edom offended, even against Israel their brother; for was not Esau Jacob's brother? Therefore God punisheth their perfidiousness to their brother with the perfidiousness of their friends to them. From whence we conclude,

That God requiteth the wicked with the same measure which they have meted to others.

3. Whereas the friends and confederates of Edom turn enemies and traitors to them, we conclude that,

There can be no true peace nor bonds of love between wicked men.

4. From all these antecedents, we may conclude that those who trust in men have no understanding.

Doct. 1. God punisheth one sin by another.

Edom first sinned against the second table of the law in wrong and violence; and then he sinned, in vain confidence in man, against the first table, and God by this severe * sin punished the first.

* Qu. 'second'?—ED.

It is the manner of Satan, after a speeding temptation to one sin, to suggest another to hide, or to defend and bear up the other; our lying comes in to conceal fraud, as in the case of Ananias and Sapphira. And so cursing and swearing come in to maintain the credit of a lie, as in Peter's denial of his Master. So there needs a great many lies to maintain one, if interrogatories do press the liar far.

If it were no more but so, that one sin doth drive us into another, even in this consideration one sin doth punish another, because the more sin is committed the more punishment is deserved; but this is much more, the sin is punished with sin. Thus Edom first breaketh the second table of the law in doing wrong to his brother, and fearing that this will one day cost blows, he sinneth another sin against the first table, and forsaketh the confidence in God, and putteth his trust in men, which turneth to his utter ruin and destruction. So even the saints of God fall, as David; for his adultery began to defile him, and then he stained himself with the blood of his well deserving and faithful subject. This is the plot of David in the matter of Uriah.

The reason why sin should be the punishment of sin, is because, nature being once corrupted, and grace withdrawn, we are then prone to those defections from God which do more and more corrupt us. And that is a great punishment; St Paul clearly sheweth it in the degrees thereof, Rom. i. 21 : 1. When they knew God, they glorified him not as God; 2. They were not thankful; 3. They became vain; 4. Their foolish heart was darkened. Thus did they run out of one sin into another, and at last, ' Therefore God gave them up to uncleanness, through the lusts of their own hearts, to dishonour their own bodies between themselves.' ' For this cause God gave them up to vile affections, God gave them up to a reprobate mind, to do those things which are not convenient.'

Sin in the heart is a fire in the bosom : Prov. vi. 27, ' Can a man take fire in his bosom, and his clothes not be burnt ? Can a man go upon hot coals, and his feet not be burnt ?'

St Gregory hath a good description of sins.

1. Some are simple, in themselves sins; such is every thought, word, and work against the law.

2. Some sins are causes of more sins, as surfeiting and fulness causeth luxury and uncleanness of the flesh.

3. Other sins are the punishment of former sins, as in my text. Edom his former sin is punished by a latter.

4 Other sins are the punishment of former sins, and the causes of latter, as in David.

His idleness was punished by his adultery, and that adultery was the cause of murder.

Query. But here is a query.

If sin be a punishment, it is of God; for all punishment is just, and is of God; but God is not author of sin, therefore sin is no punishment.

Sol. To this our answer is, that sin may be considered two ways.

1. As it is a pollution of man.

2. As it is in the effect thereof the just punishment of man.

God is not the author of sin as it is a pollution, but being committed, God in the even course of his justice turneth it into punishment of man.

And man is punished, saith Thomas Aquinas, three ways.

1. *In præcedentibus*, because God withdraweth his preserving grace from a sinner, and maketh the means of his preservation ineffectual.

For to the just he saith, I will not leave thee nor forsake thee; but to the reprobate he shutteh up their eyes, *ne videant*, he stoppeth their ears, *ne audiant*; he hardeneth their hearts, and leaveth them to their own corruptions to be wrought upon.

2. *In concomitantibus*, these are either,

(1.) Inward, the pollution of the heart.

(2.) Outward, in the calamities of life.

3. *In subsequentibus*, that is, the unrest of the conscience and the distraction of the mind.

Excellent and full to this purpose is the example of the prodigal; for,

1. God withdrew his grace from him, and left him to take his vicious and luxurious courses in the world, till he had spent all and was cast forth.

2. God punished him in his mind, by giving him over for a time to the pollution of sin; he outwardly punished him with contempt, and beggary, and famine.

3. He punished him in his conscience with the remorse of his sin, which wrought with him so effectually that he repented him of his sin and returned to his father; so this punishment was not *ad amandationem*, but *ad emendationem*. *Et quæ pæna fuit facta est medecina.*

Thus sin in the elect may be the punishment of sin, to their great good, and the recovery of them again to God, as in David's example, and in the example of Peter. But the reprobate are forsaken of grace, polluted in their minds, and tormented in their consciences, and feel crosses and afflictions in the flesh; and these be rods of their own making, wherewith God scourgeth them, sending the angel of Satan to buffet them.

The most dangerous and damnable estate is of those who, when they have sinned, do not love the word of God which should restore them; like those froward sick persons, that refuse the physic that should heal them.

The word of God is plain dealing, and telleth every one of his faults, and revealeth to them the justice of God.

When men begin to take exceptions at the word, and quarrel with the food and medicine of life, and to say, *Durus est hic sermo*, this is an hard saying, then sin groweth an heavy punishment to them, and worketh their destruction.

Use. Therefore, let all those that would not be their self-tormentors, hear what the Spirit speaketh to the churches: Let them not consult with flesh and blood, but let them order their ways according to the word of God. Let no burden seem so heavy to them as the weight of their own sins. Let no annoyance seem so stenching as the turpitude and pollution of their own sins. And then, Come unto me, ye that are weary and heavy laden, and I will ease you. Come to me, you that are defiled and polluted with your manifold corruptions, and I will wash you clean in my blood, saith the Redeemer of men.

When our sins have broken our hearts, and made us contrite, and the smart of them hath made us weary of them, then shall we see them fastened to the cross of Christ, and the grace of God will be sufficient for us.

Doct. 2. God requiteth the wicked with the same measure which they have meted others. Edom dealt perfidiously and treacherously with Israel, therefore their confederates and professed friends deal so with them. It is Christ's rule of justice, Mat. vii. 22, ' With what measure you mete, it shall be measured to you again ;' proved Isa. xxxiii. 1, 'Woe to thee that spoilest, and wast not spoiled, and dealest treacherously, and they dealt not treacherously with thee: when thou shalt cease to spoil, thou shalt be spoiled ; and when thou shalt make an end to deal treacherously, they shall deal treacherously with thee.'

It is the threatening of God, Exod. xxii. 22, ' Ye shall not afflict the widow or fatherless child. If thou afflict them in any wise, and they cry at all unto me, I will surely hear their voice : and my wrath shall wax hot, and I will kill you with the sword ; and your wives shall be widows, and your children fatherless.'

David smarted in this kind. He defiled the wife of his faithful servant Uriah. Absalom, his son, defiled his father's concubines in the sight of all Israel.

Cain feared this judgment so soon as he had killed his brother Abel, Gen. iv. 14, for he said presently, ' It shall come to pass, that every one that findeth me shall slay me.'

Adoni-Bezek confessed this justice of retaliation executed on him, for they took him, and cut off his thumbs and great toes, and he said, Judges i. 6, ' Threescore and ten kings, having their thumbs and toes cut off, gathered their meat at my table : as I have done, God hath requited me.'

So saith God to the Chaldeans : Hab. ii. 8, ' Because thou hast spoiled many nations, all the remnant of the people shall spoil thee.' And God made this judgment good against Amalek, for they sought to destroy Israel, and God by Israel destroyed them. Samuel said to Agag their king, 1 Sam. xv. 33, ' As thy sword hath made women childless, so shall thy mother be childless among other women: so he hewed him in pieces before the Lord.'

Ahab slew Naboth, and himself was slain, 1 Kings xxi. 19, Jezebel shed Naboth's blood. 'Thus saith the Lord, In the place where dogs licked the blood of Naboth shall dogs lick even thy blood also. The dogs shall eat Jezebel by the walls of Jezreel.' As Solomon threateneth, Prov. i. 31, 'They shall eat the fruit of their own way, and be filled with their own devices.'

The apostle calleth this righteousness in God: 2 Thess. i. 6, 'It is a righteous thing with God to recompense tribulation to them that trouble you.'

The word is decomposite, ἀνταποδοῦναι, and signifieth a retribution contrary to them, that in the same they shall be patients wherein they have been agents.

From this fountain of justice cometh that law judicial: Exod. xxi. 24, 'An eye for an eye, a tooth for a tooth.' Which law Christ did not abrogate, but interpret, and put it into the power of the magistrate, where it ought to be, taking it away from private persons.

Use. Let us all lay this justice of God to heart, and let us look for it at the hands of God, that he will ἀντιμισθεῖν to us our iniquities unrepented.

Let the adulterer hear Job: chap. xxxi. 9, 10, 'If my heart have been deceived by a woman, or if I have laid wait at the door of my neighbour, let my wife grind to another, and let other men bow down upon her.'

Let the cruel oppressor of his brethren look to be oppressed in himself, or in his posterity: Ps. cxxxvii. 8, If the daughter of Babel oppress, 'blessed shall he be that rewardeth thee as thou hast served us.'

It is God's own word, 'He that honoureth me, him will I honour; but he that despiseth me, shall be despised.

Doct. 3. There is no true love and peace between the ungodly.

Here hath been much confederacy between Edom and other nations; they were men of peace, they did eat and drink together, yet even those turned perfidious to Edom, and betrayed him.

Christ in his legacy of peace said, John xiv. 27, *Pacem meam do vobis, non sicut mundus dat*, 'My peace I give unto you, not as the world giveth.' For either it is *pax adulationis*, the peace of adulation, of which David saith, *Oleum peccatoris non confringet caput meum*. Ravenna's note is that in all sacrifices to God salt was used, for God cannot be flattered; when we say the most we can of him, we come short. *Adulatio quam similis est amicitiæ, non imitatur tantum, sed præcedit.*

Poor men have the advantage of the rich in this, for who flattereth them? Sinners say we need not this waste. Why should we bestow it on them that cannot requite us? We will save it, and give it to them which are mighty.

2. Or it is *pax malæ confederationis*, the peace of evil confederacy, such as is between thieves, we will all have one purse. These be, as old Jacob said of Simeon and Levi, *fratres in malo*, brothers in evil. St Augustine calleth this *nefariam amicitiam*, a wicked friendship; into their secret let not my soul come.

These tares bind themselves in bundles for the fire.

3. *Pax simulationis*, a dissembling peace, when men hide malice under a show of peace, that they may *sub amici fallere nomen*, that they deceive under show of friendship. So Judas kisseth and betrayeth, Amasa entreateth and stabbeth.

4. *Pax temporalis*, a temporal peace, when men maintain love and friendship, and exchange great gifts and tender love and service to serve a turn. So men set up the ladders that they climb by as high as they can; but when their turn is served, they lay them along upon the ground.

This is the peace which the world giveth, and there is no true friendship in it, for, Prov. xvii. 17, 'A friend loveth at all times.'

> Nec ullis divulsus querimoniis
> Suprema citius solvit amor die.

True peace is like the dew of Hermon, none but the elect of God have it. 'My peace I give to you:' it is not like the light of the sun, that shines on good and bad. This is like the light that shined on Goshen, when all Egypt else was in palpable darkness. This is like 'the precious oil poured on Aaron's head, and running down to the skirts of his raiment; for there the Lord commanded the blessing, and life for evermore,' Ps. cxxxiii. 2, 3.

Aristotle held that friendship contracted either by pleasure or profit could not hold; for the cement and glue that should tie them together is but weak. This continuation is but *hujus ad hoc*, of this to that. But the union of the faithful is *hujus in hoc*, of this in that; for they be incorporate in one body, and they are made members of Christ, and members one of another—one flesh, one body.

We see men in their greatness followed, and served, and petitioned, observed, and presented with choicest and richest gifts; if we see them decline in favour or power, we see them forsaken of their servants. We see young prodigals frequented with company, courted with compliments, feasted and swelled with all delights; but when the fountain of this friendship is drawn dry, and the means fail, who calleth those men friends, or seeketh their conversation?

This yet appeareth more plainly in the Idumeans of Rome, that have long persecuted the true church of God; for though they have laboured ever since the first corruption of the church to maintain their heretical opinions, yet could they never be at any perfect peace amongst themselves. And this offer our church may boldly make to them, that there is no tenet in our religion we maintain against them but we will renounce it, if we do not find it averred by some one, or most of eminent learning amongst themselves.

And because it will take up too much time to give instance in all particulars of our difference from the Trent church, for a taste let me refer so many as are desirous of better satisfaction to read that learned proof of this truth in the reverend Dean of Gloucester's third book of the church, at the end of it, where he nameth the agreement of our church with their best learned in points wherein the Jesuits at this day accuse us of heresy. Therefore, one observed well that the religion of Rome was like Nebuchadnezzar's image; the height of it was sixty cubits, and the breadth was but six, that is, without any proportion, for never could they make the parts of it symmetrical.

Therefore, first, we are comforted against all the enemies of our religion. Their strength may be great, and their malice greater, but they cannot unite themselves with the bond of true peace, and the God of peace is not their tutelary God. In the damnable conspiracy of the powder traitors, God, by one of themselves, diverted the treason. I deny not but Turks have had many great prevailings against Christians, papists against protestants, and their confederates have held fast with them. So had Moab and Ammon, Gebal, the Assyrians, Philistines, the Chaldeans against Israel. But God found a time to consume these nations by their own strength, and their own confederates were the ruin of them.

We have heard that war is one of the sore judgments wherewith God scourgeth offenders.

At this time a great part of the protestant church is hostilely attempted with war. We have many of our countrymen, noble, generous, and valiant volunteers engaged in that cause. I hope we shall do a charitable Christian duty to God and them, to pray God to cover their heads in the day of battle, to beseech him whom Job calls the preserver of men to save them from all evil. Thou, Lord, preservest man and beast; do thou save them: let their eye have its desire upon their enemies. And for ourselves, we say, 'O Lord, be gracious unto us; we have waited for thee: be thou their arm every morning, our salvation also in the time of trouble,' Isa. xxxiii. 2.

God is called Lord of hosts, and so he can master his enemies; the stars in their courses by their influences; the elements: fire, as in Sodom; air, as in the pestilence in David's time; water, as in the deluge; earth, as in Korah's transgression, to smite sinners. He can punish man by frogs, by flies, by lice, by grasshoppers, and such like armies of his. Yet he chose to destroy the army of the Midianites by themselves, rather than by any other means : Judges vii. 22, 'The Lord set every man's sword against his fellow throughout all the host.' He could have employed other executioners to have done vengeance upon blaspheming Sennacherib, king of Assyria, but he would shew that no bonds of society or nature can hold them together whom God hath not joined : Isa. xxxvii. 38, ' Therefore, it came to pass, as he was worshipping in the house of Nisroch his God, that Adrammelech and Sharezer his sons smote him with a sword.'

2. We are therefore taught to unite ourselves in the Lord by the bonds of true love ; for all other bonds will be like the new cords wherewith Samson was tied, break in sunder, and we shall cast them from us. The great friendship that is made by bribes cannot be sincere ; for,

1. The receiver of them knows that his love is a dear pennyworth to his friend ; it is not a gift, but a perquisite, and therefore he cannot call it sure.

2. The giver knoweth his money, and not his love, made the friend ; and if this friendship bear him out of the hands of justice, his conscience will still tell him that his money, not his innocency, acquitted him ; if this friendship prefer him, his conscience within him will say that his money, not his worthiness, had advanced him. Therefore, the friendship thus made is not sincere.

But they whom religion and the fear of God doth unite are of one heart and of one soul. Here is no lack of anything, if any of them may supply it, Acts iv. 32. The wounded man shall have both the oil and wine of the Samaritan out of his vessels, and the help of his hand, and of his beast, and of his word, and of his purse. Our Saviour Christ saith, ' Go thou and do the like.'

How can we say we are neighbours, when we are so far from healing our brethren's wounds, that we rather set them into a fresh bleeding, and open them wider ; we rather make more in the whole and sound flesh ; we rather take away their oil and wine, and beast, and money, wherewith they should help themselves ; and instead of putting them into an house, we take their houses over their heads, and expose them to storms? The God of peace sanctify us throughout, that his peace may knit us together in him!

Doct. 4. Those who trust in men, have no understanding.

Here on earth we do much value the wisdom and judgment of man, by his choice of adherence and dependence; and we judge them unwise that address themselves to such as cannot either support them as they are, or put them on farther. But the word of the Lord saith, there is no understanding in Edom to trust in man; and the psalmist, *non relinquat hominem*. He adviseth, 'Trust not in princes, nor in any son of man, for there is no help in him;' God goeth farther in my text, 'there is treason in him,' *subducet auxilium, super inducet exitium*. He will bring thee to thy uttermost borders, and there he will leave thee.

Junius reads, *cujus vulneris non erit intelligentia*, as pointing out so great a plague upon Edom, *ut ipsam nequeat mens humana comprehendere, nedum curare arte et intelligentia*.

Joannes Draconites readeth the text thus, *ante proderis hostibus quàm animadvertas*. But the sense is easy, God censureth them for fools that put their trust in man; for God himself saith, Jer. ii. 13, 'they commit two great evils, they forsake God the fountain of living waters, and hewed them out cisterns, broken cisterns that can hold no water.'

The Philistines, 1 Sam. xvii. 10, trusted in their great champion Goliath, and they defied the host of Israel, and despised David; the Aramites sent Israel word, 1 Kings xx. 10, that 'the dust of their land should not be enough to give every one of their army an handful.' The reason of this folly is, 2 Cor. iv. 4, 'the god of this world hath blinded the eyes of them that believe not; for Satan worketh strongly in the children of disobedience,' he hath strong illusions for them, to make them believe lies. 'They that trust in lying vanity,' saith Jonah, 'do forsake their own mercy.' It is a lying vanity to trust the false gods of the heathen. God upbraideth the apostate Jews so, Deut. xxxii. 38, 'Let them rise up and help you, let them be a refuge.' It is a lying vanity to trust in any confederacy against God, it is God's woe: Isa. xxx. 1, 'Woe to the rebellious children, that take counsel, but not of me; that cover with a covering, but not of my Spirit, that they may add sin unto sin; that walk to go down into Egypt (and have not asked at my mouth), to strengthen themselves in the strength of Pharaoh, and to trust in the shadow of Egypt. Therefore shall the strength of Pharaoh be your shame, and the trust in the shadow of Egypt your confusion.'

He declareth this folly in the next chapter, Isa. xxxi. 3, 'Now the Egyptians are men, and not God, and their horses flesh, and not spirit. When the Lord shall stretch out his hand, he that helpeth shall fall, and he that is holpen shall fall down, and they all shall fail together.' This sheweth want of faith, when we trust in the vain help of friends.

It is true, that we must use all good means to further God's providence, but we must not put any trust in these means; there may be help *by* them, there is no help *in* them. David setteth these two in opposition, and declareth the differing success of them: Ps. xx. 7, 8, 'Some trust in chariots, and some in horses, but we will remember the name of our Lord. They are brought down and fallen, but we are risen, and stand upright.'

Is it not folly for man to run himself upon the curse of God? God hath said it: Jer. xvii. 5, 'Cursed be the man that trusteth in man, and maketh flesh his arm, and withdraweth his heart from the Lord.' The poets, the prophets of the heathen, can tell us what ill success the giants of the earth had, with their confederacy against the gods. *Non est consilium contra Dominum.*

The use of this point is, let us all labour and pray for understanding,

1. To know the impotency of the creature, that we may not trust to it.

2. To know the omnipotency of our Creator, that we may not oppose it, but seek our rest under that shadow.

This will change our vain confidence into a strong faith; and faith is a shield in all our wars.

Ver. 8. *Shall I not in that day (saith the Lord) even destroy the wise men out of Edom, and understanding out of the mount of Esau?*

Their fourth hope despaired.

Doct. They trusted to their wisdom; God doth threaten to destroy both the wisdom and the wise men of Edom.

In this passage consider we,

1. The judgment upon Edom: *Destruam sapientes*, 'I will destroy the wise men.'
2. The assurance: *Dicit Dominus*, 'saith the Lord.'
3. The time: 'in that day.'

1. Concerning the judgment, we are taught that human wisdom and counsels without God are no fence for a state.

Here is the mother disease of human nature. Eve heard that wisdom was to be gotten by eating the forbidden fruit, and she aspired in the pride of her heart to be like God, knowing good and evil; ever since, man hath much affected wisdom; therefore God, who hath revealed the true wisdom to his church, hath ever professed himself an enemy to the wisdom of this world: it hath two titles, *inimicitiæ apud Deum, et stultitiæ*, enmity and folly.

The true and saving wisdom is Christ; he is 'made unto us of God wisdom,' and his word is sufficient to make the man of God wise unto salvation: Eccles. ix. 14, 'There was a little city, and few men within it; and there came a great king against it, and besieged it, and built a bulwark against it. Now there was found in it a poor wise man, and he by his wisdom delivered the city.' This little city is the church of God, the few men in it be the little flock of God's chosen, the enemy that assaulteth it is Satan, the prince of darkness, the god of this world. The poor wise man in it is Jesus Christ, the carpenter, the son of poor Mary, of whom the scribes and priests said, 'Is not this the carpenter?' He by his wisdom saved his church.

This wisdom directeth to the whole armour, and teacheth how to fit it to us, that we may be able to resist Satan, Eph. vi. But the wisdom that is of the world, that studieth how to carry things on without God, sometimes against God, for God is not in all their ways; and this was ever a broken reed, it doth both deceive and wound him that leaneth on it. For, Rom. viii. 7, 'The wisdom of the flesh cannot be subject to the law of God.' Yet it striveth in vain; for, Prov. xxi. 3, 'there is no wisdom, nor understanding, nor counsel against the Lord;' for it is written, Job. v. 13 and 1 Cor. iii. 19, 'He taketh the wise in their own craftiness.'

1. The reason is given by the prophet, Isa. xxxi. 2, 'Yet he also is wise,' meaning there the wisdom of direction and counsel, for that belongs to him only; the wisdom of obedience and sequence is that which we most* seek.

Therefore God resisteth and destroyeth all those that usurp his wisdom, but take counsel, and not of him, and cover with a covering, but not of his Spirit, Isa. xxx. 1; that is, seek protection and coverture against evils, but not consulting his Spirit, who alone claimeth right in that title to be *custos hominum*, the preserver of men.

2. 'God hath chosen the foolish things of the world to destroy the wise,' 1 Cor. i. 17; the reason is given, ver. 19, 'That no flesh should glory in his presence.' God is the only subject of glory properly in himself; we give it to him in our Lord's prayer, *Tuum est regnum, potentia, et gloria,* 'Thine is kingdom,' &c.

He is a jealous God, he hath sworn that he will not give his glory to any creature. Wisdom is one of his glories, for 'the foolishness of God is wiser than men,' 1 Cor. i. 25. And for this cause God will destroy the wise men of Edom, both their persons and their wisdom, as he did Ahithophel, the oracle of those times; he defeated him, for he turned his wisdom into folly, and left him not wisdom enough to save himself from the halter.

* Qu. 'must'?—Ed.

Use. Therefore by Edom's example let us learn not to trust to human wisdom, flattering ourselves that we can do anything without God; for even the wicked, when they oppress the church and hurt the saints, do it not without the counsel and wisdom of God; so he saith before, 'Thus saith the Lord, an ambassador is sent to the nations, arise ye against him in battle.' It is God that maketh their confederates forsake Edom, and the men of their peace be the sword of God drawn out against Esau. Reviling Rabshakeh, the general of Sennacherib's forces against Jerusalem, could say, Isa. xxxvi. 10, and he said truly, 'And am I now come up without the Lord against this land? The Lord said unto me, Go up against this land.' For God stirred them up, and animated them to fight his battles against Israel.

The wisdom of the world is not worth the seeking, because it may be lost and taken from us. The wisdom of God, which is from above, God giveth to his chosen, and he cannot take it away from us, because the gifts and calling of God are without repentance. But the wise men of the world, when they have most cause to use their wisdom, then it faileth them; like the seaman's cunning in a violent storm, it is gone, saith David, Ps. cvii. 27.

The wisdom of God in man is ever at the best in the greatest tempest of danger and sense of sin. The disciples, when they are brought before kings and rulers, are promised, *Dabo vobis sapientiam*, I will give you wisdom; and further, *Dabitur illâ horâ*, it shall be given in that hour. Stephen at the hour of his death, not distracted with the fury of them that stoned him, died calling upon God, calling on him for them that killed him.

God takes away wisdom from them that know not how to use it; such as are wise to do evil, but to do good have no understanding. Wisdom in an ungodly man is *armata nequitia*, armed wickedness; and therefore David prayeth against it, 'Let not their wicked imagination prosper.'

It was David's wisdom, *Audiam quid loquatur in me Deus*, 'I will hear what the Lord will say.' For he

will speak to our hearts peace and joy in the Holy
Ghost. He will uphold us with his counsel; the fear
of the Lord is the beginning of our wisdom.

2. The assurance, 'Thus saith the Lord.'

For the trust in wisdom is so confident, that the
holy prophet, though he had called his prophecy his
vision, and though he had begun his whole prophecy
with *Thus saith the Lord*, yet the more to assure the
events threatened, he resumeth this authority.

(1.) He bringeth in God himself dispersing their
first hope, 'I have made thee small, the pride of thy
heart hath deceived thee.'

(2.) In their second hope, which was in the strength
of their habitation, he bringeth in God speaking to
Edom, 'I will bring thee down, saith the Lord.'

(3.) Now again, in this third hope of theirs, in the
wisdom of their wise men, two things do meet in this
verse to fortify the assurance.

[1.] The authority of him that saith and doth those
things, 'Thus saith the Lord.'

[2.] His appeal to them; for he doth not say, I
will destroy the wise men out of Edom, but he appealeth to their own hearts, saying, 'Shall I not
destroy them? *q. d.* Do you think that I will be
over-reached by your wise men? No; they shall not
have wit enough to save themselves, much less to
save you, 'For I will destroy them.' Which peremptory declaration of the will of him who is judge of all
the world, doth leave no place for evasion; for the
psalmist saith of him, that 'He doth whatsoever he
will in heaven and in earth, and in all deep places.'

By virtue of this certain word of God, we do gather
this assurance against all the enemies of the church,
in all ages thereof; for he hath said it by the mouth
of Job, chap. xxi. 17, 'How often is the candle of the
wicked put out! and how often cometh their destruction upon them! God distributeth sorrows in his
anger.' What though the execution of this wrath be
deferred? He addeth, ver. 19, 'God layeth up his
iniquity for his children,' that is, the punishment of
his iniquity. As there is a decree against them in
the counsel of God, and word against them, declaring
the decree of God, so *dies erit*, there shall be a time.

3. The time, 'in that day.'

Our days and times be all in the hand of God, and they be hid in his own power, who in his secret wisdom hath appointed them. When that day should come, he hath not yet revealed to Edom in this prophecy.

God is so patient and longsuffering that he doth not punish presently; for vengeance is his, he may take his time when he will, and no man can resist him.

The point here considerable is, that God in his secret wisdom hath designed a particular day for every execution of his will; yea, the Scripture goeth so far as to the hour, even to a moment, the least fraction of time. This declareth that the wisdom of the world and of flesh hath but its time; there is a period fixed wherein it must determine. Ahithophel's counsels went for oracles till this day, then God turned his wisdom into folly and destruction. So God, Isa. iii. 2, threatened Jerusalem with a day in which 'the Lord would take away from them the mighty men, and the men of war, the judge and the prophet, the prudent and the ancient.'

This he doth two ways.

One, by turning all their knowledge into ignorance, and their wisdom into folly.

Another, by destroying their persons, either by his sore judgments, or by leading into captivity. Here both are threatened, for he will destroy both *prudentes*, wise men, and *prudentiam*, their wisdom, in that day.

This may remember us of that great day of which St Paul preached to the Athenians, Acts xvii. 31, that 'God hath appointed a day in which he will judge the world in righteousness, by that man which he hath appointed.' For as the day of Jerusalem, and the day of Edom, and the time of God's particular judgments, is set and fixed, so is the day of the last judgment, in which every man shall give an account to God of himself, and all our works shall come to judgment.

What manner of men, then, ought we to be, expecting this day, and providing for it?

This doctrine of the set day of particular execution of God's threatened wrath against sinners, doth teach,

1. Holy patience in waiting the Lord's pleasure; and as the apostle admonisheth, Heb. x. 35–37, 'Cast not away therefore your confidence, for ye have need of patience, that after ye have done the will of God ye may receive the promise. For a little while, and he that shall come will come, and will not tarry. And blessed is he that endureth to the end.'

This living under the rod of the ungodly, and this beholding the prosperity of the wicked, doth much disquiet even the saints of God on earth, as in the example of David we see. Therefore we have need of patience, to sweeten the sorrows of life to us, and to clear our eyes, that we may not mourn as men without hope.

2. It teacheth faith; for the same author saith, ver. 38, 'Now the just shall live by faith,' for he that hath promised is faithful, and no word of his shall fall to the ground unfulfilled.

'Faith cometh by hearing,' let us then use it as the best remedy against the oppressions of the ungodly, to be swift to hear the word of God, that we may get the shield of faith to bear off all the darts of Satan. So David in that disquiet went to the house of God, there he was taught the end of those oppressors.

3. It teacheth holiness; for, seeing the wrath of God from heaven is revealed against the enemies of the church; there is no safety but in the church of God, and that is the congregation of saints. These are safe in that day, he hideth such under his wings, 'his faithfulness and truth is their shield and buckler.' 'There shall no evil happen to them, neither shall any plague come nigh their dwelling.'

So long as we make conscience of our words, and thoughts, and ways, and labour our sanctification, and strive against sin, we need not fear in the evil day.

Holiness is our door mark, and our forehead mark, the destroying angel shall pass over.

Ver. 9. *And thy mighty men, O Teman, shall be dismayed, to the end that every one of the mount of Esau may be cut off by slaughter.*

Their last hope is in the strength of their own mighty men. This is addressed to *Teman*. Which word, as it signifieth the coast to which the Idumeans lay from Jerusalem, *i. e.* the east, so it is the name of one of the nephews of Esau, Gen. xxxvi. 11, whose posterity inhabited a part of Arabia, called also by his name. He was the eldest son of Eliphaz, the eldest son of Esau; and under his name here the whole nation of the Idumeans is threatened.

And as the hope the Idumeans had in the wisdom of their wise men faileth them, for they have trusted to false friends, and all their providence for their safety miscarrieth, so shall they fail in the hope that they have in their own strong men, for they shall not be able to preserve them from a final destruction, even so great that every one of the mount of Esau shall be cut off by slaughter. Excellently is their judgment set forth, for their confederates shall turn perfidious to them abroad, and their strong men at home shall be dismayed.

Two things make wars advantageable to a commonwealth, *consilium et fortitudo*, counsel and strength; in the former verse God befools their wisdom, in this he enfeebles their strength. The reason is, he hath decreed that every one of the mount of Esau shall be destroyed. And when God turneth enemy, neither head nor hand, neither wisdom nor force can resist him. David and his sling shall discomfit Goliath and his armour, his sword and spear, and admired strength; the two little flocks of Israel, the great armies of the Aramites.

It is worth our noting that God, working by means, and directing our operations so, even in this work of overthrow threatened to Edom, doth destroy them by disabling to them all the means of their safety, as before he turneth the hearts of their friends against them.

He destroyeth the wisdom of their wise men, and now he takes away all heart and courage from their strong men. To teach us that all the outward means strong men. To teach us that all the outward means of safety are not sufficient to keep us from ruin, except the Lord be on our side. Therefore we pray, 'Hallowed be thy name. Thy kingdom come. Thy will be done.' And we acknowledge,

'Thine is the kingdom, power, and glory.'

And this enforceth upon us the law of the first table, to have no other gods but one; to give him outward worship, to sanctify his Sabbath, not to abuse his name. And this filleth us with faith, saying, *Credo in Deum Patrem omnipotentem*, 'I believe in God,' &c. For as David saith, *Domine, quis similis tibi?* Lord, who is like to thee? 'There is no wisdom or strength,' not that which is in the god of this world, the prince that ruleth in the air, but it is a beam of the heavenly light. Can God suffer any of his own gifts to be abused against him, to turn edge and point against the author of them? There is a time when God winketh at the outrage of the ungodly, for the exercising of the patience of his servants; but when he intendeth a cutting off by slaughter of his enemies, in that day the Lord will be known to be God.

These things are written for our sakes; for the enemies of our church are here threatened to be cut off by slaughter; even antichrist, the man of sin, who sitteth in the place of God as God, and is worshipped, whom God shall scatter with the breath of his mouth, that is, by the power of his word preached; and we have comfort against him, that neither his wit nor his force shall prevail against us.

We have two examples which I hope no time will ever forget to praise God for, till the second coming of Jesus Christ.

The power of antichrist was defeated in '88, when the pope gave away the kingdoms of England and Ireland to the king of Spain, who sent his invincible armada hither, not as a challenger, but as a conqueror, to take possession of these lands. They had special revelations to assure their victory, and the prayers of the popish church were all in arms against us. But, as it is in my text, their mighty men were dismayed, their strong ships either sunk in the sea, or well beaten, or constrained to fly, because God meant to cut them off by slaughter, and the power of Spain so weakened, and the coffers of their treasure so emptied, that nothing was more welcome to them than the news of peace with England.

The wisdom of Rome had no better success in the year 1605, for when some men of blood, the sons of Belial, had laid a plot for the destruction of the whole church and commonwealth then in Parliament, by powder; we cannot deny but the serpent put his best wits to the rack, to stamp a device with his own image and superscription. Never was there *nequitia ingeniosior*, a more witty wickedness, than to bring so many precious lives to the mercy of one executioner, who had nothing to do but to put fire to the train. Yet in the very act of preparation, and the night before the intended execution, God put fire to his own train laid for them, and discovered things hidden in darkness, and cast them into the pit which he had digged for them; and their wit and policy proved hanging and quartering to the conspirators, and declared the papist our secret enemies, such whom we must carefully look to; for if, by strength or wit, he can destroy the state of the church and commonwealth, the mercies of his heart are so cruel, that we can expect no favour.

That is now the cause why His Majesty, intending a parliament, doth require so strict a survey of the land, for the detection of all popish recusants, as now is both by the ecclesiastical and civil magistrate urged. For they have given us fair warning that, if they can do anything by wit or force, they will abate nothing thereof to the prejudice of this church. But as the confounding of the wisdom of Edom, and the disabling the strength of Edom, did forerun their fall, so our faith is, that antichrist, God's enemy and ours, hath now but a short time; and every one of the mount of Esau, of the city built upon the hills, shall be cut off by slaughter. The pride of their own hearts, who think they have the keys of heaven and of hell; not only Peter's keys, but David's also; who bear the world in hand, that they can save or condemn, shall deceive them. The rock of their habitation shall prove to them like an undefenced city. Their confederates, and men of their peace, that eat bread with them, shall turn edge against them. Their wise men shall fail them, and their triple crown and the temporal power of their hierarchy shall be disabled. We have the word of God for it: 'The man of sin must be destroyed.' 'Even so let all thine enemies perish, O Lord.' Amen, amen.

Ver. 10–14. *For thy violence against thy brother Jacob shame shall cover thee, and thou shalt be cut off for ever. In the day that thou stoodest on the other side, in the day that the strangers carried away captive his forces, and foreigners entered into his gates, and cast lots upon Jerusalem, even thou wast as one of them. But thou shouldest not have looked on the day of thy brother in the day that he became a stranger; neither shouldest thou have rejoiced over the children of Judah in the day of their destruction; neither shouldest thou have spoken proudly in the day of their distress. Thou shouldest not have entered into the gate of my people in the day of their calamity; yea, thou shouldest not have looked on their affliction in the day of their calamity, nor have laid hands on their substance in the day of their calamity: neither shouldest thou have stood in the cross-way, to cut off those of his which did escape; neither shouldest thou have delivered those of his that did remain in the day of distress.*

The cause provoking God to this severe process against Edom.

This is set down,

1. In general terms, ver. 10, ' violence against their brother.'

2. In a particular description, ver. 11–14.

1. The general term is, *violence*, or as the old reading was, *cruelty;* and the word here used doth express all injury.

Either done by strong hand or force,

Or done by subtlety and cunning.

2. In the particulars of their cruelty, there is,

(1.) Their confederacy with the enemies of their brother Jacob, ver. 11. This is cruelty of combination, *stabant ex opposito;* they were rather for the enemies of Jacob than for their brother; as David saith, they take the contrary part, they were as one of them.

By the strangers that carried away the forces of Jacob captive, and the foreigners that entered into his gates, and cast lots upon Jerusalem, are meant the Chaldeans, which referreth us to the story of those times, 2 Chron. xxxvi. 17–19.

'Therefore he brought upon them the king of the Chaldeans, who slew their young men with the sword in the house of their sanctuary, and had no compassion upon young man or maiden, old man or him that stooped for age; he gave them all into his hand.'

There was direption of the sanctuary, robbing the treasury of the king, burning the house of God, and deportation of the residue into captivity.

In that day Edom was as one of them; for then, as the psalmist saith, Ps. cxxxvii. 7, 'In the day of Jerusalem, they cried, Rase it, rase it, even to the foundation thereof.'

(2.) They are charged with the cruelty of their eye, and that twice: ver. 12, 'But thou shouldest not have looked on the day of thy brother in the day that he became a stranger.' Again, ver. 13, 'Thou shouldest not have looked on their affliction in the day of their calamity.'

(3.) They are charged with cruelty of heart: ver. 12, 'Neither shouldest thou have rejoiced over the children of Judah in the day of their destruction.' The heart is the seat of affections, they joyed in the sorrow of Edom.

(4.) They are charged with the cruelty of the tongue: ver. 12, 'Neither shouldest thou have spoken proudly in the day of their distresses.'

(5.) With the cruelty of their hands, violent actions against their brother: ver. 13, 14, 'Thou shouldest not have entered into the gate of my people in the day of their calamity, nor have laid hand on their substance in the day of their calamity: neither shouldest thou have stood in the cross way, to cut off those of his that did escape ; neither shouldest thou have delivered those of his that did remain in the day of distress.'

Which chargeth them with four cruelties:
1. Invasion of their cities.
2. Direption of their goods.
3. Insidiation, lying in wait for them.
4. Depopulation, not sparing the residue.

We have seen the sin of Edom in the total cruelty against their brother Jacob. We summed up the particulars, and find that God had just cause to enter into judgment with Edom, and to execute upon them his fierce wrath.

The sin was breach of the law, and a trespass against the second table ; against Jacob, that is, the posterity of Jacob their brother. And here I note that especially two commandments of the second table are broken.

1. Thou shalt do no murder.
2. Thou shalt not steal.

For what part of their cruelty toucheth the life of Jacob, is a breach of the first.

What toucheth his estate and goods, is a breach of the latter commandment.

And this example may serve for a commentary upon those two commandments, teaching how they are broken; for Edom is a very full example of transgression.

(1.) In the cruelty of combination. They that join with others that seek the life of man, are murderers; not accessories, but principals. So did Edom, for he was even as they.

Saul, after Paul, a blessed apostle, doth charge the murder of Stephen upon himself, because, as here, he was of the other side, and sat by and kept the clothes of them that stoned him. It is a fleshing of men in cruelty to associate in blood, and to communicate with the blood-thirsty. We see it after in Saul; he was a principal actor, and got commission to persecute, and went about breathing threatenings against the church.

And as it is in the law of murder, so it is in the law of theft, for every association with thieves and robbers is the breach of that commandment; and

Edom brake both these laws, for they were even as they that robbed Israel, and sought their life. Though they commenced not the war against their brother Jacob, yet they joined with them that did, and so they are *pares culpa*, alike in fault.

Use. This teacheth us to be very careful, not only how we be authors of murder and theft, but how we be actors or abettors of the same, and helps of the wicked against the church of God; for God said to Jehoshaphat aiding of Ahab, 2 Chron. xix. 2, 'Wouldst thou help the wicked, and love them that hate the Lord? therefore there is wrath upon thee before the Lord.'

Do not think that all the blame shall light upon the authors of evil. Do not wipe thy mouth with the harlot in the Proverbs, chap. xxx. 20, and say, I have done no wickedness, for all society with sinners in their sins are forbidden; the apostle is very precise herein: 2 Thess. iii. 14, 'If any man obey not our word, note that man, and have no company with him.'

The manifest breakers of the law are despisers of the word; with such eat not. God saith that such as converse with them be as they, that is, equally culpable.

Upon this evidence we find the church of Rome guilty of the powder treason; it was secretly animated and abetted by them, and they prayed for the success thereof.

(2.) The cruelty of the eye. This is twice here urged, ver. 12, 13, for the eye of humanity doth abhor the sight of murder. To look on, and behold the wrongs done to our brethren in their life or goods, is murder and theft. Hagar was so tender, that when her son Ishmael was ready to perish for want of water, she cast the child under one of the shrubs: Gen. xxi. 15, 16, 'And she went and sat her down over against him a good way off, as it were a bow-shoot; for she said, Let me not see the death of the child.' 2 Sam. xx. 12, the sight of Amasa murdered, and weltering in his blood in the way, was a stop in the way of Joab's soldiers, 'and all the people stood still.' It was a grievous sight, and troubled soldiers, men used to acts and sights of death, for Amasa was a worthy captain. They looked on in condolement, not in rejoicing.

It is reported that, after the massacre of the protestants in France, on the Bartholmew night following, the queen-mother, with many others, went out to behold the dead carcases ; and having caused the body of the noble admiral of France to be hanged upon a gibbet, they went out of the city to feed their eyes with that spectacle.

God will one day require the blood of those men at the hands of all those whose cruel eyes delighted in that spectacle : 'For thou shouldest not have looked on thy brother in the day of his affliction with cruel eyes.'

With compassionate eyes we may; so it is foretold of the elect : Zech. xii. 20, 'They shall see him whom they have pierced, and shall mourn for him.' So Mary and John saw Christ crucified, and Christ invited to that sight : 'Have ye no regard, all ye that pass by? see if there be any sorrow like to my sorrow.' But when the ungodly of the earth perish, there is joy, as the wise man saith ; it is one of the comforts of the church against the enemies thereof: Isa. lxvi. 24, 'And they shall go forth, and look upon the carcases of the men that have transgressed against me, for their worm shall not die, neither shall their fire be quenched, and they shall be an abhorring to all flesh.' And David saith, Ps. xcii. 11, 'Mine eye also shall see my desire upon mine enemies.'

These be special executions of wrath upon the ungodly, but the general rule of charity doth convince that eye of cruelty which beholdeth the blood of man with joy, shed on the earth ; and the law of piety doth find that man guilty of murder that looketh on, whilst an Egyptian smiteth an Israelite, which Moses could not endure to see, for as Seneca, *oculi augent dolorem*, the eye increaseth sorrow : Exod. ii. 12, 'He slew the Egyptian and hid him in the sand.'

This is no example for imitation, for lookers on to become gamesters of a sudden. How justifiable that fact of Moses was I will not now dispute ; the point is, Moses could not look on and see wrong done to an Hebrew. It is a cruel eye that can see a neighbour suffer injury in his person or in his goods, and will pass by and not give him help. It is a cruel ear that will suffer a neighbour to be scandalized in his good name, and will not open a mouth to defend him. If thine eye so offend thee, Christ adviseth thee to pull it out and cast it from thee.

When Pilate had caused Christ to be cruelly whipped, he brought him forth to the people to shame him openly, saying, *Ecce homo*, Behold the man, hoping that their eyes satisfied with that lamentable sight of his stripes would have cried, Enough, let him go. But this gave their eye a new appetite to see more, and they cried out, 'Crucify him, crucify him!' Those eyes that hunger thus, let the curses of Agur the son of Jakeh fall on them: Prov. xxx. 17, 'Let the ravens of the valley pick them out, and let the young eagle eat them.'

(3.) The cruelty of the heart: 'They rejoice over the children of Judah in the day of their destruction.' This also is murder, to joy in the destruction of our brethren, though we put neither hand nor counsel to it.

This evidence doth pronounce the church of Rome guilty of that murder in the cruel massacre of Paris under Charles the Ninth before mentioned, wherein, by a cunning pretence of friendship, there were destroyed 30,000 protestants; for after the massacre there was a solemn procession throughout the city; and that this was the joy of the whole church of Rome, we may avouch it from the testimony of the head of the church. For Gregory XIII. hearing of it, caused all the ordnance of his castle of St Angelo to be shot off in token of joy, and a mass to be sung in St Lucy's church for honour of the exploit. And the parliament of Paris enacted it, that in honour thereof, every year, on St Bartholmew's day, should a solemn procession be observed through the city of Paris. The cardinal also of Lorraine, in a public oration, magnified the fact, and caused monuments thereof to be erected.

Far be it then from us, who carry the names of Christians, to rejoice at the sufferings of our brethren, for this is murder. Let Roman Christians teach Turks, and Indians, and Massagets to be barbarous, let their mercies be cruel; for so would they have joyed if their powder-treason had sped. But as dear brethren, let us put on the bowels of compassion, and love, and tenderness. Let not us rejoice in the ruin of their persons that are executed for heinous prevarications of the laws of the kingdom, but rather gush out rivers of water for them that keep not the law. The punishment of sin is the joy, but the destruction of the person of the sinner is the grief, of all them that fear God.

The heart is a principal in murder, for out of the heart cometh murder, and an evil eye to look upon it. It proceedeth from a corrupt and cruel heart, when we pass by and regard not the afflictions of our brethren to relieve them, as the Samaritan did; but when we rejoice over them, as Edom here did, and make ourselves merry with their sins, or their punishments, our hearts are murderers of our brethren; and when he cometh that will one day make inquisition for blood, he will remember the complaint of the poor. The God of our salvation is called the God of mercies, and the Father of all consolation. If we be sons of this Father, 'be you merciful, as your heavenly Father is merciful;' 'love as brethren,' comfort the heavy-hearted, strengthen the weak, bring him that wandereth into the way, and let not thy brother's blood cry from the earth for vengeance against thee. There is *vox sanguinis*, a voice of blood; and ' He that planted the ear, shall he not hear ?' It covered the old world with waters. The earth is filled with cruelty; it was *vox sanguinis* that cried, and the heavens heard the earth, and the windows of heaven opened, to let fall judgment and vengeance upon it.

The joy that the Jews had at the death of Christ, what sorrow hath it cost them ever since ! They have gone, like Cain, with a mark upon them, stigmatized and branded as murderers, and they are scattered upon the face of the earth; 1600 years almost of deportation have they endured; and who cries now, It is time for the Lord to have mercy upon Zion!

The author of the *Three Conversions of England* writes a congratulatory epistle to the catholics in England, rejoicing at the timely quiet death of Queen Elizabeth, in a full age, full of days and full of honour, and telleth them that they have as much cause of joy as ever the Christians had in the primitive times for the death of the bloody and cruel emperors. This candle of the wicked was soon put out, for ere that epistle could come to them, our gracious king was proclaimed the heir of her crowns and of her faith.

(4.) They are charged with the cruelty of the tongue: ver. 12, 'Neither shouldest thou have spoken proudly in the day of their distress.' This is another kind of breach of the law, *Non occides*, 'thou shalt not kill;' to speak proudly, or, as the original doth express it, to make the mouth great, or wide, against our brethren in their distress. For they animated the persecutors of their brethren 'in the day of Jerusalem; and said, Rase, rase it, even to the foundations thereof,' Ps. cxxxvii. They opened their mouth wide in cruelty, or, as Ezekiel speaketh for them: chap. xxv. 8, 'Moab and Seir did say, Behold, the house of Judah is like unto all the heathen,' *i.e.* God taketh no more care for them than for any other people. It is one of the provocations wherewith God was provoked against Edom: Ezek. xxxv. 10, 'Because thou hast said, These two nations, and these two countries, shall be mine, and we will possess it; though the Lord was there.' He accuseth them of anger and envy against those two nations, *i.e.* Israel and Judah; so called because the land was divided in Jeroboam's time into two kingdoms.

Anger and envy are by our Saviour declared to be murder, and the tongue is called by David a sharp sword; the poison of asps is under their lips. It is the bow out of which they shoot for * arrows, bitter words. 'Thou hast loved all the words that may do hurt.' *Verba be verbera. Venite percutiamus eum lingua,*

* Qu. 'forth'?—ED.

'Come let us smite him with the tongue,' said the enemies of Jeremiah, Jer. xviii. 18; and Saint James, chap. iii. 5, 6, saith there is *ignis in lingua,* a fire in the tongue, 'Behold how great a matter a little fire kindleth!' 'The tongue is a fire, a world of iniquity: so is the tongue amongst the members, that it defileth the whole body, and it setteth on fire the course of nature; and it is set on fire of hell. It is an unruly evil, full of deadly poison.' Prov. xii. 18, 'There is that speaketh like the piercings of a sword.'

1. In their anger they spake cruelly, instigating their enemies to destroy them.

2. In their pride they spake insolently, expressing their inward joy at their ruin, by speeches of scorn and disdain, and of triumph over them.

The Jews are a fearful example of this in their process against Christ, for they cruelly said, 'Crucify him, crucify him,' 'not him but Barabbas.' 'If thou let him go, thou art not Cæsar's friend. And after, tauntingly, when he was upon the cross, to him, 'He saved others, let him save himself;' to his Father, 'Let him now save him, if he will have him.' Which how dear it cost them, let their own tongues repeat their judgment. *Sanguis ejus super nos, et filios nostros,* 'His blood be upon us and upon our children.' It was so ever since; and as God wrote the cruelty of Amalek in a book, and vowed never to forget, so even to this day he remembereth what that Amalek did to Israel. The desolation of their city and temple, the glory, and pride, and praise of the earth, their miserable dispersion to this day, is a certain testimony of God's unappeased displeasure to them.

Sarah saw Ishmael working;* he doth not say she heard him. Peradventure it was but a scornful or proud look that she observed; but it is understood that he scoffed him with some words of disdain, that he should be the young master and heir of the house. And this provoked Sarah to solicit his casting out of the house; and the apostle doth call it persecution, and a kind of murder.

* Qu. 'mocking'?—ED.

Beloved, do you know that cursing is murder ? Do you know that bitter and scornful slandering, which toucheth the good name of a brother, is murder ? Do you know that every word you speak to animate and encourage against a brother is murder ? Do you know that those reviling speeches which anger venteth in your common scoldings, and reproachful railings one upon another, and that secret and private whispers wherewith you deprave one another, be murder ?

Saint James teacheth you, chap. iv. 11, that ' he that speaketh evil of his brother, and judgeth his brother, speaketh evil of the law, and judgeth the law ;' that is, he declareth himself to be above the law, and takes upon him to judge ; for he that judgeth the law, and thinketh that the law of God doth not bind him to obedience, he is not a doer of the law, but a judge. Christ saith, ' He that saith to his brother, *Fatue*, thou fool, is obnoxious to hell fire.' Let us all judge ourselves by this law, and we shall find that we had need to ' take heed to our ways, that we offend not with our tongue.' It is no easy work to govern the tongue, it asketh care and caution. David himself must take heed.

That was the lesson Pambus found so hard, that it was enough to take up his whole life. And in our anger and fury we do little think upon it, that ' by our words we shall be judged, by our words we shall be condemned ;' and if ' of every idle word we shall give an account to God,' how much rather of every angry word, of every lying word, of every spiteful and scornful word, every cruel and bloody word, of every profane and blasphemous word ?

This is commonly the revenge of the poor, for when they have no other way to right themselves against injuries, they fall to cursing and imprecations. Saint James telleth you, chap. i. 26, ' If a man among you seem religious, and bridle not his tongue, he deceiveth his own heart, this man's religion is in vain.' And again, chap. iii. 2, ' If any man offend not in word, the same is a perfect man, and able to bridle the whole body.' It is a master-piece to govern the tongue. Ps. xxxiv. 12, 13, ' What man is he that desireth life, and loveth many days, that he may see good? Keep thy tongue from evil.'

But of all kind of evil speaking against our brother, this sin of Edom, to sharpen an enemy against our brother in the day of his sorrow and distress, this opening of the mouth wide against him to insult over him in his calamity, is most barbarous and unchristian. Yet I deny not but that God giveth matter of joy to his church when he destroyeth the enemies thereof, and it may be sometimes lawful to open our mouths wide in the praise of God for the destruction of the ungodly; as I find joy in the camp of Israel for the devouring of proud and cruel Pharaoh and his armies in the Red Sea: Exod. xv., 'Then Moses taught them a song,' not only of thanksgiving unto God, but of insultation over those enemies, wherein they said, ' Pharaoh's chariots and his host hath he cast into the sea: his chosen captains also are drowned in the Red Sea. The depths have covered them: he sank into the bottom as a stone. The horse and his rider hath he thrown into the sea.' This was the first song that we do read of in holy Scripture, the ancientest song that is extant in the world upon record. And therefore it is a type of the jubilation of the saints in heaven for the destruction of the beast; and it said, Rev. xv. 3, that they ' sing the song of Moses the servant of God.' For there was more cause of joy in the whole church for the fall of the beast, than Israel had for the fall of king Pharaoh, for indeed that of Israel was but a type of this. But Moses was warrant enough for the one, and the same Spirit which directed Moses shall authorise the other.

Yet here is a dangerous way, and exceeding slippery, and wonderful circumspection must be used, and David's caution, ' I said, I will take heed that I offend not in my tongue.' For Christ hath put a duty upon us in his evangelical law, to $εὐλαλεῖν$ and $εὐπράττειν$, to speak well and do well.

There is in the enemies with whom we have to do a double opposition, which maketh a double quarrel.

1. They are opposite to God himself, when they oppugn the church of God, or any member of that church for God's sake. This is God's quarrel.

2. When they personally violate the servants of God in life, goods, or good name, this is our quarrel, whether in passion the case be ours, or our brothers' in compassion.

There is a double respect to be had to enemies:

1. As they are men.
2. As they are enemies.

This ground being laid, these conclusions do result concerning this point.

1. That no man ought to rejoice at the ruin and destruction of a man as he is a man, for this is a natural tie that bindeth us one to another. And religion doth not unbind the bonds of nature; rather it is *religatio*, and tieth them much faster. The reason is, for though the image of God in which man was created were much defaced in the fall of man, yet was it not wholly extinguished; for the image of the Trinity is an indelible character, it cannot be wholly lost; not in the reprobate, I may add, not in the damned, for even they also are the workmanship of God. Therefore, as they are the creatures of God, we do owe them love and pity, in honour of the image of God in them, and ought not to rejoice to see the blemishes of God's image.

So the Samaritan shewed kindness to the Jew that fell among thieves, although, as the woman of Samaria said, they converse not together. And so Jacob cursed the cruel fury of his sons for destroying the Shechemites, though aliens from Israel, and usurping their land. And so God hating both the Moabite and the Edomite, yet he avenged the cause of them against the king of Moab, saying, Amos ii. 1, 2, 'For three transgressions of Moab, and for four, I will not turn away the punishment thereof'; because he burnt the bones of the king of Edom into lime. But I will send a fire upon Moab, and it shall devour the palaces of Kirioth.' And to go lower, when the rich man in hell-fire saw Abraham afar off, and besought him for help, he answered him by that loving compellation,

'Son, thou in thy lifetime,' &c. Hell would not take that from him but that he was Abraham's son according to the flesh. And whilst we live here, we ought much rather to do all offices of humanity to our enemies, because they are men, and because only God knoweth who are his, and they may be converted, and come into the vineyard at the last hour.

2. As they are enemies:

(1.) We consider them as God's enemies, so we hate them; not their persons, but their vices; for that, as Augustine defineth, it is *odium perfectum*, a perfect hatred. And indeed it is the hatred that God beareth to his enemies; for 'the wrath of God from heaven is revealed against the unrighteousness and ungodliness of men,' Rom. i. 18,—not against their persons, they are his workmanship, and carry his image in some sort, though much disfigured; but against the unrighteousness and ungodliness of men, by which their persons do stand obnoxious to his displeasure. And thus I find the saints of God have insulted over the wicked, as Israel over Pharaoh, and the Gileadites over the children of Ammon; not rejoicing in the destruction of God's creatures, but of God's enemies, and wishing with Deborah and Barak, 'So let all thine enemies perish, O Lord.' This is no more but an applauding of the judgment of God, and a celebration of his justice; and of this we have examples both in the militant and in the triumphant church.

[1.] In the militant. Babylon, where the Israel of God were captives and despitefully entreated, and where they hung up their harps and were scornfully and sarcasmatically required to sing one of the songs of Sion, is thus insulted over: Ps. cxxxvii. 8, 'O daughter of Babylon, who art to be wasted; happy shall he be that rewardeth thee as thou hast served us. Happy shall he be that taketh and dasheth thy little ones against the stones.' Isa. xiii. 2, 'Lift ye up a banner upon the high mountains, exalt the voice unto them, shake the hand. I have commanded my sanctified ones, I have also called my mighty ones for my anger.' Jer. l. 2, 'Declare ye among the nations, and publish, and set up a standard, publish, and conceal not; say, Babylon is taken, Bel is confounded, Merodach is broken in pieces,' &c.

[2.] In the triumphant church: Rev. xviii. 20, 'Rejoice over her, thou heaven, and ye holy apostles and prophets, for God hath avenged you on her.' Yet I will not conceal from you that many learned expositors of the Revelation do understand this text of the militant church. But no doubt the saints judging the world in the last day do rejoice against the world in the execution of God's just judgment upon them; for they are then entered into their Master's joy, and all tears are wiped from their eyes. Thus, then, it is lawful, when God hath executed his judgment upon his enemies, for all the friends of God to insult over them, and to lift up their voice and hand against them, for this is part of the punishment of God's enemies: 'They that despise me shall be despised.' This is the last perpetual shame that shall evermore continue upon them, the just reward of their bold presumption, who durst advance themselves against God.

(2.) We must consider the wicked as our enemies, and this way we must be tender how we insult over them in this life, because we do not know whether their destruction here be their full punishment or no.

[1.] Because God sometimes chasteneth with temporal judgments that he may forbear eternal, and sometimes he punisheth rather *ad dignam emendationem* than *ad amandationem*, and by that temporal punishment doth, as by some sharp physic, restore them to health. It is the voice of God's church: Micah vii. 8, 'Rejoice not against me, O mine enemy, when I fall, I shall arise; when I sit in darkness, the Lord shall be a light unto me. I will bear the indignation of the Lord, because I have sinned against him.'

[2.] Because this opening of the mouth, and insulting over the adversities of men, is one of the practices of the ungodly; they use, as David saith, to say, 'Where is now their God?' So insolently did proud Sennacherib insult over the cities that he had subdued: Isa. xxxvii. 13, 'Where is the king of Hamath, and of Arphad, and the king of the city of Sepharvaim, Hena, and Ivah.'

With them is the chair of the scornful.

Rather should we commit our cause to God, and comfort ourselves in his justice, and say no more, when we suffer, than the son of Jehoiada said, when Joash, forgetting his father's love to him, put him to death. 'The Lord look upon it, and requite it,' 2 Chron. xxiv. 22. And when we see that God hath executed his judgment on our behalf, let us give God the honour due unto his equal justice, with joy therein.

Yet I love the example of Israel, when in the case of wrong done in Benjamin to the Levite in his concubine, they, by God's appointment, destroyed the most of that tribe, when they had so done, Judges xxi. 2, 'The people came to the house of God, and abode there till even before God, and lift up their voices and wept sore.'

4. They are charged with cruelty of hands.

(1.) Invasion of their city.

Ver. 13. *Thou shouldest not have entered into the gate of my people in the day of their calamity.* This Edom did, to behold the calamity of Jacob, not to help; but, as it after followeth, to rob him; for the Idumeans joined with the Chaldeans in the invasion of the city, and were as they, and entered in by the gate with them. It was a double calamity to Israel, to behold their brother Edom confederates with their enemies, and auxiliaries to them in their wars. This bringeth Edom into the former charge of cruelty of combination, and maketh them equally culpable with the Chaldeans, with whom they joined in society of war against Israel.

(2.) Of direption of their goods.

Ver. 13. *Neither shouldest thou have laid hand on their substance in the day of their calamity.* This chargeth them with theft, against that commandment, 'Thou shalt not steal;' for not only secret stealth is therein forbidden, but all depredation by violent and unjust war. As a pirate told Alexander, I am accounted a pirate, because I rob in a small ship; but thou, because thou robbest in great fleets, art esteemed a great captain!

Thomas Aquinas, *Prohibentur nocumenta quæ inferuntur facto;* and it extendeth, saith Borhanus, *ad quamlibet alienæ rei usurpationem.* And, therefore, when a company of pilling and pirting offenders were carrying a thief to the gallows, Demosthenes said, *Parvum furem a majoribus duci,* the lesser thief to be led by the greater.

This sin is so near bordering upon the sin of murder, as sometimes, and even in this case in my text, it is both theft and murder too; for to take away life is murder, and to take away the necessaries by which life is sustained, is theft and murder too; and therefore the apocryphal author of the book called Ecclesiasticus avoucheth a canonical truth, saying, chap. xxxiv. 22, ' He that taketh away his neighbour's living, slayeth him; and he that defraudeth the labourer of his hire is a blood-shedder.' He gave the reason in the former verse : ' The bread of the needy is their life; he that defraudeth them thereof is a man of blood.' When Abraham, Gen. xiv., heard that his brother Lot was taken captive, and that the four kings had taken all the goods of Sodom and Gomorrah and all their victuals, ' He armed them of his own household, and set upon the enemy by night, and brought back all the goods; he rescued Lot, and his women and people.' Melchisedek blessed him, therefore, and said, ' Blessed be the most high God, which hath delivered thine enemies into thine hand.' Here God punished theft and prey; yet he that readeth the story shall find that the quarrel of the assailant was for rebellion against him. ' Twelve years they served Chedorlaomer, but in the thirteenth they rebelled.'

This fact of Abraham, thus blessed by Melchisedek, thus prospered by God himself, doth declare the subjection of these kingdoms to Chedorlaomer to have been oppression, and their rebellion a just prosecution of their liberty, and therefore the war of Abraham a just war. And God gave the robbed their goods again.

The law of God which saith, *Non furaberis,* Thou shalt not steal, doth declare that there is *meum et tuum,* mine and thine, in the things of this world, and that God hath not left an anabaptistical community of all those things on earth, and a parity of interest in all men to all things; for then there would be no theft, seeing whatsoever any man did seize on was his own.

This was no new heresy, but a reviving of the old, of them that called themselves *Apostolici,* mentioned by St Augustine, who, in imitation of the apostles, would have all things common. True, that in those beginnings of Christ's church, when the number of Christians were yet but small, it was a voluntary, not a compulsory, communication of goods that was then, and for a small time used, as a fortifying of themselves against the common adversary. But there was no law but of their own piety and charity that did impose this as a duty upon them; so that Ananias and Sapphira were not punished with sudden death for detaining a part of the price of the field which they sold, for they might have withheld all; but they were punished for lying to the Holy Ghost, bringing but a part, and affirming that they brought all. For Peter saith to Ananias, Acts v. 4, ' After it was sold, was it not in thine own power?' Yet in that communication it was not lawful for every man to take what he would; but the apostles ' distributed to every one according to their need,' Acts iv. 35.

Surely if Edom and the Chaldeans had had as good right to the city of Jerusalem, and to the goods therein, as Israel had, God had not laid this for an evidence against Edom, that he laid hand on their substance. God is Lord of all, and he hath given the earth to the sons of men, yet not in common, nor in equal distribution. Here ' the rich and poor meet together, and the Lord is maker of them both,' Prov. xxii. 2.

The apostle learnt how to abound, and how to want; and God giveth to the rich things necessary in possession, as to owners thereof during his pleasure; he giveth them things superfluous, that their cup may run over to the relief of others, as to his stewards put in trust, to see that their brethren want not.

And there be two virtues commended in holy Scripture which make men proprietaries in the things of this world: that is, *justitia qva suum cuique tribuis*, justice, whereby thou givest to every one his own; *misericordia qua tuum*, and mercy, whereby thou givest of thine own.

The use of this point is, let every one know his own, and not lay hand on the substance of his brother; and 'let him that stole, steal no more, but let him labour,' not all for himself, but 'that he may give to him that needeth,' Eph. iv. 28; that the poor may grow up with him, as he did with Job, and that none perish for want of meat and clothing.

Godliness must be joined with contentment; the law doth not only bind the hand, *non furaberis*, thou shalt not steal; but it bindeth the heart too, *non concupisces*, thou shalt not covet, not his house, not his ground, not his wife, not his servant, not any thing of his.

There may be many ways of theft; I am limited to that of violent taking away of our neighbour's substance, for that only is here named and judged, and that is either directly by invasion, or secretly practised by oppression.

Oppression, like other sins, putteth on the habit of virtue, and passeth for good husbandry; but all stopping of the wells whereof Isaac and his cattle should drink, is oppression and theft; and whatsoever is saved from the poor by it, is the treasure of wickedness; and the wise man telleth us, Prov. x. 2, 'The treasures of wickedness profit nothing.' We shall see it clearer when we come to God's revenge upon Edom, for laying hand upon his brother's substance.

(3.) They are charged with insidiation for life.

Ver. 14. *Neither shouldest thou have stood in the cross-way to cut off those that did escape.*

Edom divided himself against Israel, some entering the city to rob and spoil their goods, and to destroy them that abode there; others attended without the city to cut off them, who, to save their lives, did escape out of the city. The Chaldeans, that came from far to invade Jerusalem, were not so well acquainted with the ways and passages for escape near to the city as the Edomites, their brethren and neighbours were; therefore that cruel office they take upon them, to declare their full malice to Jacob, and to make up a complete destruction. The history of those times doth make this plain : 2 Kings xxv. 4, ' And the city was broken up, and all the men of war fled by night by the way of the gate, between two walls, which is by the king's garden (now the Chaldees were against the city round about); and the king went the way toward the plain.' At that time the Edomite, knowing the secret ways, mingled himself with the Chaldees to cut off such as escaped.

In this passage, note,

1. The miserable calamity of war, how it maketh desolations, and filleth all places with blood; no safety from invasion in the city, and none from insidiation without the city.

(1.) When you hear of these things, thank God for the peace of the commonwealth in which you live, and reckon it amongst the great blessings of God that you are born in a time of peace, and live in peace every one under his own vine and under his own fig-tree, every one enjoying the comforts of life without the noise of invasion, no leading into captivity, and no complaining in our streets.

(2.) Let us also think of the woful calamity of that part of the church wherein we have so great a part, so much of the best blood of this land and crown in danger of this cruelty; and if either our persons or purses, or our prayers to God, may relieve them, let us not spare to comfort their distresses, as we would desire in like extremity to be comforted ourselves.

(3.) Let us learn to abhor the bloody religion of the scarlet strumpet of Rome, that maintaineth and abetteth these quarrels, and kindleth those coals in Christendom which threaten conflagration.

(4.) Let us observe all them that make contention, and move the hearts of their brethren to schism, to alienate their affections from the peace of the church, lest this fire, which beginneth but amongst thorns and brambles, inflame the cedars of our Libanus.

2. See the afflictions of Judah and Jerusalem, and search the cause thereof: 2 Kings xxiv. 3, 4, 'Surely at the commandment of the Lord came this upon Judah, to remove them out of his sight, for the sins of Manasseh, according to all that he did, and also for the innocent blood that he shed (for he filled Jerusalem with innocent blood), which the Lord would not pardon.'

Have not we provoked the God of mercies to awake his justice against our land? Did ever pride put on more forms of costly vanity and shameless disguise than our eyes behold? Did drunkenness ever waste and consume more of the necessaries of life, which many poor Christians want, than now? Were the prophets and ministers of the word rebuking the vices of the times less hearkened to than in our days? Was there ever a more curious search into men's estates and lands, or more advantage taken, or more new inventions to get wealth, than we have heard of? Was the church at any time more rent with schisms, and maimed by defections and separations, and the faithful ministers more opposed with contradictions, and depraved by unjust calumniations, by those that usurp the appearance of great professors, than now? Did knowledge ever swell and puff men up more than now? The times are foul, and the crimes thereof are clamorous; why, then, should not we expect Judah's punishment, that live in Judah's sins? Oh sin no more, lest some worse evil fall on thee!

(1.) Let us break off these sins by repentance, and seek the Lord whilst he may be found; and, seeing the light of his countenance shineth on us, let us walk worthy of this light.

(2.) Let us serve the Lord in fear, and pray to God that the thoughts of our heart, which are only evil continually, may be forgiven us.

(3.) Let us receive with meekness the word of truth, and suffer it to be grafted in us, that we may bring forth no longer our own sins with the fruits of evil works, but the fruits of the word.

(4.) Let us pray that God would pass by our offences, and establish us with grace, and pluck up sin within us, that root of bitterness which bringeth forth corrupt fruits of disobedience, that God would continue upon us the light of his countenance.

(5.) Let us not flatter ourselves and say, None of these things shall come upon us, because we have so long enjoyed the favours of God; for Judah, where God put his sanctuary, and Zion, where he made himself a dwelling, was not spared. The righteous judge of the world is not such a one as we, though he hold his peace awhile; our provocations may make him whet his sword, and prepare against us instruments of death.

Observe the cruelty of the Edomite; he not only joineth in open hostility, but in secret insidiation, to cut off all, root and branch, all in a day; he is implacable.

Such is the hatred of the Romish church to ours. Did we not see it in the attempt in '88 for invasion and possession? Did we not see the heart of antichrist in the powder treason plotted to a perfect and full destruction?

Surely David had cause to pray to God, ' Let me not fall into the hands of man.'

This is further declared in the next circumstance, ' Neither shouldst thou have delivered those of his that remained in the day of distress.'

4. Depopulation. For if any remained whom neither the invasion had met with in the city, nor the insidiation without, those the Edomite found out, and delivered into the hands of their enemies.

Of those, some fell off to the enemy, others were carried away captives, others of the poorer sort were left in the land to serve the enemy there, to be vinedressers and husbandmen. This is called sweeping with a besom, and wiping as one wipeth a dish.

Two things do aggravate this cruelty of Edom: 1, against thy brother Jacob.

For a Turk to oppress a Christian, an infidel a believer, is but a trespass against humanity; for Hebrews to strive, and one Christian to afflict another, woundeth religion also. The papist calleth himself a Christian, and pretendeth great love to Christ; he is our unnatural brother, and he casteth us out by excommunication; he hateth us in our affliction, yet he saith, Let the Lord be glorified. But for us to wound and smite one another of us, protestant against protestant, this is seven spirits worse than the former. Brethren by nation, brethren by religion, should live as brethren by nature; live as brethren, and our Father will be angry if we do not, and the God of peace will fight against us.

(2.) Another circumstance of time is much urged, and it maketh weight; for when was Edom so bloody? You shall see that in the time, and you will say with Solomon, that the mercies of the wicked are cruel. Ver. 11, 'In the day that strangers carried away captive his forces, and foreigners entered into his gates, and cast lots upon Jerusalem.' Ver. 12, 'In the day that thy brother became a stranger, in the day of their destruction, in the day of distress.' Ver. 13, Thrice named 'in the day of their calamity.' Ver. 14, 'In the day of distress.'

1. Observe in this how their cruelty is aggravated by the time; the wofullest time that ever Jerusalem had, called therefore the day of Jerusalem. When all things conspired to make their sorrow full, then, in the anguish and fit of their mortal disease, then did Edom arm his eye, his tongue, his heart, his hand, and join all those with the enemy against his brother.

2. Observe that God taketh notice not only *what* we do one against another, but *when;* for he will set these things in order before thee, for the God of mercy cannot abide cruelty.

To strengthen the hand of affliction, and to put more weight to the burdens of them that be overcharged, this is bloody cruelty; as to oppress the poor is always abominable to God, but to oppress him in his tender and orphan infancy, or in his feeble and decrepit age, doubleth the offence. To hinder the willing labourer from his labour at all times, it is a crying sin, and they are men of blood that do so; but in times of dearth, or in times of his greatest expense, to deprive him of his labour or his pay, this God considereth, for he knoweth whereof we are all made, and he observeth our carriage towards one another of us.

Ver. 15, 16. *For the day of the Lord is near upon all the heathen: as thou hast done, it shall be done to thee; thy reward shall return upon thine own head. For as ye have drunk upon my holy mountain, so shall all the heathen drink continually; yea, they shall drink, and they shall swallow down, and they shall be as though they had not been.*

This is the fourth part of this section, containing God's revenge upon Edom, which is before threatened, particularly against Edom: ver. 2, ' Behold, I have made thee small among the heathen: thou art greatly despised;' and after further declared it, despairing all the hopes of Edom.

1. The pride of their heart; 2. The strength of their confederacy; 3. The strength of their situation; 4. The hope of their wise men; 5. The hope in their own strong men. Yet further, ver. 10, he saith, ' Shame shall cover thee, and thou shalt be cut off for ever.'

But now, as Edom was not alone in that sin, but joined with others, so are they all joined together in the punishment.

The words are somewhat obscure.

For the *day of the Lord*, he meaneth the day of vengeance, to repay the violence done to his own people; called the day of the Lord, because God will shew himself, who hath lain concealed as it were all this while and been a looker on, whilst his people did suffer punishment for their sins.

The time of Jerusalem's chastisement was called *the day of Jerusalem*, because their sins deserved that day to come upon them; but the day of the heathen is here called the day of the Lord, because now God doth awake as one out of sleep, and sheweth himself clearly to his enemies.

This day, the prophet telleth them, is now at hand, and near to them.

This is near upon all the heathen; not only upon Edom, but upon all those with whom Edom joined himself against the people of God. The prophet Jeremiah, chap. xxv., foretelling this day, nameth the heathen upon whom the wrath of the Lord was to come; and the judgment is 'eye for eye, tooth for tooth.' *Lex talionis*, wherein he telleth her, 'As thou hast done, it shall be done to thee,' &c.

And after, metaphorically he expresseth the retaliation, 'As thou hast drunk upon my holy mountain.' Hereof we observe the change of the manner of speech that is here used; we shall clear the text from that difficulty that hath distracted interpreters, so that they have failed in the right meaning of these words.

For whereas before the prophet speaketh to Edom, here he bringeth in God himself speaking to Jerusalem, comforting them in the declaration of his just judgment against her enemies; for he saith to Jacob, 'As thou hast drunk upon my holy mountains, so shall all the heathen drink continually. By the metaphor of drinking, which is referred to that which is called the cup of the Lord's indignation, of which David saith, 'In the hand of the Lord there is a cup, the wine is red,' &c.; by this figure, then, the cup of affliction is understood. The phrase is used after by our Saviour, 'Let this cup pass from me:' again, 'If thou wilt not let it pass, but that I must drink thereof, thy will be done.' We use that phrase, to 'drink of the cup of God.' So the threatening runneth in this sense, that as the people of God upon God's holy mountain have drunk of the cup of God's wrath, and have had their draught thereof, which was but for a time, 'so shall all the heathen drink, and their judgment shall not have end: they shall drink continually; there shall be no end of their affliction: they shall swallow down the wrath of the Lord until they be utterly destroyed, for they shall be as though they had not been.'

In which words is contained,
1. A judgment against the heathen;
2. A consolation to the church.
1. In the judgment observe,
1. The certainty thereof: the day is set.

2. The propinquity of it: it is near.
3. The extent of it: to all the heathen.
4. The equity of it: 'as thou hast done.'
5. The certainty of it: 'they shall drink,' &c.
6. The duration of it: 'continually.'
In the comfort note,
1. He speaketh of it as of a judgment past and gone: 'as ye have drunk thereof.'
2. He calleth their dwelling, though thus punished, 'my holy mountain.'
3. He revealeth to them his severe vengeance against their enemies.
1. Of the judgment; 2. Of the certainty.

The Lord hath set down and decreed a day for vengeance. Threatenings of woe at large do move but little; but when the punishment is denounced, and the day set for the execution thereof, this cannot but pierce and draw blood. And being here called 'the day of the Lord,' that is, a day designed by the Lord for this execution, it is more quick and penetrating.

There is no sin which is committed on earth but God hath both made a law against it, to forbid the doing of it, and he hath declared his judgment against it; yet hath he given us the light of his word, or the light of the law, which his finger wrote in our hearts, to declare it to us; and he hath given us time also to repent and amend it, and he is patient and long-suffering in his expectation of our amendment. But where it is not amended, he doth set down a day for the execution of his just judgment; for he will not, he cannot, suffer his truth to fail. His patience and mercy will take their day first, and his justice will also have her day.

St James advertiseth us, chap. i. 4, 'Let patience have her perfect work.' We have a fair example of God for this, for he will not let the work of his patience be unperfect; he will forbear us till the very day of his justice designed for punishment.

Though all the masters of assemblies, all the ministers of the word, be continually striking at this nail, we cannot drive it into the head, to make men believe that God hath set a day for punishment of all our sins. The promise of grace to the penitent doth so comfort us generally, that we hope we shall have time enough to put off that day by our repentance. And then again, we often take that for repentance which is not it. For it is not enough to remember our sins with a *God forgive me!* Repentance is a putting off of sin, an hatred of it, and a change of life and manners; every sorrow is not such. But were it that this day were thought upon with that fear and trembling that is due to it, it would put sin out of countenance, and the sinner out of hope. The sinner that believes not this doth make God a liar, whose word of truth hath revealed the certainty of this day to us.

2. It armeth the lusts of the flesh against the soul; for who is he that liveth without fear, that will bridle his affections, or stop the swift current of nature in himself, but runneth into sin as an horse rusheth into the battle? But when we do consider, upon every sin that we commit, that the day of the Lord shall declare it, the day of the Lord shall punish it, this maketh us afraid of our secret sins for fear of shame, and of all sins for fear of punishment. The certainty that this day will come, the uncertainty when it will come, is the greatest motive to hasten repentance that may be.

2. The propinquity: it is near.

If our consciences be convinced of the certainty of this day, and the judgment thereof, Satan's next allusion* is to flatter us that it is afar off, and shall not come yet, and there will be time enough to repent us of our sin. If we tell you indefinitely that it is near, yet you may hope not so near but that we may prevent it. For the apostle hath told his brethren long ago of the last day: 'The end of all things is at hand,' 1 Peter iv. 7. But it is sixteen hundred years since, and where is the promise of his coming?

But let not that comfort thee in sin, for even that day is near, seeing time is nothing to eternity; but thy day, wherein God shall visit thy sins with his judgments, may be much sooner.

If we had commission to tell you it is but forty days, and the next day is the day of the Lord, as Jonah did, peradventure it would warn you; but we have no commission to say it is so. It is a good proof that it is

* Qu. 'illusion'?—ED.

near, when none can promise that this very day shall not be it.

Yet we see there were some that took the day of their death near themselves, *cras moriemur;* yet they made evil use of it, *edamus, bibamus,* as the epicure, *dum vivimus, vivamus.* For the sensual and carnal man maketh that evil use of his near end, to live more sensually. *Post mortem nulla voluptas.* In every particular man's case St John† doth admonish us all well: 'Now also is the axe laid to the root of the tree.'

I learn a parable of Christ. Do but consider thine own field, and see the corn that grows upon it, and observe if it be not white and ready for the sickle; observe thine own ways and works, and see if they do not tell that the day of the Lord cannot be far off.

There be that put this day far off from them, that is, by flattering themselves in their sins; they make themselves believe that they shall not yet come to punishment. Repentance only lengtheneth this day, and suffereth it not to approach to us. Such an one feareth not *in die malo,* in the evil day.

3. The extent of this judgment: 'over all the heathen;' meaning here all those that have joined together in war against the Jews. See Jer. xxv.

Here is a query,

Did not God stir them up against Jerusalem? In this prophecy he declareth how Jerusalem was chastened by the heathen; and doth not the holy story say, 2 Kings xxiv. 3, 'Surely at the commandment of the Lord came this upon Judah'?

Judah well deserved this punishment, and God justly inflicted it, and the heathen were the rod of God wherewith he chastened Judah; yet this execution done upon Judah by the heathen was impious in them; for they made war against God's church, and sought the ruin of religion. It was covetous, they robbed Jerusalem; it was cruel, they delighted in the blood of the Lord's people; it was proud, they insulted over them.

It is true that these heathen do not go without God to invade Judah, true that he sent them to punish the

† Qu. 'John the Baptist'?—Ed.

transgressions of his people, true that they are the rod and sword of God, for so David confessed that God bade Shimei to curse him : 2 Sam. xvi. 16, ' The Lord hath said unto him, Curse David.'

As in the creation God separated the waters from the face of the earth, and called the gathering together of the waters seas ; yet David says God hath set them their bounds, which they cannot pass, nor return to cover the earth; yet they would cover the earth. Surely the wicked are resembled to the sea in every consideration ; the church may be compared to the dry land. God holdeth the wicked in, that they cannot drown this dry land ; yet this they would do, for there is a natural antipathy in the heathen to the church of God. When the church sinneth, God openeth a gap and letteth his sea break in. He suffereth the wicked to scourge the church when it defaulteth; for both their sakes, that he may execute his judgment upon both ; and as Augustine saith, *Utitur Deus malis bene*.

In the story of the Judges, we read how the concubine of the Levite was abused to death in Gibeah, Judges xx., which being complained of to the rest of the tribes by the Levite, they sent unto Benjamin to deliver up to them those men of Belial that had done the villany, that they might put away the evil from Israel. But Benjamin would not hear their brethren, but prepared to put themselves in arms, and to go out to battle against the children of Israel : ver. 18, ' The children of Israel arose, and went to the house of God, and asked counsel of God, and said, Which of us shall go up first to the battle against the children of Benjamin ? And the Lord said, Judah shall go up first. They went, and Benjamin destroyed that day two and twenty thousand men. The children of Israel went up and wept before the Lord until even, and asked counsel of the Lord, saying, Shall I go up in battle against the children of Benjamin my brother ? And the Lord said, Go up against him. They did so the second day, and the children of Benjamin destroyed of Israel eighteen thousand men.' Here was nothing done without consulting of God ; God bade them go, and yet they prospered not ; yea, they lost in all forty thousand men. There is no clear expression in this story to declare why God punished Israel with this great effusion of blood. Plain it is that God's purpose was to punish Israel, and first the tribe of Judah; but the text sheweth,

1. That the cause of this war was a just provocation; there was villany done in Israel.
2. That the end of this war was godly, for it was to remove evil from Israel.
3. That they did nothing herein without God's express warrant, for they began to take counsel of the Lord.

Yet before God would revenge the fault of the Benjamites upon them, by Benjamin he punished the tribe of Judah first, and then the rest of the tribes, with loss of so many men, and effusion of so much blood. And I must tell you that I find not the reason thereof expressed. It may be that the Holy Ghost hath suppressed it, that we might rest in the fear of God, and not search further; it is enough for us to know what God doth, and not why; for, as Augustine saith, *Judicia Dei occulta esse possunt, injusta non possunt esse*, God's judgments may be secret, but never unjust. And we must be very tender how we call God to account for what he doth; for God is whatsoever his will is, of which we must not seek to know more than is revealed, for that is prying into the ark, and costeth death; God is accountable to none for what he doth. The third day he gave Israel a full victory against Benjamin; by Benjamin he scourged Israel, and by Israel he after destroyed Benjamin, and left of them but six hundred men. So may we say of this example in my text, God useth the heathen to scourge his church, and after destroyeth the heathen in his just but secret judgment.

Yet let me tell you what some learned judgments have conceived of that great example of justice in that story of Israel and Benjamin.

Rabbi Levi saith, that Israel might provoke God at first, because they came to God to ask who should go first against Benjamin, and did trust to their own strength, and did not beseech God to give them victory. Rabbi Kimchi saith, it was because that Israel had suffered idolatry in Dan, and had never taken the cause of God to heart, to ask counsel of God against them; but now, in a private injury done to a Levite, they were provoked, and sought revenge. Others conceive that this was the cause: they came too slightly to God at first, for they did only bluntly inquire who should go first against Benjamin; not whether they should go or not; not inquiring by what way he meant to punish their brother. But the second time they went up to the Lord, they wept till even, and then they asked counsel. 'Shall I go up again in battle against my brother?' Yet even then, being commanded to go, they lost eighteen thousand men. True; but they came not the second time with that preparation which became them, that would fight the Lord's battles, to remove evil out of Isaael; for the third day they mended all: Ver. 26, 'Then all the children of Israel, and all the people, went up, and came unto the house of God, and wept, and sat there before the Lord, and fasted that day until even, and offered burnt offerings, and peace offerings before the Lord. Then they inquired of the Lord, for there was the ark, and there was Phinehas, the son of Eleazar, the son of Aaron, standing. And they said, Shall I yet go again to battle against the children of Benjamin my brother, or shall I cease?' And then God promised them victory.

It may be that they offended in the two first days in the preparation; they were not enough humbled before the Lord, or in the manner of their consultation with God.

But I must tell you plainly, all these are the conjectures of some learned judgments concerning this question, God hath left no account to us of his proceedings therein. Neither hath he done the like in the example in my text, why he punisheth all the heathen for smiting Jerusalem, seeing himself set them a-work.

Use. Therefore let not our prevailings against our brethren swell us up with pride, making us presume that we have God our friend, because we have had the upper hand of our enemies, for God may punish our brethren, and make us his rod to whip others, and he may burn the rod when he hath done with it. This is one of God's strange works that he doth upon earth; he foretelleth one of them by his prophet Habakkuk, and saith, Hab. i. 5–12, 'Behold ye among the heathen, and wonder marvellously: for I will work a work in your days, which you will not believe though it be told you.' And what is that? 'For, lo, I raise up the Chaldeans, that bitter and hasty nation, which shall march through the breadth of the land, to possess the dwelling-places that are not theirs. They are terrible and dreadful: their judgment and their dignity shall proceed of themselves. Their horses also are swifter than the leopards, and are more fierce than the evening wolves,' &c. These are sent of God; and they prevail, and when they have done, they thank their own God for the victory. But the church is comforted against them. 'O Lord, thou hast ordained them for judgment, thou hast established them for correction.' Therefore the example of Israel having overcome Benjamin in the former story is excellent; for when they had conquered their brother, they did not say in triumph, We have prevailed, nor bragged of their victory; but the people, having fulfilled the will of God in that war, 'came to the house of God, and abode there till even before God, and lift up their voices and wept sore,' Judges xxi. 2. They were sorry that God had used their sword and arm to their brother.

4. The equity of this judgment. Ver. 15, 'As thou hast done, it shall be done to thee: thy reward shall return upon thine own head.' The law of nature written in our hearts is, 'Do as thou wouldst be done to.' For Aristotle's *abrasa tabula* is not true divinity. Seeing the heathen will not do this, the justice of God putteth it upon them. They shall be done to as they do. Of this point see before.

5. The contents of this judgment. 'They shall drink; yea, they shall drink and swallow down, and they shall be as though they had not been.' The old heathen had a fashion of capital punishment by death, to give the offender a potion of poison to drink. The

prophet here speaketh of the punishment of Edom and the heathen in that very phrase, alluding to that of David : Ps. xi. 6, ' Upon the wicked he shall rain snares, fire and brimstone, and an horrible tempest; that shall be the portion of their cup.'

And, Ps. lxiii. 8, ' Thou hast shewed thy people hard things : thou hast made us to drink of the wine of astonishment.' This is the cup that David speaketh of, Ps. lxxv. 8, ' For in the hand of the Lord there is a cup, and the wine is red : it is full of mixture, and he poureth out of the same; but the dregs thereof all the wicked of the earth shall wring them out, and drink them.'

Wine immoderately drunken doth set the body on fire; it infatuateth the brain, it maketh the parts of the body useless, that neither head, nor hand, nor foot can do their several offices.

Drunkenness is such a disabling to man, that God hath chosen to express the severity of his wrath in the similitude of drunkenness; and the prophet Jeremiah hath used the very phrases thereof upon like occasion : chap. xxv. 15, ' Take the wine of this cup of my fury at my hand, and cause all the nations to whom I send thee, to drink it. And they shall drink, and be moved, and be mad.' Yet more fully, ver. 27, ' Drink ye, and be drunken, and spue, and fall, and rise no more.'

Let drunkards behold themselves in this glass, and see how loathsome and dangerous a sin they sin. Every cup they drink immoderately is a cup of God's wrath; every health they drink drunkenly is a disease even unto death. Drunkenness maketh men the emblems of God's indignation, the very images and pictures of divine vengeance. In this phrase God often in Scripture doth express his judgment, and his fury and vengeance against evil doers. Therefore, ' be not drunk with wine, wherein is excess.' ' I beseech you, brethren, by the mercies of God, that you would do no more so.' If any of you have by occasion been overtaken with that epidemical and popular fault, do no more so wickedly, sin not against your own bodies. *Morbus est;* it is a disease. Sin not against your good name; it is a foul blemish to be called a drunkard; they that are so are very impatient of that name. Sin not against God's creatures; they were given us for use and service; not that we, abusing them, should become servants to them, and be overcome of them. Sin not against your brethren by evil example, or by tempting them to this sin. Above all, 'God forbid that you should do this great wickedness, and so sin against your God.' You see he can and will set you a-drinking off his cup, and he will make you doff it, as you call it; and do him right to drink all, even to the bottom, till you fall and rise no more, till, as my text saith, 'you be as though you had not been.'

The phrase of my text hath carried me thus far out of my way, but I must do so, if I will meet with drunkards, for they are so brain-crazed, that they cannot keep the right way.

I return to the contents of this judgment, thus expressed in the phrase of drinking. 'These nations have filled the cup of affliction full for Jerusalem, and Jerusalem hath drunk deep thereof; now God will change the object of his fury, he will take away his cup from the church, and he will give it to her enemies,' as Isaiah hath sweetly and fully declared it, to the great grief of the nations, the great joy of the church. 'Hear, thou afflicted and drunken, but not with wine. Thus saith the Lord, and thy God that pleadeth the cause of his people: Behold, I have taken out of thy hand the cup of trembling, the dregs of the cup of my fury; thou shalt no more drink it again. But I will put it into the hand of them that afflict thee, which have said to thy soul, Bow down that we may go over, and thou hast laid thy body as the ground, and as the street to them that went over.' This calleth to my remembrance the word of the apostle St Peter: 2 Peter iv. 17, 'For the time is come that judgment must begin at the house of God; and if it first begin at us, what shall the end be of them that obey not the gospel of God?' When God sent destroyers into Jerusalem, their commission was, Ezek. ix. 6, 'Slay utterly old and young, both maids, and little children, and women.' It followeth, 'And begin at my sanctuary.'

The first cruelty that was executed on earth, that is upon record, was upon just Abel, and the first death we read of was a violent death. The first that suffered in Sodom any notable affliction was righteous Lot. For, 2 Peter ii. 7, 'he lived in much tribulation, vexed with the filthy conversation of the wicked. For that righteous man dwelling among them, in seeing and hearing, vexed his righteous soul from day to day with their unlawful deeds.'

After that cruel execution done upon our Saviour Christ by the Jews and Romans, God sent his judgments abroad into the world, but he began at his own sanctuary. The first that suffered was Stephen, then James the brother of John; the apostles all but one suffered martyrdom. The church lived in persecution, then God punished the Jews by the Romans, and after that the Romans lost their monarchy.

The difference of their drinking was,

1. The church drinketh first, and tasteth of the cup of wrath, as Christ said to the sons of Zebedee: 'Ye shall drink of the cup whereof I drink, and be baptized with the baptism that I am baptized withal.' They drink some of the uppermost of the cup.

2. God punished them for a time, but he took not his mercy utterly from them.

The church have an end of their afflictions; but the next point declareth the severity of God against the enemy nations.

5. The duration, 'continually.' This sometimes holdeth in temporal afflictions; if God's curse be upon Canaan, Israel shall have their land, and they shall have charge to root them out, and to destroy them utterly. God remembereth what Amalek did to Israel: 'The Lord hath sworn, that he will have war with Amalek from generation to generation.' 'The face of the Lord is against them that do evil, to cut off the remembrance of them from the earth.' These carry their destruction about them: 'for evil shall slay the wicked,' *malum culpæ;* the evil of sin that infecteth them shall be *malum pœnæ*, to punish and torment them.

The reason hereof is, for where God once hateth, he ever hateth. He hath once said, 'I have hated Esau.'

Let the blessing of his father feed him with the fat of the earth, let his habitation be in the rock, let his neighbour nations make leagues and confederation with him, let him have all the purchase of his sword for a time, 'the right hand of God shall find him out,' and not leave smiting him till he be utterly destroyed; so he is threatened before.

His very hidden things shall be sought out; the decrees of God be like himself, 'without variableness or shadow of change.'

God hath ever given great way to the intercessions of his saints; they have so far prevailed, that Abraham, praying for Sodom, gave over asking before God gave over yielding to his petition.

God hath shewed much favour to evil places for some few righteous persons' sakes that have been there.

But when he cometh to execute judgment once upon a place, he saith three times in one chapter, Ezek. xiv., 'Though Noah, Daniel, and Job were in that place, they should deliver but their own souls by their righteousness, but they should deliver neither son nor daughter.' Therefore, the word of God is not sent in the ministry of his servants to convert reprobates; that cannot be, they cannot be converted; and if God had revealed to us whom he hateth, we might save a labour of preaching to them in hope of their conversion. But the use of preaching and prayer is, for such as are already in the church, to 'confirm the brethren,' and to build them up; further, for those sheep which are without, to bring them to the fold; for Christ saith, he hath 'other sheep which are not yet of his fold,' and them he must bring to it.

And when you read of so many 'added to the church,' it was not out of the number of reprobates, but out of the number of God's chosen who were before uncalled. This is a secret which God concealeth within the closet of his own wisdom. 'The Lord knoweth who are his.'

Let the elect of God rest in this: if the wicked of the earth, that live in all kind of ungodliness, be in the decree of his election, they cannot miscarry, though they hold out as the thief did, till they come to the cross to die. Therefore, let us despair of no man's salvation amongst us.

But if the decree of God's hatred be settled upon them, there is no hope; for Christ, the remedy of sin, undertaketh for no more than the Father hath given to him. These, howsoever they prosper on earth in things temporal, they have drank a draught of deadly wine, that ever riseth up in them, and upbraideth them, for God hath spoken it. *Nulla pax impio*, there is no peace to the wicked; but he is like the raging of the unquiet sea, ever foaming out mire and dirt, for a reprobate man dare not trust God.

2. But if we come to the after-reckoning in the day of judgment, there can be no end of the woe of them whom God hateth; their worm of conscience never dieth, their fire of torment never is quenched. There have been some, whom St Augustine doth call *misericordes illos*,* that have believed and affirmed,—

1. Some of them that the damned devils, and all after some long time of sharp punishment, shall be received into favour; these make hell but a purgatory.

2. Others say,† True, that they shall be damned to everlasting pains: but *donabit eas Deus precibus et intercessionibus sanctorum suorum*.

The illusion that deceiveth them is this: *Non credendum est tunc amissuros sanctos viscera misercordiæ, cum fuerint plenissimæ ac perfectissimæ sanctitatis: ut qui tunc orabant pro inimicis, quando ipsi sine peccato non erant, tunc non orent pro supplicibus suis, quando nullum cæperint habere peccatum.* And supposing that the saints will pray to God for them, he inferreth, *An vero Deus tunc eos non exaudiet, tot et tales filios suos, quando in tanta eorum sanctitate, nullum inveniet orationis impedimentum?*

This is further urged: for when we say the Scripture doth tell us that God will everlastingly punish the wicked; and David saith, 'He will not suffer his truth to fail;' they answer, that all those threatenings of Scripture are to be understood *in veritate severitatis*, in respect of the evil desert of the wicked, but not *in veritate miserationis*, for that must at last have honour

* De Civ. xxi. 17.   † Cap. xviii.

above all his works.

Further, they plead : God hath never more plainly and positively declared his will concerning the eternal destruction of the reprobate, than he did by his prophet Jonah declare the destruction of Nineveh. It is but forty days, and without any condition, *Ninive destrueter.* Except we allow mental reservation, *mendacem non possumus dicere Deum, et tamen non factum est.* The truth was in this, *pronunciavit eos dignos hæc pati.* Their inference is, *Si tunc pepercit eis Deus quando prophetam suum contristaturus erat parcendo; quanto magis tunc parcet miserabilius supplicantibus, quando, ut parcat omnes sancti ejus orabunt?* They add the saying of the apostle, ' God hath concluded all under sin, that he might shew mercy unto all."

To the first, and therein to both, St Augustine doth fully answer,* that if we deny everlasting death, we may as well deny life everlasting; for we have the same ground for both, the same direct word of God. *Aut utrumque cum fine diuturnum, aut utrumque sine fine perpetuum.*

To the second, he denieth that which is presumed, that the saints will pray for the damned. Here we pray for all, because we know not who be elect, who be reprobate. But when God hath revealed his will concerning these, *cessat oratio,* praying ceaseth, and the voice of the elect is,'*Fiat voluntas tua,* thy will be done. Yea, ' the saints shall judge the world then ; and those bowels of human commiseration which they had on earth are put off; they now hate where God hateth, and judge where God judgeth, and rejoice against them whom God condemneth.

And for the example of Nineveh, his answer is full and sappy. *Evertuntur peccatores duobus modis.* 1. *Sicut Sodomitæ, ut pro peccatis suis homines puniantur.* 2. *Sicut Ninivitæ, ut ipsa horum peccata pænitendo destruantur;* there was the mistake of Jonah, for that was the city which God threatened and destroyed. *Eversa est Ninive quæ mala erat, et bona ædificata est, quæ non erat. Stantibus mænibus, perditis moribus.*

* Cap. xxiii.

To the last argument, from the words of the apostle, 'He hath concluded all under sin, that he might have mercy on all.' He bids them there read the whole text; they shall there see *quos omnes intelligit, nempe eos omnes de quibus loquebatur*, that is, both Jews and Gentiles, not comprehending the whole of both, but only *vasa misericordiæ*, in both the vessels of mercy; and the very course of the text cleareth it to be so meant.

Therefore the revealed will of God hath settled this perpetuity of woe upon the ungodly: 'They shall drink, and they shall drink continually.'

The justice of this proceeding against the ungodly is taken from the merit of sin, which, being committed against an infinite majesty, must needs be also infinite. Now, the person guilty being finite, cannot bear a punishment infinite in the weight of it, and therefore it must be infinite in durance, to eternity.

Again, the hater* of God repayeth vengeance which is deserved, at least with the same measure wherewith his love giveth rewards undeserved; but the love of God giveth eternal life, therefore the hatred of God cannot give less than eternal death. This sheweth you the reason of those earnest exhortations, 'to work out your salvation,' to 'make your calling and election sure.' He meaneth in your own faith, for so long as a man liveth in fear of this eternal judgment, and seeth no way to escape it, his soul is among lions, even the roaring lion and all his whelps; it is in the keeping of the spirit of bondage. His sins lie so heavy upon him that he cannot look up.

2. The comfort implied and expressed.

1. He speaketh of the judgment on Israel as already past and over: 'As ye have drunk.'

2. He calleth Jerusalem, though thus wasted and made desolate, 'my holy mountain.'

3. He graciously revealeth to his church his just revenge upon his enemies.

1. *As ye have drunk;* that is, whenas ye have drunk of this cup of affliction, then God shall take it from you; which doth yield this comfortable doctrine.

* Qu. 'hatred'?—ED.

Doct. That though the church of God do live for a time under the cross, God will not leave it so for ever.

Afflictions are some part of that physic which God doth minister to his church, to heal the sores and diseases thereof.

Timerias in Plutarch, seeing the people very disorderly, αὐτὸς ἐβόα τὸν δῆμον ἀποτόμου χρείαν ἔχειν ἰατροῦ, ἢ μεγάλου καθαρμοῦ. But physic is not given perpetually; it ceaseth when the disease is removed. God knoweth the use of the rod to be necessary for a time; so the church confesseth: Isa. xxvi. 9, 'For when thy judgments are in the earth, the inhabitants of the world will learn righteousness.' When they have taken out that lesson, God ceaseth to afflict.

God is sharp in these visitations. Job hath not leisure to swallow his spittle. Job vii. 19.

Yet he endureth but a while in his anger: Ps. xxx. 5, 'Weeping may abide for the evening, but joy cometh in the morning.' 'For a little time have I forsaken thee, but with great compassion will I gather thee: for a moment in mine anger I hid my face from thee for a little season, but with everlasting mercy have I compassion on thee.'

1. The cause of God's favour eftsoons shining on the church after affliction is to let them see that his quarrel is not to the persons, but the sins, of men; for no sooner do men repent of their sins, but God also repenteth of his judgments. He is a father, and a tender father doth not love the smart, but seeketh the amendment of his son; and God himself, in the smiting of his church, is first weary, and he complains first: 'Why should you be stricken any more? Ye will revolt more and more; the whole head is sick, and the whole heart faint. From the sole of the foot even to the head, there is no soundness in it, but wounds, and bruises, and putrefying sores,' &c. Thus God suffereth in the passions of his children, and all our stripes ache upon him. Yet he is a God that loveth not iniquity, and therefore when he laid upon his dearly beloved Son the iniquity of us all, the apostle said, 'He spared not his own Son, but gave him unto death.'

2. He will not suffer his church to live always forsaken under the cross, in respect of his servants, and that for four reasons.

(1.) Afflictions do work upon them so that it breedeth in them contrition and sorrow for their sin; and 'a broken and contrite spirit God cannot refuse.' He will not discourage the contrite and sorrowful, but will have them to know that their groanings and sighs come up even into his ears: 'He putteth all their tears in his bottle.'

(2.) Afflictions do turn the children of God into prayers and supplications, and he will not neglect them that pray to him, that they may see the power and virtue of prayer, that upon all occasions they may prostrate their hearts before God in prayer.

God hath said of the just man, Ps. xci. 15, 'He shall call upon me in trouble, and I will hear him; yea, I will be with him in trouble, I will deliver him and glorify him.' Hosea v. 15, 'In their affliction they shall seek me diligently.' In the house of bondage he heard Israel: Exod. iii. 7, 'Then the Lord said, I have surely seen the trouble of my people which are in Egypt, and have heard their cry.' St James saith, 'If any man among you be afflicted, let him pray.' If that were not our comfort when all remedies fail us, we were most unhappy, for we can never be shut up so but we may send our prayers from us to heaven, to plead our cause in the name of Jesus Christ.

(3.) Sharp afflictions may be a strong temptation to make the children of God doubt of the love of God. It was not lawful for them in the judicial law to be immoderate in correction.

A trespasser might have forty stripes given him, but not more, lest if he should exceed and beat him above these with many stripes, then thy brother should seem vile unto thee, Deut. xxv. 3. God will not overdo in his chastenings of his church, to prevent this danger, lest his servant should think himself lost in the favour of God. We see how David was put to it in this kind. When his sore ran and ceased not, his soul refused comfort; yea, once he complained, 'My God, my God, why hast thou forsaken me?' yea, he 'thought upon

God and was troubled.' Therefore, God doth carry a favourable hand in his afflictions, to prevent the despair of his children, for he knoweth whereof we be made.

(4.) Sharp afflictions may be an occasion to harden the heart of man, and make him fall away from God to sin ; and that reason is given by the holy psalmist : Ps. cxxv. 2, 'For the rod of the wicked shall not rest upon the lot of the righteous, lest the righteous put forth their hands to iniquity.'

Indeed, some that have been well taught, and do understand well, and have lived in some measure of good life, and walked conscionably, when God hath tried them with wants, have fallen into snares, and embraced temptations.

Magnum pauperies opprobrium, jubet quidvis et facere, et pati, virtutisque viam deserit arduæ. Shifts, frauds, secret stealths, borrowings without means or hope of repayment, &c.

The wise son of Jakeh prayed to God, Prov. xxx. 9, ' Give me no poverty, lest I be poor and steal, and take the name of my God in vain.' Extremity of pain and sickness and soreness is a great temptation ; two great lights in the church of God were eclipsed by it : Job, the example of patience, fell into bitter cursings of the day of his birth ; so did holy Jeremiah, the Lord's prophet. In these respects God is tender, and suffereth not his chosen to be tempted above their strength, but doth give issue to their temptations. Yet sometimes he suffereth his elect to see their own weakness by some fall, that when he putteth to his helping hand they may be more wary to keep a better watch upon their hearts.

3. God doth not suffer his church to be forsaken in afflictions, lest the enemies thereof should too much insult over them. It is David's suit to God, ' Let them not say, We have prevailed.' When Saul and Jonathan were dead, David lamented them with great lamentation : 2 Sam. i. 19, 20, ' The beauty of Israel is slain upon the high places ; how are the mighty fallen ! Tell it not in Gath, publish it not in the streets of Askelon, lest the daughters of the Philistines re-

joice, lest the daughters of the uncircumcised triumph.' For this addeth to the ungodliness of the wicked; they grow proud upon it. 'Let not their wicked imagination prosper, lest they grow too proud.'

4. The afflictions of the church, when they do grow sharp and smarting, cause the ungodly of the earth to blaspheme the name of God. It is not for nothing that David doth pray so earnestly, Ps. cxliii. 11, 'Quicken me, O Lord, for thy name's sake; for thy righteousness' sake, bring my soul out of trouble.'

The ungodly Jews and Romans, standing by the cross of Christ, did speak contemptibly of God, and took his name in vain, in derision of his Son. It is the manner of the ungodly to blaspheme, if once they prevail against the church; then the God they serve is thought unable to protect them, and the religion they profess is scandalised for untruth.

These be great reasons why God doth not forsake his church in affliction, but giveth them a heavenly issue out of them.

This point teacheth its own use, for it serveth both to, 1, Inform; 2, convince; 3, exhort; 4, rebuke.

1. *Information.* This is a sure and infallible rule, that whom God once loveth he ever loveth; as he saith, 'I will never leave thee nor forsake thee,' 'for the gifts and calling of God are without repentance.' His love is himself, and 'he cannot deny himself.' He hath given us to his Son; and 'of them thou hast given me,' saith he, 'I have lost none,' and 'no man can take them out of my hand.' Rom. viii. 35, 'What shall separate us from the love of God in Christ Jesus?' He nameth the greatest miseries of life : ' Shall tribulation, or distress, or persecution, or famine, or nakedness, or peril, or sword ? Nay, in all these things we are more than conquerors through him that loved us.'

The love of God to his church is a banner over it, Cant. ii. 4.

2. *Conviction.* This doctrine convinceth the heathen, who deny that there is any providence, because the best men drink deepest of the cup of affliction, which maketh the profane say, 'It is in vain to serve God; and what profit is it that we have kept his ordi-

nance, and that we have walked mournfully before the Lord of hosts? Mal. iii. 14. True, that they who make conscience of their ways are despised, their soul is filled with the scorn of the proud.

Ver 15, True, that 'they that work wickedness are set up, and they that tempt God are delivered;' but the elect say, 'For thy sake we are killed all the day long.' Yet the comfort that the just have in their affliction doth assure that ' verily there is a reward for the righteous, doubtless there is a God that judgeth the earth.' And though for a time the wicked insult over the just, the day will come when they shall see their ruin.

3. *Exhortation.* This doth admonish us to trust in the Lord, for he never faileth them that put their trust in him. Trust is best expressed in a storm, when the waves rage horribly, when the sorrows of death compass, and the floods go over our soul. In fair weather, when health, and youth, and plenty, and power, and pleasure, make a calm in our life, and we have the desire of our hearts, it is no trial of us to say, 'Surely God is good to Israel.' But in the furnace seven times heated, in the den of lions, in the belly of the whale, in the valley of the shadow of death, they that then trust in the Lord, they declare their faith more than victorious. In sickness, and smart, and pains of the body, in want and misery, those that then say to God, Thou art my rock and my fortress, my stronghold, and the God of my salvation: though thou kill me I will trust in thee,—these are more than conquerors by faith, for they do not only conquer fear and all the temptations to despair, but they do advance instead thereof joy in the Holy Ghost, rejoicing in tribulations, and giving thanks to God for all their sorrows.

(2.) This teacheth us patience, for 'tribulation bringeth forth patience,' and patience must have a perfect work to hold out to the end. 'By our patience we possess our souls,' for the impatient man is not his own man. Impatience is like drunkenness; it so staggereth our reason and drowneth our understanding in the deluge of passion and perturbation, that our tongue speaketh, our heart thinketh, our hand worketh things that in the next calm we have cause to repent.

(3.) Affliction is *cos orationis*, the whetstone of prayer, it turneth us all into prayer, as I have taught, and maketh us call upon him who is *Deus liberator*, God our deliverer.

(4.) Affliction is *cos obedientiæ*, the whetstone of obedience; so 'now I keep thy commandments,' saith David, *quia bonum est me affligi*, because it is good for me to have been afflicted; I have gotten that good by it.

(5.) It teacheth us commiseration of the sorrows of our brethren, and filleth us with comforts, wherewith we comfort them, according as we have received comfort ourselves in our sorrows. So, when we visit one another in sickness, if we have had either some other or some like pains ourselves, we tell them how we found ease; so the apostle saith, 2 Cor. i. 2–5, 'Blessed be God, even the Father of our Lord Jesus Christ, the Father of mercy, and God of comfort, who comforteth us in all tribulations, that we may be able to comfort them which are in any trouble, by the comfort wherewith we ourselves are comforted of God.' For as the sufferings of Christ abound in us, so our consolation also aboundeth by Christ.

4. *Rebuke*. This doctrine chideth those that can receive good at the hands of God, and not evil; who upon every affliction fall out with God, and murmur at his visitations, and doubt of his favour, as if temporal ease and prosperity were the measure of his love.

There is a root of bitterness in us, and the best of God's saints have declared themselves to be but men in this trial. Afflictions are too strong for us; we cannot well endure pain, we cry to our chirurgeon, *Tolle quia urit*, take it away, it paineth me, the plaster paineth us; he telleth us, *Non tollam quia sanat*, I will not, because I would cure you; we see that this pain is soon over: God continueth but a while in his anger. This is the only purgatory of the elect, and this fire is but for our dross, and this medicine is but for our disease.

2. He calleth Jerusalem, though thus wasted and overthrown, 'my holy mountain.' David saith, 'he

loved the gates of Sion more than all the habitations of Jacob.' God said of it, 'Here will I dwell, for I have a delight therein.' The former doctrine declareth that God did not mean to cast off his people for ever, and the next words, ver. 17, promise restoration.

Two things had met on this mountain, to corrupt it and unsanctify it.

1. The grievous and crying sins of the people of God, provoking wrath.
2. The barbarous cruelty of the enemies of the church, executing wrath.

These made no difference between holy and unholy, but first robbed and pillaged the sanctuary, and carried away the treasures and utensils, the ornaments of the temple, and all that might yield them any profit, and then put fire to that admirable pile of the curiousest structure for art and cost that ever the bright eye of heaven looked upon.

I cannot but stay your thoughts upon the way, to consider with me what desolations sin may make upon the earth.

Here is blood spilt in Jerusalem, the holy city; no respect of the grey hairs, no compassion of the fairest virgins, no tenderness either to new-born or unborn children. Here is deportation of others in numerous multitudes into captivity, to become vassals to the proud conqueror the Assyrian monarch. Here is the city of God demolished, the very ring and jewel of the world; the psalmist calleth it, 'The joy of the whole earth.' Here is the temple, the rich diamond of that ring, the place wherein God was served, and offerings were burnt therein to his name, that now made an holocaust and burnt-offering itself, and sending forth *lambentes sidera flammas*, flames ascending to the stars; the specious spacious courts of that house, God's own enclosure, and all the holy mountain, the glebe-land of the church, laid common; the land emptied of her native inhabitants, save some few reserved to be the drudges of the Chaldeans, to plough their grounds and to dress their vines. Beloved, a greater example of the provocation of sin, or the execution of justice, no time, not all the books of time, have ever shewed.

And what shall we say? Hath sin lost the sting that it had wont to carry; or hath God lost his feeling, that we should equal that city in sins, and not expect equal vengeance? Every man shuns it, to be a prophet of ill news, and men had rather exhort than correct. If we come with the rod which Paul threatened, we may chance handsel it ourselves. Sinners be too bold to be under the check of God's ministers; but there is one aloft that saith, 'But I will reprove thee, and set in order before thee the things that thou hast done.'

The comfort yet is, that this mountain of Sion, though thus punished, is called God's mountain still; God vouchsafeth to own it, and call it his. The enemies thereof have gotten the possession of it, yet God will not lose the right of his inheritance there, for he meaneth to build up again what the enemy hath destroyed, and return again those whom the enemy hath carried away captives; as the next section declares fully.

Let the brethren of schism and separation lay this to heart, who fall from the communion of the church of England, pretending the great corruptions that be, some in the doctrine, but most in the discipline thereof. Is Sion the mountain of the Lord still, although both sin and vengeance have left it desolate? Did Christ call the temple his Father's house, when the ungodly profaners of it had made it a den of thieves? I dare not say now, though that mountain of the Lord, and the place where God's honour did sometimes dwell, and wherein God took delight, hath almost endured sixteen hundred years' desolation, and is now the cage of unclean birds, inhabited by Turks and Saracens, and for the profit of both, by popish idolaters, which make prize of pilgrims resorting to visit the places sometimes hallowed by the presence of Christ and his mother, and his holy servants; I dare not say that God hath lost his interest therein, or resigned all his right thereto. *Nullum tempus occurrit regi.*

I remember the prophecy of Zechariah, chap. xiv. 7, 8: 'But it shall be one day which shall be known to the Lord, nor day, nor night: but it shall come to pass, that at evening time it shall be light. And it shall be in that day, that living waters shall go out from Jerusalem.' A prophecy not yet fulfilled, for though interpreters do commonly attribute this to the coming of Christ in the flesh, and the light of the gospel, beginning at Jerusalem and shining over all the world, the words of the text do directly confute that exposition, for this prophecy is determined to the evening-time, that is, to the latter end of the world, and Christ came in the fulness of time. And at the coming of Christ in the flesh it was not as here is said, 'nor day, nor night,' for then *lux magna orta est*, the Sun of righteousness arose in our hemisphere, the very night was lighted to the shepherds with an extraordinary clarity; and such a light shone in Jerusalem as not only lighted them, but it was a light to lighten the Gentiles; it shone to the east upon the Magi there, and all the ends of the world soon saw the salvation of their God.

Therefore I conclude that this prophecy is to be fulfilled towards the end of the world, when God shall call again his people from far, and his dispersed from the ends of the earth. When the fulness of the Gentiles is come in, then shall God call again his people, and 'remember the oath that he sware unto Abraham, and the sure mercies of David.' Then shall he set his name again in Jerusalem, and displant the intruders upon his possession, and settle his habitation once again upon the holy mountain, at the end of the world.

Yet I do not affirm that there shall be again a commonwealth of the Jews, or a distinction of tribes, as heretofore; that wall of partition is taken down, and the bond of Christian religion shall be the bond of peace, and God hath said it.

 Tros Tyriusve mihi nullo discrimine agetur.

Both Jew and Gentile, all shall be alike.

But God hath laid such claim to this mountain, and professed so much love to it, that I dare not believe that he can forget it for ever; but that when the time, the appointed time, shall come, he will have mercy upon Sion, and will pity the ruins and dust thereof.

But when here Sion is called *mons sanctus meus*, 'my holy mountain,' here is a *quære*, how any place can be called holy, and what kind of holiness it is, which is ascribed to any place.

Surely if it be *sanctus quia meus*, what place is it where God is not? He is in the valley of the shadow of death; he is present over men in the nethermost hell.

But God is said to sanctify some places here on earth, because he is present there;—

1. *Secundum specialem curam*, in respect of his special care and protection.

2. *Secundum specialem cultum*, in respect of his special worship.

Jerusalem was the place which God took into his special protection, and where he placed his special worship; for 'the Lord God was well known in Sion; at Salem was his tabernacle, and his dwelling in Sion.'

1. And for the special care that he had of that place: 'He loved the gates of Sion more,' &c.

And 'though the earth was the Lord's, and all that therein is, yet of Sion he said, Here do I dwell: I have a delight herein.'

And this *spiritualis cura*, spiritual care, so sanctified that place, that when Israel had polluted the worship of God, and heathen came in upon God's inheritance, and defiled his sanctuary, yet ceased not that place to be holy, not by any inherent holiness, as the Roman church suggesteth, but only *secundum specialem curam*, because it was not yet out of God's special protection; and only thus it is holy at this day.

2. *Propter specialem cultum*, for his special worship. When any place is dedicated to God's worship, and separate from common use, it is an holy place, and God vouchsafeth there *specialem præsentiam*, a special presence. For I am not of Mr Calvin's mind, who saith, *Templa non sunt propria Dei habitacula, unde aurem propius admoveat.* For God hath a special interest in those places which are separate to his special worship, and the very place is fearful to them that have any sense of religion; and as Damascene saith, *plus participat gratiæ et operationis Dei*, they partake more of the

powerful operation of God. For why is heaven the throne of God more than the earth, but because God doth there more express his glory than he doth here?

And for the interest that God hath in those consecrated places, consider God's challenge in my text. Sion, though in the hand of the Chaldeans, is the mount of God.

Churches and lands once given to God, do remain his for ever; for unless God shall manifestly reveal his resignation to man, what man on earth hath any assignment from him of his right? Beloved, we have power to give to God of his own, but we have no power on earth for revocation; when it is once sacred, and God hath enclosed it, no man can lay it common. But the fat of the church hath set so many of all degrees in this land to that growth and strength that this doctrine is a paradox, and we are but laughed at when we plead the right of God to things sacred. For if sacrilege be a sin, what rank of men in this or our neighbour kingdom doth not live in sin and by sin?

The mount of Sion is challenged here to be the holy mountain of God, in whose hand soever the possession thereof be, and all that invade the right of God in things sacred shall hear him complain, 'Ye have robbed me;' and though they make it strange, and ask, 'Wherein have we robbed thee?' Solomon will tell them, Prov. xx. 25, 'It is a snare for a man to devour that which is sanctified, and after the vows to inquire.'

3. It is a great favour of God to his church to reveal to them his will concerning both their own short punishment and the long affliction of their enemies.

For themselves, they shall see in this revelation that God will not give them over utterly; and affliction doth never shew intolerable when we can look beyond it, and see fair weather after it. This had need be preached to the church of God, to keep them from fainting in their patience and falling into sin. David confessed, Ps. xxvii. 13, 'I had fainted unless I had believed to see the goodness of the Lord in the land of the living.' The prophet having given us his own example, doth also give us his good counsel: ver. 14, 'Wait on the Lord, be of good courage, and he shall strengthen thy heart: wait, I say, on the Lord.'

You see the use of this doctrine is to put mettle into us, that we be not cast down with the present sense of God's judgments, but that we courageously do bear them, and patiently expect our deliverance from them. Of this before.

2. It is a comfort and joy to the church to know that God will execute their judgments upon their enemies, and pass the cup of his wrath from them to those that hate them.

1. Because it stoppeth the way to an high and grievous sin, which is murmuring against God. Let every man suspect himself for this, for God's own Israel did often fall this way; but when God revealeth to us his purpose, we cannot find fault; though we feel where judgment beginneth, we know where it shall end.

2. It allayeth all thoughts of revenge on them that trouble and persecute us, for to what purpose should we fret ourselves at the instruments of God's vengeance, when we know the end of these men, how ' God hath set them in slippery places,' and that he will take the matter into his own hand to revenge it?

And this is a necessary doctrine for us, because the pursuit of private revenge is one of the crying sins of the time. We have poor men, that, to molest a neighbour, will swear the peace against them to put them in bonds, when it is to be feared that it is rather revenge than fear that makes them swear; and this upon a little cooling of blood appears clearly.

Just laws are made to do men right against wrongs. We must go to judges as children to their father, to seek justice in charity, not in the spirit of revenge. God hath declared himself to be *Deus ultionum*, a God of revenge, and hath promised to judge our cause. Let us commit the matter to him, and give our souls rest, possessing them with patience.

Israel shall see their cup, that they have but tasted, drunk up, and swallowed down of their enemies: the mouth of the Lord hath spoken it. Ps. xcii. 11,' Mine eye shall see my desire upon mine enemies.' David maketh this use of this point, Ps. xli. 12, ' By this I know that thou favourest me, because mine enemy doth not triumph over me.' But it is a good sign of God's love to his church, that he suffereth not the ungodly to insult over them.

And for the enemies of the church, they may have victory, they cannot have a triumph ; for the cup of wrath is no sooner taken from the church, but it is presently given to her enemies to pledge them, as the prophet saith, ' When thou hast done spoiling, thou shalt be spoiled ;' the drink shall not pall in the cup. You see that David made that use of the fall and punishment of his enemy, only to rejoice in the Lord and his favour, and not to insult over his enemy ; for the wise man adviseth, Prov. xxiv. 17, 18, ' Rejoice not when thine enemy falleth, and let not thine heart be glad when he stumbleth ; lest the Lord see it, and it displease him, and he turn away his wrath from him.' Thy patience doth heap coals of fire on the head of thine enemy, and thy favourable forbearance of him in triumphing over him, holdeth the cup still to his mouth. We cannot do our enemy a greater pleasure than to be glad at his afflictions, for God seeth it, and abateth his displeasure against him ; but we may rejoice safely and boldly in the love and favour of God to us.

Ver. 17. *But upon mount Sion shall be deliverance, and there shall be holiness ; and the house of Jacob shall possess their possessions.*

The second part of the prophecy, containing the comfort of the church against all her enemies, *ad finem capitis,* to the end of the chapter.

1. A promise of restitution of them to their own, ver 17.
2. Of victory against their enemies, ver. 18-20.
3. The means ordained for this, ver. 21.
1. Of their restitution of their own.

Mount Sion literally doth signify the seed of Jacob, the whole nation of the Jews, taking name from the most eminent part of their kingdom, as mount Sion* denoteth Esau and his issue. This shall be delivered from the captivity of Babylon ; that is the deliverance here promised.

Qu. ' Seir ' ?—Ed.

And the holiness here mentioned is the renewing of the people, by repentance and new obedience, to the pure worship of God, and then the house of Jacob shall recover the possessions which the army of the Chaldeans took from them.

Allegorically and typically this prophecy doth foretell the deliverance of the church from all the enemies thereof in the end of the world, which shall be performed by the Spirit of sanctification fitting them to the same.

That the church shall not alway be under the rod of correction, we have formerly declared.

1. The point now considerable is, what our God requireth of us, even holiness.

2. That God performeth his mercy of deliverance first, that after he may sanctify us to himself.

1. That God requireth holiness of us: Micah vi. 8, 'He hath shewed thee, O man, what is good, and what the Lord requireth of thee : surely to do justice, and to love mercy, and to humble thyself to walk with thy God.' This is holiness. This is no earthly wisdom, which is 'carnal, sensual, and devilish;' it is 'the wisdom which is from above,' and therefore, 'He hath shewed thee, O man.'

Holiness is not learned in the school of nature, nor to be seen by the light of reason; it is the inward light of the Spirit of God that enlighteneth our darkness, which openeth to man the way of good life, not moral and civil only, but religious and spiritual, which teacheth justice mingled with mercy, both built upon a good foundation of humility ; and these not as before men, but as in a walk with God himself.

For such as these God keepeth a book of remembrance, as the prophet saith : Mal. iii. 16, 'Then they that feared the Lord spake often one to another : and the Lord hearkened, and heard it; and a book of remembrance was written before him for them that feared the Lord, and that thought upon his name. And they shall be mine, saith the Lord, in that day when I make up my jewels (or special treasure); and I will spare them, as a man spareth his own son that serveth him.' What can a man desire more of God, than to be esteemed amongst his jewels and precious treasure? Such are the holy; and what trouble can it be to them to be despised of the world, and cast out of them, when God shall take them in as his jewels and treasure? God himself giveth holiness in precept, and giveth the reason in that injunction : ' Be ye holy, for I am holy,' 1 Peter i. 16, *ex* Lev. xxi. 44. And St John saith, 1 John iii. 3, ' That every man that hath hope of eternal life purifieth himself, even as he is pure.' So that God's holiness is the motive that must induce us, and the precedent and pattern that must conduce us, to holiness.

1. The motive, because, he being holy, nothing ungodly and unclean may approach him; therefore all the legal purifications and sanctifyings of the people, before any special worship and service of God, were types of that holiness which must fit us for God's service, because ' without holiness no man shall see God.' Again, because the favours which we desire from God be holy, and Christ saith, *Nolite dare quod sanctum est canibus*, give not that which is holy to dogs; surely he will not do so himself.

2. It must be our pattern and example, because holiness is never accepted but where it hath three properties, as it hath in God.

(1.) That it be sincere, and not in hypocrisy. There is a sin of hypocrites, and there is a portion with hypocrites. False holiness is like counterfeit gold, it will not go for pay; it is high treason against God to counterfeit his image and superscription, for holiness is the image of our God stamped in us in our creation, therefore hell is called the portion of hypocrites.

(2.) That it be total: holiness in the face, and outward gesture proceeding from holiness in the heart and inward affections; holiness of the tongue, that it speak not lewdly, falsely, or profanely; holiness of operation, that we do nothing but what becometh the saints of God; holiness at church, and holiness at home; holiness in our private conversations, and in our private retirings, that is, in the whole man, in the whole time of his life, and in all places.

(3.) That it be guided with knowledge; for the ignorant holiness of the church of Rome, which is implicit, and knoweth not what it doth, is the sacrifice of fools; like the Athenians' worship, directed to an unknown god.

This is the way to come again to our own possessions, and to cast out that strong man armed, that hath led us into captivity; this is the old way and the good way to the new Jerusalem. 'Many walk, of whom I have told you often, and now tell you weeping, they be enemies of the cross of Christ, whose end is damnation, whose belly is their god, and whose delight is in their shame, which mind earthly things.' But our conversation must be in heaven; an holy conversation is an heavenly conversation, and maketh heaven upon earth. 'And if we be risen with Christ,' to this conversation, 'then we seek those things which are above, and not those things which are beneath.' It must, therefore, be our care to look to those things which hinder holiness, and to keep good watch upon our life, that none of those things do corrupt us.

These are, as the apostle doth enumerate them:
1. The lusts of the flesh.
2. The lust of the eye.
3. The pride of life.

1. Carnal desires do make us unholy; not only fornication and adultery, which do make the members of Christ the members of an harlot, of which sin the apostle saith, that 'adulterers and fornicators God will judge,' but carnality also in our affections, labouring more for the body than for the soul, for the flesh, to fulfil the lusts thereof; studying meat and drink for the belly, stuff and fashions for the garments, more than to please God in the exercise of religion, and duties of charity and piety; carnality also in the very service of God, of which the apostle also speaketh; for while 'one saith, I am of Paul, another I am of Apollos, are ye not carnal?' For the truth of God and the wisdom of God, is valued, not in itself, but in respect of persons. And so those that be the greatest pretenders to holiness, that pretend most of the Spirit, unawares do serve the flesh; and are men in religion carnal, yet think they do God good service.

2. The lust of the eye is another great enemy to holiness, for that coveteth an evil covetousness. How easily is flesh and blood carried away from God with the wings of worldly desires! I would I were as well housed, as well placed, as well landed, as well friended, as well moneyed, as such and such are. Who wisheth, I would I were as holy as the prophets and apostles were? When we must needs die, Balaam would wish his latter end like theirs.

3. The pride of life, affecting place and court above others, trim and rich bravery beyond others, power and authority over others, these things do corrupt religion, and make us unholy; and all these things do perish in the use of them.

There be two things which make the life of man proof against these darts of Satan.

1. Godliness, that fixeth our hearts on God, and fasteneth our trust on him, which giveth us assurance that we shall never want things sufficient for us; and therefore fear not to lose by it, if we bestow our time, and strength, and means in his service.

2. Contentedness, which respecteth rather a supply of wants, than a fulness to look upon, considering that of all that we have in possession, no more is truly ours than what serveth for use, and that is little ; and seeing we brought nothing with us, and we leave all, but what our wants have spent, behind us, let a little content us, lest much do distract us from the service of our God, or corrupt our holiness.

2. This teacheth to embrace all the good means by which holiness may be preserved and increased in us; that is,

1. Diligent hearing the word of God, upon which must attend, 1, private meditation ; 2, conference.

This is not the service of God itself, but a candle lighting us the way to the worship of God. David saith, *Verbum tuum lucerna pedibus meis*, thy word is a lantern to my feet. And they are much deceived, that think they have sanctified a Sabbath to the Lord if they have only heard sermons, and meditated, and conferred on them. That is neither *opus diei*, nor *opus loci*, the work of the day nor place. All this is but receiving from God. The worship of God must have somewhat from us to God, to which preaching doth direct us; therefore we must add,

2. Our worship of God, which chiefly doth consist in, 1, thanksgiving; 2, prayer.

Thanks for the graces already bestowed, prayer for the continuance and increase of them. This is the worship which is immediately directed by Christ to himself, and for himself only, that is, for his glory. And in this the Holy Ghost helpeth our infirmities, for being the greatest duty of Christian worship, we cannot, without great help, perform it; and great help we have, the whole Trinity joining with us: the Holy Ghost, in conceiving and uttering our prayers, and putting life into them; the Son, in carrying them up to the Father; and the Father, in receiving of them. 'Pray continually;' 'in all things give thanks.'

2. God performeth this mercy of deliverance to his church first, and then there shall be holiness. God is ever beforehand, and he would have us know that our holiness is rather a fruit and effect of his deliverance than a cause of it, procuring or meriting it. And so the Lord's deliverance of us is a free as well as a full favour, it is no wages for our work, as the church of Rome doth not only erroneously but blasphemously teach.

So doth Zachariah confess: *Ut liberati a manibus inimicorum serviamus ei*, that being delivered from the hands of our enemies, &c.; not *ut servientes liberemur*, not that serving we should be delivered, *ut liberandi* serviamus*, but he doth all his favours for us to win us to his service.

The church of God was punished for not serving of him as it should, and now it is restored to her own possessions, that it may serve him hereafter in holiness.

1. It is an excellent use that we make of the good favours of God, when they make us the more holy and the more careful to serve him: Rom. vi. 22, 'But now, being made free from sin, and become servants

---

* Qu. '*liberati*' —Ed.

to God, ye have your fruit unto holiness, and the end everlasting.' 1, Delivered and made free from sin ; 2, then our fruit unto holiness ; 3, and then everlasting life.

1. This deliverance, a motive to holiness.
2. This holiness, a fruit of our deliverance.
3. This everlasting life, a reward of our holiness.

It is a great sign that God is not with us when his favours do corrupt us, as when our knowledge doth beget in us spiritual pride, and our riches and temporal preferments bring forth carnal pride; when the many affairs of the world do make us neglect the church service, or break God's Sabbath, which ought to be religiously consecrated to God's worship; and when any temporal happiness doth work in us any relaxation of the service of God, for the true sanctification of all these doth consist in this, that we do make them motives and provocations to holiness.

2. This doth make holiness our chiefest study and care, because God, in the promise of restoring Israel to his possessions, doth not say, Then shall be outward peace, and prosperity, and wealth, and ease, but then there shall be holiness, as the proper fruit of God's favours; for peace, and health, and plenty may be lost again, but holiness cannot be lost, because that is a work of the Holy Ghost in us which cannot perish, for that Spirit shall abide in the church for ever.

This doth also shew whereby we may settle our possessions to us; namely, by embracing of holiness; for the enemy hath no power against us, so long as we be holy, and when Israel shall see that their unholiness was their sin, God restoring them, they shall make conscience of sinning any more, lest some worse judgments overtake them. For God doth promise to restore religion, and his holy worship, which is the only safety of his people, which, whilst they formerly corrupted, they brought upon themselves deportation, ruin upon their city, and fire upon the sanctuary of God.

You see all the earnestness of holy Scripture to persuade us to holiness doth aim at our own safety, and God for our own good persuadeth it; for what good will our holiness do him ? or what do we hurt him, if we be unrighteous ? Our well-doing extendeth not to him, to add any thing to him; our ill-doing is no prejudice to him : the benefit of our holiness redoundeth to ourselves, and the word, that teacheth it, is given to profit us withal. God give us all grace to make a right and profitable use thereof to his glory. Amen.

Ver. 18–20. *And the house of Jacob shall be a fire, and the house of Joseph a flame, and the house of Esau for stubble, and they shall kindle in them, and devour them ; and there shall not be any remaining of the house of Esau, for the Lord hath spoken it. And they of the south shall possess the mount of Esau, and they of the plain, the Philistines : and they shall possess the fields of Ephraim, and the fields of Samaria ; and Benjamin shall possess Gilead. And the captivity of this host of the children of Israel shall possess that of the Canaanites, even unto Zarephath ; and the captivity of Jerusalem, which is in Sepharad, shall possess the cities of the south.*

2. Their victories.

These are expressed two ways :

1. In the conquest of their enemies.

2. In the dilatation of their kingdom, by taking in their possessions.

The kingdom of Israel, in Jeroboam's time, was divided into two kingdoms, Judah and Israel, and the kingdom of Judah is here called the house of Jacob; the kingdom of Israel is called the house of Joseph, and these two are promised this victory.

There were also two captivities.

The Israelites were carried away captives by Shalmanezer, Judah by Nebuchadnezzar. God promiseth that fire shall go out from those, to consume Esau utterly, till there be none of them remaining.

He promiseth them also victory over the Philistines, their ancient enemies, so that Ephraim's portion shall come again to them, and Samaria, wherein the king of Assyria having removed the inhabitants thereof, and led them captives into his land, and settled Assyrians in the possessions of their land, that shall be recovered from them. And Benjamin, confining upon enemies, should have quiet possession of Gilead. This victory, with the extent of their kingdoms here promised, doth shew, that the people after their return shall have more room, more glory and power, than they had before their deportation.

From whence these comfortable doctrines do arise:

1. That the afflictions of the church do turn to their greater good.

2. That God punisheth the enemies of his church, even by those against whom they have prevailed.

3. That the church hath good warrant to settle their faith in this assurance, 'for the Lord hath spoken it.'

1. The afflictions of the church turn to their greater good.

And here a double benefit is expressed:

(1.) Spiritual good; he will endue them with holiness.

(2.) A temporal. [1.] Of restitution; [2.] Of dilatation.

(1.) Of the spiritual good. So David said, 'It is good for me that I was afflicted, for now I learn thy statutes.' Afflictions have their good uses; for though afflictions for the time seem grievous in the bearing thereof, yet they serve,

1. To take down the heart, and to humble men under the mighty hand of God; for the afflicted man cannot but, like the mariners in the ship with Jonah, being in a storm, search for whose sake the storm ariseth. When Manasseh was carried captive into Babel, and there put in chains, he soon found where the fault was, and he fell to confession and prayers, *humiliavit se valde,* 2 Chron. xxxiii. 12. The church of God under the cross said, Lam. iii. 4, 'Let us search and try our ways, and turn to the Lord.' In health, liberty, plenty, ease, we find something else to do; we have no leisure to search our ways; therefore God layeth his rod upon us; and when the smart of affliction doth make us weary of the world, and

putteth us out of the way of our delights, then we can consider, and try our hearts within us, and our ways without us: as Peter, when he begins to sink, can cry for help; and the disciples in a storm will awake their Master. The heart must be first broken, and our stout stomach taken down, before we can enjoy the sweet fruits of liberty. 'Behold, his soul, which is lifted up, is not upright in him,' Hab. ii. 4. Proud persons have crooked souls; they do not look up, but like the woman that had the spirit of infirmity, they are bent to the earth, to see how many they can overtake. But sickness, disgrace, imprisonment, will make our bulls of Bashan as tame as lambs, and then a poor man's tale may be heard.

We have seen examples of great falls in our time; and in them that stand now, and look up where they did sit, it is as easy a matter to behold as great a change of their hearts, as of their fortunes. Truly, so do men rise or fall indeed, as their heart riseth or falleth; for an humble man keeps the same posture always; he knows how to abound and how to want, and no prosperity can soar him up higher, no adversity can cast him lower than his pitch, for his heart is not exalted.

2. Afflictions do serve to breed in us a conscience and fear of sin, when we see what smart it bringeth; as here, it turned Israel out of house and home; it fired their city, and their holy temple, and carried them away captives to a strange land, and fed them with the bitter bread of banishment. It filled their souls with the despite of the wicked, and the reproach of the proud. This affliction saith unto them, 'Sin no more, lest some worse thing fall upon thee.' But who makes that use of sickness, imprisonment, disgrace, to cast it upon the merit of his sin? That maketh the hand of God so heavy upon us, and that returneth judgment so often to us. But here Israel is brought to holiness by it, and let us mistrust ourselves that we stand not in a state of grace with God, except our afflictions do mend us, and bring us to repentance of our sins, and to holiness of life.

3. Afflictions do bring us to an awe and reverence of the worship of God, for they do declare God to be just, and not to be dallied with; he is whetting his sword whilst we are in our sins; he is bending his bow, and preparing instruments of vengeance. He is still turning over the book of remembrance, wherein all our sins are recorded, and perusing the inventory of his graces, which we have received in vain, and of his gifts which we have abused, of his talents which we have misemployed, teaching us to fear him, and to fear all our ways before him. So David will be wiser hereafter : ' Against thee only have I sinned, and done this evil in thy sight.'

These three, humility, conscience of sin, and of the majesty of God, will bring us to holiness of life, which is the way of peace, and it is good for Israel to be afflicted, to come to this.

(2.) The church here was the better for this affliction that they sustained, even in their temporal estate.

[1.] In the restitution of their possessions ; for it is a rule of truth, though it shew a very great imperfection in our judgment, as great corruption in our affections, *carendo magis quam fruendo*, by waiting* rather than by enjoying, we come to know the true worth of God's favours ; and that *carendo*, by wanting, not so much in an *ante-want* as in a *post-want*.

In an *ante-want*, when we rise from poverty to wealth, from baseness to honour, from labour to ease ; commonly, as our good, so our blood ariseth ; and it is a great grace of God if the rising of our fortunes be not the sinking and falling of our faith and obedience to God ; for many in low estate have been humble whose pride in high estate have been importable, many in poverty have had tender hearts who in wealth have turned great oppressors of their brethren, and many in labour have been content with a little who in ease have grown resty and idle.

But in a *post-want*, when men fall from wealth to poverty, from honour to the dust, from ease to labour, then they can look back and recount the sweetness of

* Qu. 'wanting'?—ED.

these outward favours. Holy Job hath two whole chapters. In one he confesseth his former estate, the fulness, and the power, and the ease, and the glory thereof; he begins it with an *optative*: 'Oh that I were as in months past, as in the days when God preserved me; when his candle shined upon my head, when by his light I walked through darkness, as I was in the days of my youth,' Job xxix.

Few of us in health do feel the favour of God to us therein, few in wealth do taste the sweetness of God's open and giving hand, few content with their portion; but in sickness, every little mitigation of our pain is sweet, and we are ready to fall on our knees before God to thank him for it; in poverty, every alms given to us thankfully received; and then, if we were as in months past, how much better would we use wealth. For Job in the next chapter doth feel the change, and findeth bitterness in it; and he endeth that chapter, 'My harp is turned into mourning, and my organs into the voice of them that weep,' Job xxx.

Therefore, when we once come to want that which we have formerly possessed, we whose ambitious desires gave us no rest, either to be thankful for that we had, or content with it, would desire no more than to be as in some months before, that God would but light that candle again, and restore us to what we have lost.

As in the spiritual state of the soul, David, that neglected the day of his salvation, which God gave him before his fall, and sold it for a little carnal pleasure, when he came again to himself, he only prays, 'Restore to me the joy of thy salvation.' And the church, revolting from God, remembereth herself, and saith, Hosea ii. 7, 'I will go and return to my first husband, for then was it better with me than now.'

Therefore it is a great favour of God to his people to restore them their own possessions again, that they may be as in years past; for now they, having wanted them, do better know the favour of God than they did before in the use of them. They would have esteemed it a greater favour in their captivity to have had but some ease of their burdens, some liberty to have eaten the fruits of their labours. In great miseries, every little breathing of ease is sweet and comfortable, but here is a full restitution of them to their former possessions promised.

[2.] But here is much more promised, even dilatation of their borders; they shall have more than they had; they may call their place *Rehoboth*, as Isaac called the well when he had room to dig in, Gen. xxvi. 21.

The Lord hath an open and a filling hand even in this also; *multiplicat benefacere;* here is *copiosa redemptio, copiosa restitutio.* For as it is another degree of favour to rise from restitution to dilatation, so it may stand for a degree that he enlargeth their bounds out of the possession of their enemies, and giveth away their land to his people.

Let no man charge God with injustice herein; for ' the earth is the Lord's, and all that therein is;' he giveth it where he will. And Jesus Christ his Son hath promised the meek the inheritance of the earth; for by right none but the elect are true owners of the earth; the ungodly are but intruders and usurpers thereof.

Thus much added to their own, to make them more territory, and thus much taken from their neighbouring enemies, the Edomites and Philistines, and given to them, makes them gainers by their loss. Their banishment was a sowing in tears, this is a reaping in joy.

David was so reasonable, that he only desired of God, saying, Ps. xc. 15, ' Make us glad according to the days wherein thou hast afflicted us, and the years wherein we have seen evil.' God is a more bountiful giver, for he maketh his people glad not only with that which they lost, but with much more ; he impoverisheth their enemies to enrich them, that they may take the labours of the people into their possession.

Job would have wished no more than to be as he was in some months past, and God not only restoreth him what he formerly had, but he giveth him twice so much as he had before : Job xlii. 10, ' So the Lord blessed the latter end of Job more than his beginning,' which St Gregory doth apply to the state of the church in the last day, when they shall receive full glory both in their souls and bodies in this kingdom.

For in things temporal, this doth not always hold, that God repaireth thus the losses of his children, neither do they expect it, for they have learned how to want; but what wanteth in outward things is restored to them in spiritual graces, in the gifts of patience and contentedness, in thankfulness, and the spirit of supplications.

2. *Doct.* God punisheth the enemies of his church by those against whom they have prevailed : ' for the house of Jacob shall be a flame, and the house of Joseph a fire.'

Not transubstantiate into fire and flame, as a papist might prove as well out of this text, as he hath the corporeal presence of Christ out of *Hoc est corpus meum*, this is my body, but by way of similitude, and by reason of the effect that shall follow ; for ' they shall consume the house of Edom,' whom God will make as stubble for them, easy to take fire.

It was Balaam's prophecy of the people of Israel then in distress: Num. xxiii. 24, 'Behold, the people shall rise up as a great lion, and lift up himself as a young lion ; he shall not lie down till he eat of the prey, and drink the blood of the slain.' Which was begun to be performed by Moses, continued by Joshua, further prosecuted by David, fully accomplished by Christ, whom God made to rule in the midst of his enemies, Ps. cx. 1, 2.

The elect are built upon a rock in the sea of this world : all the men of war that assault it shall dash themselves in the end against this rock ; so Solomon, Prov. xi. 8, ' The righteous escapeth out of trouble, and the wicked cometh in his stead.' And again he saith, Prov. xxi. 18, ' The wicked shall be a ransom for the righteous, and the transgressor for the upright.' The reason of this is the equal law of God's justice before mentioned, that as it hath been done by them, so it may be done to them, and that their reward may fall upon them. ' For he will avenge the blood of his servants,' and yield vengeance to his adversaries, but he will be favourable to his own land, and be merciful to his own people, Deut. xxxi. 43.

Even this also must pass for a further degree of his love, to overthrow the enemies of Israel by Israel; for not only this prophet, but Balaam foretold it; even this particular: Num. xxiv. 18, 19, 'Seir shall be a possession for his enemies, and Israel shall do valiantly. Out of Jacob shall he come that shall have dominion, and shall destroy him that remaineth of that city.' In Amos God saith, chap. i. 12, 'I will send fire upon Teman, which shall devour the palaces of Bozrah.' Here Obadiah sheweth what fire Amos meaneth: the house of Jacob shall be that fire, and the house of Joseph that flame. Both expounded in plain terms by the prophet Ezekiel: Ezek. xxv. 14, 'I will lay my vengeance upon Edom by the hand of my people Israel, and they shall do in Edom according to mine anger, and according to my fury; and they shall know my vengeance, saith the Lord.'

And what God threateneth the temporal and carnal enemies of his church, the same hath he also threatened to the spiritual enemies thereof: Rom. xvi. 20, 'The God of peace shall tread Satan under your feet shortly.' It had been enough for us if God had trodden him under his own feet, but God will cover his enemies with shame and grief as well as smart and pain.

All the elect have their part in this victory of the world, for he that overcometh hath this promise, Rev. ii. 26, 'Such shall have power over nations, so that they shall rule them with a rod of iron, and as the vessels of a potter they shall be broken.' Which promise doth assure the church, that although here her enemies prevail against her, yet her spouse, whose power shall put down all rule and all authority and power, shall conquer for her, and she, united to him by her faith, shall by faith overcome all.

This admonisheth us,

1. Not to be troubled at the power and prevailings of the enemies of God's church, though we see and hear evil news daily that toucheth us to the quick, and all them that love the peace of this land, and the

liberty of the gospel; for the church of God and the patrons of his truth are under the banner of God's love, and their latter end must be peace; let us by daily prayers commend them to the tutelary protection of God, and let him hear *vocem fidei*, the voice of faith, of those that fight his battles; and *vocem sanguinis*, the voice of blood, of those that die in his quarrel.

2. It furnisheth us with patience to tarry the good pleasure of God, for when he shall arise, his enemies shall be scattered, and they that hate him shall fall before him. He hath promised his church victory, and he will not suffer his truth to fail. Excellently is this comfort expressed by the prophet Isaiah, chap. xxx. 18–20, 'And therefore will the Lord wait, that he may be gracious unto you; and therefore will he be exalted, that he may have mercy upon you: for the Lord is a God of judgment: blessed are all they that wait for him. For the people shall dwell in Sion at Jerusalem; thou shalt weep no more: he will be very gracious unto thee at the voice of thy cry; when he shall hear it, he will answer thee. And though the Lord give you the bread of adversity, and the water of affliction, yet shall not thy teachers be removed into a corner any more, but thine eyes shall see thy teachers.'

3. The assurance which the church of God hath in all this: 'The Lord hath spoken it.'

They build sure that build upon the word of God; for heaven and earth shall fail and perish, but no word of God shall be unfulfilled. 'Ye have a sure word,' saith the apostle, for God hath magnified his name and his word above all things: 'This is my comfort in mine afflictions; thy word hath quickened me,' Ps. cxix. 50. 'Remember thy word unto thy servant, upon which thou hast caused me to hope.'

The best faith hath many fears and terrors joined with it to shake it, and the faithful do sometimes want the feeling of the favour of God. We are directed here, like wise men, to let rather our understanding, spiritually enlightened, than informed by sense, govern us. The natural man's understanding is wholly led and instructed by the outward senses, and as they suggest, that apprehends; when the sense feeleth pain, the understanding apprehends cause of fear and grief, and stirreth the affections that way. But the spiritual man doth not value God's love by what the sense feeleth, but by that which the word of God suggesteth. In pain, the flesh smarteth, the sense complaineth, and Satan saith, God hath forsaken thee; but the spiritual man saith, No, for God's word saith, 'I will never leave thee nor forsake thee.' Therefore, in all afflictions, the soul of man hath no better remedy than to resort to the word. 'Thou art my hiding-place and my shield; I hope in thy word:' this is the pool of healing waters, God's *Bethesda* for all infirmities; and he hath sent his angels, his ministers, to stir these waters, by exposition of the word, exhortation, and consolation, to heal the diseases of his saints.

Ver. 21. *And saviours shall come up on mount Sion to judge the mount of Esau; and the kingdom shall be the Lord's.*

3. The means ordained for the performance of all this. *Vid. divis. supr. p.* 70.

Mount Sion here doth signify the whole church of God in the two houses of Jacob and Joseph, as they are before distinguished; that is, the two kingdoms of Judah and Israel, as they were divided under Rehoboam; for mount Sion was at first *caput imperii*, the head of the empire. The saviours here mentioned are those that God employed for the re-establishment of the state of his church; and that

Either in the procuration thereof,

Or in the execution of the same.

First, In the procuration.

1. Cyrus, king of Persia, had the honour of the means of this favour; for God stirred up the spirit of Cyrus, king of Persia, and he confessed that God, the Lord of heaven, gave him all the kingdoms of the earth, and charged him to build him an house at Jerusalem which is in Judah, and therefore by proclamation he gave a large commission to this purpose, Ezra i. 1, &c.

2. The chief fathers of Judah and Benjamin had the same motion from God to undertake this design,

ver. 5. But Artaxerxes, by a contrary edict, made this work to be given over, chap. iv. 17.

3. Then God, by the prophecy of Haggai, stirred up Zerubbabel and Joshua the son of Jozedek to attempt the work. This also was opposed, and Darius, then king of Persia, was solicited against the Jews to hinder their building so.

4. Darius came in as a saviour to help the people, and confirmed the decree of Cyrus, according to that he found in the rolls, chap. vi.; and the work went on, and the house of God was finished and dedicated.

5. Ezra moved Artaxerxes and prevailed, for a full grant both for the return of the people out of captivity, and for the re-establishment of the worship of God at Jerusalem.

6. Nehemiah moveth Artaxerxes, for the building again of the city of Jerusalem; he prevaileth, and they go to work, and their enemies, who by scornful speeches and violent opposings hindered their building, lost their labour, Neh. ii. These be the saviours, who by procuration did advance this work of God in his church.

2. By execution, all these concurred.

1. Cyrus gave leave and means; so did Artaxerxes and Darius, restoring them the treasures of the temple which Nebuchadnezzar had taken away, and arming them with full commission for all the helps that might advance that work.

2. The prophets of the Lord encouraged the work, and Ezra the scribe prayed and wept, and mediated with the kings.

3. Zerubbabel, Nehemiah, and Joshua, and the chief fathers of the people, laboured to hasten the execution of that work; and for this all these are called here saviours, because God used them as his instruments in his preservation of his church, giving them the honour of his own proper appellation; for in the fitness of the word, and in the fulness of sense, God only is properly, and by peculiar prerogative, capable of that great title, as himself hath laid claim to it. Isa. xliii. 11, 'I, even I, and there is no

saviour besides me.' And he gave this title to his Son, Hosea xiii. 4, who 'thought it no robbery to be equal with God;' for 'he shall save his people.'

These saviours shall come upon mount Sion to judge the mount of Esau.

By the mount of Esau, Edom, or the Idumæans, the posterity of Esau is understood throughout this prophecy; that people who, as you heard, dealt so cruelly with their brother Jacob in his posterity.

To 'judge this people,' is to execute those judgments upon them which God hath in this prophecy threatened, and elsewhere, as you have heard from other prophets, especially that of Balaam and of Ezekiel, for God spoiled Edom by his people whom they preserved.

And the kingdom shall be the Lord's; that is, God will declare himself to be king in the government and protection of his church, and in the victorious conquest of the enemies thereof; he will settle his church and worship at Jerusalem as in former times; for then is God said to have the kingdom, when his word is a law to his people, to rule them, and when the people live in the obedience and awe thereof. As appeareth performed by them of the return from the captivity, who made a covenant with God, and sealed the same. For we read, Neh. ix. 18, that the children of Israel did assemble themselves with fasting and sackcloth, and earth upon them: 'They stood up in their place, and read in the book of the law of the Lord their God one fourth part of the day; and another fourth part of the day they confessed, and worshipped the Lord their God.'

Note here how hearing and worshipping are distinguished; they do hear first, and thereby they learn to worship.

Then followeth their commemoration of the great mercies of God to their fathers, which David calleth God's mercies of old, and his former mercies; they do also, to the praise of this mercy, confess the transgressions of their fathers. Then they confess their own sins for which they were carried away captive, they acknowledge the just judgment of God upon them.

And now, being restored again to their possessions, they make a sure covenant with God: chap. x. 29, 'They entered into a curse, and into an oath, to walk in God's law, which was given by Moses, the servant of God, and to observe and do all the commandments of the Lord, and his judgment and statutes.'

In particular, they vowed not to give nor take daughters to wife with strangers, which I understand to be in respect of the difference of religion, because there can be no good marriage between believers and infidels, between the sons of God and the daughters of men, between the sons of God and the daughters of Belial, that was the same that first corrupted the old world, and at last followed the flood; God is not acknowledged king where such marriages are.

2. For observation of the Lord's Sabbath: they covenanted to keep it strictly, and not to buy anything of the people of the land on that day; for where the Sabbath is not kept, there God is not acknowledged king.

3. For forgiving of debts every seventh year: which was a judicial constitution, and did only bind them; yet the equity of that constitution remaineth in the church, that men should lend freely; and where there is no ability of repayment, extremity must not be used, if God be our king.

4. They charged themselves yearly every man with the third part of a shekel for the maintenance of the service of the house of God; for God is denied his kingdom there where his holy worship hath not fit maintenance to support it from every person according to his ability; for they conclude, ver. 39, 'We will not forsake the house of our God.'

And this they vowed to perform,

1. In the maintenance of the material temple.

2. In the just provision for the offerings of all sorts to be made unto God there.

3. In the true payment of tithes for the maintenance of the Levites that served at the altar.

This was the sum of the covenant which the people made with God, and bound themselves by a vow, with a curse, to observe it, as the apostle saith, taking God to record against their souls, if they observed it not, that the curse of God might come upon them. And they sealed this covenant to bind themselves the more; yet was all this no more than they were bound before to do by the law of God; yet they vow, to make the bond greater.

This is the literal and historical exposition of these words. The learned interpreters of this prophecy have well conceived that this prophet, this seer, did look further into the purpose of God for his church; and they say that mount Sion doth here also signify the whole church of God all the world over.

St Augustine* understandeth by mount Sion the church of the Jews, and by Edom the church of the Gentiles; and meeting with an ill translation, and not understanding well the original, he perverteth the meaning of the prophet, as if the salvation of God should go out of Sion to the Edomites, whereas there is a plain prophecy of judgment against Edom in particular. And therefore Edom, whom God did threaten to destroy utterly in this prophecy, cannot be a figure of that part of the church which was by the preaching of the gospel to be gathered together out of the Gentiles.

Lyranus gives another exposition; for by Sion he understandeth Jerusalem; by the saviours he understandeth St Peter and St Paul, and the chief of the apostles, as he calleth them; by the mount of Esau he understandeth Rome; and by judging the mount of Esau, he understandeth their application to Constantine, the first Christian emperor, who settled Christianity in the Roman empire. And by the kingdom which shall be the Lord's, he understandeth that Rome shall be head of the church; for that point of learning they can collect from all texts, to make the church of Rome the only true church!

I like nothing in that exposition but his resemblance of Rome to Esau, for that doth fit most properly; for they are the persecutors of Jacob, even of all true worshippers. And God hath promised them a destruction: 'The mouth of the Lord hath spoken it.'

* De Civ. Dei, lib. xviii. 31.

Master Calvin hath a learned observation upon this place; for understanding it of the state of the church under the gospel, he saith, that these saviours here spoken of are but ministerial, and so this place pointeth out the Messiah, to whom these saviours are subordinate. For the expected Messiah is such a one as by whom all the other saviours are sent, and for whom all others work, whom all others do serve and observe. And this is the extent of this prophecy in the judgment of M. Calvin, Junius, and Arias Montanus, that Christ shall leave in his church his apostles and ministers of the gospel, to shew unto men the way of salvation, in such sort as that the kingdom of God shall be advanced in the church, God ruling by his word.

Others by saviours on mount Sion judging the mount of Esau, understand the last and final judgment, wherein the saints shall judge the world, and then the kingdom shall be the Lord's; of which St Paul saith, 'He shall deliver up the kingdom to God, even the Father, when he hath put down all rule, and all authority, and power.'

I like those expositions that take the wings of a dove, and fly to the uttermost part of the text, *et non relinquit locum;* surely this is God's promise to the church, that it shall judge the world.

The parts of the text are three:

1. A gracious promise to mount Sion concerning itself: *servatores*, 'saviours.'

2. A further promise concerning their enemies: *judicabunt montem Esau*, 'shall judge the mount of Esau.'

3. The issue and effect of both: *et regnum erit Jehovæ*, 'the kingdom shall be the Lord's.'

Doct. 1. Saviours shall come upon mount Sion.

This gracious promise revealeth to us a comfortable and cheerful doctrine, that God, howsoever he punisheth, yet he still loveth his people.

Which is thus proved:

1. Because God doth not look downwards upon his people to see what they do deserve, but he looketh upward to the decree of his own election, and the

counsel of his will. If God should look downwards toward men, even to his elect, who could stand in his sight? He looketh with pure eyes, and he found imperfection in his angels. Moses hath cleared this point to this people of Israel: Deut. vii. 5–7, 'For thou art an holy people to the Lord thy God; the Lord thy God hath chosen thee to be a special people to himself, above all people that are upon the face of the earth. The Lord did not set his love upon you, nor choose you, because you were more in number than any people, for ye were the fewest of all the people, but because the Lord loved you.' From this fountain of his love did flow all those streams that made glad the city of the great king; as Ps. cv. 12, 'Albeit they were few in number; yea, very few, and strangers in the land; and walked about from nation to nation, from one kingdom to another people; yet suffered he no man to do them harm, but reproved even kings for their sakes; saying, Touch not mine anointed, and do my prophets no harm.'

Therefore, let all afflicted consciences, which are overcharged with the burden of their sins, 'look up to these hills, from whence their help cometh;' let them, as Christ biddeth, 'lift up their heads.' Let them chide themselves as David did: Ps. xliii. 5, 'Why art thou cast down, O my soul?' The remedy is, 'Hope in God; he is the health of my countenance, and my God.'

Faith and fear work together. Faith doth take up the decree of election, and the just is bold as a lion; fear looketh down upon the corruptions of nature and propension to sin, and trembleth under the mighty hand of God; and the more we fear, the faster hold we lay, and the surer we tread on the steps of that ladder by which we scale heaven. Thereupon doth the apostle give this precept, 'Make your calling and election sure;' that is, having a strong faith of these. And then the many failings in your obedience, your lapses and relapses into sin, may breed your grief, they cannot bring forth despair.

2. The decree of God is a secret, and peradventure Satan will suggest that thou art not within this decree.

Therefore God hath revealed his decree to his church, and sealed it with gracious promises, for so Moses saith to Israel: Deut. vii. 8, 'Because he would keep the word which he had sworn unto your fathers.'

This oath, as we do learn from old Zacharias in his *Benedictus*, hath two branches: one concerning God, another concerning his people: Luke i. 73, 'The oath which he swore to our father Abraham, that he would give unto us, that we, being delivered from the hands of our enemies, might serve him without fear,' &c.

(1.) God bindeth himself by his oath, to deliver his church from their enemies.

(2.) The same oath bindeth him to the procuration of his own service for us; for only he must grant *ut serviamus*, that we may serve; by him we are *liberati*, delivered, for we cannot think a good thought without him. In him we live and move; and Christ saith, *Sine me nihil potestis facere*, 'without me you can do nothing.'

This promise of God to his church he hath sealed, by giving to us the Spirit of promise; which Spirit he hath deposited in his church, to abide with it for ever; and he hath given to all the elect of God his Spirit, the earnest of this covenant. This Spirit serveth for a light in us, to discern our salvation afar off, for a witness to testify to our spirits, that we are the sons of God; and God is faithful, he will not suffer his truth to fail.

This also doth settle the faith of the elect in all the tribulations of life. I am the son or daughter of God; I know it by the Spirit which he hath given me, which leadeth my understanding into the way of truth, which converteth my affections, and frameth them to his love, which directeth my ways, and ordereth them to his obedience. This Spirit doth teach me to lay hold on the promises of grace, and to challenge my part in them; these promises do lift me up as high as to the decree of my election, and therefore I will not fear.

David goeth farther: 'I am thine, O save me.' For the interest that we have in the love of God, doth send us to him for salvation.

Doct. 2. Though God love his people, and have all power in his hand to save them, yet he doth use means, and raiseth up out of themselves saviours.

The providence of God worketh by means, even from amongst ourselves, to effect our preservation.

1. Because his immediate operations are full of terror, and therefore we cannot so well endure them; therefore the people prayed Moses to speak to them, and desired that God might speak no more to them. The angel that brought word to Mary, that she should conceive a son by the Holy Ghost, began his message with 'Fear not.' The angel that proclaimed the birth of Christ to the shepherds, said to them, 'Fear not.' We have so much cause to fear in respect of our own unworthiness, that if God did not abate somewhat of the splendour of his glorious majesty, by the employment of means familiar to us, we could not abide it.

2. God using weak means to effect his will, doth magnify his own strength; for 'his strength is made perfect through weakness,' whereby we are taught,

1. To content ourselves with the means, in the wisdom of God ordained for our preservation, not expecting miraculous and extraordinary subventions. The rich man's brethren, Luke xvi. 27, &c., shall not have a preacher come to them from the dead, to give them warning that they come not to that place of torment where their brother is: 'They have Moses and the prophets, let them hear them.' God, that sent his Spirit on the apostles, could have done so upon the whole church; and when the eunuch was reading Isaiah in his chariot, he could have opened his understanding to have known what he had read, but he chose rather to use the ministry of an apostle; and therefore he commanded Philip to join himself to that chariot, and by him he taught and baptized the eunuch. So was Cornelius directed to Peter, Acts x. 16, to be taught by him what he ought to do. And to the apostles Christ saith, Luke x. 16, *Qui vos audit, me audit*, 'he that heareth you heareth me.'

2. This teacheth us, looking on the weak means which God ordaineth for the good of his church, not to rest in them, but beyond them to look to that high

wisdom and power by which those means are enabled, for the church of Rome hath overshot that way.

John, when an angel talked with him, was ready to worship him; we are naturally prone to give undue honour to the means, because we are more led by sense than by faith. But the faithful must walk by faith, not by sight; from this sensual and carnal eye upon the means, the honour of God is given in the church of Rome to the mother of our Lord, to angels, to saints; yea, to very images and pictures, and so idolatry is committed. Therefore Peter and John, after they had raised the cripple that lay at the porch of the temple, finding the people amazed, and fearing lest any carnal opinion might wrong the glory of God, prevented any undue ascriptions to themselves, and directed them where to fasten them: Acts iii. 12, 'Ye men and brethren, why marvel ye at this? or why look ye so earnestly on us, as though, by our own power or holiness, we had made that man walk?' He attributeth this work to Jesus: ver. 16, 'His name, through faith in his name, hath made this man strong.'

Doct. 3. We are taught to give honour to all the means of God, ordained and used for our good. You see that God himself doth so; for although none but God is properly a Saviour, yet he hath given the honour of that great attribute to the means of his people's safety, and calleth them here by the name of saviours.

This title he giveth to those temporal deliverers, who saved Israel from the hands of their enemies. So Othniel is called a saviour, Judges iii. 9, and Ehud hath the same title, ver. 15. And Joshua was a saviour, he had even the name of Christ, of whom he was a type. The ministers of the gospel have this high title also given to them. St Paul to Timothy: 'So doing, thou shalt save thyself, and those that hear thee.' St James: 'If any man err from the truth, and another convert him, let him know that he shall save a soul from death.' So the layman may be a saviour too. St Jude, directing his epistle to all at large that are sanctified by God the Father, and preserved in Jesus Christ, and called, admonisheth them.

1. To 'build up themselves in the most holy faith, praying in the Holy Ghost,' &c.

2. 'And of some have compassion, making a difference; and others save with fear, pulling them out of the fire.' Also the apostle saith, 1 Cor. vii. 14, 'The unbelieving husband is sanctified by the wife, and the unbelieving wife is sanctified by the husband.' So Christ to his apostles, 'Whosoever sins ye remit, they are remitted.'

We do all know that all those be but the means by which God worketh, and yet they are graced with the attributes and effect of him that useth them.

At this day God hath left no other outward means of salvation but by our ministry; if we be not your saviours, you cannot be saved. He that employeth us in this great service, and honoureth us with his own title, will both see and avenge the contempt of his messengers.

The eye of the world is too much fixed on the earthen vessels, and regardeth little the treasure that is sent therein. God's own people did offend that way, in neglect of God's prophets, who were sent from God to them; and it lay heavy upon their consciences, and they felt the sorrow and smart of it upon themselves and their children.

Ezra prayeth and confesseth, chap. ix. 10, 11, 'We have forsaken thy commandments, which thou hast commanded by thy servants the prophets.' Daniel prayeth and confesseth, chap. ix. 6, 10, 'Neither have we hearkened to thy servants the prophets, which spake in thy name.'

The great preserver of men useth the ministry of men for the salvation of his people. To us hath God committed the ministry of reconciliation, as if God by us did speak to his church.

Your faith is begun in you by our ministry, and we exhort you to increase more and more, as you have received of us how you ought to walk and to please God, therefore 'despise not prophesying.' The Grecians in St Paul's time called preaching foolishness, but he saith that God, by this foolishness of preaching, saveth such as do believe.

The reason why God giveth this honour to the means by which he worketh any good to his church, is to instruct us by his example to do the like, for thus it must be done to the man whom the king will honour.

Haman thought these five things necessary to express the honour of a king done to a servant that he delighted in :—

1. That he be clothed in royal apparel, such as the king useth to wear.

2. That he be set on the horse that the king rideth on.

3. That the crown royal be set upon his head.

4. That this be done to him by one of the king's most noble princes.

5. That he proclaim before him that he is one whom the king will honour.

The apostles and their successors have all this honour done to them.

1. That apparel which the king useth to wear is put upon them, for he giveth them his own attributes : he calleth them teachers and pastors, and saviours of his church.

2. He setteth them upon his own horse, for they ride upon the wings of the wind. The wind is the Holy Ghost. *Alæ Spiritus*, the wings of the Spirit, by which it flieth over the church, be the two Testaments, which holy men wrote as they were inspired. They 'ride prosperously, because of truth, meekness, and righteousness,' Ps. xlv. 4. *Propter veritatem quam prædicant, propter mansuetudinem qua prædicant, propter justitiam quam parturiunt.*

3. Thirdly, the king's crown is set upon their heads, for the people of God whom they teach and convert are their crown : 1 Thes. ii. 19, 'For what is our hope, or joy, or crown of rejoicing ? Are not ye in the presence of our Lord Jesus Christ at his coming ?'

4. This is put upon us by the most noble of all God's princes, even the Son of God himself, who sendeth us abroad and saith, 'Go unto all nations.'

5. He proclaimeth this, *Sicut misit me Pater, sic ego mitto vos,* 'As the Father sent me, so send I you ;' not only sending us forth to do his work, but

in some measure also to partake of his honour, as ambassadors of princes are received and esteemed honourably for their sakes whom they represent. This the apostle confessed to the praise of the Galatians, that they 'received him as an angel of God, even as Christ Jesus,' Gal. iv. 14.

God hath left no other saviours upon mount Sion, his church, but his faithful ministers : therefore,

1. We are taught to make conscience of our holy employment, to be faithful in it, that neither by our negligence in preaching, nor by unsound doctrine, nor by our evil example, we become destroyers of our brethren ; for we are all God's ministers, and the chaplains of Jesus Christ, who will call us to severe account of the talent which he hath committed to our trust.

2. The people committed to our pastoral charge are taught where to seek salvation, and from whom to require light. The Colossians may call upon Archippus to look to his charge ; and the minister Archippus may call upon them to walk in the light, saying, 'To you is this word of salvation sent,' be 'swift to hear ;' again, 'Take heed how you hear,' and see 'that ye be not hearers only, deceiving your own souls.'

Thank God that, by men like yourselves, he corrects the hearers, and cometh down to you, and preacheth to you the way of salvation ; and howsoever you esteem of our persons, touch not our calling, for that is holy and heavenly.

2. *To judge the mount of Esau.*

This part of the promise doth concern the enemies of God's church ; and seeing those saviours shall not only have employment to preserve the church, but they shall also have power of judgment to destroy the enemies thereof, we are taught,

Doct. That the enemies of the church shall not always prevail, though they do stand it out long, but the church of God at the last shall have the victory. The blood of Abel shall judge Cain, for it crieth unto God out of the earth against him ; and Cain shall smart for that murder whilst he liveth, and God shall give another son for Abel, whom Cain slew. Israel is a full example; for being in the land of Egypt, in the house of bondage, they had a promise to keep them in heart: Acts vii. 7, 'And the nation to whom they shall be in bondage I will judge, saith God: and after that they shall come forth, and serve me in this place.' The Jews, by reason of Haman's plot against them, were in great danger. It is said, Esther iii. 15, 'The king and Haman sat down to drink, and the city of Shushan was perplexed.' But God turned their mourning into a feast; and Haman died upon his own tree, and the distressed Jews had one holiday the more for that. Sennacherib, a troubler of Israel, died a great many of deaths; for neither could the privilege of the place, the temple of his god, nor the service that he came to do there, nor the god of the temple, protect him from death; and which was most fearful and grievous to him, his own bowels rebelled against him, and they to whom he had been the author of life were the ministers of his death. Adrammelech and Sharezar, his sons, slew him with the sword. For you have heard, that though 'judgment begin at the house of God,' it doth not end there;' so David, 'Mark the godly, and behold the just; for the end of that man is peace,' whatsoever all the rest of his life be; and we truly say, *All is well that ends well.*

Christ to his disciples, Mat. x. 16, 22, 'Behold, I send you as sheep in the midst of wolves,' &c.: 'but he that endureth to the end shall be saved.'

The apostle saith, Rom. viii. 37, 'We are more than conquerors.' Conquerors overcome by force and strong hand, or some cunning stratagem; the saints overcome by patience, and weary their persecutors with their sufferings; for, *Vincit qui patitur.*

The reason of this happy end of the labours and sorrows of the church is,

1. That the narrow way to glory may be frequented; for who would put himself to the rugged severity of a strict life, into the hatred of the world, to make himself as the way of the street for the proud to go over him, if he did not persuade himself that his heaviness should endure but for a night, and that he should have joy in the morning?

No, there is not heaviness all night; for the servants of God do 'believe to see the goodness of God in the land of the living.'

And this is that same *carmen in nocte*, song in the night, that David speaketh of; *lætitia in tribulatione*, joy in tribulation, as St Augustine doth expound it.

And thus doth God comfort the church often, by taking away either perfidious and unsound friends, that live in the church to betray it, or by removing corrupt and bribing retailers of preferments in church and commonwealth, or by committing* of cruel and unmerciful oppressions of their brethren, as bad as the task-masters of Egypt, to lay burdens upon them to keep them down. This is some refreshing to the church of God, to behold this just hand of God against the ungodly of the earth, and it is an earnest of that purging of his floor, when he will fan away the wicked as the dust and chaff of the earth; for when the wicked perish, there is joy.

2. Another reason is, because God will have the enemies of his church know that their power is borrowed; and he that lent it to them can resume it to himself, and extinguish it in them at pleasnre. So Christ told Pilate that he could have no power against him, except he had it from above; whereupon grows that consolation of the church, 'Fear not them that can kill the body, and can go no further.'

The wicked are compared, in respect of their tumultuous rage, and the manifold scourges* of their wicked attempts against the church, to the raging of the sea. The comparison doth hold out thus far: God hath set this sea bounds, and the proud waves may come thus far, and no further; so hath God limited the fury of his enemies, and set them their *non ultra*, no further.

The use which the church maketh of this experiment is,

1. It taketh away fear of outward enemies. Fear of man is a dangerous perturbation, and such as en-

* Qu. 'by removing those who are guilty of committing'? —Ed.

* Qu. 'surges'?—Ed.

dangereth faith, against which Christ giveth his disciples warning, 'Let not your hearts be troubled, nor fear.' *Quid timet hominem homo in sinu dei positus? Tu de illius sinu non cadere potes; quicquid ibi passus fueris, ad salutem valebit, non ad perniciem.*

Scripture setteth forth the power of the outward enemy in these and such like phrases: there is *rugitus leonis*, the roaring of the lion; there is *unguis leonis*, the lion's paw; there is *cornu unicornium*, the horn of the unicorns; there is *pes superbiæ*, the foot of pride; there is *oculus nequam*, an evil eye; there is *manus violenta*, a violent hand; and *iniquitas manuum*, the iniquity of the hands; *os sepulchrum*, the mouth an open sepulchre; and *venenum aspidum sub labiis*, the poison of asps under the lips. 'The mercies of the wicked are cruel; but I will not fear what man can do unto me.'

> 'Multos in summa pericula misit
> Venturi timor ipse mali; fortissimus ille est,
> Qui promptus metuenda pati.'

The fear of evil to come hath endangered many; he is the most valiant that is ready to suffer what is feared.

2. It trieth our faith. Christ said to Peter, *Cur times, exiguâ fide præditus?* when he so felt himself sinking in the waters; God promised, 'I will not leave thee, nor forsake thee.' Do we believe him, dare we trust him, as Christ? 'Do you believe in God? believe also in me.' James i. 2, 'My brethren, count it all joy when you fall into divers temptations; knowing this, that the trying of your faith worketh patience. But let patience have her perfect work, that ye may be perfect and entire, wanting nothing.' 1 Peter i. 7, 'That the trial of your faith, being much more precious than of gold which perisheth, though it be tried with fire, might be found unto praise, and honour, and glory, at the appearing of Jesus Christ,' &c.

3. This setteth before our eyes the great appearance that our enemies shall make before us, either in this world, when our eye shall have our desire on them that hate us, or in the last day, when the saints shall

judge the world; which serveth to admonish us with
the prophet, to 'commit our ways to the Lord, and
to trust in him, for he shall bring it to pass.'

Excellent is the story of Elisha, whom the king of
Syria sent an army to take, and they beset Dothan,
where he lodged; but Elisha prayed, and God smote
the whole army with blindness, and he whom they
sought offered himself to them to be their guide, and
he brought them into Samaria; and then God opened
their eyes, and they saw themselves in the hand and
power of their enemies. Thus doth God blind the
eyes of the enemies of his church, and when their
malice is at the height, they find themselves set at
the bar to be judged by his saints; then Jacob ' shall
judge the mount of Esau.'

Methinks I see the great appearance of the boisterous tyrants of the earth, whose eyes did sparkle fire
in the faces of God's servants, whose tongue spake
proud words, whose foot trode upon God's saints,
whose hand spared them not, whose countenance
darted against them scorn and disdain, and whose
swords were made drunk in the blood of God's holy
ones. With what a fearful trembling and horrible
dread they come to this judgment against their wills,
where they shall see the saints, all in long white robes,
like a flock of sheep that come from the washing; in
whose glorified faces they shall behold their own
shame and dishonour; in whose peace and joy they
shall behold the bloody persecution wherewith they
have oppressed them in their life, and in whose settled
happiness they shall read their doom of eternal woe.
And as St Peter saith, ' How shall the wicked and
ungodly appear?' there needs no more evidence against
them; bring them to judgment, and that sight shall
convince them.

3. The issue and effect of all: ' And the kingdom
shall be the Lord's.'

This is the proper fruit of our deliverance from the
hands of our enemies, that the kingdom of God may
be established on earth in God's church.

1. For so long as the enemies of God do tyrannise
and fill all with their gross actions, the face of the

church is covered, the temples of God are defiled and demolished, the worship of God seeketh private corners, and sheweth not itself, the saints of God fly from the sword of persecution, wandering here and there, from one nation to another people : and it is hard to say where the church of God is.

During the persecution under the cruel emperors, till Constantine arose and restored the kingdom to God, the kingdom of God on earth was not abolished quite, but it was in some sort invisible ; not that it was then hidden from all the faithful, as it was from the world. Therefore, concerning the invisibleness of this kingdom, we do affirm,

(1.) That though this kingdom of God be so established on earth, that the gates of hell shall not prevail against it, because God gave to his Son that asked him the heathen for his inheritance, and the utmost part of the earth for his possession ; and Christ promised to give the Holy Ghost to his church to abide with it for ever : yet at some times the faithful may be so few in number, and they so separated one from another, in the pursuit of their own safety, that the world cannot easily discern the face of a church. This, some of the church of Rome have confessed, affirming that about the time of Christ's passion, and the dispersion of his disciples, the true faith remained only in the blessed Virgin Mary. But untruly ; for the disciples, though they fled from the persecution of that time, they fled not from the faith of Christ. But was it not so in Elijah's time, when he knew of no more but himself alone that served the true God ? yet God had knees that had never bowed to Baal, even then.

(2.) We affirm that Satan's kingdom may so far dilate itself in power and spreading, that the external government of the church may cease, the succession of bishops and pastors may be interrupted, the discipline of the church hindered, and the outward exercise of God's worship suspended ; the sun of righteousness may suffer eclipse; and thus much the Rhemists do confess in their notes upon 2 Thes. ii. 2.

(3.) That which the common opinion doth embrace

for the kingdom of God, may be Satan's kingdom, whose doctrine is poison, whose pastors are wolves in sheep's clothing, whose children are bastards of the strumpet of Babylon.

This appears in the church story, for when Rome forsook her first love, and began to turn faith into action, and religion into carnal policy, to establish a transcendent greatness on the face of the earth, and to tyrannise over all that stood for the truth revealed in the word, then was the candle of the church put out so far as they could prevail, and the word of God, the light of our steps, was taken away from the people. Then did the faithful subjects of God's kingdom hide themselves from the sword, and the fire, and the sundry persecutions which Rome devised to oppress them. Then their heresy passed for truth commonly, their usurpers for lawful bishops, their mercenaries for pastors, their legends for gospel, and they boasted themselves the only true church of God, and spouse of Jesus Christ. And when by the ministry of Dr Luther the church began to lift up the head again, and that one single man opposed the pope, and was a burning and shining lamp, to whose light many daily resorted, we see that ever since that time the church hath come more and more in sight, and grown both in number and strength. Kings have been nursing fathers, and queens have been nurses, and the kingdom of God hath been gloriously advanced on earth. Then did England cast off the yoke of Rome, and God caused a light to shine in darkness, and ever since a face of the church hath appeared, gathering more and more fresh beauty; and now we may say truly of our times, the light never shone more clear in this land than now it doth; never more learning, and never more communicated than now.

But, beloved, this will not serve our turn; God must have as well a rule of our hearts as of our ears, of our hands as of our heads. Let us look to our example in my text: when God had restored this people to their land, they established his kingdom. With public assemblies, with fasting and humbling of themselves before God, with confession of sins, with weeping and mourning, with solemn vows to perform all the commandments of God; they spent their time, not all in hearing, but in worshipping also of God. They vowed not to make any marriages with such as were no professed subjects of the kingdom of God, such as was the marriage of Solomon with king Pharaoh's daughter. They vowed to keep the Sabbath holily to the service of God, to deal charitably with their poor brethren; to honour God with their riches, setting apart a portion to maintain the worship and public service of God. And all this must we do if we will advance the kingdom of God amongst us, not only in outward profession, but in inward subjection.

You may know a true subject of God's kingdom by his walk, and by his pace; for he walketh,

1. Circumspectly, fearing danger before him to meet him, behind him to follow him, above him to press him down, under him to blow him up; temptations on his right hand, provocations on the left hand; therefore he loseth no time, but redeemeth it to the service of God.

2. He walketh in holiness, as in the sight of God, who searcheth the hearts and reins, and cannot be deceived with false semblances and empty shadows, and seemings of false and hypocritical shows, but requireth truth in the inward parts. He walketh in righteousness, that is, in the obedience of the second table of the law, living in the practice and exercise of his knowledge to the uttermost of that measure of grace that is given to him, as it becometh the saints. For these know that they were therefore delivered from the hands of their enemies, that they might more freely attend the service of God, and the saving of their own souls.

Amongst such as these God reigneth, and hath put on his glorious apparel, and is acknowledged as God their king. Idolatry and false worship doth unking and dethrone God, and trespasseth the majesty of our King; swearing and blasphemy maketh the name of God (which is the safety of his subjects, for our help is in the name of the Lord) like to a broken hedge.

Breach of the Sabbath, which is God's holy day, is a trespass against his moderate prerogative, claiming some part of our time for his public service and the exercise of religion. Contempt of the word is a trespass against the laws of this kingdom. Injury in any kind to our brethren, is breach of peace amongst the subjects of this kingdom. Gluttony, drunkenness, pride, be wasteful sins, and consume the outward treasures thereof, and they also seem to quench the Spirit of God, and to kill all good motions in ourselves and others.

Let us remember our prayer, *Adveniat regnum tuum*, Let thy kingdom come. And seeing God hath graciously established a church amongst us in peace, which he hath watered with early rain in the first coming thereof in this land, and with a latter rain in the government of two incomparable princes, truly called defenders of the faith against heresy and schism; let the kingdom be the Lord's, let our obedience to his law bear witness of our faith, and let our peace amongst ourselves give testimony of our charity, and let us walk all one way, like the horses of Pharaoh's chariot; let us all fight as one man against sin and Satan, against the devil and the pope, *tanquam acies ordinata*. For if the Lord be our king, we shall have cause to be glad thereof: for 'Blessed are the people that are in such a case; blessed are the people that have the Lord for their God.'

2. Let us look as far as we can by Saint Paul's prospective. There will be a time when Christ, our grand captain, shall overcome all his enemies, even death, which is the last enemy; and then shall he deliver up the kingdom to God, even his Father; then Israel shall have judged Esau, the church, the world. Then Christ resigneth his office of a mediator, and then God is all in all. For then all his enemies shall be in prison in the chains of darkness; all his elect shall be fastened together, and united with Christ their head in glory. God shall then have none to contest with him for sway and domination: his glory shall then be great in the salvation of his church, and in the victory of his enemies.

Thus have I in a few months gone through this short but full and pithy prophecy of Obadiah: I know with what great comfort, light, and delight, in mine own meditation; I hope not unprofitably for you.

If you desire many hours' work in a few minutes of time, this is the analysis of it.

It was divided into two parts, { 1. *Titulus*, the title. 2. *Vaticinium*, the prophecy.

1. The title shewed, { 1. *Whose:* Obadiah. 2. *What.*

1. *Whose;* Obadiah.

Doct. God stirreth up his servants the prophets to give warning of the anger to come.

2. *What:* a vision.

Doct. The faithful minister must see before he say, and take instructions from God before he undertake to teach others.

2. The prophecy: this hath two parts:

1. Against Edom, *ad finem*, ver. 16.
2. For the church, ver. 17, *ad finem*.

In the first, observe three things:

1. The subject of this prophecy, Edom.
2. The suggester of it, the Lord.
3. The prophecy itself.

1. Of the subject, Edom.

Doct. Riches, strength, honour, victory, are not so precious things as many do value them. Oftentimes they go away with them all a long time whom God hateth: he saith, 'I have hated Esau;' yet he had all these.

2. Of the suggester of the prophecy. The Lord saith thus.

Doct. God's ministers must deal faithfully with the church, saying no more or less, and in the same manner as God speaketh to them.

3. The prophecy, that hath four parts:

1. The judgment intended against Edom, ver. 1, 2.
2. The despair of all Edom's hopes, ver. 3 *ad* 9.
3. The cause provoking God, ver. 10 *ad* 14.
4. God's revenge, ver. 15, 16.

1. The judgment intended contains:

OBADIAH

1. The discovery.
2. The rumour itself.
3. The effect.

1. The discovery, by a rumour from the Lord, an ambassador sent among the heathen.

Doct. 1. The decrees of God's judgment upon the wicked be constant and unchangeable.

Doct. 2. The consent of ambassadors, all declaring the same judgment, sheweth that the Lord's trumpet *dat sonum certum*, gives a certain sound.

Doct. 3. The preaching of all true and faithful ministers and prophets accord to their instructions is *rumor a Domino*, a rumour from the Lord; and because weak and distressed consciences do often hear suggestions of fear, they must examine the rumour, *si a Domino*, if it be of the Lord.

2. The rumour was, that God would punish Edom by war.

Doct. 1. All wars are ordained by God.
Doct. 2. God punisheth one evil nation by another.
Doct. 3. War is one of God's rods to punish sin.
Doct. 4. The people of God may lawfully make war.

3. The effect of this war, ver. 2.

1. From God, 'I have made thee small.'
2. From man, 'Thou art greatly despised.'

In both,

Doct. God giveth warning of his judgments to those whom he foreseeth such as will not take warning to amend.

In the first, God maketh small his enemies:

Doct. 1. God casteth down the proud.

In the second, thou art despised:

Doct. 2. They that despise God shall be despised.

2. The despair of all their hopes; five hopes:
1. In the pride of their own hearts.
2. In the safety of their dwelling, vers. 3–6.
3. In the strength of their confederates, ver. 7.
4. In their wisdom, ver. 8.
5. In the strength of their own men, ver. 9.

1. Hope in their own pride:

Doct. God resisteth the proud. Pride is an abominable sin in the sight of God, and it deceiveth man.

2. Hope in the strength of their dwelling:

Doct. No place is safe without God's protection; for the hidden things of Esau shall be searched and found out.

3. Hope in their confederates:

Doct. 1. God punisheth one sin by another; for the sin of Edom in casting off their trust in God is punished by their trusting in men.

Doct. 2. God requiteth sinners with the same measure that they have measured to others.

Doct. 3. The falling out of these confederates with Edom, sheweth that there is no true peace between the ungodly.

Doct. 4. Those who put their trust in men have no understanding.

4. Hope in their wise men.

Doct. Human wisdom and counsel against the Lord are no fence for any state.

5. Hope in their strong men:

Doct. Vain is the help of man against God.

3. The cause provoking God to this severe prosecution of Edom:

1. Set down in general terms, ver. 10.
2. In a particular description, ver. 11–14.

1. In general, they are charged with cruelty to their brother Jacob.

2. In particular, they are charged,

1. With cruelty of combination.

Doct. They that join with others in action of murder or robbery are actually culpable as aiders, abettors, and maintainers of cruelty and wrong,

2. With the cruelty of the eye:

Doct. They that look upon the injuries done to their brethren with delight, and without compassion or relief of them, be equally culpable with them that wrong them.

3. With the cruelty of the heart; they rejoiced against their brethren:

Doct. The heart of man affected to wrong, though neither the head of counsel nor the hand of assistance join with it, doth break the law of charity.

4. With the cruelty of the tongue:

Doct. The proud words of the enemies of God do break peace, and transgress the current of charity.

5. With cruelty of hands shewed in these things:
1. Invasion of their city.
2. Direption of their goods.
3. Insidiation for life.
4. Depopulation, not sparing the residue.

Doct. Whatsoever is done against our brother, in his person or in his goods, breaketh the law.

The fourth part, God's revengement.

This containeth two things:
1. A judgment of God revealed against the ungodly.
2. A sweet consolation of the church.

In the judgment, I note six things:
1. The certainty: the day set.
2. The propinquity: near at hand.
3. The extent: to all the heathen.
4. The equity: as thou hast done, &c.
5. The contents: they shall drink.
6. The duration: continually.

1. *Doct.* God hath set a time to punish every sin of the impenitent.

2. *Doct.* That time is at hand.

3. *Doct.* God doth punish those whom himself hath stirred up to be his instruments to punish others.

4. *Doct.* God doth punish by retaliation.

5. *Doct.* Though the judgment of God do begin at the house of God, the wicked shall not go unpunished.

6. *Doct.* The judgment of the wicked and unmerciful is without all mercy.

2. The comfort of the church.

1. He speaketh of their judgment as past:

Doct. Though the church of God do live under the cross for a time, it shall not be ever so.

2. He calleth Sion, though thus laid waste, his holy mountain.

Doct. Where God loveth once, he loveth ever; and though he afflicteth, yet he loveth still.

3. He revealeth to his church their own deliverance, and the destruction of their enemies:

Doct. The cup of wrath shall pass from the church

to her enemies, the knowledge whereof is a great settling to the church in comfort.

The second part of the prophecy,

Containing the consolation of the church against all her enemies; wherein observe,

1. A promise of restitution to their own.
2. Of victory against their enemies.
3. The means ordained for this.

1. In the promise of restitution:

1. *Doct.* God requireth of them whom he delivereth from evils holiness of life.

2. *Doct.* That God delivereth his church first, that after they may serve him.

2. The victories of their enemies:

1. *Doct.* The afflictions of the church do turn to their greater good.

2. *Doct.* God punisheth the enemies of his church by his church, against which they have formerly prevailed.

3. *Doct.* The church hath good warrant to settle their faith in the assurance of this, because the mouth of the Lord hath spoken it.

3. The means to effect this:

1. Here is a promise of saviours to them.

1. *Doct.* Though God do long punish, he doth ever love his people.

2. *Doct.* Though God have all power and means under command, yet he doth choose to make us instruments of his favour to one another, men-saviours.

3. *Doct.* We are taught to give due honour to the means of God's favours, by the examples of God's communicating to his instruments his own great title of saviours.

2. Here is a promise of victory to his church, full victory: they shall judge the mount of Esau.

Doct. Though the enemies of the church do resist long, yet God at last will give his church a complete victory over them all.

3. The issue and effect of all.

'The kingdom shall be the Lord's.'

Doct. This is the proper work and fruit of all God's favours to his church, to advance the kingdom of God on earth, and to submit ourselves as faithful subjects to his dominion.

Thus have I drawn the two breasts of this prophecy, and milked it to you: *venit ad mulctram;* for it hath two parts, *binos alit utere fœtus.*
1. Here is the doctrine of God's justice.
2. The doctrine of his mercy.

I have done more, I have gathered the cream of this milk; for these doctrines which I have collected be *flos lactis.*

I confess that I have studied this prophecy with singular delight, which hath turned the pains I took in it into sweet and gracious recreations; for in this short only chapter of his prophecy,

Here is a sweet meeting,
1. Of the majesty and authority in the sender, and fidelity in the messenger.
2. Of great substance and weight of matter, with admirable oratory of words and sentences, and with sweet disposition of order and method.

Righteousness and peace have kissed each other.

Righteousness, punishing Edom and the heathen, and avenging the cause of Sion: peace, establishing the kingdom of God in the restoration of his church.

The prophecy is like a seasonable March; it comes in like a lion to end winter, it goes out like a lamb to bring in the cheerful spring.

For it begins at *Bella, horrida bella;* it ends with, 'Peace be within thy borders, and plenteousness within thy palaces.'

In the title of this prophecy, which is called the vision of Obadiah, I can shew you the best book in my study, and the light of all my meditations, even the vision which God by his Spirit revealeth in my understanding, to discern what his will is, and to suggest what I shall preach in his church.

Great are the helps of a plentiful library to furnish us for this service; but he that hath not the help of vision from him that giveth eyes to the blind, shall walk in the dark, and not know whither he goeth; I may say with St John,

'What I have seen and heard, that have I delivered unto you.' And I have no more to say of it, but I wish the good will of him that dwelt in the bush to second his outward ordinance of semination with a blessing of increase, without which, he that planteth is nothing, he that watereth is nothing. To him let us give the honour due to his name, and say,

Gloria Patri et Filio et Spiritui Sancto. Amen, Amen, Amen.

HABAKKUK

EDWARD MARBURY

HABAKKUK

The burden which Habakkuk the prophet did see.

HABAKKUK I. 1

THIS first verse tells us what we shall find in the ensuing prophecy, and it openeth to us three things which give light to that which followeth:
1. The minister of God in this prophecy.
(1.) By his name, Habakkuk.
(2.) By his function, the prophet.
2. The manner how he came by it, vision.
3. The matter of it, the burden.
1. Of the minister; first, of his name.

The name *Habakkuk* is rendered by Philo the Jew *amplexans*, embracing; so doth Pagnine give it; our English, a *wrestler;* for they that wrestle do embrace and hold fast one the other: a name well expressing the office and employment of this prophet, who wrestled with the sinners of those times, and their horrible iniquities to cast them. 1. But as God wrestled with Jacob, that he might leave behind him a blessing. His tribe, Dorothæus saith, was Simeon; I know not upon what information, for the silence of the holy Scripture doth argue it to be conjectural.

Concerning the time when he prophesied, it is not particularly expressed, but it appears to be before the deportation into Babylon; for the Chaldeans' invasion is here threatened, and therefore Junius thinks him contemporary with Jeremiah, and referreth his prophecy to the end of Josias his government. Others, after the Hebrews, refer it to the time of king Manasseh.

Mr Calvin very truly affirmeth it before the time of Zedekiah.

Arias Montanus gives a probable conjecture by comparing that which is said, 2 Kings xxi. 12, 'Therefore, thus saith the Lord God of Israel, behold I am bringing forth an evil upon Jerusalem and Judah, that whosoever heareth of it, both his ears shall tingle.' That in the 11th verse it is said, 'Because Manasseh king of Judah hath done these abominations, and hath done wickedly above all that the Amorites did, which were before him, and hath also made Judah to sin with his idols.' And this commination is almost in the same words in the 5th verse of this chapter.

St Jerome, in his Prologue to this prophet, saith that he is called a wrestler, *quia certamen ingreditur cum Deo*, because he wrestled with God. *Nullus enim prophetarum ausus est tam audaci voce Deum ad disceptationem justitiæ provocare*, none durst so boldly provoke God to vindicate his justice, as it appears, ver. 2. But he doth violate the text of canonical Scripture and history to verify that Apocrypha tale of Habakkuk's bringing food to Daniel by miracle, which destroyeth the truth of the history to make faith of a legend.

For either there must be two Habakkuks, or this one must live, as Arias Montanus doth cast it up, three hundred years, if he lived to feed Daniel in the captivity; a long time of life then, or this must prophesy before he was born. Bellarmine hath found out two Daniels: one the prophet, of the tribe of Judah, and another of the tribe of Levi, that heard the cause of Susanna; and Ribera, a Jesuit, two Habakkuks.

But we lose time in this question, for they that have not the light in the word do go in the dark, and they that go in the dark know not whither they go. The best use of this is to limit our search to the holy canonical Scripture, and to take all our light from thence; so shall we not go astray.

2. The function of this man is set down in the name of a prophet, that is, a man enlightened by divine revelation to understand the will of God in some things, and appointed to declare the same.

Secondly, the manner how he came to it: *vision*, that is, divine revelation, assuring him of the truth of God's will so fully as if he had seen the same with his eyes accomplished. (*De his consule conciones super Obadiam.*)

Thirdly, the matter of the prophecy, the burden; in which two questions are moved:

1. Why this prophecy is called a *burden*.
2. *Whose* burden this is.

To the first; it is called a burden, in respect,

1. Of the sin here punished, which is *onus*, a burden.
2. Of the punishment here threatened; that is, *onus*.
3. Of the word of God threatening; that is, *onus*.

1. *Peccatum onus*, sin a burden: 1. *Deo*, to God. 2. *Hominibus*, to men.

1. *Onus Deo*, a burden to God.

God complaineth of the sins of his people, that they are a burden to him: 'Behold, I am pressed under you, as a cart is pressed that is full of sheaves.' The very service that these sinners do seem to perform to God is a burden to him, as he complaineth, 'Your new moons, your appointed feasts, my soul hateth: they are a trouble unto me; I am weary to bear them.' *Laboravi sustinens*, so the prophet Malachi complaineth: chap. iii. 17, 'Ye have wearied the Lord with your words: yet ye say, Wherein have we wearied him? When ye say, Every one that doeth evil is good in the sight of the Lord, and he delighteth in them; or, Where is the God of judgment?' Three things weary God:

1. When we multiply our own sins.
2. When we tender God service continuing in sin.
3. When we justify sinners, and flatter them in their sins, as though God had accepted them.

2. *Peccatum onus est hominibus*, sin is a burden to men. Christ calleth none to him but such as are weary of this burden of sin; to such he promiseth

refreshing. Ask the first sinners if they found not their sin their burden, when they hid themselves from the presence of God. Ask the first murderer if any place were safe for him, who thought and said that whosoever met him would kill him. They that think that Lamech killed Cain, read the text, *occidi hominem in vulnus meum.* Ask Joseph's brethren, when they saw their sad constraint in Egypt, both at their first coming to buy corn, and after the death of their father, if the trespass against their brother Joseph did not lie heavy upon them. Ask the tender conscience of any of God's children, if any weight or burden be like unto that of the body of sin, and if he do not cry with Paul, *Quis liberabit me?* 'Who shall deliver me?'

Till we come to this, to feel the burden of sin, and to be weary of it, we are the sons of wrath; and every man may call himself Ταλαίπωρον, a wretched man.

Here is pride and vanity, clothing of us; here is gluttony and drunkenness, feeding of us; here is the mouth full of evil words, the hands of violence or bribes, giving or taking; the day, the night, the year, spent in pleasure and recreations; God's Sabbath is neglected, God's word not regarded; the time served, the humours of sinful men observed; and when these things are no burden to the bearers thereof, there is wrath gone forth from the Lord against them; and if timely repentance do not stand in the gap, it will break in upon them that do such thing like a flood, and no man shall escape that is pursued by this judgment.

Let me therefore entreat you to hear a word of exhortation. Give not the members of your bodies servants to sin. Give not; for, indeed, what have you to give, seeing you brought nothing with you into the world? And what have ye that you have not received? Or if you will needs be giving, hands off, give not the members of your body; for your body is the temple of the Holy Ghost, or should be, if you would give so comfortable a guest welcome; or if you will give your bodies away, do them not the wrong to put them out to service, for they are bought with a

price, the dearest pennyworth that was ever bought;
their liberty cost the binding, their sanity the breaking, their ease the smart and aching, their life the
death, of the holiest body that ever lived upon earth.
Or if you will needs give your body a servant, let it
not be to sin; for that is ponderous in the weight,
noisome in the stench, bitter in the smart; the burden
of sin is the wrath of God.

Here let me awake your thankful hearts to an acknowledging consideration of that great redemption
performed by Jesus Christ to his church, who came
to take this burden upon him, and to ease us of it;
Agnus qui tollit peccata, the Lamb that taketh away
sins from us, that he might wash us in his blood.
Upon himself he bore our infirmities, and God made
the iniquity of us all to meet on him.

He did not rob us, as Israel did the Egyptians, of
our jewels of silver and jewels of gold; he only took
our infirmities and our sins from us; and whereas
once we might have said with Cassiodore, *Quantitas
delicti mensura est repudii*, the quantity of the fault is
the measure of the judgment,—for by our sins we might
have taken measure of the wrath and judgment of
God,—now there is an unscaled height, an unsounded
depth, an unbounded breadth, of love, which hath
said to the church, of the whole burden of sin,

' Cantantes ut eamus, ego hoc te fasce levabo,'

let us sing as we go, I will ease thee of this burden.

2. The punishment here threatened is a burden to
man.

Issachar, under his double burden, saith, that rest
is good; he found rest among his burdens. But
there is no peace to the wicked man. A sinner that
hath any sense of sin will say as David, *Non est pax
ossibus meis propter peccatum:* ' There is no rest in
my bones, because of my sin.' He was so overcharged with the fear of God's judgments, that
sometimes he doubted that God had forgotten to be
merciful, and that he would be no more entreated.
' Who can stand in thy sight when thou art angry?'
I can tell you who could not stand; not the angels that

kept not their first estate; heaven was too hot for them; God cast them down, *ejecit, conjecit, dejecit, rejecit, subjecit;* and that anger is yet their burthen, and shall be for ever. The first tenants of paradise could not; they fled from the face of God, and the curse of God lay heavy upon them. Cain confessed his punishment more than he could bear; the old world, all but eight persons, sunk under this wrath, and were drowned in the great deep. The transgressing cities suffered the consuming and tormenting flames of fire and brimstone: Ps. xviii. 7, 'The very earth trembled and shook; the foundations also of the mountains moved and quaked, because he was angry; smoke went out at his nostrils, and consuming fire out of his mouth.'

Beloved, let me tell you what I fear: never any times did more put almighty God to it to reveal his anger from heaven, and to rain down burdens upon the sons of men; for the clearer the light of the gospel shineth, the more his expectation is of walking in the light; but our knowledge is rather floating in the brain than working in the obedience of our life. Christ saith, ' It shall be easier for Sodom and Gomorrah in the day of the Lord than for those of that generation' to whom the light appeared in his ministry so clear and glorious; and yet they ' love darkness better than light, because their works were evil.' Great is the weight of a millstone hanged about our neck, and we cast therewith into the bottom of the sea; yet the burden of God's wrath, he sayeth, is much heavier than that. And yet we make no care nor conscience, and live without fear of this anger; we do this and that great wickedness, and sin against God, and provoke him to anger with our actions and inventions, as if the Lord saw not this, as if there were no knowledge in the Most High; as if he could not pluck his hand out of his bosom; as if we had stolen away his sword, and his quiver full of deadly arrows.

I beseech you, my brethren, do not so wickedly; your oaths and blasphemies, your pride and vanities, your cruelty and oppressions, your frauds and circumventions, your abuse of God's good creatures in excess and wantonness, they are all gone up to heaven, and awake vengeance, and challenge the God of mercy to declare his justice.

Doth not some part of the church now in the Palatinate and in Bohemia groan under the burden of war? wherein the goods, the liberties, the lives of men, Christian men, professors of the same faith with us, do lie at the stake, and blood toucheth blood. Doth not our neighbour church in France tremble for fear of a new massacre? Hath not the sword of violence tasted already of protestant blood? Do not the Jesuits, the incendiaries of the Christian world, blow the coal and incense the king thereof to grassation and destruction of all that have not the mark of the beast either openly in their foreheads, or secretly in their hands? And dare we anger our God, who gives us the early and the latter rain, who crowns our land with peace, and the daughter of peace—plenty! Shall we flatter ourselves, and say that although we do wickedly, this burden shall not fall upon us? Let us pray for them, and amend our own lives, and sin no more, lest some worse judgment do fall upon us; for we shall else find too late that the wrath and judgment of God is too heavy a burden for us to bear.

2. The wrath and judgments of God: they are a burden to God; he professeth it. 'As I live, saith the Lord, I delight not in the death of a sinner.' He calleth upon his Israel, 'Why will ye perish, O house of Israel?' When he punished his people, how heavy was the burden of their punishment upon him! He smarted under his own rod; the burdens that he put upon his people wearied him: Isaiah i. 5, 'Why should you be stricken any more? The whole head is sick, and the whole heart is faint. From the sole of the foot to the head, there is no soundness in it,' &c. Truly God doth bear with us in a double sense, for he doth forbear our punishment in expectation of our amendment, and he doth suffer with us in our sufferings; he is our Father, and every stripe he layeth on us smarteth upon him. Oh grieve not the Spirit of God, by whom you are sealed up to the day of your redemption.

3. The word of God threatening sin is a burden.
1. To God.
2. To the prophet.
3. To the people.

1. It is a burden to God to threaten judgment. He loves to speak us fair, and to speak and treat kindly with us ; to draw us with the cords of men, and with the bands of love ; to be as one that taketh off the yoke : for he knoweth whereof we be made, for he made us, and not we ourselves. He will allure and persuade Japhet to dwell in the tents of Shem.

If Adam do transgress his one commandment given to him in paradise, he tarrieth, expecting when Adam will come to him to acknowledge his fault, and cast himself at his feet to seek mercy. If Adam will not, he will come to him, but it shall be the cool of the day first; and he will call him to account, but yet so fatherly that he cannot execute the law without preaching the gospel; he cannot banish him the earthly paradise till he have opened to him an heavenly. He cannot threaten till he have promised ; he cannot punish till he have pardoned.

2. This is a burden to the prophet, and that three ways :

(1.) In respect of his fidelity to him that sendeth him.
(2.) In respect of his zeal.
(3.) In respect of his charity and compassion to them to whom he is sent.

(1.) In respect of his fidelity. It is a burden to him to keep in the word of this prophecy ; he cannot conceal it. When Jeremiah found the people incorrigible, and that the word of God in his ministry was despised and made his reproach, ' Then I said, I will not make mention of him, nor speak any more in his name : but his word was in my heart as a burning fire shut up in my bones, and I was weary with forbearing, and I could not stay,' Jer. xx. 9.

Some carnal men do confess that it is true that we must preach the judgments of God against sin—that is our trade ; but let children fear those bugbears ; they know as well as we can tell them that God is merciful, and his mercy is above all his works. It is true that we must preach judgment against sin, for we have fear of the burden of all those sins of others which we reprove not, to fall upon ourselves : Ezek. iii. 18, 'If thou givest him not warning, his blood will I require at thy hands.' Therefore this word of excommunication is our burden, and we must not conceal it.

(2.) In respect of his zeal. For the prophets of the Lord and his holy ministers, beholding the sins which they do daily reprove to come up so fast, as though they had never laid the axe of God's judgment against the root of that corrupt tree ; the zeal of God's glory so stirreth them that they cannot hold, but they must strike with the sword of the Spirit ; they must lift up their voices like trumpets ; they must tell the house of Jacob their sins. Jeremiah doth express this to the life : chap. vi. 11, ' Therefore I am full of the fury of the Lord ; I am weary with holding in ; I will pour it out upon the children abroad,' &c. Let not the sensual and carnal man call our threatenings of sin our own ravings and railings, and our comminations of judgment the intemperate issue of our own choler. Jeremiah calleth it ' the fury of the Lord.' And so long as we reprove justly, and mingle none of our own heat with the fire of God's altar, we shall kindle a fire in the bones of the sinner which shall give him no rest, but his conscience shall say to him, as Nathan said to David, ' Thou art the man.'

(3.) In respect of his compassion. Do not think that it is any joy to us to reprove or to threaten. St Paul is loath to use the rod. Jonah will rather run away from God than he will carry the news to Nineveh that it must be destroyed. ' Many walk, of whom I have told you often, and now tell you weeping.' We shall find, as soon as we are past this first verse, that this prophet did feel the burden which he did see ; and the grief he took for them turned his harp into mourning, and his organs into the voice of them that weep. Every tender heart avoideth being a messenger of evil news, but their feet be beautiful that bring glad tidings—tidings of peace.

3. The word of threatening is a burden to the

people to whom it is sent. *Judæis non Chaldæis.*
(1.) To the penitent.
(2.) To the impenitent.

(1.) To the penitent. It is an heavy burden to them to think how they have provoked God to anger, and have drawn out his sword against themselves. They that truly fear God, when they hear their sins threatened, do retire themselves into their chambers; they weep and deplore their iniquities. Hezekiah, hearing the prophet threatening his life, Isa. xxxviii. 2, 3, ' He turned himself to the wall, he prayed to the Lord; and Hezekiah wept sore.' Never think that you hear the threatenings of God with any profit till you feel the burden of them oppressing, and the edge of them drawing blood on you. *Lachrymæ* be *sanguis animæ.*

The lion roareth, and all the beasts of the forest do tremble. A tender son that hath done a fault, and heareth his father threatening to punish him, findeth that threatening so great a burden to him that he can give himself no rest till he have recovered his father's favour.

(2.) The very impenitent, who have any sense of the terror of the Lord, feel God's threatenings heavy. It will make Ahab, that sold himself to do wickedness, put on sackcloth, and crown his head with ashes, and go mourning, if he hear that God's anger is stirred to bring evil upon his house. Even Absalom, an ungracious son, is impatient of living out of his father's presence; and he setteth Joab's corn on fire for neglecting the mediation which might bring him to his father's face. Esau will seek his father's blessing with tears; and what would not Balaam give that he might die the death of the righteous? Surely God is a consuming fire; and if coals of this fire are kindled in the bosom of the impenitent, and their damnation doth not sleep, but is awake in them, in the accusation of their guilty consciences to begin their hell even here on earth.

Verse 2. *O Lord, how long shall I cry, and thou wilt not hear! even cry out unto thee of violence, and thou wilt not save!*

Here this Habakkuk, this *wrestler*, doth begin his wrestling; for what is this whole chapter but a serious expostulation and complaint? wherein the prophet,

1. Contesteth with God himself, ver. 2–4.
2. He bringeth in God denouncing his own intended judgments against Judah and Jerusalem, 5–11.
3. He returneth again to expostulate with God, ver. 12–17.

1. He contesteth with God, wherein

(1.) He challengeth him for not hearing his prayer, ver. 2.

(2.) For shewing to him the sins of the people, ver. 3, 4.

In the first observe,

1. What the prophet did: (1.) He cried; (2.) He cried long; (3.) He cried to him.
2. What cause he had: of violence.
3. What success: (1.) Thou wilt not hear; (2.) Thou wilt not save.

To give some light to that which followeth, let me first admonish you that it may well be gathered, by the title that is here given to Habakkuk the *prophet*, that he was sent by almighty God to preach to the Jews to reclaim them from their evil ways, and to still the noise of their crying sins; and prevailing nothing with them to bring them to repentance, he prayeth and crieth to almighty God for his judgment upon this people, to punish their many sins; and God not hearing him, nor giving way to his anger to correct them, the prophet, moved with the zeal of God's glory, wrestleth with God, and contendeth with him for his rod upon them.

1. What the prophet did: (1.) 'I cry;' he lifteth up his voice against this people, his brethren; for it is twice expressed. 1. He crieth; then he resumeth it; he saith, he crieth out. This is a thing that God doth use to take special notice of, *expectavi justitiam, et ecce clamor.* It is said of Abel, that being dead he spake. Moses saith, it was *vox sanguinis*, a voice of

blood; and God said that voice cried to him out of the earth for vengeance. The cry of a prophet, one of God's secretaries, to whom he revealeth his will; one of God's chaplains, to whom he committeth the ministry of the revelation of his will; one of God's saviours, to whom he committeth the office of saving his people; the crying, the vociferation of one of God's seers, who cries not out of passion or human perturbation, but from a secret inspiration illuminating him, and shewing him things to come; one of God's holy ones, whom the zeal of God's glory doth inflame with this earnestness, the grief of man's rebellion doth provoke to that loudness: such a cry cannot spend itself all into air and sun, and perish with the noise it makes.

(2.) He was no son of thunder, to make some sudden rattling noise, and then cease. He cried loud, he cried long: 'How long shall I cry?' If the weakness of his voice could not penetrate the ear of God *vi*, by force, here was *sæpe cadendo*, by often calling. So David got an hoarseness in throat with crying loud and long to the Lord; and our Saviour hath commanded that kind of importunity in prayer. And the prophet will give God no rest till he hear and answer; for the prayer of the just, if it be fervent, prevaileth with God. Zeal is an holy fire, the flame of it ascendeth to heaven, and penetrateth all the passages till it come to God. Cold and perfunctory devotions, intermitted and given over, do not prevail with God; they please him best that use most violence, for the kingdom of heaven suffereth violence.

(3.) *Unto thee.* He directeth his prayers aright; for Baal's priests may cry from morning to night, and may cut and lance their flesh, and make many signs of zeal and earnest importunity without success, because their god heareth not, his eyes see not, his ears hear not, his hands handle not; there is no breath in his mouth to give them answer.

But the cry of the prophet went up to God, who beholdeth ungodliness and wrong, that he may take the matter into his own hand.

Thus far we have seen what the prophet did: (1.) He cried; (2.) He cried loud; (3.) To God.

2. What cause had he to cry? For violence. This is fully and largely expressed in the second part of his contestation with God, ver. 3, 4.

I therefore only observe here two things:

(1.) That he complained not without great provocation, for violence was God's own complaint and quarrel against the old world: Gen. vi. 13, 'The earth is full of violence, and behold I will destroy them with the earth.' It was God's quarrel against Edom: Obad. 10, 'For thy violence against thy brother Jacob, shame shall cover thee, and thou shalt be cut off for ever.'

(2.) We consider where this violence was; not of Esau against Jacob, but of Jacob against Jacob, as Isaiah describeth it: 'Every man eating the flesh of his own arm, Manasseh Ephraim, and Ephraim Manasseh, and both of them against Judah,' Isa. ix. 21. Civil and domestic wars in the bosom of the church, grievances and vexations one of another, these differences it is likely that the prophets had laboured to compound, and used all means to settle peace there; but it appeareth that they prevailed not, therefore he complaineth.

3. With what success. (1.) 'Thou wilt not hear.' The cry of the prophet was to awaken the justice of God, to chasten his people for this violence; for so desperate was the disease of the church, that they needed the sharpest physic to heal it, even the rod of God to correct them. Yet God is so slow to wrath, and so long-suffering, that he would not hearken to the voice of his prophets as yet, to pull his hand out of his bosom, though they said with David, 'It is time for thee, Lord, to put to thine hand.'

(2.) 'Thou wilt not save;' *i. e.* thou wilt not succour them that suffer violence against the hand of their oppressors. As his not hearing is to be imputed to his mercy and patience, so his not saving is to be imputed either to his wisdom, putting his children to the trial of their faith by afflictions, or to his justice, making one of them, who have corrupted their ways, a rod to scourge the other, neither of them being as yet worth the saving, till he had humbled them.

The text thus cleared, the doctrines which grow upon this stem and first branch of the prophet's contestation are these:

1. That the weapons wherewith the holy servants of God do fight against sin, are their prayers to God.

2. That one necessary ingredient in our prayers, is earnestness and importunity.

3. That the zeal of God's glory, and the love of peace, cannot dispense with tumult and combustion in the church of God.

4. That God sometimes suspendeth the desired success of the earnest prayers of his most faithful servants, when they do pray according to his will, and doth not hear them by and by.

Of the first of these first.

1. *Doct.* The weapons wherewith the holy servants of God do fight against sin, is their prayers.

I find that this people, to whom God had sent his prophets, rising early and sending them, were grown incorrigible; and therefore even the prophets, that loved them, and wished them well, having no other way to reform them, were now put to it to pray against their violence to God. They that had wont to stand in the gap, to turn away ingruent judgments, do take such offence at their ungodliness, that they are put to it to pray to God against them. Thus Joseph carried the evil report of his brethren to his father, and made them to be shent, wherein he did a brotherly office, to seek their reformation.

The spleen of Habakkuk is not against the persons of his brethren, they are not so much as named here: he crieth out of violence; and so St Paul saith, 'The wrath of God is revealed from heaven against all unrighteousness and ungodliness of men.' David did thus in a case of violence: Ps. cix. 3, 4, 'They compassed me about with words of hatred; and fought against me without cause. For my love they are mine adversaries; but I give myself unto prayer,' *ego oro.*

Quære. How doth it stand with the rules of charity to complain to God of our brethren, and to stir up his indignation against them?

Sol. I confess that this asketh an especial tenderness in the servants of God; for to begin here, without using other means to reclaim our offending brother, may shake the walls of our charity, and may accuse us of want of love; therefore all those ways of charity must be first tried, as to admonish privately; or not speeding so, join another with thyself in the private chiding of his sin; after failing, to communicate the matter to the church. If all these supports which we do owe to our brother will not keep him up, then let him be as an heathen; and then is David's prayer in season, 'Let the heathen know that they are but men.'

But in my text here was the body of the church diseased; the members and parts of the body in arms one against another; only some few of God's holy servants lived with grief in their righteous souls, to behold the ungodly conversation of men nefariously wicked and careless of religion; therefore what other way was left them, but that of David? 'I will yet pray against their wickedness; take away their ungodliness, and thou shalt find none.'

The prophets and seers of former times have had special revelations of the will of God, concerning the ungodly of the earth, whereby they might as boldly use imprecation, as deprecation or supplication. We that come short of their measure of the Spirit, must not dare to go to the farthest extent of their liberty in prayer, to pray against our brethren; only thus far we may with Habakkuk cry out unto God, and make our moan to him for violence.

1. Committing our cause, and the care of our safety unto him, as to a faithful creator; and so the care and safety of our brethren.

2. Desiring God to bring to an end the wickedness of the ungodly, and to finish their sins. This serveth,

1. To settle faith in God, and to seek our repose only in him in all cross opposals, because he is the sun and shield, and there is no rest but in him. He only overruleth all, and evacuateth the counsels, and frustrateth the works of wicked men; he only shall bring it to pass.

2. This serveth to reprove the means that are in use amongst us, to reform sin as we pretend; but they are unlawful and ungodly.

(1.) By public blazing and detecting of offenders, to put them to open shame in the world; for the loss of a good name doth more often harden a sinner, and cause impenitency, than reclaim him; for what hath he to boast that hath lost the good opinion of men? Love covereth a multitude of sins, and therefore that is an evil tongue that is the trumpet of another's shame. It is charity to make the best of everything.

(2.) The same offence is committed in private whispers and secret detractions, and the fault is aggravated by concealing ourselves, as unwilling to justify our accusations.

(3.) By cursing and bitter calling upon God for his vengeance on them that offend, if the offence touch us or our friends; for God knoweth without us how to manage his judgments; and cursing, it returneth and smarteth at home. For the apostle saith it twice, 'Bless, curse not.'

(4.) By public plays and interludes, to represent the vices of the time, which, though it were the practice of the heathen, which knew not God but afar off, yet in Christian states, it is no way tolerable nor justifiable to act the parts of evil doers, since the apostle saith it is a shame to name them, much more to act and personate them.

(5.) By private conceived libels, after divulged by secret passage from pocket to pocket, from one bosom to another, for which the devisers thereof have no warrant, and to which they have no calling.

(6.) By satires and poetical declamations; for who hath sent these into the world to convince the world? Is it not to put the Spirit of God out of office, who is sent to convince the world of sin? And who but the Lord's prophets have warrant to lift up their voices like trumpets to tell the house of Jacob their sins? Every empiric man may not profess and practise physic. There is a college of soul-physicians, who have a calling to this purpose, and are sent to heal the sores of the people;—

[1.] By their diligent preaching of the word of God to them.

[2.] By drawing against them, and exercising upon them the sword of ecclesiastical discipline.

[3.] By continual prayer unto God to give end to their sins, whereby they do trespass God and good men.

3. This serveth to discourage men from doing evil, for fear of offending the prophets and ministers of the Lord, whose righteous souls cannot but be vexed to see their good seed cast away upon barren, stony, or thorny ground.

For howsoever basely and unworthily we be deemed, if the incorrigible iniquity of men do put us to it to move almighty God by our earnest prayers against them, they shall find that as Job can do his friends good by his intercession, because he is a prophet, so the Lord's ministers may awake judgment against such as go on still in their wickedness, and will not be reformed.

2. *Doct.* Our prayers must be importunate.

The prophet cried, yea, he cried out to the Lord. This importunity is expressed two ways:

1. In the ardency and zeal of his prayer, it was not *oratio*, a prayer, but *vociferatio*, a crying.

2. In the continuance of time. 'How long.'

Thus must we pray with fervour of spirit. Our tongue is the piece of ordnance, our prayer is the shot, the zeal of our heart is the powder that dischargeth it; and according to the strength of the charge, such is the flight of the shot. Nineveh crieth mightily to God, Jonah iii. 8. Christ our Saviour cried earnestly to his Father, yea, with strong crying and tears. Solomon spread his arms abroad; the publican beat his breast; Christ fell on the ground; David said, Ps. xxxviii. 9, 'My sighing is not hid from thee.' The Israelites' weeping is thus described: 'They drew water and poured it out before the Lord.' The Holy Ghost doth not furnish us so much with words and phrases in prayer as with sighs and groans, which cannot be expressed. Paul prayed three times against Satan's angel; Abraham moved God six times for Sodom; Nehemiah had so spent himself in watching and prayer for his people, that the king observed his countenance changed.

Beloved, it is not prayers by number and tale, as in the Romish church, nor prayers by rote, or by the ear perfunctoriously vented in the church, and for custom said over at home. It is not much babbling and multiplicity of petitions, or vain repitions, that will send up our prayers to heaven: Isa. i., 'Though you stretch out your hands, I will hide mine eyes from you; and though you make many prayers, I will not hear you.' The Pharisees wanted powder to their shot; for they prayed in their synagogues, and in the corners of the streets, but, as God saith, *Quis requisivit ista*, Who requireth these things?

The soul that actuateth and animateth prayer is *fervor spiritus*, the holy zeal of him that prayeth.

2. Duration of time is another testimony of zealous importunity; when our prayer is not a passion, but a deliberate and constant earnestness, holding out, as the apostle saith, 'Pray continually;' not as the Euchites, to do nothing else; but to entertain all occasions to confer with God, and to prostrate our suits before him.

Christ spent a whole night together often in prayer; David, day and night; Daniel, twenty-one days together, during the time that he ate no pleasant bread, and was in heaviness, Dan. x.; Jonah, three days and three nights in the belly of the whale, made it his oratory and chapel, from whence he prayed to the Lord.

If our sore run, so long we can pray whilst we smart; or if our necessities do press us to importunity, we can hold out long for ourselves. But in my text, the cause is God's; zeal for God's glory cannot contain itself in the cause of God; the Lord's people do break his law, and will not be reformed; the prophet of the Lord cannot stand and look on, as in the next verse he doth, and see the glory of God thus suffer, but he must awake in the cause of God to bring him to correction. So David: 'Rise, Lord, and let thine enemies be scattered; let them that hate thee fly before thee.'

And thus, for God's glory's sake, we may, with reservation of those that do belong to the election of grace, pray to God earnestly for the confusion of all Sion's enemies, and of all that would fain see Jerusalem, the true church of God, in the dust.

Shall our fervency and heat be only for ourselves? If it be, the grant of our requests doth quench it, and putteth us to silence; but if the glory of God be that we seek and aim at, the more God heareth our prayers and granteth our requests, the more he inflameth our zeal, and even, as it were, transforms us into prayer. And what better motive can we give of Christ's so frequent, so durant prayers, than this, 'I know that thou hearest me always'?

Now, because long and frequent prayers are a weariness to the flesh, the flesh is no good friend to this exercise; and we do find ourselves in no exercise of religion more tempted than in this. For this cause watching and fasting are so often joined with prayer, as the best means to disable the rebel flesh from resisting.

Doct. God sometimes suspendeth the success of the prayers of his servants.

There is a case wherein God will not hear at all, though Moses, Samuel, Noah, Daniel, Job, do pray to him. In some cases God will hear, but not yet; for he that keepeth the times and seasons in his own power, knoweth best when it is fittest for him to hear.

And that was the case of this prayer. God did, 1, give them yet more time to repent and seek his face, that he might preserve them, and sent his prophets to them to reclaim them.

2. He did expect, if not the conversion of them by fair means, then, that after the full taste of the fruits of his patience, they might by the rod be brought to him, when he should change his right hand. *Mutatio dexteræ.*

3. Or he did expect the filling up of the measure of their sins, that they might have no plea to excuse their ungraciousness.

4. He forbore, to stir up the prophet so much the more to this importunity, that it might be seen that

not only their sins, but the prophet's prayers, had awaked vengeance.

5. To declare how acceptable a sacrifice prayer is, he will delay us that we may pray, for with such sacrifices God is pleased; but if we withdraw ourselves, God's soul will have no pleasure in us.

Let no man think the worse of this holy service of God because he presently feeleth not the success thereof; but as the woman of Canaan, Mat. xv. 22, would not be put off by the disciples, or by Christ himself, so that both her request was granted, and her faith commended.

If we remember our Saviour's limitation, all will be well: 'Father, if thou wilt.' Let us set those bounds to our prayers.

1. What thou wilt; 2, in what measure; 3, when thou wilt; 4, in what manner, *sicut tu vis*, as thou wilt.

Ver. 3, 4. *Why dost thou shew me iniquity, and cause me to behold grievance? for spoiling and violence are before me: and there are that raise up strife and contention. Therefore the law is slacked, and judgment doth never go forth: for the wicked doth compass about the righteous; therefore wrong judgment proceedeth.*

2. He contesteth with God for shewing to him the sins of the people, ver. 3, 4.

For the opening of that text.

Why dost thou shew me iniquity? The prophet doth hereby declare,

1. That it is not his own curious search to look into his brethren. I do not say so scrutinously as the hypocrite in the gospel, who, with a beam in his own eye, could yet discern a mote in his brother's eye; no, not to behold their gross iniquity. He did not look upon his brethren like an informer, to see what fault he could find in them to complain of; he had something else to do: he saith that God shewed him the iniquity of his brethren. So he freeth himself of suspicion of malice and evil affection to his brethren. For there may be malice in looking into the vices of brethren, though it pretend desire of reformation.

2. This cleareth the prophet that he is not as one of them, no partner with them in their iniquity; seeing they that live in the society of evil practice, and do not communicate* with the evil in evil, cannot behold the evil, the object is too near them or gone out of sight.

It sheweth that God doth not only himself take notice of the evils that men do, but he acquainteth his prophets and ministers therewith, which he doth to that end that he may prove their fidelity to him, whether they will discharge their duty to him and their people to whom they are sent, in telling the house of Jacob their sins, and in labouring to bring them to the knowledge thereof, that they may repent.

It followeth, '*Thou dost cause me to behold grievance.*' Wherein he resumeth what he hath spoken before, and rhetorically amplifieth it; for it is one thing to shew, another to cause him to behold. This is an effectual demonstration, as the prophet David doth pray: Ps. li. 8, 'Make me to hear joy and gladness.'

God hath sent his gospel, which is the voice of joy in the tabernacles of the righteous, all the world over: 'Have they not heard? Their sound is gone out into all the world, and their word to the ends of the earth.' But that is not enough, except God do cause us to hear the same.

We preach this gospel of peace, and we shew unto men their righteousness; that is, *viam justitiæ*, how they may be justified in the sight of God. We declare unto men their sins, and shew them how the law of God is broken; but if God do not cause our* hearts to behold this, if God do not turn their eyes into themselves, and into their own ways, to see them, we spend our strength in vain. The scorner goeth away from church, and wipeth his mouth, as the harlot in the Proverbs, and saith, This is nothing to me, because God doth not make his heart smite him for it. God doth not cause him to behold; God doth not open our eyes to see our† sins for ourselves only that we may declare them, but for you, that we may give

* Qu. 'do communicate'?—Ed.

* Qu. 'their'?—Ed.   † Qu. 'your'?—Ed.

you warning of the anger to come.

And what did God shew him?

1. Iniquity; that is, the unjust dealing of the people one with another, as it after followeth.

2. Grievance; either the grievance which that unrighteousness doth bring upon their brethren, or the grievance wherewith the righteous soul of the prophet is vexed day by day, in seeing and hearing the evil conversation of them to whom he is sent.

For spoiling and violence are before me. 1. Here is spoiling; that is, robbing one another, invading one another's goods and lands, and that done in the commonwealth of the Jews, where God himself was so careful to establish the right of propriety in several, that he divided the land himself, to every tribe their part, and by a judicial law set every man his bounds, and taught every man to be content with his own.

The commonwealth cannot long last in prosperity where this spoiling is in practice, whether it be by corruption of the magistrate stopping the course of justice, or by the covetousness of the private man taking advantages to make his brother a prey.

This is commonly the worm of peace; for when external wars do cease, then internal digladiations do commonly succeed; then wit, and policy, and power, do put themselves to it to see what they can get; and this is a sin which God taketh notice of, and which he declareth to his prophets, that they may reprove it.

2. Here is violence also added; for where, by fraud, and circumvention, and secret conveyance, this spoiling cannot be wrought, there, like the priest's servant that came for flesh for the priest, they will take by strong hand and by violence that which they would have. This is commonly the war between the superior and inferior, between the strong and the weak; for the weakest here go to the wall.

These be signs of a drooping and decaying commonwealth, when cruelty and violence is its own carver, and the poor have their faces ground between the tearing millstones of oppression; when the poor flock pines and starves with hunger; when,

'Alienas oves custos bis mulget in hora.'

For they be called *filii alieni*, 'strange children,' that do oppress their brethren, when things are not carried by the law of justice, but by the power of violence. And the commonwealth of the Jews were even sick to the death of this disease, at this time when Habakkuk prophesied; for shortly after followed their deportation, and the destruction of Jerusalem, and desolation of the temple.

Let all the kingdoms of the world take warning by this fearful example, and let not private persons transgressing in this kind forget what the Lord did to this people.

3. The prophet addeth, *before me ;* wherein he declareth a double boldness of these sinners.

1. That they professed their opposition, and cared not who saw it; for the holy men of God search not so deep into the manners of men to seek out their faults, neither do they profess themselves students in the affairs of the commonwealth, as to observe how things are carried; but if God declare it to them, and cause them to behold it, and if the workers of this wickedness be so bold and open that they care not who see it, this doth prove the sin deeply rooted and high-grown in amongst them.

2. It proves their boldness in sinning, that they durst commit those crying sins before the prophet, the messenger of God sent of purpose to reprove them, and coming from almighty God to dissuade them from it. Sin at first is bashful and modest, and doth fear the sight of any good man. Seneca, the learned preacher, thought it a good thing to keep in unruly desires, and any intemperancy in young men. *Prodest sine dubio custodem sibi imposuisse, et habere quem respicias ;* and to live *Tanquam sub alicujus boni viri semper præsentis oculis.* But when men grow to that height of sinning that they dare commit their iniquities in the sight of God and men; in the sight of the minister that carrieth the sword of God's Spirit, the word of God to reprove it and threaten it; or in the sight of the magistrate that carrieth the sword of God to punish it, then, to use the apostle's word, ' Sin is out of measure sinful.'

Such are they that swear, and blaspheme the name of God, that talk scurrilously and lewdly, that deprave their brethren maliciously, that drink drunk even before us, the ministers of God's word, as if God had sent us to bid them sin on, and as if we had no commission to find fault out of the pulpit. They save their own stakes by confining us to the pulpit, and shutting up our power there; for there they know we may not tax personally, and they think themselves free enough if we smite at sin only in general terms; for such reproofs have no edge but what particular application doth give them, and therein they are wise enough to favour themselves.

It is not nothing that the prophet doth say that this spoiling and violence was done before him; for his words of reproof will prove them guilty of wilful transgression, and contempt of the divine majesty, as it presently followeth. And he will be both a fearful imprecator against them, as he proveth in this chapter, to call down God's judgments upon them; and he will be a full witness to testify against them before God.

And there are that raise up strife and contention. This is a further complaint of the prophet against this people; that they are so far from peace, that they do pick quarrels one with another, and make matter of strife and contention. This is contrary to the apostle's precept: Rom. xii., 'If it be possible, as much as in you is, have peace with all men.'

There be some of that froward nature, and wrangling disposition, that cannot contain themselves within the bounds of peace, but they must be ever searching where they may find fault, thinking it best fishing in troubled waters. You see that God taketh notice of such unquiet persons, and detecteth them to his prophets, that they may chide them for it; as the apostle saith, Rom. xvi. 17, 'Now I beseech you, brethren, mark them which cause divisions and offences.' You see God marketh them; for it is one of the six things which God abhors, Prov. vi. 19, 'him that soweth discord among brethren.' There is great cause why God should abhor such as stir up strife.

1. Because God is called 'the God of peace,' and his gospel is called 'the gospel of peace;' and his natural Son became *pax nostra*, 'our peace,' and his adopted sons be 'children of peace.' Therefore those sons of thunder, those boisterous and tumultuous natures, must needs be abominable to him whose ways be *viæ pacis*, the ways of peace; for contraries do expel one the other.

Contention doth derive itself from two very offensive corruptions in men, which are abominable to God, as Solomon sheweth.

1. Only 'by pride cometh contention,' Prov. xiii. 12; and indeed they that think themselves wiser than their brethren, and overween the graces of God in themselves, and think themselves worthy to sit at the helm, and to direct all, if they cannot have their own wills in everything, then they quarrel, and contend with all that oppose them.

The proud man God resisteth, for he encroacheth upon his sovereignty; therefore David saith that God abhorreth him.

2. 'Hatred stirreth up strife,' Prov. x. 12; that is another corruption in man which God cannot dispense with, because he is charity; and only 'he which dwelleth in charity dwelleth in God, and God in him.'

There be many distastes and dislikes that do grow even amongst friends, because we either want the wisdom to know, or the patience to consider, when time is, that there can be no peace between us, except we can bear with one another, and forgive one another some infirmities, which the apostle calleth 'bearing one another's burdens.' It is not that sin of infirmity in our nature that is here complained of, but when men be so perverse and unquiet that they will stir up strife and contention; as David complaineth, 'They stir up strife all the day long.' And when there is not only contention, as in those that secretly work one against another, but there is *jurgium*, a chiding and scolding too; and that they go so far in it, that when the prophet speaketh to them of peace, they prepare themselves to battle; this is hostility to peace.

Here all those that disquiet the peace of their brethren, by secret whispers and by open detractions, and all those that molest one another in needless suits of law; all tale-bearers, that carry fire about them to inflame a brother against a brother, do see who takes notice of them, even God himself; and they make the prophets and ministers of God, like Joseph, to carry their evil report to their father, and to complain of them as enemies unto peace.

All those, that when a contention is laid asleep, do awake it with new suggestions, and stir it up afresh, and put fuel to it to inflame it; all which proceeds from an evil root of bitterness in us, and witnesseth against us, that surely the fear of God and the love of brethren is not in that place.

The apostle telleth us, that 'if we be led by the Spirit of God, we are the sons of God.' But it is clear that contention, and strife, and debate, are fruits of the flesh, and declare us to be carnal; and 'flesh and blood cannot inherit the kingdom of heaven.'

Those contentions do make us unfit for the service of God, and to perform all Christian offices to one another; and God, seeing it for the good of his people, he detecteth it to his prophets of purpose, that they may seek reformation thereof. But these did strive even with the prophets.

How far this unquietness did stretch in this people, the next words declare.

Therefore the law is slacked. By the law here he meaneth the law of God that *labefactata est*, is weakened; or, as others read it, *lacerata est*, is torn in pieces; others, *dissolvitur*, is dissolved, that is, the law of peace and charity; for the whole sum of the law is love: that is broken, and no man maketh conscience thereof, or careth to be rued* by it. Here observe,

1. This goeth near the heart of God's prophet, when he seeth that God is no more set by, and his law no better regarded; so doth the prophet complain, Ps. cxix. 158, 'I beheld the transgressors, and was grieved,

---

* Qu. 'ruled'?—ED.

because they kept not thy word.' This complaint, then, was no human perturbation, but a sad complaint for the injury done to almighty God in his law. And herein we shew our zeal of God's glory, when we are moved and troubled at the contempt of his law; for commonly we are full of heat and provocation in personal injuries when ourselves are touched; but we are too cold in the quarrel of God. The holy psalmist cries out, ' Away from me, all ye that work iniquity; for I will keep the commandments of my God.' This is to be angry without sin, when we are provoked against them that violate the holy law of God.

2. Note how licentiousness was overgrown in this people, and to what an height their sin was come up. When the law of God, which was by God given to them, deposited with them, given with such a charge of keeping it, with such terrible threatenings of all declining from it, given with such promises annexed to the keeping of it, was now neglected; the lantern and light to their feet put out, of purpose, because they love darkness more than light.

These two things, *mutuo se generant*, do mutually beget each other; for from the contempt of the law of God doth arise licentiousness and custom of sinning, and from that licentiousness doth grow a further contempt of the law.

When men live out of the awe of God's commandments, and will not be kept within the bounds and limits which the law of God doth set them, there can be no hope of their conversion; their estate is desperate; the prophet must repair to God; this is *dignus vindice nodus*. ' It is time for thee, Lord, to put to thine hand; for they have destroyed thy laws.'

Judgment doth never go forth. 1. Some understand this of the impurity of those wicked men, that God doth see their violence, and how his law is broken, and yet he keepeth in his judgment, and doth not punish the transgressors; which maketh them to sin boldly; for ' because sentence is not speedily executed against the wicked, the heart of the children of men is wholly set in them to do evil.' In which sense the prophet doth challenge God of remissness in execution of his judgment, and quickeneth him by this complaint.

2. Others do understand these words of the corruption of all judicial authority amongst them; for where the law of God faileth, and is not regarded, there can be no seat of justice; no man can expect that judgment should come from thence; *expectavi judicium et ecce clamor*, there is the stool of wickedness. And that sense doth best agree with this place and the coherence of the text; for where religion is despised, the courts of justice must needs be corrupt. Justice is either turned into wormwood, if the judge be incensed, and carry a spleen; or if the judge be servile, and live in fear of some great power, he must take his directions from them, and he must decree as he is commanded; or if he be covetous, justice is a prize, then win it and wear it; or if he be partial, as the parties are befriended, so the cause is ended. So that judgment, that is, upright and uncorrupted judgment, never goeth out; and so the best causes speed worst.

You see here was great cause of complaint, when there was neither religion nor justice left in that land. It followeth,

'*The wicked doth compass about the righteous.*' So David complained, Ps. xii. 8, 'the wicked walk on every side.' And again, Ps. xxii., 'Be not far from me, for trouble is near; for there is none to help.' He complaineth of the ungodly, and calleth them bulls and lions; strong bulls, ravening and roaring lions. 'Dogs have compassed me.' Where the law of God is neglected, authority and power degenerateth into oppression and tyranny; men lay aside humanity, and are transformed into brute beasts that have no understanding. There is nothing more dangerous than to be an honest man, and one that feareth God and maketh conscience of his ways amongst the wicked: 'They came about me like bees,' as the Sodomites came about Lot; and they cry, Down with them, down with them, and let them never rise again. The prophet Isaiah describeth it well: chap. lix. 14, 15, 'And judgment is turned away backward, and justice standeth afar off; for truth is fallen in the streets, and equity cannot enter. Yea, truth faileth, and he that departeth from evil maketh himself a prey: and the Lord saw it, and it displeased him that there was no judgment.'

Christ told us long ago, in his disciples, 'If you were of the world, the world would love you;' for the world loves all her own : 'but because you are not of the world, but I have chosen you out of the world, therefore the world hateth you.' You see how they compass about the just men in whom any religion appears, or any care of a good conscience, or any fire of holy zeal; the wicked come about such to quench this fire, and beset such round about that they may not escape them.

Let Lot say to the Sodomites, 'I pray you, brethren, do not so wickedly,' Gen. xix. 9; they will press upon him, and threaten him, 'Now will we deal worse with thee than with them; then they pressed to break the door.'

Therefore wrong judgment proceedeth. Because things are carried by the licentious and unbridled will of power, without religion or conscience of equity, therefore there is wrong judgment. I understand the prophet thus: That private injuries and oppressions between man and man were frequent, and the wicked used all means to molest the just; and when they did fly for remedy to the courts of justice, they were also so corrupt, and did so favour the cause of the wicked, that there they had wrong judgment. The judges and magistrates that should execute the judgments of God upon the wicked, and should deliver the oppressed out of the hands of the oppressor, they were guilty,—

1. Of favouring and animating and abetting the wicked in their ungodliness, which they should have punished, for which also they were ordained.

2. Of unjust judgment, punishing where they should spare, and oppressing whom they should defend.

Here was a corrupt commonwealth, and this was the grief of the prophet, and he had no remedy but to put the scroll of their sins and to spread it before the Lord; and in behalf of the oppressed, to appeal from the courts of men to the tribunal of God.

The words thus opened, and the sense cleared, let us consider this text,

1. In the total sum : it is a very serious complaint of the prophet to God.
2. In the particulars of which he complaineth.

He complaineth of two things.

1. Of the corruption of the state of the commonwealth of the Jews.
2. Of God's declaring the same corruption to him.

The corruption is expressed in three things.

1. In the conversation.
2. In the religion.
3. In the justice of that nation.

1. In the total. The prophet doth complain to God seriously, and out of a grieved heart, of the people.

Doct. Complaint is a part of prayer.

Prayer is a pouring forth of the heart to God, wherein we prostrate all our desires to God, and crave his help. Sometimes we call to remembrance the mercies of God, and sum up his benefits, which, though it be joined with prayer, and doth pass under the name of prayer, yet is it rather a special and distinct part of God's worship in itself, than properly any member or part of prayer. Sometimes we beg of God supply of our wants, and that we call petition. Sometimes we plead the cause of our brethren, and beg for them; that is intercession. Sometimes we pray against judgment and sin, and that is deprecation. Sometimes we have cause to complain to God of the sins and transgressions of our brethren, when either the honour of God or the peace of brethren is violated : so here ; this is imprecation. For when we see that the outward means of reclaiming men from giving offence to God, to the church, and to Christian religion, do not work effectually to reform them, yet we must not forsake the cause of God so, but make our complaint unto him, and put the matter into his hand.

Thus, when there was a council held against the apostles, Acts iv., and therein consultation for the quenching of the light of the gospel, then beginning to shine more clearly, Peter and John went aside from the council, dismissed with a strait and severe charge to speak no more in that name. They came to their brethren and informed them of these things, and 'they lifted up their voice to God with one accord.'

In that prayer they complain of their enemies: 1, For that which they had done already. 'For of a truth, against thy holy child Jesus, whom thou hast anointed, both Herod and Pontius Pilate, and the Gentiles, were gathered together.' 2. For that which they meant to do. 'And now, Lord, behold their threatenings.' This also is twice included in the Lord's prayer; for when we desire that the kingdom of God may come, we do complain of the enemies of that kingdom, and desire God to arise and scatter them, and defeat all their designs against the same. And when we pray not to be led into temptation, but to be delivered from evils, we do secretly complain of all those evils which Satan and his wicked instruments do plot against the body of the church, or any particular members thereof.

1. The reason is, because vengeance belongeth to God; and we must remember of what spirit we are, and must not take the quarrel of God into our hands, but leave it to God to see and require.

2. Because the times and seasons are only in his power; and we must leave it to his wise justice to take the fit time for the conversion or confusion of his enemies, in the mean time resting ourselves on his sure protection and faithful care of us.

3. Because we may have enemies for the present, who may come to a sight and sense of their sins, and may by our complaint of them to God, receive his saving mercy to reconcile them to the church, as he did Saul at the prayer of Saint Stephen, who shortly after became an apostle, and proved a chosen instrument of God's glory.

4. We must complain of these things to declare our zeal of God's glory, and our holy impatience to see his commandments despised of men.

5. To shew our charity to our brethren, who do suffer by this cruel and wicked world, whose estates

we pity, and we go to God as a common Father to us all, to take the matter into his own hands.

From whence we conclude that it ever ought to be a part of our prayer, to call upon the name of God by way of complaint of the iniquity of the times in which we do live, that God may give an end to it, and that it may not prevail against his church, lest the enemies thereof do grow too proud.

This manner of complaining and calling upon God for justice against the ungodly doth not die with us here; the separated souls parted from earth, and from their bodies, do retain it: Rev. vi. 9, 10, 'I saw under the altar the souls of them that were slain for the word of God, and for the testimony which they held. And they cried with a loud voice, saying, How long, O Lord, holy and true, dost thou not judge and avenge our blood on them that dwell on the earth.'

This doctrine yieldeth this fruit of application to our profit.

1. If we ought to complain to God of the wickedness of our brethren when they do grow incorrigible, it is a fair warning to us to walk warily and with a good conscience before God and man; and that in two respects.

1. That we do not offend our brethren by any means, lest we give them occasion to complain to God of us. It is a dangerous thing to give occasion of offence to any of those little ones that trust in God, and woe be to them that give the offence. It is the praise of Zacharias and Elizabeth, Luke i. 6, that they were ἄμεμπτοι. The apostle doth require this of the Philippians, chap. ii. 15, ἵνα γένησθε ἄμεμπτοι καὶ ἀκέραιοι. *Sine querela, sine cornibus*, of μέμφομαι, *conqueror*.

You shall find it a great contentment in your heart, and peace in your bones all your life through, but especially upon your deathbed, when you can comfort yourselves with this: that your brethren, with whom you have lived, have had no cause to complain of you. But it will be an ornament to your memory, and a second life to your good name, when you are departed hence.

Let no man neglect the complaints of his brethren, especially of God's ministers; for where they be just, they have swift passage and easy admittance, and most gracious auditors.

2. That we do not so defile ourselves with our sins that we may complain, and God will not hear us; for there be many more that complain and are not heard, than of those that complain and have audience and redress. For this is much more anger than holy zeal.

They had need be very innocent that complain of others. *Turpe est authori cum culpa redarguit ipsum.*

This teacheth us by all means to seek the reformation one of another; for if by our good counsel, or by our good example, or by brotherly reproofs, or by the mediation of friends, or by the sharp coercion of the laws, we cannot destroy sin in them, yet we must not give them over; we must complain to God of them, and leave them to his justice.

2. Let us now review the particulars of the prophet's complaint.

1. Of the corruption of the state of the commonwealth of the Jews, and therein,

1. Of their corrupt conversation generally, expressed in these words, *grievance, spoiling, violence, strife,* and *contention;* all of them against the law of the second table, 'Thou shalt love thy neighbour as thyself.'

Doct. The sin of uncharitableness corrupteth a commonwealth, and maketh all the faithful servants of God complain; it is a crying sin. Observe the prophet's words:

1. *Grievance:* If we do anything, or say anything whereby we do grieve our brother, and alienate his affections from us.

2. *Spoiling:* If we by any means hurt him in his maintenance, either by taking from him that which he doth possess, or by preventing him in that which he should possess, by withholding from him the wages of his labour, or by denying the labourer work whereby he should live, or by undervaluing his labour to make it unsufficient to support him, or by bringing up an evil report of him, or by any alienation of his friends from him.

3. *Violence :* Using strong hand to any of these purposes, which is called sinning with an high hand and stiff neck, abusing power and place to oppression and wrong.

4. *Strife :* Disquieting our brethren's peace.

5. *Jurgium :* Provoking them with proud and imperious speeches.

These sins corrupt a commonwealth, and overthrow charity, and grieve all such as fear God.

1. Because they impeach the authority and power of God, who hath reserved to himself the dispensation of his own gifts here; for the earth is the Lord's, and all that therein is, and he hath given it to the sons of men. Whatsoever either honour or wealth any man possesseth, which is not of his gift, that is achieved by unlawful means, it hath not his blessing, and it is held by intrusion and usurpation.

He hath not put man into the world, as he did the people of Israel into Canaan, to be his own carver, and to take what he can get by strength or policy; they had warrant for what they did there, we have a law of restraint, to confine us to lawful ways and means of living; therefore all such violence as invadeth the goods of our brethren is a wrong to him who openeth his hand and filleth with plenty, and doth not bid us arise, kill, and eat, and get what we can, no matter how.

2. This uncharitable practice doth destroy society; for seeing God for peace sake hath made a difference between men on earth, some superior, others inferior; some rich, some poor; that there might be a need of one another, to maintain the state of a commonwealth, all they that engross to their own heap, and do only study themselves and their own house, they corrupt and destroy that common society which ought to be in the members of the body.

I read that Pope Adrian the sixth, a monkish man, demanded once of John of Salisbury, his countryman, what opinion the world had of the church of Rome. He answered that the church of Rome, which should be a mother, was now become a step-mother, and gathered and got all from her own children. The pope replied with a tale : all the parts of the body did conspire against the stomach, and thought much to labour for that, whereupon they resolved to feed it no longer ; but within few days, there grew such a general decay in the state of all the parts of the body, that at last, finding their error, they laboured as before for the stomach, and found then that that maintained them all. The pope's application was, that the pope is the stomach in the body of the church, and that though all the members of the body do feed him, yet he gathereth not for himself, but for the whole body.

It is true, that the father of a commonwealth is the stomach, from whence all the body, as from the root, deriveth sap and nutriment, and therefore all must labour for him. But one body must have but one stomach ; and therefore when every man shall rob and spoil and swallow up what he can, the body must needs perish.

Again, where that one stomach is good, the body thrives ; for that hath not only an appetitive faculty to desire food, and receptive to entertain it, and a retentive to keep it, but a digestive also to distribute it into all the parts of the body.

But if the stomach be appetitive and rapine, and devour all, as in some disease, *caninus appetitus*, which is a greedy devourer ; or if it be retentive and will part with nothing, but is the hell and grave of all that it receiveth, as in covetousness ; or if it be defective in the retentive faculty, and cast up all, as in prodigality and waste ; or if it be ill affected in the digestive faculty, that it feedeth nothing but ill humours, to overthrow the contemperament of the complexions ; that is, if it feed the sanguine only, and so maintain all kind of wantonness, pride, and vanity ; if it feed only choler, and so support tyranny and violence ; or if it support only melancholy, it feedeth sullen and busy projecting wit ; or if it feed phlegm, it sustaineth idleness ;—if it do not nourish the temperament of these humours in the body, it feedeth diseases and destroyeth the body.

Thus was the commonwealth of the Jews at this time diseased, and only the choler was fed, which brought forth grievance, spoiling, violence, strife; so riches became the faculties of evil doing, and power was the mother and nurse of violence.

Use. Our lesson therefore is, if we love the state of the commonwealth in which we live, and would have the body thrive, of which we are members, we must observe the law of the Christian charity and common justice.

Justitia tua suum cuique tribuit, charitas tua tuum, we must do all men right, and know our own from another man's, and we must distribute to the necessities of our brethren, that there be no complaining in our streets; the elder must labour by good counsel and good examples to support the younger, the younger by their strength and labour to give subvension and help to the elder, each to know their own, and to think nothing theirs which is not lawfully gotten.

Let us remember the severe prohibition of the law, which not only bindeth our hearts and affections, saying, 'Thou shalt not steal,' *nec actu, nec affectu,* neither in act nor in desire; but it restraineth our very first thoughts and motions of the mind: 'Thou shalt not covet any that is thy neighbour's.'

Let us remember how much violence, and spoiling, and grievance, and strife displeaseth God, and let our brother dwell in peace by us; let us not so much as look upon our brethren with an evil eye, to envy their thriving, or with a covetous desire to enrich ourselves with their spoils.

We see the danger of this commonwealth of the Jews because of their oppression, and we see the remedy here used, to complain thereof to God; therefore if we with Solomon, Eccles. iv. 1, 'Turn and consider all the oppressions that are wrought under the sun, and behold the tears of the oppressed, and none comforteth them; and the strength is of the hand that oppresseth them, and none comforteth them;' I know no remedy that we have but our prayer to God, for he only is the refuge of the afflicted.

If the minister complain that he cannot be entertained to execute the priest's office without simoniacal contracts, or being in the execution of the same, cannot keep the tithes and profits of his place from spoil and depredation; if the soldier complain that in time of peace he is despised; if the merchant be hindered in his commerce, the husbandman overracked in his rent, the labourer either not found work, or not paid their wages; if the common man be exhausted by impositions and exactions, and the rich man milked by borrowings, while the most idle and unprofitable moths of the commonwealth, and the rust of peace, doth devour all, and build their nest on high, full of the spoils of their brethren: these things tell us, that they that are dead in the Lord are happy; as Solomon saith, they hear not the voice of the oppressor, and they shall not see the evil which this crying sin shall bring upon the living, for you shall see that God heareth the complaints of his holy ones, and visiteth the land that transgresseth in these things.

The corruption of religion, even the contempt thereof, is complained of. The law of God slacked, weakened, despised.

Doct. It is a diseased and a desperate state where religion is contemned, and where the law of God is not cared for.

Reason 1. The cause is, because we hold nothing temporal in this life by any other right than upon condition of our obedience to the law and will of God: Isa. i. 19, 20, 'If thou consent and obey, thou shalt eat the good things of the land: but if ye refuse and rebel, ye shall be devoured with the sword.'

Moses, repeating the law of the ten commandments to the people, Deut. v. 2, calleth it the covenant which the Lord made with them in Horeb; and the conditions of the covenant were these: 'Ye shall observe to do therefore as the Lord your God hath commanded you; you shall not turn aside to the right hand nor to the left; you shall walk in all the ways which the Lord your God hath commanded you, that ye may live, and that it may be well with you, and that ye may prolong your days in the land which ye shall possess.'

The very introduction into the law, 'I am the Lord your God, which brought thee out of the land of

Egypt, out of the house of bondage,' sheweth why God delivereth us from the hands of our enemies, that we may serve him, and that we may thrive and prosper in his service.

Therefore, where the law is slacked, and religion set at nought, the despisers thereof have no lawful interest in anything that they possess, but are intruders and usurpers, and such as encroach upon God's rights without any plea of right; they are robbers of the just, to whom the earth is given, and with whom only the covenant of God is made.

The psalmist saith, Ps. cxix. 1, 'Blessed are the undefiled in the way, who walk in the way of the Lord.' The idle speculations of secular wise men, and the corrupt affections of carnal men, have sought felicity in other ways, but have not found it. The way of religion, and keeping the law of God, never failed any man; for though the faithful man be not justified by his obedience and keeping of the law, yet the faith of the man is so justified; as St James saith, 'Shew me thy faith by thy works.'

The way of temporal fulness hath misled many, and corrupted the very Jews of God's people; for why did they oppress, and spoil, and grieve, and contend with their brethren, but to mend their own heap? And riches are not but for use. By riches they might have their heart's desire in anything here below, they might buy it out.

Every one observeth the way of his time; if he see that there be no way of rising or thriving in the world but by such a mediation, the whole address is that way, and that means is wholly studied. If a man see that there is nothing to be had without money, for money anything, then money is his whole study: *quærenda pecunia primum*.

And sure if men did see that nothing but virtue, and religion, and the fear of God did prefer men, and sufficient worth for the place that they seek, men would study virtue and honesty, and all those parts which might make them worthy of what they seek.

But it is no matter; let the men of this world share amongst them things temporal, and let them break and slack the law of God to humour the present times, as those Jews at this time did, of whom the prophet doth complain, 'I will give them sauce to their meat.' For three things well considered will call us away from these temporal desires, and make us despise the world.

1. Though one man had all that this world affordeth delightful, yet all this could not satisfy his unbounded desire; he could not take use of it all, he should have but the beholding of some of it with his eye, and that the least part of the whole.

2. All these things could not give rest and peace to the conscience, or heal the diseased soul, or comfort at the dying hour; they cannot stand in the gap to turn away the judgment of God, they cannot so much as cure the headache, or the toothache, or any disease of the body.

When our sins be ripe and ready for the gathering, all the wealth of the world cannot keep out the sickle of vengeance.

3. None of all this sublunary happiness can extend itself to eternity; we brought it not with us, and we must leave it behind us; and, as Zophar said, Job xx. 15, 'He that hath swallowed down riches shall vomit them up again; God shall cast them out of his belly.' Neither do all men tarry till they die to lay down these things. We have heard with our ears, and seen in our own times, how some have outlived great honours, and seen them conferred upon others; we have seen great esteemed rich men break, and their poverty come upon them like an armed man.

On the contrary, the man that keepeth the law of God with his whole heart, and doth his best to walk conscionably before God and man, that man hath three benefits, which would encourage any man to embrace the law of God with obedience, and they are the three things in this life most of all to be desired:

1. Safety from evils.
2. Comfort within himself.
3. Estimation abroad.

1. Safety.

The greatest danger that the just man feareth in this life is the wrath of God; for all other evils be the exercise of his virtue, that evil of God's displeasure is the wound of the soul; for there is no peace where God is angry, but only the terror of the Lord. From this, he that keepeth the law of God is safe; for he knoweth that whom God loveth once, he loveth for ever, and the grace of election cannot be lost.

He may chasten such with the rods of men, but his mercy he cannot utterly take away; for the foundation of the Lord is sealed with this seal: 'The Lord knoweth who are his.' 'Whom he knoweth he electeth, he predestinates, he calleth, he justifieth, he sanctifieth, he glorifieth.' They cannot sin unto death. He will cover them under his wings, and they shall be safe under his feathers.

2. Comfort within himself.

This cometh from a pure fountain of grace: 'The Spirit of God witnessing to our spirit that we are the sons of God;' and then the answer of a good conscience to that spirit, which hath this effect, that the more we do see and feel the failing of all our temporal comforts, the more we cleave to God, and seek our comfort in him.

3. Estimation abroad.

1. They are dear to God, who loveth them, and declareth them heirs of his promises.

2. They are dear to the Son of God: he bought them with a price, and he thought it well bestowed on them; he gave them his word in the Holy Ghost to abide with them for ever, and he is gone to prepare a place for them.

3. They are dear to the angels of God: they pitch their tents about them living, and minister unto them; and when they die, they carry their souls into Abraham's bosom.

4. They are dear to their mother the church of God, who saith to them as Solomon's mother, Prov. xxxi. 2, 'What, my son? what, the son of my womb? what, the son of my vows?' And she is ready to tender her children to God, saying, 'Lo, here am I, and the children which thou hast given me.'

5. They that live in the obedience of the law of God have the testimony of the wicked, for they cannot complain of them; if they do them wrong, they suffer it without seeking revenge; if they need the help of the godly, they give it them without respect of persons; if they be sick, the faithful pray for them; if they do evil, they reprove them friendly; and when they die, they will rather cast the care of their estates and children upon such as fear God than upon other men whom they have loved more for their similitude of manners.

And note this, they that walk severely in the obedience of God's law, are at the most taxed but for hypocrisy, which sheweth that even the world cannot blame them, if they be sincere, and truly and really answerable to their outward profession.

To all this we may add, as the full comfort of all, that 'godliness hath the promises of this life, and the life to come.'

1. Of this life. We hold that which we possess in a good right, by our obedience to the law of God, and we have God's word and promise for it, that nothing shall be taken from us, if that we do enjoy here but for our greater good.

2. Of the life to come. That is double:

1. Here; in our good name, in our posterity, a sure house.

2. Hereafter; in glory, in fulness of joy.

I do not doubt but God hath wrought that sad* effect by the plentiful ministry of his word in our church; that he hath many holy souls here amongst us which hold the commandments of God more dear than all that they possess, or that the world hath to give them; and for their sakes God is merciful to our land, and gives us that peace and plenty which many of our neighbour churches do want. And if God should shut up these in the chambers of death, the candle of the wicked would be soon put out.

But we cannot but see that papists do grow both more and more bold than they have been; whence

---

* Qu. 'said'?—Ed.

they have their encouragement, God best knoweth. We see that schismatics and separatists are increased, and much of the knowledge that is gotten turneth into swelling, and pride, and contention. We see that the Sabbath of God is most neglected, even of those that owe God most service, for the abundance of things temporal; we see that profit, and pleasure, and company, and custom of sinning, hath brought the law of God into contempt with such as are profane.

Let such see and consider how God dealt with his own people in such a case, as the next part of this chapter sheweth, and let them fear. For us; let us know that in keeping of the law of God there is great reward; and let us learn to love this law, and put our whole strength to the keeping of it, that we may live. And this,

1. In sincerity; not with eye-service, to be seen of men; against hypocrisy.

2. In zeal and fervency of spirit; his word in our hearts must be as a burning fire, Jer. xx. 9, against cold and perfunctorious profession, which is the general disease of professors.

3. With perseverance to the end, without any intermission or cessation; against apostasy and backsliding, even as our great example did, who was obedient to the death; even he bowed down his head, and gave up the ghost. This, and nothing else, doth make this life peace, and the next life glory; this is the old and good way; walk in it, and you shall find rest for your souls.

3. The corruption of justice is another of the prophet's complaints.

Doct. Corruption of justice is a dangerous sign of a drooping commonwealth.

Reason 1. The magistrate sitteth in the place of God, and he is the common father of the people; and God hath put his own sword into his hand, and commanded him to judge justly between man and man.

If either there be no magistrate, as when there was no king in Israel, the people did what seemed good in their own eyes, then every man is his own judge, and the stronger prevail against the weaker. Or if the magistrate be corrupt, there goeth forth wrong judgment; and good causes have unequal hearings, and right taketh no place. Solon in the Athenian, and Lycurgus in the Lacedæmonian, commonwealth, got them honour in the books of time for their justice; and Herodotus reporteth, that amongst the Medes, when they yet had no king, Deioces being but a private man, by compromising contentions betwixt man and man justly and equally, got that reputation amongst the people, that in short time all the causes of the country were referred to his hearing, which got him such a name of doing justice, that when they found it necessary to put themselves under the government of a king, they found no man so fit to invest in that honour as Deioces; and they with one consent chose him to be their king. And Solomon saith, Prov. xvi. 12, 'The throne is established by righteousness.'

Therefore, where justice faileth, God's ordinance is made an instrument of cruelty, and the king's throne is set on a slippery place; as we find it exemplified in this kingdom of the Jews, whereof Zephaniah complaineth, chap. iii. 3, 'Her princes within her are roaring lions; her judges are evening wolves.' And Micah, chap. iii. 10, 'They build up Zion with blood, and Jerusalem with iniquity. The heads thereof judge for reward. Therefore shall Zion for your sakes be ploughed as a field; and Jerusalem shall become heaps, and the mountain of the house as the high places of the forest.' For God cannot long endure that his sword shall be drawn against his people, and that his gods (for he giveth judges his own title) should become lions, and bears, and bulls, and wolves, and devils, amongst the sheep of his pasture.

He did the government, then, a great honour, who bore in his shield the picture of justice, having in one hand the sword, in the other the states,* with this word, DUM ILLA EVINCAM.

But when *tribunalia* may be called *tributalia*, where judgment is given according to the gifts and rewards that are given; or where corrupt affection serveth its

---

* Qu. 'scales'?—ED.

own turn any way from the way of justice, God seeth it, and is angry that there is no judgment, *et qui videt requiret.*

Reason 2. Corruption of justice is a sign of a drooping commonwealth, because it not only is contrary to religion, and the written law of God, but it is contrary to the law of God written in the heart of man.

For, as Lactantius† saith well, *Radix justitiæ et omne fundamentum æquitatis est illud, vide ne facias ulli quod pati nolis.* This counsel is good. *Transfer in alterius personam quod de te sentis, et in tuam quod de altero judicas.* And if this law of nature must bind all men to do justice one to another, much more must it oblige those to whom the office of administration of justice is committed; let them make it their own case, and so no wrong judgment shall go forth.

For this same *jus naturale* is the fountain of all justice; which religion hath so enlightened, that God, having planted true religion in his church, the prophet saith, Isa. v. 7, 'He looked for judgment.'

Use 1. The proper application of this text is to the magistrate, to admonish him to execute the judgments of God justly, that neither the people may have cause to complain of wrong, but may know where to have right done them; neither the prophets of God may have cause to awake the justice of God against those that manage the sword of justice cruelly or partially, or any way corruptly. But I have none such in this audience to admonish, and therefore I omit that exhortation, as unproper for this hearing.

Use 2. For us, if we hear the cry and complaint of our brethren, or feel the smart of oppression in ourselves, we see the danger of it to the state in which we live, threatening it with ruin; and it ought to stir us up, as the apostle doth admonish, to pray to God for his help: 1 Tim. ii. 1–3, 'I exhort therefore, that, first of all, supplications, prayers, intercessions, and giving of thanks, be made for all men; for kings, and all that are in authority; that we may lead a quiet

† Divin. Instit.

and peaceable life in all godliness and honesty. For this is good and acceptable in the sight of God our Saviour.'

Insurrection against the magistrate, and deposition of kings, and violence offered to their persons, even unto death, is a presbyterian doctrine. Buchanan, the Scottish chronicler, our king's first schoolmaster, in his book *de jure regni*, was the first broacher hereof, who maketh kings to derive their authority from the people, and giveth power to the people to take away the same if he govern not justly.

Against this we have God's own word, saying, 'Touch not mine anointed,' where he calleth kings his anointed by a special title, not given to any other persons but such as exercise regal authority all the Scripture through. And if they may not be touched, much less may they be deposed, or their persons violated.

And this title is not only given to David but to Cyrus: 'Thus saith the Lord to Cyrus, mine anointed,' Isa. xliii. 1; for, as Irenæus saith, lib. v., '*Inde illis potestas unde Cyrus;* for so the apostle, 'The powers that be are ordained of God.'

Therefore the presbytery and papacy, like Herod and Pilate, are friends to do a shrewd turn, when they both put power on the people to right themselves against kings that do not execute judgment.

The apostle is a better guide; he bids pray for them, and if you consider what kings then reigned, you will say there could not be worse.

I must therefore with the apostle admonish: let every soul submit itself; let no man, let not a confederacy of men, seditiously and maliciously advance themselves against the Lord's anointed. Hand off, offer him no violence, use not the tongue to curse him, use not the pen against him to libel him; curse him not in thy heart, touch him no noxious and offensive way; and if subordinate magistrates do let wrong judgment proceed, appeal from them to him that sitteth on the throne of justice, who doth drive away all evil with his eye. If he will not do thee right, go in the prophet Habakkuk's way, wrestle with God by thy prayers, and make thy complaint to him, 'He heareth the complaint of the poor.'

2. He complaineth and chideth with God for shewing him all this iniquity and violence; from whence we are taught,

Doct. It is lawful in our prayers to expostulate and contest with God.

Habakkuk goeth far in this, you have heard. Jerome saith, *Nullus prophetarum ausus est tam audaci voce Deum provocare.* Yet we shall find that others have gone very far this way, David for one: Ps. xxii. 1, 'My God, my God, why hast thou forsaken me? why art thou so far from helping me, and from the words of my roaring? O my God, I cry in the day, but thou hearest me not; and in the night season I am not silent.' And he professeth it. Ps. xlii. 9, 'I will say unto God my rock, Why hast thou forgotten me? why go I mourning because of the oppression of the enemy?'

David is very frequent in these expostulations; so is holy Job, so is Jeremiah, and both these are very much overgone in passion, and therefore examples rather of weakness, which we must decline, than rules of direction to imitate.

St Paul doth give us good warrant for this wrestling with God; it is his very phrase: Rom. xv. 30, 'Now I beseech you brethren, for the Lord Jesus Christ's sake, and for the love of the Spirit, that ye strive together with me in your prayers to God.' He useth a word that signeth such striving as is in trying of mastery who shall have the best. And Jacob is a type hereof, who wrestled with the angel till the break of the day; and though he got a lameness by striving with his over-match, yet would he not let him go till he had gotten a blessing. Representing the fervent petitioners that come to God in the name of Christ, as the woman of Canaan did for her daughter, neither the disciples nor Christ could make her turn aside or be silent.

Quer. But here is a *quære*, for the apostle doth say, Rom. ix. 20, 'O man, who art thou that repliest against God?' When once God hath declared himself in anything, how dare we call him to account, and ask him a reason for anything he doth? And again the prophet Isaiah saith, chap. xlv. 9, 'Woe unto him that striveth with his maker.' Further, is it not contrary to that petition in the Lord's prayer, *fiat voluntas tua;* for doth not the prophet declare here a dislike of that which God did, as seeming to wish it had been otherwise, when he asketh, 'Why dost thou shew me iniquity, and make to behold violence?'

Sol. The best way to clear this doubt is to behold this passion in some chosen servant of God, and see what he makes of it. We will take David for our example, and let us hear him first complaining and then answering for himself. His complaint is passionate: Ps. lxxvii. 7–9, 'Will the Lord cast off for ever? and will he be favourable no more? Is his mercy clean gone for ever? doth his promise fail for evermore? Hath God forgotten to be gracious? hath he in anger shut up his tender mercies?' He recovereth himself, saying, ver. 10, 'And I said, This is mine infirmity: but I will remember the years of the right hand of the Most High.'

Surely there be infirmities in the saints of God, and this expostulation with God is an effect of infirmity. Yet shall you see that this doth no way weaken the doctrine before delivered, that it is lawful to expostulate with God in our prayers.

The infirmities of God's servants are of two sorts: 1, natural; 2, sinful.

We must so distinguish, for when Christ took our nature into the unity of his person, with it he took upon him all our infirmities, but not our sinful ones; for he was like man in all things but sin.

Three especially are noted in the story of the Gospel; that is to say,

Sorrow, fear, anger.

1. Sorrow; for he wept and mourned.
2. Fear; for he was heard in that he feared.
3. Anger; for he did often chide and reprove.

These affections be natural, and so long as they be affections, they are without blame; when they exuberate and grow into perturbations, then they are faulty, for there is ἦθος, which is the inclination, and there is παθος, which is the inflammation of nature. God, who in creation gave these affections to nature, hath not denied us the use of them, yea, he hath ordained them as excellent helps for his work of grace in us; therefore we find fear mingled with faith to keep it from swelling into presumption; that fear is not a sin in the elect, as some weak consciences ignorantly mistake it, but it is *cos fidei*, the whetstone of faith, to give it the more edge, as in that complaint of David, ' My God, my God, why hast thou forsaken me?' Where the first part of that complaint is *vox fidei*, the voice of faith, *My God, my God;* the second is *vox timoris*, the voice of fear, *quare me direliquisti?* And we say fear is a good keeper, it makes us lay so much the faster hold on God by faith; yea, it is a warning to us to avoid anything that may do us hurt. 'The wise man feareth and departeth from evil,' Prov. xiv. 16.

Sometimes we find fear mingled with joy, as, for example, Ps. cxxvi. 1, ' When the Lord brought again the captivity of Sion, we were like them that dream.' They were overcome with joy for their deliverance and restitution, and yet they felt withal a fear that it was too good to be true, and doubted that it was but a dream. We do not receive any good news, but before the hearing of it we fear. The angel that appeared to Zacharias the priest found him afraid, Luke i. 13. The angel that came to the Virgin Mary found her afraid, so did he that brought the news of the birth of Christ to the shepherds; for all men know that we have no cause to expect any news* from heaven, we are so evil and sinful.

And although the comforts of God do remove that fear for a time, yet God would not have it quite extinguished in us, for the prophet biddeth us, Ps. ii. 11, ' serve the Lord with fear, and rejoice with trembling;" and the apostle doth bid us, too, 'work out our salvation with fear and trembling.'

Sometimes grief is mingled with faith, as in the poor man in the Gospel, of whom Christ said, 'Dost thou believe?' He answered first with his tears, then with his words, saying, 'Lord, I believe: help thou my unbelief.' So in the publican, beating his breast, and saying, 'Lord, be merciful to me a sinner.'

Sometimes indignation is mingled with faith, as in all the imprecations of the prophet, which, as they are prophecies, and so proceed from the Spirit of God, so are they passions in these holy men, and are vented with that indignation of which the prophet saith, 'Be angry and sin not,' and which the same prophet justifieth, 'Shall not I hate them, O Lord, which hate thee?' And this holy indignation you see in the very separate souls: Rev. vi. 10, 'They cry with a loud voice, How long, Lord, dost thou not judge and avenge our blood on them that dwell on the earth?' *Tantæne animis cœlestibus iræ!*

To come now to the point in question:

This zeal of the prophet is not a dislike of, or an opposition to, the will of God by way of contradiction, but a dislike of the thing done, according to the express will of God, wherein the prophet doth not offend.

The example of our Saviour Christ is full, and giveth testimony to this truth; for coming of purpose to lay down his life for his church, and knowing it to be his Father's will that he should so do, yet in the garden he three times prayed that if it were possible that cup might pass from him. He did not resist the will of God, for to that he submitted himself, but he disliked that which he was to suffer according to that will. The reason is, because it was evil and a punishment, and he who taught us to pray, *Libera nos a malo*, 'Deliver us from evil,' did so himself.

So, though he knew the will of God to be peremptory for the destruction of Jerusalem and the rejection of the Jews, he sorrowed and wept for the same, which shewed his dislike of the thing decreed, though he approved the decree itself, and resisted it not.

Sorrow is a grief taken by a natural dislike of that for which we grieve. When our parents, wives, children, or friends die, we grieve. The apostle doth not forbid that affection : he limiteth and regulateth it ; he would not have us sorrow as men without hope. And when he took on him our natural infirmities and affections, he did not so undertake them to remove them from us or to extinguish them in us, but to correct and temper them ; as St Cyril saith, *ut sic natura nostra reformaretur ad melius,* that so our nature might be bettered.

In this very example in my text, of the prophet's dislike that God should shew him this iniquity and violence of the Jews, which was a grief and a burden to him to see, remember what is said of Lot by St Peter : 2 Peter ii. 8, 'For that righteous man dwelling among them vexed his righteous soul from day to day with their unlawful deeds.' Here was not only an holy grief for, but an holy indignation against, the sight of these things which God shewed him, and that in the righteous soul of a righteous men.

I conclude this point as before, with David's words. I deny not that this was the prophet's infirmity ; I deny it to be his iniquity, it was no sin in him. And I again urge my former point of doctrine, it is lawful for the holy servants of God to expostulate and contest with God in their prayers.

Reason 1. Because hereby we declare our dislike of those things against which we contest, as here the prophet sheweth that it is to him very hateful and offensive to behold the sins of the people, which both corrupt and endanger the state of the commonwealth. So when the prophet complaineth often of God's longsuffering toward the wicked, he sheweth it to be an offence to the children of God, that the enemies of God should be so long forborne. And when he awaketh God, ' Up, Lord, why sleepest thou ?' and stirreth him to revenge of his own cause, therein he declareth his zeal of the glory of God, of which he must be careful especially.

Reason 2. This public expostulation, used in this case to awake the justice of God against the wicked, doth seem to terrify the ungodly from their wicked ways ; for when they see that they that fear God, and walk before him, and with him, are up in arms against them, and bandy their imprecations against them, they cannot but see their estates in great danger.

Reason 3. This expostulation of the just doth declare that their yielding to the will of God in these things, which they do without offence to God's dislike, is not out of natural principles and reasons incident to humanity, but from a supernatural dedition and yielding of themselves to the transcendent will of God, whereby they do approve even what they do dislike, because they find the will of God that way.

The profit which we may make of this point is,

1. To teach us zeal in the cause of God; for there is no life in the service that we perform to God without zeal. There is not only the Spirit of God required in us, but fervency of the Spirit by the apostle; and that the same apostle calleth the Spirit ' dwelling in us plentifully;' and in another place, ' The Spirit sanctifying us throughout.'

This giving our bow the full bent, that it may have the full strength, and this to be drawn home, when we send our prayers up to heaven, that they may reach the mark, this is, ' So run, that ye may obtain.' It is called striving to the mark.

Zeal only used in matters of form and ceremony, and in outward things, makes us, like Agrippa, almost Christians; but zeal against the evil life and crying sins of the time, is discreet and necessary; for these do hack and hew the bough we stand upon, these underdig the ground we walk upon.

These put it to an *if, si Filius Dei es*, if thou be the Son of God. Let them that love righteousness and peace be troubled at these things, and quench this common fire first; that is the apostle's method. For having taught the doctrine of the sacrament of the Lord's supper, and of holy preparation to the communicants, he concludeth: 1 Cor. xi. 34, ' And the rest will I set in order when I come,' $διατάξομαι$. First, he directed them in the prayers of piety; he reserveth the $τάξις$, the order, till his coming to them, shewing that he had apostolical power for that; but that must be done after this.

In religion, that is now the double complaint,

1. Of want of zeal where it most should be.
2. Of inordinate zeal in other things.

The want of zeal in many professors of religion is such, that both popery, and anabaptistry, and other schismatical and sectarious professors, are suffered to grow up together with the profession of the gospel, which could not be if we had zeal proportionable to our knowledge, such as was in David, 'All false ways I utterly abhor.'

We see also great corruptions in manners, which holy zeal might soon eat out, and without which religion may bring us to church, and to the font, and to the Lord's table, and may rank us with outward professors ; but till we grow to such an hatred of sin, as the very patience, and forbearance of God toward those that do abominably, and will not be reformed, doth disquiet and grieve us, and make us complain, we fail and come short of duty to God.

2. Another complaint of the church is, of inordinate zeal, which is,

(1.) Either in persons without a lawful calling seeking to reform things amiss.

(2.) Or in respect of the things, when men, carried with the strong current of opinion, find fault where no fault is, or make the fault greater than it is.

(3.) Or in respect of times, when men prevent the time, and exasperate the judgments of God, and provoke his justice against their brethren, before they have done all that can be done by the spirit of meekness.

(4.) Or in respect of time, when they express their zeal first against those things that may with least hurt to the church be forborne, till more concerning affairs of the church be advisedly thought upon.

(5.) Or in respect of the measure of zeal, if it be more or less than the cause of God requireth.

(6.) In respect of the mixture of it, if it be commeded with any of our own corrupt and furious perturbations.

2. Seeing, therefore, we may make so bold with God, as the prophet here doth, we are to be taught that God is so slow in the execution of his judgments,

even upon them that do ill, that till he find that his patience is a burden to his church, and till he be even chidden to it by his faithful ones, he cannot strike.

Wherefore we must both stir up ourselves and our brethren to a serious consideration of this goodness of God, and that which the apostle doth call ' the riches of his patience;' that we despise it not, that we spend not such riches unthriftily, but bestow it upon our repentance, and making our peace with God.

3 Seeing we may thus call God to account, as the prophet here doth, and chide his remissness, let us not take it ill at the hands of God if he chide us for our sins, which do well deserve it, and he contest with us for our neglect of our duties, either to him or our brethren.

4. Seeing we have so good warrant for it, when we see any unremedied evils which do threaten ruin to our church or commonwealth, which perchance the minister may be forbidden to reprove or to dissuade, such as these in my text, violence and oppression, corruption of religion, and corruption of courts of justice, which the minister in general terms may reprove, but he must not with Nathan say, *Tu es homo*, Thou art the man, to any delinquent in any of these kinds.

This, then, is the remedy: we may go to God himself, and chide with him for it, without any fear of *scandalum magnatum;* and in holy indignation and zeal of God's glory, laying aside our own corrupt passions, we may call him to account for shewing us, and making us to see such things.

And I do not doubt but we shall have as good success as this prophet had, as the next section of this chapter doth declare.

Vers. 5–11. *Behold ye among the heathen, and regard, and wonder marvellously; for I will work a work in your days, which you will not believe, though it be told you. For, lo, I raise up the Chaldeans, that bitter and hasty nation, which shall march through the breadth of the land, to possess the dwelling-places that are not theirs. They are terrible and dreadful: their judg-*

ment and their dignity shall proceed of themselves. Their horses also are swifter than the leopards, and more fierce than the evening wolves: and their horsemen shall spread themselves, and their horsemen shall come from far; they shall fly as the eagle that hasteth to eat. They shall come all for violence: their faces shall sup up as the east wind, and they gather the captivity as the sand. And they shall scoff at the kings, and the princes shall be a scorn unto them: they shall deride every stronghold; for they shall heap dust, and take it. Then shall his mind change, and he shall pass over, and offend, imputing this his power unto his god.

These words are the second section of this chapter, and do contain God's own answer to the former complaint of the prophet, wherein God declareth how he will be avenged on his own people, for the oppression and violence which they have used, for the corruption in manners, in religion, and in the administration of justice.

Let us begin at the words, and search the will of God revealed therein.

Ver. 5. *Behold ye among the heathen, and regard, and wonder marvellously.* Here is God himself speaking to his sinful people the Jews, and awaking them to behold the anger to come.

Here is first the roaring of the lion, as in Amos, chap. i. 2, 'The Lord will roar from Sion, and utter his voice from Jerusalem.'

This is the thunder; the thunderbolt doth after follow.

1. He biddeth them behold; that is, to take this threatening of God's judgment, and to spread it before their eyes, and to peruse the sad contents thereof.

2. *Behold ye among the heathen.* He turneth their eyes to the heathen, whom God will now make their sharp schoolmasters to instruct them; for seeing they will learn nothing by the ministry of his prophets, whom he hath sent to them to chide them, and guide them; and seeing they are not moved with the lamentable complaints of their brethren, groaning under their oppressions, and grievances, and injustice;

now he biddeth them to look among the heathen, as to the quarter from whence the following tempest is like to arise; for by them God intendeth to punish the Jews.

3. He addeth *Regard;* for beholding without regarding, and taking the matter into due and serious consideration, is but gazing. As the apostle presseth an exhortation, 'Consider what I say.'

God hath sent his prophets to instruct them, and they heard them, but regarded them not. Now he will not be so neglected.

4. He addeth, *and wonder marvellously: attoniti este et obstupescite.* Here he prepareth their expectation for some extraordinary judgment. This is that which the apostle doth call *terror domini,* and *ira ventura,* the terror of the Lord, and the wrath to come.

5. He addeth in general terms the matter of their fear and consternation. For,
1. There is a work to be done.
2. God himself professeth to be the worker.
3. The time is at hand, 'in your days.'
4. The wonder is, that though God himself foretell them thereof, *non credetis,* you will not believe.

The work to be done is, ver. 6, God threateneth to raise up the Chaldeans against the Jews; he calleth them a bitter and a hasty nation; those shall go all the land over, and drive out or destroy the Jews, and take possession of their land.

Chaldea lay from Jerusalem north. It was a mighty kingdom, and the chief city thereof was Babylon. Nebuchadnezzar was king thereof. They are to be stirred up by God himself, who, as you heard out of Obadiah, doth use to punish one nation by another, and sometimes his church by the heathen.

He gave Israel the promised land upon condition of their obedience to his law; and now, finding them rebellious, he giveth away their land to the heathen; and as before he drove out the posterity of Canaan to plant Israel there, now he will remove them, and give their land to the Chaldeans.

God is very terrible in his threatenings; for a great part of the chapter is spent, as you see, in description of that nation of the Chaldeans, to fill them full of horror.

Ver. 6. For the people of that land, he calleth them 'bitter and hasty.' Bitter in the execution of that wrath whereof God had made them his ministers, and hasty in the speed thereof; for the wicked are limited, and if God stayed them not, they would soon swallow up the church of God; but when God enlargeth them, and suffereth them for the sins of the church to break in upon them, they will come in like a flood that overfloweth and breaketh the banks, and cover all with inundation.

Ver. 7. They are described to be 'terrible,' and 'dreadful;' and therein he declareth that he will put the Jews out of heart, that they shall have no courage to resist this invasion; for God will smite them with fear of the adversary's power, which fear in them shall open the enemy an easy way to victory.

He proveth this, for he saith, 'their judgment and their dignity shall come of themselves.' His meaning is, that God will not restrain them, but give the Jews into their hands, and leave the Chaldeans to be both judges and executioners in their own cause, and to follow the leading of their own will. No law of God shall awe them, no law of nature or nations shall limit them, their own will shall carry them to give judgment upon the Jews, and to get them dignity and honour over them.

The reason why God will put them into so merciless hands is given by the prophet Jeremiah: chap. xliv. 16, 17, for the Jews have said to Jeremiah, 'As for the word that thou hast spoken to us in the name of the Lord, we will not hearken unto thee: but we will certainly do whatsoever thing goeth forth out of our own mouth.' For this wilful stubbornness God doth now purpose to put them into the power of such as shall be as wilful as they, whose judgment, by which they shall judge the Jews, and whose dignity, by which they shall exalt themselves, shall follow their own will.

Ver. 8. He proceedeth to shew what preparation they had for war; and herein first of their horses, in which kind of strength some put their trust; as David saith, 'Some put their trust in chariots, and some in horses.'

These horses of the Chaldeans he doth make terrible in two things:

1. 'They are swifter than the leopards;' he compareth them not with the roebuck and the hind, so much mentioned in Scripture for speed, nor with the hare, whose speed is to save themselves, but with the leopards, persecuting with swiftness the beasts on which they prey, as he addeth,

2. 'They are fiercer than the evening wolves;' those wolves whose hunger not only leadeth them out to seek prey, but such is their cruelty, that they will destroy whole flocks if they can.

The Chaldeans did breed horses for the war, whose speed and fierceness is such, that, as Jeremiah saith, describing the turning of men to their own ill ways, it was like as an horse rusheth into the battle.

Yet this were no great terror, but that it followeth, their riders shall be such as shall put them to it.

1. They shall spread themselves; for they were to pass throughout the breadth of the country, that there will be no escaping them by resistance.

2. They shall come from far to set up the army, so that they shall be terrible in their number.

3. They shall fly as the eagle that hasteth to eat; no man shall escape them by flight, all shall be a prey.

Ver. 9. He proceedeth to describe the easy victory that the Chaldeans shall have over the Jews: 'They shall come all for violence.' *Tota gens ad rapinam veniet;* not *ad pugnam,* but *ad prædam.* The whole nation shall come to spoil, not to fight, but to prey.

Their faces shall sup up the east wind. The east wind, it seemeth, was the most unwholesome breath of heaven upon that land, within short time withered and destroyed the fruits of the earth, and the hopes of the spring. The Lord saith that the faces of the

Chaldeans, the very sight of them shall be as baneful and as unresistible as the east wind.

They shall gather the captivity as the sand. 1. They shall gather together the people of that land to carry them away into captivity, with no more pain than one would take up his vessel full of sand out of the heap; or they shall carry multitudes of the Jews into captivity, without number, as the sand.

Ver. 10. *They shall scoff at the kings, and the princes shall be a scorn unto them.* Either he meaneth that he shall make nothing of the power of any kings, either in the land against which he cometh, or amongst their confederates, but shall laugh them to scorn that come to help the Jews, as his vassals. Or he shall easily subdue them, and lead them in triumph whithersoever he goeth, and proudly insult over them.

Some extend it so far, as that the Chaldean conqueror shall make kings his jesters and parasites, and make himself sport with them. And whereas the strongholds and castles are wont to be a terror to the invader, the Chaldeans shall deride every stronghold.

For they shall heap dust and take it; i. e. they shall raise up of the earth near unto their strongholds such fortifications as shall defend them and offend the enemy, the very earth of the Jews shall they use against the Jews to overcome them.

Ver. 11. *Then shall his mind change, and he shall pass over.* These words do declare that the Chaldeans, full of victories, and full of pride after this great conquest, shall change their mind, and pass over to some other quest of glory, big-swollen with their former prevailings; and he sheweth how these enemies of the Jews shall run themselves upon the just displeasure of God, who stirred them up to this war.

He shall offend, imputing this his power unto his God. From hence cometh the ruin of the Chaldeans; for being puffed up and proud of their victories, they shall not acknowledge the great God of heaven, the God of their war, or esteem themselves his agents to chasten the Jews, but shall give the glory of their conquest to their own idol god.

Now in these words thus interpreted, observe,
1. The total.
2. The particulars.

1. The total is the answer of God to the grievous complaint and expostulation of the prophet.
2. The particulars are two.
(1.) The judgment threatened.
(2.) The executioners of this judgment, very fully and rhetorically described.

1. The total. God answereth the prophet's complaint, yieldeth this doctrine, that,

Doct. God doth hear the complaints of such as have just cause to complain of violence, to execute his judgments upon them that offend.

The story of holy Scripture is full of examples of this truth. Cain for Abel, *vox sanguinis,* the voice of blood.

The whole old world was punished with a general inundation for the cruelty that was upon the earth; their violence made the Lord repent that he made them.

You have heard out of Obadiah how the cruelty of Edom was intolerable, and God heard the cry of the church and delivered them, and punished Edom with desolation.

And when Israel was in the land of Egypt, in the house of bondage, God saith, ' I have seen, I have seen the affliction of my people which is in Egypt, and I have heard their groaning, and am come down to deliver them,' Acts vii. 34.

Even Israel his own people is not spared; Zion his holy mountain, Jerusalem his holy city, is punished for oppression. He doth this,

Reason 1. First, In regard of his servants that do complain to him, to let them see the power of their prayers, that he may stir them up in all grievances to commit their cause to him, and not to seek private revenge, as Tertullian, *Si apud Deum deposueris injuriam, ipse ultor est; si damnum, restitutor est.*

Use. Therefore let not the oppressed wrong their own cause with vexing, and disquieting their own hearts at them that lie heavy upon them; for St

James tells us, chap. i. 20, that 'the wrath of man worketh not the righteousness of God.'

Let them not vent their spleen in bitter cursings and execrations, which be the voice and language of impatience and impiety, and turn upon us, and all to tear us; but let them seriously complain to God, and he will hear them, and do them right. Let them tarry the Lord's good leisure, and they shall see that he will take the matter into his own hand.

1. Either he will take the oppressed out of the world, and give them rest from their labours, and lay them in the beds of ease, and lock them in the chambers of peace till all storms be over, and then he will say, 'Return ye sons of Adam.'

2. Or he will change the heart of the oppressors, and for stony hearts, give them hearts of flesh, and fill them with compassion and tenderness.

3. Or he will restrain the power of the wicked against his chosen, and suffer no man to do them wrong, but will reprove even kings for their sakes; the rage of man will he restrain.

4. Or he will give the oppressed such a measure of patience and charity, as he shall bear injuries without murmuring, and bless them that hate and persecute him.

5. Or he will pour forth his wrath upon the oppressor, and let him feel the weight of his hand: either upon his body, by inflicting diseases upon it; or upon his mind, by the troubles of an unquiet conscience; or upon his family, by cursing the fruit of his loins, that they shall be his sorrows by taking ill ways; or upon his estate, by cursing all his gatherings, that though all the streams of profit run every way into his bags, nothing shall make him rich, like the Caspian sea, into which many waters do pour in water continually, yet is it never the fuller, rather like the lean kine, never the fatter; or upon his life, by taking him out of the world, and thereby giving occasion to the afflicted to rejoice.

Therefore, art thou afflicted? pray and complain, and expostulate with God, for he will hear thee.

Reason 2. God heareth the complaint of the just against the oppressors for his name's sake, for so

David urgeth him. 'Hear me, O God, for thy name's sake;' for it toucheth God in honour when his faithful servants do appeal from the school of unrighteousness, where they are oppressed, to the tribunal of his judgment, where they should be relieved, and cannot be heard.

You remember when Christ was on the cross, and his enemies had their cruel hearts' desire against him, they contented not themselves to be cruel and scornful to him, but they blasphemed also the name of God, saying, Mat. xxvii. 43, 'He trusted in God, let him deliver him now if he will have him.' The very thieves that were fastened then to the cross, on either hand of him, cast that in his teeth.

When the wicked prevail against the just, the next word is, 'Where is now their God?'

Use. Let us then know the name of God is himself; he cannot deny himself, he hath a name above all things, and a special glory due to that name; he cannot suffer that name to be blasphemed: 'He will not hold him guiltless that taketh his name in vain.'

Therefore, in all grievances, let us say with David, 'Our help is in the name of the Lord, who hath made heaven and earth.'

It is our comfort in trouble that we do suffer together with the name of God, and if we do lay fast hold on that, we shall be delivered together with it; we may well cast our trust upon that name, for, *in hoc vinces*, in this thou shalt overcome, is the motto and word thereof, it is a strong tower to all that trust in it.

Reason 3. God will hear the complaints of the just, for his truth's sake; for he hath promised the just, 'I will not leave thee, nor forsake thee.' And he hath said, 'He shall call upon me, and I will hear him. I am with him in trouble, I will deliver him, and he shall glorify me.'

And David saith, 'He will not suffer his truth to fail.' We have more than his promise, we have his oath against the ungodly: Ps. xcv. 11, 'I have sworn in my wrath that they shall not enter into my rest.'

Use. Let us build, then, upon this promise, for God is faithful that hath promised. The violent and the oppressor hath part in the wrath of God, as he saith : Mal. iii. 5, 'And I will come near to you in judgment ; and I will be a swift witness against the sorcerers, and against the adulterers, and against false swearers, and against them that oppress the hireling in his wages, and the fatherless, and the widow, and that turn aside the stranger from his right, and that fear not me, saith the Lord of hosts. Here is God's threatening against two of the sins of this people, violence, and the want of the fear of the Lord, whereby the law is slacked. And for corruption of justice, they that turn judgment into wormwood have their doom. Judgment without mercy shall be shewed to them that have no mercy.

Let us not, therefore, fear them, or be troubled at them that go in these wicked ways ; for the judge of all the world will do justly. 'The cry of the oppressed shall prevail against them. He also will hear their cry, and will help them.'

The Lord is king, the earth may be glad thereof, and the multitude of the lands may rejoice; for he is known by executing judgment ; he is the husband of the widow, and the father of the fatherless. The poor committeth his cause unto him, for he relieveth the oppressed.

2. The particulars of this judgment threatened contain two things :

1. The judgment threatened.
2. The executioners thereof.

1. The judgment threatened is, that he will punish them by the conquering hand of the heathen. This calleth to our remembrance divers points of doctrine delivered out of the prophecy of Obadiah.

1. That the decrees of God's judgment upon the wicked are constant and unchangeable.

2. That God useth war as one of his rods to punish sin.

3. That all wars are ordained by God ; for he stirreth up this war against the Jews.

4. That God punisheth one evil nation by another.

5. That God giveth warning of his judgments to those whom he foreknoweth to be such as they will take no warning to amend.

6. That God requiteth sinners in the same kind in which they offend. The Jews' sin was violence, and violence is their punishment.

7. That the judgment of God upon the wicked and unmerciful shall be without all mercy.

Doct. The point that I will now add is, that the justice of God doth not spare his own people, if they provoke him. The Jews shall have no favour, if the prophets and holy men have cause to complain of them. All the promises that God made to Israel are limited by the condition of their obedience, and the law given to them is called the Lord's covenant, because all those promises did follow the obedience of that law, otherwise God stood free to withdraw his mercy from them.

So Moses, Deut. v. 2, 'The Lord made a covenant with us in Horeb.' The covenant is, 'You shall walk in all the ways which the Lord your God commanded you, that ye may live, and that it may go well with you, and that ye may prolong your days in the land which ye shall possess.'

God himself confesseth, Ps. lxxxix. 3, 'I have made a covenant with my chosen ; I have sworn unto David my servant : thy throne will I establish for ever, and build up thy throne to all generations.'

But yet with condition of obedience, for, vers. 30–32, 'If his children forsake my law, and walk not in my judgments; if they break my statutes, and keep not my commandments, then will I visit their transgression with the rod, and their iniquity with stripes.' So that no promise or oath of God doth give privilege or immunity to any to offend the law of God. And such is the equal justice of God, that David, though a man after God's heart, although a servant of God's finding, a king of God's own anointing, doth confess, 'If I regard wickedness in my heart, the Lord will not hear me.' Moses his sister Miriam must be a leper, and shut out of the camp for murmuring. Moses and Aaron shall not go into the promised land for their want of sure trust in God ; for God is no accepter of persons.

Reason. Those who are sealed with the Spirit of promise have their infirmities, lapses and relapses ;

but as they sin not unto death, *i. e.* the second death, so they cannot suffer any other than temporal chastisement; yet these they cannot stop, for by this physic God doth often purge them and restore them to health: in this fire of tribulation he doth often purge their dross.

For some, water will serve to wash them if they be taken in time; for some, that have taken rust with God's long forbearance, and their own custom of sinning, fire is necessary to burn out their dross. But none escape; of this all are partakers: and as personal sins have personal chastisements, so epidemical sins have popular punishments. When a commonwealth is diseased, what though it be a people as Israel, whom God hath chosen out of all the nations of the world; what though he have rooted out the heathen to plant them in, although he have given them a land flowing with milk and honey, settled the priesthood and his worship, given them his word, continued them in peace many generations; yet if they shall use violence and oppression, if they shall break the law of God, and corrupt the seat of judgment, the Lord will see it, and be angry; and Noah, Daniel, and Job shall not keep out judgment, rather the complaints of the just shall help to hasten the coming of wrath against that land.

We have heard also that judgment beginneth at the house of God, 1 Peter iv. 17. When God sent destroyers into Jerusalem, their commission was, Ezek. ix. 6, 'Slay utterly old and young, both maids and the children, and the women; and begin at my sanctuary.'

Use. We may say that England hath been for many years, since the restitution of our religion, God's pleasant plant; he hath given it rest, he hath hedged you, walled it with his providence. He hath given us peace within, he hath given us victories abroad, he hath kept out the Chaldeans, the Spaniards, whose invincible strength came to possess and divide the land. He hath spoken the word, and we have had multitude of preachers, religion, and all kind of learning; all mercature hath flourished, and we have traded to the ends of the world; mechanical and manual arts have come up to their full growth ; we may say, *Non fecit Deus taliter*, we have peace now with all the world, at least in show and pretence.

Let not these favours of God swell us, and make us presume in our hearts that our God cannot be lost to us, to encourage sin. If the sins of the Jews be found amongst us, violence, contempt of religion, and corruption of justice, God will do a thing in our days which he that heareth will not believe, by reason of our long rest.

All the favours of God came in with true religion, and the contempt thereof will carry them out again; for God is no accepter of persons. As we are *Angli*, if we were *angeli*, he would cast us out of our heaven upon earth, and give our land to strangers that shall punish us, and make them that hate us to be lords over us.

2. The executioners of this judgment ; wherein observe,

1. By whom God will punish.
2. How far the punishment shall extend.
3. What shall become of them whom God doth use as his rods in this execution.

1. By whom? By the Chaldeans. These are described,

(1.) By their own fitness for their design.
(2.) By their preparation to accomplish it.
(3.) By their intention in it.

2. How far the punishment shall extend,

(1.) To a full conquest.
(2.) To a proud triumph.

3. What shall become of them ?

(1.) They shall change their mind.
(2.) They shall offend in imputing their victories to their own idols.

1. By whom God shall punish the Jews.

(1.) Of their fitness for this execution. They are described to us by these notations :

[1.] They are bitter.
[2.] They are hasty.
[3.] They are dreadful.
[4.] They are wilful.

[1.] Bitter in their harsh and cruel natures.
[2.] Hasty in their participation* and speed.
[3.] Dreadful in their power and strength.
[4.] Wilful in taking their own ways; for their judgment and dignity proceedeth from themselves.

To be bitter and slow gives warning to resist, and affordeth the benefits of time, a great friend to defence.

To be bitter, and hasty, and weak, is but a lightning, a flash and away.

To be bitter and hasty are dreadful, but to admit advice gives time of breathing; but when the nature is inflamed with bitterness, and the action is accelerated with haste, and fortified with strength, and followed with wilfulness, this makes up a full danger, especially where God setteth such a work.

These be evil affections in this people, and prove their minds set upon mischief; yet God maketh rods of these twigs, and whips of these cords, to punish the sins of his own people.

The point of doctrine here is,

Doct. That God can make good use of the vices of men, and can make wicked men serve him as the instruments of his will, as Augustine, *Deus bonus utitur malis nostris bene.*

So Mr Calvin judiciously observeth on the text, *Hæc quidem non fuerunt laudanda in Chaldæis, amarulentia et furor; sed potest Deus hæc vitia convertere in optimum finem.* St Augustine,† treating of the pro-semination of the gospel, and the quick spreading thereof, hath two chapters to our purpose.

In the 50th, he sheweth, *Per passiones prædicantium illustrior facta est prædicatio,* by the sufferings of preachers preaching is made the more famous.

In the 51st, *Per dissensiones hæreticorum fides Catholica roboratur,* by the dissensions of heretics the Catholic faith is strengthened.

He is so full to this purpose, to shew what good God works out of evil, that I cannot suppress his words.

Inimici ecclesiæ, quolibet errore cæcentur, si accipiunt potestatem corporaliter affligendi, exercent ejus patientiam. Si tantummodo malè sentiendo adversantur, exer-

---

* Qu. 'preparation'?—Ed. † Civ. dei. 18.

cent ejus sapientiam. Ut diligantur, exercent ejus benevolentiam. But when the church of God grows foul, and when people of God forsake God and go in their own ways, then God useth the wicked *ad vindictam*; then, as David saith, Ps. xvii. 13, 'the wicked are the sword of the Lord.'

And that is the reason why God doth suffer so many evils in the world, because they be his rods to chasten evil.

Even in this example, Jeremiah the prophet of the Lord doth threaten the same judgment: chap. xxxvii. 8, 'The Chaldeans shall fight against this city, and take it, and burn it with fire. Thus saith the Lord, Deceive not yourselves, saying, the Chaldeans shall depart from us, for they shall not depart. For though you had smitten the whole army of the Chaldeans that fight against you, and there remained but wounded men amongst them, yet they should rise up every man in his tent, and burn the city with fire.' Thus God doth, because he will declare his own perfection of wisdom and goodness, that he can work good out of evil, and dispose the very vices of men to good.

And thus the examples of foul sins in our brethren do move us,

1. To a loathing thereof. As we read, the Lacedæmonians would make their slaves drunk, and then shew them to their children to make them loathe drunkenness; and all that have the fear of God, when they see and hear the evil conversation, and the evil and profane words of the wicked, they behold in them the ugly face of sin, and are touched at the heart with a detestation of the same.

2. They move us to charity.

1. *Charitas incipiens*, at ourselves, to take warning by their example, that we, when we see a thief, do not turn to him, nor be partakers with the adulterers.

To make us set a guard upon our whole life, a zealous purpose to eschew evil.

To use the means for our preservation from evil, which are hearing, and meditation of the law of God, and frequent and fervent prayer.

2. *Charitas proficiens*, to pray God for our brethren, that he would direct their paths, forgive their sins, and mend their lives, and preserve others from being corrupted by their evil example.

Reason 2. God bringeth forth the effects of his own good will out of the ministry of the vices of men, to declare his true justice in punishing sin by sin, that sinners may see that they serve for rods, one to whip another of them, whereas the just do not, cannot, hurt one another, for all evil is noxious, holiness is humble.

Reason 3. God declareth himself King and supreme Lord of the earth herein; for, as David saith, *fecit quicquid voluit*, 'he hath done whatever he will.' He will not let either the sinner that acteth, or Satan that suggesteth, evil, to have the managing thereof; for howsoever it seemeth that they serve their own turns therein, he will dispose their evil to his own proper ends, and they shall unwillingly work for him, though both the bent of the suggestions of Satan, and the promise of the intention of the sinner, and the fuel of the affection, and the whole force of the action, be diverted against him. So Joseph's brethren, full of envy to him, sold him into Egypt. What a charity did God work out of it! So the Jews for envy pursued Christ to the cross. All the godly fare the better for the good which was effected by it.

Israel is here punished by the Chaldeans, and God maketh use of these briars and thorns to prick and gore his people. He suffereth them to be carried into captivity.

All the force of Satan and his instruments prevail no further against his church than for correction and burning out the dross; God doth still do all things for the best.

Use. The consideration whereof serveth,

1. To pacify us against evils, and to lay that storm which either human passion or inordinate zeal may stir up against sin and sinners. Though all punishment in its nature be evil, yet God may work good of it; and the Son of God saith, Resist not evil; let it have its course, and expect God's end in it.

You see how much Habakkuk was troubled at the sins of the Jews, how he did even chide with God for his patience and remissness toward them. You see from thence it is a burden to men to bear the impieties of their brethren, and to behold their uncharitableness, and therefore it is lawful to complain to God of such, and to awake his justice against them.

And here in God's answer you see that God can make use of men of evil natures and ungodly lips to execute his will.

Observe the faults of these Chaldeans;

1. Idolatrous; therefore religion and the whole worship of God, and the house of his worship, and the priests and the ministers of it, were like to pay for it.

Woful is that state that giveth any way to idolatry to enter into it, for Amaziah cannot endure Amos to prophesy near the king.

2. Fierce and cruel, and therefore no mercy to be expected where they may use the sword.

3. Proud and imperious, so that to serve them was the basest vassalage that might be. Such a nation as this will always make a good sharp rod to scourge the church when it rebelleth against God.

And let that land into which such a nation doth come, either in a storm by force, or in a calm by treaty, to have power therein, persuade itself that God owes it a whipping, and will not be long in debt.

But in all fears and smart let the comfort of this doctrine season our hearts, that God doth use the evils that be in men well, and all things shall come to the best to them that fear God.

Let us remember our lesson, let us live in the learning and practice of it, fear God and keep his commandments, and let Satan do his worst; and let the Catholic bishop, and the Chaldeans, his idolatrous, cruel, and proud sons, use either their wit or strength against us; *si Deus pro nobis*, if God be for us, all is well.

These thorns shall bear us grapes, and these thistles figs. We had need to consider that in all machinations and actions of mischief against the church, there is also the right hand of the Most High, *dextera excelsi.*

Let us take heed that we do not sin too boldly with that. Rather let us await the good issue that his holy will shall produce, for all things do work together for our good if we do fear and serve him.

Use 2. This serveth to soften that hard doctrine of our Saviour's, which goeth so much against the heart of flesh and blood, to bless those that curse and persecute us, and to pray for those that hate us, to love our enemies; for, seeing all their actions be governed and disposed by the providence of God, who loveth us so well that he spared not his own Son, but gave him up to the death for us, we may promise ourselves good out of all evils that they imagine to execute against us.

There be two things which must be considered in our enemies to quicken this charity:

1. The person of our enemy, which beareth (though much defaced) the image of God, and is the same nature with us, flesh of our flesh, and bone of our bone, which we must not hate nor wish ill to.

2. The employment of God in his actions which do offend us, for we see that God stirreth him and setteth him a-work, and manageth the whole operation to his own purpose. Therefore, think not our Saviour's precept an hard saying, who commandeth charity even to an enemy, and love to such as hate us. For even in the injuries they do to their brethren, they do service to God.

Yet is not God author of the evil done, but of the good extracted out of that evil, and applied to the benefit of his church.

2. Their preparation to accomplish this will of God,
  (1.) In their own persons. [1.] Terrible. [2.] Wilful.
  (2.) In their military forces.
  [1.] Their horses, fierce, speedy.
  [2.] Their riders, numerous, speedy, cruel.

  (1.) For their own persons. No doubt but they should bring with them all the appearance of danger and horror that might be, that God might cast the fear of them upon the Jews; that is, number, choice of soldiers, strength of arms.

(2.) For the forces here named, horses trained up to the field, fleshed in blood, with horsemen to manage that fierceness, to the destruction of the Jew.

This is their preparation, wherein we are taught that,

Doct. When God undertaketh to do a work, he accommodateth all fit means for a full execution. πάντα συνεργεῖ, all things work together; for when he beginneth, he will also make an end.

You all know that God hath no need of means to execute his will; his will is a law to his creature. Yet he chooseth in his great wisdom, by visible and sensible means, to chasten the rebellion of the Jews, that his ways may be known upon earth, even the ways of his judgments, that the earth may stand in awe of him. God would have his church know, that if he once take displeasure against them, he hath the command of armies to fight against them; for he is ' LORD OF HOSTS.'

Men, partners with them of the same nature, shall be fearful and terrible to them; they shall lay aside all humanity, and shall arm themselves with malice and cruelty to destroy them; they shall see that God can put mettle into them, and into their horses, and make all their military provisions mortal to destroy them; for who is so great a God as our God?

Edom had made peace, as you heard out of Obadiah, with his neighbour nations, yet the men of his confederacy put a wound under him.

Let us not put our trust with all the world, especially with them whose religion is a warrant to them to break with us when they see an advantage.

Let us make and keep peace with our God, and put our sins to silence, which cry out for judgments against us; for if he be on our side, we need not fear the arm of flesh: the horse and the rider too will fall, and fail, as in the example of Israel; he hath a red sea, a judgment of vengeance to follow them: one shall chase a thousand: Ps. xci. 7, ' A thousand shall fall on thy side, and ten thousand at thy right hand, but shall not come near thee.' There is, there can be, no danger to them that have the God of Jacob for their refuge.

When armies fight his battles, they are terrible and dreadful; when he is on our side, there are more with us than against us.

The name of the Chaldeans, their fierceness, their hasty violence, their number, their horses, their riders, their whole preparation for war, do all borrow terror from *Ego excitabo*, I will stir up; it is God that setteth them a-work, which putteth this mettle into them.

Let me learn of the apostle St Paul to apply this terror to the common use of all those that are the despisers of the threatenings of God: Acts xiii. 40, 'Beware, therefore, lest that come upon you which is spoken of by the prophets.' And there he citeth these words, ver. 5, 'I will do a work in your days, which ye will not believe,' &c., whereby he sheweth,

1. That the provocation which moveth God to this severe judgment is contempt; therefore St Paul saith, 'Hear, ye despisers,' for it was spoken at first to such as did slack the law of God, and had no awe or reverence of his threatenings and judgments.

2. That this was no singular judgment proper to that nation of the Jews, but common to his people all the world over; for God seeing religion contemned, and justice corrupted, that neither a Christian nor a moral conversation is regarded, he will find Chaldeans, more fierce and hasty and violent nations, to overrun and destroy such a people. Our sins are the edge and point of their weapons.

3. The intention of the Chaldeans.

God worketh as he professeth in this invasion, and his end is, to punish the overgrowing sins of the Jews; and the Chaldeans they work, their end is spoil, and enlargement of their dominion.

God, for his own end, giveth way to them, and suffereth; that is not all, he worketh with them, and accomplisheth their desire.

The papist and the anabaptist do both charge the protestant church that we maintain God to be the author of sin.

Campian saith for us, *Volens, suggerens, efficiens, jubens, operans, et in hoc impiorum scelerata consilium gubernans.* And this is one of our paradoxes.

Cardinal Bellarmine doth maintain that all evils are done on earth only *permittente Deo*, by God's permission. Our answer is,

That in all sinful actions two things are to be considered, as Aquinas well teacheth:

1. *Ipsa actio*, the action.
2. *Vitium actionis*, the fault of the action.

We confess that God is *volens, suggerens, efficiens, jubens, operans, et gubernans in actione*; for *omnis actio quatenus actio est bona*, for *Deus omnia operatur*. In him we live and move, and without his power no action can be performed. It is blasphemy to say or think that anything is or can be done against the will or without the power of God, or that God doth lend his power to any against himself and his will, for that destroyeth the omnipotent providence of God.

But for the evil that is in a wicked action, that deriveth itself from the corrupt root of man's sinful nature.

St Augustine, handling this point, doth thus exemplify it:* *Quum Pater tradiderit Filium, et Dominus corpus suum, et Judas Dominum, cur in hac traditione Deus justus est, et homo reus, nisi quia, in re una quam fecerunt, causa non una est ob quam fecerunt?*

In the example in my text, God himself hath cleared this truth, for here are the Chaldeans:

1. Out of a natural fierceness of evil nature, apt to do mischief, and hasty to execute it.
2. Out of a covetous desire to enrich themselves, making no conscience to invade the goods of their neighbours.
3. Out of an ambitious and proud desire, longing to possess a land that is not theirs.

Doth God approve these unchristian desires in this idolatrous and wicked nation? We say and believe that God hateth wickedness, neither shall evil dwell with him.

Yet for the action of violence. God seeth his people of the Jews, for contempt of religion, and for corruption of justice, and for violence to one another, worthy of

* Ep. xlviii. ad Vincent.

punishment; he holdeth them worthy to be punished with violence, and therefore he stirreth up a violent nation against them. He seeth that they live by oppression, and therefore he sendeth oppressors to strip them out of all. He seeth that they live in unbridled licentiousness, and therefore he taketh away their liberty, and sendeth them into captivity. He findeth them unworthy of the land which he gave them, and therefore he giveth it away to strangers, and putteth their enemies into possession thereof. Consider all this as *malum pœnæ*, the evil of punishment, and so God is author, suggester, and operator herein.

But consider how the Chaldeans work in this affair, and God himself acquitteth himself in this text, and putteth it off upon them: ver. 7, 'Their judgment and their dignity shall proceed from themselves.' That which they seek is a project of their own, they know not what God would have done; and as they advise not with him, nor understand that he stirreth them, they acknowledge nothing to him, as it followeth, for they thank their own god for the victory.

You do now see God's good end and their evil, and in this one action. And St Augustine saith, *Deus quasdam voluntates suas utique bonas implet, per malorum hominum voluntates malas.* (Vide Whitak. contra Camp. ratione 8.)

From hence it cometh that they which, fulfilling the will of God, which they know not, do fulfil their own will, which they aim at, have no reward of their service; but rather are after punished for the same. As Hugo de Sancto Victore saith, *Quoniam non suâ voluntate, ad implendam Dei voluntatem diriguntur, sed occulta ipsius dispositione.* And thus doth Master Calvin* teach men, in those places which Campian doth slanderously traduce to this paradox, that God is author of sin. The title is, *Deum ita impiorum opera uti, et animos flectere ad exequenda sua judicia, ut purus ipse ab omni labe maneat.*

It sufficeth that we see the intention of the Chaldeans evil, for that condemneth them; and his judg-

* Inst. i. 18.

ment upon them, which followeth in this chapter, doth prove that their intentions make their whole service corrupt, so that though it pleased God that evil was done against the Jews, they did not please God that did execute the same.

The rule is true, that all evil actions are justly judged by the intentions of their agents. Good actions are not so, for every good intention will not justify an action to be lawful, as in Rebekah and Jacob her son; it was a good intention to seek the blessing which God had decreed, but the act whereby it was attained was merely unlawful; but an evil intention is sufficient to corrupt any action, though it carry never so specious a show of good. Jacob's sons went about a good action, to draw the Shechemites into a conformity with the Hebrews in religion. The intention of the Shechemites, which made them embrace the motion, was the enriching of themselves by this correspondency; the intention of Jacob's sons was to bretray them to death, and God punished them both—the Shechemites with death, the sons of Jacob with their father's curse.

And* the Chaldeans punished the Jews, and sought therein the glory of God only, and gave him the praise of their victory of whom they borrowed the power of their strength, they had been blameless; but their hands concurred with the just will of God, their hearts did not, yet God is just in employing them.

The rule therefore is, that he that willeth the same thing which God willeth, and doth the same thing which God would have done, sinneth, except he willeth and doth the same thing in the same matter and for the same end which God projecteth. 'Let the same mind be in you that was in Christ Jesus;' 'Arm yourselves with the same mind,' 1 Peter iv. 1.

That mind is an armour against the wrath of God; we know we cannot displease him, so long as there is an harmony of our mind with his. That mind is an armour against the revenge of men, for, if we be abundant always in the work of the Lord, we know that our labour is not, cannot be, in vain in the Lord,

* Qu. 'had'?—ED.

Eph. iv. 23, for we must be renewed in the spirit of our mind, we must not be like the axe and hammer in the hand of the artificer, which knoweth not who useth it, nor what he doth, nor why; we are living instruments, and our minds must set our hands a-work; we must know what we do, for whom and why, or else our work is against ourselves.

We do nothing, but as God doth guide the hand, so he frameth the heart and affections to it; if he do not also enlighten our understandings, and apply our minds to it, we are carried as brute beasts, we are not led as men.

So, then, I leave those Chaldeans, though the armies of God at this time, and doing the will of God ignorantly, yet for the corruption of their intention culpable, and in as ill case as they whom they persecute and overcome.

Use. All the injuries that we do by word or deed to our brethren, they are done with God's privity; he knoweth thereof, he disposeth them to their punishment who suffer by us, or for the exercise of their patience, or the trial of their charity to them that hurt them, or their constancy in obedience to him.

Let us not so much consider what good God doth work out of us to them as what evil breedeth in our heart, and so no thanks to Joseph's brethren that he is the second man in Egypt. All the fat of the land of Goshen, and the sweet exchange of their pinching famine for a swelling plenty, will not still the clamorous accusing voice of their guilty conscience for the sin of their evil intention against their brother; for as soon as their father died their fear revived: they doubted that Joseph would revenge that fault.

The old word was *Animus cujusque, is est quisque,* every man's mind is himself; and so when David saith of the just man, ' the floods of many waters shall not come near him,' it is expounded it shall not come so high as his mind, to the disquieting thereof: it shall not come so high as his faith, to the weakening thereof.

Remember this when you pray, *fiat voluntas tua,* thy will be done; that you desire of God not only a correspondence with his hand, that you may do that which he would have done, but correspondence of will that you may do it for the same cause.

2. How far the punishment shall extend. (Divis. p. 34.)

(1.) To a full conquest.
(2.) To a proud triumph.

(1.) The full conquest is set forth, ver. 6 : ' They shall march through the breadth of your land, to possess the dwelling-places, that are not theirs. They shall come all for violence, and shall gather together the captivity as the sand.'

Wherein is described a full possession of the land of the Jews, and a deportation of the people, a loss even of the birthright and the blessing.

The land of Canaan is called the land of promise, for God promised it to Abraham, and swore to him that his seed should inherit it, but by way of covenant which had reference to their obedience of the law of God, for so Moses forewarned them : Deut. viii. 19, ' If you forget the Lord thy God, &c., I testify unto you this day, ye shall surely perish, as the nations which the Lord destroyeth before you ; so ye shall perish, because ye would not be obedient unto the voice of the Lord your God.' Deut. xi. 26, ' And Moses saith unto them, Behold I set before you this day a blessing and a curse : blessing, if you obey the commandments of the Lord, &c.; and the curse, if you will not obey.'

Now God is free of his promise and oath that he made to them, for they have disobeyed him ; they have corrupted their ways, they have contemned and slacked the law of God, therefore they have forfeited their estate in that good land, and their persons stand obliged to the punishment of their disobedience.

Doct. The lesson is, that all the promises of God's favour to men are not absolute, but conditional, and are referred to the obedience or disobedience of men.

Reason. For man is mutable. God is unchangeably just; he must not, he cannot favour disobedience; his love goes not in the blood, but in the faith of Abraham. Israel, the posterity of Abraham, is no more to him than the posterity of Canaan, who had his father's curse, except that Israel do serve him better than they do. He hath told them so by Moses, for seeing there was no merit in them to deserve his love at first, and no means for them to continue his love, but their obedience; that failing, they are to him as heathens.

Christ teacheth us that if any be wilful, and will not obey the church, he must be to us as an heathen and a publican; we can never excommunicate such *ex communione charitatis*, out of the communion of charity, for as much as in us lieth we must have peace with all men, and we must never hide ourselves from our own flesh, and we must do good unto all men; but we may, we must exclude them, *ex communione ecclesiæ*, from the communion of the church; we must not admit them to our congregations, nor esteem them members of the church, till they be reconciled.

Religion is the knot of true union, that knitteth us to God, that uniteth us to one another; that once dissolved, farewell fair weather, we must turn all into chiding and reproof, and, as the apostle saith, come to them with the rod. We must complain of them to God, and awake his justice upon them. So that if we would keep our land from invasion and depopulation, our persons from captivity and deportation, our goods from direption and deprecation, let us serve the Lord in fear and obedience, in holiness and righteousness before him all the days of our lives.

(2.) The punishment shall extend to a proud triumph, which is expressed, ver. 10: 'They shall scoff at the kings, and the princes shall be a scorn to them; and they shall deride every stronghold.'

Doct. This is another of God's rods: he punisheth the despisers with scorn and contempt, as you heard out of Obadiah: 'Behold I have made thee small; thou art greatly despised,' ver. 2.

Therefore St Paul, repeating this prophecy, Acts xiii. 40, doth, by way of exposition, to shew to whom this judgment doth belong, say, 'Behold, ye despisers, and wonder, and vanish away, for behold ye amongst the heathen.' This is God's own word, 'He that despiseth me, shall be despised.' Yea, as the psalmist saith, 'He poureth contempt upon princes.'

Two things that are most privileged from contempt shall here suffer it.

1. The majesty of kings.
2. The strength of fortifications.

But when the supreme majesty of God is offended and despised, these cannot escape both destruction and contempt.

This the generous nature of man doth more fear than any temporal evil: let me ache, and smart, and lose all, but let me not be despised.

When the Jews began, after their captivity, to build again the walls of the city, they had strong opposition by their enemies, Tobiah, and Sanballat, and others, who laboured to hinder the building all they could. But when they despised the Jews, and scorned their work, Nehemiah took it to heart, and grew very earnest with God in complaint against them. For, Neh. iv. 1, Sanballat mocked the Jews, and said before his brethren and the army of Samaria, 'What do these weak Jews? will they fortify themselves? will they sacrifice? will they finish it in a day? will they make the stones whole again out of the heaps of dust, seeing they are burnt? And Tobiah the Ammonite was beside him; and said, Although they build, yet if a fox go up, he shall even break down their strong wall.' This sends Nehemiah to God, saying, 'Hear, O God; we are despised: and turn their shame upon their own head.' This heavy judgment shall God inflict upon the Jews.

Reason. The reason is, because this is the fittest punishment for their pride. Now they shall see, that so long as a people walketh humbly before God, so long they live in glory and reputation; but when God faileth them for their sins, their enemies do prevail against them, and cover them with disdain.

When God tried Job with all kind of corporal and temporal calamities, in the agony and smart of his passion, he looketh back to the former mercies of God; wherein I observe, that he giveth the first place of his temporal happiness to that respect that was given to him: Job xxix. 7-11, 'When I went out to the gate through the city; when I prepared my seat in the street! The young men saw me, and hid themselves; and the aged arose, and stood up. The princes refrained talking, and laid their hand on their mouth. The nobles held their peace, and their tongue cleaved to the roof of their mouth. When the ear heard me, then it blessed me; and when the eye saw me, it gave witness to me.'

But in the next chapter, recounting the miseries which had come upon him, he gives the first place to contempt: chap. xxx. 1, ' But now they that are younger than I have me in derision, whose fathers I would have disdained to set with the dogs of my flock.' Ver. 8-10, ' They were children of fools, yea, children of base men; they were viler than the earth. And now I am their song; I am their by-word. They abhor me, and fly far from me, and spare not to spit in my face.' (Read on at leisure.)

But thus did the Jews abuse Christ: 'Is not this the carpenter?' And after they put on him a purple garment, and put a reed in his hand, and crowned him with thorns, and saluted him scornfully, ' King of the Jews.' They spit on his face, and even, hanging on the cross of pain and shame, they laughed him to scorn. Some refer the *non sicut* to this especially: Lam. i. 12, ' Have ye no regard, all ye that pass by the way? consider and behold, if ever there were sorrow like my sorrow, which was done to me.' For the grief of contempt must needs be the greatest humiliation, because of the eminency and excellency of his person.

And for Christian religion in the primitive times of the church, the common evil opinion of it was, that it was heresy; but the learned Grecians did call preaching foolishness: *Ubi sapiens? ubi scriba?*

Use. The way to avoid this contempt is humility, a virtue unknown to the moral wise men of former ages; it is the proper virtue of the Christian. *Discite à me quia mitis et humilis.* This is the virtue, and he the only teacher of it, the best example of it, the fullest reward of it. You heard from Obadiah to Edom, ver. 3, 'The pride of thy heart hath deceived thee.' The pride of life is the queen of vices, as you heard then; it trespasseth the majesty of God; it turned angels into devils, and cast men out of paradise (Hugo). *Superbia mihi Deum aufert.*

Humility doth make us think reverently of God, and charitably of our brethren, and worse of ourselves. St Paul, 'Of whom I am chief.' Humility makes us think all the least favours of God too good for us, and so joineth contentedness with godliness.

Contempt cannot smart upon the humble in respect of themselves, but in respect of God, who is despised in them. Study and pray to God for this grace; this keeps peace in the church, and quietness in our common conversation, for only of pride cometh contention. Let me once say with Jacob, 'I am not worthy of the least of thy mercies,' and we shall value the very crumbs that fall from the children's table. The least of God's favours will be sweet to us, and God shall be praised for them. And with such as be of a contrite and lowly spirit God will dwell; God himself boweth the heavens, and cometh down to such to visit them, *Atque humiles habitare casas,* 'Behold I stand at the door and knock.' Not at the door of the proud, for their self-love keepeth him out.

The humble man is the Lord's temple, and he saith, 'Here will I dwell, for I have a delight therein:' 'I will satisfy their poor with bread,' 'the holy ones shall rejoice and sing:' 'I took David from the sheepfold,' 'there will I make the horn of David to flourish; I have ordained a lanthorn for mine anointed.'

Ver. 11. *Then shall his mind change, and he shall pass over, and offend, imputing this his power unto his god.*

3. What shall become of the Chaldeans thus victorious?

1. They shall change their mind.
2. They shall pass over.
3. They shall offend.
4. Their fault.

1. *They shall change their mind.* The prosperous and victorious success of the Chaldean shall so infatuate the Chaldean, that he shall be transported with the pride thereof, and God shall give end unto his violence. God shall change his mind, for their sakes whom he reserveth as his remnant amongst the Jews.

Doct. The rod of the wicked shall not rest on the lot of the righteous. The wicked are the sword of the Lord; he will not always chide nor strike, but he will put up his sword in his sheath, his arm in his bosom.

He guideth the hearts of all men, like rivers of waters, which way he pleaseth. It is a doctrine which I lately taught out of Obadiah. Though the church of God do live under the cross for a time, it shall not be always so; for, as here it is declared, ' their mind shall change that afflict her.'

1. Because God's quarrel is not against the persons of men, but against their sins; therefore he punisheth *non ad vindictam,* but *ad emendationem vitæ,* and it is no pleasure to God to punish his children; therefore he will not always punish, because afflictions are of excellent force to bring forth in his children, 1, contrition; 2, supplication.

2. He will not always punish, lest the extreme passions of his servants should breed in them a doubt of his love, and so weaken their faith.

3. Lest the righteous should put forth his hand unto sin.

4. Lest the enemies of his church should grow too insolent.

Further we are taught, that those whom God useth as his rods are limited; when they have executed his will, they shall then change their minds. The mind of the Chaldean was cruelty, and oppression, and covetousness, and ambition; this victory shall change their mind into pride and insolence, so that, as the wise man saith, ' The prosperity of fools shall destroy them.'

It is a true saying for the most part, that as the good, so the blood riseth. Men of low degree, when they rise to high places, men of poor estate when they grow to plenty, even nations when they overflow their own banks and overrun others, do change their minds; they have not the same hearts and affections that they had. It is a singular wisdom to use the fulness of prosperity well. The paradise of God did not content our first parents; the forbidden fruit seemed to Eve the fairest fruit of the garden; that changed her mind from the obedience of the law of God, to be both a prevaricator and a tempter.

The sons of God, living in prosperity in the favour of God, set their eyes on the daughters of men; and because they looked fair, like Eve's apple, they changed their mind from living under the religious awe of God, to take them wives, by whom the service of God was corrupted; for they that marry with tempters, and take them to their bosoms, either presume too much on their own strength, and they tempt God therein; or else they change their minds and religions with them. 'Can a man carry fire in his bosom, and not be burned? Or walk upon burning coals, and not be scorched?' The author of the book of Wisdom saith well of the righteous, chap. iv. 11, 'That he is speedily taken away, lest wickedness should alter his understanding, or deceit beguile his soul.'

There is a great measure of grace needful to him that would use prosperity well: he must not be wicked; for where the good Spirit of God is wanting, there is nothing but unstaidness and inconstancy. But David prayeth, 'Establish thou me with thy free Spirit.' David's victories and peace and prosperity did change his mind; he grew wanton; and to hide that, cruel, and to live in that sin of uncleanness, irreligious, till God sent Nathan to him.

Hezekiah, having rest, changed his mind, and proud of his treasures, shewed them to his own disadvantage, and provoked God's anger against him.

Experience shews us how the world, and the wealth and honours thereof, do corrupt men of good minds before, and changeth their understandings: that Demas will forsake Paul, whom he hath long served; and some disciples will no longer walk with Christ.

Reason 1. The cause hereof is because outward things, unsanctified to the owner and user thereof, have no power to establish the heart; for the heart is established by grace, and not with meats, nor with any outward things.

Reason 2. Because there is no peace with the wicked man; he must be as violent and as inconstant as the sea, casting up also foam and filth.

Reason 3. Because iniquity knoweth no measure, but runneth into all extremes, *virtutisque viam deserit arduæ:* their mirth is madness, their music vanity. So their sorrow is sullenness and discontent. Conquered, they are base, and lick the dust from the enemy's foot: conquering, they are proud, and tyrannise over them whom they have subdued.

Thus the mind of the wicked changeth in them.

Use. The profit that we may make of this point is great.

1. It discourageth us from greedy seeking of temporal prosperity, because it hath this danger in it, to change our minds, and to shift us from vice* to vice: wherefore it is a good petition in our holy Litany, ' In all time of our wealth, good Lord, deliver us.' And that of Agur, Prov. xxx. 9, ' Give me not riches, lest I be full and deny thee, and say, Who is the Lord?'

2. It comforteth the oppressed, that their oppressors are not always of the same mind, but they may hope for fairer weather in the greatest storms that do arise, because the minds of their enemies shall change; as David saith, ' He made them that led them away captive to pity them,' for God hath a power in this change, which is *mutatio dextræ excelsi.*

2. They shall pass over them.

Either to some further quest of glory, or they shall exceed their commission and go beyond the bounds appointed them, either in punishing whom God would have to be spared, or in time, continuing the punishment beyond the time designed.

God only knoweth how far he would have his judgment to pass; the Chaldeans do transgress and pass over this measure, whereby they grow intolerable, and their malice punishable.

* Qu. ' virtue '?—Ed.

Or *pertransibunt* may be referred to their own short domination; for the Chaldeans were a few years after conquered by the Medes and Persians, as the learned Jesuit Ribera observeth. And we find that Nebuchadnezzar, the king of the Chaldeans, felt the smart of this prophecy in his own person.

For, Dan. iv. 33, he changed his mind, and passed over, when he became as a brute beast, and was driven from men, and did eat grass as oxen, and his body was wet with the dew of heaven, till his hairs were grown like eagles' feathers, and his nails like birds' claws. Thus, he that passed the bounds of justice in the oppression of the Jews, and the bounds of modesty in the pride of his victory, is changed in his understanding, and passeth the bounds of common humanity. All this proves that God's employing the wicked to punish others doth not move them or derive the favours of God upon them, they cannot keep within any compass.

1. If *pertransibit, pass over*, do signify a further quest of glory, we are taught hence that the ungodly are insatiable in their desires, nothing will content them, every victory encourageth to a new war, as we find in all examples of the greatest monarchies of the world, till their own weight ruin them.

2. As this passing over doth signify their going beyond their bounds, we are taught that they whom God employeth without their knowledge and privity, do only seek their own ends, neither is God in all their ways.

3. As this passing over signifieth the short joy of their victory, so it teacheth that an ungodly man can never be a happy man, nor a sinful man a wise man; for in short time he will lose that what he hath unjustly gotten. For though God intended the taking away of the Jews' land from them, he intended it but for a time; he meant the Jews a sharp chastisement, not an eradication.

I understand those words of a cessation from any further prosecution of this war against the Jews; for he shall carry away some captive into his own land, and the meaner sort he shall leave behind to husband

Judea, and so shall cease. And this doth strengthen our former doctrine, that those whom God useth as instruments of his justice, shall at length desist; God will not suffer them beyond his decreed time.

3. *They shall offend.* Let no man mistake this place, as if God did lay upon them a necessity of offence ; but he doth, out of his prescience, foretell that they will offend God, as with all their other sins, so particularly with this, their service done to him.

Doct. 1. They are stirred up to this war by God, and it is his just will to punish the Jews ; yet the Chaldeans, that execute this will, do offend, which was before proved by their evil intention, and will after more appear in the close of this text ; wherein we have charged the action upon God, and the evil of the action upon the Chaldeans.

Doct. 2. God foreknoweth the sins of men.

He foreknew the fall of Adam, and provided a remedy for it in his eternal counsel. He foreknew the sins of the old world, and provided a judgment to punish them. He foreknew the sins of his Israel, and therefore he made all his promises conditional, and referred them to their obedience. He foreknew the trespass of Judas, the cruelty of the Jews, the injustice of the Romans against his Son; and he made his death medicinal and cordial for his church, and a ruin to the enemies thereof. The same stone which was the corner-stone of the church, was a rock of offence to her enemies.

This is the ground of God's justice against the Chaldeans in the next section of this chapter ; for foreseeing how they would offend, he did also fore-decree how he would punish them.

He is called Θεος, *a seer*,* for all things are manifest in his sight ; the eye of the Lord is over all the world, he seeth both the good and the bad. God foreseeth offences before they be come into the hearts of men, as Christ knew Judas would be a traitor before Judas knew it himself; and God, by his prophet, 2 Kings xiii. 8, told Hazael how cruel he should be, before Hazael was king; and when Hazael thought such

* This is on the supposition that Θεος is derived from Θεαομαι, *video.*—ED.

wickedness could not have bred in him, 'Am I a dog that *I* should do this great thing?' And Christ told Peter that he would deny him, when Peter protested against it very strongly.

1. Because he knoweth the heart in which sin breedeth, and knows how apt it is to conceive sin. He knoweth whereof we be made.

2. He foreseeth the temptations wherewith man shall be tempted.

3. He knoweth what measure of strength and virtue is gone out from him to man, to enable him against these temptations.

Use 1. Let no man, therefore, flatter himself that he can commit any sin so secretly that the eye of God shall escape it; he knoweth our thoughts long before, there can no darkness hide us from this eye; but the darkness is as light as the day to him, darkness and light are both alike. And if God foresee offences to come, much more doth he remember sins past, and observe sins present.

Use 2. Let this stir us up to the fear of the Lord, which is a continual putting of us into the presence of God, and filleth us with fervent prayers to God to keep us from sin, either from the desire of it, or from the committing of it, or from the punishment of it, by giving us strength to resist sin tempting us, or at least to hate the evil which we do against the law of our mind, transported by the law of our members; or to give us the grace of repentance, that we may turn to him, and break off our sins by righteousness and godly life.

This is that petition in our Lord's prayer, ' Lead us not into temptation.' Which petition followeth that former, ' Forgive us our trespasses;' for whom God pardoneth, them Satan tempteth most, both because he despiteth God, and because relapse into sins once pardoned, is a double danger. And he prayeth God not to lead him into the temptation, because we must not only remember with grief the sins we have committed, but we must consider with fear what sins our infirmities may fall into. Into which God leadeth us, by withdrawing his grace from us, or from which he keepeth and preserveth us by his assisting grace. The foresight of God is, in respect of himself and his own perfect knowledge, infallible and certain ; that will come to pass which he foreseeth, and this is his wisdom ; though man have a free will to do evil, yet he knoweth how far this his free will shall mislead him. And for that cause he hath set a guard of angels about the just, to keep them in all their ways that they fall not, to take them up again when they fall ; and he hath given his word and lantern to their feet, to guide and direct their paths.

Yet we may say, that this foresight of God may be, in respect of the means, conditional; and so God may foresee such an event upon some secret condition, which yet by means may be prevented, and not succeed.

A great example hereof in David's story, 1 Sam. xxiii. He heareth that the Philistines do rob Keilah, David goeth against the Philistines, and overcometh, and saveth the men of Keilah. Saul, hearing of it, arms his forces to surprise Keilah secretly. David asketh of God : ver. 12, ' Will the men of Keilah deliver me and my men into the hand of Saul ?' The Lord said, ' They will deliver thee up.' Here God foresaw a sin in the men of Keilah which was never committed, but Saul had sent, and God knew the corruption of the heart of these men, and gave warning. Here his foresight in respect of himself was certain, which was, that David should take this warning to escape. But in respect of the sucesss, it was conditional, because it hath reference to the means of evasion.

So God foresaw the death of Hezekiah, by his conditional will, deferred; but by his revealed will, present; and his revealed will doth not always make necessity of event, but sometimes it is a warning to escape it.

Thus God foreseeth the spawning of sin in man's life, in the seed or root thereof, which is lust; yet he revealeth means to keep the just from falling into these sins. But for the wicked, he leaveth them to the stream and current of their own free will, and leadeth them into temptation; for temptation is their punishment.

This may stir us up to husband the means of grace to the best advantage of our souls, to keep us undefiled in the way, that iniquity may not have dominion over us. For God's certain knowledge of our evils will bring forth a certain judgment to punish them.

4. *Wherein he shall offend, imputing this his power to his god.* The Chaldeans were not without their god. Nebuchadnezzar their king had made them a god of the best metal, and had set it up in the plain of Durah, in the province of Babel, and called all the people in his dominions to worship the god which Nebuchadnezzar the king had set up. This god must have the glory of the Chaldeans' conquest; and what greater dishonour can they do to the living God than to give his glory to lifeless and senseless stocks?

1. Yet it appeareth that those people, although they knew not the true God, yet they had a knowledge of the Divinity. And so we do hold that no man is *simpliciter atheos*, that is, without knowledge or acknowledgment of some divine power ruling and governing all things. For this is the finger of God in the heart of the natural man, who, though he do not perceive *quæ Dei*, the things of God, yet he perceiveth *quod Deus*, that there is a God.

2. It appeareth that they did confess a debt of glory due to the Deity. Whatsoever they would think worthy to be esteemed their god, they would think it worthy of all ascriptions of honour and glory; which is another truth of the law of God written in the heart of every man, and it is a good principle of nature, it is a lineament of the image of God in man.

3. It also appeareth that they believed the ordinance and moderation of great affairs to depend on the power and strength of their god, because they gave him the honour of this victory; for this power, the power which he calleth his, he confesseth to be borrowed, for he imputeth it to his god, which also is another beam and ray of heavenly light. But the Lord saith here, they shall offend herein; for God's glory is given away from him, and horrible idolatry is committed.

This light of nature doth serve to convince the Chaldeans that Nebuchadnezzar's golden image is not, cannot be, God; for that is fixed, it moveth not. What wealth it hath in the matter, is the king's gift; what proportion or form it hath in the fabric and form of it, it hath from the hand of the workman.

But, beloved, let me lay open to you the true cause of all idolatry, not only that of the heathen, but even that of them that call themselves Christians; it is want of faith. For seeing God is an invisible essence, and they are loath to worship what they cannot see, and they walk by sense and not by faith; the invisible Deity is by them worshipped in some visible form; and I cannot judge more hardly against them than that they have too much weakness in their understanding to make it necessary that their god must be visible, yet not so much weakness of sense as to judge that idol to be God which is of their own making.

But see how God punisheth them; for seeing they will not worship a god whom they cannot see, he leaveth them to worship that which they can see to be no god.

Yet give me leave to commend the Chaldean for one thing, he doth not assume the glory of this victory to himself, and he findeth the honour of it above human nature. Therein teaching us to give the glory of all our good successes to him whom we know and believe to be our God, and not to overween ourselves herein; for before this chapter shall pass us, we shall find that the Chaldean will learn to be his own god, and thank himself for his victories; as it followeth, ver. 26, 'Therefore they sacrifice to their net;' for *nemo subito fit pessimus*.

Yet, some interpreters, applying this to Nebuchadnezzar, do think that this imputing of the power to his god was assuming of it to himself, and that he was his own god; as we read of Alexander, that after his many victories he was so full of himself as to suffer himself to be flattered with that high appellation. And Daniel's story sheweth the pride of Nebuchadnezzar high grown; and this sacrificing to their own net, which followeth, doth favour this exposition.

When I put these things together, *they shall offend, imputing this their strength to their god,* I find here,
1. Idolatry, imputing this to his god.
2. That idolatry is an offence to God.

1. Idolatry. That the Chaldean is justly charged with idolatry here, I thus shew. Dr Rainold, de Idol. lib. ii. 1, 1, ' Whosoever gives divine worship to a creature is an idolater; *Quisquis creaturæ divinum cultum exhibet idololatra est, at Chaldæus hoc facit,* but the Chaldean doth so, *ergo.*

The first proposition is cleared, for whatsoever is honoured with the honour of God is put into the place of God, against that law, *Non habebis Deos alienos,* ' Thou shalt have no other gods.'

That the Chaldean is thus guilty, the text convinceth him; he imputeth the force of his war and victory to his god. This is *deus alienus,* this is an idol.

It is the proper honour to the true God to be *custos hominum,* the preserver of men—to be *Dominus exercituum,* the Lord of hosts. This honour the Chaldean gave to his god.

When Rachel said to Jacob, Gen. xxx. 2, ' Give me children, or else I die,' Jacob was very angry with her, whom he loved dearly, that she should despoil God of his due glory, and seek it from a creature; and he answered, ' Am I instead of God?' for Plato, an heathen philosopher,* did confess, *Quamvis in mortali animante fiat, res tamen divina est prægnatio, et ab immortalibus est.*

So, when the king of Syria wrote to the king of Israel in the behalf of Naaman the leper, that he might be cured of his leprosy, the king of Israel rent his clothes at that idolatrous demand, and said, ' Am I a god, to kill and give life?' so that the honour of God given away from him to any creature is the setting up of an idol in the place of God.

The Nicene Synod did condemn the Arians of idolatry, because they denied the divinity of Christ, and yet acknowledged divine worship to him; and because Nestorius did affirm Christ to be a mere man, and not God, both the Ephesian and Nicene Synods condemned them of anthropolatry.

* In Sympos.

We do usually offend too much in our ascriptions to the means of any good to us, wherein we wrong God's glory, if we look not up to him as the supreme agent working in that means. Thus, in the church of Rome, angels by God employed for the service of man, by the overdoing thankfulness of man, were honoured with the honour due to him that sent them.

Those that leave the service of God and study men, and apply themselves wholly to their humours to better their estates, do set up new and strange gods against the true God, and give his glory to creatures, and make their means their idols, do commit idolatry, and break the first great commandment of the law.

The Romanists cannot clear themselves of this trespass, though Bellarmine their champion do his best to excuse it. He distinguisheth between *images*, which he calleth *verus rerum similitudines*, the true similitudes of things; but he calleth *idols* false representations of things that are not.

But not to trouble ourselves to examine his frivolous distinction, the image itself of a true thing subsisting is a creature, and to give that the honour due only to God is gross idolatry; for example, that in their Roman breviary, which is directed to the cross, be it not to the image and representation of the cross before their eyes, but in it to the cross itself, is it not idolatry? *O crux ave spes unica, hoc passionis tempore auge piis justitiam, reisque dona veniam!*

2. This text chargeth them that they offend, whereby it appeareth that idolatry is an offence. You see how high it reacheth, even to the ungodding of the Almighty, and we shall shortly see how sore it smarteth upon the offenders.

Reas. 1. The devil is the author of idolatry, for, when God had buried Moses secretly to prevent idolatry, the devil would have discovered the place, to move the people to idolatry. That was the strife which St Jude mentioneth between Michael the archangel and the devil about the body of Moses, wherein the archangel prevailed against him.

Reas. 2. The devil is a great tempter to idolatry, for he assaulted Christ so, Mat. iv., *si procidens adoraveris me*, 'if thou wilt fall down and worship me.'

Reas. 3. The devil is the chief agent in the ministry of the idolatrous priests, as the evil spirit, 1 Kings xxii. 22, offered his service to be a lying spirit in the mouths of Baal's prophets, four hundred of them at once.

The promise of Satan is that which he professed to Christ, to draw men from the worship of God to worship him; and there is no mean: all worshippers that do not worship the true God worship Satan. So the Chaldean imputeth their force to Satan, for he that is not with him is against him.

Use. The use of this point is taught by the apostle St John: 1 John v. 21, 'Babes, keep yourselves from idols;' give not the glory of God to creatures.

It is an admirable thing in the whole course of the story of Israel, and after of the Jews, Moses could tell them, Deut. iv. 7, ' For what nation is there so great, who hath God so nigh unto them, as the Lord our God is in all things that we call upon him for ?' Yet was idolatry their national sin, although upon all occasions they might advise with God, though they had the pillar of fire, the pillar of cloud, the ark, the law, the priesthood, the temple, and all the oracles of God committed to them; therefore no wonder if the Chaldean, who had none of this, did commit idolatry.

These are examples for us; and because we have no fear but of the idolatry of the church of Rome, we must take warning to keep ourselves from their idols and their idolatry.

This, we understand, is now the study and care of the religious patriots in the honourable and high court of parliament. Let us join with them in our prayers to God for the rooting out of the Romish religion; let us give God our hearty thanks that he worketh by his Spirit such zeal of the glory of his truth in the godly faithful hearts of the commons of this land, to stir and rouse up themselves in a matter so much concerning the honour of our God as this doth.

For who delivered us from the Spanish violence in '88 ? and who delivered us from the bloody powder treason in *An.* 1605 ? If the gods that our enemies serve could have prevailed against our God, had we not been as Sodom and Gomorrah?

Therefore let us pray God to preserve us from idols, and from them that love and serve them, of whom I may say truly with David, Ps. lv. 21, 'The words of their mouths are smoother than butter, but war is in their heart: their words are softer than oil, yet are they drawn swords.'

There can be no hope that those men which will rob God of his glory, and give it away to creatures, will ever be true to us. Let every one in the zeal of God's glory shew and profess his hatred to idolatry and his love of the true worship of God; and as they need the sword of the Lord and of Gideon, so let us cry, The sword of the Lord, his word in the mouths of his faithful ministers, and the sword of Gideon— the sword of the religious court of parliament against them!

Vers. 12–17. '*Art thou not from everlasting, O Lord my God, my Holy One? we shall not die. O Lord my God, thou hast ordained them for judgment; and, O mighty God, thou hast established them for correction. Thou art of purer eyes than to behold evil, and canst not look on iniquity; wherefore lookest thou upon them that deal treacherously, and holdest thy tongue when the wicked devoureth the man that is more righteous than he? And makest men as the fishes of the sea, and as the creeping things, that have no ruler over them? They take up all of them with the angle, they catch them in their net, and gather them in their drag; therefore they rejoice and are glad. Therefore they sacrifice unto their net, and burn incense unto their drag; because by them their portion is fat, and their meat plenteous. Shall they therefore empty their net, and not spare continually to slay the nations?*

After God had denounced his judgment upon the Jews, contained in the former section, now the prophet beginneth a new wrestling with God in the behalf of the afflicted members of his church.

The prophet's speech is addressed to God himself, wherein he first ascribeth to God eternity : ' Art not thou from everlasting, O Lord my God ?' He ascribeth to him holiness : ' My Holy One.' And this pronoun possessive, *my*, doth lay hold upon a special interest that Habbakuk by faith claimed in God.

From which consideration he draweth this cheerful conclusion, ' We shall not die, O Lord ;' speaking of himself and of the afflicted in the church of the Jews, that though God had threatened such an invasion by the hand and power of the Chaldeans, yet shall it not proceed to their ruin. God will keep his church ; there is a remnant that God will save from the stormy wind and the tempest ; as David saith, ' The flood of many waters shall not come near them.' This faith he builds upon a good foundation, for,

1. From the eternity of God we may conclude that the love wherewith he loveth the church is an eternal love, and therefore not to be subject to the power of time.

2. From the holiness of God he may conclude that all the faithful Jews, being an holy seed, shall have his favour.

Against this it may be objected that God hath revealed himself to the contrary, for he hath before threatened to raise up the Chaldeans, a fierce and terrible nation, that shall go through the breadth of the land, and shall run like an eagle and an evening wolf only for prey. What hope then can there be against these ?

The prophet answereth that objection : ' Thou hast ordained them for judgment, and, mighty God, thou hast established them for correction ;' that is, God, by his might hath armed them against the Jews to execute his judgment on them, and for castigation and correction of them, not for eradication.

He proceedeth then to expostulate and dispute with God concerning this judgment to be executed upon the Jews by the Chaldeans : ' Thou art of purer eyes than to behold evil, and canst not look on iniquity.'

There is a further confession of the holiness of God, to whom he attributeth pure eyes, such as cannot behold evil and look upon iniquity, because that holiness cannot approve ill, and that justice cannot wink at it and leave it unpunished.

Otherwise, *videre malum non est malum*, to see evil is not evil. God's general view of all things doth set his eye upon the good and evil. So the sun shineth upon the just and the unjust, but God is a God that loveth not iniquity, neither shall evil dwell with him: he abhorreth all them that work wickedness. David saith, his soul abhorreth them. So that the prophet here acquitteth God from any hand in the evil of these Chaldeans, although he stirreth them up against the Jews. He is wise to use them as instruments of correction, but he is too pure and holy to be partaker in their sins.

From hence groweth the expostulation following: Seeing thou art so pure and holy that thou abhorrest evil, and hatest all the workers of iniquity, why dost thou look upon them that deal treacherously? Why dost thou, O holy and just God, look on whilst the Chaldean betrayeth thy people? Mr Calvin reads *transgressores*, Montanus *prævaricatores*, Jun. *perfidos*, whom the king's Bible followeth.

This the prophet Isaiah, chap. xxi. 2, calleth a grievous vision: 'The treacherous dealer dealeth treacherously, and the spoiler spoileth.' For the Chaldean did invade the Jew, both cunningly by treason, and violently by force.

He urgeth God further: 'Why holdest thou thy tongue when the wicked man,' that is, the Chaldean, an idolater and a bloody man, 'devoureth the man that is more righteous than he?' that is, devoureth the Jew, who, as bad as he is, is a better man and more righteous than the Chaldean. He wondereth at the softness and forbearance of God, that can see and be silent to behold so much iniquity.

He proceedeth in his complaint: ver. 14, 'Thou makest man as the fishes in the sea,' where the great ones do prey upon the small ones, 'and as the creeping things that have no ruler over them,' and therefore feed upon one another, who have no law to awe them; but *quo quis est valentior, eo violentior*, so the Jews are to the Chaldeans a prey.

But the words following do shew another thing intended, not a reference of these creatures one to another, but all of them to the fishermen; so the sense is, thou seemest to esteem the Jew no more than thou dost the fishes on the sea, or the creeping things on the earth; for it followeth, ver. 15, 'They take up all of them with the angle, they catch them in their net, and gather them in their drag.' The Chaldeans are the fishermen, the Jews the fishes; and for these they have,

1. *The angle*, whereby is meant their fishing for a single person.
2. *Their net*, let fall to catch more.
3. *Their drag*, for whole shoals of fish. So that here is no evasion. He that escapeth the angle shall fall into the net; or if he escape the net, the drag shall sweep him away, and bring him to the shore.

So that hereby all way of evasion seemeth stopped against the Jew; he is put into the hand and power of the Chaldean, as a draught of fish into the hand of the fisherman; and all this while the fisherman thinketh he doth no man wrong, as the poet saith,

Nec patitur Tyrrhenum crescere piscem.

For the fish of the sea is esteemed his that can catch him; so shall the Chaldean fish Judea, as if the Jews were fishes, not men, and as if there were no providence to take care of them, no owner to call them his.

Therefore they rejoice and are glad. There is no compassion in them of Chaldea toward the Jew; but as the fisherman rejoiceth in his draught of fishes, and never looketh upon them with any pity of their lives, but is glad that he hath gotten them, so shall the Chaldean be glad when the Jews are in his net, that they may carry them into captivity.

This victory doth not only make the Chaldean glad, but he is proud too, and boasteth in his own strength, and attributeth his prevailings to his own power, as it followeth.

Ver. 16, *Therefore they sacrifice unto their net, and burn incense unto their drag;* that is, they do thank their own arm and armies for their victories; and, as Job saith, 'They kiss their own hands, because thereby they come to have a fat portion and plenty of meat;' so that they give no glory to God; yea, before the prophet saith from the mouth of God, that they would ascribe the prosperity of their wars to their god, *i. e.* to their idol, now they will grow so proud that they will thank their own wit and power for all.

The prophet concludeth with a passionate expostulation: ver. 17, ' Shall they therefore empty their net, and not spare continually to slay the nations?' Seeing they are a people so lawless, so merciless, so proud, O Lord, wilt thou give way to them still? and shall they possess all that they catch? which he calleth emptying their net, and shall they not spare continually to slay the nations? Shall they pass thus from nation to nation, and shall they still conquer? Is all fish that comes into their net?—(*De verborum interpretatione hactenus*).

In the further handling of this section I observe, as in the former, two things:

1. The sum and contents of the whole section.
2. The parts thereof.

1. The sum hereof is this: whereas the prophet at first beholding the sins of the Jews, was moved with an holy indignation against them, and with zeal of God's glory, which turned him into a chiding expostulation with God for bearing so much with them, and therefore did stir up God to judgment, to chasten them in the first section of this chapter.

Now that God hath answered him in the second, with declaration of his purpose to punish the iniquities of the Jews by the Chaldeans, whom God would stir up to fight against them, and to prevail; now in this third section, the prophet is as much troubled and grieved at their punishment as he was before at their sin. Now he chides as fast, and disputes as hotly against the remissness and patience of God towards the Chaldeans, as he did before towards the Jews. Before, he pleaded the cause of the glory of God's justice, in punishing the iniquity of the Jews; now he pleads the glory of God's mercy in sparing them. The first part was imprecation. And herein the prophet doth declare his mixed affection to the Jews; for out of his hatred to their sins he desired their correction; but now out of his love to their persons he prayeth against their punishment, so far that it may be moderate, as in Jeremiah's prayer, 'Correct us, O Lord, yet in thy judgment, not in thy fury, lest we be consumed and brought to nothing.' Which teacheth us that,

Doct. Religion hath the bowels of compassion. Truly they have no true religion that have no mercy.

Reason 1. This is given us in precept with a *sicut*, 'Be ye merciful, *as* your heavenly Father is merciful,' Luke vi. 36. There is nothing wherein the image of our God doth more shine in man than his mercy, because that is the heavenly nature; the wisdom of God is too high for us, the power of God too great for us, the justice of God too strict for us: all these virtues of the Godhead be out of reach of our imitation.

The furthest that our Saviour goeth in the pattern and precedent of wisdom is, *estote prudentes ut serpentes,* 'Be wise as serpents;' in innocency, *innocentes ut columbæ*, 'be ye innocent as doves;' it is not *estote prudentes ut Pater vester*, 'be ye wise as your heavenly Father.' Concerning fortitude, the mother of Samuel saith, *non est fortis sicut Deus; sicut leo,* Solomon hath it; *sicut quercus,* Amos hath it. Concerning justice, let us take the righteous men at their best, and then *justi fulgebunt ut sol,* the righteous shall shine as the sun, but be *misericordes ut Pater vester*. We must strive to imitate him in mercy, that is, the divine nature, because it is *super omnia opera Dei,* above all the works of God; and that is the human nature also, because it is called *humanity,* and therefore well becometh the man of God.

Reason 2. There is nothing that every one of us doth more stand in need of than mercy, without which all the frame of nature would shake and dissolve. It is *anima mundi,* the soul of the world; it is the juncture of every limb thereof; it is the garment that hideth our nakedness; it is the grave, the sea that burieth, that swalloweth all our reputed sins; it is the tailor to our backs, the caterer to our bellies, the soul that quickeneth us, the strength that supporteth us, the grace that saveth us, the power that raiseth us, the glory that crowneth us. And they that shew no mercy shall have none.

Reason 3. The consideration of our own infirmities doth plead for our mercy to our delinquent brother, not to make the most of their faults, and screw their punishment to the uttermost; rather to save our brethren, and to pull them out of the fire, lest we also be tempted, Gal. vi. 1. For we have many suits to God for pardon of our own sins; and therefore by the law of justice, let us do as we would be done to, that is, solicit the favour of God for our brethren. And although the zeal of God's glory do put us to it to pray for their correction, that they may be amended, yet considering how bitter the medicine is that healeth sin, let us entreat the physician to look but on the corrupt humours in the body of the church, to purge them, to take no more blood from the body thereof than may stand with the health of the body.

Reason 4. It is a more easy suit to obtain the mercy of God than to stir up his anger; for as he is slow to wrath, and longsuffering, and when he doth begin to chide he will not keep his anger continually, so he is rich in mercy, abundant in goodness. *Oleum supernatat vino*, the oil swims about the wine. Christ his Son, the character of his Father's glory, of his mercy, the true copy of that *sicut Pater vester qui est in cœlis*, as ' our Father which is in heaven.'

Of whom Saint Augustine,* sweetly commenting upon his *Pater ignosce eis*, ' Father, forgive them,' saith he left them not *quousque ejus jam sanguinem possent bibere credentes quem fuderant sævientes*, [till] they know how to drink believing, the blood which they shed raging, which is called in the psalmist *multitudo dulcedinis*.

Saint Hilary † upon the parable of the parable in the vineyard saith, *Ad spem omne tempus est liberum, et mercedem non operis sed misericordiæ undecimæ horæ operarii consequuntur*.

* De utilit. pæn. l. i. † In Ps. cxxix.

God loves to be solicited for mercy.

Reason 5. Because in the contrary Jonah had a chiding from God himself, that he stood more upon the credit of his office than he did upon the honour of his God that sent him, being so angry at God's sparing of Nineveh. Wherein God himself pleaded the cause of his own mercy, and justified his suspense of the threatened judgment against Jonah, &c.

David had good cause to choose to fall into the hands of God, rather than into the hands of men, for 'with God there is mercy.' And had Nineveh been in the hand of Jonah, their fasting with sackcloth and repenting should not have cleared nor calmed the storm threatened. God said, in Nineveh there were more than six score thousand persons that knew not the right hand from the left; there were a great many more in the nation of the Jews, many also that served God with a true heart, many that was not yet come to the height of sinning, of whom there was hope; many that had drunk deep already of the cup of affliction by the sins of others, who had thereby provoked God. Therefore Habakkuk could do no less than stand in the gap now, and keep out some of this wrath.

Use. To make use of this doctrine, and of the holy example of this prophet, let me use the words of the apostle to you: Col. iii. 12–14, 'Put on therefore, as the elect of God, holy and beloved, bowels of mercies, kindness, humbleness of mind, meekness, longsuffering; forbearing one another, and forgiving one another, if any man have a quarrel against any man: even as Christ forgave you, so also do ye. And above all things put on charity, with the bond of perfectness.'

As it is a welcome suit to God, when, out of a zeal to his glory, you do call upon him for his judgments, to chasten the overgrown sins of the time in which ye live, so it is a pleasing intercession which soliciteth for mercy in justice; for the pure justice of God will endure an allay of mercy, and we shall have the better interest in his favour by how much the more we desire more sharers in it.

There be good authors of opinion that the prayer of Stephen, 'Father, forgive them,' was no weak means of the conversion of Saul, who was one of his persecutors.

The point is moderation, that neither we should so favour high-grown sinners as not to complain to God of them, nor yet so delight in their punishment, as not to pray against the whole and full displeasure of God; that neither the zeal of God's glory do extinguish Christian compassion, nor the tenderness of pity quench the zeal of God's glory, but that at once we do shew our obedience to the whole law, that he that loveth God may love his neighbour also.

God himself directed Abimelech to Abraham to pray for him, and the friends of Job to use Job's intercession, because he loves to be treated to shew mercy. And the rich man in hell would not have his brethren come to that place of torment.

Complain, then, that is holy passion; but beg easy punishment, that is charitable compassion. The children of God have as many tears to shed for the punishment of their brethren as for their sins.

2. The parts are two :
1. The prophet's resolution concerning the church and commonwealth of the Jews.
2. The prophet's dispute with God.
The first containeth an argument.
1. The antecedent : 'Thou art from everlasting, O Lord my God, my Holy One.'
2. The conclusion : 'Therefore we shall not die. O Lord, thou hast ordained them for judgment; O mighty God, thou hast established them for correction.'

The proposition, that God is eternal and holy, needs no proof to such as know God; both are clearly maintained through the whole body of Scripture.

1. The eternity of God.

'And Abraham planted a grove in Beersheba, and called there on the name of the Lord, the everlasting God,' Gen. xxi. 33.

Moses : 'Before the mountains were brought forth, or ever thou hadst formed the earth and the world, even from everlasting to everlasting, thou art our God,' Ps. xc. 2.

Saint Paul, speaking of the mystery of the gospel long kept secret: ' But now is made manifest, and by the scriptures of the prophets, according to the commandment of the everlasting God, made known to all nations,' Rom. xvi. 26.

' Hast thou not known, hast thou not heard, that the everlasting God, the Lord, the Creator of the end of the earth, fainteth not?' &c., Isa. xl. 28.

Plato defined God to be, *æterna mens, sibi ad omnem felicitatem sufficiens, summe bona, et omnis boni efficiens in natura.*

Neither can we rest in the search of causes till we come to one supreme eternal cause of all things, the *Alpha* and *Omega* of other things, of himself without *Alpha* or *Omega*.

2. The conclusion from hence issuing is, ' Therefore we shall not die,' saith Habakkuk.

For as God is eternal in himself, so is he to his church; and from the eternity of God doth the eternity of angels and men derive itself; for eternity cannot flow from anything that is not itself eternal; and we know that the nature of angels and men is eternal, both of them being by the eternal God created to abide for ever: the elect angels and men in eternal glory, the reprobate angels and men in eternal shame and pain.

Yet is the judgment of the reprobate in Scripture called by the names of *death, destruction, perishing*, because these be titles of the greatest horror and dismay that the heart of man can conceive.

Now we have two hopes built upon this foundation of God's eternity, *non moriemur*.

1. Temporal. That God will still reserve a remnant of the Jews to return again to the possession of their fathers, and to build again the city and the temple, and to renew the face of a church and commonwealth; so, *non moriemur, hoc est, omnes*, we shall not die, that is not all.

2. Eternal. That God will not utterly cast off his people from his favour, but that, although he scourge

them with the rods of men, even to a temporal loss of their land, their liberty, and their lives, yet *non moriemur*, we shall not lose our interest in his promise of a better life.

So that the prophet doth teach us the right use of the doctrine of God's eternity, to assure us against all temporal and eternal evils.

And this doth Moses conclude for this antecedent: Ps. xc. 2, ' Before the mountains were brought forth, or ever thou hadst formed the earth and the world, even from everlasting to everlasting, thou art our God.' Ver. 3, ' Thou turnest man to destruction ; again thou sayest, Return, ye sons of Adam.' From the power of God's eternity there is a return for the sons of Adam ; as David saith, ' Thou renewest the face of the earth.' *Non moriemur;* death, our last enemy, shall be destroyed and perish, we shall be translated from death to life ; this is clear, because God hath in eternal wisdom appointed an eternal redemption for some to an eternal inheritance of eternal glory.

This eternity of God is twofold :

1. *Eternitas essentiæ*, eternity of essence in himself.
2. *Eternitas providentiæ*, eternity of providence in respect of his creatures.

From the first we conclude the second ; for if God be in his own nature eternal, he hath also an eternal providence by which he governeth all things ; his word by which he governeth is also eternal in the heavens.

Saint Augustine* proveth this point of God's eternity thus, *Quod incommutabile æternum est.*

That he proveth, *Quod semper est ejusdem modi est incommutabile.*

Such is our God, without variableness or shadow of change, and therefore eternal.

And whereas from this eternity our prophet doth conclude *non moriemur,* Saint Augustine doth therefore call our eternity *immortalitatem,* rather than *æternitatem.*

2. Another argument is here enforced.

Thou art holy. Therefore this punishment of the Jews by the Chaldeans is for their correction only.

* Quest. lxxxiii. l. c. 19.

Of the antecedent, *God is holy.* The choristers of heaven do attribute it to God three times; in some Greek copies we read it three times three, nine times ἅγιος, holy.

The song of Moses is sung in heaven, Rev. xv. 4; and that saith, 'Who shall not fear thee O Lord, and glorify thy name? for thou only art holy.' The seraphims say each one to another, Isa. vi. 3, 'Holy, holy, holy, is the Lord of hosts; the whole earth is full of his glory.'

It was his law. 1. For his Godhead, that none other but he should be called God, or esteemed.

2. For his worship, not to be given to creatures.

3. For his name, not to be taken in vain.

4. For his Sabbath, to be kept holy.

And it is our first petition, *sanctificetur nomen,* 'hallowed be thy name,' and for our conformity with him: Levit. xi. 44, 'For I am the Lord your God: ye shall therefore sanctify yourselves, and ye shall be holy; for I am holy.' So there is, 1, *sanctitas increata,* an increate holiness in God.

2. *Creata,* created, in man as a beam of that heavenly light, a stream of that full fountain in our God.

This uncreated holiness, which is the attribute of God, is the absolute perfection of God's nature and attributes, his full goodness; not only that wherein he is good in himself, but in his operations also.

The consequent. From hence the prophet concludeth, that God cannot do more to his church than correct it; he cannot utterly destroy it, because he is holy, so is his church; his correction of the elect is only a fire to purge out their dross, which will go out of itself when the combustible matter is spent. Hear God himself: Isa. xliii. 15, 'I am the Lord, the Holy One, the Creator of Israel, your King.' Ver. 21, 'This people have I formed for myself; they shall shew forth my praise.'

Ay! but our sins spoil all. He addeth, ver. 25, 'I, even I, am he that blotteth out thy transgressions for mine own sake, and will not remember thy sins.' The church of God is *semen sanctum,* an holy seed; God cannot forsake it; he is *sanctus Creator,* an holy

Creator, and he is *sanctus Redemptor*, an holy Redeemer of it, as the holy text styleth him.

Application. You see here that, as Christ saith, 'This is life eternal, to know thee.' Let us study God and his attributes, for from thence we derive whatsoever we are or have; they are our light of direction, our staff of supportation.

From the wisdom of God, we have all intellectual illumination.

From the justice of God, all our integrity.

From the holiness of God, all our sanctification.

From the eternity of God, our immortality.

From the omnipotency of God, our strength.

And as by our faith we cleave to him, so we are made partakers of the divine nature.

The juice of this text is the prophet's faith, which, from the holiness and eternity of God, doth resolve,—

Doct. That this judgment of God, threatened against the Jews, is no more than a temporal chastisement, according to the doctrine taught out of Obadiah. Though God afflicteth his church, yet he loveth her still.

This persuasion of deliverance from evils is found in natural men; but either it is grounded upon an opinion that they have of fortune,—such make chance their god,—or it is built upon the consideration of the vicissitude of things which maketh sundry mutations.

> 'Informes hyemes reducit
>   Jupiter; idem
> Summovet.   Non, si male nunc, et olim
> Sic erit.'*

God sendeth foul weather and fair; if it be ill now with us, it will not be so hereafter. This is but cold comfort, to hope only in the change of times, and so to look for better days.

Some acknowledge a deity, and ascribe all alterations to that, not knowing the true God, as Æneas comforted his company,

> Durate et vosmet rebus servate secundis.

* Hor. Car. ii. Od. 10.

Continue and reserve yourselves for better times. *Dabit Deus his quoque finem,* God will put an end to these your sufferings.

But that which comforteth the saints of God in afflictions is their faith in the eternity and holiness of God, from whence they gather assurance that they shall not miscarry under the rod of God. He is eternal, therefore they shall not perish; he is holy, therefore he will but correct, not destroy; and hereof they make this use:

1. They do not limit God to a set time when he shall deliver them. So Daniel waited for the deliverance of Israel from Babylon seventy years. The church waited till the fulness of time for the promised Messiah.

2. They do not limit God to any set means of deliverance. Mordecai did see that the preferment of Esther was a likely means to save the Jews from the fury of the decree which Haman had procured against them, and he putteth her to it, to use her mediation with the king for it, but he builded not his hopes in that means; for he said to her, Esth. iv. 14, 'If thou altogether hold thy peace at this time, then shall there enlargement and deliverance arise to the Jews from another place.'

The promise made to Abraham concerning his seed was in nature despaired by the old age of Abraham and Sarah, yet was not Abraham out of hope; but when Isaac, the son of promise, was come, God afterward commanded him to be offered in sacrifice, yet did not that weaken the faith of Abraham; for he built upon the word of the promise, and not upon the possibility of the means. For he that promised was faithful.

3. They do not limit God to the measure of affliction; for they know that whatsoever the judgment be which God inflicteth upon his church, it cannot exceed a fatherly correction. So Job, chap. xiii. 15, 'Though he kill me, yet will I trust in him.'

4. They are not discouraged in the faith of God's mercy, though they feel the contrary; and therefore, being in one contrary, they do believe another. Thus, even when they feel the burden of their sins, they be-

lieve their justification; for the heavy laden seek Christ for ease. When they feel misery, they believe blessedness; for they know 'Blessed are they that mourn.' When they feel correction, they believe; for he chasteneth every son whom he receiveth. When they feel themselves forsaken of God, they believe themselves interested in his favour; as David and Christ: 'My God, my God, why hast thou forsaken me?' both forsaken in respect of their feeling, neither in respect of their faith.

5. They by faith are ever in the presence of God. So David, Ps. xvi. 8, 'I have set God always before me, for he is at my right hand; therefore I shall not be moved.' So it is said of Moses being in danger in Egypt, Heb. xi. 27, 'By faith he forsook Egypt, not fearing the wrath of the king; for he endured as seeing him who is invisible.' Thus strongly do they build, whose foundation is not laid in any possibility of their own merits to deserve deliverance, and of their own wit and cunning to decline evils, or of their own strength and power to resist them, or evade them, or the vicissitude of things to change them, but trust in the living God, and make him their hiding-place.

Doct. 2. Whereas the prophet saith that God had ordained the Chaldeans for judgment, that is, for the execution of his judgment, and hath established them for correction; *Docemur*, we are taught that God is the author of punishment; God himself assumeth it to himself: Amos iii. 6, 'Shall there be evil in a city, and the Lord hath not done it?' *Malum pœnæ*, the evil of punishment. So Moses: Ps. xc. 7, 'For we are consumed by thine anger, and by thy wrath are we troubled.' So David: Ps. xxxix. 11, 'When thou with rebuke dost correct man for iniquity, thou makest his beauty to consume away like a moth.'

Reason 1. Because every sin is a trespass against God; as David, *Tibi, tibi soli peccavi*, 'Against thee only have I sinned;' for every sin is $\dot{\alpha}\nu o\mu i\alpha$, a transgression of the law, and therein God is offended, and he is 'a jealous God, visiting the iniquity of the fathers upon the children.'

The trespasses against our brethren, in the breach of the second table, be immediate sins against God. For as when the plate is not cut for the mint, to clip it is no breach of the law; but when it hath the stamp impressed, and is coin, then to clip or wash, it is treason, not for the matter, but because of the stamp. So the matter of our brethren is but earth, and the violation of it is but the defacing of earth; but bearing the image of God in it, it is a trespass against him whose image is therein insculped, to wrong it.

Reason 2. Because every punishment, as it is *pœna*, a punishment, so it is *vindicta*, a revenge, and God layeth claim to that by prerogative, *vindicta mea*, my revenge; no man can take the sword out of his hand: it is *virga tua*, saith David, thy rod.

Reason 3. Because none but God can search the heart, where sin breedeth, and knoweth how to proportion punishment to the sin. Punishment is the physic of the church: as Augustine, *Quod pateris medicina est, non pœna*, that thou sufferest is thy medicine, not thy punishment. He only knoweth how to temper the medicine for the health of the patient, for he knoweth whereof we be made; he only can work good out of evil.

Reason 4. Because there is none but God that doth whatsoever he will, none but he can ordain or establish judgment. The judgments are called *Judicia Dei*, the judgments of God. In that cruel execution done upon Christ in our flesh, as there were the wicked hands of the Jews and the Romans, so there was the determinate counsel and foreknowledge of God, Acts ii. 23.

Use 1. Let us not therefore sin against God, and make an idol of him, by making him all mercy; for though we call him Father, doubtless there is a God that judgeth the world, who upon the wicked will rain snares, storms, and tempest: this shall be their portion to drink. Rather meet a temptation with Joseph, and say, ' How then shall I do this great wickedness, and so sin against God?' For ' our God is a consuming fire,' and ' it is a fearful thing to fall into the hands of the living God.'

Use 2. Let us not fret at the means ordained by God for our correction, remembering that God hath established them for our chastisement; but let us rather say with David, Ps. xxxix. 9, ' *Obmutui et non aperii os meum, quia tu domine fecisti*, ' I was dumb, &c., because thou, Lord, hast done it :' let us know and confess who it is that smiteth us, and say, ' Thou hast smitten me, and thou wilt heal me.'

Use 3. Let us remember, when God taketh off his hand and restoreth us again to the cheerful light of his countenance, to acknowledge his mercy to us, and, as Christ saith, to ' sin no more, lest some more heavy judgment fall upon us.' Let us, with David, remember the vows which we made to God in our affliction, and spend the time of our sojourning here in fear.

Use 4. Lastly, seeing God hath comforted us, let us also comfort our brethren, as the apostle saith, 2 Cor. i. 9, ' for God comforteth us in all our tribulations, that we may be able to comfort them which be in any trouble, by the comfort wherewith ourselves are comforted of God.' So, as Christ said to Peter, when we ourselves are converted, we shall strengthen the brethren, and the God of peace and all consolation hall give unto us the blessing of his peace.

2. The prophet's dispute with God.

The prophet seemeth amazed at the course of God's proceeding against the Jews by the Chaldeans. And the remainder of this chapter doth contain his expostulation with God, wherein,

1. He layeth a ground of this argument : the eyes of God are pure.

2. He questioneth God how these inconveniences following are borne withal by him, which are these :

Grievances.

1. How God should look on whilst men deal treacherously, ver. 13.

2. How God should hold his tongue whilst the wicked devoureth the man that is more righteous than he, ver. 13.

3. How God can expose the Jews, his people, as a prey to the Chaldeans : ver. 14, ' And thou makest men as the fishes of the sea, and as the creeping

things that have no ruler;' from which liberty given to them, they break forth into all extremes of cruelty: ver. 15, 'They take up all with their angle; they catch them in their net, and gather them in their drag.'

4. They insult over the conquered: ver. 15, 'they rejoice and are glad.' They commit self-idolatry: ver. 16, 'Therefore they sacrifice to their net, and burn incense to their drag, because by them their portion is made fat, and their meat plenteous.'

5. How God can so long dispense with the enemies of his church, and whether he will so forsake them: ver. 17, 'Shall they therefore empty their net, and not spare continually to slay the nations?'

1. Of the ground of his contestation, 'Thou art of pure eyes.' This phrase is according to the capacity of human understanding, and it is doubly figurative:

1. In that eyes are attributed to God.
2. In that they are said to be pure.

1. It is a thing frequent in Scripture, to give the parts of a man's body to God: the eye, the ear, the hand, the heart, the foot, the bowels, the arm, the face, the back-parts; whereupon certain heretics, literally understanding those phrases, have believed and taught that God is like to man in shape of body, and that the image wherein God made man was corporeal. These heretics are called anthropomorphites, because they ascribed to God the image and corporeal likeness of man, whom some ignorant persons have used to paint in the representation of a grave old man, against the clear text of Scripture and warrant of truth.

Of this I will only tell you what St Augustine,* writing to Fortunatianus, a bishop, concerning the judgment of another bishop who maintained this heresy, saith, The text of Scripture attributing the parts of human bodies to God must not be literally understood, for then we must allow God also to have bodily wings, for we read also often of the wings and feathers of God. But, saith he, as by the wings of

* Epl. i. 11.

God we do understand divine protection, *sic cum audimus manus operationem ; pedes præsentiam ; oculos visionem ; faciem justitiam ; brachium potentiam :* so by hands, divine operation; by feet, presence; by eye, vision ; by face, justice; by hands, divine power. And to shew that *neque solus*, neither alone, *nec prior*, nor first he is of this opinion, he citeth St Jerome, St Gregory Nazianzen, St Ambrose, St Athanasius, all of the same judgment.

And surely because this error is yet in the minds of many simple and ignorant people of the world, it will be fit that you do learn that when you do either give thanks to God, or pray, or think on God, you do not conceive him in your thoughts in any such manner, but as he hath revealed himself to us in his word. God is a Spirit, eternal, immortal, invisible, infinite in wisdom, justice, holiness, power, mercy, goodness; seeing and foreseeing all things ; doing whatsoever he will in heaven and in earth, and in all deep places ; governing all things by the word of his power.

Moses, who searched as deep into this sacred and secret mystery of God, found that the face of God, that is, his heavenly nature, could not be seen, only his back parts ; that is, the effects of his attributes might be seen. No doubt God took that occasion in Moses to teach the church how they should conceive him in their thoughts: Exod. xxxiii. 23, 'Thou shalt see my back parts.'

Gregor. Nyssene. We must follow after God ; for he goeth before us, and guideth us ; as David, 'He teacheth the way that we should choose.' *Qui autem sequitur, non faciem sed tergum aspicit* (Procopius). *Invisibilia Dei videntur ex creatione.* For we must remember how tender God was of appearing in any form which might have been represented in picture or sculpture, for fear of idolatry : Deut. iv. 15, 16, 'Take ye therefore good heed unto yourselves (for ye saw no manner of similitude on the day that the Lord spake unto you in Horeb out of the midst of the fire), lest ye corrupt yourselves, and make you a graven image, the similitude of any figure,' &c.

Neither is it necessary for adoration, that we do assign any set figure to God in our thoughts, seeing every one of us doth believe that he hath a living soul in him, whereby all the parts of the body are both directed and enabled in their several offices, yet no man can conceive any set form or similitude whereunto it may be resembled.

2. Another figurative speech here is, where the prophet calleth these eyes of God pure eyes; for wickedness and evil cannot defile the sight. It is said of the fair eye of heaven, that it shineth upon the just and unjust. And David saith that God 'seeth all the thoughts of man's heart.' Why, he then seeth much vanity and much iniquity. But those are called pure eyes which do behold nothing that is evil, to approve it in itself, to abet it in our brother, to imitate it in ourselves; and in this sense the eyes of God are said to be pure, that is, abhorring sin. Again, the purity of God's eyes doth import the clear judgment of God, which is of such penetration as nothing can conceal itself from him: in which sense David saith, Ps. xi. 4, 'The Lord is in his holy temple, the Lord's throne is in heaven; his eyes behold, his eyelids try, the children of men.' Upon which words St Augustine saith, that there is *apertio* and *opertio oculorum Dei,* an opening and a covering of God's eyes.

He is said to see with his eyes when he declareth himself to see and take notice of anything; but he doth try with his eyelids, when he maketh as though he slept and considered not, winking for a time at the iniquities of men.

Our lesson from this double figure of speech is,

Doct. That God is a severe searcher and punisher of sin. For search, he 'trieth the hearts and reins;' for punishment, 'judgment begins at his own house.' This certain rule of truth we must lay hold and believe, that the justice and truth of God cannot fail. The whole course of Scripture, the experience of all times, doth make this good.

The sin of the angels that kept not their first estate was soon found out and punished. The first news we hear of them was that one of them was a tempter, and deceived our first parents.

There was a light shining in darkness, which the darkness comprehended not. The Manichees, seeing the devil went so early against God, thought and taught that there were two *principia*, two beginnings: one good god the author of all good, another evil god the author of all evil, not knowing the fall of the angels, and the mischief that they attempted against God after their fall. But they were the first example of the severe vengeance of God, of whom St Jude saith, ver. 6, 'And the angels which kept not their first estate, but left their own habitation, he hath reserved in everlasting chains, under darkness, unto the judgment of the last day.'

And for our first parents, the pure eyes of God saw their nakedness after their fall, and came himself into the garden in the cool of the day, and convinced the delinquents, and examined the fault, and gave judgment against them all, and presently executed that judgment.

Then Cain, when his sin was yet but in the bud, at the first putting forth thereof, in the casting down of his countenance, was called to account for it, God disputing the matter with him; and after, when he came to the execution of his abominable wickedness, God again well examined the evidence, convicted the prisoner, and brought him to confession of his fault, and banished him from his presence.

In all these examples, God was a speedy and a severe judge, as was fit for terror in the beginning; but after he grew more remiss, and, as the apostle saith, 1 Peter iii. 20, 'The long-suffering of God waited in the days of Noah, while the ark was a-preparing.' So that God declared himself patient and longsuffering, who had before shewed and revealed his severe justice, that the terror of his righteousness might discourage sin, and yet his gentle forbearance might invite to repentance.

Therefore, throughout the whole course of holy Scripture, we have examples of both sorts, both of quick vengeance and of favourable sufferance, that

God may be known both to be just and merciful. The reason whereof is,

1. That the danger might breed terror; for who can promise himself mercy when our just God may and doth take such quick vengeance? 'Remember Lot's wife,' that she was Lot's wife whom God favoured; that the angel pulled her out of Sodom to hasten her from their judgment; that her offence was no more than looking back, whether out of curiosity to see what God would do to Sodom, or out of unbelief, doubting the truth of the threatening, or out of love to the place, or to some persons left behind to the woe, she was made an example of present calamity, and turned into a pillar of salt. Therefore remember Lot's wife for terror, to strike fear in thee that thou sin not, lest thou be smitten so soon as thou hast offended; this to prevent sin.

2. That such as sin and find not the present wrath of God avenging sin, may make use of that patience of God to repent, lest a lingering judgment be but the whetting of a sword to a sharper cutting when it cometh. For the remissness of God doth not proceed from any respect of persons, nor from a liking of any kind of sin, but out of free and undeserved favour, and for the glory of his own mercy, that he may be feared.

Use. Who knoweth the mind of the Lord, or who hath been of his counsel? Who can tell when he is tempted to any sin, and embraceth the temptation, and committeth the sin, whether God will make him an example of his patience and mercy and long-suffering, by giving him both the time and grace of repentance, and open to him the fountain for sin and for uncleanness, to wash him and cleanse himself from his sin; or whether he will make him an example of his severe justice, in chastening his trespass with some speedy vengeance, as he did the rebellion of Korah, or the lying of Ananias and Sapphira?

Therefore our care must be to keep our heart with all diligence from conceiving sin, to take heed to our ways that we offend not in our tongue; to take heed to our foot, to our hand, that they act not sin, ever remembering that God is a jealous God, and that loveth not iniquity, and that he hath pure eyes, which cannot behold evil to allow thereof.

Herein the example of Christ is good, Ps. xvi. 8, 'I have set the Lord always before me;' for godly fear doth put God always in sight of us, and of all our ways. Let us set ourselves always in the sight of God, and answer every temptation to sin with this answer, 'Thou, O Lord, art of purer eyes than to behold evil.'

For therefore hath God so clearly revealed his majesty, power, and justice to the sons of men, Exod. xx. 20, 'That his fear may be before your eyes, that you sin not.'

The king on earth chaseth away all evil with his eye, because men fear the wrath of a king as the roaring of a lion; and shall the pure eyes of God, seeing all our ways, being about our path, and about our bed, understanding our thoughts long before, nothing awe us! Christ saith, 'Fear not them that can kill the body, and can do nothing more; but fear him that can cast both body and soul into hell fire.'

This God, that hath this power over the work of his own hands, as he hath pure eyes, from whose sight nothing can hide or conceal itself, so he hath a right hand, *inveniet dextra ejus inimicos ejus*, his right hand will find out his enemies; yea, strong is his arm, and the sword that he wieldeth is sharp; for David saith, 'he hath whetted it of purpose, to cut off from the earth the ungodly thereof;' he hath also a bow, and that is bent; he hath a quiver, and that is full of deadly arrows; and howsoever we shall slight him, our God is a consuming fire. To the elect he is *ignis in rubo*, a fire in the bush, burning, but not consuming; but to the ungodly, that make no conscience of sin, he is *ignis devorans*, a fire devouring; as David saith, 'the flame shall burn up the ungodly.'

The crying sins of our times, injustice in the courts of judgment, contempt of religion, oppression of the poor, breach of the Sabbath, profane swearing, beastly drunkenness, abominable wantonness, contentions, and such like, do give evidence against us, that there is no fear of God before our eyes, that we fear not the presence of God, we regard not his pure eyes.

We would have cured Babel of those diseases, and she is not healed; the word, which is the proper physic for these maladies, is either not heard with attention, or kept with retention; we mingle it not with faith when we hear it, so that we heap up wrath against the day of wrath. My brethren, do not so wickedly; sin not against God, sin not against your own souls, for so Moses calls Korah and his company, Num. xvi. 38; he calls them sinners against their own souls, and that are ensamples recorded for the perpetual use of the church, even for them upon whom the ends of the world shall come. When the judgment of Korah and his company was in sight, it is said, ' all Israel that were round about them fled at the cry of them;' for they said, ' Lest the earth swallow us up also.'

These records of former times are kept for us, that we might always have them in sight, that we might make it our own case, and fear before the Lord, and fly from the tents of such wicked persons, who make no conscience of the pure eyes of God beholding all their ways, lest we perish with them.

2. Upon this ground he doth dispute; for, seeing he resolveth that God is most just, and there can be no shadow of changing in him, he inquireth of him how it comes to pass that so many evils be suffered in the world, in the eye and sight of God.

Doct. From whence we are taught that in all our considerations of the carriage of things under the government of God's providence, howsoever strange the effects may seem to us, yet we must take heed that we never question either the wisdom, justice, or goodness of God. Let us resolve on that, and we may safely sit down and wonder at the effects of his will; for David saith, *Tu facis mirabilia solus*, ' Thou alone dost wonders.' And Augustine saith that God doth manage things *judicio sæpe arcano, sed semper justo*, often by secret, but always by just judgment.

And upon this holy resolution of the prophet, which giveth God his due, and no way doth tax him, but pronounceth him to be himself, I dare not receive the judgment of Mr Calvin upon this passage, because I am persuaded that he is too harsh in his censure of this prophet; and yet I find it so much against his will to find fault, that he doth what he can again when he hath wounded him to heal him again.

I honour the memory of Mr Calvin, as of a clear light set up in the church of God, and am as unwilling to tax him as I find him unwilling to tax the prophet, and therefore I wish his reader to read him out upon this place, and he shall find that it is not *motus violentus*, but *trepidationis*, not a violent, but a trembling motion that carries him. For,

1. He saith, *descendit ad humanos affectus*, he descendeth to human affections; so he may do and yet not offend.

2. He addeth, *ostendit se quodammodo vacillare*, he shews himself somewhat wavering. That cannot be defended; for the motto of a just man is *semper idem*, always the same; and it is the ungodly man who is unstable in all his ways; his heart is not established.

3. But he smiteth home when he saith, *verum quidem est, secundam partem versus affinem esse blasphemiæ*, the second part of the verse to be near akin to blasphemy; *quia obmurmurat et insimulat Deum nimiæ tarditatis*, because he murmured, and accused God of too much slackness.

Yet Mr Calvin healeth him again. Pardon him in this; for he was *in angusto*, in a strait, jealous of having the honour of God touched by the prophet, and yet tender of any touch of the charity that he did owe to the prophet; and therefore having declared his holy love to God, he doth his best to excuse the prophet, saying of him, *frænum sibi injicit et occurrit mature. Se temperat ut præveniat nimium fervorem*, he tempers himself that he might allay this too great heat. And in the end he confesseth, *quia non potest se expedire rebus tam confusis, disceptat potius secum quam cum Deo*, because he could not get out of this maze, that he reasoned with himself rather than God.

For my opinion, I acquit the prophet of any suspicion of inordinate affection in this his complaint, so long as he doth do God the right to acknowledge him both eternal and equal. I wonder not if he, and all that consider him aright in his ways, be swallowed up in the depth of admiration of them. Let any man observe that which followeth in the prophet's complaint, and he shall see great cause of wonder; but whensoever such occasion is offered to us to behold the like, let us do our God the right to confess him holy and just, and to resolve that, which way soever things go, there can be no fault in him. Therefore let us say with David, Ps. iii. 18, *Domine, tu justus es, et justa sunt judicia tua,* ' thou art just, and thy judgments are just.'

It is a good saying of old Eli the priest, when Samuel told him of the judgments of God upon his house, ' It is the Lord, let him do what seemeth him good.' Yet is it not unlawful for the children of God reverently to consider the ways of God; yea, it is a work for the Sabbath, to take the works of God into regard: Ps. xcii. 5, ' O Lord, how great are thy works, and thy thoughts are very deep. A brutish man knoweth not, neither doth a fool understand this.'

It argueth a great defect in judgment when we shall think a thought which may derogate anything from the glory of our God. For it is true, *fecit quicquid voluit,* he hath done whatever he would; so it is true *omnia bene fecit,* he hath done all things well. And we say truly of him, He hath done all things for the best; for so he doth even then when his ways do cross ours, and when those things that he doth do seem to us and to our reason as most opposite. To help which our weakness we are taught to pray, *fiat voluntas tua,* thy will be done.

Let us come then to a view of the particulars which the prophet recounteth, which God doth behold and not yet punish. And herein we shall find the prophet an orator, setting forth the iniquity of the times and the miseries of the church then, so as we may say his heart hath indited a good matter, and his tongue is the pen of a ready writer.

Here be the prophet's grievances:

1. The first is treason: ' Wherefore lookest thou upon them that deal treacherously?' Mr Calvin ren-

ders it *quare aspicis transgressores?* And so doth the Geneva translation render it, ' Why lookest thou upon the transgressors?' But that is somewhat too large, for that includeth all sorts of sinners.

Jun. *Cur intueris perfidos?* So the Chaldeans, of whom the prophet complaineth here, are set forth, as you heard, by the prophet Isaiah.

Dolus an virtus, quis in hoste requirit?

Treason is not wrought by a professed enemy in times of open war and proclaimed defiance, neither do we call the secret practices of enemies working underhand by the name of treason, they are military stratagems; but it is called treason when by corrupting some of the opposite side, the enemy doth take advantage. And this is commonly one of the mines which is carried under the states of great kingdoms, to destroy them and blow them up.

And the Author and Finisher of our salvation, though he was assaulted by professed war of the chief priests, scribes, and pharisees, yet he was put into their hand at last by treason; one of his own twelve betrayed him.

And it is the chief use of the new order of Jesuits in foreign states to corrupt the affections of subjects *ut prodant*, that they may betray.

This is a great grievance, for treasons be commonly carried with great secresy; yet the prophet saith that God looketh on, he beholdeth all the conveyances, both of projection and execution. And that is it which amazeth the prophet, that God, who loveth not treason, should look on and behold it in all the ingress and progress of it, and not stop it.

Beloved, we have a lesson from hence.

Doct. The Lord seeth treason.

Not only the great treasons wrought against states and kingdoms, but the particular falsehoods in common friendship; the private insidiations for the goods, the chastity, the good name, the life of our neighbours.

It is not any negligence in God's government of the world, or any oversight, or any forgetfulness, or any approbation of evil, that doth keep God so quiet that he sitteth in heaven; he keepeth Israel, and he neither

slumbereth nor sleepeth. Yet he looketh on while
thieves come in the night and break open a way into
men's houses, gather together and rifle, and carry away
their goods. He seeth while the secret enemy watcheth
his brother upon the way, or goeth forth with him, as
Abel did with Cain. God knew that Abel was to be
killed that day. When Joab and Amasa met, God saw
it a death; he knew that embracing would prove a stab.
Sometimes God doth detect and defeat these treasons
betimes, sometimes he letteth them go on to the very
moment of execution, yet then he disappointeth them;
but sometimes he looketh on and seeth them performed,
and hindereth them not.

This is that which the prophet would fain know, why
God, that loveth no evil, and hath power at hand to
prevent it, doth look on and see it done; for amongst
us *qui non vetat peccare cum licet, jubet*, he that when
he may hindereth not a fault, commands it. And for
man it is a true rule, that all the evil which we might
have hindered and did not, shall be put upon our account. This rule holds indeed with us, but God is
not so limited. He maketh both evil creatures, that
is, devils and wicked men, to be his servants to do his
will, and he maketh the very sins of men rods to scourge
both themselves that commit them and others.

2. The second grievance of the prophet: 'The
wicked devoureth the man that is more righteous than
he, and God holdeth his tongue.' That is, the Chaldean, who worshippeth strange gods, devoureth the
Jews, the posterity of Abraham, who, though they be
much to blame, yet they are more righteous than the
Chaldeans; and God seeth and saith nothing, whilst
the Chaldeans doth spoil Israel.

This indeed is a great grievance, to behold the afflictions of the church, and the power of the wicked against
them. It was that which put David into an extreme
ecstasy for the time; and till he went to the house of
God, and was there taught the end of such men as hurt
their betters, his foot had well nigh slipped. Our experience sheweth us much more; for the wicked sons of
Belial, the moths of our commonwealth, the rust of
our peace, how have they fed upon the fat of the land,
and by fair pretexts of common good, even devoured

the commonwealth, and made more righteous men than
they their prey, assaulting their goods, their liberty,
and peace of life, disturbing their honest callings
with dishonest encroachments, to the great prejudice
of the state! And God held his tongue many years,
although he saw it; but now he hath set open the
eyes of the politic body to detect them, and he hath
opened the mouth of that body to accuse and to condemn them.

David saith, 1 Sam. xxiv. 13, 'It is a proverb of
the ancients, Wickedness proceedeth from the wicked.'
This is wickedness in a grown degree, for the godly
be the holy ones of God. And God saith, *nolite tangere*, touch not. They do not only *tangere*, but *angere;*
yea, *devorare justiores se*, devour juster than they.

There is a natural antipathy between the seed of the
woman and the seed of the serpent. Sinners cannot
abide them that carry any face or show of religion, or
the worship of God; hating, and touching, and biting
will not serve nor satisfy, they must devour and
destroy.

Solomon saith, Prov. xii. 10, 'The tender mercies
of the wicked are cruel;' *viscera crudelia*, cruel bowels.
The wicked is ever the devourer. Observe it as a sure
rule, that church or that commonwealth which devoureth and maintaineth slaughter and effusion of blood, is
the synagogue of the wicked.

The true church is no smiter, no traitor, no plotter,
no abettor of invasions; it was ever true, *arma ecclesiæ
preces et lachrymæ*, the weapons of the church are
prayers and tears.

The church of Rome, the mother of murders, and
the nest wherein treasons breed; the nurse of Jesuits,
the incendaries of Christendom; the mint of facinorous
machinations; the cathedral and dogmatical defenders
of the lawfulness of anything that is done for their
own good, hath discovered herself to be antichristian
by this infallible mark of cruelty; she is a devourer.
It is the religion of Rome that armed the Spaniards
against Queen Elizabeth and her land in '88; the
blessing of the pope and the curse of God was upon
that enterprise. For they came to devour them that
were then more righteous than they.

It is the religion of Rome that digged the vault, that hired, that freighted the cellar under the Parliament House to blow up all; *os sepulchri*, the mouth of the grave; *os inferni*, the mouth of hell; the mouth of Rome shall gape and swallow with the best of them. Surely this is a great grievance and vexation of spirit here on earth, to see the worst sort of men prevailing, and better than they swallowed up. This is also aggravated in the manner of it, which is fully and rhetorically amplified by the prophet.

3. The next grievance amplified by a comparison, which is double, ver. 14.

(1.) They are compared to the fish of the sea.

(2.) To creeping things which have no governor.

In the first resemblance he insisteth, ver. 15. The Chaldeans are the fishermen, the Jews the fish, as you have heard; and these fishermen use, 1, the angle; 2, the net; 3, the drag, which sheweth a full devouring: as in Isa. xiv. 22, 'I will sweep it with the besom of destruction, saith the Lord of hosts.'

Compare this text with that of Joel, chap. i. 4, 'That which the palmer-worm hath left hath the locust eaten; and that which the locust hath left hath the canker-worm eaten; and that which the canker-worm hath left hath the caterpillar eaten.' For what the angle leaveth, the net taketh; and what escapeth the net, the drag doth sweep it up. Observe here with me,

1. This manner of teaching, by familiar resemblances, is much used in both Testaments; and it is a smooth and easy kind of teaching, which doth bring things to the understanding by some sensible demonstrations.

And may we not justly charge the church of Rome with cruelty to her children, that when the Spirit of God hath so laboured in both the Testaments to open himself to the understanding of the simple, the oracle of Trent shall put out the candle, and turn men to seek the way of life darkling, without the light of the word, which they shall not be suffered to read, for fear of understanding by it their impostures. It can be no good religion, wherein they that know the least, and believe the most, are made to believe they are in the best case.

2. I find here that there is a wisdom of God to be learned out of the natural and moral ways of life: as the stork for natural affection; the ant for providence; the spider for industry; the bee for art, industry, and providence. When we see dogs pursuing an hare or a deer, thus do the projectors of our time hunt the commonwealth. When we see fishermen cast in their nets, thus do the oppressors of their brethren; all is fish that comes into their net. A wise and sober judgment may make good use of all that his eye seeth, to behold therein either the goodness of God to man, or the good or evil that cometh from one man to another.

3. In that he doth use two comparisons and resemblances, to fishes on the sea, and to creeping things on earth, we see that both sea and land do afford examples. And the prophet is very near touched with the calamities of his brethren, that which way soever he looketh, he beholdeth some representation of their woe. It is the manner of grief to take all occasions to figure and represent to itself its own sorrow.

4. Where he resembleth them to creeping things which have no ruler over them.

Two things do aggravate the calamity represented thereby:

(1.) That which God brought upon Edom, 'I have made thee small;' for these creeping things of the earth are of small strength, and are subject to the foot of man and beast to tread on them. Thus God hath made the Jews the very earth for their enemies to go over them; and this is the punishment of their pride; for pride must have a fall, and these towering fowls of the air must be turned into creeping worms of the earth.

(2.) They have no ruler over them. This is here set forth as a point of especial note, to express the unhappiness of a people to be without a ruler; and therefore anabaptists are wise politicians, that would have no magistrate; but the punishment of the Jews is just, that they should be without a ruler.

Because they did so much abuse authority and rule, that the very seat of judgment were corrupted; the wicked is plaintiff, and the godly defendant: 'The wicked compasseth about the righteous, therefore wrong judgment proceedeth.'

Better no rulers at all, than such as David describeth, 'Thou seest a thief, and thou consentest with him.' A companion of thieves, whose justice is like that on Salisbury Plain, Deliver thy purse. Perchance on both sides.

But rule and magistracy is the ordinance of God, as St Paul teacheth; and God, by his subordinate rulers on earth, carrieth a sword, and not in vain. Without this, as when there was no king in Israel, every man doth what seemeth good in his own eyes; which doth utterly destroy the body, not only disfigure the face of a commonwealth.

5. Observe also here, the outrage of the ungodly when they find any way open for their violence; for they come in like a flood, that hath made itself way through the weak banks, and deluge all.

Here is angle, and net, and drag, as before: 'The wicked compasseth about the righteous.' Which way shall the righteous escape? 'As if a man did fly from a lion, and a bear met him; or went into an house, and leaned his hand on a wall, and a serpent bit him,' Amos v. 19. This made David so earnest with God not to fall into the hands of man.

There is nothing more cruel than a multitude of ungodly men, that have no fear of God before their eyes.

Certum est in silvis inter spelæa ferarum malle pati; the teeth of these dogs, the horns of these bulls of Bashan, the horns of these unicorns, the tusks of these wild boars, the paws of these lions and bears are mentioned in Scripture often, to express the fury and outrage of the wicked.

As Edom cried in the day of Jerusalem, Raze it. 'If the foundation be destroyed, what can the righteous do?' Ps. xi. 3.

Judge now, is it not a great grievance to see and feel the force and fury of the wicked carry all before them, and neither their own conscience nor the laws of men restrain them, and God sit still, look on, and hold his peace ? This is that which grieves the prophet to the heart. But God that seeth it hath pure eyes, and hath a right hand that will find out all his enemies.

Amos will tell us that God hath his angle too, and his net, and his drag: chap. ix. 11, 'I saw the Lord standing upon the altar; and he said, I will slay the last of them with the sword: he that fleeth of them shall not fly away; and he that escapeth of them shall not be delivered. Though they dig into hell, there shall my hand take them; though they climb up into heaven, thence will I bring them down: and though they hide themselves in the top of Carmel, I will search and take them out thence; and though they be hid from my sight in the bottom of the sea, thence will I command the serpent, and he shall bite them: and though they go into captivity before their enemies, thence will I command the sword, and it shall slay them: I will set mine eyes upon them for evil, and not for good.'

Let us not be discouraged, for the wise man saith comfortably to us: Eccles. v. 8, 'If thou seest the oppression of the poor, and violent perverting of judgment and justice in a province, marvel not at the matter: for he that is higher than the highest regardeth; and there be higher than they.'

Our commonwealth grew foul, the hand of the oppressor was stretched out, and they that pretended to be the physicians of the diseases of this state gave it a potion of deadly wine, that it grew sick, and drawing on even to death, the hearts of true patriots failed them. The poor cried out; the rich could not say of that which he possessed, *Hæc mea sunt*, these are mine; seats of justice, instead of judgment, yielded wormwood, *et ecce clamor*, and behold a cry, even the loud voice of grievances. But God awaked, as one out of sleep; and what the angle of the magistrate and the net of the king could not take, the drag of the parliament is now cast out to fetch it in; and we have gracious promises that we shall see religion better established, and justice better administered, the moths that fretted our garments destroyed, the caterpillar, the cankerworm, and the palmer-worm, the projectors of our times that devoured the fruits of the earth, and drew the breasts of the commonwealth dry into their own vessels, both detected and punished; yea, that we shall see Jerusalem in prosperity all our days. It is the music of the voices of both houses of parliament, and he that is *rector chori*, the master of the choir, doth set for them both, 'Let peace be within thy walls, and plenteousness within thy palaces.'

This fills our mouths with laughter, and our tongues with singing. The keeper of Israel is awake, and hath not been an idle spectator of those tragedies that have been acted here amongst us; he hath but tarried a time, till the abominable wickedness of the sons of Belial was found worthy to be punished.

6. One note more remaineth. The prophet doth find that all this evil doth not come upon the Jews by chance, by the malice of Satan, or the proud covetous cruelty of the Chaldeans; for he saith to God, 'Thou makest men as the fishes of the sea.' Here is the hand of God, and the counsel of God in all this.

And God taketh it upon himself, as you have heard before: vers. 5, 6, 'Behold ye among the heathen, and regard, and wonder marvellously; for I will work a work in your days, which you will not believe. Lo, I raise up the Chaldeans,' &c.

For though sin brought in punishment, yet God's justice is the author of all evils of this kind, and the inflicter of punishment. *Tu domine fecisti,* saith the psalmist, Thou, Lord, hast done it.

And I have taught you that the wisdom and goodness of God can make use of evil men for the correction of his church; they be ingredients in the dose that God giveth to his diseased people to purge them.

Therefore let not our hearts fret at those rods, which have no strength to use themselves, but rather stoop to the right hand of God, who manageth them for our castigation. We have no fence against these judgments, but a good conscience endeavouring to serve God sincerely, for that either diverteth the judgment, that the sun shall not smite us by day nor the moon by night, or it maketh us able to bear it, as from the hand of a father that cannot find in his heart to hurt us.

You heard the faith of this prophet concerning this point, 'We shall not die: thou hast ordained them for judgment, thou hast established them for correction; only let us not be incorrigible, nor faint when we are rebuked, ' for he chasteneth every son that he receiveth.'

4. The fourth grievance is the pride and vainglory of the proud Chaldeans; expressed in two things:

1. In the joy of their victories, ' They rejoice and are glad.'

2. In their attribution of this glory to themselves, which is self-idolatry.

1. They rejoice and are glad.

The enemies of the church have their time to laugh; the wise man calleth it the candle of the wicked; it lighteth them for a time; it is *unius diei hilaris insania;* they dance to the pipe, and drink their wine in bowls; they eat of the fat, and they remember not the affliction of Joseph to pity it: they remember it to result* over Joseph.

The king and Haman sat drinking together when the edict was gone forth for the destruction of the Jews, and then the city Shushan was perplexed, Esther iii. 15.

The grief of the church is the joy of the ungodly; it is David's complaint, Ps. xxxv. 21, ' Yea, they opened their mouth wide against me, and said, Aha! our eye hath seen it.' They have David's deprecation, ver. 25, ' Let them not say in their hearts, Ah, so we would have it: let them not say, We have swallowed them up.' They have David's imprecation, ver. 26, ' Let them be ashamed, and brought to confusion, that rejoice at mine hurt: let them be clothed with shame and dishonour that magnify themselves against me.' He was in the very passion of this prophet for this: ver. 17, 'Lord, how long wilt thou look on?'

St Augustine upon these words saith, *Quod capiti,*

* Qu. ' insult '? or ' exult '?—ED.

hoc corpori, what was to the head, that to the body, for thus did the Jews rejoice in the cross of Christ; they had their will of him; it is *vox capitis*, the voice the head: 'But in mine adversity they rejoiced, and gathered themselves together against me.'

St Augustine's comfort against this calamity is, *Quicquid faciunt, Christus in cœlo est: honoravit ille pœnam suam, jam crucem suam in omnium frontibus fixit*, which hath reference to the signing with the sign of the cross in the baptism of Christians, then in the use of the church.

Reason 1. The reason of this joy in the wicked at the sorrows of the church is because the wicked do want the knowledge and fear of God; they do not know that God is the protector of the church, but because they see them in outward things most neglected, they judge them given over of God and forsaken. David's complaint, 'For mine enemies speak against me, and they that lay wait for my soul take counsel together, saying, God hath forsaken him: persecute and take him, for there is none to deliver him.' For they measure the light of God's countenance according to the scantling of outward prosperity.

Reason 2. The wicked want the unity of the Spirit, which is the bond of peace; for the God of peace is not in their ways; they love not, they call not upon God. Charity is a theological virtue; where there is not true religion, there can be no true love.

I am sure this is a true rule in divinity, whatsoever human policy have to say against it. Christ foretold his disciples, John xv. 17-19, 'In the world ye shall have affliction. These things I command you, that ye love one another. If the world hate you, ye know it hated me before it hated you. If ye were of the world, the world would love his own.' Charity is the bond of peace only to the children of peace; and they that in religion do stand in times of contradiction, it is not possible to fit them with a girdle.

This point is thus made profitable to us.

Use 1. For ourselves. Seeing religion is the best bond of brotherhood, and where no religion is, there can be no sincere love, let us labour to grow up more and more in the knowledge and love and obedience of the truth, that we may be fortified throughout both in our bodies and in our souls and spirits, for this maketh us all one body; and we can no more fall out than the members of our natural bodies can disagree one with another. The orator spake ignorantly of the union of affections by the same country: *Patria omnes in se charitates complexa est*, the love of country comprehends all love; for we know that we have had many unnatural fugitives which have abandoned their country and plotted treasons abroad against it, and have returned full of foreign venom and poison to corrupt the affections of the natural subjects of their sovereign, with hatred of religion and peace.

That is only true of religion, for that so sweeteneth the affections of men, that, as they are content to do anything they can one for another, so they can be content to endure anything one for another, to bear for one another's sakes, and to put up at one another's hands many things, to forgive ' not seven times, but seventy times seven times.' For the true church, as Bernard saith, doth *suspendere verbera, producere ubera*, hide the rod and lay forth the breasts.

2. For our children, we must instruct them betimes in the knowledge and fear of God, that they may learn the doctrines of piety and charity, and may be taught to be members one of another.

3. This setteth a mark upon the enemies of God, because where there is strife and envying, where there is hatred and malice, are not they carnal?

If it be our duty to rejoice with them that rejoice, and to weep with them that weep, they belong not to the fold of Christ that rejoice at the weeping, or weep at the rejoicing, of their brethren.

4. This declareth the vanity of the joy of the world, for seeing their rejoicing is evil, it cannot be long lived; and therefore it is said, that ' the candle of the wicked shall be put out,' but ' the joy of the elect shall no man take from them.' Therefore, ' woe to them that laugh here,' for their ' harp shall be turned into mourning, and their organs into the voice of them that weep;' but 'blesssed are they that mourn, for they shall be comforted;' and the time shall come

when they shall rejoice over them who have joyed at their pains; and 'rejoice over her, O heaven, and ye holy apostles and prophets, for God hath avenged you on her.'

2. They attribute the glory of the conquest to themselves, they understand not who raised them up against the Jews, who gave them strength to fight, and who gave them victory; therefore they burn incense to their own nets, and kiss their own hands, and thank themselves for all. Here is the growth of iniquity; for first they exercise all cruel inhumanity against the Jews, then they rejoice over them, and then doth their sin grow out of measure sinful, for they forbear not to provoke God himself by their pride of heart, robbing him of the glory of his own work, and ascribing it to themselves.

This even the light of nature hath detected to be most injurious to God, and most dangerous to men, for they that have any natural notion of the Deity, know that the whole glory of all achievements belongs to that supreme Power which ruleth all.

In the great consultation wherein Xerxes* made a proposition of war against Greece, having a special grudge at the Athenians, Mardonius was an earnest persuader to the attempt, but Artabanus, son of Histaspes, the uncle of Xerxes the king, a grave, aged man, dissuaded it. His great argument was drawn from a consideration of the danger of greatness to which the king, his nephew, aspired to be lord of all, and urgeth that old observation which Horace the poet since used, *Feriuntque summos fulmina montes*, the lightning strikes the highest tops. His rule is, *Gaudet Deus eminentissima quæque deprimere, quia Deus neminem alium quam seipsum sinit magnifice de se sentire.* The point here notable is,

Doct. The prosperity of this world doth fill the hearts of men with pride and vain estimation of themselves.

At the first, when things succeeded well with the Chaldean, he gave the honour thereof to his idol god, as you have heard, but now he taketh it all upon

---

* Herod. l. 7. Polyrrima.

himself; his own net, that is, his wit and strength, hath done all, and he is now his own god. The wise man saith, Prov. i. 42, 'The prosperity of fools shall destroy them.'

They that worship strange gods, and do ascribe all their fair betidings to them, do commit idolatry and sin grievously; yet these do confess a Deity, and acknowledge the power though not the person of God in supreme agency; but they that assume all to themselves deny a Deity, or disable it, so as that they may work without any borrowed help from thence; so that the greatest idolatry that is or can be committed is that pride of heart which assumeth to itself the glory of prosperous success. And let men take heed of this temptation, for it is flattering and fair spoken, and our corrupt nature is very prone to give it entertainment. This is one of the two things that Agur, the son of Jakeh, did pray against: Prov. xxx. 8, 9, 'Remove far from me vanity and lies.' This opinion of ourselves is well termed vanity, for nothing can be more empty and void than it is; and it is as well called *lies*, for nothing can be more untrue than that we should be able as of ourselves to do anything for ourselves.

The danger, ' Lest if I be full I deny thee, and say, who is the Lord ?

Here are two things in the Chaldeans, which Job doth protest against, and imprecate himself if he be guilty of either of them.

The former evil, Job xxxi. 29, ' If I rejoiced at the destruction of them that hated me ;' and this, ver. 27 ' If my heart hath been secretly enticed, or my mouth hath kissed my hand,' this also were an iniquity to be punished by the judge, for I should have denied that God that is above.

It is saint Gregory's note upon that text : *Per manum operatio, per os locutio designatur; manum ergo osculatur ore suo, qui laudat quod facit et testimonio propriæ locutionis soli virtutem tribuit operis.*

Let us remember our *sicut in cælo,* ' as in heaven.' For in heaven the twenty-four elders cast their crowns before the throne, which, as St Gregory saith, is, *Certaminum suorum victorias non sibi tribuere, sed authori, ut ad illum referant gloriam laudis, à quo se sciunt accepisse vires certaminis.*

To arrogate to ourselves God's glory, this in Job's judgment is *iniquitas maxima*, the greatest iniquity; for *peccatum ex infirmitate spem non perdit*, sin of infirmity loseth not hope, but presumption destroyeth hope utterly, and so faith also, ' for faith is the ground of things hoped for.' Against this let us hear the apostle: Gal. v. 26, ' Let us not be desirous of vainglory ;' this is that dangerous sin of pride, which doth put ourselves into the place and room of God, and usurpeth his rights.

Our Saviour hath sufficiently discouraged this sin in a few words to such as do rightly understand him; for when the disciples returned to him, Luke x. 17, and said, ' Lord, the devils are subject to us through thy name,' Christ answered, ver. 18, 'I beheld Satan as lightning fall from heaven.' Greg., *Ut in discipulis suis elationem premeret ; judicium ruinæ retulit, quod ipse magister elationis accepit.*

The very way to begin the true worship and service of God in us, is to put off ourselves by an humble and true confession, that of ourselves we are able for no good work. I do not say to demerit God, but not to do ourselves any good. The wisdom that guideth us is from above, the strength that enableth us is *dextra excelsi*, the right hand of the Most High. This shews which way the glory and praise of all must go.

Considering then the fault of these Chaldeans in this vanity of boasting themselves,

1. Let us come to decline it as a disease.
2. Let us embrace the remedies thereof.

Use. 1. Decline it.

(1.) Because it trespasseth that same *primum et magnum mandatum*, the first and great commandment; for it robbeth God of his glory, and assumeth it to ourselves ; and God hath sworn that he will not admit any partner or sharer with him in glory.

(2.) It connumerateth us with the children of Satan, for he is the father of all the sons of pride.

(3.) It exterminates charity ; for it maketh a man's own will the rule of his actions, and not the will of

God, which maketh us the prevaricators of the second like commandment to the first, *diliges proximum sicut teipsum*, Thou shalt love thy neighbour as thyself.

(4.) It maketh us liable to the severest vengeance of God, for God resisteth the proud; and if they perish whom God doth not assist, what hope can they have whom God doth resist?

(5.) It strippeth us out of all those graces and common favours of the Holy Ghost which we have; for when God seeth that we employ his talent to our own advantage, he will surely take it from us, seeing he took from him that employed not his talent to his advantage; for it is a greater sin to be a false than to be an idle servant.

(6.) There is no vice that becomes a man worser than self-opinion. We esteem one poor and proud very odious; and such are they that ascribe anything to themselves, because we are not able of ourselves, to think, to move, to live, to subsist, without our God.

(7.) There is no vice that pleaseth Satan better than self-confidence, for that quitteth God's part in us, and separateth us from God, which is all that Satan seeks, for then he hath sure possession, and all that he holdeth is in peace.

(8.) A proud man, that ascribeth all to himself, must needs be unthankful. I may stir up all the inconveniences of self-opinion with this, for it is an old truth, *Ingratum si dixeris, omnia dixeris*, Say he is unthankful, and you have said all. This is a full imputation; and St Bernard saith, *Ingratitudo est ventus urens, siccans sibi rorem misericordiæ, fluenta gratiæ*.

2. The remedies.

These we may reduce to these few.

(1.) A frequent and serious consideration of ourselves, what we were by creation, what we are by our fall; for so we shall find how poor and impotent we are in ourselves, how we have no strength to do anything, but we are debtors to God for all. All that we have is borrowings; *quid habes O homo quod non accepisti?* We have lost the freedom of our will to anything that is good; we do carry about us *legem membrorum, corpus peccati*, so that our strength is weakness, our wisdom is folly, our friendship with the world enmity with God.

(2.) The clearest mirror to behold ourselves in, is the holy word of God, which reporteth to us the story of our creation, and of our fall, which openeth and revealeth God to us in his justice, holiness and wisdom, and power and mercy.

(3.) Let us set God always before us, and the nearer we approach to him, the more shall we perceive whereof we are made, and we shall then remember that we are but dust; we shall perceive wherefore we are made, namely, to live in the obedience and service of our Maker; to bestow all our time constantly therein, even to the end, to glorify God in our bodies and in our souls.

We shall see how unable we are to perform any part of this duty without God, and how we stand obnoxious to the curse of the law, for either omitting the duties which we should perform, or committing anything against that just law. What have we then to be proud of, seeing 'in him, and for him, and by him are all things'?

(4.) Let us often revolve and recount the good favours of God to us, and remember all his benefits, and consider what he hath done for us; and we shall find that there is a full stream of favour coming towards us, whether we sleep or awake, whether we drink of that brook in the way or not.

The apostle joineth two precepts together, which do sweetly serve to exercise a godly and Christian life: 'Pray continually; in all things give thanks;' which do shew that all good gifts come from above to us, and therefore all our holy duties must direct themselves that way; and as our help cometh from those hills, so our eyes must be ever to those hills. 'It is not bread that man doth live by, but by every word that proceedeth from the mouth of God;' it is not the letter of the word that quickeneth us, but the Spirit.

Our whole help is in the name of the Lord, who hath made heaven and earth; 'hallowed be that name,' 'we are his people, and the sheep of his pasture; let us go into his gates with thanksgiving, and into his courts with praise; let us be thankful to him, and speak good of his name.' Let us do this faithfully, and we shall see it is no thank to our own net, or drag, that our portion is fat, and our meat plenteous; for none but he filleth the hungry with good things. Peter and his company, though they had their nets, and fished all night, yet they caught nothing, when at Christ's word they let fall their net and made a great draught, they knew whom to thank for it. *A domino factum est hoc*, this is the Lord's doing, is the voice of the church; therefore, *non nobis, non nobis*, twice he putteth it from ourselves, *sed nomini tuo da gloriam*, 'not unto us, but unto thy name give the glory.'

5. *Grievance.* Ver. 17, 'Shall they therefore empty their net, and not spare continually to slay the nations?'

He continueth his former figurative manner of speech, and presseth his grievance; shall those fishing Chaldeans, when they have filled their net with fish, empty it, and return to another fishing? will it hold out that they shall go from nation to nation, and make all theirs as they go?

The grievance is, that the prophet doth not see any end of their cruel persecutions as yet, for the lingering afflictions, which gather increase of strength by time, do threaten final ruin, whereas violent extremities spend themselves into vanity and nothing.

Two things are here feared.

1. The hurt that they may do, if they may fill and empty, and fill again their net as often as they will.

2. The pride of heart, that they may gather by the vain-glory of their conquests. The point here considerable is, that,

Doct. The ungodly man hath no bowels.

Cain must kill Abel his own natural brother, and Judas must betray innocent blood. They that be once fleshed in the blood of men, can make no spare thereof; there is *oculus in sceptro*, but not *oculus in gladio*, an eye in the sceptre, not in the sword. Agag's sword made many women childless. The growing monarchies ruined all before them as they went, and overflowed all as a deluge; nations and kingdoms that prevented not sacking and destruction with timely dedition, perished before them. But it is a sign of an unestablished state, when the foundation thereof is laid in blood; and such as must be watered in blood to make them grow, shall have an informer against them; *vox sanguinis fratris tui clamat de terra*, the voice of thy brother's blood crieth from the earth.

This makes all that love the gates of Sion, and take pleasure in the prosperity of our Jerusalem, to give God no rest in their earnest devotions, praying him not to deliver our church into the hands of papists, because it is a bloody religion, such as doth hazard princes more than common men; which doth bear them out in murders, and legitimateth massacres for the safety and increase of their church.

2. It is wisdom out of the present state of things, to forecast what may come hereafter, as the prophet doth; the Chaldeans must come and invade the land, they shall fill their net with fish. God hath spoken it; it is like to be a merry time with them, they shall rejoice and be glad. They are like to grow very proud upon it, *sacrificabunt lagena sua*, &c. They shall sacrifice to their net. But shall this conquest so flesh them, that they shall empty their nets, and fish again amongst the nations, and not cease to shed blood?

Hezekiah hath the name of a good king; he prayed to God, 'Let there be peace,' or, as the king's Bible reads, 'Is it not good that there be peace and truth in my days?' But careful princes will look beyond their own days, and fit their designs to the good of posterity. Present evils, being in their growth, threaten future dangers; and we say of them as our Saviour doth, 'These are but the beginnings of sorrows,' and there is fear that there will be *semper deterior posterior dies*, the latter times will be the worser. The best remedy is to awake the tender love of God to his church, with an expostulation, Shall they do this, O Lord? Thy will be done. Shall they do it continually? Wilt thou suffer it? When the time is come, he will have mercy.

CHAPTER II

VER. 1. *I will stand upon the watch, and set me upon the tower, and will watch to see what he will say unto me, and what I shall answer when I am reproved.*

In this chapter God answereth all the prophet's grievances, and it containeth two parts.

1. The prophet's attendance upon God for his answer, ver. 1.
2. The Lord's answer, in the rest of the chapter.

In the first,
The prophet having disputed with God, and as his name importeth, having *wrestled* with him, doth re-resolve,

I will stand upon the watch, and set me upon the tower, alluding to the military practice of soldiers, who appoint some in some eminent place to observe the enemy, and to give timely warning of their doings.

And seeing God hath declared himself an enemy to the Jews, by all those evils which he hath threatened to bring upon them, the prophet watcheth him, and attendeth to receive further advertisement from himself concerning his purpose toward them.

I will watch to see what he will say unto me; for the secrets of the Lord are revealed unto them that fear him. 'And God spake in the mouth of all the prophets, which have been since the world began.'

Neither doth the prophet attend God out of a curiosity, *scire ut sciat*, to know only, as Bernard speaks; but that he may know what to answer for God when he is reproved, or as the margin saith much better, when he is argued with, and others come to dispute with him upon those grievances, as he hath done with God; for you must understand, that in all the former complaints this prophet hath not argued as a particular man, but as undertaking the cause of the church, and sustaining the persons of all his afflicted brethren, for whose sakes, that he may satisfy them, and for God's sake, whose minister he is, that he may know how to maintain to them the cause of God's wisdom and justice, he doth now attend God's answer.

By this standing upon the watch and upon the tower, in this place, is meant the prophet's attending upon a further revelation of the will of God concerning these grievances, because in those times God did speak to his prophets by visions, and dreams, and secret inspirations. And holy men then had access to him immediately, whereby they knew the mind of God, and he did communicate to them his counsels. Yet so as he put them to it to await his good leisure, and to expect his answer. So David, in his own case, 'I will hear what the Lord God will say unto me.'

These words do well express the whole duty of a faithful prophet, and minister of the word, consisting of two parts.

1. His information of himself, *implet cisternam*, he fills the cistern.

2. His instruction of others, for then he will turn the cock.

In the first observe,

1. His wisdom: he will borrow all his light from the sun. 'What will he say unto me?'

2. His vigilancy: 'I will stand upon the watch.'

3. His patient expectation: 'I will set me upon the tower.'

4. His holy care, to see what will be said to him.

1. His wisdom.

He will take his information from the mouth of God; teaching us,

Doct. That the faithful minister of God must speak only in the Lord's message. He must see before he say. He must first be a seer and then a speaker, and he must not go from the instructions which God shall give him, to speak more or less.

This is our wisdom and understanding, to take our light from the Father of lights, to gather our wisdom from him that is wisest; 'Whose foolishness is wiser than man,' as the apostle telleth us.

Reason 1. Because of our nature which is corrupt, so our reason and judgment; subject to errors and mistakes, as we see in Nathan, who encouraged David in his purpose of building a temple, which in his human reason seemed a good intention, and David a fit person to undertake it. But God directed him to repeal that commission, and to assign that work to Solomon, David's son.

Reason 2. Because we are ambassadors from God; and ambassadors go not of themselves, but are sent; and they must remember whose persons they bear, and be careful to speak according to their instructions.

Use 1. This as it is a direction to us to limit our ministry, that we may not do more or less than our errand;—

Use 2. So it is a rule for you to whom we are sent, to receive or refuse our ministry, accordingly as you shall justify our preachings by the will of God, revealed in the sacred canon of Scripture; searching the Scriptures as the men of Berea did, whether those things which we teach be so or not. And if any shall in the name of God broach or vent the doctrines of men, you may say to him, as Nehemiah said to Sanballat, Neh. vi. 8, 'There are no such things as thou sayest, but thou feignest them out of thine own heart.'

But take heed you exceed not this example of Nehemiah; for he did not charge Sanballat thus, till he perceived that God had not sent him, but that he pronounced this prophecy.

For many hearers are so seasoned with prejudice against their teachers, that if any thing sound not to the just tune of their own fancies, they will suddenly quarrel it. Yet, as Gamaliel saith, 'If the counsel be of God, it will stand, whosoever oppose it.'

Use 3. This reproveth those forward intruders into the Lord's harvest, who come unsent, and bring not their sickle with them; they will work without tools, and they will teach before they have learned. Like the foolish virgins, they would spend of the wise virgins' oil; they do *sapere ex commentario*, and take their sermons upon trust, hearkening what God hath said to others, and not tarrying till God speak to them. It is no wonder if these merchants do break who set up without a stock; they be but broken cisterns; though some water run through them, they hold none.

The faithful minister must not only observe *quid dicit Dominus*, what the Lord saith, but *quid dicit mihi*, what he saith to me. He must have the warrant of his own mission from a special illumination of his own understanding, or else his trumpet will never give a certain sound.

Use 4. This bindeth the hearer to affection. For if the Spirit speaketh to the churches, then *qui habet aures audiendi audiat;* 'He that hath ears let him hear.' *Est Deus in nobis*, God is in us. They do not flatter us as they did Herod, and we shall never die of the worms for receiving that testimony of our ministry, if we deal faithfully, that say of our preaching, 'The voice of God, and not of man;' for St Paul testifieth of the Thessalonians, 1 Thes. ii. 13, 'For this cause also thank we God, because, when ye received the word of God which ye heard of us, ye received it not as the word of men, but, as it is in truth, the word of God, which effectually worketh also on you that believe.'

Beloved, it is true that we that are now the witnesses of God, have not that open access to him that the prophet had, to receive immediate instructions from his own mouth. But Christ saith, *Sicut misit me Pater, ita et ego mitto vos,* 'As the Father sent me, so send I you.' And he telleth his Father how he hath provided for his church till his second coming: John xvii. 8, 'I have given them the word which thou gavest me, and they have received them;' and having so done, he said unto them, *Ite et docete,* 'Go and teach.'

When thou comest then to church, and hearest Moses and the prophets, and the psalms, which was the manna wherewith God fed the fathers before the incarnation of Christ, when the veil of the temple was up, remember what Abraham said to the rich man, *Habent Mosen et prophetas, audiant eos,* 'They have Moses and the prophets, let them hear them.' That is the way to keep out of hell. When thou hearest the voice of the Son of God in the gospel, the veil of the temple being torn from the top to the bottom, Christ now revealed to thee with open face, take heed thou despise not him that speaketh to thee in the ministry of a mortal man. This is a treasure which is brought unto you in earthen vessels; value the vessels at their own worth in themselves, but yet regard them above their worth for their use, for they bring you the treasures of wisdom and knowledge, enough to make you wise unto salvation, sufficient to beget faith in you, by which you may overcome the world: enough to make you perfect, throughly perfect, to all good works. This is done by our ministry, if you will hear God in us; and what would you desire more than to be taught how to become wise and honest? for such are not afraid of the parliament, and say with St Paul, 1 Cor. iv. 3, 'With me it is a very small thing that I should be judged of you, or of man's judgment.'

2. The vigilancy of the prophet, 'I will stand upon the watch.'

Amongst the great titles of honour and service that are given to the ministers of the word in Scripture, this is one; they are called *watchmen*. It is God's word to Ezekiel, chap. iii. 17, ' Son of man, I have made thee a watchman unto the house of Israel: therefore hear the word at my mouth, and give them warning from me,' which is repeated in the same words, chap. xxxiii. 7, as the margin of the king's Bible directeth you. This correspondence must be between God and his minister; for if God do make us watchmen over the house of Israel, then, with Habakkuk, we must stand upon the watch.

Let not us plead the trust of God committed to us, except we can plead our faithfulness in the discharge of that trust.

This is indeed an honour done to the prophets and ministers of the church, to commit the church of God to our care; but the burden of this care, to keep watch, is exceeding great. 'A necessity is laid upon me, and woe be to me if I preach not the gospel.'

Here be two things in this office:

1, To watch; 2, To give warning.

1. Some can watch, but they can give no warning, ministers of good and preaching lives, but not apt to teach, which St Paul requires in his ministers, of whom St Jerome saith, *Innocens sine sermone conversatio, quantum prodest exemplo, tantum nocet silentio.*

2. Some will sometimes give warning, but they cannot always watch; preach learnedly when they preach, but they have not learnt out all their lesson of the apostle: *Cave tibi et doctrinæ, in his persta,* ἐπίμενε. Continue in all things; it requires incumbency, as the law calleth it.

3. But if we will do our duties, we must do both. Some would fain do both, and cannot get a watchman's place: there is none void; for, be the people never so empty, yet *ecclesia est plena*, the church is full. All is not well that way: the church complains, and they that have laboured abundantly to enable themselves for this watch are too much searched and examined too narrowly for their gifts.

Others have a watch, but they do not with the prophet stand upon it: either they sit at ease, or they sleep it out soundly. This prophet promiseth to stand in readiness for action and execution of his charge.

Beloved, many will not believe it, but we feel it: if we make conscience of our duties in our calling, that our vocation is laborious, this watching in all weathers, and this robbing of our temples of their timely rest, to attend the watch over your souls, as those that must give an account to God for ourselves and for you, is an honourable burden, τις ἱκανος, who is sufficient?

1. *Vigilat hostis*, the enemy watcheth; he compasseth the earth to and again; he goeth about like a roaring lion; he is ever either reaching out an apple of temptation, as to Eve, or stretching out an arm of provocation, as to the blessed virgin; *gladius pertransibit animam tuam*.

We must keep you waking, that he bring not upon you the spirit of slumber; we must awake you if you sleep in sin, that he surprise you not. *Custos Israelis non dormit*, 'the keeper of Israel slumbereth not;' Alexander lies down to sleep without fear, because he leaves Parmenio, his faithful counsellor, waking; David will lay him down in peace, and take his rest, seeing God doth make him dwell in safety: *Dominus dat dilectis suis somnum*.

Yet let us observe two things concerning our sleep, for the apostle saith, 1 Thes. v. 6, 'Therefore let us not sleep as do others,' ὡς οἱ λοιποί, as unbelievers; Lyranus, *qui sunt increduli*, λοιποί, such as are left out of the church, and out of God's fold to the world, let us not sleep so. How then?

1. Before our sleep let us take David's example for our *donec*, until: 'I will not give sleep to mine eyes, nor slumber to mine eyelids, *until* I find out a place for the Lord,' Ps. cxxxii. 4, 5; that is, saith Augustine, *Donec inveniam locum Deo meo in me*, till I find a place for God in me; for God doth delight to dwell with the humble, and such as are of a contrite heart, Isa. lxvi. And Christ saith, 'Behold, I stand at the door and knock; if any man open to me, I will come

in to him.' In the letter, David sweareth to take no rest till he have found out a place for the building of the temple ; that was David's care.

This is our *donec*, until, till we have done our especial service to God, which concerns us in our calling; let us not think of sleep till we have consecrated ourselves as temples for the Holy Ghost to dwell in.

2. Let us in sleep take the example of the church, Cant. v. 2, 'I sleep, but my heart waketh ; it is the voice of my beloved, saying, Open to me ;' that is, let our sleep be moderate, so sanctified by our prayer that we may say with the church, Cant. iii. 1, ' By night on my bed I sought him whom my soul loveth.'

Thus doth the faithful watchman of Israel take heed to himself and to his doctrine, to himself and to his flock, as the shepherds to whom the angels appeared, giving them notice of the birth of Christ, ' They kept watch by night because of their flock ;' ' Blessed is that servant whom the master, when he cometh, shall find so doing.'

3. His patient expectation, 'I will set me upon the tower, and will watch to see.'

God doth not always reveal himself and his will to his minister : he must tarry God's leisure and wait his times.

Sometimes God doth withdraw his light from the minister for the punishment of the people, and will not let him see a danger that is coming, that he may chasten the sins of his people with the rods of men. Sometime he doth shut up the door of utterance, and will not let them give warning of the wrath to come to punish their sin. Therefore Saint Paul willeth the Ephesians, chap. vi. 18, 19, ' Praying always with all manner of supplication for all men, and for me, that utterance may be given me.'

Beloved, we watch for you, we pray for you, we preach to you ; whilst we stand upon these towers to give you warning, pray you for us that God would be pleased to make us sufficient for this holy service. When Paul and Silas went to preach, Acts xv. 40, they were ' commended of the brethren to the grace of God ;' ' pray the Lord of the harvest, *ut mittat operarios*, that he would send forth labourers.'

We do not stand upon these towers to keep watch for ourselves only, but for you ; and whensoever we come into a pulpit, your thoughts must be ready to say to us, as Cornelius did to Peter, Acts x. 33, 'Now therefore we are all here present before God, to hear all things that are commanded thee of God.'

The care imposed on us is greater than the care of the king and the magistrate. To which of them hath he said at any time, Feed my sheep, feed my lambs ? ' Obey them that have the rule over you, and submit yourselves, for they watch for your souls as those that must give an account,' Heb. xiii. 17.

Wonder not at our infirmities, and do not make the worst of our weakness, for we stand upon the tower, and suffer many a blast which cometh not near you. No sort of men lie so open to Satan's force and fury as we do ; he vexeth us with all his storms. When Joshua stood before the angel of the Lord to receive his commission, Satan stood at his right hand to resist him, Zech. iii. 1. He desired to winnow Peter. God sent the angel of Satan to buffet Paul. When Christ lived a private life, little is said of him ; but so soon as he was baptized, and entered into the execution ef his ministry, he was tempted of Satan in the wilderness forty days together. It was the policy of the king of Aram to bend all his forces against the captains of the Lord's army, 1 Kings xxii. 31. ' We are not able of ourselves to think anything as of ourselves ; all our sufficiency is of God, who hath made us able ministers,' 2 Cor. iii. 5, 6.

Therefore whilst we attend the opening to us of the whole counsel of God, we have great need of your prayers, that we faint not in our expectation, that we shrink not in the execution of our duty ; for through God only we are mighty, 2 Cor. x. 4.

I conclude this point in the apostle's words of exhortation, seeing we stand upon the tower and keep watch till God will put a word into our mouths : 'You also helping together by prayer for us, that, for the gift bestowed upon us by the means of many persons, thanks may be given by many on our behalf,' 2 Cor. i. 11. The apostle doth confess that our gifts are bestowed on us by the means of many persons, by the prayers and supplications of many of God's good servants. Therefore, that we may stand it out in all weathers, that we be not idle and drowsy in our watch, that we may be full of the strength of God to do the work of evangelists; pray you to God without ceasing for us.

For we have many discouragements, and standing so high upon the tower, we have many eyes upon us; and Satan on our right hand to resist us, and the world on the left hand to tempt us; and the great difficulty of our service and employment in the church to dishearten us; yet, *audiam quid loquatur Deus,* yet I will hear what God will say to me.

4. His holy care in his office.

It is not to study what his own brains will suggest, but to hear what God will say to him; for this is *dignus vindice nodus,* a knot worth the loosing. Many observing the state of the church, and seeing the best men on earth suffer most, and possess least; and beholding the wicked and ungodly gather all, live in peace of the world, in fulness, heaping up riches, rising to honours, and having the monopoly of this life present, have staggered in the faith of God's providence. David's feet upon this slippery ground had well nigh slipped, and there were some that professed it: Mal. iii. 14, 15, ' It is in vain to serve God; and what profit is it that we have kept his ordinance? And now we call the proud happy; yea, they that work wickedness are set up; yea, they that tempt God are delivered.' Therefore it is high time for the prophet to seek his information and light from God himself.

The light of human reason cannot penetrate this thick cloud; David confesseth so much, the sweet singer of Israel could not hit upon this tune, for he saw how prosperously everything succeeded with the ungodly of the earth: Ps. lxxiii. 16, 17, ' When I thought to know this, it was too painful for me, until I went to the sanctuary of God; then understood I their end.' Which teacheth us in these great deeps of the wisdom of God, not to resolve anything out of human reason, but to consult God himself, and to hearken what he will say to the matter, to speak after him and follow him.

Our experience telleth us that there hath been much opposition, much injustice here in our land, that the commonwealth groaned under the burden thereof. The ways of God are not like our ways ; did not God see this ? Did not the cry of the poor and the oppressed go up to him, even to his ears ? Is he not come down to visit the transgressors, and to take the matter into his own audience ; even now, in the cool of the day he is come at last to keep a sessions, and to search Jerusalem with a candle and lantern; now his eyelids do begin to try the sons of men, and the joyful church and commonwealth cry to him saying, Ps. xlv. 3, 4, ' Gird thy sword upon thy thigh, O most Mighty, with thy glory and thy majesty. And in thy majesty ride prosperously, because of truth, and meekness, and righteousness ; and thy right hand shall teach thee terrible things.'

2. His instruction of others.

He will not only hearken to satisfy himself, but he will furnish himself from the mouth of God with answers to satisfy them that shall dispute and argue with him against the providence of God.

That is the use of our study and labour in our ministry :

1. To teach the truth.
2. To convince contradicters.

This second part of our duty the prophet had now special use of, for the church foreseeing the fearful judgments of God upon the Jews, did argue the matter with the prophet, and all those former grievances they objected as arguments against God's government of his church. The prophet holdeth the foundation, and seeketh to inform himself how he may be able to maintain the same against opposition and strife of tongues.

Docemur, We are taught.

Doct. In the church of God there will be ever some that will argue and dispute against God.

Reason 1. Because men are first taught by the wisdom of the world, and that is enmity with God. This proceeds from our original pravity of nature, corrupt in the first derivance from our parents, which albeit it hath the seasoning of the law of God written in the heart, yet the law of the members, which is contrary to the law of God, doth prevail against that law, and leadeth us captive unto sin.

Reason 2. Because, as the apostle saith, for 'who hath known the mind of the Lord?' Rom. xi. 34. Ignorance of the ways of God doth breed in us many sinister opinions, as we find in David in this very case; for he confesseth that the prosperity of the wicked troubled him, till he went into the house of God: there he learned the mind of God, and then he was well satisfied.

Even this prophet knew not how to answer them that would argue with him against God, till he had called to account and disputed the matter with him.

Reason 3. Because the apostle saith of the elect, 2 Cor. v. 7, 'For we walk by faith, and not by sight.' Now in many of God's chosen, the sight and sense is full, the faith is weak and imperfect; and when we come to hear of the equal justice of God in punishing sinners, and feel the smart of his rod upon the church, it is an hard matter to assure the heart by believing against that which is suffered in feeling.

Reason 4. Because Solomon saith, Eccles. vii. 29, 'God hath made man upright; but they have sought many inventions;' for surely the equal and constant ways of God are suspected by the unequal and inconstant inventions of men, who, in favour of themselves, spare not to cast the afflictions of the church rather upon the will of God, of which they are not able to give the reason, than upon the evil deservings of their own sins.

Use 1. The minister must learn of the prophet, to apply himself to the remedy of this inconvenience, to maintain the cause of God against all contradiction and strife of tongues; for as we are the people's orators, to plead their cause with God, so are we God's orators, to defend him against the corrupt and perverse censures of men, by proclaiming his constant justice, and wisdom, and truth, and by teaching them, as the psalmist saith, 'He will not suffer his truth to fail.' We need not strain ourselves much for this, for wisdom will be justified of her children, and he whom we defend against the calumniations of profane, or against the distrustfulness of the ignorant and weak, will fill our mouths with arguments in his own defence.

Job saith to his friends: Job xiii. 7, 'Will ye speak wickedly of God? and talk deceitfully for him?' The cause of God is an upright cause, we shall not need to be put to our shifts to defend him against the dispute and arguing of men. It is enough that we rest in this principle of undeniable truth : 'Surely God is just, and there is no unrighteousness with him,' as Abraham : Gen. xviii. 25, 'That be far from thee, to do after this manner, to slay the righteous with the wicked : and that the righteous should be as the wicked, that be far from thee. Shall not the Judge of all the earth do right?'

Use 2. The people that are our hearers are taught to hearken to the voice of our message, and to learn this lesson of the justice, wisdom, and truth of God, that they may rightly know God, and sincerely love him ; that if any thoughts of distaste of God's government, or distrust of his justice, shall arise in their hearts, they may presently call to remembrance our pleadings for him, and confess that, how admirable soever the ways of God are in our judgments, yet they are always equal ; how secret soever they be, yet they are always just.

It is a malicious suggestion, when Satan shall belie us to God, as he did Job, when he said Job served not God for nothing, Job ii. 25 ; but there is no great danger in it, for he knows Satan to be a liar and a murderer, and 'he needeth not that any should testify of man ; for he knoweth what is in man.'

It is a dangerous suggestion, when he shall belie God to us. *First*, Either flattering us with an overweening of his mercy, to encourage sin ; as when he told Eve, 'You shall not die at all.' *Secondly*, Or shall affright us with the terror of his justice, as if there were no hope of favour, as he did to David, setting some a-work to tell him, *Non est tibi salus in Deo tuo,* there is no help for thee in thy God. *Thirdly,* Or shall tax to us the government of God, as if he were either negligent of the affairs of the sons of men, or ignorant altogether of the sufferings of his church, or partial in administration of justice, or directly unjust in suffering his own servants to be oppressed with the injuries of men.

The minister must diligently preach, the hearer must reverently hear, and faithfully believe the truth concerning the providence of God, or else all religion will sink, and want foundation.

Ver. 2, 3. *And the Lord answered me, and said, Write the vision, and make it plain upon tables, that he may run that readeth it. For the vision is yet for an appointed time, but at the end it shall speak, and not lie: though it tarry, wait for it; because it will surely come, it will not tarry.*

Here begins the second part of the chapter, which contains the Lord's answer to the prophet's expostulation. Containing,

1. A direction to the prophet, vers. 2, 3.

2. A declaration of his holy will in the general administration of justice.

1. Concerning the direction given to the prophet.

And the Lord answered me, and said. For the manner how God maintained intelligence with his holy prophets, we are not very particularly informed; we find inspiration, and revelation, and vision, mentioned; he that made the light that is in us, and gave us our understanding, can best make his ways known to his holy ones; and as I do not think that Habakkuk's contestation with God was verbal and vocal, but rather a wrestling and striving of his spirit and inward man, neither do I think this answer of God was audible, presented to the ear, but by some secret divine illumination suggested.

And where he saith, 'The Lord answered, and said,' these phrases do express so plain an answer, as is made in conference between man and man.

Write the vision. That is, set down in writing my answer. It is our manner, for the better preservation of such things as we would not forget, to set them down in writing.

But because this request of the prophet's doth concern others that he may inform them, God addeth, 'make it plain upon tables, that he may run that readeth it.' That is, write my answer in a table in great characters, that though a man be in haste, and run by, yet he may read as he runneth; shewing that he was desirous to satisfy all such as the prophet spake of before, who should argue against him. As our manner is to fix public proclamations and edicts on walls, or on posts, in ways of common passage, that any passenger may take notice thereof, seeing it concerneth every one; to that the Lord alludeth in this place, giving the prophet great charge for the declaration of his holy will in this great matter, so to express it that every one of his people may receive information thereof. *Vult aperta esse verba et aperte scribi,* saith St Jerome.

For the vision is yet for an appointed time. The time is not yet fulfilled for the execution of the will of God; but it is in the holy wisdom and purpose of God determined when it shall be fulfilled.

At the end it shall speak, and not lie. That is, in the time prefixed by almighty God it shall take effect, and the counsel and decree of God shall be executed; for God that hath promised cannot lie.

The answer of God is full, as it after will appear, and doth not only clear the justice of God in the present cause of the oppressed Jews against the Chaldeans, but it maketh a further and more general overture of God's decree against all unrighteousness and ungodliness of men; so that this prophecy shall not only comfort that church and those times, but it is directed to the perpetual use of the church in all the ages thereof. He therefore addeth, 'Though it tarry, wait for it;' do not think, by any importunity, to draw down the judgments of God upon the ungodly, or to hasten the deliverance of the church. God doth all things *tempore suo*, in his time, and the servants of God must tarry his leisure.

Because it will surely come, it will not tarry. He giveth assurance of the complement of his will in the proper and prestitute season thereof, which nothing shall then hinder.

The parts of this text, containing God's direction given to his holy prophet, are three :

1. The care that God takes for the publishing of his will to the church, ver. 2.

2. The assurance that he gives of the performance thereof in the time by him appointed.

3. The patient expectation which he commands for the performance thereof.

1. The law* that he takes for publishing it.

The prophet must not only hear God speak, the seer must not only behold the vision, but he must write the same ; *litera scripta manet*, the written letter abideth.

I will not stand to search how ancient writing is, wherein some have lost time and labour. I know that many do make God the first immediate author of it, and do affirm that the first scripture that ever was, was God's writing of the law in two tables, Exod. xxxii. But because I find, in Exod. xxiv., that Moses wrote all the word of the Lord, and Josephus doth report a tradition of the Hebrews for writing and graving before the flood, I hold it probable that both scripture and sculpture are as ancient as the old world. I will not question Josephus his record of the two pillars erected before the flood, engraven for the use of posterity, with some memorable things to continue in succeeding ages, whereof one remained in Syria in his own time.

It is frequent in Scripture to express a perpetuity of record by writing. In the case of Amalek, Exod. xvii. 14, ' Write this for a memorial in a book ;' Job, chap. xix. 23, 24, ' Oh that my words were now written ! that they were printed in a book ! graven

---

* Qu. ' care '?—ED.

with an iron pen, in lead, and in the ink* for ever!' Isaiah the prophet, 'I heard a voice from heaven, saying to me, Write, all flesh is grass'; John, *Audivi vocem dicentem, Beati mortui,* 'I heard a voice from heaven saying, Blessed are the dead.'

Beloved, thus have we the light that shineth upon the church, and guideth our feet in the ways of peace by writing; for all Scripture is given by inspiration; holy men wrote as they were inspired. It was given to them by inspiration to know the will of God; they impart it to the church of God by writing, and that boundeth and limiteth us, τὸ μὴ ὑπερ το γέγραπται φρονεῖν, 1 Cor. iv. 6. Thus hath God revealed himself to his church, both sufficiently, that we need no more knowledge for eternal life than what is contained in Scripture, and so clearly, that the word giveth understanding to the simple.

And as this word from the immediate mouth of God doth warrant this particular prophecy, so doth the apostle say of all the body of canonical Scripture, that all Scripture is given by inspiration; and God's care is double:

1. That it be written to continue.
2. That it be written plain to be read.

1. It must be written that it may remain; for in the old world, because of the long life of the fathers, the oracles of God were committed to them without any mention of writing, because they were both wise and faithful in the custody and transmission of them; for Adam himself living nine hundred and thirty years to teach his children, had under his teaching Seth, Enoch, Kenan, Mahalaleel, Jared, Henoch, Methuselah, and Lamech, the father of Noah. And Noah lived wi h Abraham fifty-seven years; but after the flood, when the church, in the posterity of Jacob, increased, and no doubt had many corruptions by dwelling in Egypt, then was Moses appointed both to be the deliverer of the people of Israel from Egypt, and to be the penman of God, to write those things which God would have to remain in the church for all

* Qu. 'rock'?—ED.

succeeding times; and after him successively holy men wrote as they were inspired.

And a better argument we cannot give for the danger of unwritten traditions, which the church of Rome doth so much commend, even above Scripture, than this.

God saw that men had corrupted their ways, and he found the imaginations of men's hearts only evil continually, and that the church was a very few; therefore he stirred up Noah to be a preacher of righteousness, in whom the light of truth was preserved: he destroyed the old sinful world, and by Noah and Shem, he began a new church to the restored world. Yet, after Noah's death, the worship of strange gods were brought in, so that to heal this grief, and to prevent the danger of traditions, God caused the word to be written by holy men for the perpetual use of his church, whose books were faithfully preserved in all ages thereof. Then came the Son of God, and he left his Spirit in the church, to lead the church into all truth, by which Spirit the New Testament was indited and written. So that now all things necessary to salvation are so clearly revealed, that traditions of men have no necessary use in the church in the substance of true religion, for that which is written is sufficient.

The church of Rome denieth the sufficiency of Scripture. Many of their great learned men write both basely and blasphemously thereof. But they are not agreed upon the point; for Scotus, Gerson, Occam, Cameracensis, Waldensis, Vincentius Lerinensis, do all confess what we teach of the sufficiency of Scripture, as the learned Dean of Gloucester, Dr Field, l. iii. de Eccles., c. 7, hath fairly cited them.

And Dr White, in his Way of the Church, addeth Tho. Aquinas; Antoninus, archbishop of Florence; Durandus Alliaco, a cardinal; Conradus Clingius; Peresius, divinity reader at Barcelona, in Spain; and Cardinal Bellarmine, of whom Possevinus writeth, that he is one of the two that have won the garland: *De verbo Dei,* l. i. c. 2. *Sacra Scriptura regula credendi certissima et tutissima est: per corporales literas quas cerneremus et legeremus, erudire nos voluit Deus.* Writing against Swenckfield and the Libertines, this is a legal witness : *Pro orthodoxo heretici testimonium valeat.* I know to whom I speak, and therefore I forbear the polemical bands of arguments to and fro upon this question, which in print and in English is so fully and learnedly debated.

Our lesson is, seeing God's care of his church, for the instruction thereof, is here expressed, in commanding his revealed will to be written, that

Doct. God would have his church to be taught his ways in all the ages thereof.

Reason 1. Because the ways of God, and the saving health of God, cannot be parted. None can have the saving health of God without the knowledge of his ways ; no ignorant man can be saved. It is said of Christ, Isa. liii. 11, ' By his knowledge shall my righteous servant justify many ;' *per scientiam, qua scitur.* Therefore David's prayer is, ' that thy way may be known upon earth, thy saving health among all nations.'

Reason 2. Because the promise of God doth run *in semine,* in the seed : ' I will be thy God, and the God of thy seed.' Our children are the Lord's inheritance, his care extendeth so far. Deut. v. 33, ' That ye may live, and that it may be well with you, and that you may prolong your days.' But that is not all : ver. 29, ' That it may be well with them and their children for ever.'

Reason 3. For his own sake, that his wisdom, power, and justice may be known to men, that they may be able to plead the cause of God against such as either ignorantly, through unbelief, or maliciously and blasphemously, shall dispute and argue against God, for therefore God doth condescend to this apology of himself, that he may instruct his church how to plead the cause of his justice against all strife of tongues, that the name of God be not evil spoken of.

To make profit of this point.

Use 1. Herein let us consider what the Lord hath done for our souls ; for he hath given us two means to communicate to us his holy will, hearing and reading ; and he hath used to this purpose both the voice and the pen of holy men, for he spake by the mouth of all the holy prophets since the world began, and holy men wrote as his Spirit directed them. 'Let him that hath ears to hear, hear, *quid Spiritus*,' ' and seek ye out the book of the Lord and read :' but then add this caution, 'Whoso readeth, let him understand.' It was Philip's question, *Sed intelligis quod legis ?*

Use 2. Seeing God hath written to us, and the whole body of holy Scripture may well be called God's epistle or letter to his church, let us bestow the reading of God's letter. St Augustine saith,* *Quæ de illa civitate unde peregrinamur venerunt nobis literæ, ipsæ sunt Scripturæ.* It was St Gregory's complaint of Theodorus,† that he was so over-busied with secular cares: *Et quotidie legere negligit verba redemptoris sui ; quid est autem Scriptura sacra, nisi quædam epistola omnipotentis Dei, ad venturam suam.*

It is a question in our times whether printing has done more hurt or good; for Satan, finding this a means to keep things alive in the world, hath employed the press in all sorts of heresies, in all sorts of idle and lascivious, false and dicterious, slanderous and blasphemous books. The remedy is to refrain such readings, and, as Dr Rainold tells Hart, his adversary, that he hath no book allowed him to read but the Bible, it is likely then that he is perfect in that book, and that physicians do well when they find their patient surfeited with too much variety of meat, to confine him to some one wholesome diet. So shall we do well to limit ourselves to the reading of God's letter, and know his mind ; for he is wisest, and the wisdom that we shall gather from thence is wisdom from above ; it is 'able to make us wise unto salvation,' as the apostle saith.

Use 3. Seeing God teacheth us by Scripture, we must learn to carry a reverent opinion of God's written word, and to esteem it as God's great love to his church, and as a means ordained by him to bring us all to him. Therefore David saith in one psalm, Ps.

---

* In Ps. xc. 2. † Regist. iv. 841.

lvi. 4, 'In God will I praise his word,' ver. 10, twice. He hath reason for it, Ps. cxix. 50, 'For thy word hath quickened me.'

This word is now written, and 'whatsoever things are written, they are written for our learning, that we, through patience and comfort of the Scriptures, might have hope,' Rom. xv. 4.

It was Christ's shield by which he bore off the fiery darts of Satan, discharged against him in the wilderness, *Scriptum est*, 'It is written.' They that know not the Scriptures, know not the power of God; this is a sure word, because it is upon record from the Spirit of God, the charter of our heavenly inheritance.

2. It must be written plain, so that not only he that comes of purpose may read it, but even he that comes along by it may read it as he goes. When we come to examine this writing, we shall find it to contain the sum and abridgment of the whole Bible, and all that is written may be referred to it.

From this no man may be excluded, none forbidden to read it; it must be set forth to public view, and put into the common eye.

Doct. This sheweth us, that are the ministers of the word, what our work is, to write the word of God in a fair and legible hand, in great characters; that is, to open to the church of God the whole counsel of God.

Reason 1. Because this is the lantern to men's feet, and faith cometh by hearing and understanding this. And this is the office of our ministry; none can be saved but by our ministry; for this we have the great title of saviours given us in holy Scripture. And seeing the apostle saith, 'God would have all men to be saved, and come to the knowledge of his truth;' that is, saved by coming to that knowlege; we must be faithful, we must hide none of this light from men. Christ gave a full commission to his apostles, Go ye into all the world, preach ye to every creature. St Paul saith, 'Woe is me, if I preach not.'

Reason 2. Because there is a natural blindness in man, and the god of this world, by outward temptations and our own inward corruptions, do cast so thick a mist of darkness before our understandings, that the natural man doth not well discern those things which are of God. Therefore, as decayed sight is helped by a fair and great letter, so by our easy and familiar handling of the holy Scriptures, we must labour to help the weak understandings of the ignorant.

Reason 3. We must consider the true end why God gave his word, both spoken and written in Scriptures. 'The word was given to profit withal;' for so saith God: Is. lv. 10, 'As the rain cometh down, and the snow from heaven, and returneth not thither, but watereth the earth, and maketh it bring forth, and bud, &c., so shall my word be that goeth forth from my mouth; it shall not return unto me void.' It doth no good on stony ground, where it is not received in, nor where it is kept off from falling upon any ground. It must be our care to see that the seed be good, and fit for the ground where it is sown, that it may come up again in fruit. And because some have weak eyes, we must write very plain characters; and because some have running and gadding wits, we must write so as they that run may read.

Use 1. This teacheth the minister to have a special regard of his audience, that they may profit by his ministry; for we are ambassadors from God to man: let us deliver our message so as man may know what the good and perfect will of God is.

Five words thus spoken do more good, as the apostle saith, in the church than a hundred spoken in strange tongues. Saint Bernard saith that it is better *apta quam alta sapere*. Christ our Master, that set us a-work, and whose συνεργοί we are, told his disciples, John xvi. 12, *Multa habeo vobis dicere, sed nunc non potestis portare*, 'I have many things to say, but you cannot hear them now.' It must be our discretion to let our preachings run like the waters in Ezekiel, xlvii. 3, 4, &c., which were at first going into them up to the ankles, then to the knees, then they rose up to the loins, then they grew fit only for good swimmers.

And it must be your discretion that are hearers of our preachings, to remember your own measure and

Christ's rule, *qui potest capere capiat;* let no man ὑπερ-φρονειν, be over-wise, nor exercise himself in things too high for him. Let not such as be mere waders adventure to swim in deeps, but content themselves in those shoals where they may have sure footing, till God, the giver of wisdom, reveal more to them. They preach most profitably to a mixed auditory, consisting of several scantlings of understanding, who serve them all as Joseph's brethren were served in Pharaoh's house, Gen. xliii. 33, ' the eldest according to his age, and the youngest according to his youth,' that the weakest understanding may gain some light, the weak understanding may gain more light, the good understanding may better itself, and the best may not think the time lost; to make rough things plain, and to write in a full hand and a legible character.

This is God's own manner of teaching, as he saith: Isa. xlviii. 17, 'I am the Lord thy God, which teacheth thee to profit, which leadeth thee by the way that thou shouldest go.' And Saint Paul saith, 1 Cor. vii. 35, ' This I speak unto you for your own profit.'

Use 2. Seeing God would have his word so fair written that he that runneth might read, we are taught the power and efficacy of the word plainly delivered. They that run, and have something else to do and think on, yet cannot escape the power of this word, they shall read this writing although it be *in transitu*, in passing by.

Belshazzar was a runner, for being amongst his cups, and drinking in the vessels of God's house amongst his princes and concubines, and praising his own idol gods, he saw an handwriting upon the wall; it was so fairly written, that he could not but read it; and it was so full of terror, that though he had all the means to move delight before him, Dan. v. 6, yet ' The king's countenance was changed, and his thoughts troubled him, so that the joints of his loins were loosed, and his knees smote one against another.'

The messengers whom the chief priests sent to entangle Christ in his words were runners; they came with purpose to do Christ wrong, but his preaching was like a table so fairly written, that they could not but read; and they returned, saying, 'Never man spake like that man.'

If they that run from the word may be taken thus with a glance upon it, you may soon conceive what effect it may work in those that run to it, that are swift to hear, that hunger and thirst after righteousness. If they that hear or read the word immediately, *aliud agentes*, may perceive the mind of the Lord by the plain opening thereof, much more they that come of purpose and run to it, that come with appetite and desire after it, with delight in it, with purpose to profit by it, and with due preparation of the heart by earnest prayer, for the holy blessing of God upon the ministry, and hearing of it; therefore, *Quid Scriptum est? Quomodo legis?* What is written? How readest thou?

2. The assurance that he gives of the performance of his purpose in due time. 'The vision is yet for an appointed time, but at the end it shall speak and not lie.' Next verse, 'It will surely come, it will not tarry.'

This is rhetorically set down; for,

1. Here is *veritas decreti*, the truth of the decree: 'The vision is yet for an appointed time.'

2. Here is *veritas verbi*, the truth of the word: 'It shall speak, it shall not lie.'

3. Here is *veritas facti*, the truth of the deed: 'It will surely come, it will not tarry.'

1. *Decretum*, the decree. The vision is here put for the thing seen, as you have heard, and that is the declaration of God's just judgment in the cause of his church against the Chaldeans; for he saith the time is appointed, meaning in his own holy and fixed decree, which is unchangeable.

2. *Verbum*, the word. God will speak his mind by this vision, and declare what he intendeth against the Chaldeans, and therein he will deal truly and faithfully; for he is truth, he cannot lie. For these be two premises or antecedents to one conclusion, for we may conclude both ways.

1. The decree of God is passed. *Ergo veniet, non tardabit*, he shall come, he will not tarry.

2. The word of God is passed: *Ergo, &c.*

From thence we are taught,

Doct. That whatsoever God hath decreed or spoken shall certainly take effect in the appointed time.

The holy word of Scripture confirmeth this. Indeed, who should alter God's decrees? for he himself will not, I may say truly he cannot, change them, for the apostle saith, Eph. i. 11, ' he worketh all things after the counsel of his will.' And the will of God is himself; and ' he cannot deny himself,' 2 Tim. ii. 13. Neither can he repent, as Samuel told Saul: 1 Sam. xv. 29, ' The strength of Israel will not lie nor repent, for he is not a man that he should repent.'

And if God himself be without variableness and shadow of change, his will being established by his counsel and wisdom, we may be sure that there is no power beneath him that can swerve him from his own ways; for the wise man saith, Prov. xxi. 30, ' There is no wisdom, nor understanding, nor counsel against the Lord.'

One reason may serve of this doctrine.

God is equal, infinite in his wisdom, justice, and mercy. To conceive him infinite in power to do whatsoever he will, and not infinite in wisdom to decree whatsoever he will do, were to make him a tyrant, not a king; but David saith, ' The Lord is King,' and we do ascribe it to him, *Tuum est regnum et potentia,* ' thine is the kingdom and power;' for power without equal proportion of wisdom must needs degenerate into cruelty. This wisdom forseeth all things that shall be; this wisdom decreeth all things that he will do, which his power after in the times appointed doth perform and bring to act.

Obj. Against this doctrine is objected,

1. Why then do so many texts of Scripture tell us that God repenteth?

Sometimes he repenteth of the good that he hath done; for to make man upon the earth was a good work; yet it is said, Gen. vi. 6, ' And it repented the Lord that he had made man on the earth, and it grieved him at his heart. So to make Saul king over Israel was a good work, for it was his own choice; yet himself saith, 1 Sam. xv. 11, ' It repenteth me that I have set up Saul to be king.'

Sometime God is said to repent of the evil that he hath done; *malum pœnæ*, the evil of punishment is there to be understood. So after the great plague. when David had made a fault in numbering the people: 2 Sam. xxiv. 16, 'When the angel stretched out his hand upon Jerusalem to destroy it, the Lord repented him of the evil, and said to the angel, It is enough, stay thy hand.'

And concerning his word, we have frequent examples in Scripture of events contrary to the letter of his word. For example, his word was to Hezekiah by Isaiah, 'Set thy house in order, for thou shalt die,' *non vives*. Yet Hezekiah did live fifteen years after that. His word was to Nineveh by Jonah, 'Forty days, and Nineveh shall be destroyed;' yet it fell not out so; and the story saith, Jonah iii. 10, 'God repented of the evil that he had said that he would do to them.'

Sol. To all we answer:

1. That the will of God, that is, his counsel decreeing what he will do, is constantly the same, and unchangeable, as we have taught.

2. Where it is in Scripture charged upon God that he doth repent, we say with Chrysostom,* it is *verbum parvitati nostræ accommodatum*, a word accommodated to our weakness, for we are said to repent when we change our minds. Now the God of wisdom and power never changeth his mind, but sometimes he doth change his operations. There is not *mutatio mentis*, but *mutatio dextræ Excelsi*, as Augustine, *pœnitudo Dei est mutandorum immutabilis ratio*, by which he, without changing of his own decree, maketh alterations in the disposition of things mutable.

This, for want of understanding in us to comprehend the ways of God, is called repentance and grief in God; but, as Augustine saith, *Non est perturbatio, sed judicium quo irrogatur pœna;* as St Paul, 'I speak after the manner of men, because of the infirmity of your flesh.'

3. I approve that received distinction of the will of God;—

* Hom. 22 in Gen.

(1.) *Voluntas signi,* of the sign.
(2.) *Voluntas beneplaciti,* of his good pleasure.

(1.) God doth reveal his ways to the sons of men, and sheweth them what he would have them do, and openeth to them the knowledge, and tendereth to them the use of fit means to perform that which he would have them; and so it is said he would have all men to be saved, and to come to the knowledge of his truth. According to this revealed will of God, he doth offer mercy to all, and he doth withal threaten judgment to such as forsake their own mercy, as Jonah saith. And when he seeth cause to call in either his mercy from them that abuse it, or to stop the course of his justice to them whom correction doth amend, then we say he repenteth him of that which he hath either promised or threatened. For clearing whereof, understand,

That God never changeth in promise or in threatening, but only in things concerning this life; as in all the examples repeated, all those promises and threatenings be used as motives to induce obedience; and therefore they are not absolute, but conditional. For it is no good argument to persuade a man to be religious, and to fear God, abstaining from all the pleasing delights of the world, to promise him his heart's desire, if he know that that promise doth bind God, that whatsoever he do, he shall be partaker of the promise. And it is no inducement to dissuade sin by the commination of judgment, if the judgment must of necessity be inflicted. Therefore this revealed will of God is conditional, and hath reference to our obedience, and faith, and good life, and use of the means ordained by God, and tendered to us. This is the rule of life, and by this will is the church of God governed; for by this he doth reveal himself, both in his word, and in his permissions, and in his operations.

[1.] God signifieth his will by his word; for that doth declare in precepts, prohibitions, and examples, what God would have to be done, what not to be done; it revealeth both rewards and punishments, and it useth both promises and threatenings.

[2.] God signifieth his will by permissions, because he declareth thereby, that what he suffereth to be done, that he willeth to be effected.

[3.] By operations; for what God doth he doth according to his will.

(2.) *Voluntas beneplaciti* is the secret will of God reserved in himself, in which,

[1.] There is *consilium*, the wisdom of God, foreseeing what is to be done.

[2.] There is *decretum*, determining it; and herein the counsel of God is not the rule of his will, for there is nothing in God above his will; but willing all things to be thus as he hath decreed, he foreseeth in wisdom what he willeth, and therefore the rule is not with God, *This is good, therefore I decree it;* but *This I decree, therefore it is good.*

Now sometimes there seems to be an opposition between these two wills of God, which is thus reconciled.

The will of God is revealed to man,

1. Either for necessary and absolute obedience, as in the whole moral law of God.

2. For probation and trial; as in the commandments given to Abraham to offer up Isaac, wherein God concealed his secret will, which was to preserve Isaac; and concealed the purpose of his commandment, which was to try the faith of Abraham. So on the contrary, he sent to Pharaoh commanding him to let Israel go, yet it was not his secret will that Israel should go yet; but the commandment was given to convince Pharaoh of hardness of heart. And as in Abraham the commandment did cause him to declare his faith, so in Pharaoh did it convince him of rebellion to the will of God.

So all our preaching, wherein we persuade repentance, and promise life eternal, it serveth to direct all that look for salvation in the way of life, and it serveth to convince the world of unrighteousness if they obey not.

The answer then is, that whatsoever God willeth and decreeth *voluntate beneplaciti,* by the will of good pleasure, doth take effect. What God willeth *voluntate signi,* by the will signified, not always.

Reply. How then shall I know what to do, seein the signifying will of God is my rule, and that seemeth uncertain, and not agreeable to the secret will of God's good pleasure?

Sol. Do as Abraham did, prepare to offer thy son. Do as thou art commanded, leave the event and the disposition of thy obedience to God, who will further reveal himself unto thee. Do as Hezekiah did, set thine house in order, yet use the means by repentance and prayers to prolong thy life. Do as the Ninevites did, fast and repent, and call upon the name of the Lord, and 'try him,' as the prophet saith, 'whether he will shew thee mercy or not.'

But to bring this home to my text, when God pronounceth the decree of judgment against the enemies of the church, and promiseth mercy to his church, believe him in both; for neither can God's enemies repent to change the course of his justice, neither can his church sin unto death, that he should take his mercy utterly from it.

So then, the argument holdeth strong; God hath said and decreed what he will do against these Chaldeans, what for his church, therefore it shall come to pass.

Quest. But if this be true, what need then is there of prayer? Doth it not argue in us a kind of distrust in the favour of God when we do not take his word, but are still importunate to solicit his favour?

To this our answer is, that this cannot discourage prayer, because the decree is past and unchangeable; this is the proper foundation of prayer; for the apostle saith, 1 John v. 14, 'And this is the confidence that we have in him, that if we ask anything according to his will, he heareth us.' So that it is a necessary knowledge before we undertake to pray, to know what is that good, that acceptable and perfect will of God. For we not only lose our labour, but we do also offend God, if we ask anything against or beside his will; therefore, that we might not run into the error of the sons of Zebedee, *nescitis quid petatis*, you know not what you should ask, our Saviour hath set down a form of prayer so absolute, as that we cannot justify the asking of anything according to the will of God that hath not reference to one of those petitions.

Obj. If then we prevail in our prayers, why do we commend prayer, seeing all events do follow God's will and decree, and not our prayers?

Ans. Our answer is, that though the supreme agent in all operations be the will of God, yet the hand of operation, in many things, is prayer, which God hath ordained and commanded as a means to draw forth his will to execution. So God giveth every good gift : yet we are, without any wrong to God, thankful to men, by whose means any good cometh to us. So that the doctrine doth remain firm ; whatsoever God hath promised to his church, or threatened the perverse enemies thereof, that he will surely perform ; for the decrees and the word of God are unchangeable.

Quest. But when God threateneth me punishment, and denounceth judgment against me, how shall I know whether it be *voluntas signi,* or *beneplaciti ?* Is there not an hope left me, that God may repent him of the evil that he threatened ?

It is a note of the evil conscience to fear where no fear is, *i. e.* where there is no cause of fear. An elect man fearing judgment threatened, which shall not come near him, feareth where no cause is of fear.

Sol. To this I answer, let not us dispute the will of God, or search beyond that which is revealed ; if God have revealed his will to us, that must be our guide. That revealed will hath threatened nothing in us but sin, and sin carrieth two rods about it, shame and fear.

There be two things in a regenerate elect man :

1. A conscience of his sin.
2. Faith in the promises of God through Christ.

So long as we do live, we do carry about us *corpus peccati,* the body of sin ; and as that doth shake and weaken faith, so doth it confirm and strengthen fear.

Use 1. We are taught from hence to believe the word of God ; the apostle saith, ' He is faithful that hath promised.' The faithful servants of God have this promise, 'I will not leave thee, nor forsake thee.' David believes him, *in convalle umbræ mortis non timebo:* 'In the valley of the shadow of death I will not fear.' Job believes him: 'Though he kill me, I will trust in him.' David believes verily when he smarts: 'I shall see the goodness of God in the land of the living.'

It is a sweet content of the inward man, when the conscience pleads not guilty to the love of sin, though our infirmities miscarry us often, that we may say with Nehemiah, chap. xiii. 14, 'Remember me, O my Lord, concerning this, and blot not out the loving-kindness that I shewed to thy house, and to the officers thereof.' And with Hezekiah, 'Remember, Lord, now, I beseech thee, how I have walked before thee in truth, and with a perfect heart, and have done that which is good in thy sight:' but it followeth, 'And Hezekiah wept sore.' If he were so good a man, why did he weep? If not so good, why did he boast?

Surely we carry all our good amongst a multitude of infirmities, and therefore we cannot rejoice in our own integrity with a perfect and full joy; yet is it a sweet repose to the heart, when God giveth us a peace of conscience from the dominion of sin.

So on the other side, believe God threatening impenitent sinners with his judgments; for he is wise to see the sins of the ungodly, he is holy to hate them, just to judge them, and he is omnipotent to punish them.

Let me give one instance.

The third commandment in the first table of the law saith, 'Thou shalt not take the name of the Lord thy God in vain.' What needs any more?

1. Put these two one against another, *Thou, the Lord thy God*.

2. Consider what the law concerns, God's name; wherein standeth his glory, our help.

3. What is forbidden, taking it in vain, and we pray, *Sanctificetur*, let it be hallowed.

But where all this will not serve, yet this is *murus aheneus*, a brazen wall, one would think; God doth make yet another fence about his name, an hedge of thorns : 'The Lord will not hold him guiltless that taketh his name in vain.'

The laws of God be unreversible decrees ; heaven and earth shall pass, ere one of these words shall sink or lose strength. Yet the blasphemer feareth nothing; that is a crying sin in this land ; not the houses only, the streets and highways resound the dishonour of God's name ; this sin is growing incorrigible. 'The land mourneth because of oaths.'

  Hoc dicunt omnes ante Alpha et Beta puellæ.

And believe God, who cannot lie, 'He will not hold him guiltless that taketh his name in vain.'

Thus we make use of this doctrine, to restrain, if not overcome, and to destroy the dominion, if not the being, of sin in us.

Use 2. For the better rectifying of our judgments, and reformation of our lives, let us observe the consonancy of God's practice in the world with the truth of his word. He hath declared himself an hater of evil; and do we not see daily examples of his judgments upon wicked men, how ill they prosper in their estates, what shame, and disgrace, and loss of all that they have unrighteously gotten cometh upon them ; how their posterity smarteth, according to that threatening in the second commandment, God bringing the iniquity of the fathers upon the children, and visiting it to the third and fourth generation of them that hate him ; that we may say, 'Let him that thinketh he standeth, take heed lest he fall.' Whence cometh all this, but from the constant truth of God's unreversible decrees, because the word is gone out of his mouth ? And though the ungodly do not believe it, though it be told them, 'Verily there is a reward for the righteous; doubtless there is a God that judgeth in the world.'

We may say of our times, as Hecuba did of hers, *Non unquam tulit documenta fors majora quàm fragili loco starent superbi ;* for we live in the school of discipline, and the rod of correction is not only shewed, but used with a strong hand, that all men may fear **to** be unrighteous. We have not only *vigorem verborum*, the vigour of words, chiding sin in our ministry of the word; but *rigorem verberum*, the rigour of stripes, in the administration of justice. Never did any age bring both fuller examples of terror than we have heard with our ears, and seen with our eyes; for the wisdom of God's decrees and the word of God's truth is justified in our sight. Therefore, seeing sentence executed upon evil works, let* the hearts of the sons of men be wholly set in them to do evil.

Use 3. Let us consider the vain confidence of the ungodly, and compare it with the constant truth of the decrees and word of God. Isaiah expresseth it fully: chap. xxviii. 15, 'Ye have said, We have made a covenant with death, and with hell are we at agreement; when the overflowing scourge shall pass through, it shall not come to us: for we have made lies our refuge, and under falsehood have we hid ourselves.' They are answered and confounded: ver. 20, 'The bed is shorter than a man can stretch himself on it; and the covering narrower than he can wrap himself in it.' He that is to lodge so uneasily, cannot say, 'I will lay me down in peace and take my rest.'

The Chaldeans invade the church; they kill, and take possession, and divide the prey; they oppose better and more righteous men than themselves; their trust is in their strength, and riches, and power, *nec leves metuunt Deos*. What care they who weeps, so they laugh; or who bleeds, so they sleep in a whole skin; who dies, so they live. 'They trust in lying vanities.'

Solomon saith, Eccles. viii. 12, 13, 'Though a sinner do evil an hundred times, and his days be prolonged, yet surely I know it shall be well with them that fear God, which fear before him: but it shall not be well with the wicked, neither shall he prolong his days, which are a shadow; because he feareth not before God.'

God hath made an act against them; their judgment is sealed, they have nothing but vanity and lies to support their staggering and reeling estate of temporal felicity. God is not in all their ways, nor the direction of God to manage them, and therefore not the pro-

* Qu. 'yet'?—ED.

tection of God to defend them. He leads them into temptation, but he doth not deliver them from evil. But God is a rock for foundation, and a castle for defence, to all such as put their trust in him.

3. The patient expectation which he requireth in the prophet for the performance of this promise: 'Though it tarry, wait for it.'

Doct. We must not think long to tarry the Lord's leisure. It is the prophet's rule, Isa. xxviii. 16, 'He that believeth shall not make haste ;' and it is David's precept, Ps. xxxvii. 34, 'Wait on the Lord, and keep his ways.' And we have Job's example, 'All the days of my appointed time will I wait.'

The promise of the Messiah was made in paradise: 'The seed of the woman shall bruise the head of the serpent.' This was the gospel that God himself preached to the serpent; and all the sacrifices of the old law, and all the prophecies of former ages, and all the types in the Old Testament, were commentaries upon this text. The fathers in all ages of the church before Christ, rested on this; the apostle saith of them, Heb. xi. 13, 'These all died in faith, not having received the promises, but having seen them afar off, and were persuaded of them, and embraced them.'

Reason 1. Because this doth best fit the constant decree of God, that we do rest in it; for it were in vain for us to serve a God whom we might not trust, and upon whose word we could not build assurance. It is the apostle's rest, *scio cui credidi*, I know whom I have believed.

Reason 2. Because this doth best declare our faith; for faith being of things not seen in themselves, the apostle saith, here we see in a glass. Faith is a Christian man's prospective, through which he beholdeth all things far off as if they were near at hand.

Reason 3. Because this is an exercise of our patience: Heb. x. 36, 37, 'For ye have need of patience, that, after ye have done the will of God, ye might receive the promise. For yet a little while, and he that shall come will come, and will not tarry.'

Reason 4. This also doth exercise our hope, for hope is nourished and fed with future objects, as sense is with present; and hope hath that wise forecast, that as soon as the seed is cast into the ground, hope is at work to gather in the harvest: 'Rejoice in hope.'

Use. Saint Bernard doth teach us to make use of this doctrine, of awaiting God's leisure; for, first, he layeth a good foundation; *tua considero in quibus tota spes mea consistit :*
1. *Charitatem adoptionis.*
2. *Veritatem promissionis.*
3. *Potestatem redditionis.* Upon this he buildeth.

Dicit fides parata sunt magna inexcogitabilia bona à Deo fidelibus suis. Dicit spes, mihi illa servantur. Dicit charitas, curro ego ad illa.

We must be very tender how we do invade the royalties of God. Christ saith that his Father hath kept the times and seasons in his own power, he will have the alone managing of them.

They that cannot tarry the Lord's leisure do commonly fall into one of these two evils:

1. Either they murmur impatiently at God, and quarrel his delay, as Israel did when they came out of Egypt;

2. Or else they seek unlawful means to accomplish their desires. So the woman of Endor gets customers.

Against these: 'Let patience have her perfect work, that ye may be perfect and entire, wanting nothing,' James i. 4. This work is thus perfected.

1. Let us not be too busy to search into the ways of God, to know things to come. It pleased God, before the coming of Christ in the flesh, to reveal much of his purpose concerning the time to come, by the ministry of his prophets; and the devil finding men taken with this desire of the knowledge of future events, did erect his oracles, whose giddy and dubious predictions did so infatuate the world, that few did undertake any matter of moment without consulting the oracle. The devil grew rich by the offerings and presents that were given him for divination, when the success sorted; and he lost nothing of reputation or belief when it failed, because all his oracles were of ambiguous sense, for to carry, if need were, contrary constructions.

And it is a thing admirable, which the wisdom of observation hath recorded to the honour of Christ, that at his coming into the world all oracles grew speechless, to shew that he that should dissolve the works of the devil was come. The head of this serpent being now by his coming bruised, the way to establish our hearts is to rest in the Lord, and not to be too busy with the key of his closet, and to content ourselves with so much knowledge of things to come, as either,

1. The wisdom of foresight may read in the volume of reasonable discourse.

2. Or the faith of God's holy ones may read in the written word of holy Scripture.

3. Or the judgment of those scholars of nature may find by searching the great book of the creatures; for these open things are for us, and here, *qui potest capere capiat*, he that can let him receive it.

It hath been the fault of many, that they have so anxiously discrutiated themselves with the solicitous inquisition of the future, that they have too much neglected the present; and desiring to know what God would do for them hereafter, both themselves lose the sense, and God the thanks of that good that he was then doing. God hath his ways and his paths where his footsteps are not seen.

2. Let us take the word of God for his promise and threatenings, whatsoever appearances do put in to countersuade.

In the case of my text, the oppressed church must tarry, they have two promises: one of their own deliverance and restoration; another of their enemies' confusion and ruin. God hath promised both; yet against this promise, the church which hears of comfort feels smart, and their threatened enemies rejoice and divide their spoil. The assurance is, God cannot lie, and repentance is hid from his eyes.

Why should man desire better assurance than the word of God to fix and establish his heart; seeing all things had their being from the word, and no man now in being 'doth not live* by bread only, but by

---

* Qu. 'doth live'?—ED.

every word that proceedeth from the mouth of God.'

3. To perfect our patience. That we may wait the Lord's leisure, we must beforehand consider that the vision may tarry; the promises of God, which shall be fulfilled in their fulness of time, may be foretold long before. Christ was promised in paradise, some do think the first day of the world, to man, *i. e.* in the day of man's creation, the eve of the first Sabbath; but he was not born till almost four thousand years after, yet the faithful in those times waited for the coming of Christ, and tarried with patience till he came.

4. God himself waited one hundred and twenty years for the repentance of the old world, all the while the ark was preparing. It is the apostle's phrase, 1 Peter iii. 20, 'The longsuffering of God waited.' If God have the patience to wait on us for our good, this may perfect our patience in our waiting on him for our own good.

Saint Paul, Rom. ii. 4, calleth this 'the riches of his goodness, and forbearance, and longsuffering;' and saith that 'the goodness of God leadeth to repentance.' If we consider his provocation, and how our daily sins tempt him to repent that he either did make us or do anything for us, all which are in his sight, and all which his soul abhorreth; and if we compare this his patience with our passionate bitterness upon the least provocation, and consider how ready we are to call for fire from heaven to consume them that anger us: we shall see that God doth wait for our repentance with much patience. And who would not wait upon such a Lord?

5. Let us consider how willingly we do attend and observe those that can do us any good; how early we rise, to be sure to prevent their hours; how well our hopes do support us and stay our stomachs, though many delays interpose their stop and threaten failing; yet the success of expectation in things temporal depending on men is always uncertain, for there are no bounds that can oblige human favour, not merits, not rewards, not promises, not oaths; but 'the promises of God are yea and amen,' as he saith: 'The vision is yet for an appointed time; at the end it shall speak, and not lie:' it will surely come.

This assurance that we have from the word doth make expectation easy; it is no pain to tarry for that which shall not fail us. Jacob thought the seven years a short time bestowed for Rachel, because he loved her, though he served and was not his own man till he had fulfilled the time. Neither doth that of Solomon discourage our tarrying the Lord's leisure, because he saith, Prov. xiii. 12, 'Hope deferred maketh the heart sick.'

1. Because, if that hope be of some things temporal, depending upon the favour of the times, or persons of men, there may be a failing; therefore delay is a disease in such cases, and maketh the heart sick.

2. But hope in the promises of God, determined to their certain time, cannot be said to be delayed; for his hope is in vain who hopeth anything before the time.

3. And again, where hope resteth in the word and promise of God, neither the alterations of persons, nor the vicissitude of times, nor the intercurrence of impediments can any way cross the purpose, disable the means, or defeat the end of God's decree.

Further, if we understand Solomon, of hope rightly grounded on the promise, and construe the deferring it, not to any protraction beyond the time, but to the long expectation of it *in tempore suo*, which desire of fruition doth make long, that that hope maketh the heart sick, we must not understand this sickness as a disease of the heart; for when the church saith, Cant. ii. 5, 'Stay me with flagons, and comfort me with apples, for I am sick of love,' let no man think that this sickness was any disease in the church; we may say of it as our Lord did of Lazarus's sickness, 'This sickness is not to death.' This is but fervour of the spirit, and earnestness of desire; as Bernard saith, it is *tædium quoddam impatientis desiderii* he means, and holy impatience, *quo necesse est affici mentem amatoris absente eo quod amat, dum totus in expectatione quantamlibet festinationem reputat tarditatem.*

This is an wholesome sickness; it is the disease of the whole creation, and of all the elect: Rom. viii.

22, 23, 'For we know that the whole creation groaneth and travaileth in pain until now; and not only they, but ourselves also, which have the first-fruits of the Spirit; even we ourselves groan within ourselves, waiting for the adoption, to wit, the redemption of our body.' This, verse 19, is called the earnest expectation of the creature, waiting for the manifestation of the sons of God; this is not weakness of the flesh in the elect, but fervour and strength of the spirit.

So David longed; as he professeth, Ps. lxxxiv. 2, 'My soul longeth, yea, even fainteth for the courts of the Lord; my heart and my flesh crieth out for the living God.'

And this desire goeth with us to heaven; for even there the souls must wait; and they are full of this holy desire, which proves that their happiness is not consummate till the resurrection. For the souls under the altar cry with a loud voice, saying, Rev. vi. 10, 'How long, O Lord, holy and true, dost thou not judge and avenge our blood on them that dwell on the earth?'

This desire is *cos orationis*, the whetstone of prayer; for the more our hearts are established in the assurance of the truth of God's promises, the more is the fire of this desire kindled and inflamed in us, and then it breaketh forth into prayer, and the prayers that are fired at the altar of zeal ascend the next way to the throne of grace.

Christ himself kindled this heat in us when he taught us to pray to our Father, *fiat voluntas tua*, thy will be done: for we may tarry the leisure of the *fiat* in faith, and yet desire it with fervency; for in nothing do we more declare our concurrence with the will of God, than in our earnestness in prayer to him to fulfil his will.

For application of this point, let us look back to the vision. It is double; for God revealeth,

1. The purpose of his fierce wrath against the enemies of his church, whom he threateneth to consume.

2. His promise of mercy to his church, that he will restore it to the joy of his countenance, and give it rest from all her enemies.

This promise of God holdeth to the world's end; even the whole vision is for appointed times.

Therefore the distresses of the church must ever be comforted with those comforts; for these the apostle doth call 'the comforts wherewith we are comforted of God.' All other comforts spend themselves into breath, and vanish and leave the heart oppressed as it was; the vision of God's revealed comfort establisheth the heart, for this telleth us where we may have rest for our souls, namely, in the decree and promise of God.

And needful is this comfort now; for though our church, by the good favour of God, do enjoy the liberty of the word in peace, under the gracious government of our king, whom God hath anointed defender of the faith, the protestant and reformed churches in other parts of the world do at this present smart for it. Long have they lived under the rod of the Spanish inquisition; long subject to the sugillations of the Jesuits, their mortal enemies. But now the sword of massacre is drawn against them; before there were some attempts made upon the persons of some few of the religion, or some encroachment made upon their goods. They thought it gain to lose all for Christ, so that they might win him, and be found in him; but now the poor, distressed church heareth the voice of the daughter of Babel crying out against her, *Nudate, Nudate;* first discerning them, and then, but who can tell what then? The true church, lying at the mercy of Rome, shall find her mercies cruel.

We cannot but take notice of it, that the church of Rome is both a strong and a bloody enemy; she is not yet stupannated, nor past teeming; she aboundeth in continual succrescence of new seed. Cardinal Bellarmine, under the name of *Tortus*, doth wonder why our king should fear the cruel dominion of the pope, under whom all his tributaries do so well.

And the humble supplicants to his Majesty for the liberty of conscience, as they call it, and for toleration of the Romish religion, have urged the peaceable state of our neighbours in France, where the papist and protestant do exercise their religion in peace.

We now see that they feel and smart for it; that there can be no peace with Jezebel of Rome, so long as her whoredoms and her witchcrafts are so many, 2 Kings ix. 22. She lieth lurking in the secret places, to murder the innocent; her patience is limited with no other bounds but *donec adsint vires*, till they have strength. *Nunc proximus ardet Ucalegon*, they have declared themselves here what they would have done. Our comfort is in this vision, and we must tarry and wait the Lord's leisure.

Haman, the Jesuit, hath got a decree against the reformed church in France to root it out, and the sword is now drawn against them; the Protestants in Bohemia have felt the edge of the Romish sword; she that calls herself mother of the Christians, *ostendit ubera, verbera producit*, she pretendeth love. *Sævus amor docuit natorum sanguine matrem commaculare manus*. And the church makes pitiful moan, saying, Hab i. 17, ' Shall they, therefore, empty their net, and not spare continually to slay the nations ?' But we know that God is good to Israel, to such as be true of heart. God hath a sword too, and he is whetting of it; he hath a quiver, and it is full of arrows; he is bending of his bow, and preparing his instruments of death, and he hath a right hand, and that shall find out all his enemies.

How shall we wear out the weary hours of time, till God come and have mercy upon Zion? We have many ways to deceive the time.

1. The idle think the time long. Whilst we have, therefore, time, let us do good. We have work enough, to ' work out our salvation with fear and trembling,' to ' make our calling and election sure,' to ' seek the Lord whilst he may be found,' to ' wash us and make us clean, to put away the evil of our works,' to ' cease to do evil, to learn to do well,' to get and keep faith and a good conscience, to walk with our God.

They that well consider what they have to do, borrow time from their natural rest, from their meats, from their recreations, to bestow it on the service of God.

There be that overcharge themselves with the businesses of the world, with the care of gathering riches, with ambitious thoughts of rising higher, with wanton desires of the flesh, with sensual surfeits in gluttony and drunkenness, and the day is not long enough for these children of this world, to whom I say with the shepherd,*

Quin tu aliquid saltem potius quorum indiget usus.

Are these the things you look upon? *Non relinquetur lapis super lapidem,* There shall not be left a stone upon a stone ; ' Walk circumspectly, not as fools, but as wise, redeeming the time, because the days are evil.' Remember your creation to good works, that you should walk in them, and, whilst you have the light ; walk in the light, *Ambulate in luce, ambulate digni luce.*

2. To sweeten the delay of the vision, and to shorten the time of our expectation, let us hear our Saviour saying, ' Search the Scriptures.' There,

(1.) We shall find the promises of God made to his church in all ages thereof, beginning in paradise at *semen mulieris,* the seed of the woman, and so continuing to the fall of the great strumpet, the ruin of Babylon in the Revelation; wherein we shall find God to be ' yesterday, and to-day, and the same for ever.'

(2.) We shall read the examples of God's mercy to his church, and judgment of the enemies thereof, all the Bible through.

It is a work for the Sabbath, as appeareth in the proper psalm for the day (Ps. xcii.) ; to praise God for this, to sing unto the name of the Most High. The church professeth it: ver. 4, 'Thou, Lord, hast made me glad through thy work ; I will triumph in the works of thy hands.' The works of God are these : ver. 7–17, ' When the wicked spring as grass, and when all the workers of iniquity do flourish ; it is that they shall be destroyed for ever. For, lo, thine enemies, O Lord, for, lo, thine enemies shall perish ; all the

---

* Virg. Alexis.

workers of iniquity shall be scattered. But my horn shall be exalted like the horn of an unicorn: I shall be anointed with fresh oil. Mine eye shall see my desire upon mine enemies; mine ears shall hear my desire of the wicked that rise up against me. The righteous shall flourish like a palm-tree; he shall grow like a cedar in Lebanon. Those that be planted in the house of the Lord shall flourish in the courts of our God. They shall bring forth more fruit in their age; they shall be fat and flourishing.' The use of all, 'To shew that the Lord is upright; he is my rock, and there is no unrighteousness in him.'

These be meditations of a Sabbath or rest, and the word of God giveth full examples of this truth, and daily experience in our own times assureth it.

(3.) The Scripture doth put into our mouths, 'psalms and hymns, and spiritual songs, teaching us to sing and to make melody in our hearts.'

Excellent to this purpose are the Psalms of the Bible; and if we sing merrily to the God of our salvation, this will pass away the time of our waiting for the promise of God cheerfully; we shall not think it long. For this did David desire to live. 'Oh, let me live, and I will praise thy name.'

(4.) The Scripture is full of heavenly consolations to establish the heart, that it shall not sink under the burden of this expectation, for in the Scriptures the Spirit of God speaketh, 'Let him that hath ears to hear, hear what the Spirit speaks to the churches.' This Spirit hath Christ left in his church to be the comforter of his church, to abide with it for ever. We have the earnest of this Spirit to bind the bargain of eternal salvation. We have the first fruits of this Spirit.

We have the testimony of this Spirit 'witnessing with our spirits, that we are the sons of God; and if sons, then heirs, and co-heirs with Christ.'

3. To spend the time of our waiting here for the promise of God, we have the holy exercise of prayer. This doth bring us to a familiar conference with God; and, as in hearing and reading of holy Scripture, we say, *Audiam quid loquatur Deus*, so in prayer God

saith, 'He shall call upon me and I will hear him; I will be with him.' In prayer we may challenge God of his promise, as the Psalmist, 'Ps. cxix. 49, 'Do well, O Lord, unto thy servant, according to thy word. Remember thy word unto thy servant, upon which thou hast caused me to hope.' Faith and feeling are not always joined together; therefore in the want and expectation of God's promises we pray, building upon the word of God, because we know, ver. 89, 'For ever, O Lord, thy word is settled in heaven.'

St Augustine saith of prayer, it is *oranti subsidium*, an help to him that prayeth; *Deo sacrificium*, a sacrifice to God; *dæmonibus flagellum*, a scourge to the devils.

1. It helpeth us, for it setteth us in the face of God, and bringeth us into his conference; and the time can never seem long to us that is spent in that company.

2. It is a sacrifice to God; for it is the performance of a duty by him commanded.

3. It is a scourge to the devils, and to all his agents; for when we pray against the evil, our God heareth us, and delivereth us from evil.

Ver. 4. *Behold, his soul which is lifted up is not upright in him: but the just shall live by faith.*

God having directed the prophet concerning the vision in the two former verses, 1, for the publication, and then for the expectation thereof, he cometh now to the vision itself, which containeth a ' declaration of his holy will in his general administration of justice,' and so doth not only serve those times and persons present, but may be extended to all times and persons so long as the world endureth. And God's shewing hereof maketh it a vision to his prophet, and so to his church, and so it begins at *Behold*.

Now the answer of God doth first prevent an objection which might arise out of God's former words; for when he saith of the vision, that the time is appointed for it, and though it tarry, the church must wait; as implying that it might be long before it were fulfilled;

the prophet might inquire, But what shall the people do in the mean time? How shall the afflicted hold out till that time appointed?

Therefore, in the rest of the chapter,

1. He cleareth that objection, ver. 4.
2. He revealeth the proceedings of his justice against sundry sins in all the rest of the chapter.

For the first, let us examine the words.

Behold. Here he openeth the eyes and cleareth the sight of the prophet and of the church to see the vision, requiring us to take the matter into serious consideration, as the apostle saith, Consider what I say. 'Let him that hath ears to hear, hear what the Spirit speaketh unto the churches;' so is this word often used in Scripture to move attention.

His soul which is lifted up in him is not upright. Interpreters do two ways understand these words: either thus, ' He that is not upright, his soul is lifted up' ; or by conversion, ' He that is lifted up is not upright.' This last we follow, and this I take to be God's meaning.

It is true, in the first sense, that the ungodly man seeketh trust elsewhere than in God, and doth strengthen himself in the malice or pride of his heart. But God would shew here that whosoever is thus big swollen in the pride of his heart, hath not *rectam animam*, some read *quietam*, or *tranquillam animam*, a right or a quiet soul. It agreeth well with the prophet's complaint of the insolency of the Chaldeans, that they being now lifted up with the glory of their many victories, their souls are not upright; wherein he declareth them horrible offenders, and therefore obnoxious to his high displeasure.

Mr Calvin doth understand this place thus, that God declareth his just judgment against the Chaldeans, that because they have trusted in themselves, they shall have no peace in their souls, but some new suspicions shall still arise to disquiet them, or new hopes to put them on upon fresh adventures, or some new fears to discruciate them, so that they shall never rest in their souls.

Arias Montanus, and Ribera, a Jesuit, do both follow a corrupt translation. *Ecce quia incredulus est non erit recta anima ejus.* Whereas he speaketh not of unbelief, but of pride of heart, which yet doth include infidelity; because such do translate the trust that they ought to place in God alone unto themselves, and their own means of accomplishing their intendments; but our reading doth much better agree with our copy.

It followeth in the second part of the antithesis, 'But the just shall live by his faith.'

And here let me first tell you that this sentence is cited in the New Testament often. (1.) Rom. ii. 17, 'As it is written, the just shall live by faith.' (2.) Gal. iii. 11, 'But that no man is justified by the law in the sight of God, it is evident; for the just shall live by faith.' (3.) Heb. x. 37, 38, 'For yet a little while, and he yet shall come, will come and will not tarry. Now the just shall live by faith; and if any man shall draw back, my soul shall have no pleasure in him.'

In all these four places, the words have one and the same sense. The just man, that is, he who is justified by a saving faith, shall be supported by that faith; so as whatsoever either outward or inward calamities shall assault him, his faith shall carry him through all: because, putting his trust only in God, in the confidence of the mediation of Jesus Christ, he shall have peace of conscience, and shall take all that befalls him in good part. So then,

1. By *the just*, we do understand not any legal righteousness, such as standeth in the performance of obedience to the whole law, which no man but Christ, God and man, could perform; but an evangelical righteousness, which doth consist in a godly zeal, and holy endeavour of obedience to the law, according to the measure of that grace which God hath given to men, and whereunto is joined both repentance of all sins, and an holy sorrow that we do come so short of that full obedience which in duty we do owe to God.

And where he saith *vivet*, he shall live, he doth mean both a natural, a spiritual, and an eternal life.

1. A natural life; for faith doth make that to be a life which else were a death, for the wicked are dead in trespasses and sins. So Christ saith, 'Let the dead bury their dead,' and the wanton widows are said to be dead even whilst they live. But by faith our natural life hath life put into it, as the apostle saith: Gal. ii. 20, 'And the life which I now live in the flesh, I live by the faith of the Son of God, who loved me and gave himself for me.' And surely this comfort must be applied in my text, so, though not so only, to cheer the natural life of the distressed Jews against the many oppressions of the Chaldeans, that their faith in the promise of God must be their life: as David saith, 'I had verily fainted, but that I believed to see the goodness of God in the land of the living.' There faith preserved the natural life of David.

2. This includeth also a spiritual life, which is the conjunction of our soul with God by Jesus Christ; for what doth quicken us but our faith? for by faith Christ dwelleth in us, and by faith we are rooted and grounded in him, Eph. iii. 17, Col. ii. 7.

3. This includeth an eternal life; for how do we come to be where Christ is, but by faith? Christ first testifieth of the faith of his church, then he prayeth, 'Father, I will that they which thou hast given me, may be with me, that they may behold the glory that I had with thee,' &c. They that overcome this world do overcome it by faith; and such as have this faith do grow boisterous and violent: 'they take the kingdom of God perforce.' And this, perchance, gave occasion to the various lection, some reading in the present *vivit*, doth live, some in the future *vivet*, shall live; some understanding the natural and spiritual only, others only the eternal life. But I understand the promise extended, as the apostle saith, to both; for godliness hath the promises of this life and that which is to come. This sheweth what is meant here by faith, not the historical faith, by which we understand what the will of God is; not a temporary faith, which trusteth in God for a time, and after falleth off from him; not the faith of miracles, which even some wicked persons whom Christ will not

know at the day of judgment, had; not the faith of hypocrites, which seemeth and is not: but a justifying and saving faith. For we must live by the same faith here by which we must be saved hereafter. And this faith is called the ground of things hoped for.

Cicero defineth the Latin word *fides* of *fiat*; for it implieth performance. Saint Augustine, of the word *fides*, saith, *Duæ syllabæ sonant: fides, prima à facto, secunda à dicto*, which may have a double construction.

1. With reference to God; for his *dictum* doth assure *factum*, and that is our *fides*.

2. With reference to us; for, as Augustine saith, *fac quod dicis et credis*, do what thou sayest and thou believest. I will not conceal from you the dissection of this word *fides*, as a witty ancient hath anatomized it into five several letters, by which he collecteth the ingredients which must meet in a saving faith.

1. *F* implieth *facere*, to do, as the apostle saith, Rom. ii. 13, 'Not the hearers, but the doers of the law shall be justified.' And Christ saith, Mat. vii., 'Not every one that saith unto me, Lord, Lord, shall enter into the kingdom of heaven, but he that doth the will of my Father which is in heaven.' For a man must not be of the number of them who confess God with their mouths, and deny him in their works.

2. *I*. This importeth *integritatem*, integrity, which doth express itself in believing all the articles of Christian faith; for that faith which is not entire doth not hold fast, and there is no trusting to it.

3. *D*. That implieth *dilectionem*, love; for, Gal. v., our faith must work through love. And Saint Bernard saith, *Mors fidei est separatio charitatis*, faith without love is dead. And again he saith, *Ut vivat fides tua, fidem tuam dilectio animet*. And in the school, that faith which is not joined with love is called *fides informis*, an unformed faith. It is St Augustine's saying, *Cum dilectione fides est Christiani, sine dilectione fides est dæmonis*. For we find that the devils confessed Christ. *Confitebantur*, saith Saint Augustine, *Dæmones Christum credendo, non diligendo; fidem habebant, charitatem non habebant*.

4. *E* implieth *expressè*, expressedly; for it is not sufficient to retain faith in the heart, but we must also strive to express it two ways.

(1.) In the fruits of faith, good life.

(2.) In the outward profession, as the apostle doth join them together: Rom. x. 10, 'With the heart man believeth unto righteousness, and with the tongue he confesseth to salvation.' Against those Nicodemites, which come to Christ by night, and all those who think it enough to reserve the heart for God, though their outward deportment be fashioned to the time, and place, and persons, where, when, and with whom they do live.

5. *S*, which standeth for *semper*, always, which doth express perseverance; for it is no true faith if it do not hold out to the end.

Let us now put all together. A true faith must be entire, working always by love, ' so that men may see our good works, and glorify God which is in heaven.' In a word, the faith here mentioned is an holy apprehension, and a bold application of the favour of God to his church, in the mediation and merits of Jesus Christ, by whom we do believe that ' God is in Christ reconciling us to himself,' and the just man doth live by his faith. *(De verbis hactenus.)*

The words thus cleared, we come now to the division of this text.

It containeth an antithesis, wherein two contraries are set in opposition one against the other.

1. The man that is lifted up.
2. The just man.

1. Of the first he saith, *Non recta est anima ejus*, ' his soul is not upright.'

2. Of the second he saith, *Ex fide vivet*, ' he shall live by faith.'

In the first I note two things:

1. His notation: *elevatus*, lifted up.
2. His censure: *non recta est anima*, his soul is not upright.

1. His notation: *elevatus*.

This is a thing that God loves not; for it is said, ' God resisteth the proud:' that is the point of doctrine in this place.

Doct. God taketh offence at such as are lifted up.

It was the fall of the angels that kept not their first estate, *ero similis altissimo.* It was the fall of man: 'Behold, man is become like one of us, knowing good and evil.'

Some think this part of the text meant of Nebuchadnezzar, the proud king, whose heart was so big swollen with his great victories, that in the ruff of self-opinion he ascribed all to himself, and therefore was turned to graze, as in the story of Daniel's prophecy we read.

Remember the fearful quarrel of Christ with Capernaum: Luke x. 15, 'And thou Capernaum, which art exalted to heaven, shalt be thrust down to hell.' It is one of the works of the preaching of the gospel; I may call it one of the miracles of the power of our ministry. 'Every mountain and hill shall be brought low,' Luke iii. 5. Chrysostom, *Elatos et superbos nomine montis denunciat,* he calls the proud by the name of a mountain; the early and the later rain that falleth on them doth slip off and fall into the under valleys, and the valleys (as the psalmist saith) do abound with corn. The power of the word extendeth to the humiliation of many that are lifted up; for it revealeth unto us Christ, without whom we can do nothing, without whom no man cometh to the Father. And this leaves us nothing to lift us up.

I have spoken of this sin out of the former chapter, where the Chaldeans, proud of their victories, do rejoice, and ascribe the glory thereof to themselves. And from the mouth of an heathen man,* Artabanus, the uncle of king Xerxes, I take it, *Gaudet Deus eminentissma quæque deprimere;* his reason, *Quia Deus neminem alium quam seipsum sinit magnifice de se sentire.* Yea, sometimes we find, when God doth owe a man a shrewd turn, he will lift him up himself, that he may throw him down; as David complaineth, 'Thou hast lifted me up, and cast me down.' But the lifting up here understood, is the pride of heart which maketh men to esteem of themselves above all

* Herodot. Polymnia.

that is in them. Such are their own parasites; and the wise man saith, 'There is more hope of a fool than one of these.'

In this argument, I went so far in the former chapter, as to teach you two things:
1. To decline this as a disease.
2. To embrace the remedies against it.

Eight reasons I give against it to persuade declining of it. :
1. It trespasseth *primum et magnum mandatum legis*, the first and great commandment of the law, &c.
2. *Connumerat nos filiis Sathanæ, patri filiorum superbiæ.*
3. *Exterminat charitatem; voluntas dominium exercet.*
4. *Subjicit nos oppositioni divinæ; Deus resistit superbis.*
5. *Tollit à nobis talentum dum nostra quærimus.*
6. *Male nos decet*, poor and proud.
7. *Nullum vitium Sathanæ magis placet.*
8. *Superbus ingratus,* and so *omnia dixeris.*

The remedies: 1. Serious consideration of ourselves.
2. Studious searching in the word of God.
3. Putting ourselves often in the sight of God.
4. Frequent casting up the favours of God to us.
5. Earnest and devout prayer.

This is a sly and cunning insinuation of Satan to lift us up in our own opinion; there is a tang of our hereditary corruption that runs in the same channel with our blood. We are all apt enough to value ourselves above the lone price. Few of the mind of Agur, the Son of Jakeh, 'I am more brutish than any man.' Few of the mind of St Paul, 'Of whom I am chief.' It is a great victory that a man hath gotten of himself if he be once able to keep himself under; for whether we do increase in outward goods or spiritual graces, we shall have much ado to avoid this sin.

2. The censure, *Non est recta anima ejus*. This physician doth search the disease to the bottom, he finds where the fault is; the soul is naught, the inward man is corrupt. 'And if the light that is in us

be darkness, how great is that darkness!' It is the Searcher of hearts and reins that findeth this fault; who but he can examine and try the inward man?

We see what body, what complexion, what stature man hath; we may see what honours he attaineth in the world; how he increaseth goods; what delights a man useth for recreation; we cannot see what souls men have, *rectas an obliquas*. But if we see and observe men proud and lifted up high in their own opinion, we see there is cause of fear, that they have not *rectas animas*, right souls. And though the judgment of our brethren belong not to us, yet let us judge ourselves by this; for if we do find in ourselves an elevation above our pitch, that either the opinion of our wisdom and strength, or riches, or honours, or friends do swell us, it is a certain symptom of a diseased soul.

Reason 1. Because this lifting up doth dislodge God from the soul. He will not dwell with a proud man, he hath so declared himself: Isa. lvii. 15, 'For thus saith the high and lofty One that inhabiteth eternity, whose name is Holy; I dwell in the high and holy place, with him also that is of a contrite and humble spirit, to revive the spirit of the humble, to revive the spirit of the contrite ones.'

Now, as Augustine saith, *Vita corporis anima, vita animæ Deus*. If he say to our soul, 'I have no delight in thee;' we may complain, *in pace mea amaritudo*, our soul is sick even to the death.

Reason 2. Because this pride of life which lifteth us up, is not able to keep us up; for the elevation of our souls is like the violent casting up of an heavy body into the air, which will fall down again with its own weight; it is a man's own lust that draweth, and driveth, and forceth him up, James i. 14. And if Satan do put his help to it to lift us up, he will be the first that will put hand to the casting of us down again. When he had lifted up Christ to the pinnacle of the temple, the next temptation was, 'Cast thyself down.'

Reason 3. Because this pride of life filleth the soul so full of itself, that there is no room for the spiritual graces of God to dwell there. Christ lodged in a stable, *quia non erat locus in diversorio*.

Reason 4. Because, as the eating of some things doth put the mouth out of taste, that it cannot relish wholesome food, so the pleasing of the soul's palate with the luscious sweetness of temporal vanities, doth make the soul out of taste with the bread of life, that wholesome diet which should keep our souls in health.

Use. Let us make profit of this doctrine.

1. Let it be the main and chief care and study and endeavour of our whole life to get and keep *animam rectam,* an upright soul. To keep your accounts straight, to keep your estate upright, to keep your body in health by a regular observation thereof, to keep your interest in the love of your friends, all these be lawful cares of life, and this is an incumbent duty which obligeth and engageth all men; but let not these cares swallow us up, and devour our whole life. These things perish in the very using of them. The soul of every man, that is, the man, if that be not kept upright, ' What profit will it be to a man to win all the world, and lose the soul?' In the last day an upright soul will be able to stand it out before the judgment-seat, when they that have kept all things upright but their souls, shall see that none but upright souls are happy.

Use 2. Let us, therefore, not stand wishing, I would I had such a soul; as Balaam, I would I might die the death of the righteous; but let us study and use the means to get such a soul. These are,

1. The word; for in that the Spirit speaketh. There is a sound of the voice that cometh to the ear, that is not enough; there is the Spirit speaking to the soul; that is the sermon, the Spirit of God is the preacher, the souls of men are the audience. So the psalmist, ' I wait for the Lord, my soul doth wait, and in his word do I hope.'

2. The sacrament of the Lord's supper; for that is spiritual meat and drink, the *pabulum animæ,* it is both meat and medicine, worthily received; it is '*Emmanuel,* God with us.'

I may say to you, my brethren, as Christ said to the woman of Samaria, John iv. 10, ' If you knew the gift of God,' and understood what grace is offered you in the word and sacrament, and how beneficial they are, how nourishing, how cordial to the inward man, you would not come to the word when your leisure served, but you would put by all businesses, and make them attend that service; you would not receive the sacrament once a year, if so much, but your word would be *desiderio desideravi comedere hoc pascha.* I only say with Christ, 'If you know these things, happy are ye if ye do them.'

3. Confession to God is another good means; keep the soul upright, we say, even reckonings make long friends.

There is a threefold confession:

(1.) *Confessio fraudis: quid omisi?*
(2.) *Confessio facti: quid feci?*
(3.) *Confessio laudis: quid retribuam?*

Here is work enough to take up the whole life of man, and this keeps our account with God even.

4. I must never leave out prayer; that must make one in all the exercises of Christian life: 'pray continually.' And let our petitions be that God would give us wisdom from above to direct us in the ordering of our souls, so as we may ever keep them upright, for it is not in man to order his ways, much less to govern his own soul. Let us therefore pray to him who challengeth interest in all souls, who is called 'the Father of spirits,' and who saith, All souls are mine.

We have a good encouragement from St James: chap. i. 5. 'If any of you want wisdom, let him ask of God, who giveth to all men liberally.' And Christ hath promised that whatsoever ye shall ask the Father in his name, he will do it.

5. It will help to keep our souls in integrity, to have regard of our conversation, of our calling, of our recreations, of our time, of our means.

(1.) That we keep good company, which may not corrupt our manners, either *consilio* or *exemplo*, by counsel or example.

(2.) That we live in a lawful calling, that we may have the testimony of a good conscience, that the means of our maintenance are honest and lawful, and that we do not spend the wages of unrighteousness, that defileth the soul with an indelible pollution, all your prayers and alms will not purge you.

(3.) That your recreations be both lawful and moderate, such as may make you fit for the service of God, not such as may make you suspend the time wherein God should be served, not such as may provoke you to impatience or to blasphemy, and abusing the name of God.

(4.) That your time be spent by weight and measure, as those that are to be accountants to God for it.

(5.) That our means that we enjoy in this life be so gained and managed that they may seem as faculties of well-doing, and may by no means stoop the soul to any departure from God for love of them or by abuse of them.

Use 3. Let us learn humility; decline pride, for that doth corrupt the soul. To such God giveth grace. He that is *humillimus** should be *humillimus*. But the just shall live by faith. This is the second part of the antithesis, that contains in it the whole sum of the gospel. There be three words in it that carry the contents thereof:

1, Righteousness; 2, faith; 3, life.

Righteousness and faith are the way of life; they are two special pieces of that spiritual armour which the apostle doth advise all the children of God to use against their enemies, Eph. vi. 14, 'the breastplate of righteousness,' and 'the shield of faith.'

1. Of righteousness. This is that virtue which denominateth a man just and righteous, and it is a virtue which doth give *suum cuique*; to God in the obedience of the first table of the law; to man in the obedience of the second table.

This is given, 1, legally; 2, evangelically.

For the first, which is legal righteousness, it is the fulfilling of the whole law, in every part of it, by the whole man, in body and soul, the whole time of his life; and Adam, who was created in the image of God, was clothed with this righteousness, as the apostle saith, created in the image of God, and in righteous-

---

* Qu. 'excelcissimus'?—ED.

ness and true holiness. And this righteousness was lost by Adam's fall, and was never found in any man since but in the man Jesus Christ, who is called ὁ δίκαιος, 'that just one,' Acts xxii. 14. And of him it is said, Isa. lix. 17, that he 'put on righteousness as a breastplate.' And this righteousness the saints in glory have; so the apostle calleth them, Heb. xii. 23, 'the spirits of just men made perfect.' But on earth, Rom. iii. 10, 'there is none righteous, no, not one.'

The church of Rome doth directly contradict the Spirit of God speaking in Scripture concerning this righteousness, for the council of Trent* hath set it down for a canon : *Siquis dixerit Dei præcepta, homini justificato et sub gratia constituto, esse ad observandum impossibilia, anathema sit.*

Let me then clear the church tenet concerning this point, that legal righteousness is altogether impossible to man in the present state of desertion from our creation. Our argument is this : whosoever sinneth, breaketh the law of God ; but every one that liveth sinneth ; *ergo*, every one that sinneth breaketh the law.

The first proposition is proved by the definition of sin given by the apostle, ἁμαρτία is ἀνομία, 1 John iii. 4. But every man that liveth sinneth. St James will make that good : *In multis offendimus omnes,* 'in many things we offend all.'

The conclusion followeth, *ergo omnis prævaricatur legem*.

Andradius answereth with a distinction to the minor, Every man sinneth. Sins are of two sorts :

1. Mortal ; so every man sinneth not ; for he that is born of God sinneth not, nor can sin.

2. Venial ; so every man sinneth ; but this kind of sinning, saith he, doth not break the law of God, because they deserve not the wrath of God and condemnation. Lyndanus, *Levicula vitiola lapsuum quotidianorum aspergines et nævuli sunt, qui per se non maculant et contaminant, sed quasi pulvisculo leviter aspergunt vitam humanam*.

* Sess. 6. Can. 18.

Yet as light as they make of this pollution, it is no way to be purged but by the blood of Christ; and Christ is answerable to the Father, and to the justice of his law, even for the least of these. Therefore the prophet saith, 'God hath laid upon him the iniquity of us all,' and all our sins meet in him. This cannot but include venial sins, for the elect have no mortal sins.

Yet our tenet is, that all, even the least obliquity of thought, *primi motus ad peccata sunt peccata*, the first motions to sin are sins, and directly against the tenth commandment; and he that breaketh the least of the ten is guilty of all, for he breaketh the law.

So then the veniality of sin is not in the nature and merit of sin, but in the favour of God by Christ, he suffering and satisfying for it, and we by faith applying this to ourselves, and it will follow; for in its own nature every sin is mortal, deserving death. And the just are not said to be blessed because they have no sin, but because their iniquities are forgiven and their sin is covered, and because God imputeth not their sin to them, as some are quit by proclamation, because no evidence is given in against them.

2. We must then fly to evangelical righteousness, which hath two parts.

The one is called the righteousness of faith, the other of a good conscience, Rom. x. 6. 'Pray for us; for we trust we have a good conscience in all things, willing to live honestly,' Heb. xiii. 18.

1. The righteousness of faith. This is Christ's righteousness by faith received of us, by grace imputed to us, as the apostle saith, 'Christ is the end of the law for righteousness to every one that believeth,' Rom. x. 4. The end of the law is to save those that fulfil it. This, by reason of the body of sin that we do bear about us, none of us can perform; but Christ hath fulfilled the law for us, and his obedience is by the favour of God imputed to us, and by our faith applied, and we justified and saved thereby. For what the law exacteth of us is accepted for us, as if we in our own persons had done it, because we believe it done by Christ for us.

2. The righteousness of a good conscience. This is a work of the Holy Ghost in us, by which we do approve ourselves to God and man, and by our endeavour to do that which the law commandeth; and such a righteous person David describeth, Ps. cxix. 3, 'Surely he doth no iniquity, but walketh in the way of God.'

Object. If any man object, then is he no transgressor of the law, because he doth none iniquity; then is his obedience full, because he walketh in the way of the Lord.

Sol. St Paul doth answer for himself, and therein for all the elect of God, and sheweth wherein his innocency consisteth, and saith, Rom. vii. 15-22, 'For that which I do I allow not; for what I would do, that I do not; but what I hate, that do I. If then I do that which I would not, I consent unto the law that it is good. Now then it is no more I that do it, but sin that dwelleth in me. I delight in the law of God in the inward man.'

Here γνῶθι σεαυτον, know, if thou be an elect child of God, thou consistest of a double man so long as thou livest here on earth.

1. There is in thee an outward man, the unregenerate part of thee.

2. There is an inward man, that is, the regenerate part; for we must know and confess that we are not capable in this life of a total and full regeneration, which is an utter abolition of the body of sin.

There is *corpus peccati*, the body of sin; there is *lex membrorum*, a law of the members; there is concupiscence, which doth carry us into the evil which we know in our understandings to be against the law of God, and our conscience trembleth at it. This is an inward man, which in Peter is called κρυπτὸς τῆς καρδίας ἄνθρωπος, 1 Peter iii. 4. So that the inward man which keepeth the law is the understanding and conscience, and the outward man that breaketh the law is the will and the appetite, and the instruments thereof in the act of sin. So then I shall now describe to you whom the prophet here meaneth by the just man, even him who in his understanding apprehendeth the good and perfect will of God, and maketh conscience of obeying it according to the measure of grace given to him, for this is an evangelical righteousness.

The use of it is great, for the prophet saith of Christ Jesus, that 'he put on righteousness as a breastplate,' Isa. lix. 17. He that came to loose the works of Satan, and therefore to bid him battle, did not come into this life, which is *militia super terram*, a warfare upon earth, unarmed; he is the general of God's forces against the kingdom of darkness, against the prince that ruleth in the air, against the god of this world, against principalities and powers; and no sooner was he baptized, and began to appear to his employment, but the Spirit led him into the field to a duel with Satan for forty days together, where this breastplate of proof was a sufficient wall about his vital parts, and did preserve him against Satan's fury and force. And we that are his soldiers, who must *ambulare sicut ille*, walk as he, we are taught by the apostle both to get and put on this righteousness as a breastplate.

The benefits that this righteousness doth bring with it are many.

1. It is a proof against temptations; for howsoever our affections do receive some titillations from the outward senses to affect them with evil, our understanding, like Goshen, will always see the sun, although the rest of our Egypt be benighted. Howsoever our will may be corrupted for a time, our conscience will continue zealous of good works. In our minds we shall serve the law of God, and this will keep our heads always above water, that though we be put to it to strive and labour hard for life in the deep waters both of temptations and afflictions, yet through many dangers and painful strugglings, we shall at length recover the shore.

The distressed conscience troubled with the terror of sin, though it cannot escape Satan's sifting and buffeting and wounding, yet can it not fall into final despair, because this righteousness cannot be lost.

2. This maketh our calling and election sure; for, if we be truly regenerate, we shall be saved certainly, and this righteousness is a full assurance of our rege-

neration, as the apostle saith, 1 John ii. 29, 'Ye know that every one which doth righteousness is born of him,' so that righteousness is the earnest of our salvation. It is *salus in semine*, salvation in the seed here; it is *salus in messe*, in the harvest, hereafter; for St James saith, James iii. 18, 'The fruit of righteousness is sown in peace;' for where righteousness is once rooted, there is peace and assurance both of grace and glory.

3. This righteousness doth honour God in this world, for when men live in the conscience of their ways and in the holy fear of God, abstaining from evil all they can, doing all the good they can, rather suffering and forgiving than doing and revenging injuries, striving to bear themselves uprightly before God and men, our Saviour saith, 'Others seeing their good works will glorify their Father that is in heaven.'

4. This righteousness is the only witness of our sincerity in the love and service of our God, for let no unrighteous man say he loveth God or serveth God. The proud, the covetous, the wanton, the breaker of the Sabbath, the drunkard, let them come to church, and hear and receive the sacrament now and then; let them not deceive themselves: without this righteousness no man shall please God, neither shall the church esteem such as members of the body of Christ, for we are taught that no adulterers, fornicators, covetous persons, &c., shall inherit the kingdom of heaven: 1 Peter iii. 15, 16, 'But sanctify the Lord God in your hearts: and be ready always to give an answer to every man that asketh you a reason of the hope that is in you with meekness and fear: having a good conscience; that, whereas they speak evil of you, as of evil-doers, they may be ashamed that falsely accuse your good conversation in Christ.' Let men hunt for fame and reputation in the way of honour and high place, in the way of great dependence or of riches; if they be ungodly and want this righteousness, they want the salt that should pickle them to keep. The just shall be in everlasting remembrance; their candle doth not go out by night; their name shall be like to

precious unguent. But let the ungodly do what they can, 'the name of the wicked shall rot.'

5. This righteousness upon a deathbed will comfort, when neither meat nor medicine will down with us; for there follows after righteousness a gracious train, a comfortable sequence: Rom. xiv. 17, 'The kingdom of God is righteousness and peace, and joy in the Holy Ghost;' Ps. xxxvii. 37, 'Mark the upright man, and observe the just, for the end of that man is peace.'

What a joy of heart was it to Hezekiah! Isa. xxxviii. 3; he did not say, I have reigned a king over thine inheritance so many years, I have gotten so much riches and treasure, I have subdued so many enemies, but, 'Remember, Lord, I beseech thee now, how I have walked before thee in truth, and with a perfect heart,' &c.

Thus, having learnt what this righteousness is, and having surveyed the benefits that attend it, let us take a few necessary cautions to order and regulate both our judgment and our life:

1. Let us not take that for righteousness which is no such matter, for all that glittereth is not gold; Satan hath good skill in varnishing, and gilding, and painting, to make things that are not seem as though they were. I do not think but the pharisees thought themselves just men, and that opinion was held of them abroad, and that Christ seemed a strange preacher, that told the people, 'Except your righteousness exceed the righteousness of the scribes and pharisees,' &c., for St Paul, Acts xxvi. 5, doth call their sect ἀκριβεστάτην αἵρεσιν. We must exceed that, or else no salvation; yet if that righteousness, which consisted in great chastisement of the flesh, in great austerity of life, in so many real acts of devotion, would not serve, beloved, that cheap and soft and tender religion, that eats and drinks of the best, and wears soft garments, and lies easily, and consisteth only in hearing much and knowing something, and talking of good things, and an outward formal representation of goodness, will never pass for righteousness before God. This doth not come near the righteousness of the scribes and pharisees. Their doctors were never out of Moses's chair; they were faithful and painful in

teaching the law. Alas, many of our labourers loiter. Their auditors were frequent and attentive; when they knew of the sitting of their rabbis, they would tell one another, and call one another to it, as Jerome saith, saying, Οἱ σόφοι δευτεροῶσι, the wise repeat; and they would hasten thither. They compass sea and land to make proselytes to their sect; we by our evil conversation lose many from our congregations.

It is the complaint of them of the separation, that our evil life is one great cause of their forsaking of us; and though that do not excuse them, yet it doth accuse us, and we cannot plead not guilty to that indictment.

They gave God a quarter of their life in prayer. Let every man's own conscience speak within him how far he outgoeth them in this. They read, they studied, they repeated, they carried about them always some part of the law, and were expert in the understanding of it. And do not pamphlets of news, vain poems, and such like froth of human brains, devour much of the time the holy Bible should have bestowed upon it?

Beloved, the righteousness that should be in us, to fill us with true love of God and our neighbour, is wanting in most, it is imperfect in the best, in too many it is but seeming. In religion, zeal is gone; some false fires there are yet in the church, that boast themselves to be zeal, and are good for nothing but to find faults and pick quarrels; true devotion, which had use to shew itself in all outward holiness and reverence, is so retired, that many are more homely at church, in presence of God and the holy congregation, than they dare to be in the private houses of many that are here present. Our heads are grown so tender, that even boys must be covered at church; in prayer, our knees are too stiff to bend; we grow drowsy in hearing; the very face of religion hath lost the complexion that it had, when knowledge was yet but coming out, as if we would revive that Romish fancy, that ignorance is the mother of devotion. In civil conversation, how is righteousness turned into a cry! The words once past of our forefathers, though ignorant, were faster ties than bonds, recognisances, statutes, oaths, now are. It was once the imputation of one nation, as Tully chargeth the Greeks, *Da mihi manuum testimonium*. It was once Rome's shame, *Omnia Romæ venalia: templa, sacerdotes, altaria*. It was once the Grecian's infamy, Titus i. 12,

Κρῆτες ἀεὶ ψεῦσται κακὰ θηρία, γαστέρες ἀργαί.

There have been many national sins which one country hath upbraided another withal.

But how is it that, since the light of the gospel in our land, we have made prize of the sins of all nations, and made them free denizens amongst us? Schism in the church, corruption of justice, bribes, gluttony, drunkenness, contention, pride, outlandish manners, oppression; that Tyrus and Sidon will appear more innocent than Chorazin and Bethsaida; and Sodom and Gomorrah are like to make a better reckoning in the day of audit than Capernaum.

Therefore try your ways, and make your paths even and straight, before he come *qui justitias judicabit*. If your righteousness be not right, the light that is in thee is darkness; and then *quantæ tenebræ!* how great is that darkness!

2. When you have examined your righteousness, and find it to be a sincere reddition of due to God and man, take heed that you trust not in it.

When Jacob came to a new covenant with Laban for wages, he said to him, Do this, Gen. xxx. 33, 'So shall my righteousness answer for me in time to come, for my hire before thy face.' Our upright dealing with men may justify us to the face of man, but our righteousness in the court of heaven is a poor plea; let no man retain it for an advocate to answer there for him, it will be speechless in that presence.

So much of it as is ours is foul, and immerent, deserving no favour at the hand of God.

We have two things to do:

(1.) A debt to pay to God.

(2.) A kingdom to be purchased in heaven.

We are broken for the debt; our righteousness cometh nothing near the clearing of the debt; and can we hope of doing anything toward the purchase?

Nature itself cannot wish them more unhappy than they are that trust in their own righteousness; for the reed they lean upon will first wound them, and then break under them.

3. Yet let it go for a caution too; do not so undervalue thy righteousness as to think there is neither need nor use of it, because it meriteth nothing at the hands of God; for God is gracious to accept from us that which deserveth no such good liking from him.

Thus he accepted the humiliation of Ahab, and he rewarded it; thus he accepted the repentance of Nineveh; and the thief upon the cross that confessed Christ, and shortly after died, received a promise to be with Christ in paradise. John vi. 37, Christ speaketh comfortably, 'Him that cometh to me, I will in no wise cast out.'

Righteousness is the way to him. This is the song and jubilation of the church: Isa. xxvi. 1, 2, 'We have a strong city: salvation will God appoint for walls and bulwarks. Open ye the gates, that the righteous nation which keepeth the truth may enter in.'

For God keepeth a book of remembrance, such as Malachi saith, chap. iii. 16, 'A book of remembrance was written before him for them that feared the Lord, and that thought upon his name;' for, Ps. lviii. 11, 'The Lord loveth the righteous; and verily there is a reward for the righteous.'

Yea, beloved, I dare go so far, and I am sure that I tread on ground that will carry me through; it is not faith, it is sin, it is presumption, to trust in the righteousness of Jesus Christ only, without a care and conscience, and practice of righteousness in ourselves. For Christ redeemeth us, not to idleness, but to work out our salvation; we are delivered from the hands of our enemies, *ut serviamus ei*, that we might serve him. Redemption doth not destroy, but renew our creation; and 'we were created to good works,' and we are called to holiness.

Let no man think that Christ needeth the help of our righteousness to satisfy his Father; but we do need our righteousness to declare our faith in Christ, and to make application of the righteousness of God to ourselves.

Though the full strength of Scripture be bent against merit of righteousness, there is no ground there for idleness to stand upon; we must not cast all upon Christ, and make him who came to redeem us from the punishment of our evil works a redeemer of us from the necessity of good works.

Our very union with him is enough to necessitate operative righteousness; for he saith, 'My Father worketh as yet, *et ego operor*, and I work;' and it is his word, 'Thus must we fulfil all righteousness.' Therefore, that Christ may see he paid the debt for such as would have paid it if they could, and did their best to pay all, let us not neglect our own righteousness in our quest of salvation, but being only by Jesus Christ delivered from the hands of our enemies, let us serve him in righteousness and holiness before him all the days of our life.

4. Let it go also for a caution, that seeing the necessity of righteousness, we do look well to the integrity thereof; as the apostle admonisheth us in his testimony of the Corinthians, 1 Cor. i. 5, 7, 'That in everything ye are enriched by him, so that ye come behind in no gift.'

It is noted of the saints of God in glory, that they do wear long white robes; these be the garments of righteousness. There is our *sicut in cœlo*, we must not wear our righteousness like a short garment; it must be entire, covering the whole body to the foot; that is the integrity of the whole man. For whosoever maketh conscience of his righteousness in some things, and not in all, is but a hypocrite; that man makes conscience of nothing at all. That professor that for his profit will do anything contrary to the revealed will of God, or if for pleasure, or for revenge, he will go out of the way of God's law, that man's righteousness is but vain; for St James saith, chap. ii. 10, 'Whosoever shall keep the whole law, and yet faileth in one point, is guilty of all.' Sin is like leaven, a little of it soureth the whole lump of righteousness.

5. Knowing the necessity of this righteousness, and the continual use of it, and that our whole life is a perpetual warfare here on earth, we must know that this righteousness must never be put off or laid aside all our life long; it must not be worn in our colours *ad pompam*, but in our armour *ad pugnam*, to the fight. This righteousness is not for show, but for service.

There be some temptations that take their aim at us, and come forth to assault us; there be others that are shot at random, and yet may hit us. As he that killed Ahab directed not his aim at him, so a man sometime by occasion falleth into temptation. If a man at those times have not his righteousness to seek, but that he wear it as a breastplate, it may preserve him. Had David received two such mortal wounds in the body of his religion, and fear of God, if he had kept on his righteousness? Uriah's wife was not more naked.

These be Satan's advantages for keeping watch, as he doth; no sooner are we disarmed, but *fulmina mittit*. But as Elihu told Job, Job. xxxiii. 23, 24, ' If there be a messenger with him, an interpreter, one among a thousand, to shew unto man his uprightness; then he is gracious unto him, and saith, Deliver him from going down into the pit; I have found a ransom.'

That is then the use of our ministry, to be as Noah was to the world, *præcones justitiæ*, preachers of righteousness, to shew men which way they shall walk uprightly. He that is fit for this service must have the warrant of a minister, a *messenger*, and he must have the learning of an *interpreter;* and such a man is a rare man, one of a thousand; and his lecture is, *discite justitiam moniti*. Lose no time from it, for only righteousness hath the blessing of this promise, *justus ex fide vivit*, the just doth live by his faith. See what rate you will set upon life, so much it concerneth you to be righteous.

2. Faith. When the apostle doth come to this point concerning faith, Eph. vi. 19, he saith, ἐπὶ πᾶσι, '*Above all things*, take the shield of faith.' As Solomon saith, ' Keep thy heart above all keeping,' for indeed there is

no doctrine so necessary to salvation as the doctrine of faith.

You remember in the Acts of the Apostles, chap. xix. 8, when St Paul came to Ephesus, and continued there three months, both disputing and persuading the things that concern the kingdom of God, but after many oppositions, yet he abode there two years. His preaching had so put the gods of the heathen out of countenance, and had so advanced the glory of the true God, that Demetrius, a silversmith, which made silver shrines for Diana, called the workmen of his trade together, and said, ' Sirs, ye know that by this craft we have our wealth;' and, ' So that our craft is in danger to be set at nought.' And presently upon it there was a great cry, *Magna Diana*, ' Great is Diana.'

Beloved, look well about you, and you shall see that by faith we have our welfare, we get our being by it, both here and in heaven; therefore let us join in the cry, to cry up faith, *Magna est fides Christianorum*, great is the faith of Christians.

1. Great is the good that it is.
2. Great is the good that it does.

1. In that it is.

Faith is a certain persuasion wrought in the heart of man of the truth of all God's promises, and a confident application of them is made to the believer, both which are wrought in the believer by the Spirit of God.

(1.) So it is great in respect of the Author of it in us; for it is not αὐτόφυτον, growing of itself. This is a seed which the Lord hath sown, a plant which God's own right hand hath planted; for faith is the gift of God.

(2.) Great is the object, for it aimeth at the promises of God, which are yea and amen.

(3.) Great in the extent; for it spreadeth to all the promises of God, and all the benefits that do arise to us from him, as wisdom, righteousness, sanctification, redemption, salvation.

(4.) Great in the operation; because it layeth hand upon all those, and challengeth a right to them, saying, *Hæc mea sunt*, these are mine.

(5.) We may add also this to the excellency of faith, that it is a mother grace, the root of all other graces; for from faith they do derive themselves.

[1.] Repentance; for 'by faith God purifieth the heart,' Acts xv. 9.

[2.] Love; for 'faith worketh by love.'

[3.] Fear; that fear which is 'the beginning of wisdom.' For if we do not believe the truth of God's word, and promises, and comminations, we would not so much stand in awe of God, or fear and distrust ourselves.

[4.] Obedient; for knowing that we have no subsistence in the favour of God but by Christ, that swayeth all our observance that way, and biddeth us hear him: Heb. xi. 6, 'And without faith it is impossible to please God.'

2. For that it doth it is great.

(1.) No grace of God in us doth more honour to God than our faith doth, for none but the believer doth confess God aright; for as the apostle saith, 1 John v. 10, 'He that believeth not God, hath made God a liar.' Make that breach in the holy chain or knot of God's attributes, and all fail, for truth is the girdle of them all; so make him a liar, and make him unwise, impotent, cruel, profane, all evil. Abraham, 'strengthened in the faith, gave glory to God,' Rom. iv. 10.

(2.) No grace to us more profitable; for it is not said of any of all the other virtues and graces that we do live by any, by all of them, but only by faith, because faith doth unite us with Christ, in whom we are knit to God; for 'all fulness dwelleth in him,' and 'of his fulness we receive grace and grace,' John i. 16. And by faith only Christ dwelleth in our hearts, Eph. iii. 17. By faith we are reconciled to God in Christ: 'Whom God hath set forth to be a propitiation through faith in his blood, to declare his righteousness for the remission of sins that are past, through the forbearance of God,' Rom. iii. 25. By faith we are justified: ver. 28, 'Therefore we conclude that a man is justified by faith, without the deeds of the law.' By faith we are sanctified; for God doth 'purify our hearts by faith,' Acts xv. 9. By faith we are saved, Eph. ii. 8; for 'by grace ye are saved through faith, and that not of yourselves, it is the gift of God.' Faith bringeth peace of conscience in the assurance of all this: Rom. v. 1, 'For being justified by faith, we have peace with God, through our Lord Jesus Christ.' Ver. 2, by faith 'we have access to God into the grace wherein we stand, and rejoice in hope of the glory of God.' Ver. 3, by faith 'we glory in tribulations, knowing that tribulation worketh patience; patience, experience; experience, hope: and hope maketh not ashamed; because the love of God is shed abroad in our hearts by the Holy Ghost which is given us.'

And thus the church of the Jews is comforted against the oppressions of the Chaldeans by faith.

Lastly, faith is commended to us for a shield, by which we defend ourselves against the fiery darts of Satan, Eph. vi. 16.

Therefore to make the necessary doctrine of faith profitable to us, let us consider,

1. How faith may be gotten.
2. How it may be proved.
3. How it may be preserved.
4. How it may be used.

1. How faith may be gotten.

Herein we must needs observe two things: 1, the author; 2, the means.

1. The author. We must go to him from whom every good and perfect gift doth proceed, to seek faith.

Here I must admonish you that faith is given without seeking at first, for it is a free gift, and it is the glory of God, 'I am found of them that sought me not.' Do not think that the gift of faith is acquired, *that* is freely given; but the increase of our faith is acquired by means. I prove it thus:

The Spirit of God is given in the womb, it is given to infants, therefore faith is also given; for the Spirit is never unfruitful, and faith is one of the fruits of the Spirit: 'And the apostles said unto the Lord, Increase our faith.' The grace of God, which moveth in the generation of them that fear the Lord, is the seed of all virtues; and first of faith, the mother virtue, which issueth all the rest, that is given early. And the gift of faith doth so lie hid in the elect of God, that themselves know not of it till God be pleased, not to *put* his Son *into* them, but to *reveal* his Son *in* them. This magnifieth the free grace of God, and teacheth us to say, 'It is so, Father, because thy good pleasure is such.' And this excludeth all boasting on our part, seeing we have it of mere and free gift. And it ascribeth the glory of all to God.

2. The means to get faith. These, as I have said, do not lay the foundation of faith in us; that is the free gift of God; but these means do advance the building, they do help to increase our faith.

I will refer you to one place to declare to you the acquisition of more faith: Acts xvi. 14, 15, 'And a certain woman named Lydia, a seller of purple, of the city of Thyatira, which worshipped God, heard us, whose heart God opened, that she attended unto the things that were spoken of Paul. And when she was baptized, and her household, she besought us, saying, If ye have judged me faithful to the Lord,' &c.

Observe the whole passage:

1. Here was a woman living in an honest and lawful vocation; she was a seller of purple.

2. Here were some beginnings of faith in her, for she worshipped God.

3. The outward means to increase her faith: she heard us.

4. The inward means: the Lord opened her heart. After which followeth:

1. More attention to Paul.
2. Baptism.
3. A desire to be esteemed faithful.
4. Hospitality: she welcomed her teachers.

So that for the increasing of faith she heard the word; and the more she believed, the more attentively she heard; and for confirming of faith she was baptized. 'Faith cometh by hearing; for how shall they believe on him of whom they have not heard?' Here let me admonish you:

1. But when I say *by the word* with the apostle, I do understand, and would be understood to speak of

the word, not as it is the voice of a mortal man, nor as it is a dead letter, but as the Spirit doth speak to us in the word. For this the apostle biddeth us 'be swift to hear,' it concerns us much; but that you may see that faith is not begotten in us by hearing, hearing doth us no good without faith; and we must have a grain of faith to season our hearing, or else our hearing will add nothing to our faith: Heb. iv. 2, 'The word preached did not profit them, not being mixed with faith in them that heard it.' So do we see some at first pour water into a pump to set it a-work, that it may yield water plenteously; for faith poured into our hearing, doth make our hearing bring forth more faith.

And so in prayer. Fulgentius saith of faith, *Incipit infundi ut incipiat posci.* A man cannot have faith without asking, neither can he ask it without faith.

2. When I name the word for a means to beget an increase of faith, I mean the written word, to exclude all unwritten traditions, and all written legends, which the tell-tale church of Rome hath coined to gull the swallowing credulity of the misled ignorants; that is, the books of canonical Scriptures of the Old and New Testament, of which the apostle saith, 'They are able to make a man wise to salvation, and perfect, throughly perfect to every good work.'

3. When I name the word a means of faith, I must mean the word understood by us; for the eunuch learns nothing of Isaiah the prophet by reading him without understanding. And I wonder that ever the church of Rome could so befool and infatuate the judgments of men, to believe that either hearing a form of service, or praying in a strange tongue, could carry any validity in them, except they did conceive, or do believe that such hearing and praying have power of incantation.

Therefore there is required a translation of the word into our natural language, or some other that we understand, if we understand not the original.

And herein I must stir you up to a thankful consideration of their profitable labours, who have taken pains to translate the Bible to English for the common benefit of you all, that you may read the Scriptures, and exercise yourselves in the study of them, and examine the doctrines that you hear by them. Blessed be the Lord God of our fathers, who put such a thing as this into the heart of our king's majesty, to set this work a-foot, and to see it finished.

Herein also I must commend unto you the easiness and perspicuity of Scripture; for if God had not left the way of salvation open, but had shut it up in such clouds of obscurity, that we must needs have a guide to light us the way to the lantern, why would David have called the word itself 'a lantern to our feet'?

Therefore let no man be discouraged from his own private studying of Scriptures, for fear of their hardness. It is no better than idleness and shuffling, to say the Scriptures are too deep for me, I will not meddle with them. Christ commandeth, 'Search the Scriptures'; is he not antichrist that saith, Do not, thou shalt not search?

I say and believe that the word only read over by us or to us, without the help of any comment, or sermon, or exposition of it, is a lantern, and giveth light to the simple. Much more the word with good commentaries and written expositions. Much more the word preached by learned and judicious preachers, which know how to divide the same aright. Those be called fellow-labourers with God, angels of God, the salt of the earth, the light of the world, and even saviours of men; and because of their labour in the word, and oversight of the people, honour, double honour is allowed to them by the apostle St Paul.

This point is of great use.

1. To us that are ministers of the word, for it layeth a necessity upon us, and woe be to us if we preach not the gospel. I am sure the apostle putteth it home to Timothy: 2 Tim. iv. 1, 'I charge thee before God and the Lord Jesus Christ, who shall judge the quick and dead at his appearing and his kingdom; preach the word; be instant in season and out of season; reprove, rebuke, exhort, with all longsuffering and doctrines.' God hath given and committed to us the ministry of the word of faith, by which we

must live; and if we be not found faithful in the dispensation thereof, our souls shall answer for the sins of the people, which are committed by our negligence, and for want of our giving warning.

2. To you it is a provocation of you to be swift to hear, to take heed how you hear, to hear with meekness, to hear willingly, to hear attentively, to meditate in the word that you hear, to search the Scriptures, to believe the word spoken, to be obedient to the form of doctrine delivered, not to despise him that speaketh in our ministry; it is said of Lydia, that 'she heard us.'

This was the outward means of her faith. This had never done good alone; for 'he that planteth is nothing, and he that watereth is nothing, but God that giveth the increase.' He is nothing, saith the apostle, that planteth; that is, the minister of the word is nothing.

There were two things much amiss amongst the Corinthians at that time.

1. One was, they did too much depend upon their ministers, and ascribe too much to them, wherein he that sent them had wrong.

2. They were partial in their estimation of their ministers, some affecting and preferring one, some another, that it came to a schism.

To remove which double disease in the church, the apostle telleth them, that the minister is not anything; his meaning is not to disgrace the ordinance of God, to defile his own nest, to dishonour his own high calling, but to bring them to true judgment of it, and to let them understand that the ministry of men is outward, that God hath no need of it, he can convert and establish souls without it.

And further, whatsoever the minister doth, it is by the suggestion and help and efficacy of the Holy Ghost. The purpose of the apostle is to withdraw us from dependence on outward means; he doth not seek to discourage the use or to disparage the honour of them, or to question their necessity, but to shew that, as planting and watering of a tree are to the bearing of fruit, so is our preaching to your good life;

except God do give the increase, the means in itself is not anything.

Therefore let us search deeper for the power of God in the increase of our faith, and we shall find it a special work of the Holy Ghost; and so St Paul, speaking of the spirit of faith, 2 Cor. iv. 31, doth give us to understand, that faith is wrought in us by that Spirit of God which bloweth where he listeth. So it is said of Lydia, that 'the Lord opened her heart.'

The manner of the operation of this Spirit in the work of faith, is thus:

1. It worketh upon the supreme part of the soul; that is, the understanding.

2. Upon the inferior part; that is, the will and affections.

1. Upon the understanding; and there it openeth to us three things:

(1.) The excellency of our creation.

(2.) The misery of our fall.

(3.) The remedy thereof.

(1.) The excellency of our creation.

For man was made in the image of the Trinity, that is, in holiness and righteousness; he had free will to have continued that happy estate, and he had the tree of life whereof he might have eaten, and lived for ever in the state of his creation. It is necessary that we be instructed in the story of man's creation, that we may understand the power, wisdom, and goodness of God shewed in man, who, out of so base a matter, composed so excellent a frame as this of man's body, and inspired it with a reasonable soul, endowing it with heavenly light, and giving to man the lordship of the works of his hands, leaving it in his own freewill to perpetuate the tenure of his happiness.

This is called man's state of innocency, wherein,

1, His knowledge, 2, his holiness, was full and perfect.

1. His knowledge was full. (1.) Of God; (2.) Of himself; (3.) Of the creatures.

(1.) Of God; knowing him so far forth as a frail creature was capable of the knowledge of an infinite nature; and therein man was no whit inferior to the angels of God; for God created men and angels in his own image, and this knowledge is the image of God : so saith the apostle, Col. iii. 10, ' Created in knowledge, after the image of him which created him.'

(2.) Of himself; for he was then sensible of all that God had done for him, and I cannot doubt but that light which God set up in this excellent creature did shew him the τὸ γνωστὸν of himself, so that he knew the secret of his own composition, the admirable faculties of the intellectual and animal part, of the symmetry, the anatomy, the use of every part of the body, the end and use of his creation.

(3.) Of the creatures; for as all the creatures were brought before him to declare to him his dominion over them, so for more expressure of his lordship, he gave to every creature a name; surely the light of his understanding penetrating so deep as to the secret nature of all things sublunary, as also well read in the great volume of the celestial bodies, and furnished with all science whereby either the content of the mind, the honour of his high place, being lord of all, or the use of his life, or the glory of his Maker, might be maintained or procured.

Such was man in the state of innocency in respect of his knowledge; and though his fall eclipsed that light very much, and much of that particular knowledge which Adam had perished in him, yet sure that which remained after the fall, which was the stock wherewith he set up in the world, did give the first rules, and lay down the grounds of all arts and sciences; which being perfected by observation, study, and experience in the long life of the fathers, descended upon succeeding times, like rivers which gather in some brooks to mend their stream as they hasten to the sea, and so improve their strength in current, and dilate their banks.

Much of this maketh much against man; for in this excellency of his knowledge, extending itself so to the creature, no doubt but he knew the angels also, and knew of their fall. I cannot suppose that so excellent a creature as man, bearing the image of God that made him, and of the angels that stood and kept their first estate, could be ignorant, or that God would conceal from him such an example of weakness in so excellent a creature, of justice in him. I cannot suppose but that he knew into what condition the fall of angels had dejected them, and how far their sin had corrupted them; he could not but know them, hating of, and hateful to God, and therefore no friend to man.

He might have suspected the forbidden fruit to have had some poisonous quality, when God said, *Quâ die comederis, morte morieris;* but he knew by that full knowledge that he had of the creatures, that it was good and wholesome for meat.

But the more we honour God in the perfection of his creation, the more we dishonour man in the precipitation of his fall. Surely he stumbled not, he fell not for want of light; he fell in the day, as it will after follow. But much of this knowledge survived his innocency, and no doubt but the angels that fell had, and have, much more knowledge than men now have.

2. His holiness was also complete; for that Maker is not author *imperfecti operis*, of an imperfect work; he did nothing but it was *bonum valde*, very good. Surely I doubt not to affirm, that there was as full and as great perfection of holiness and righteousness in Adam, in the state of his innocency, as was in Jesus Christ, for God was well pleased in them both. The difference was this: Adam was a mere creature, and his height of honour was the image of his Maker; but Christ was man, not united by way of similitude with the image of God, but by way of personal union with the nature of the Godhead, so that Adam's holiness was changeable, but Christ's holiness was not. This holiness and righteousness consisted in a sincere purity of the creature within himself, and in a total conformity to the will of God. The exaltation of God's favour to him went no higher. So high did it go, Adam might have kept him so to this day, and for ever, if he would. The reason of this mutability in the state of man was, because he was made of earth, which was made of nothing, and therefore could not participate of the immutability of God, as it did of his goodness and holiness.

Considering man thus in his state of innocency, we shall find that all Adam's posterity was then in him, and in his person was the whole nature of mankind. So that the whole nature either stood or fell in him, and was either in his standing to hold the innocency of creation, or in his fall to lose the same.

By this light we see the goodness, and love, and wisdom of God in the creation of man, and here is the ground laid of his justice also; for there is no necessity laid upon man that he must fall; and being thus set up, he cannot break but by his own ill husbandry of the talent of grace that is given to him; for what would he have more? God may say of this vine, 'What could I have done more to it than I did? He may be eternally and unchangeably happy if he will.

2. The misery of our fall, and therein,
1. How we may know it.
2. What it is.

1. How we may know it.

It is properly the work of the law to declare to man how miserable he is. So saith the apostle: Rom. vii. 7, 'I knew not sin, but by the law; for I had not known lust, except the law had said, *Non concupisces*, Thou shalt not covet.'

Therefore, to work faith in us, the Spirit of God doth preach the law to the conscience, and teacheth us to examine and try our ways by the law, not literally as they of old did, whom Christ reproveth, but according to the full scope of the law, which aimeth not at the boughs and exuberant branches of sin, but is an axe laid to the root thereof, and telleth us how miserable we are, declaring,

2. What this misery is, (1.) in the infection; and (2.) in the wages.

(1.) In the infection. Thus the law declareth us guilty.

[1.] In original sin.
[2.] In sins of omission.
[3.] In sins of evil motion.
[4.] In sins of evil affection.
[5.] In sins of evil action.

[1.] In original sin. The law declareth Adam a transgressor, and therein a corrupter, not only of his own person, but of the whole nature of mankind; because, having free will to have kept the good estate in which he was created, by prevarication of the law he fell from the chief good, and thereby infected and polluted his posterity, so that ever since no clean thing could derive itself from that which is unclean. This sin hath produced these effects in man;—

First, The image of God is much blemished in him; for, instead of that full knowledge which he had, he retaineth only some principles, which be called 'the law of God written in the heart,' which do serve to make a man without excuse in the day of his judgment, because he cannot deny but that he knew a Godhead, and knew good and evil in some measure. *Video meliora proboque.* For 'the invisible things of God, his eternal power and Godhead, are seen by the creation of the world,' Rom. i. 19, being considered in his works. And that law, 'Do as thou wouldest be done to,' serveth us to distinguish between good and evil in many things. So though there be* a total privation of our light, yet is there a dark cloud overshadowing us. 'For now,' 1 Cor. ii. 14, 'the natural man perceiveth not the things of the Spirit of God, neither can he know them, because they are spiritually discerned.' 2 Cor. iii. 5, 'Not that we are sufficient of ourselves to think any thing as of ourselves.'

And from hence it cometh that we mistake our way often, and that is not always the nearest and best way that is the fairest and broadest, and most trodden: Prov. xiv. 12, 'There is a way that seemeth good in the eyes of men, but the end thereof is death.' Rom. viii. 7, 'For the wisdom of the flesh is enmity to God, for it is not subject to the law of God, neither indeed can be.'

Secondly, The image of God in the will.

There followeth a natural inclination rather to evil than to good, and men naturally do bestow their wits rather to project evil than good; for the mind and

---

* Qu. 'be not'?—Ed.

conscience is defiled, Titus i. 15; for there is naturally a vanity in the understanding, Eph. iv. 17. So it may be said, Jer. iv. 22, 'They are wise to do evil, but to do well they have no knowledge.'

In the will, the image of God is blemished.

For we shall find in ourselves a reluctation against God; all the service of God naturally doth bring a weariness upon us, and nothing doth terrify so much with fear of difficulty as good works.

This is called original sin, because it runneth in the same stream with our blood, and we derive it from our faulty progenitors, which the apostle calleth, Heb. xii. 1, 'the sin that hangeth so fast on.' Saint Paul, Rom. vii. 17, calleth it *peccatum habitans in me,* 'sin dwelling in me;' *corpus peccati.* *Lex membrorum.* *Concupiscentia.* And the whole corruption of man deriveth itself from this head, so that we are born by nature children of wrath; for who can draw that which is clean from that which is unclean?

Therefore the Spirit of God, working faith in us, doth set our eyes upon the quarry out of which we were digged, and pointeth us to this first corruption.

There is great use of this looking back, that we who think ourselves brave creatures, to whom God hath put so many of our fellow-witnesses into service, 'may know that we are but men,' so it serveth to humble us under the mighty hand of God. It is Augustine's saying, *Magna pars humilitatis tuæ, est notitia tui.*

I find it also urged by the prophet Isaiah, chap. li. 1, 'Hearken to me, ye that follow righteousness; ye that seek the Lord, look to the rock whence you were hewn, and to the pit whence ye are digged.'

This, to consider the small beginnings of the church; for God called Abraham, being one, and from him is the house of Israel.

I find it urged, to remember our unworthiness, and to establish the faith of God's free grace: Ezek. xvi. 3, 'Thus saith the Lord unto Jerusalem, Thy birth and thy nativity is of the land of Canaan; thy father was an Amorite, and thy mother was an Hittite,' &c., to chide the rebellion of Israel, to whom God hath shewed mercy, being so unworthy. Three good uses of this point, if these virtues do follow : 1. Humility ; 2. Thankfulness ; 3. Repentance.

This doctrine of original sin hath found some heretical opposition, though the voice of Scripture and reason doth speak out loud and clear for it. The Pelagians long ago denied propagation of sin, and ascribed all to imitation. The Romanists deny it to be *peccatum mortale*, a mortal sin. But the Anabaptists of our times have revived both the Pelagian and the popish heresy. For in their last book, printed 1620, they do deny that infants traduce sin from their parents, and therefore are not born in sin. I only admonish you, if any such corrupt suggestions shall obtrude themselves to your judgments, that you waive them as contrary to the express word of holy Scripture, that you never forget the pit out of which you were digged.

[2.] Sins of omission.

This is another corruption of nature ; for our original imperfection doth so incline us to evil, that we are ready to leave the duties undone which the law of God requireth to be done.

The Spirit of God working faith in us, doth shew us that whatsoever holy duty we omit, we transgress the law, which in every precept doth bind the conscience to obedience, and leaveth them guilty before God, who do not those things which the law commandeth. Note it, that in the process of the last judgment it is said, *Non pavistis me, non amicivistis me, non visitastis*, ye fed me not, &c. And in the parabolical example of the rich man and Lazarus, it is declared that the rich man went to hell for not feeding Lazarus. 'Consider this, ye that forget God.' How often have you neglected public prayers when you have had no just occasion to detain you ? How often have you neglected to hear, to come to the sacrament ? When the table of the Lord hath been prepared for you, you have turned your back and gone away. To such the Master of the feast saith, *Non sunt digni, et non gustabunt cœnam meam*, they are not worthy, they shall not taste of my supper.

God doth offer occasions every moment to praise him, or to pray to him; it is part of man's misery that he is negligent, and taketh not the benefit of these occasions to serve God. He was adjudged to utter darkness who hid the talent of his Master in the ground. 'Take that unprofitable servant and cast him into utter darkness:' yet was this but a sin of omission.

The law saith, *Hoc fac et vives*, do this and live; and not only they that do *contrarium huic*, contrary to this, but they that do not *hoc facere*, are prevaricators of the law. 'To do good, and to distribute, forget not;' he doth not say, forbear to do evil, or omit not to do good, but *forget not*: it is a sin to forget our duty, more to omit it willingly, but most horrible to do the contrary.

[3.] Sins of evil motion.

These are against the tenth commandment, *non concupisces*, thou shalt not covet; for there is a conception of sin, a vegetation, and a putting forth. The conception of sin is the first motion thereof, the first titillation of the sense, as Galasius, *Quamvis non plane assentiamur desiderio, si tamen nos titillat, sufficit ad nos reos peragendos.*

So Chrysostom, *Aliud est concupiscere, aliud velle.*

St Bernard doth distinguish our cogitations thus:

1. *Sunt cogitationes otiosæ*, idle thoughts, *et ad rem non pertinentes;* these he calleth *lutum simplex*, that is, a thin clay which cleaveth not, yet it coloureth.

2. *Sunt cogitationes violentæ et fortius adhærentes*, violent and faster cleaving thoughts; these he calleth *lutum riscosum*, a viscous clay, stickfast.

3. *Sunt cogitationes fœtidæ*, filthy thoughts, *quæ ad luxuriam, invidiam, avaritiam, &c., pertinent*, which belong to luxury, &c. *Cœnum immundum*, foul mud.

The first of these, *cogitationes et motus primi*, may be either in phantasy only, so they defile not; or *in voluntate*, in the will; a little infecting that, so they break the law.

St Chrysostom, *Si concupiscentiæ non consentit voluntas, sola concupiscentia non condemnat*, if the will consenteth not, the concupiscence condemns not.

I dare not embrace his judgment. St Paul found by the law, and he could find it by no law but this of the tenth commandment, that *concupiscentia est peccatum,* concupiscence is sin. This is part of the misery of our fall from God, we cannot think a good thought of ourselves.

[4.] Sins of evil affection.

The Spirit doth detect this further misery, when the consent of the will, and the bent of desire, doth affect evil; in which kind our Saviour, the best interpreter of the law, doth call anger murder, and unchaste desires adultery, and desires of our neighbours' goods theft. These are not only sins *in proventu ex corde,* but *in corde,* as Christ saith, ' out of the heart cometh murder, adultery, theft.'

[5.] Sins of evil action.

These are evil prevarications, and actual transgressions of the law, such as the erecting of another god against the true God, worshipping of idols, swearing and blasphemy, breach of the Sabbath in the first table of the law. Disobedience to authority, murder, adultery, theft, false witness in the second table. They that do these things have not God in their ways: *Hæc sunt quæ polluunt hominem,* saith Jesus Christ.

It is a principal work of the Spirit of God in man, to make him sensible of the pollution of sin. It is a thing natural to fear punishment, and to decline it; but the perfect hatred of sin is in respect of the pollution; so that if there were no further danger, yet because it fouls my soul and defiles my body I abhor it. This is an high degree of holiness.

Saint Paul, who had an inward assurance and certain persuasion of the salvation of his soul, as he declareth, *reposita est mihi corona.* And he knew whom he had trusted; yet how doth he complain! ' To will is present with me, but I can do,' &c. ' Of sinners I am chief.' ' But I am carnal, sold under sin,' ' wretched man that I am!' Those sorrowful bewailings of himself, those confessions and deplorings of his sin, do not proceed from fear of punishment; he knew that he was past the rod. They proceed from the horror of the infection of sin. It grieved him that he was so foul and unclean in the sight of him that hath so pure eyes.

2. This misery appeareth further in the punishment of sin, which in the justice of God is *ite maledicti*, the curse of God, as it is written, Deut. xxvii. 26, 'Cursed is he that confirmeth not all the words of this law to do them.'

To live under the curse of God containeth all the crosses and tribulations of this life, outward, in our bodies, our estates, our liberty, our friends; inward, in the surges of our own vexations; in the winds of temptation without us, and death itself. It containeth also the second death, *pœnam damni*, depriving us of all comfort, and *pœnam sensus*, possessing us of all fulness of woe. Two things make weight in this woe.

1. That the Judge hath booked the full evidence against us. Nothing can be either suppressed or excused by us; nothing can be defended.

2. That there is no power in us as of ourselves to satisfy the justice of God; so that we are at Saint Paul's pass, *Quis me liberabit?* Who shall deliver me?

And herein the law doth us a favour; for it is our schoolmaster to bring us to Christ, which is the next point which the Spirit revealeth.

3. The remedy; wherein consider,

1. How the law doth shew us the remedy.
2. How the gospel doth declare it.

1. The law is our schoolmaster.

So saith the apostle: Gal. iii. 24, 'Wherefore the law was our schoolmaster to Christ.' In the school of God there are three forms:

1. *Incipientes*, beginners, in the lowest form, for the most part taught by their fellows. Such were they before the law, taught by their fellow-creatures, reading and learning both the glory of God in the speculation of the works of God, and finding the use of their life in the constant obedience of the creatures to the ordinance of God.

2. *Proficientes*, proficients, taught by the usher of the school, that is, Moses and the prophets.

3. *Perfecti*, perfect, taught by the chief schoolmaster, that is, Christ.

The law is our usher, and makes us come fit to come into the uppermost form, and that two ways.

1. By representing Christ in figures and types, in sacrifices and ceremonies. This is the ceremonial.

2. By shewing us our misery, that in ourselves there is nothing but matter and merit of condemnation; so the law is a sharp schoolmaster, and doth severely correct us. And no man cometh to Christ that hath not lived under the rod of the law, and been truly humbled in his soul with the consideration of his sins, in such measure that he despaireth of his salvation in himself, and findeth himself in his own ways hateful to God, as Job, 'Therefore I abhor myself.' This done,

2. The gospel revealeth to us the full remedy of our misery in Christ, saying, 'Unto you is born a Saviour, which is Christ the Lord.' Gal. iv. 4, 5, 'God sent his Son, made of a woman, and made subject to the law, that he might redeem them that were under the law, that we might receive the adoption of sons.'

Against our ignorance, Christ is made our wisdom.

Against our guiltiness, he is made our righteousness.

Against the infection of sin, our sanctification.

Against the punishment of sin, our redemption.

The remedy thus sufficient, Christ, God and man, is a person able to satisfy the law; and being without sin, able to recover us the favour of God; and being victor of all our enemies, able to open paradise to us.

Thus far in the work of faith, the Spirit of God worketh upon our understanding; and there can be no faith in us except we be rightly informed in these three things, our excellent creation, our miserable fall, and the comfortable remedy. (See division, *supra*, p. 97.)

2. To settle us in the faith, the Spirit of God must also work upon our will; that is,

1. In respect of the glorious creation of man, to move us to three duties:

(1.) Of thanksgiving to God for it.

(2.) Of sorrow for our fall from it.

(3.) Of holy desire again to recover it.

2. In respect of our misery, it moveth us,

(1.) To know it by searching and trying our ways.

(2.) To deplore it with godly sorrow, the effects of which sorrow are named by the apostle, 2 Cor. vii. 11.

[1.] Carefulness. [2.] Clearing ourselves.
[3.] Indignation. [4.] Fear. [5.] Desire.
[6.] Zeal. [7.] Revenge.

3. In respect of the remedy, it moveth us,
(1.) To know it.
(2.) Hunger and thirst after it.
(3.) To endeavour, both all our time and with all our strength, to attain it.
(4.) To use all the means to procure it.

And howsoever we find ourselves most miserable in ourselves, yet must we not so far undervalue as to think ourselves unworthy of eternal life.

The Jews are charged, Acts vii. 51, that they resisted the Holy Ghost, and would not admit the gracious suggestions thereof; they would not hear the voice behind them whispering in their ear a return from their evil ways. Paul and Barnabas tell them, Acts xiii. 46, ' It was necessary that the word of God should first have been spoken to you; but seeing ye put it from you, and judge yourselves unworthy of life everlasting, lo, we turn to the Gentiles.'

Quest. But are we not all unworthy of eternal life?

Ans. True; but it is one thing by our evil deeds to give sentence against ourselves that we are unworthy; another thing it is, out of the conscience of sin, to confess ourselves unworthy. Yet in this confession and contrition there is hope, that though in ourselves we be both unworthy and incapable of heavenly life; yet having an eye to the remedy of our misery, we despair not in him, because we hold upon sure and precious promises, which are precious,

1. In regard of the promiser, whose power and love doth make him able and willing to perform all good to us.

2. In regard of the motive that moved God to promise, expressed by the apostle to be his own goodness, the good pleasure of his will so free.

3. In regard of the fulness of his favour: ' For God, who is rich in mercy,' Eph. ii. 4, hath promised. ' Abundant in goodness,' Exod. xxxiv. 6.

4. In regard to the extent, *gaudium quod erit omni populo*, joy unto all people, Luke ii. 10; for this brazen serpent is lifted up, that whosoever looketh thereon may have help.

What, then, should keep thee from this remedy?

1. Consider that there is no man in better case than thou by nature; for all have sinned, and are deprived of the glory of God.

2. Consider that this remedy is without thyself. If it were of thyself, thou hadst cause to distaste it; but it is the free offer of God's grace to thee.

3. Consider that the giver of the remedy is the giver of faith also, by which the remedy is apprehended and applied; and if thou do not feel this faith in thyself, do not judge thyself void of it; for there may be and is faith often where is no feeling thereof.

4. Tarry the Lord's leisure, as before; wait, for the vision will not lie. How long lay the poor man at the pool of Bethesda? And though still hindered, yet was he not without hope.

We must not part the truth of God, and his justice and mercy; for the truth of God bindeth both the threatenings of his judgment, and the truth of his mercy.

Thus is the faith of the elect given and nourished in us.

2. How our faith may be proved.

Because there may be a show and seeming of faith, where the true substance thereof is wanting. The best way to try our faith is by the true touchstone; for as gold is tried by the touch, so faith, which 'is much more precious than gold that perisheth,' 1 Peter i. 7, hath a proper touchstone to try it.

1. That is, the conscience of man within, for that doth declare to himself his faith.

2. That is, good conversation and godly life; for that doth declare our faith to men.

1. A good conscience.

For ' being justified by faith, we have peace toward God,' Rom. v. This peace a wicked man cannot have; *Non est pax impio*, saith God, ' No peace to the wicked.'

Against this is a double objection.

Obj. 1. Many wicked men have quiet hearts and ail nothing, they are not humbled like other men, they are not poured from vessel to vessel, therefore their scent remaineth in them.

Sol. The effect of true peace is joy in the Holy Ghost. The wicked man's joy is not such, it is but a flash; it is neither sound, for when any trial cometh it faileth; neither is it lasting, for it perisheth in time; neither is it growing and increasing, neither is it excusing.

Obj. 2. Many of the best of God's servants have their minds troubled, and suffer great distresses in their conscience for sin; yea, such a winter there is upon their souls, that they feel not any life of grace at all in them.

Sol. True; but observe from whence this wrath ariseth: even from the war of the spirit against the flesh, the world, and the devil; in which conflict oftentimes the spirit is daunted and dismayed for a season; but there is ever joy in tribulations, and joy arising and growing out of sorrows, whereas the hearts of them that have not faith die in them. And this fire is from heaven: the covering of it with oppressions doth make it to burn so much the hotter; and the stirring of it up with temptations doth make it shine the clearer; so that peace of conscience is a sure sign of a good faith.

2. Another touchstone for this gold, this faith, is an evidence of godly conversation, to approve ourselves to God and man, both by doing all the duties of a godly life and avoiding the contrary. This is the only * work of faith in us.

1. The pit whence we draw this water of life is deep; the bucket by which we fetch it up is faith; for whatsoever desire or strength we have, or endeavour to live godly, it is an extraction drawn by our faith from Jesus Christ. I live by faith in the same† God.

* Qu. 'only the'?—ED.   † Qu. 'Son of'?—ED.

2. Faith only doth assure to us the loving-kindness of God : ' God so loved the world, that he gave his only begotten Son,' &c. *Ecce quantam charitatem*, what eye shall behold this, but the eye of faith ?

3. Faith worketh love ; that is, it breedeth a correspondence between Christ and us ; for the believing soul, assured of Christ's love to it, doth cast about within itself, *quid rependam ?* and, finding nothing to recompense that love, it seeketh how God may be pleased, and walketh in that way so near as he can. So it is said of the faithful, that they walk with God, and they answer every temptation to evil as Joseph did, ' How shall I do this, and sin against God ?' Or if by infirmity they fall, they cry God mercy, and they groan and grieve within themselves that they cannot perform better service to God : 1 John iv. 19, thus ' we love God, because he loved us first.' And Christ said, Luke vi. 47, ' Many sins are forgiven her,' *quia dilexit multum.* This is a fruit of the Holy Ghost, shed abroad in our hearts by faith.

Observe it, when faith doth lie concealed in us, that ourselves cannot discern it, yet may we discern in ourselves our love of God, and of such as love God ; and this proves God's love to us, for we could not love him, except he loved us first.

4. Faith maketh us sincere ; for it is the notation of our faith, it is called ' faith unfeigned ;' and Christ saith, ' Blessed be the pure in heart.' Faith purifieth the heart, as the apostle saith.

These are not the generation of them that are pure in their own eyes, of which Solomon spake, but the other of which David his father spake, *Hæc est generatio quærentium faciem tuam.*

Seeing there cannot be *perfectio operis*, the perfection of works, God is pleased if there be *puritas cordis*, purity of heart, which the apostle, 2 Cor. i. 12, calleth ' simplicity, and godly pureness.' And that is known by these signs.

1. If a man be humbled in true contrition for sins which he knoweth himself guilty of, and hath no peace in his heart till he hath comfort in his conscience that God hath forgiven them.

2. If he consider his own weakness, so far as to acknowledge that he committeth many sins that he knoweth not, and prayeth earnestly, and often with David, *à secretis meis munda me,* cleanse me from my secret sins.

3. If he find in his heart a present strife of his spirit against the flesh, wrestling with his own corruptions, and not suffering sin to reign in his mortal body, 'leading him captive to the law of sin.'

4. If he find him watchful to prayer, and fasting, and watching, and all exercises of mortification, striving to bring his body in subjection to the law of God.

5. If he be willing to hide the word of God in his heart, to arm him against Satan's temptations, as Christ did with *Scriptum est,* it is written.

6. If he find a desire of perseverance therein to the end, which is discerned by his spiritual growth from grace to grace, bringing forth more fruit even in age, as Christ testifieth of the church of Thyatira, Rev. ii. 19, 'more at the last than the first;' for, John vii. 38, 'he that believeth in me, out of his belly shall flow rivers of the water of life.'

These be sure proofs of sincere faith, which, though it be weak, yet it will gather strength; and being able to fight, will in the end be made able to overcome all our enemies.

3. How faith may be preserved.

This seemeth a needless question, because we have clear evidence of Scripture, that sincere faith cannot be lost.

True, it cannot finally be lost, it is assured to God; but we must preserve it, so as that in temptations and afflictions we may not be cast down with fear that it is lost. Neither that we do bear ourselves too bold upon it, so far as to presume. Therefore we are bound to the use of all those means ordained by God to preserve faith.

If it be an hypocritical or a temporary faith, it may be lost; if it be a true faith, this is one certain sign of it. The same means that breed faith in us, the same means do nourish it: therefore, Rom. xi. 20, If 'thou standest by faith, be not high-minded, but fear.'

It is a tenet of the church of Rome, and it is now revived of late by the Anabaptists, in a book of the last year, that a man may finally fall away from saving grace ; and many false shows are made out of scriptures not rightly understood, to maintain this heresy.

I say no more, but as the apostle doth, 1 Cor. x. 12, ' Let him that thinketh he standeth, take heed lest he fall.' He that is once assured of his standing, cannot fall, because the same Spirit which witnesseth to our spirits that we are the sons of God, doth also teach us all things, and bring all things to our remembrance which Christ hath taught us.

The means are, the word, the sacraments, prayer.

1. The word; for as we are born anew by the immortal seed of the word, so we must, ' as new born babes, desire the sincere milk of the word, that we may grow thereby.'

2. The sacraments of baptism and the Lord's supper ; for these also serve to strengthen faith.

(1.) By visible representations to the sense of the inward graces of God's Spirit, that, walking here by faith, and not by sight, we may have something to fasten our eye upon, which may be to us as the brazen serpent lifted up.

(2.) By the virtue of the consignation, because these sacraments are the seals of God's covenant of grace, obliging God the giver to continue his love to us, and reciprocally binding us to return duty, and love, and obedience to him.

(3.) By the efficacy of mediation, because they be the means, in the ordinance of God, whereby he doth convey his spiritual graces to us; so that baptism is called the laver of regeneration, and by baptism Christ is put on. The supper of Christ presenteth Christ to us our spiritual food, and therein we do eat and drink his body and blood. This admonisheth us to be swift to hear, and to neglect no opportunity for the same ; to renew our baptism by often repentance, to frequent the table of the Lord as the feast of our souls.

This advanceth our ministry of these, by which this serpent is lifted up on high, and set on a pole for all that desire health to look upon it.

They that are careless and negligent in these things will soon make shipwreck of that temporary faith that they seem to have; for they that live in the neglect of these things do forsake their own mercy, and declare plainly that their faith is not sound and sincere, but their whole righteousness is like the morning dew, soon dried up.

3. Prayer; for, 1, that shews of whom we hold, not of ourselves, but of God; 2, that bringeth us into God's acquaintance and familiar conversation, whereby we do more perceive God's love to us and declare our love to God.

4. How faith must be used.

The handling of this point draweth in the third word of my text, which is life, 'The just shall *live* by faith.' The right use of faith is to live by it, as I have shewed in the exposition of the words.

1. There is use of it in the natural life.
2. In the spiritual life.
3. For the eternal life.
1. In the natural life, for,
1, in prosperity, 2, in adversity, there is use of it.
1. In prosperity.

1. Faith is a shield to bear off all the flattering temptations of the flesh, the world, the devil; so it is said of Moses, Heb. xi. 24, 'By faith Moses, when he was come to years, refused to be called the son of Pharaoh's daughter'; and by faith Joseph, when he was tempted by his unchaste mistress, whose offer tendered him all sensual delight, refused her, and would not sin against God.

2. Faith is the contentment of the righteous in those things that they possess; they believe them to be the gifts of God, and they are satisfied with his allowance; so by faith Daniel was content with his pulse, and refused the king's meat. They that do believe that God knows better than they what is good and sufficient for them, are content with what they have.

3. Faith is the acknowledgment of all our good from God, for thanksgiving is a work of faith, and giveth God his due.

4. Faith dependeth upon God for the time to come, as David saith, Ps. xvi. 5, 'Thou maintainest my lot;' ver. 8, 'I have set the Lord always before me: he is at my right hand, I shall not be moved;' upon which ground the faithful do build things hoped for, and commit their ways to the Lord; they 'cast all their care upon God, for he careth for them.' And surely it is for want of faith that the *filii sæculi hujus*, the men of this world, do rise so early and go so late to bed, and eat the bread of carefulness, robbing God of his service, and breaking the Sabbath, and often doing wrong to their brother, to build up themselves; it is a sign that they dare not trust God. A strange inference!

1. For we brought nothing with us into the world.
2. We cannot deny but that whatsoever we have or possess in the world, it is the gift of God, for *aperiente manum de* implet omnia*, we have no interest in anything; being born in sin, the right is in him, the gift from him.
3. We must confess that very little will serve our necessities whilst we do live in the world.
4. We shall carry nothing away with us, and why should we discruciate ourselves with cares for others, seeing that is the care of God? Our children also are his inheritance.

I know and believe that our children are under the covenant and promise of grace, *ero Deus tuus et seminis tui*. Let us study to breed them to the love and service of God; let us not waste unthriftly what we may spare from our own necessities, and for the charge of their education; let us use all honest and lawful means to provide for them.

Thus are we discharged of our duty; *permitte Deo cætera*, leave the rest to God. Faith now doth all that remains to be done: Heb. xi. 20, 21, 'By faith Isaac blessed Jacob and Esau concerning things to come. By faith Jacob, when he was dying, blessed both the sons of Joseph.'

2. In adversity.

* Qu. '*aperiens manum Deus*'? or '*aperiendo manum*'?—ED.

Thus it serveth to furnish us with, 1, patience ; 2, hope.

1. With patience, to bear the present distress without murmuring at God.

David is a notable and full example of this faith. I shall shew you him in distress, 1 Sam. xxx. For when the Amalekites had burnt Ziklag, and had carried away captives all the people therein, and amongst them David's two wives, Abinoam and Abigail, David was greatly distressed ; so were all the people. 'They lift up their voice and wept, until they had no more power to weep.' David, beside this sorrow of his loss, and compassion of the loss of his people, &c., feared. 'For the people speak of stoning him, because the souls of all the people were grieved, every man for his sons and his daughters.' No remedy against all this sorrow but faith. But 'David encouraged himself in the Lord his God.'

The like example of Jehoshaphat, 2 Chron. xx. When some came and told the king of an army coming against him to invade him, instead of mustering his men, surveying his armour, sending out for auxiliaries to resist this army ; or instead of sending a messenger to treat of peace to divert the enemy, and to prevent war, ver. 3, Jehoshaphat lets the enemy come on. Jehoshaphat feared, and set himself to seek the Lord, and proclaimed a fast throughout all Judah ; he goes to church and prays, ver. 12, 'O our God, wilt thou not judge them ? for we have no might against this great company that cometh against us ; neither know we what to do : but our eyes are upon thee.'

In the very distress to which this remedy is applied, God hath threatened the Jews with an invasion by the Chaldeans ; he hath declared the enemy insolent and violent : what shall the Jews do in the misery ? Observe,

God takes no care of the wicked. Let him sin ; let the Chaldeans do his worst to him : but 'the just man shall live by his faith :' for he shall possess his soul in patience.

Beloved, we hear of distresses abroad ; if we do but cross the water, the sword is drawn against the professors of the gospel of Jesus Christ, and they that have arms put them on to save their lives, and stand upon their guard. The bloody Jesuits cry to the French king of our religion, Raze it, raze it! We know not how God may visit us hereafter, when the light of Israel shall be quenched; although there go over neither men nor money to relieve the distresses of our own mothers' children, *filios ecclesiæ*, children of the church. Such consultations are far above us; yet let us pray for them to God, that God would give them faith to depend upon him; and the just amongst them shall live by that faith.

There is an example nearer kin to this land, the daughter of Great Britain, and her root and branches, for whom many a loyal heart in this kingdom acheth, in whose quarrel the honourable house of parliament have, in the name of the Commons, offered to unlock all the treasures, to put on arms, and to adventure the lives of all faithful patriots in the just cause of restoring them to their rightful inheritance, and all such honours as their just claim shall challenge. In their distress I know no other comfort but my text : 'The just shall live by faith.'

In a word, where these three great and crying sins do reign, which in this prophecy are threatened, that is, corruption of conversation; when there is no honesty nor truth left amongst men, but that every man studieth the building of his own house, he cares not where he hath the brick and the mortar. Corruption of religion, that schism and heresy do carry it from peace and truth. Corruption of justice, that honours, places of service in the commonwealth, and justice itself, are sold for money; good men punished, evil men rewarded. Comfort : *Justus ex fide sua vivet*, 'the just shall live by his faith.'

2. Faith furnisheth us with hope.

That also, 1, in prosperity; 2, in adversity.

We have hope through faith that God will continue his loving-kindness to us, and not take away from us the light of his countenance. So David, Ps. xxiii. 6, 'Surely goodness and mercy shall follow me all the days of my life; and I will dwell in the house of the Lord for ever.'

Observe in David's hope two things :

1. The ground of it. Faith in God's protection, for that is the part of the whole psalm : ' The Lord is my shepherd : he shall feed me, he restoreth my soul. In the valley of the shadow of death thou art with me : thou preparest my table ; thou anointest my head with oil ; my cup runneth over.'

2. The means by him used to continue the assurance thereof, even by dwelling in the house of God continually ; that is, by consecrating his whole life to God's service and worship.

2. In adversities. We have hope that either God will strengthen us to bear it, or give issue out of it.

This is grounded upon that promise of God to his church, ' I will not leave thee, nor forsake thee.' And, Rom. viii. 25, ' If we hope for that we see not, we do with patience wait for it.'

There is no such comfort in the sorrows and distresses of life as reading the holy Scriptures for the support of our hope ; for, Rom. xv. 4, ' They are written for our learning ; that we, through patience and comfort of the scriptures, might have hope.' This hope keeps the heart from breaking ; for building upon the truth of God, it cannot be shaken.

2. How faith must be used in the spiritual life.

(1.) For this the apostle doth call it ' the shield of faith ;' and it serveth for defence against the fiery darts of Satan to keep off the evil that is yet without us, either in temptation or provocation.

(2.) It serveth also to purify our hearts from that evil which we do bear about us in the infection thereof.

(3.) It serveth for a provocation to stir us up to resist the power of the enemy ; for so St Peter saith, 1 Peter v. 8, 9, though ' Satan go about like a roaring lion, seeking whom he may devour : whom resist stedfast in the faith.'

(4.) It serveth for victory : ' This is the victory by which we overcome the world, even our faith.'

(5.) Many that return out of the field victorious, yet may bring home some dangerous wound that they have received in the battle ; and there is another good use of faith, to cure and heal all the wounds ; for our faith maketh us whole.

(6.) It serveth for the effectuating the means, hearing, sacraments, prayer.

3. For our eternal life. 1 Tim. iv. 8, faith is 'profitable unto all things, which hath the promise of the life present, and of that which is to come.'

The manner how it worketh this assurance is,

1. It assureth us that there is a life eternal; for that is an article of Christian faith, the close and sweet conclusion of our creed.

2. It assureth us that we are they who shall, by the free gift of God, be made heirs of this heavenly kingdom, *reposita est mihi corona justitiæ.*

3. It applieth all the promises of God to those several graces in us. Thus, I mourn, therefore I shall be comforted; I am pure in heart, being washed in the blood of Christ, therefore I shall see God; I hunger after righteousness, *ergo*, satisfied; I love God, *ergo*, all things work together for my good; I believe, *ergo*, I shall be saved.

4. It assureth our perseverance to the end in our love and obedience, yea, faith assureth our faith to us; for believing in the author is believing in the finisher of our faith.

5. It stayeth us in expectation of the fruit of our faith, that though the vision do tarry, yet we think it not long to wait for the performance of it.

Having heard of the excellent use of faith, you cannot but observe the reason why Satan doth aim all his fiery darts at our faith; because all our obedience, and righteousness, and holiness, is quickened and strengthened by faith, without which it is impossible to please God. There is nothing in a Christian man that so much provoketh Satan against him as his faith; for faith keepeth us from being devoured of this roaring lion. Therefore two assaults we must provide for:

1. Satan's labour to keep us from getting this shield of faith.

2. His fond care, when we have gotten it, to rob and spoil us of it.

1. Assault. Satan, knowing that our faith makes us too strong for him, and quencheth all his fiery darts, doth therefore all he can to keep us from the means

by which faith is increased in us; that is, from hearing the word and receiving the sacrament, from meditation, from prayer; and as often as you find yourselves tempted to neglect these, know it to be Satan's malice against you to keep you from faith. The breastplate of righteousness, without a shield of faith, is not sufficient to keep off the fiery darts of Satan from wounding us; but faith quencheth them.

They therefore that live in the love and in the use of those means may comfort themselves that Satan shall not be able to hinder them from obtaining a comfortable vegetation and growing up in faith.

2. Assault. And whereas he laboureth to wrest our faith from us, we shall find that both his cunning and strength will fail him, for saving faith cannot be lost.

To establish our faith, let us know that imperfect faith may be a sound and true faith, for we cannot attain to perfection in this life; but if we have 'a good conscience in all things, willing to live honestly,' Heb. xiii. 18, we may have boldness with God. For as Christ prayed for Peter that his faith might not fail, so he prayeth for his whole church, even for all that shall believe in him through his word, that the love wherewith the Father hath loved him may be in them, and he in them, John xvii. 26; which love will keep us that we fall not off quite from him.

We are not denied the use of riches, honours, or lawful pleasures; these be ornaments and comforts of life; but we cannot live by them, they perish in the using of them.

Our obedience and good works are the fruits of faith; we live by faith, faith lives in obedience, for without works faith is dead. Did we but know the invaluable price of faith, we would seek it more than all other things; and like the merchant in the parable, Mat. xiii. 44, we would part with all we have to purchase faith. I conclude with St Bernard, *Dicamus fidem vitem, virtutes palmites, botrum opus, devotionem vinum*.

Our vineyard hath bestowed much digging, and planting, and composing, and fencing upon this vine;

let it put forth, and let the clusters call it fruitful, and let the vine please both God and men.

Now that we have searched this gracious mine of comfort, and found the rich vein which maketh us able to live both here and hereafter, let me admonish you what is objected against the doctrine delivered out of this place.

Ribera, a learned Jesuit, when he cometh to this text in his full commentary upon this prophet, saith, *Incidimus in locum qui est lapis offensionis duabus domibus Israelis, hoc est orthodoxis, et hæreticis qui recesserunt à domo David.*

It grieves the church of Rome that we have so clear a text in this prophet, and that so much urged in the epistles of the apostles, for our justification by faith alone; and Ribera is much deceived if he mean us under the title of heretics, for this place is no offence to us. It is the most comfortable doctrine that we can embrace, nothing doth more set forth the excellency of faith, nothing doth more assure to us our eternal life. Fain would Ribera have shifted off the clear evidence of this place with this illusion, that the prophet's meaning is this: the just man, that is, the man that desireth to be just, shall live the life of grace by the faith which he hath in Christ Jesus. We understand that a man is justified only by faith, and that without the law, as the apostle doth also teach. And it were a poor comfort to the church in their distress to tell them, that the just man should live by his faith, except the Lord in that promise did assure them the comforts, not only of the natural, but of the spiritual and eternal life.

Neither would the apostle urge this text, but with these contents. For examine the places where these words are urged, and it will appear.

The apostle professeth: Rom. i. 17, 'I am not ashamed of the gospel of Christ,' &c. 'For therein is the righteousness of God revealed from faith to faith: as it is written, *Juxtus ex fide vivet*, The just shall live by his faith.'

The gospel is said to reveal the righteousness of God. He cannot mean the essential righteousness by which God is justice itself in his divine nature; but he doth understand that righteousness of which the apostle speaketh, 'who is made unto us wisdom, righteousness,' &c., that is, 'Christ our righteousness,' and this is called the grace of God which bringeth salvation. This is revealed now in the clear light of the gospel in real performance, which was before exhibited in visions and dreams, and types and ceremonies, whilst the veil was up.

It is revealed from faith to faith. As Origen and Chrysostom truly enough, but not enough fully, *Ex fide veteris testimonii in fidem novi;* as Ambrose, *Ex fide Dei promittentis in fidem hominis credentis;* but most fully, *Ex fide incipiente in fidem proficientem.* For as Clemens saith, *Apostolus unicam tantum fidem annunciat, quæ crescendo proficit.* Till it grow up to be πληροφορία τῆς πίστεως a fulness of faith, Heb. x. 22.

And so this text is well cited, for the just man, who is made just by faith, doth live in it and by it.

For how can the gospel be the power of God to salvation, except it revealeth to us the life of faith, seeing it is so only to such as do believe?

This first place cleareth the point, that the apostle doth understand God's word in my text, so as that the means of life is faith only; for so it is further urged by St Paul, who saith, Gal. iii. 11, 'But that no man is justified by the works of the law in the sight of God, is evident: for, The just shall live by faith.' Here these words are brought in to prove, that faith only doth justify in the sight of God, which is thus proved;—

Life eternal comes only by faith; therefore righteousness comes only by faith.

The antecedent is God's own word in my text.

The consequence is thus proved, for 'righteousness is the foundation of life eternal.' Rom. v. 17, 'They which receive the abundance of grace, and of the gift of righteousness, shall reign in life.'

And in the next verse it is called 'justification of life.'

And this sequence doth the apostle make in his own comfortable persuasion of himself: 2 Tim. iv. 8,

'I have fought a good fight,' this is the great fight with principalities and powers ; 'and I have kept the faith,' this is the shield which beareth off the fiery darts discharged against him in this fight; his comfort is, 'From henceforth is laid up for me a crown of righteousness.' This righteousness is not of the law, which he hath fulfilled, but the righteousness of the faith which he hath kept. It is not the breastplate of righteousness, but it is the shield of faith that beareth off all the fiery darts of Satan, and therefore the just man doth not live and come out of this battle victorious by righteousness, but by faith.

This place thus applied by our apostle, is the ground of our church tenet, against which the gates of hell cannot prevail, namely, that *sola fides justificat*, faith alone doth justify. That which the Romanists do lay to our charge is, that we exclude good works, and upon that slanderous imputation, both Drs Stapleton, Harding, Bellarmine, Campian, Bishop, and indeed generally all popish writers, do proclaim us heretics ; and they will not hear us, saying that the justifying faith which we preach must be such as worketh by love. They, like the pharisee, trust in themselves that they are perfect ; we, with the publican, cry out in faith of Christ's sufficient satisfaction, *Domine, miserere,* 'Lord, have mercy ;' upon whose example St Augustine saith, *Videte fratres, magis placuit humilitas in malis factis, quam superbia in bonis factis.* The cause is in sight : the humility of the one was with faith, the pride of the other was in presumption ; and 'God resisteth the proud, but giveth grace to the humble.'

I conclude this point, wherein I have held you long ; I know with how much comfort and profit to myself, I hope without your loss of time. What man is he that desireth life, who would live as a man, as a good man, and as an happy man ? I answer in the words of the Son of God, 'As thou believest, so shall it be unto thee.' Or in the words of the Father of that Son in my text, 'The just man shall live by his faith.'

Ver. 5. *Yea also, because he transgresseth by wine, he is a proud man, neither keepeth at home, who enenlargeth his desire as hell, and is as death, and cannot be satisfied, but gathereth unto him all nations, and heapeth unto him all people.*

Now that God hath declared what rest and comfort his church hath in the manifold oppressions of the enemies thereof, they shall live by their faith; in all the rest of this chapter, he declareth his own just providence in the government of the world, and in the severe execution of his judgments upon impenitent offenders, that the prophet may inform himself and others, that God hath not forgotten to be just. The last verse of the chapter is the total of the chapter: ' The Lord is in his holy temple, let all the earth keep silence before him:' that he sitteth not there idle, but is awake; that his eyes do see, and his eye-lids do try the sons of men; that we shall hear from his own mouth.

Concerning the words of this fifth verse, ' Yea also, because he transgresseth by wine, he is a proud man, neither keepeth at home.' These words are read diversely both by translators and by expositors.

Our first English church Bibles read thus : ' Like as the wine deceiveth the drunkard; even so the proud shall fail, and not endure.' The Geneva followeth the same sense : ' Yea, indeed, the proud man is as he that trangresseth by wine, therefore shall he not endure.' Arias Montanus: *Et quo modo vinum potantem decipit, sic erit superbus, et non decorabitur.* In his Interlineary he followeth the text in the original, but in his commentary he followeth the vulgar Latin authorised for the canon by the Council of Trent. Pagnine : *Quanto magis potator vini qui prævaricatur, qui est vir superbus, non permanebit?* So Mr Calvin, *Etiam certe vino transgrediens, vir superbus non habitabit.* The LXX have no mention of wine. Ὁ δὲ κατοιόμενος, καὶ καταφρονητὴς, ἀνὴρ ἀλαζων οὐθὲν μὴ περάνη.

Here be three words to express pride fully :

1. To think too well of ourselves.
2. To think contemptibly of others.

3. To boast and glory in vain ostentation.

It seemeth to me that the purpose of this place is to express the insolency and pride of the king of Babel, proud Nebuchadnezzar, and generally of the enemy of the Jew, the Chaldean; and that the scope of the place is to resemble them big swollen in their own self-opinion, to a man that is drunk with wine. This hath good coherence with the former words, for shewing how the just man and the proud man do stand in opposition. 'His soul which is lifted up is not upright in him: but the just shall live by faith;' faith shall establish the just man. But the proud man, who is drunk with the vain over-weening of himself, he shall not continue, *non habitabit*, he shall not be established.

And here I forsake the king's Bible, for I cannot find either sense or coherence in it.

The words following are plain enough; for God therein doth express that he taketh notice of the insatiable desire of the Chaldean, who, encouraged by his victories, doth covet to be monarch of all the world.

And this is now the partition of the rest of this chapter.

1. Faults.
2. Punishments.

The first fault here named, insatiableness.

The punishment, ver. 6, 7, 8.

1. The ground and note of this disease of insatiableness is pride of heart.
2. The disease itself is insatiableness.

1. Of the ground: it is pride.

This is resembled to drunkenness. It is a spiritual giddiness, wherein men lose themselves; and as the drunkard doth both think and speak, and do those things which betoken madness, his reason, and understanding, and judgment, and memory failing, and is wholly governed by his fancy, so the proud man, made drunk with the wine of his overweening, as a man beside himself, is transported with his own self-opinion to do things as unseemly as the drunkard doth.

The prophet, reproving the pride of Ephraim, doth use this resemblance, Isa. xxviii. 1, ' Woe to the crown of pride, the drunkards of Ephraim.' And again, ver. 3, 'The crown of pride, the drunkards of Ephraim, shall be trodden underfoot.' And after, chap. xxix. 9, 'They are drunken, but not with wine; they stagger, but not with strong drink.' Thus doth pride rob us of our wits, and we say of the proud man that he doth not know himself.

Wine and strong drink moderately taken do comfort the heart of man; but when we overdrink, we cease to be ourselves. So is it with self-love; for every man, by the law of charity, is bound to love himself, and to love himself first. When this love doth not overflow the banks, it is charity; when it exuberateth, it is pride. All sober men do esteem drunkards vile, and account drunkenness a loathsome sin. Let the proud man see himself in that glass, for the drunkard is the picture of the proud man.

1. Drunkenness makes men think themselves very wise, and such as fly the conference of their betters when they are sober, in their drink care not with whom they do contest, and regard no man's presence. So the proud man is wise in his own opinion. Solomon saith, 'There is more hope of a fool than of him.'

2. Drunkenness maketh many apt to quarrel. 'Who hath contentions?' Prov. xxiii. 29; the answer next verse, 'They that tarry long at the wine.' And so it is with the proud man: Prov. xxviii. 25, 'For he that is of a proud heart stirreth up strife.'

3. The drunkard, whilst he is in his cups, is not to be admonished. Abigail durst say nothing to Nabal whilst the wine was in his head. And the proud man is too full of himself to hear any good counsel.

4. David hath two complaints: Ps. cxix. 51, 'The drunkards made songs of me. The proud have had me exceedingly in derision;' so both of them sit in the chair of the scornful.

5. They are alike in their punishment in this world, for the drunkard and the proud man are both rewarded with contempt; all that walk in good ways are ashamed of them, and avoid their company. 'A man's pride shall bring him low,' Prov. xxix. 23. 'He that loveth wine and oil shall not be rich,' Prov. xxi. 17.

6. They are alike in the last judgment; for, Prov. xv. 25, 'The Lord will destroy the house of the proud.' And the apostle, 1 Cor. viii. 10, saith of drunkards, that none such shall inherit the kingdom of God. You see how like they be both *in culpa et in pœna*, fault and punishment.

Therefore humility is our lesson, and we shall find it an hard lesson to take out now in the overgrown pride of our times, wherein contrary examples do grow so thick. It is a great part of the study of many to outshine their neighbours in glorious buildings, gay apparel, rich furnitures of their houses. This kind of pride hath done much hurt, especially in the ruin of

(1.) Charity, which had wont to clothe the naked, feed the hungry, refresh the thirsty, and minister to the necessities of the poor brother.

(2.) The ruin of justice, which gives every one his own. I fear, if many proud and gay persons, that flaunt it in bravery of rich show, should do so, their feathers restored, they would be found naked.

(3.) The ruin of temperance, which prays, Give me not poverty, give me not riches, give me things convenient for me; for they be fools, in the judgment of the wise man, that die of prosperity.

(4.) The ruin of religion, for godliness is not itself without contentedness.

You have heard how deceitful a vanity pride is. 'The pride of thy heart hath deceived thee.'

I hasten to the second point, the disease: insatiableness.

It is set forth in two resemblances.

1. The proud man is resembled to hell.
2. He is resembled to death.

These are two things that cry 'Give, give,' and are never satisfied.

Observe whereinsoever any man or woman is proud, if they do know any bounds.

Is it pride in apparel? Who was ever fine enough? Do we not see the richest stuff laid and overlaid, almost hidden, with rich adornment of trimming? and when the stuff may call the wearer proud, the trim and fashion may resemble them to the grave and hell, and shall testify against them that nothing can satisfy them; and yet to this they add often change.

I do not say much change of rich apparel, but changing often in the wearing. I have heard of two or three shifts in a day. These be they that entertain every foreign fashion, and naturalise outlandish forms amongst us. Christ will one day tell somebody, 'I was stark naked, and ye clothed not me.'

The ambition that all sorts and degrees of men and women are sick of is a desire to exceed their own rank in show. The country striveth with the city, as far as their markets will bear it out; the city with the court. These encroachments put pride to shifts; for when mechanicals come so fast upon the ancient gentry of the land, usurping both their show and title, almost ashamed of the name of their trades and occupations that have made them so fine, the gentry are put to it to strain their tenant one note higher to enable them to the start; and their rising and growth must put on the nobility, and make them mend their pace. Thus insatiably do we strive to outgo ourselves, that goodly inheritances are worn out, and vanity doth end in misery in many; in them it continueth with scorn and disdain.

And when you have made yourself as fine as you can, you will come a great many degrees behind Solomon in his royalty; yet Solomon was not clothed like one of the lilies of the field.

Thus insatiable is the pride in buildings, a vanity which ladeth the earth here and there with specious, spacious piles of brick and stone, whereof the owners have scarce the pleasure of beholding the same with their eyes, being afraid of the hospitality that should correspond that great show of room.

The proud in beauty declare themselves insatiable in striving to mend God's work by art. *In pretio quondam ruga senilis erat*, the aged wrinkles were wont to be held in honour. But if there be any help for it now, time shall be spent in study how to hide and conceal the ruins of time.

The pride mentioned in my text is of power, which every one desireth, and few do know how to manage. The Chaldeans, having obtained some victories, are now ambitious to be lords of all the earth.

It is said of Pyrrhus, king of the Epirotes, he sits studying how he may get the next kingdom to him, to make himself strong enough to bid the next king battle, and to get the conquest of him, that the fear of his power may make the next king yield himself; and Alexander, when he had conquered the world, sat down and wept, that there were no more worlds left for him to conquer.

The bishop of Rome, from a diocesan jurisdiction, hath swelled by degrees, partly by his own ambition, partly by the connivance of princes, to an universal hierarchy, and his parasites make him the man to whom belongs *omnia subjecisti pedibus ejus, thou hast put all things under his feet.* His eldest son hath fairly dilated his empire. We know that in '88 he had not enough; he would have fain been dividing of Shechem, and meting out the valley of Succoth.

In inferior places, how are men transported with desire and power of command, and how insatiable in that desire! Witness the many offices, the various employments, which some have desired and obtained to be congested on them.

I say no more of this insatiable gulf of desire than my text saith: it is like two things that they love not, hell and death. Death is not satisfied but with all. It is named last in my text as the greediest of the two. Hell desires all the ungodly of the earth; it is a pit digged for the ungodly; but death swalloweth all: *Statutum est omnibus semel mori,* what man liveth and shall not see death? So insatiable is the desire of power.

This resemblance doth shake the strength of that desire much, if we think upon it well. I labour and strive to get many under my command, and death is labouring together with me to bring me to the grave; and if I do not use my power to the glory of God and the good of my brethren, hell is as busy and as greedy to devour me.

This is one of the crying sins of our land, insatiable pride. This makes dear rents, and great fines; this takes away the whole clothing of many poor to add one lace more in the suits of the rich; this shortens the labourer's wages, and adds much to the burden of his labour. This greediness makes the market of spiritual and temporal offices and dignities, and puts well-deserving virtue out of countenance. This corrupts religion with opinions, justice with bribes, charity with cruelty: it turns peace into schism and contention, love into compliment, friendship into treason, and sets the mouth of hell yet more open, and gives it an appetite for more souls.

The use of all is the doctrine of contentation, as we profess that we have our being, not of ourselves, but of God: 'In him we live, move, and have our being:' 'He made us, and not we ourselves;' so let us be content with his provision for us.

It was Satan's first suggestion to Adam; for so he had formerly corrupted himself and lost his first estate. To suggest pride, he would shew man a way how to be like God, and then all the fruits in the garden would not content him; he must taste also of the forbidden fruit. Haman was as high as the favour of the king could advance him, and yet he confessed, Esther v. 13, 'All this doth me no good.' Pope Julius the Third was forbidden to eat pork by his physician, and no other dish would please him. He commanded it to be set before him in despite of God; therefore hear the apostle: Heb. xiii. 9, 'It is good to have the heart stayed or established with grace, and not with meats which have not profited them,' &c,

The grace of contentment is like the ballast of the ship, which gives her her trim, and makes her strong and jocund upon the great waters. Faith doth bring us to God; it stoopeth us to him, it fasteneth us upon him. Pride maketh us shift for ourselves, and divideth us from God. He offereth his wings to such, and they will not be gathered together.

Let us know that we are never past the wings of God's protection here, and therefore let us resort humbly to them, for there is safety, and rest, and sufficiency of all good things. Let us remember we call him our Father, and therefore we may cast our care upon him. Let us know and remember that nothing but God can fill us. We are like broken vessels, that can hold nothing, without he fashion us behind and before; we are like fusty vessels, that corrupt all things we receive, without he purify our hearts by faith; we are leaking vessels, that let go all things, without he caulk us and make us tight; we are bottomless bags, wide-mouthed to take in, but unbottomed to retain anything, except he do give us contentment to stay our stomachs, and to remove from us,

1. An inordinate love of that which we have.
2. An inordinate desire of more.
3. An inordinate use of all.

The punishment will be *terror Domini*, the terror of the Lord.

Ver. 6–8. *Shall not all these take up a parable against him, and a taunting proverb against him, and say, Woe to him that increaseth that which is not his! how long? and to him that ladeth himself with thick clay! Shall they not rise up suddenly that shall bite thee, and awake that shall vex thee, and thou shalt be for booties unto them? Because thou hast spoiled many nations, all the remnant of the people shall spoil thee; because of men's blood, and for the violence of the land, of the city, and of all that dwell therein.*

2. The punishment of pride now followeth.

Concerning the words,

Shall not all these take up a parable against him?

By *all these*, he meaneth all those whom the king of Babylon and his Chaldeans have troubled and persecuted, and all lookers on also.

By taking up of a parable, which word is rendered by *apophthegma*; a grave and wise speech is here meant, declaring that the wisdom of men shall check the pride of the Babylonians, and proclaim them vain.

The *taunting proverb* which the Seventy render here προβλῆμα, signifieth *dicterium*, a bitter quip uttered in an enigmatical manner of speech, a secret gird full of salt and sharpness, where, under some obscurity of words, is secretly couched some galling and cutting tartness of meaning.

We must search this speech for two things, for here must be ἀπόφθεγμα, a wise saying, and here must be a taunt and salt taxation in some obscure and enigmatical speech.

The first is in the former words, wherein he denounceth a woe to him that makes up his heap with other men's goods; and he crieth to him 'How long?' taxing his insatiableness. The sharp and salt reproof is in these words, 'and to him that ladeth himself with thick clay.'

For, first, wherein he thinketh to gather an happiness, he reapeth nothing but woe.

2. Wherein he hopeth for ease and relaxation of his cares, he getteth a burden, which the word of *loading* implieth.

3. He is charged that he is author to himself of that burden; he loadeth himself; as David, 'he disquieteth himself.'

4. That for which he doth himself so much hurt, bringeth on himself so much danger, it is no better than thick clay.

The gold and silver of the earth is sharply and scornfully mentioned as no better than thick clay; and indeed as it cometh from the melting to the eye, gold seemeth such, even like to a thick and massy clay, hath no beauty in it to affect the eye.

And seeing the world prizeth this rich metal at so high a rate, that the Babylonian doth make no conscience of cutting the Jews' throat and breaking all laws of nations to get their gold, God doth in this smart quip shew how the Chaldean shall be censured and taxed abroad for his scraping, when all that he hath gotten is but thick clay.

If we go to our *principia naturæ*, principles of nature, we shall find that God made the earth, and whatsoever after that, either mineral, growing within the earth, grass or pearl, flower, tree, or fruit, growing on the earth, beast or bird, fish or fowl, worm or fly, living on the earth or in the water, and man, the lord of all, all are made of earth. Earth the chiefest material in their building; therefore to Adam said God, *Terra es*. If man, the most excellent of creatures, in the composition of his body be but thick clay, the style is high enough to give that title to any, either mineral or vegetable whatsoever.

Ver. 7. *Shall they not rise up suddenly that shall bite thee, and awake that shall vex thee, and thou shalt be for booties unto them?* Some interpreters think this verse also a part of that taunting speech which many shall use against Babylon and the Chaldeans, wherein they shall declare that they do look pride should have a fall.

The manner of speech frequent to the Hebrews by interrogation, *Shall they not rise up?* &c., hath more weight in it, and implieth both vehemency in the commination and assurance of the judgment threatened, more than if he had said, 'They shall arise that shall bite thee.'

Read Isaiah xiii. and see the burden of Babylon, and pass to the 14th, for this verse is but a short abridgment of that full prophecy, and expoundeth these words of my text, that the Medes and Persians shall very shortly arise to destroy Assyria, and all the Chaldeans. The same judgment is threatened by the prophet Jeremiah, chaps. l., li., a nation coming out of the north to make their land desolate; for Media is a city north from Babylon, whence Cyrus came against it. And for the manner of the taking of Babylon, it is here set down to be sudden: 'They shall rise up suddenly that shall bite thee.'

Herodotus reports that upon one of their great holidays, when all the city were in their dancing and disports, *ex inopinato eis Persæ astiterunt*, on a sudden the Persians came upon them; they came into the city, and took a part of it, when the other part sung out their song, and danced on, and knew not that the enemy had surprised them. So they were bitten, and vexed, and taken; and the mighty and glorious great city of Babylon was made a booty and prey to the Persians.

The greatness and riches of this city of Babylon, is by Herodotus thus expressed: The whole dominion of the Chaldeans being laid and assessed to maintain the king's wars for defence of his state, for the twelve months in the year, the charge of four months was imposed on Babylon, and all the rest of Asia bore the charge of the eight months; so that one-third of the imposition lay upon Babylon.

Ver. 8. *Because thou hast spoiled many nations.* The first monarchy that we read of in holy Scripture is that of the Assyrians, begun by Ninus, of whom Nineveh took name, and by Nimrod, whom histories call Belus, and after him succeeded by Semiramis his wife. This monarchy grew, by continual wars and violations of their neighbours, to an exceeding height and strength. So that the exaltation of that monarchy was the ruin of many nations in power, and their subjection to the Assyrians; and this monarchy lasted, as some write, *annos* 1300.

St Augustine, *de Civ. Dei*, lib. xvi. cap. 17, speaking of this monarchy, saith, *In Assyria prævaluerat dominatus impiæ civitatis, hujus caput erat illa Babylon.* He calleth it *nomen aptissimum, confusio,* confusion, actively, for it confounded all the parts of Asia, bringing them under one regiment, and it came itself after to a shameful confusion.

This victorious grassation of the Assyrians, overrunning all like to a deluge of waters, did so swell them with the pride above reproved, and here threatened, that the prophet Isaiah doth call this monarchy Lucifer: chap. xiv. 12, 'How art thou fallen from heaven, O Lucifer, son of the morning!' As in the judgment of the ancient learned fathers, alluding to the fall of the angels that kept not their first estate.

Nimrod their founder is called, Gen. x. 9, 'a mighty hunter before the Lord;' that is, a mighty tyrant and a great oppressor of men. The blood of men was not precious; the land, the city, and the inhabitants, all bent to spoil and to violence; therefore it is said, 'The remnant of the people shall spoil thee.'

There was not such an universal subjection to the monarchy of the Assyrians, but that there were a remnant left to come upon them, and to overcome them. These, as hath been said, were the Medes and Persians, whom God calleth his sanctified ones, his mighty ones for his anger; because he hath called them, and set them apart from others, to be ministers of his vengeance for the destruction of this proud nation. For he will make inquisition for blood, and they that have smitten with the sword shall now perish by the sword. (*De verbis hactenus.*)

In these words, which are the declaration of God's just judgment against the Chaldeans, before we proceed to the full handling of them,

We must first take notice of the just process of God against this pride of the Chaldeans; for it pleaseth God to give us here an account of his provocation, and he giveth in evidence against them, that their pride went not alone, but was accompanied with many sins.

1. Their gripple covetousness, in seeking to increase their own heap; and covetousness is a sin that God abhorreth. St Paul doth call it 'the root of all evil.'

2. Their violent invasion of the goods of others by injury, oppression, and extortion; for he increaseth that which is not his. Not to be content with our own is ungodliness, but to spoil and rob others, and to be our own carvers to take what we can get, is wrong to our brethren. Covetousness corrupteth ourselves, but oppression doth violate our neighbour, of whom the law giveth such charge, *ama proximum ut teipsum*.

3. Their folly; for what is this great stock which they have gathered, and what is the rich heap that they have caught? It is but thick clay. And what have they done with all their labour and travail, but made a burden thereof for themselves?

4. Their cruelty is charged upon them, which is expressed in sundry circumstances of amplification; as,

(1.) In the extremity of it, no less than spoiling, which comprehendeth all kinds of hard measure that can be offered.

(2.) In the extent of it, which is amplified by two circumstances.

[1.] Not persons, nor societies, towns, cities, but whole nations.

[2.] Many nations.

(3.) In the effect of their cruelty, which also brake forth into blood, the blood of men, a thing that God holdeth at such a price, that he not only made severe laws for preservation of life, but he maketh a curious inquisition for blood, when contrary to his law it is unjustly spilt, unto which God hath given a voice; for there is *vox sanguinis*, a voice of blood, as we see in Abel's story, and to which voice he lendeth an ear, for that blood crieth unto him.

(4.) In the general infection of this cruelty, which hath corrupted the whole land of the Chaldeans; the city, the great city of Babylon, and all the people that dwell therein.

The prophet in the former chapter did complain to God of the pride, and cruelty, and covetousness of the Chaldeans, in which as they exceeded, so the poor church of God smarted; and the patience of God forbearing to punish them, made them think that God gave no regard to them; and it made many even within the church stagger, fearing lest God had taken no notice of their sufferings, and their enemies' injuries. Do you not now receive it from the mouth of God himself, that he hath all those things written in his book, that he keepeth an exact account both of the offences done, and of the offenders?

(5.) To shew that they have abused his patience and longsuffering, by continuing in the evils abovementioned, he saith, How long? to shew that he hath contended with them in patience all this while, and that no forbearance will recover them from their evil ways, no spoil nor cruelty will satisfy them in their evil ways; therefore he proceedeth to judgment against them.

The argument of this text is the punishment of the pride of the Chaldeans, punished,

1. With just reprehension of all.
2. With derision, they shall be taunted.

3. *With spoil and destruction.*

Here we must first take notice of the justice of God's process against them; for he giveth account of his provocation, and rendereth a reason of his judgments.

Our lesson is, whensoever God punisheth, there is a fault deserving that punishment, for God is just, he doth not punish the innocent. Thus he began with the first sinners that we read of in the holy story, Gen. iii. 14. With the serpent, *quia tu hoc fecisti,* 'Because thou hast done this.' So to Adam, 'Because thou hast hearkened to the voice of thy wife,' &c. And to Cain, 'If thou do evil, sin (that is, the punishment of sin) standeth at the door.' And for the process against the old world: first, God saw the fault thereof, before either he repented the making of it, or resolved the punishing of it; and so forth, all the Scripture through, and through the experience of all times.

Reason 1. Because God is just,. and justice is a virtue that giveth *suum cuique,* every one his own. Now rods are for the back of fools, and all sinners are fools, and all men are sinners, and therefore none past the rod in the justice of God.

Reason 2. Because punishment, in the nature of it, is evil, though in the use of it it be good, for the good it doth; and sin brought it into the world, it is contemporary with sin, it cleaveth to it, it cannot be parted from it; as the mortality of man is joined with the nature of man.

Therefore we may conclude, whensoever we feel any punishment in ourselves, or see any inflicted on others, *subest culpa,* there is a power that deserveth this punishment.

Against this it may be objected that,

1. God doth chasten some of his own beloved children with punishments for their trial, that they may come forth as gold fined.

2. God doth some time correct his own for example of others.

3. The wicked and ungodly vex and torment the righteous, even for the serving the true God; many have lost their goods, their liberties, their lives for the

testimony of the truth. Thus did all those holy confessors, and all those glorious martyrs, suffer the cruelty of the enemies of God.

4. The corruption of justice, and the abuse of power, doth sometimes turn into tyranny; and so evil men are cherished, and good men punished; as the prophet Isaiah saith, 'He that abstaineth from evil, maketh himself a prey.'

5. Sometimes good princes are abused by their flatterers and lying informers, who possess them of an evil opinion against better men than themselves, as in the example of Mephibosheth, 2 Sam. xvi. 3, 4; for Ziba his bailiff accused him falsely of treason to David; and David, though a king of God's choosing, was not at leisure to search into the matter, but presently, not hearing the just defence of Mephibosheth, gave away to Ziba all that pertained to Mephibosheth.

6. Sometimes just persons, in execution of justice, are *nimium justi*, over wise; and such justice is injury; as Solomon saith, ' Be not just over-much:' and the light of nature taught the heathen to say, *Summum jus est summa injuria*.

7. Sometimes judges are swayed by the affection they bear to others, to regard rather the satisfying of their envy, whom they love, than the execution of justice, and so wrong may be done where it is not deserved; as Herod cut off John's head, for no dislike of him in himself, but to please his minion.

In answer to all these objections, put the case how you will, I am sure God is just, and will neither himself punish, nor cause, nor suffer any to punish, but where so much punishment is well deserved.

Peradventure, he that inflicteth the punishment may offend in it, and there may be a fault done in the manner of it; or that for which the punishment is inflicted may be no just cause, or the person may be mistaken; but still I say God is just, *subest culpa*, there is a fault; the hand of God, the will of God is in every punishment, and they never do anything without the justice of God. Job, that justified his integrity so stoutly, as we read in his story, did never deny himself to be a grievous sinner, and to deserve the punishment that he suffered, though he still did stand upon it, that he was not therefore punished.

If the punishment be for trial, the gold that is tried will be divided from the dross, and that dross deserveth a melting. If the punishment be for example, know that God will never give so ill example as to punish an innocent. If men do like men in the execution of God's judgments, know that God knows why he suffereth them so to do, for he searcheth the hearts and reins. Thus, many condemned to death by the law, according to probable evidence, profess their innocency at their death; yet can find in the book of their conscience evidence enough to condemn them worthy of death for something else.

Use. The use of all is, seeing God is just, and punisheth not but where he findeth sin; stand in awe, sin not, do your best to keep from the infection, lest you come under the dominion of sin; abstain from all appearance of evil, from the occasions and means of offence; resist Satan; quench not the Spirit, that should help your infirmities, redeem the time in which you should do good, and strive to enter into that rest. Thus doing, what punishment soever we suffer, it is rather the visitation of peace than the rod of fury, and God will turn it to our good.

The punishment here threatened:

1. Just reprehension. Shall not all these take up a parable against them, and say, 'Woe to him that increaseth that which is not his!' $\dot{\alpha}\pi o\varphi\theta\epsilon\gamma\mu\alpha$. I remember the question of our Saviour to his disciples, 'Whom say men what I, the Son of man, am?' It is wisdom for any private man, more for a great state, to inquire what fame it hath abroad.

The wisdom of state is such, as one government hath an eye to another; I speak not only of confederate nations, which have lidger* eyes in each other's commonwealth, but even of enemy-states, and such as stand neither in terms of hostility nor in terms of confederacy; they have their secret intelligence, and thus they know and judge each of other.

---

* That is, 'the eyes of leigers, or ambassadors.'—ED.

Nebuchadnezzar was a most potent prince, yet his neighbours did not approve his wisdom; they did condemn his violence, and cry out, Woe be to him. I understand this to be a great punishment to this mighty king, to be justly condemned for injustice, and to deserve the curse of his neighbouring nations. For extremes do ever carry the evil words, and the evil wishes of all that love virtue; and they cry woe to him that increaseth greedily and covetously that which is not his; and woe to him that wasteth prodigally that which is not his. The wisdom of policy doth hold violence and oppression hateful in great princes, and it calleth them pusillanimous and idle that will not stir in the just defence of their own.

But there is *sapientia sæculi hujus*, the wisdom of this world, which calleth all his own which he can compass directly or indirectly, justly or unjustly, which St Paul doth call enmity with God. Just princes are tender in that pursuit, holding that axiom of Cæsar irreligious and unjust, *Si jus violandum, regni causa;* and therefore, *sapientia quæ est desuper*, the wisdom from above crieth, Hand off, invade not, usurp not *aliena jura*, other men's rights; be content with thine own, for woe be to him that increaseth *non sua*, that which is none of his own.

Princes that manage the sword of justice, which is *gladius Dei*, the sword of God, must be tender how they draw that sword against God that committed it to them; and every attempt that their power maketh for that which is not theirs, doth arm itself against God.

Mr Calvin observeth well, *Manent aliqua in cordibus hominum justitiæ et æquitatis principia; ideo consensus gentium est quædam vox naturæ:* there abideth in the hearts of men certain principles of justice, therefore the consent of nations is a certain voice of nature.

Those princes that care not what nations do think and speak of them, but pursue their own ends against the stream and tide of *jus naturale*, natural right, do run themselves upon the just reprehension of other states, which wise and religious princes do labour to avoid.

1. Because the private conscience in these public persons can have no inward peace, where public equity is violated.

2. Because the old rule of justice is built upon the divine equity of nature, and confirmed by experience of time, that *male parta facilè dilabuntur*, evil gotten goods soon consume.

3. Because all that love this *jus naturale*, will soon find both will and means to resist encroachments, fearing their own particular, as all hands work to quench a fire.

But what cares Nebuchadnezzar, or Alexander, or Julius Cæsar, so they may add kingdom to kingdom? And what cares his holiness of Rome, so that he may be universal bishop, what other kings and bishops say of them?

To make this point profitable to ourselves, for we speak to private persons. The rule is general.

All that increase their own private estate by oppression and injustice, multiplying that which is not theirs, making prize of all that they can extort from their brethren, buying them out of house and home, wearying them with suits of molestation, spending the strength of their bodies with immoderate labours at so short wages as will not sustain them with things necessary; such, though their power do bear them out in their injustice, yet do they undergo the hard opinion and censure of all that love righteousness, and they do bear the burden of many curses. Let them lay this to heart, and take it for a punishment from the hand of God.

2. The derision, *taunted*.

What do these men but lade themselves with thick clay? This also may pass for a sharp punishment; kings and great persons are not privileged from the tooth of a satire, from the keen edge of an epigram, from the bold affront of a libel.

We live in the age of fresh and quick wits, wherein it is not an easy thing for eminent persons to do evil, and to escape tongue-smiting and wit-blasting, pens and pencils, a hand up to blazon great ones and their actions, and inferior persons want not eyes upon them to behold them, nor censures to judge them, nor rods to whip them. I must not draw from this place any authority to legitimate contumelies and disgraces, and that which we call breaking of bitter jests upon another, selling our salt cheap.

1. Therefore understand that bitter taunts, satires, and libels may be evil and unlawful, and yet God may make a good use of them to lash and scourge those that deserve ill; and they that are so girded and jerked shall do well to do as David did, to confess that God sent Shimei to curse; and as for Shimei, he shall see that God will find a time to pay him too. That this is a punishment sent from the hand of God we have full evidence from the witness of holy Scripture, even in this case.

The prophet Isaiah threateneth the Chaldeans with this judgment, 'Thou shalt take up this proverb'— the margin readeth this taunting speech—'against the king of Babel: how hath the oppressor ceased, the golden city ceased!' &c., Isa. xiv. 4. You see in derision she is called the golden city. And after, ver. 10, 'All they shall speak and say unto thee, Art thou also become weak as we? art thou also become like unto us? how art thou fallen from heaven, O Lucifer!' &c. Thus the great glory of the mighty monarchy is become *ludibrium vulgi, et fabula mundi*, the scoff of the vulgar, and the tale of the world.

So Jeremiah declareth that this shall be one part of the punishment of Babylon, she shall be laughed to scorn. Read at your leisure the 50th and 51st of Jeremiah; amongst many salt and sharp taunts spent upon Babel, this is one for a taste: chap. li. 8, 'Babylon is suddenly fallen and destroyed: howl for her, take balm for her pain, if she may be healed.' It is David's phrase, Ps. lix. 8, 'But thou, O Lord, shall laugh at them; thou shalt have all the heathen in derision.'

It was no small part of the passion of Jesus Christ, the subsannations and scornful derisions of his enemies; they made sport with him, as the Philistines did with Samson: 'Thou that couldest build the temple, come down,' &c.

It pleaseth God sometimes to suffer his good servants to be tongue-smitten, as we see in the example of David, and of Jeremiah, and Job, and others. And have many examples of his permission of it in the punishment of the wicked. This doth not justify contumelies, or make libels and scandalous derisions lawful, but it declareth them to be the rods of God.

Therefore let men tender their reputations, and do that which is right in their places, be they high or low, that they may not deserve ill of the times in which they live, that they may have good report of all men, and of the truth itself.

Amongst other things which, by way of caution, we may take warning of,

1. Let them that would live out of the danger of scorn and derision, apply themselves to glorify God in their bodies and in their souls, and to honour him, for God hath spoken it, 1 Sam. ii. 30, 'He that honoureth me, him will I honour; but they that despise me shall be lightly esteemed.'

2. Let such take care that they be no despisers of their brethren, that they sit not in the chair of the scornful, for the wages of the scorner is scorn, and they that trust in themselves and despise others go away from the sight of God unjustified. Can pride have a fall, and the lookers-on not laugh them to scorn?

3. Let such keep a good tongue in their own heads, for many fair pretenders of religion and outward professors are as long as Pambo in Eusebius taking out of that lesson from David, *Servabo circa os meum capistram ne peccem lingua,* 'I will set a watch,' &c.

It was in fashion while that they that sought (as they pretended) reformation of the church, sought it in the way of libelling, and breaking jests upon the prelates and malignants of the church. But St James telleth us, chap. i. 26, that 'if any among us seem to be religious, and refraineth not his tongue, that man's religion is in vain.'

4. Let such take out the lesson of the apostle: Col. iv. 6, 'Let their speech always be with grace, seasoned with salt, that you may know how to answer every man.' This is the seasoning of wisdom from above.

which, being the breath of the Holy Ghost, which is the spirit of meekness, doth rather put the burdens of our brethren upon us in Christian compassion than heap burdens upon them in spite and disdain.

2. Yet I do not determine all sharp and satirical tartness of speech unlawful; the acrimony of a taunt hath sometimes due place, and it may be some of the fire from God's own altar, when they do not proceed from anger, envy, desire of revenge, vain ostentation of wit, flattery of others whom it may please, pride of our own hearts. When Adam had transgressed, and God had laid his curse upon him, God said, Gen. iii. 22, 'Behold, the man is become like one of us, to know good and evil.' St Augustine saith, *Verba sunt insultantis, quòd non solùm factus fuerit qualis esse voluit, sed nec illud quod fàctus fuerat conservavit.*

God derideth the folly of man fallen away from him. It is said of Elijah, 1 Kings xviii. 27, 'And it came to pass at noon, that Elijah awaked* them, and said, Cry aloud; for he is a god: either he is talking, or he is pursuing, or he is in a journey, or peradventure he sleepeth, and must be awaked.' So the prophet Isaiah plays upon the idol makers and idolaters as if he had one of our papists in hand, for he sets a man upon the stage, having cut down a tree: Isa. xliv. 16, 17, ' He burneth part of it in the fire; with part thereof he eateth flesh; he roasteth roast, and is satisfied: yea, he warmeth himself, and saith, Aha, I am warm, I have seen the fire: and the residue thereof he maketh a god, even his graven image: he falleth down to it, and worshippeth it, and prayeth to it, and saith, Deliver me; for thou art my god.' You see what sport the prophet maketh with idolaters, and sure he had the Spirit of God. The apocryphal book of Baruch, chap. vi., is a very pleasant bitterness against idols and idolaters.

Surely this example in my text is justifiable, for it taxeth the covetous oppressors of the earth for fools, that take so much pain, and do so much wrong to load themselves with thick clay.

---

* Qu. 'mocked'?—Ed.

Obj. But is it not an injury to almighty God to set no higher price, and to give no better title, to the richest of all metals, that which God himself was pleased should be used in the choice vessels and ornaments of his own house, than thus to indignify it?

Sol. I answer, the prophet doth not indignify the creature, but as God said to man, *Pulvis es*, thou art dust, and he told him true out of what materials the frame of his body was built, so it is no disgrace to gold to call it thick clay, it being no other in the matter of it.

And howsoever good use may be made of these outward riches, yet are they never to be esteemed for themselves, but for their use, which, if men on earth could once understand and believe, they would not set their hearts upon them. St Peter, 1 Peter i. 18, calleth them 'corruptible things;' St Paul, 1 Tim. vi. 17, calleth them 'uncertain riches.'

Every man is easily drawn to study and labour to the getting of this burden, and so insatiable in desire that few say with Esau, 'I have enough.'

There is a singular wisdom in the use of riches, which few do seek, because they do not understand for what this thick clay serveth. In the Latin phrase, all those things which we use are called *impedimenta*, impediments: for as the baggage of an army is of necessary use, yet hindereth the speed of their march, so do our riches; they are the faculties of well-doing, yet we can hardly attain the wisdom to keep them from being hindrances and lets to us in our journey homewards. They serve us for fame and reputation, for they support our credit in the world. They serve us for show, for they furnish the table with dainties, the back with bravery, &c. They serve us for custody, to lay up for posterity. They serve for dole and distribution, to be bestowed upon good uses. They serve to buy out dangers, and to deliver us from evils. They serve to make us friends. And they that can plaster their walls with this thick clay may keep off many a storm, and much foul weather.

Yet we have seen that all rich men are not happy,

even in the things of this life. Tully saith of Rabirius Posthumus, *In studio rei amplificandæ, non avaritiæ prædam, sed instrumentum bonitati quærebat;* that is the best use of them.

We see in this example that the walls of Babel, though plastered, and the roofs tiled with this thick clay, so as it was called the Golden City, could not privilege it from ruin and contempt. Therefore let us not strive and study by indirect means, nor take too much and immoderate care by direct means, to overload ourselves with this thick clay; we shall carry none of it away with us when we die, and we are not sure that they shall enjoy it to whom we would fainest leave it.

The third punishment of Babel doth shew that this thick clay hath wings. It is subject to spoil. It makes Babel a good booty; for when those sponges have sucked in their full draught, many of them come to the wringing and squeezing till they be left dry. There be such in the world as study the emptying of those full vessels, and find means to spring a leak in them. This fall from plenty and fulness to want, from honour to low condition, from power and command to subjection and awe, makes the proud man a scorn to the world; for to outlive riches and honour and power, and to see others decked in our trappings, whereof we had wont to be so proud, this pricks our bladder, and lets out all the wind, and leaveth us lank and empty.

This is the justice of God's proceeding against the proud, whom he resisteth, as you heard out of Obadiah in the example of Edom, and see now in the example of the Chaldeans. As they that despise others are now punished with contempt, so they that spoiled others are now punished with spoil. One while the hand is receiving bribes as fast as it can to get all, and in a moment the same hand is giving of bribes as fast, if it be possible to save some. If, therefore, there be no better hold to be taken of these outward things which make many so proud, if riches increase, set not thine heart upon them; use them rather than keep them.

Yet this is a great comfort to all that are oppressed by the proud tyranny of men, 'God is still good to Israel, even to all that have true hearts,' Ps. cxxv. 3; and 'the rod of the wicked shall not rest upon the lot of the righteous.' God will find a time to spoil the spoiler, and to strip him out of all. There is neither wisdom, nor counsel, nor strength against the right hand of God, and that right hand will find out all his enemies.

Greatness and power are fearful to the common man, yet nothing can restrain either the thoughts of men and their judgments, but that they will search into the actions of the highest, and observe what is done according to the rules of justice, and wherein religion and justice are wounded. Nothing can hinder but that where men may dare to communicate their thoughts to faithful ears, there the scroll of grievances will be unfolded, and the injustice of tyrannical oppressions will be laid open.

Nothing can hinder the vengeance of our just God, the king of all the earth, but that he will take the matter into his own hands, and deliver the oppressed, and spoil the spoiler. Oppressors must die; then will their names stink and be abhorred of posterity, and there will be black records made of them in the books of time. When God putteth his hand to the spoiling of them, he will spoil them in all that they trusted in.

1. In their friends: they shall fall off, and be the first that shall help to strip them.

2. In their honours: every man shall put an hand to the casting of dust upon them.

3. In their reputations: their names shall be hateful upon the face of the earth.

4. In their posterity: God shall curse their seed, and never trust any of them again with his power, or the execution of his judgments.

Only let the oppressed wait the leisure of God for this: 'the vision is for an appointed time; but it will come to pass, it will not fail.'

Ver. 9–14. *Woe to him that coveteth an evil covetousness to his house, that he may set his nest on high, that he may be delivered from the power of evil! Thou hast consulted shame to thy house by cutting off many people, and hast sinned against thy soul. For the stone shall cry out of the wall, and the beam out of the timber shall answer it. Woe to him that buildeth a town with blood, and stablisheth a city by iniquity! Behold, is it not of the Lord of hosts that the people shall labour in the very fire, and the people shall weary themselves for very vanity? For the earth shall be filled with the knowledge of the glory of the Lord, as the waters cover the sea.*

These words do tax the Chaldeans with another sin, and denounce a punishment against it. Concerning the words, *woe to him that coveteth an evil covetousness to his house,* there is a good covetousness, which engrosseth the treasure of spiritual graces, of which the apostle, Ζηλοῦτε δέ τὰ χαρίσματα τὰ κρείττονα, 'Covet the best gifts,' 1 Cor. xii. 31. Here is desire with intention; it must be zeal, and zeal with emulation, striving to be before others, that no man get precedence of us therein; but the things desired be χαρίσματα, that is, such gifts are given of free grace.

But that covetousness is evil to a man's house, that is, to his estate, and family, and posterity, which is joined with ambition of height: that he may set his nest on high to be above others, which is joined with distrust in God, and trust in things temporal; that he may be delivered from the power of evil, believing that honour and high place will set him out of the reach of misery.

Ver. 10. *Thou hast consulted shame to thy house in cutting off much people.* Here is another sin added to covetousness and ambition, cruelty and shedding of blood, to make their own portion fat; and whereas they have studied honour and greatness, all turns to shame abroad in the world, and to the burden of a guilty conscience within them: 'Thou hast sinned against thy soul.'

Ver. 11, 12. For the stone shall cry out of the wall, the beam out of the timber shall answer it. Woe to him that buildeth a town with blood, and establisheth a city by iniquity. Here God bringeth in inanimate and senseless things accusing and upbraiding them. They cannot look upon either the stone-work of the walls or the timber work on the floors and roofs of their buildings, but they shall hear the voice of their upbraidings speaking to their consciences that these are ill gotten : rapine and cruelty put them together, and married them in that frame without a licence. The voice of their clamour is woe to him that hath done so.

Ver. 13. Behold, is it not of the Lord of hosts that the people shall labour in the very fire, and the people shall weary themselves for very vanity ? I understand him thus : it is God's own hand against them that they shall endure hard and extreme labour, as it were in the fire, to compass their own ends ; and when they have crowned themselves, they shall reap a crop of vanity, as David, ' Man disquieteth himself in vain.'

Ver. 14. For the earth shall be filled with the knowledge of the Lord, as the waters cover the sea. That is, God, who by his long forbearance and remissness, is forgotten in the world, shall now declare himself in the execution of justice, that he shall be known : as David saith, ' God is known by executing judgment, *ut aquæ*, as the waters,' *i. e. sine mensura*, that is, without measure.

The sum of this section is the denunciation of that judgment of God against the Chaldeans, wherein we consider,

1. *Peccatum*, the sin.
2. *Pœnam*, the punishment.
3. *Effectum*, the effect.

1. *Peccatum*, here is a chain. For,

(1.) Here is infidelity : he would be delivered from the power of evil, but he will not trust God with protecting him from it.

(2.) Here is ambition, desire of high place to build his nest on high, for more security.

(3.) Here is covetousness, to get the means of this high rising.

(4.) Here is cruelty, to break through all impediments that stand in the way.

2. *Pœna.*
   (1.) Shame to his house.
   (2.) Sin against his soul.
   (3.) Loss of labour.

3. *Effectus.* 'The earth shall be filled with the knowledge of the glory of the Lord,' &c.

1. *De peccato.* One observation I gather from this whole point concerning this sin of the Chaldeans. It is St Augustine's, *Peccatum nunquam est solitarium*, sins grow in clusters. It is a stream that runneth in the channel of nature; and the further it runs, the more corruptions send in their currents into it; and, as rivers, the further they run the wider they grow, so doth sin, *viresque acquirit eundo.* 'When lust hath conceived, it bringeth forth sin;' and lust may say of that birth, as Leah did, when Zilpah also bare Jacob a son: Gen. xxx. 11, 'A troop cometh, and she called his name Gad;' for sin is sociable.

In the temptation which corrupted Eve, 1. Satan suggested infidelity, shaking her faith in the truth of God's word. 2. He gave a touch upon the justice of God, that it was scarce equal that God should except any tree, and not give Adam unlimited power.

3. He suggested a titillation of pride, making her believe that they might be like God.

4. Wherewith is joined a suggestion of discontent with their present state.

5. There went with this a tang of gluttonous desire.

So in Gehazi's sin, who was Elisha's servant, 2 Kings v. 20.

1. He grudged that Naaman, the Syrian, should go away with such a favour done him, and carry away the whole present that he rendered to his master.

2. He had a covetous desire to have some of it.

3. He went after, and told Naaman a lie: 'My master hath sent me.'

4. Another lie followed: 'There be two young men of the sons of the prophets.'

5. He was sent to demand a talent of silver, and two changes of raiment for them.

6. He dissembled. He must be urged to take two talents.

7. He made a cunning conveyance. He bestowed them in the house, and let the young men go secretly.

8. He shut up all with another lie : 'Thy servant went no whither.'

David's sin had many sins in it.

1. A sin against God in the disobedience of his law.

2. Sin against his own body, in defiling it.

3. A sin against the body of his neighbour's wife.

4. A sin against the religion which was so scandalised.

5. A sin against his neighbour's life, (1.) *Inebriavit eum;* (2.) *Jussit occidi.*

6. Which followed all these, a neglect of God's service for ten months together, in which he continued impenitent.

St James saith, chap. ii. 10, 'Whosoever shall keep the whole law, and yet offend in one point, is guilty of all.'

Quest. How can a man keep the whole, and yet break the whole law of God ?

Sol. He is called here a keeper of the whole law, either,

1. By supposition, and so it is but a case put thus. Put the case a man could keep the whole law, save only in some one thing.

2. Or by his own opinion of himself.

3. Or by his endeavour to keep all.

Yet this man offending in one, breaketh the whole law.

1. Because there is such a concatenation of the duties of religion and justice, that he which offendeth in one breaketh the chain.

2. Because any one sin unrepented, violateth love and obedience, which, if it be not full, it is no love, no obedience at all.

For the breach of one commandment doth distaste all the rest of our obedience, as a little leaven soureth the whole lump; therefore, though we cannot say that he which breaketh the Sabbath committeth adultery, or that he that stealeth is a murderer, yet we may say that he that doth break the least commandment of the law, is guilty of the breach of the whole law in omission, though not in commission, seeing the obedience that the law requireth failing in one duty corrupteth all that we do, say, or think.

Let us now behold the concurrence of sins in the Chaldean, and begin,

1. At his incredulity, for he would be delivered from evil; but he trusteth not God with it, but goeth his own way to it. This is the mother sin of all evil ways and means unlawfully used to accomplish men's ends here on earth, distrust in God. For when we use fraud, and lying, and dissembling and concealing of the truth, and bind untruths with oaths, to gain credit to what we say untruly; when we make no conscience of injury, which may be hidden with cunning, or borne out with violence, all this proceeds from distrust in God. And so we grow guilty of the two great evils of which God himself complaineth: Jer. ii. 13, 'For my people have committed two evils: they have forsaken me, the fountain of living waters, and hewed them out cisterns, broken cisterns, that can hold no water.' Again this: Heb. iii. 12, 'Take heed, lest there be in any of you an evil heart of unbelief, in departing from the living God.' The heart that distrusteth in God, departeth from him; therefore he saith, 'It is a people that do err in their hearts, because they have not known my ways.'

The corruption, then, is in the heart; for if that did love truly, it would trust God wholly; for where we love faithfully, we trust boldly. 'But the god of this world hath blinded the minds of them which believe not,' 2 Cor. iv. 4. That answereth his question, 'Who hath bewitched you, that you should not obey the truth?'

Infidelity is the root of all evils in us; for we cannot fear any threatening, where we do not believe any danger. We cannot hope for any benefit where we do not believe any promise; for infidelity doth take away all wisdom from us. This makes us to withdraw ourselves from the Lord, and it is a note of the wicked man, 'neither is God in all his ways.'

Thus saith the Lord, Jer. xvii. 5–8, 'Cursed be the man that trusteth in man, and maketh flesh his arm, and whose heart departeth from the Lord: for he shall be like the heath in the desert, and shall not see when good cometh; but shall inhabit the parched places in the wilderness, in a salt land and not inhabited. Blessed is the man that trusteth in the Lord, and whose hope the Lord is: for he shall be a tree planted by the waters, and that spreadeth out her roots by the river, and shall not see when heat cometh, but her leaf shall be green; and shall not be careful in the year of drought, neither shall cease from yielding fruit.'

I need not say more of this argument. Here is reason enough given why you should commit your way to the Lord; why you should cast your care upon him; why you should not leave him, to trust to yourselves. David saith, 'He made us, and not we ourselves:' he saw us imperfect in the womb: he fashioned us. 'Thy hands have made me, and fashioned me;' 'he took me from the womb.' He addeth, 'Upon thee have I depended ever since I hung upon the breasts of my mother.' When we are hungry, he giveth bread that strengtheneth man's heart. When we had not wit and understanding to shift for ourselves, who fed and clothed, and preserved us then? 'Surely his hand is not shortened, but his arm is stretched out still.' Suppose that without him we could get bread, 'man liveth not by bread only.' Suppose that without him we could sow much seed, 'it is only he that giveth increase.'

Let us observe the examples of God's judgments upon such as forsake God, and trust their money, or their friends, or corrupt means, to preserve them: 'One day telleth another.' The Chaldeans trust not in God: their own net is their god, their own yarn is their idol, they kiss their own hands. But 'fear ye the Lord, all his saints, and trust in him; for he never faileth them that trust in him.'

I have blamed some for buying and selling on the Sabbath; they have answered that they are poor, and are forced to it, to help to feed them. Is not this infidelity? They dare not trust God for their meat; they dare trust to their own ways against the precise commandment of God.

Unlawful recreations on the Sabbath are so defended; poor labouring men, that work all the six days, must have some time to refresh themselves. But I would fain know by what indulgence they may dispense with the law of the Sabbath. God hath bidden thee to remember to keep the whole day holy; if thy recreations be holy, thou keepest the law; if unholy, thou breakest it.

When some are detected of fraud and theft, their plea is their necessity. Here is a root of infidelity; for doth God lay a necessity upon any man to break his law? He hath laid on thee a necessity of labour; if that will not do, he hath given the rich charge of thee.

The truth is, that this root of infidelity doth yet remain in the hearts of most of us, and is the cause of all the sins that are committed. For the light of the gospel doth shine much more clear now than ever it did in this land, and the knowledge of the truth is more spread than ever before here. Yet never was there greater corruption of manners, nor more cunning shifts devised for the advancing of men's particulars.

The crying sins of the Jews, injuries done between man and man; corruption and contempt of religion; corruption of justice; to all these our land doth plead guilty. Where is the fault?

Have you not heard, have you not been taught, the ways of the Lord? Have you not been admonished of your duty? Have you not been chidden and threatened for these things? Hath not the seal of God's judgments, written within and without with lamentations, mourning, and woe, been opened and read to you?

Hath not God rained examples thick of his justice and judgment against high and low for these things? Why, then, is not this amended?

There is a root of infidelity; we do not, we dare not, trust God; and from hence comes,

1. In some atheism; they live without God in the world.

2. In others epicurism ; they live all to delight.

3. In others temporising, and following and serving men.

4. In others heresy, embracing their own opinions.

5. In others apostasy from religion and faith.

6. In others hypocrisy, seeming what they are not.

7. In most carnal security, not caring for threatenings.

8. In many wilful ignorance, not caring for the knowledge of God.

But thou, man and woman of God, fly these things, and know the Lord. The more thou knowest him, the more thou lovest him ; the more thou servest him, the more thou trustest him, and the more he blesseth thee.

2. Ambition : ' that he may set his nest on high.'

Ambition is a limb of pride, and it is well set forth in my text. It is a building of a nest on high ; it is but a nest that the ambitious man doth set up, but he would have it high, to overlook all ; yet that doth not make it safe, for there be clouds that can carry fire from below to consume it, and there is lightning from above to inflame it, and there is tempests and strong winds to shake it. And the axe is laid to the root of the tree in which the nest is built, and with the fall of that tree the nest comes to the ground. The highest tree for a subject to build his nest in is the favour of the prince ; yet David saith, ' Trust not in princes, for there is no help in them : their breath departeth, they return to the earth, and their thoughts perish.' It may be that he that sitteth next in the chair of sovereignty will be no tree for the same birds to build in.

Ambition is an inordinate desire of honour. St Gregory hath a rule which would stop the mouth of suitors and competitors for honours : *Locus regiminis desiderantibus negandus est, fugientibus offerendus. Virtutibus ergo pollens, coactus ad regimen veniat.*

Naturally, the love that every man beareth to himf and the good opinion that pride putteth into him of himself, doth make him desire to set his nest high ; and therefore every man observeth the course of the times in which he liveth, to see which is the readiest way to rise.

The king is called the fountain of honour, for from the ruler of the people all subordinations of rule derive themselves; and therefore, Prov. xxix. 26, 'Many seek the face of the ruler.' The way of preferment is soon found, and ambition hath a foot for it. The prophet's phrase, *Pes superbiæ*, the foot of pride. If only virtue were the way, only virtue would be studied.

But I look not so low as the throne of earthly princes for the fountain of honour. I hear the psalmist say, Ps. lxxv. 6, 7, 'For promotion cometh neither from the east, nor from the west, nor from the south. But God is judge: he putteth down one, and setteth up another.'

Many are ambitious of high places who have both friends and means, and yet cannot climb; many more unlikely speed before them; and I can ascribe this to nothing but the supreme hand of God, from whom all promotion cometh; he will have his will done.

Some he raiseth to their own ruin, others to the punishment and correction of the sins of the time in his anger; others for the good of men, in favour of his church and the commonwealth.

It becomes not us to censure the powers that are ordained of God, as the apostle teacheth, or to envy their high nests; but let every soul be subject to the ordinance of God, and rest in his will, by whom princes reign, and by whom they advance where* he pleaseth to set up.

But ambition of high nests is the theme of our discourse, which is an inordinate desire of honour; and that is a sin. It corrupted the angels which fell, and they impoisoned our parents with it in paradise; both desired to be like God, neither stood content with the glory of their creation. Concerning which, understand that the state of creation did give man no further dominion than this: Gen. i. 28, 'Replenish the earth, and subdue it; and have dominion over the fish of the sea, and over the fowls of the air, and over every living thing that moveth upon the earth.' Here is no dominion given to man over man; but all mankind is

* Qu. 'whom'?—ED.

endowed with equal dominion over all these things, and man is to acknowledge no sovereign lord but God his Maker. But presently after the fall, for the punishment of the woman, who had brought the desire of her husband subject to her, by tempting him to eat of the forbidden fruit, God said to her, Gen. iii. 16, 'Thy desire shall be subject to thy husband, and he shall rule over thee.' Yea, when God saw Cain's countenance cast down, he called him to account for it; and knowing his discontent to be against Abel, he said to Cain, Gen. iv. 7, 'Unto thee his desire shall be subject, and thou shalt rule over him;' which St Chrysostom doth expound, *de privilegio primogeniturœ*.

But as sin brought in the law, for *justo non est posita lex*, so sin brought in magistracy for execution of the law, and brought down the sword of God amongst men; and the equal condition of mankind in his creation by sin was changed into male and female, not in sex, but in subjection, high and low, rich and poor, bond and free. So that this ambition of an higher nest came in with sin, and being so brought in at first, it cannot be without sin.

St Jerome speaks bugs* words, *Cave honores quos sine culpa tenere non potes; sublimitas honorum magnitudo scelerum.* And St Augustine complains of nothing more than that he was made a bishop; he was an holy man, but a man, and his passion transported him. *In nullo sentio Deum ita iratum mihi quam in hoc, quod cum indignus essem poni ad remum, positus sum ad amplustre, sive gubernaculum ecclesiœ.* But howsoever his humility unworthied him to himself, it was God's great blessing to his church, not only then, but in all succeeding ages, that God so promoted him.

One thing among the rest maketh ambition an unmanly sin, for two contraries meet in the ambitious, that is, pride and a base mind: pride striving to climb high, and a base mind servilely attending the means of rising, waiting and observing such as may help him up, as one that climbeth embraceth every bough, and huggeth in his arms what he shortly treadeth under his foot.

* Qu. 'big'? Or is it words that may frighten us, as a bugbear?—ED.

But Seneca saves me a labour, for he doth describe such a man to the life: *Ambitiosus semper est pavidus. Timet quod dicat vel faciat, quid oculis hominum displiceat; honestatem mentitur, humilitatem simulat, cunctis adulatur, cunctis inclinat, omnium est servus et tributarius, gravem habet in se pugnam.*

The end of the Chaldean's ambition to set his nest so high, is that he may be delivered from the power of evil. Herein is a great fallacy, for be high nests the safest, and is greatness security? May not we that have lived to see in few years great changes, say that high preferments be giddy and slippery, *feriuntque summos fulmina montes?*

The reasons why ambition maketh men unhappy.

1. The ground of it is pride, which is an over-weening ourselves and our own worth; and this robbeth God of glory; for *quid habes quod non accepisti*, therefore God resisteth the proud.

2. The whole operation of ambition is by the wisdom of this world, and that is folly. Petrus Ravenna doth set it out well:

Ambitio est quædam simia charitatis: charitas patiens est pro æternis: ambitio patitur omnia pro caducis: charitas benigna est pauperibus, ambitio divitibus: charitas omnia suffert pro veritate; ambitio pro vanitate; utraque omnia credit, omnia sperat, sed dissimili modo.

3. It is altogether uncharitable; for *charitas ut teipsum*. It is Job's phrase of the fatherless, he was brought up with me as with a father; so doth charity bring up inferiors, and equals grow together; but ambition doth not, cannot affect *magnitudinem suam, sine parvitate aliena.*

4. It is before expressed to be insatiable, *quis enim modus adsit honori?* A man desireth first to be eminent in the street wherein he lives, and then in the city; and yet having attained his desire, as Seneca saith, *Navis quæ in flumine magna est, in mari parvula est.* One that is high and great in the city, in the country where he lives, in the university, let him come to the court, and he shall see how many spheres of greatness do move above him. Here is more work for ambition: if we remember the law, *proximum ut*

teipsum, 'thy neighbour as thyself,' we will no more desire to exceed one the other in the state wherein we live, than a man desireth one hand or one leg, in proportion of strength and bigness, to exceed the other in his body.

5. We have a fair example in our elder brother, for though he was such as to whom it was said, Heb. ii. 17, *Adorent eum omnes angeli ejus*, 'worship him, all ye angels,' yet to become our brother; 'In all things it behoved him to be made like unto his brethren.' He could not do this without humiliation; there was no power above him to humble him, and 'he thought it no robbery to be equal with God;' the power that did it was in himself, *humiliavit semet ipsum*, he humbled himself.

Ambition, therefore, putteth us out of the way of life. Christ humbled himself: *Et qui vult esse discipulus meus sequatur me*, 'He that will be my disciple must follow me.'

The doctrine of contentedness doth still offer itself to us, commanded in the last of the ten, for *non concupisces aliena* saith, *sorte tua contentus*, be contented with thy lot. This also serveth for the next point.

3. They are charged with covetousness, of which Christ saith, 'Take heed and beware of covetousness,' giving us a double caution against it.

The apostle giveth a reason, because it is the root of all evil, 1 Tim. vi. 10; but that reason doth not draw blood, for where the conscience is not tender, *malum culpæ*, the evil of punishment[*] is not feared. But it followeth, 'Which while some have coveted after, they have erred from the faith, and pierced themselves through with many sorrows.'

Ambition hath this handmaid to attend it, this factor to negotiate for it; for ambition is not supported without great charge. Our own times tell us so, and ambition cannot be a great spender, if covetousness be not a great getter. Covetousness is an inordinate desire of the wealth of this world, and is many ways culpable.

[*] Qu. 'sin'?—ED.

1. Because God hath given man dominion of the earth, and hath put all things under his feet, let not us remove them, and, as David saith, let us not *cor apponere*, set our heart upon them.

Gold and silver are lower put under us than the surface of the earth, for they grow within the bowels of the earth, nearer to hell, to shew the danger that is in them. Therefore the apostles had these things not put into their bosoms, or into their hands, but laid at their feet.

2. Because the Scripture hath expressed the woe of God belonging to the covetous, as you have heard, *Væ homini qui congregat non sua*, woe to the man which gathereth not his own.

They that are covetous do carry *stateram dolosam*, a deceitful balance, Hosea xii. 7, for, lay the conscience in one scale, and the least gain that is in the other, the conscience is found too light, as St Augustine, *Lucrum in arcâ, damnum in conscientiâ*.

For St Paul, Eph. v., calleth covetousness idolatry; and Christ calleth Mammon the god of the covetous: 'Ye cannot serve God and Mammon.' This is clear; for where doth the covetous man bestow and place his faith, hope, and love, but in his wealth, which we do owe to God?

The rich man sang a *requiem* to his soul, Luke xii.: 'Now my soul, make merry, for thou hast goods enough laid up for many years.'

3. Because covetousness is a fruitful sin; the daughters thereof are commonly

(1.) Usury; (2.) rapine; (3.) fraud; (4.) bribes; (5.) simony.

(1.) Concerning usury, let me out of the word say only to you, that he shall dwell in the Lord's tabernacle, that is, shall rest under God's protection on earth; and he shall dwell in the holy hill, that is, possessions in heaven, who 'putteth not his money out to usury,' Ps. xv. Where he shall dwell that doth so, you may easily conclude.

If you will hear the judgment of a parliament, the

statute* concerning the forbidding of usury doth begin thus: 'Forasmuch as all usury by the laws of God is sin, and detestable, Be it therefore enacted,' &c.

If thou wilt know the judgment of learned divines, fathers both of the eastern and western churches, councils, later divines have written against it, and detected it unlawful, so that it is of all learned evil spoken of.

But the covetousness of the Chaldeans was not of this sort, therefore not of purpose to be handled, but incidentally to be remembered; yet *non sine morsu in transitu*, yet not without a lash in the way.

(3.) Fraud is another of the daughters of covetousness, when we by any wit, or the art of seeming, do over-reach one another in matter of negotiation, of which the apostle, 1 Thes. iv. 6: 'That no man go beyond, or defraud his brother in any matter, because the Lord is the avenger of all such, as we also have forewarned you, and testified.'

(4.) Bribes is another daughter of covetousness. It was part of Samuel's purgation of himself: 1 Sam. xii. 3, 'Of whom have I received bribes to blind mine eyes therewith?' For Solomon saith, Prov. xvii. 23, 'A wicked man taketh the gift out of the bosom, to pervert the ways of judgment.' Micah describeth more than his own times: chap. iii. 11, 'The heads of Sion judge for reward, and the priests thereof teach for hire, and the prophets thereof divine for money: yet will they lean upon the Lord, and say, Is not the Lord among us? no evil can come upon us.' Read on.

(5.) Simony is another daughter of covetousness. I say no more of it, but leave it with St Peter's blessings, *Pereat argentum tuum tecum*, 'let thy money perish with thee.'

But rapine was the proper and natural daughter of the covetousness of the Chaldeans; they had their angle, and their net, and their drag; nothing could escape them. The great fish did eat up the little ones; oppression was the crying sin of Babylon, all their neighbours did groan under it.

* An. 14 Elizab.

(1.) This sin doth destroy *jus naturale*, natural right, which is, *quod tibi fieri non vis, alteri ne feceris*, do as thou wouldst be done to; out of which principles these two do arise:

1. *Ne cui noceas*, hurt none.
2. *Ut communi bono deservias*, serve the common good.

(2.) It offendeth the written law, which doth not only restrain *actum rapinæ, non furaberis*, the act of rapine, thou shalt not steal, but *voluntatem rapinæ, non concupisces*, but the will, thou shalt not covet.

Agur the son of Jakeh saith, Prov. xxx. 14, 'There is a generation whose teeth are as swords, and their jaw-teeth as knives, to devour the poor from off the earth, and the needy from among men.' This generation is not yet grown barren. Christ saith, *Pauperes semper habebitis vobiscum*, you shall have always the poor with you; and this generation of oppressors will be ever teeming so long as they have such matter to work upon, for the rich and mighty will shift for themselves.

(3.) It incurreth the severe censure of God's justice; for if God say, 'Go, ye cursed,' to them that did not *dare sua*, give their own, *quid faciet eis qui rapuerunt aliena?* woe to them that take that which is none of theirs.

(4.) This sin of rapine doth incur the curses of them that are robbed; for every man crieth woe to such as congest that which is not their own.

(5.) This sin doth hinder the ascent of the prayers of them that commit it. God will not admit them to his presence, for so God saith, Isa. i. 18, ' Relieve the oppressed; judge the fatherless; plead for the widow. Come now, and let us reason together.'

(6.) The time shall come when those that suffer wrong shall judge their oppressors, for ' the saints shall judge the world.'

Therefore let every man make conscience of doing violence. 'Doubtless there is a God that judgeth in the world.' Let us value men as our brethren, and seek their good; let us direct our intentions and subventions to that only end, that he that loveth God may declare it by loving his brother also; let our brethren grow up with us, and let us joy in their prosperity.

4. Cruelty is charged upon them.

For they build in blood, and cruelty is also one of the companions of ambition and covetousness. If Ahab have a desire for Naboth's vineyard, either Naboth must part with his vineyard or his life.

They are not all innocent of this great offence that keep themselves from shedding of blood. They that invade the means of the maintenance of life, that pinch the labourer in his wages, or that make the hireling work for nothing, or that let their hire sleep in their custody, whilst he pineth for want of things necessary, are all guilty of this accusation of blood. It was the provocation wherewith God was provoked against the old world, for which he brought upon them the great flood that destroyed them all. This was Edom's sin in Obadiah.

There is a manifold cruelty, as you then heard.

1. Cruelty of combination, when we make ourselves strong in a faction, to oppress all that oppose us, and go not our way.

2. Cruelty of the eye, when we can be content to look on, to see injuries done to our brethren, without any compassion or subvention.

3. Cruelty of heart, when we rejoice against them that suffer wrong, and make ourselves merry with their afflictions.

4. Cruelty of the tongue, when we insult over them and brand them with taunts.

5. Cruelty of the hands, when we

(1.) Either persecute their persons with molestation;

(2.) Or touch their liberty with unjust restraint;

(3.) Or rob them of their goods by cruel direptions;

(4.) Or hinder the course of justice that should do them right;

(5.) Or procure their death because they do stand in our light, and hinder our rising. Of all these I have spoken heretofore. We now hasten to the declaration of God's just vengeance against this ambition.

2. The punishment.

1. They consult shame to their own house.
2. They sin against their own souls.
3. They labour in vain, and without success.

1. They consult shame to their own house. Ambition doth affect to build up an house, to establish a name that may continue in the blood and posterity in succeeding generations with glory and honour. David hath a cross prayer, which is in the hearts and mouths of many that hate such pride: 'Let not their wicked imagination prosper, lest they grow too proud.' These words do shew that ambitious pride shall not prosper; and whereas they study honour, and consult glory, in their aim and intention, God turneth it all to shame in the event.

The words of my text are the words of God; he knoweth what he meaneth to do, and he saith, 'they consult their own shame,' because he purposeth to turn all their glory into shame.

Shame is the thing that an ambitious man doth desire to decline above all things; all his studies bend their strength against it, and pursue glory, which is the contrary to it. To this purpose covetous men gather riches, and then with money purchase great offices and great titles to make great houses, and nominous families upon earth to survive them.

But where this greatness is begun by ambition, maintained and supported by rapine and cruelty, pride will have a fall; he that meaneth to give it the fall saith so. God, whose power none hath ever resisted, he will turn that glory into shame.

The wise man saith, Prov. xv. 27, 'He that is greedy of gain troubleth his own house.' For, Prov. xiv. 11, 'the house of the wicked shall be overthrown.' He doth not mean *domus*, the house, but *familia*, the family, the whole name and posterity, the glory; all shall perish and come to shame.

And Prov. xv. 25, Solomon tells us who shall do it: 'The Lord will destroy the house of the proud.' This is their shame, to come down again, when men have been aspiring, and settled their nest on high, and made themselves believe that their honour shall be established upon their house; for then,

1. God shall laugh them to scorn, the Lord shall have them in derision, saying, Behold, the man is become as one of us.

2. Men shall laugh at them and say: Ps. lii. 7, 'Lo, this is the man that made not God his strength; but trusted in the abundance of his riches, and strengthened himself in his wickedness.' For Solomon saith, Prov. xi. 10, 'When the wicked perish, there is shouting.'

3. The Lord shall be glorified in the shame of the proud, covetous, cruel man; for every man shall say, Rev. xviii. 8, 'Strong is the Lord God who judgeth them,' as over Babel. Thus is God praised: ver. 20, 'Rejoice over her, thou heaven, and ye holy apostles and prophets; for God hath avenged you on her.'

This point is of excellent use.

Use 1. For doctrine, it teacheth us that which Solomon hath said, Prov. x. 24, 'The fear of the wicked shall come upon him.' The proud man feareth nothing so much as shame, the covetous man feareth nothing so much as want, the cruel man nothing so much as revenge, the glutton nothing so much as hard fare, the drunkard nothing so much as a cup of cold water; and God hath threatened these offenders with all these judgments.

Use 2. It commendeth to us wisdom, and righteousness, and humility, and all holy virtues, for they be all builders, and raise up houses, and lay the foundation sure. Ps. cxii. 7, *Ab auditione mali non timebit.* 'The just man is bold as a lion,' as Solomon, Prov. xxviii. 1. 'The wicked are overthrown, and are not: but the house of the righteous shall stand,' Prov. xii. 7. Humility layeth the foundation of it low. Faith worketh by love to furnish it. Honour and much glory are the roof of it; peace is the fence about it, and prosperity the demesnes belonging to it. And the guard of angels pitch their tents round about it. This house is built upon a rock, yet it must endure the winds and waves.

Use 3. This hath deceived many, for they have thought unrighteousness the better and safer way, because they have seen the wicked flourishing, and spreading like to a green bay tree. Job disturbeth them in their ruff, and glory, and fulness, and fatness: Job xx. 9, 'Their houses are safe from fear, neither is the rod of God upon them.' It goeth pleasantly for two or three verses, but, ver. 13, 'in a moment they go down to the grave.'

It is an admirable wisdom that Job hath recorded to direct our observation of such: ver. 16, 'Lo, their good is not in their hand.' They are not masters of their happy estate; which he proveth: ver. 17, 'How oft is the candle of the wicked put out;' it is but a candle, and it is put out often; 'for God distributeth sorrows in his anger.' God is angry; he doth not cover them over with sorrows, and overwhelm them with woe here, but he distributes sorrow, giving them some *lucida intervalla*.

This varnish, and paint, and gilding of unrighteousness with temporal happiness, doth make it deceive many: Ps. xcii. 6, 'A brutish man knoweth not; neither doth a fool understand this. When the wicked spring as the grass, and all the workers of iniquity flourish, it is that they shall be destroyed for ever.' Who would have thought it? every man saith when he seeth pride have a fall. No; for the psalmist saith, 'Thy thoughts are very deep.'

Here God himself declareth that ambition shall end in shame; and the candle of the wicked, when it is put out, will end in a foul and stinking smoke.

Use 4. This admonisheth and exhorteth all that love their houses, and study their own honour, to seek it in the way of piety and charity; let such serve God, let them not neglect the Lord's house, the Lord's day, the Lord's table; let them suffer their brethren to dwell in peace by them, and to grow up with them, and to be the better for them.

It is not the riches that we leave behind us to our heirs that doth build our house, but that we bestow well to the honour of God, and the good of our brethren where we live. You shall see it in our Saviour's sentence: Mat. xxv. 35, 'I was hungry, and you fed me: I was naked, and ye clothed me,' &c. Not the meat that we do eat ourselves, nor the clothes that we do wear ourselves, nor the money and land that we demise to our posterity, maketh us friends in the day of the Lord, but what we dispose.

A worthy citizen of our city, that had been his own steward of his goods, and disposed them to many charitable uses, was his own poet for his epitaph, and caused this line among others to be insculped on his grave,

THAT I GAVE, THAT I HAVE.

Which calls to my remembrance a story that I read in Peraldus, bishop of Lyons in France, how a great lord, thinking his tenant somewhat too rich, and meaning to share with him, required of him a true inventory of his estate, and what his wealth was. He answered, it was in all six hundred crowns. It was objected that he dissembled his estate: such a grange, such a house, such a farm, and many other things of good value belonging to him were not named; he answered: *Illa non sunt mea, sed domini mei, qui quando voluerit potest ea accipere; sed quod dedi pro Deo in manus pauperum in salvâ custodiâ posui, ita quod nullus potest mihi illud auferre.* These are not mine, but my lord's, who, when he please, may take them from me; but what I have for God given to the poor, I have laid that in safe custody, so as none is able to take that from me.

The riches wherewith we honour God do build our house, always provided that they be riches well gotten; for if charity have been violated in the getting of wealth, the charity of giving it away to the poor will not redeem the breach of justice. Justice must ever go before charity in the dispensation of our goods. First, *suum cuique*, to every one his own; then *tuum*, thy own; so Zaccheus, he began at *reddo*, I restore; and from thence went to *do*, I give.

2. Punishment. 'And hast sinned against thy soul.'

The meaning, as I take it, is, that all this evil shall one day smart upon the soul of the Chaldeans. The doctrine is,

Doct. All sins committed against the law of God, are done against the souls of them that commit them.

The committers of sin are of two sorts :
1. The elect ; 2. The reprobate.

The elect sin against their souls. 1. *Culpa*, in the fault. 2. *Pœna*, in the punishment.

1. *Propter culpam*, in regard of the fault.

1. Because every sin that a man committeth doth defile the soul, and polluteth the temple where the Holy Ghost should dwell; so that Christ saith to every soul, 'Except I wash thee, thou hast no part with me.'

2. Because every sin that a man committeth doth hinder the influence of grace, and maketh the soul the more uncapable of light and heat from the Sun of righteousness; for every sin is an eclipse of that Sun, which is thus proved.

1. In our hearing of the word ; if we be either like the highway, where the seed is lost quite, Mat. xiii. 3 ; or like the stony ground, where the seed cannot take root; or like the thorny ground, where it may take root and spring up, but is choked in the growth ; the good seed never cometh to an harvest. Our sins must be removed, to make the soil good and fruitful.

2. In our prayer: Ps. lxvi. 18, 'If I regard wickedness in my heart, the Lord will not hear me.'

3. In our receiving the sacrament: 1 Cor. xi. 29, 'If I eat and drink unworthily, I eat and drink damnation.'

4. In alms : Mat. vi. 1, If I do it to be seen of men, I lose my reward ; for I have it here.

Sin is leaven, it corrupteth the whole soul of man, and maketh it a trespasser in all that it doth ; so that the elect man, in respect of his fault, doth sin against his own soul, and defileth it.

2. *Propter pœnam*, in respect of the punishment.

1. Because it bringeth forth guilt of conscience, which maketh us confounded and ashamed in ourselves, so that we dare not lift up our eyes to heaven, nor look our God in the face, whose mercy we have abused, whose anger we have provoked, whose goodness we have offended.

2. Because sin maketh matter of sorrow in the soul of the offender ; and a godly sorrow troubleth

and disquieteth the soul within us. In that case was Job, Job vii. 20, *Peccavi, quid faciam tibi? Quid feci?* 'I have sinned, what shall I do unto thee?'

3. Because the soul hath no peace till it hath wrought a revenge upon itself, and upon the body too in which it committed sin.

David's *Humilavi animam meam*, Ps. xxxv. 13; and St. Paul's *Castigo corpus meum*, 1 Cor. ix. 27.

There must be *afflictio*, and *amaritudo animæ*, Isa. xxxviii. 17; we carry rods about us for the nonce; even our own hearts will smite us, as David's did. This brings God home to us again: 'For I dwell with the humble and contrite,' Isa. lvii. 15; and then salvation is come home to our house once again.

2. *Impii autem non sic.* Not so with the wicked; they sin against their souls, because all the evils of their whole life are written in the book of God's remembrance, and folded up in the roll of their own conscience, which shall be opened against them in the last day, and they shall be judged according to all that is written in those books; and there shall be 'judgment without mercy to them that shewed no mercy,' James ii. 13.

This doth not exclude temporal punishments; for so shall they smart also, they shall have no peace in this life, for ever and anon, as Job saith, 'their candle shall be put out, and God shall distribute his sorrows amongst them.' They shall have many great shames, many great fears, many sad affronts of care and discontent, though commeddled with some fair weather, good cheer, ease, delights, and such sweetenings as the flattery of the world and the favour of the times shall yield them. Yet, in the end, all the evil that they have studied and intended against others, shall fall upon their own heads. But still, the worst is behind; their souls and bodies shall smart for it in the last day, and the hand of God shall then pay home.

For them I take no care; be it unto them as they have deserved, and the Lord requite it at their hands, and requite it upon them.

But for so many as follow righteousness, and fear God, and would walk in his ways, let us stir up one another in the fear of God, to seek the Lord whilst he may be found, and to tender our souls. The sins that we commit with such delight will cost us many an heart-breaking sigh, many floods of salt water, tears of bitterness, which are *sanguis animæ*, the blood of the soul, hanging down of the head, beating of the breast, fasting from our full fare, and stripping our bodies out of their soft raiment into sackcloth, and changing our sweet powders into ashes.

There is no such disease incident to man as this *tremor cordis*, the trembling of the heart for sin; this *anima dolet*, the learning of the physician, the art of the apothecary have no receipt for it.

As Saint Paul saith of the law, that it is the strength of sin; so I may say, that at first, in the beginning of the cure, the very remedy is the strength of the disease, and makes the disease double the distress thereof, as in David.

1. The prophet came to heal him, and he saith, Ps. cxvi. 11, 'I said in my haste, All men are liars,' prophets and all, if they speak of any comfort to me.

2. God himself presented himself to his thought, and that would not do. 'I thought upon God, and I was troubled; my fear came, and ceased not; my soul refused comfort.'

Yea, there is such a sweetness in revenge that a penitent man doth take upon himself, that he hath a kind of delight in his own self-punishment, as in Isaiah's example: Isa. xxii. 4, 'Look away from me; I will weep bitterly, labour not to comfort me.'

There is nothing that makes us sin with so much appetite and so little fear as this. We have banished confession, which bringeth shame upon us, and penance, which bringeth smart; we have taken the matter into our own hands, and no man hateth his own flesh. Repentance is rather matter of discourse and contemplation than of practice and passion; and so we sin, and our souls are not much troubled at it. But whosoever is touched in conscience throughly with the remorse of sin will say, There is no disease to a wounded spirit, and the costliest sacrifice that a man can offer to God is a contrite spirit and a broken heart.

3. Punishment, labour in vain. 'Is it not of the Lord of hosts, that this people shall labour in the very fire, and weary themselves with very vanity?'

1. Here is labour; it is *labor improbus*, that useth to carry all before it. It is amplified, for here is 'labour in the fire;'

>Multa tulit fecitque puer, sudavit et alsit;

labour even to weariness.

2. Here is much ado about nothing; for all this is vanity, 'very vanity.'

3. Who crosses them? 'Is it not of the Lord of hosts?'

Annon ecce a Jehova exercituum? Calvin. *Nonne ecce à cum Domino?* Interlin.

From the first, here is labour. This sin is very painful.

Doct. Covetousness to gather wealth together, and cruelty to destroy so many to strip them, and ambition to purchase high place hereby. We may truly say, *Hic labor, hoc opus est.*

Is it not strange? The way to hell is all down the hill, yet it is very uneasy and very weary travelling thither. Christ calleth to him all that are weary and heavy laden, and promiseth to refresh them, Matt. xi. 28. And God sheweth his people a rest, saying, Isa. xxviii. 12, 'This is the rest wherewith you may cause the weary to rest, and this is the refreshing.'

But this rest is not promised to them that weary themselves, and work in the fire, rising early and going late to bed to work shame for their own houses, and to sin against their own souls; such shall one day complain,* 'We have wearied ourselves in the ways of wickedness and destruction; yea, we have gone through deserts where there was no way; but as for the way of the Lord, we have not known it.'

Πονηρὸς, which signifieth a wicked man, cometh of πόνος, which signifieth labour; for it is a great deal of labour that they take that live in pursuit of honour,

* Wisdom v.

in the oppression and molestation of their brethren, in the racking vexation of covetous congestions of wealth. Cain vexeth himself. Nimrod must be a mighty hunter before the Lord. Lamech must kill a man. The earth must be full of cruelty to have their own will. This is labour in the very fire to do mischief. The head of wickedness must be always plotting and projecting. They imagine wickedness upon their bed; it will not suffer them to sleep. The hand of wickedness must be always working. The foot of pride must be always climbing. The eye of envy is ever waking.

Shall I give you a full description of the labour of the unrighteous drawn to the life? Deut. xxviii. 65, 'The Lord shall give thee there a trembling heart, and failing of eyes, and sorrow of mind. And thy life shall hang in doubt before thee, and thou shalt fear day and night, and thou shalt have none assurance of thy life. In the morning thou shalt say, Would God it were even! and at even thou shalt say, Would God it were morning! for the fear of thine heart which thou shalt fear, and for the sight of thine eyes which thou shalt see.'

Here is unquietness even upon the bed of rest. The reason is given: Isa. xxviii. 20, 'For the bed is shorter than a man can stretch himself on it, and the covering narrower than he can wrap himself in it;' for 'there is no peace to the wicked man.'

It is one of Satan's suggestions, that the way of righteousness is painful, and denieth a man the content of his heart. And from hence arise these flattering temptations, Shall I labour and travail all my days to sustain my life with mine own pains, when a little violence will strip my neighbour out of all that he hath gotten together, and make it mine own? Shall I make conscience of an oath or a lie, when it may get me more wealth in an hour than my labour shall earn in a year? Shall I work myself when I may make prize of the labours of other men, and drink down merrily the sweat of others' brows? Shall I sit low and be despised in the world, when I may lay my neighbours on heaps under me, and raise up myself upon their ruins? Shall I undergo the charge of a

family and the care of posterity, when rich gifts and
fair words may subdue change of beauties to my welcome desires and lusts of the flesh? Shall I expect a
slow and lingering advancement by the worth of virtue
in the service of God, when I see the servants of
mammon carry all honours and preferments before
them? Shall I be humble when I see the proud
happy? Mal. iii. 15, Shall I live a godly life, when
they that work wickedness are built?

Let us here observe how these wicked ones do work
to compass their ends; they labour in the very fire,
the fire of hell. 'The way of peace they have not
known.'

2. The next point casteth up the account of their
gettings, and it is a nought, a mere cipher in arith-
metic; vanity, very vanity.

Is it riches? Then is it a thing corruptible; it is
a thing uncertain, and little of it is for use; and what
profit hath the possessor thereof in the surplusage but
the beholding thereof with his eye? When a man
considers his wealth gotten by oppression and injury,
how can he but think it may be so lost as it was gotten?

Is it in the favour of princes and great men? True,
they be gods upon earth; but they die like men at
last, and they change their minds often before they
die. One day Haman rides about in pomp; he is
ὁ μέγας, and Mordecai waiteth at the lane gate.
Another day Mordecai is set upon the king's beast,
and Haman leadeth the horse, and proclaimeth him
honourable; and the next day Haman is hanged, and
Mordecai rules all under the king.

Is it honour that thou labourest for? That also is
vanity. Honour is *in honorante*, as Aristotle saith.
It is very unhappy for a man to have his honour
without himself, his pride within him, and his happiness without him.

Wise Solomon, that had all temporal felicity in the
fullest measure, and all of the gift of God, yet called
all those things 'vanity of vanities.'

I will shut up this point in the words of David, Ps.
xxxix. 6, 'Doubtless man walketh in a shadow, and
disquieteth himself in vain.'

3. Is it not of the Lord ?

Many cross betidings befall the ungodly, and they never observe who opposeth them. It is the Lord that bringeth all the labours of the ungodly to loss and vanity, that when they come to thrash their crop of travail in the world, they find nothing but straw and chaff. To express his power to do this, he is here called the God of hosts, for all things serve him, and he resisteth the proud, he and his hosts. He layeth their honours in the dust ; he disperseth their riches, and giveth them to the poor; he spoiled them of all their treasures ; he that exalted them made them low, he that gave to them taketh away. They had need be made to see this ; therefore he saith, *Nonne ecce à Domino hoc*, is it not of the Lord ?

In the time of the persecutions under the bloody emperors, if at any time they succeeded not in their wars, they cried, *Christiani ad furcas, ad leones*, Christians, to the gallows! to the lions! They saw not the hand of God against them ; this makes Balaam smite his ass : he seeth not God's angel. In the process of human affairs, they that go on in these sins which God himself threateneth with woe, though they find these sins profitable and to afford them large revenues, that they live plentifully upon the wages of unrighteousness, yet have they many crosses in their ways, many great losses they sustain ; these they impute to second causes, and lay great blame upon those whom they do oppress, because they stand not to it whilst oppression grindeth them ; they observe not the hand of God against them, yet saith God, ' Is it not of the Lord of hosts that they weary themselves for very vanity ?'

It is a great matter to know who it is that protecteth his servants, that crosseth the designs of their enemies. David, Ps. cix. 27, prayeth for God's saving help to them, and that they may know that this is thy hand, that thou, Lord, hast done it. For let all offenders in this kind of oppression, and indeed in all kinds of bold and presumptuous sins, know that they sin with an high hand. They are ' a people that provoke God to anger continually to his face,' Isa. lxv. 3.

If you observe the text well, you will find two things in it, and they are two great judgments, and both of the Lord :

1. 'Is it not of the Lord of hosts that the people shall labour in the very fire, and shall weary themselves?'

2. 'Is it not of the Lord of hosts, that the people shall labour for very vanity?'

For the hand of God is in both for their punishment, both in putting them to extreme labour, and in turning all their labour into vanity.

He asketh the question as if he should say, Come now, and let us reason together; to what do you impute it that this people take such pains and prosper so ill? Do you not perceive that God's hand is in it, and that I the Lord do undo all that they do?

1. It is of the Lord that they labour in the fire.

For God saith, *Ego creo malum*, labour and travail is the curse of man, the wages of sin; *In labore vesceris, in sudore vultus*, Here is fire that melteth and dissolveth us into water.

All the pains that is taken here on earth to do evil is of the Lord.

1. In respect of the strength and wit used therein, for in him we live and move : he planted the ear, &c.

2. In respect of his permission, for he hath chains to bind up Satan and his instruments, and he can carry snares when he will to catch sinners. This is not approbation, but toleration for a time.

3. It is of the Lord in respect of his will, for he scourgeth a man with his own sins in just judgment, and letteth the wicked wear out themselves with extreme labours for their punishment; whereas if he have a favour to any he calls upon them, Ps. cxxvii. 2, 'It is vain for you to rise up early, to sit up late, to eat the bread of sorrows; for he giveth his beloved sleep.' And our Saviour saith, *Nolite soliciti esse*, 'Be ye not careful.' But the Egyptians shall gather jewels of silver and jewels of gold together : it is of the Lord, Exod. xiv. 25, and they shall pursue Israel into the sea; and to make them work, he took off their chariot wheels, that they drave them heavily.

2. It is of the Lord that all their labour is lost.

For the jewels of gold and jewels of silver which the Egyptians have gathered, the Israelites shall carry away. And they and their chariots which they have driven long, shall all be covered with the sea.

The prophet putteth them together: Micah vi. 15, 'Thou shalt sow, but thou shalt not reap; thou shalt tread the olives, but shalt not anoint thee with the oil; and sweet wine, but thou shalt not drink wine;' for God professeth it, Lev. xxvi. 24, 'I will walk contrary unto you, and punish you seven times for your sins.'

It is a great wisdom in our labour to consider whether God be with us and walk with us, or walk contrary to us; for if we fear God and walk in his ways, we are said to walk with God; but if we do that which is evil in his sight, and covet an evil covetousness, to build our nests, and to gather riches by unlawful means, such as God in his word hath forbidden, we shall see and find that God will walk contrary to us. The proud man shall find that when he is at the highest, God can cast him down. The extortioner shall find that no bonds nor statutes will hold his debtors; they will say, We will break these bonds, and cast away these cords from us. The wanton shall find that the sins of his youth shall ache in the bones of his age, and they that sow in wickedness shall reap in shame.

There be many that meet with grievous inconveniences in their life, manifold crosses in their health, in their friends, in their children, in the affairs of life, especially such as concern their estate, and they do not observe two things most of all to be heeded:

1. That God walketh contrary to them, and crosseth them.

2. The cause why God doth so.

Here it is plain that these crosses are of the Lord, and the Lord himself revealeth the cause, and giveth account of his judgments, for pride and covetousness, &c. Observe how the prince of darkness hath blinded our eyes!

Suggest. 1. The sins that bring in profit and make the pot seethe, though Moses and his prophets, Christ and his apostles, do tell them that they are sins, and such as lead the offenders to hell, they will not believe them all against their profit, but cry, as the Ephesians did for Diana, Great is mammon; this is called, Mat. xiii., 'the deceitfulness of riches.'

Oh who hath bewitched the heart of man, that he should value his soul, for which Christ died, at so low a rate, that he will sell it for corruptible things? So St Peter calls gold and silver: 1 Peter i. 18, 'Forasmuch as ye know that you were not redeemed with corruptible things, as gold and silver.'

Suggest. 2. These sins be thought little sins where they be confessed, because they make a man able to make God some part of amends in alms and good works; so the oppressor of his brethren turneth his oppressions into sacrifices, as if oppressions of injury could be sacrifices of righteousness. This suggestion seemeth supported by the words of Christ: Luke xi. 41, 'Give alms of such things as you have, and behold all things are clean to you;' so that he which hath congested wealth by oppression shall purify all his goods by giving alms of part thereof.

They mistake our Saviour there; observe him well: he found the pharisees faulty in this sin here threatened with judgment, for their outside was a fair profession of religion, their inside was full of rapine and wickedness.

1. Our Saviour opposeth alms against rapine. Rapine corrupteth all the goods that we possess, even the fruits of our honest labours in our callings, the fruits of our inheritance from our parents. Goods unlawfully gotten from our brethren, against the law and word of God, do make all unclean; they defile all, and bring a rust and canker upon our treasure, but charity by distribution of alms doth purify and keep clean all our wealth.

2. This charity must have matter to work upon, and that is $\tau\grave{\alpha}$ $\dot{\varepsilon}\nu\acute{o}\nu\tau\alpha$, that is, such things as are in our power; we may give no alms *de alieno*, of what is another's, and there is nothing in our power to

dispose of but what we may rightly call our own. This utterly despaireth the hope of the oppressor, that he may make a sacrifice of his rapines.

And further, whereas the custom of gathering wealth by injury which robbeth our brethren doth pass it over lightly as a small sin, let me tell you that ill gotten goods do bring such a sin upon a man as cannot be purged but with two pills : 1, unfeigned repentance ; 2, just restitution.

Observe it in Zaccheus, Luke xix. 8 ; he joined charity and restitution ; his charity was of his own goods, *dimidium bonorum meorum*. It is theft whatsoever is not God's gift, and nothing is the gift of God but what is warrantable by the law and word of God.

For this, a man that feareth God will rather be God's *Lazarus*, and beg crumbs, than the devil's *Dives*, and fare deliciously.

Suggest. 3. The oppressors of their brethren that live at ease and rest in plenty, and surfeit drinking the sweat of their brethren's faces, and, to use the phrase of David, 'drinking the blood of their brethren,' when any cross or loss betideth them, because they observe some formal customary profession and practice of religion, they smooth it over with this comfort, that God doth exercise the patience of his servants in this life with some trials.

To whom I say, take heed, be not deceived, take not that for an exercise of thy patience, which is a punishment of thy sin.

1. Thou mistakest God ; he is not thy friend, but is contrary to thee.

2. Thou mistakest thyself. Thou callest thee the servant of God ; no, mammon is thy god, for thou goest against the word of God to gather wealth. It is but a false worship that thou givest to God : God loves no divided hearts.

3. Thou mistakest the cause of thy disease and thy physician, for thou thinkest it to be some propension in thee to sin, which needeth some preventing physic, whereas it is a corroding plaster to eat out dead flesh; yet flesh and blood hath many inventions. We use to shoot another arrow after the first, and, like Balak, try in another place and see if it will prosper there.

Ver. 14. *For the earth shall be filled with the knowledge of the glory of the Lord, as the waters cover the sea.*

3. The effect (*vide supra*, page 119).

It is plain that God's remissness in the execution of his just judgments upon the proud and cruel Babylonians, and the miserable state of the church, disfigured with tears, her voice hoarse with roaring for help, her throat dry, her heart aching, and no relief appearing; all this had not only made the ungodly and profane confident that there was no such thing as Providence, but it appeareth by this prophet that the faith of God's children was staggered hereby.

But when God shall declare his justice against these his enemies, then he shall recover his glory. Then shall they both know that Christ is the Lord; both the oppressor shall know it, and the delivered shall know it, and they that are no parties to the cause of any side shall all understand.

The words of God in this text are full of marrow and fatness, for God is rich in mercy, *aperit manum et implet*, so he dilateth his favours.

1. In the latitude, *all the earth over.*
2. In the plenitude, *the earth shall be filled.*
3. In the magnitude, *the knowledge of God's glory.*
4. In the profundity, *as the waters cover the sea.*

Doct. We are taught from hence that the delivery of God's church from the power of the enemies, and his vengeance upon them, doth give honour to the name of God upon earth: so David, Ps. lxxix. 9, 'We are in great misery. Help us, O God of our salvation, for the glory of thy name, and deliver us.'

Reason 1. Because, if the wicked overcome the church, they will triumph against God: so Moses, Exodus xxxii. 12, 'Wherefore shall the Egyptian speak and say, He hath brought them out maliciously to slay them?' Rabshakeh, the general of Sennacherib's forces, proudly insulteth, Isa. xxxvi. 20, 'Who is he among all the gods of these lands that hath delivered their country out of my hands?'

But God, delivering his church and punishing the enemies thereof, is magnified thereby, as Hezekiah did pray, Isa. xxxvii. 20, 'Now therefore, O Lord our God, save thou us out of his hand, that all the kingdoms of the earth may know that thou only art the Lord.'

Reason 2. Because, as the school saith, *gloria est clara notitia cum laude*; and what doth more make the name of God known with praise than his present help to his church, his quick vengeance upon the enemies thereof? The heathen shall say, 'The Lord hath done for them great things.'

Reason 3. Because this declareth the justice of God, for,

First, He is just and faithful in performing the gracious promises that he hath made to his church.

Secondly, He is just in the punishment of oppression and iniquity, which his soul abhorreth.

Use. The use of the point is to teach us that whensoever we see the church or any part thereof delivered from the hands of their enemies, and so the righteous God taking vengeance upon them, that we ascribe glory to God for the same.

Moses' song is a good example of this duty; for when the Egyptians that pursued Israel into the Red Sea were covered and destroyed by the return of the waters of the sea upon them, Exod. xv. 1, ' Then sang Moses and the children of Israel this song unto the Lord, and spake saying, I will sing unto the Lord, for he hath triumphed gloriously : the horse and his rider hath he thrown into the sea.'

This deliverance was a type of the final deliverance of the church from all her enemies; and therefore in John's vision it is said, Rev. xv. 3, 4, ' They sang the song of Moses the servant of God, and the song of the Lamb, saying, Great and marvellous are thy works, Lord God Almighty; just and true are all thy ways, thou King of saints. Who shall not fear thee, O Lord, and glorify thy name, for thou only art holy; for all nations shall come and worship before thee, for thy judgments are made manifest.'

We have great and gracious examples at home of this. Our blessed queen, of happy memory, Queen Elizabeth, *anno* 1588, after the defeat of the Spanish Armada, came in person to the chief church in her kingdom, where, having upon her knees devoutly given the glory of that deliverance to God, she heard the sermon at Paul's Cross, and taught her people by her godly example to know the glory of God; for in those days Spaniards loved us not, and we thought it a great favour of God to be delivered from them.

The like public declaration did our sovereign that now is make of the glory of God, for the deliverance of his royal person, crown and posterity, the religion and peace of the kingdom, in the last session of that first parliament, delivered by the hand of God from the bloody design of the papists, whose religion was also in those times thought dangerous to this commonwealth. His speech and recognition of the protection of God is extant in print.

And as states and great commonwealths have their dangers and deliverances, wherein as every one that is a member thereof hath their share of benefit, so from every one is growing a debt of duty to acknowledge the same; so that Hezekiah saith, Isa. xxxviii. 19, 'The father to the children shall make known the truth of God.'

So in our particular estates, we have many tastes of the sweetness of God, in our deliverances from dangers at sea, on shore from sickness, imprisonment, infamy, and many other evils which annoy our life; in all which God revealeth to us the knowledge of his glory, and we shall do him but right, to give him, as David saith, 'the glory due to his name;' and to invite our brethren, as David did, 'I will tell you, *quid Deus fecit animæ meæ*, what God hath done to my soul.'

Doct. 2. Seeing God promiseth to fill the earth with the knowledge of the glory of God, we are taught that God is glorious, and so we ought to conceive of him. Our Saviour hath taught us so, to acknowledge in the close of the Lord's prayer, *Tua est gloria*, 'thine is the glory.' St Stephen saith, Acts vii. 2, 'The God of glory appeared to our fathers.' And of this God is so jealous, that he saith, Isa. xlii. 8, 'My glory will I not give to another.' Hold this fast.

Reason 1. The devil, when he tempteth us to sin, doth not find an easier way to fetch us about, than to blemish the glory of God, and to dim that to our sights and opinions. As in the first temptation, he told the woman, 'Ye shall not surely die, for God doth know that when ye eat thereof ye shall be as gods;' bringing the woman into divers dishonourable thoughts of God, as concerning his truth, his justice, his love to man. For in tempting her to eat against the press and precise commandment of God,

1. She must think that God would not bring death upon her for her fault, as he had threatened, which toucheth the truth of God.

2. She must suppose that the offence of eating, taken at the worst, is a small offence, and so not likely to be avenged and mulcted with any such punishment, which toucheth the justice of God.

3. She must suppose that God, who shewed so much favour to man, to give him all the fruit for his meat, but that, had he loved man as he made show, would not have left that fruit for a snare to catch him and bring him to ruin; or if he did so, he was too loving to man to work upon the advantage.

Yet in this very suggestion, wherein he infuseth so many dishonourable thoughts into the heart of the woman, to dim the brightness of God's excellent glory, observe how he doth secretly confess that God is jealous of his glory, for he saith, Gen. iii. 5, 'He doth know that in the day that you eat thereof you shall be as gods.' That is to say, as well as he loves you, he would not admit you into the society of his glory, for man was created in the likeness of God's holiness and righteousness, but not in the similitude of his glory. That Satan knew well, and therefore suggested that ambition which he knew would ruin mankind, for that had cast him out of heaven.

Here by the way, let me shew you the sting of the first sin: God had said to Adam, 'Thou shalt not eat.' 2. *Qua die comederis, morte morieris*, 'what day thou eatest thou shalt die.'

1. In the eating the forbidden fruit, the commandment of God was broken; therein man rebelled.

2. In the eating, being threatened with death for punishment of their eating, there must either be,

(1.) Presumption upon the goodness of God, which should make him merciful against his truth and justice; or,

(2.) Unbelief of his power to inflict that punishment; or,

(3.) Contempt of his power; or,

(4.) A carelessness. I will taste, come of it what will.

And in all these the glory of God is much defaced.

3. In the eating, to be as gods, that most nearly touched the glory of God, for it was a base opinion of God in the heart of the woman, to conceive him such as she might come to be as wise as he; this laid home upon the crown of God's glory.

In which passage let me commend one observation of mine own upon the text to your judgments.

Satan tempted the woman only, not the man; and he sugared his temptation with these two arguments only: 1. *Non moriemini*, ye shall not die; 2. *Eritis sicut dei*, ye shall be as gods. There was *aculeus in cauda*, a sting in the tail, for that last stung her to the quick.

When she came after to tempt her husband, it seemeth that her inducements were three:

1. It was good for food.
2. Pleasant to the eye.
3. To be desired to make one wise.

Here is no mention of this temptation, to be like God.

Which makes me think that Adam's sin did not violate the glory of God so much as the woman's did, and that therefore the apostle saith, 1 Tim. ii. 14, 'Adam was not deceived, but the woman was deceived, and was in the trangression.' For though I cannot clear Adam from doing injury that way, yet as the school saith, he that cannot be excused *a toto*, may be excused *a tanto*.

But the point which I wish terrible in your remembrance, is that suggestions to sin do lay their foundation in some unworthy opinion of God, which trespasseth his glory here spoken of.

God himself declares as much to the ungodly : Ps. l. 21, ' When thou sawest a thief, thou consentedst with him,' &c. ' These things thou hast done, and I kept silence ; then thou thoughtest that I was altogether such a one as thyself.' Ps. xiv. 1, ' The fool saith in his heart, *Non est Deus*, there is no God,' that he may sin the more securely.

David stirreth up God the avenger against the ungodly : Ps. xciv. 5–7, ' That boast themselves in evil, that break in pieces God's people, and afflict his heritage ; that slay the widow and the stranger, that murder the fatherless.' How dare they do all this ? ' Yet they say, The Lord shall not see, neither shall the God of Jacob regard it.'

Augustine to such : *Infelix homo, ut esses curavit Deus, non curat ut bene esses ?* is not this a great trespass against the honour of God, to deny his providence?

There be presumptuous sinners that go on in very great sins, sins which God's word detecteth, and reproveth, and threateneth ; yet, as the prophet saith, Micah iii. 11, ' They will lean upon the Lord, and say, Is not the Lord among us ? no evil shall come upon us.' Thus they dishonour God, that make him the patron of their persons and their sins.

But they that have true knowledge of the glory of God, they behold him in majesty, and that not only opening his hand, and giving and filling, but stretching out his arm and striking ; and so, in that one sight, they behold both, *Ecce quantam charitatem*, and *scientes terrorem Domini*, ' behold how great love,' and ' knowing the terror of the Lord.' In the due consideration of his justice and mercy, both governed with wisdom, to moderate exuberancy, consisteth the knowledge of God's glory.

Use 1. This point serveth to good use. For first it assureth us, that the God whom we serve is the true God ; because he is so jealous of his glory, that he will have none to share with him therein. For the gods of the heathen were such good fellows, as they would admit society. Baal, and Melchom, and Moloch, and Rempham, the god of Ekron, Dagon, the devil and all, I do not hear of any great jealousy between them; but the true God is impatient of co-rival in glory.

Use 2. Because God claimeth glory in such extent all the earth over, which none of the gods of the heathen did, but were content with their territories; and knowing him to be the true God, we are taught that there ought nothing be so dear to us as the glory of God.

Do but observe what remembrancers we have to put us in mind of this.

The law begins, 'I am the Lord thy God, who brought thee out of the land of Egypt.' That implies, who brought thee into the land of Egypt.

The Lord's prayer: 'Our Father which art in heaven;' and the first petition, *Sanctificetur nomen tuum;* then *adveniat regnum;* then *fiat voluntas;* all glory.

The Creed: *Credo in Deum, Patrem omnipotentem*, all beginning to season us with a reverent estimation of God, and to infuse into us the knowledge of his glory; therefore do all to the glory of God.

Doct. 3. This also serveth to shew how excellent a knowledge it is to know the glory of God, seeing God maketh such account of it, that he will have it spread all the earth over.

Reason 1. To animate us so much the more earnestly, and with appetite to seek it; and indeed there is no knowledge to be compared to it.

1. In regard of this life. For if man know no better nature than that of the creatures beneath him, though that serve to shew him how great a lord he is, and how much is subject to him, yet in them he beholdeth a society that he hath with them, in much evil, in all weakness, and in a certain mortality, which can be no great comfort to him if he stay there.

But if he look up to heaven above him, and behold *meliorem naturam,* a better nature; that of the angels, and himself but a little lower; and above them, *naturam naturantem,* the naturating nature, the glorious author of all being; this puts mettle into him, and teacheth him how to preserve the image of his Maker in him, which advanceth him above human frailty.

Hence are those ejaculations : that of Paul, *Cupio dissolvi*, ' I desire to be dissolved ;' ' Our conversation is in heaven ;' *Veni cito*, ' we walk by faith, and not by sight.'

Reason 2. In the life to come, this is the happiness of the blessed souls, they shall see God ; for this Christ desired, that the elect might be where he was, that they might see his glory.

And this maketh all those that wisely apprehend this joy in the glory of God to love the very earthy house which we call the church of God, because it is ' the place where his honour dwelleth,' because ' every whit of it speaketh of his honour ;' because thither the tribes go up to testify to Israel, to give testimony of their faith and zeal ; because there the voice of God's promise is heard, and the whole house is filled with his glory.

It was the blessing of God given in the consecration of Solomon's temple : 2 Chron. v. 14, ' The glory of the Lord filled the house of God.' But it was *gloria in nube*, glory in a cloud. That cloud is much removed in our church since the veil of the temple rent ; for Christ hath made all things more clear, and removed the veil. Let us therefore love the church well, for the glory of God revealed therein.

Much more do such long after the house of God's clear glory in heaven, wherein one day in those courts is better than a thousand otherwhere, and where they shall behold a full revelation of the glory of God.

Use. Let us all labour for this knowledge of the glory of God, for the purchase whereof we must study both the creatures of God and the word of God. For in these two books the wisdom of God is set forth to the soul, that we may say, if we be students in these books, *Vidimus gloriam ejus*, we have seen his glory ; for the heavens declare the glory of God to the eye, and God is glorious in the least of his creatures, *magnus in minimis ;* so that every part of his work doth declare him a wise omnipotent Creator, a wise and faithful preserver of all things.

And for the book of God, he that saith, ' This is life eternal, to know thee,' and saith, that he ' came to give life eternal,' saith also, *Dedi eis verbum tuum*, 'I have given them thy word.'

There is no labour that better rewardeth itself than the pursuit of the knowledge of the glory of God. For there is *libertas gloriæ*, the liberty of glory, which the creature doth even long after, and travaileth with the burden of corruption, desiring to be quit of it, Rom. viii. 22.

There be *divitiæ gloriæ*, riches of glory, Rom. ix. 23, made known upon the vessels of mercy; for God will declare his glory in shewing mercy. There is also *æternum pondus gloriæ*, 2 Cor. iv. 17, 'an eternal weight of glory;' there is *splendor gloriæ Dei patris*, 'the brightness of the glory of God the Father;' and this is the true light that enlighteneth all that come into the world, that lights us the way to this glory.

But to know the glory of God here on earth, we must observe the course of his judgments, and we shall therein see both his favour to his church, howsoever it be distressed, which, though it be *gloria in nube*, 'glory in a cloud,' the faithful will see through the cloud.

We shall also see his certain truth and justice in his hatred of sin, and in the sharp revenge that he taketh upon those that disease his church; which, though it be slow, for God is slow to wrath, yet he that believeth will not make haste. God 'giveth this light of the knowledge of the glory of God in the face of Jesus Christ,' 2 Cor. iv. 6.

1. Mercy. *Crucifixus, mortuus, sepultus*, crucified, dead, and buried.

2. Justice. *Venit judicare vivos*, he cometh to judge the live and dead.

Ver. 15–17. *Woe to him that giveth his neighbour drink, that puttest thy bottle to him, and makest him drunk also, that thou mayest look on their nakedness! Thou art filled with shame for glory: drink thou also, and let thy foreskin be uncovered: the cup of the Lord's right hand shall be turned unto thee, and shameful spewing shall be on thy glory. For the violence of Lebanon shall cover thee, and the spoil of beasts, which made them afraid, because of men's blood, and for the violence of the land, of the city, and of all that dwell therein.*

Now doth God rouse up his justice against another sin, the great and crying sin of drunkenness.

1. Concerning the words.

Woe to him that giveth his neighbour (socium or *amicum* others read) *drink, that puttest thy bottle to him.* Some read *Constringens calorem tuum;* others, *adhibens venenum tuum;* others, *iram.*

He meaneth, woe be to him, that when he sees his neighbour in drink, comes in with his pot, or pint, or quart, to inflame him.

Thou makest him drunk, that thou mayest look on their nakedness. For it is said that the king of Babylon did use in his conquests to bring forth great quantity of wine, and to make the people drink drunk, that he might make sport with them; for in those drunken fits many shameful and bestial acts of lasciviousness were publicly shewed, drunkenness inflaming them with lust.

Mr Calvin doth interpret all this figuratively, not of drunkenness with strong drink, but of immoderate desire of augmenting their dominions; of which kind of drunkenness he spake before, comparing the Babylonians to such as transgress with wine.

So doth Ribera, a learned Jesuit, understand this, of the insolent triumph of the Babylonian king, making sport in the conquest of kings, and exercising on them cruelties to discover their nakedness, how he hath stripped them out of all. But Saint Jerome reporteth that Nebuchadnezzar did abuse Zedekiah the king at a banquet in a very foul manner.

And because that kind of drunkenness was before touched to the quick, I follow Arias Montanus in the literal exposition of these words, which I have before delivered, that the king made his associate kings, and his conquered enemies, drunk, to make him sport. Which sin of his is threatened.

Ver. 16. *Thou art filled with shame for glory;* for this turned to the shame of the Babylonians.

Though Mr Calvin expound it, *satiatus es probro non tuo sed alieno,* that the Babylonian did even satisfy himself with the disgrace done to his enemy, rather I take it for a punishment inflicted on the Babylonian, that shame should come to him for this sport that he made himself, as it also followeth, 'Drink thou also, and let thy foreskin be discovered. The cup of the Lord's right hand shall be turned unto thee, and shameful spewing shall be on thy glory.'

This, I take it, was not only figuratively revenged upon Nebuchadnezzar, when the glory of his conquests ended in the shame of his transformation, the most wonderful example that we do read in all the book of God: Dan. iv. 33, 'The same hour was the thing fulfilled upon Nebuchadnezzar; and he was driven from men, and did eat grass as oxen, and his body was wet with the dew of heaven, till his hairs were grown like eagles' feathers, and his nails like birds' claws.' For thus did the king continue in this shameful punishment the whole term of seven years.

But literally this was fulfilled in Belshazzar, Dan. v. 1, who made a great feast to a thousand of his lords, and drank wine before the thousand; in which drunken feast, wherein the consecrate vessels of the temple were abused in quaffing and carousing, the fingers of an hand were seen on the wall over against the king, writing the doom of his shameful downfall. For observe the end: ver. 30, 'In that night was Belshazzar the king of the Chaldeans slain, and Darius the Median took the kingdom.' So he did drink also, and his nakedness was laid open, and the Medians came in and took away all their glory.

Ver. 17. *For the violence of Lebanon shall cover thee, and the spoil of beasts which made them afraid.* This overthrow of the Chaldean monarchy he calleth the violence of Lebanon covering them.

Junius doth understand this place thus: that the enemy should come upon the Babylonian with the same violence that hunters use, who, pursuing the wild beasts in the forest of Lebanon, having pitched their nets and tents for them, do suddenly set upon them, and drive them into their nets; so sudden a surprise shall the Babylonian suffer.

Master Calvin doth give this as a cause of their punishment, and understandeth the words thus, that God will cover the Babylonian with shame for the violence that he offered to Lebanon, and to the beasts thereof, foraging Judea, and destroying not only men and women in towns, but the very wild beasts of the forest of Lebanon, which was near to Jerusalem. So that this expresseth the cause of God's provocation against the Babylonian, and withal the comfort of the church, that God would revenge the wrong done to their land, not only to the people thereof, but to the very wild beasts of the forest. *De verbis hactenus.*

The parts of this text are two: 1, *Peccatum*, sin; 2, *Pœna*, punishment.

1. *Peccatum*, in which,
    1. *Quid ; potant amicum vel socium.*
    2. *Ad quid ; ut videant nuditatem.*
       1. *Potant vicinum ;* two faults. 1, Drink drunk; 2, make drunk.
       1. They be drunk.

Drunkenness itself is an horrible sin; it is one of the fruits of the flesh: Gal. v. 21, ' Of which I tell you, as I have also told you in times past, that they which do such things shall not inherit the kingdom of heaven.' Drunkenness is confessed of all men to be a sin; and they that love it best, and use it most, will be very angry with you if you call them drunkards. For it is not agreed upon as yet what drunkenness is. Our statute law doth impose a penalty of five shillings upon every one that is convicted of drunkenness. Our articles given to sworn men do charge them to inquire if there be any drunkards in our parishes, and to present them. But neither the ecclesiastical canon nor the act of parliament doth direct the inquisition, by describing what persons must be esteemed drunk.

I will tell you whom the Scripture denoteth.

Lot was drunk when he committed incest with his daughters, Gen. xix., and so overgone with wine that he neither knew of their coming to his bed, nor of their going from him. Noah was drunk when he lay uncovered in his tent, Gen. ix.; these were far spent in the highest degree. Uriah, the husband of Bathsheba, was drunk too, 2 Sam. xi. The text saith, David made him drunk; yet he was so much master of his own thoughts, and of his charge committed to him, that he would not go home to his own house, as the king would have had him. Amnon, the son of David, was drunk, 2 Sam. xiii. 28, yet it is said of him, his heart was merry with wine. Elah, king of Israel, made himself drunk, 1 Kings xvi. 9, and Zimri his servant killed him. Nabal made a great feast, 1 Sam. xxv. 36, and was so drunken that Abigail thought not fit to tell him of the danger that his churlishness had like to have brought upon him, till he had slept it out. A king that drinketh wine is described then to be drunk, when they drink and forget the law, and pervert the judgment of the afflicted, Prov. xxi. 5. So that to drink so deep as to forget the law of our lawful calling, and to do things contrary to the same, is to drink drunk. Christ calleth the overcharge of the heart with drink drunkenness, Luke xxi. 34. His word is $\beta\alpha\rho\nu\nu\theta\tilde{\omega}\sigma\iota\nu$, signifying the laying on of a burden upon the heart. For so much as we drink for necessity, or for moderate refection, doth cheer and refresh and lighten the heart; but excessive drinking doth lay an heavy burden upon it. Therefore, Eph. v. 18, ' Be not drunk with wine, wherein is excess.'

Now, what is excess? Not so much as layeth us under the table only, not so much as makes us stagger and reel as we go, and taketh away the use of our memory, speech, and good manners; but they are drunkards that ' sit at the wine till it inflame them,' Isa. v. 11. Wine is allowed to warm the stomach, not to set it on fire.

Some man excuseth himself that he drank not above his strength, but was able to carry it. Ver. 22, ' Woe unto them that are mighty to drink wine, and men of strength to mingle strong drink!'

This shews that all excess in drinking, which is beyond the measure which maintaineth health, is drunkenness; call it good fellowship, or making merry, or keeping good company, or whatsoever fair colours you will lay upon it, it is drunkenness. It turns grace into wantonness, and medicine into disease; it maketh the body, which should be the temple of the Holy Ghost, the very cellar of Bacchus.

The evils that grow out of this sin are many.

1. The great commandment is broken, which biddeth us to love God above all things; for the drunkard makes his belly his god, and delighteth in his shame, neither is God in all his ways. Of whom doth the name of God more suffer than of the drunkard; and who do make less conscience of the Sabbath than such do, who make that day of all others the most licentious, the most lascivious, despising the commandment of God?

2. It is a sin against himself who committeth it; for he shameth himself to beholders, he wasteth his estate, hurteth his own body, drowneth his understanding, judgment, memory, and depriveth himself of the use of reason; as Solomon saith, Prov. xxiii. 29-35, 'Who hath woe? who hath sorrow? who hath contentions? who hath babbling? who hath wounds without cause? who hath redness of eyes? they that tarry long at the wine. At the last it biteth like a serpent, and stingeth like an adder.'

It corrupteth the affections, and inflameth lust: 'Thine eyes shall behold strange women.' It corrupteth the speech: 'Thine heart shall utter perverse things.' It maketh a man insensible of his punishment: 'They have stricken me, and I was not sick; they have beaten me, and I felt it not.'

It groweth into an habit, and cannot be easily given over. Drunkenness is like a quartan, the dishonour of physicians; so it is the dishonour of preachers, they cannot cure it. We would have cured the drunkard, and he would not be healed: 'When shall I awake, I will yet seek it again.' As St Gregory saith, *Qui hoc facit, non facit peccatum, sed totus est peccatum*.

3. It is a sin against our neighbour, for it is a waster and consumer of the provisions which God hath given to nourish and sustain many; and so he becomes a thief, robbing the hungry and thirsty. For it is *panis pauperis et vinum dolentis*, the bread of the poor and the wine of the sorrowful, that is thus swilled and swallowed.

It toucheth upon the commandment of murder; for to take away life, and to take away the means that should support life, are so set, that we can hardly draw a line between them.

It inflameth lust; as Ambrose, *Pascitur libido conviviis, vino accenditur, ebrietate inflammatur.* It filleth the tongue with all kind of evil words which corrupt good manners, *turpiloquium, multiloquium, vaniloquium, fasiloquium;* and where be the good names of men more foully handled than upon the ale-bench, when a drunken senate meeteth?

And, to conclude, it dishonoureth parents; for the laws of the church and the laws of the commonwealth do forbid it, and design punishment for it.

Yet this sin is the Diana of our Ephesus; and if all the preachers of England do cry it down in pulpits, the court of good fellowship will cry it up again. Though we shew you the scroll of God, and open all the folds of it, and read it to you written within and without, with nothing but lamentations, mourning, and woe against this sin; though we bind the sinners in this kind by the power given to us by Christ, saying, 'Whose soever sins ye retain, they are retained;' yet do men run headlong into this sin, without fear or wit.

But when sin is once grown into fashion, we may stretch out our hands all the day long against it, and spend our strength in vain; yet I will not despair of a blessing upon our faithful labours against it; and thus much I will undertake to do, as the apostle saith, 'I will yet shew you a more excellent way.'

I will yet shew you approved remedies against this sin, and there is no time of the year unseasonable for the soul to take physic.

Remedia:

Remedy 1. Take David's physic: 'I have kept thy word in my heart, that I might not sin against thee,' for that word will answer the temptation, as Joseph did, 'How then shall I do this great wickedness, and so sin against my God?' Remember the fearful threatenings of woe and judgment against this sin; remember the day of judgment, wherein every man must give account to God of himself and of all his ways; remember the bitterness of the latter end thereof, all this is clearly denounced in the word of God; remember that 'it is a fearful thing to fall into the hands of the living God, for our God is even a consuming fire.'

2d Remedy is, a constant practice of mortification; for they that humble their souls with fasting, and chasten their bodies, and bring them in subjection, that watch and pray, and call their sins every day to account, and examine their consciences by the law of God, he that doth these things well, shall soon come to their diet, of whom the psalmist speaketh, Ps. lxxx. 5, 'Thou feedest them with the bread of tears, and givest them tears to drink in great measure.' Then thou wilt go mourning all the day long.

3d Remedy is, withdrawing thyself from such company as use drunkenness, from such places wherein it is used; as Solomon adviseth, Prov. xxiii. 20, 21, 'Be not amongst wine-bibbers, amongst riotous eaters of flesh; for the drunkard and the glutton shall come to poverty, and drowsiness shall clothe a man with rags.' So St Paul chargeth the Corinthians, 1 Cor. v. 11, 'But now I have written unto you not to keep company, if any man that is called a brother be a fornicator, or covetous, or an idolater, or a railer, or a drunkard, or an extortioner, with such an one, no, not to eat.' It is company that corrupts many; there are few that love drunkenness so well that they will sit down and drink themselves drunk, as Elah king of Israel did, 1 Kings xvi. 9; but good fellowship spoils all, and one pot draweth on another.

4th Remedy is, 1 Cor. vii. 20, ' Let every man abide in the calling wherein he was called.' God hath given his angels charge of thee to keep thee in all his ways. So it is said of the drunkard, that he is out of the way; for did he exercise himself in his calling within his way, he could not miscarry: Prov. xxi. 25, 26, ' The desire of the slothful killeth him: for his hands refuse to labour; he coveteth greedily all the day long.'

5th Remedy is, a consideration of the hunger and thirst which Christ sustained on earth for thee, and of the hunger and thirst which Christ yet in his members doth suffer. Remember what he hath done for thee; do not waste that unthriftily which would serve to relieve Jesus Christ. He hungered to satisfy thee, do not thou surfeit to make him hungry; he thirsted, it was one of the last words that he spake on the cross, *Sitio*, I thirst; do not thou make thyself drunk with that which should quench his thirst, lest thy last draught be, like his vinegar, mingled with gall.

6th Remedy is, a consideration that we are required to pray continually, and in all things to give thanks, which holy duty we cannot perform so long as we are in our cups. These duties require a sound judgment, a clear understanding, 'an heart established with grace;' as the apostle saith, 'Not in gluttony and drunkenness, not in chambering and wantonness; but put ye on the Lord Jesus, and have no care to the flesh, to fulfil the lusts thereof.'

We were created to glorify God in our bodies and in our souls, for they are God's; and therefore, 'whether you eat or drink, or whatsoever you do, do all to the glory of God.'

7th Remedy. Consider that we are bidden guests to the supper of the Lamb: Rev. xxii. 17, 'And the Spirit and the Bride saith, Come; and let whosoever heareth, say, Come, and take of the water of life freely.' We cannot tell when this supper time is, till God's messenger, death, cometh and telleth us all things are prepared; come now, let not us overcharge our hearts with surfeiting and drunkenness, lest that day come upon us unawares, Luke xxi. 34; they that are drunk already, and full gorged with wine and strong drink, have left no room for the waters of life; *vas plenum plus non recipit*. It is a work for our life on earth to travail and take pains, and to exercise our souls to godliness, and all to get us a stomach to this supper of the Lamb. Here is meat enough, the fatness of God's house, we shall be fed as it were with marrow; here is the hidden manna for bread; here is *calix inebrians*, we shall be made to drink of the rivers of God's pleasures; 'for at his right hand are pleasures for evermore.' Here are good guests; for, Mat. viii. 11, 'Many shall come from the east and west, and shall sit down with Abraham, Isaac, and Jacob in the kingdom of heaven.' They that come there, let them drink and spare not, but let them keep their stomachs till then. I conclude this point in the words of our Saviour, John xiii. 17, ' If ye know these things, happy are ye if ye do them.'

2. They gave their neighbours drink, and put their bottle to him, adding heat to heat.

Drunkenness, as you have heard, is a grievous sin; but this is a degree of fuller unrighteousness, to make others drunk. Amongst all the sins that David did commit, nothing sat so close to him, nor left so foul a stain upon the honour of his memory, as did his carriage toward the Hittite Uriah: 1 Kings xv. 5, ' David did that which was right in the sight of the Lord, and turned from nothing that he commanded him all the days of his life, save only in the matter of Uriah the Hittite.' This excuse of David in all other things wherein through human frailty he failed often, doth shew how God passeth over the sins of the elect, as the apostle saith, ὑπεριδών, which through infirmity they do commit; but this special notice taken of the matter of Uriah the Hittite, declareth it to have been *peccatum primæ magnitudinis*, a sin of the first magnitude, in a vessel of glory, because so many sins met together in it. To name the most eminent: first, adultery; then the making of Uriah drunk; then the murdering of Uriah; wherein you see that this foul sin doth make weight in the burden of David.

The Holy Ghost, to declare how foul and hideous a sin drunkenness is, hath not spared to leave the dishonour of God's good servants upon record, offending therein; as of Noah, who is much to be excused, because, having planted a vine, and out of the grapes having pressed the first liquor that we read made of grapes, and not knowing the strength thereof, being also old, he was overtaken with it once, and no more. Surely it was the will of God so early to let the danger of wine appear, even at the first drinking thereof, that all succeeding times might beware.

So the example of David, who made Uriah drunk, against whom the matter of Uriah is upon record, for terror that men should fear this great sin of making their neighbours drunk, for that is part of 'the matter of Uriah the Hittite.'

Will you hear the decision of the canon law* in their cases of conscience concerning this sin: *Ille qui procurat ut quis inebrietur, mortaliter peccat, quia consentit in damnum notabile proximi.*

This is now the crying sin of our land; court, city, country, all defiled with it; and I must confess a truth which the sun seeth, not all innocent of it who should by authority from God reprove it by the word, and punish it by the sword; it is a sin in fashion.

Yet at the great feast which Ahasuerus made to his princes, it is specially noted: Esther i. 8, 'And the drinking was by an order; none might compel: for so the king had appointed to all the officers of his house, that they should do according to every man's pleasure.' Lyran his note is, *Nolebat rex ut in aula sua aliquis uteretur modo incomposito et irrationabili, more barbarorum, qui nimis importune inducebant homines ad bibendum.*

Reason 1. It is our duty to stir up one another, and to provoke one another to all Christian duties; of these, to act sobriety in the moderate using of meat and drink, and fasting, in the abstinence from them for a season. St Paul, 'Whether ye eat or drink, do all to the glory of God;' Christ, *quando jejunatis*.

To omit this duty is a great sin, to commit the contrary evil is most abominable. This the prophet sheweth, Isa. xxii. 12, 13: 'In that day did the Lord God of hosts call unto weeping and mourning, &c. And behold joy and gladness, slaying oxen and killing sheep, eating flesh and drinking wine,' eating and drinking, *cras moriemur;* and it was declared in the ears of the Lord of hosts, ' Surely this iniquity shall not be purged till ye die.'

How then shall they appear before God, who, instead of calling to fasting, call to drinking, and press the drinking even to the making of their neighbour drunk?

* Summa Anglica, *Ebrietate.*

Reason 2. If we contrive against our neighbour's life to take it from him, we are murderers; if against his wife to defile her, we are adulterers; if against his goods to rob him of them, we are thieves; if against his good name, we are false witnesses. Consider then what thou dost when thou attemptest thy neighbour to make him drunk, for thou seekest to perish his understanding, to rob him of the use of reason, which should distinguish him from a brute beast, to expose him a spectacle of shame and filthiness to all beholders, and to make him a transgressor of the law of God, the church, and the commonwealth.

Yet they that are thus overtaken, do commonly excuse themselves that they have been amongst their friends; but this pot-friendship, which hath the power to divide a man from himself, will scarce prove a glue strong enough to unite and knit him to another. The kisses of such friends betray thee, and thou mayest say rather, 'Thus was I wounded in the house of my friends.' It was David's prayer, let it be thine, Ps. cxli. 5, 'Let the righteous smite me, for that is a benefit; and let him reprove me, and it shall be a precious oil, that shall not break my head;' but 'Incline not mine heart to evil, that I should commit wicked works with men that commit iniquity; and let me not eat of their delicates, nor drink neither.' It is a good observation of Cardinal Bellarmine here, *ubique nocet conversatio malorum, sed nusquam magis, quam in conviviis, et compotationibus.*

This is no new danger, but a disease of former ages, infectiously transmitted by imitation to our times, and in them grown epidemical.

St Ambrose describeth a surfeiting and drunken meal: *Primo minoribus poculis velut velitari pugnâ præluditur; verum hæc non est sobrietatis spes, sed bibendi disciplina; ubi res calere cæperit, poscunt majoribus poculis, certant pocula cum ferculis. Deinde procedente potu longius contentiones diversæ, et magna certamina quis bibendo præcellat. Nota gravis si quis se excuset.*

All you that call God father, and do desire either the honour of his name, or the coming of his kingdom, or the fulfilling of his will, make conscience of this great sin, call it no longer good-fellowship; for St Ambrose saith, *Vocatis ut amicos, emittitis inimicos. Vocas ad jucunditatem, cogis ad mortem; invitas ad prandium, efferre vis ad sepulturam; vina prætendis, venena suffundis.*

Say to him that tempteth thee to drink drunk, *Vade retro me, Sathana,* Get thee behind me, Satan; 'the kingdom of God is not meat nor drink,' God shall find thee out, thou hast his woe upon thee, and thou shalt see anon how he will punish thee.

2. *Ad quid? ut videant nuditatem.* It is the boast of brave drunkards, how long they have sat at it, how many pots and pottles they have swallowed, how many they have made drunk; this is thy nakedness.

Literally drunkenness doth make men do things uncomely. Some use this lewd practice to make way for their lust, some to take advantages otherwise. Modesty cannot utter what unclean provocations do arise from drunkenness, what lewd and unchaste actions are done, what profane and filthy words are spoken. Noah himself, full of wine, doth lie uncovered in his tent, and sheweth his nakedness.

St Ambrose complaineth of women that, full of wine, did come immodestly into the street, singing and dancing: *Irritantes in se juvenum libidines. Cœlum impuro contaminatur aspectu, terra turpi saltatione polluitur, aer obscenis cantibus verberatur.*

Oh the miserable state of man in whom sin reigneth! He is not only tempted to do evil, horrible and shameful evil, to drink drunk, but to be his neighbour's devil, to draw him into evil by making him drunk; and also this *propter malum,* even to discover the nakedness of his brother.

Some shew themselves in their pots like lions, furious and quarrelsome; others are dull and heavy, only serving for whetsones to sharpen the wits of the company; others drowsy and sleepy; others talkative, every man in his humour, all in their nakedness. To do evil that good may come of it is an heinous sin, for God needs not Satan's help. But to do evil ourselves to draw others into evil, for so evil an end, this doth make sin out of measure sinful.

1. Take nakedness literally, for the discovering of those parts which modesty doth hide out of sight. So after the transgression the man and woman saw that they were naked, and they were ashamed, being but themselves alone in the garden; and they sewed fig-leaves together to hide their nakedness from each other's sight. So much remained in them, that, having left *primas sapientiæ*, they yet retained *secundas modestiæ*, and could not for shame behold each other's nakedness. The apostle saith, 1 Cor. xii. 23: 'These members of the body which we think to be less honourable, upon these we bestow more abundant honour, and our uncomely parts have more abundant comeliness.' The honour here meant is the decent hiding of their nakedness, and the modest covering of our shame. Where the apostle doth declare the care that is in the natural body; the comely parts, which need no hiding from sight, do cover the uncomely parts from sight. Therefore they that uncover nakedness do shew themselves to be no members of the body; so that such drunkards as give strong drink to their neighbour, to this end to discover their nakedness, declare themselves to be no parts of the body of the church.

Surely much nakedness is discovered in many drunken meetings; and no marvel, when men and women, having laid aside reason and temperance, religion and the fear of God, if they then turn beasts, and do those things that are uncomely.

2. Take this nakedness in a spiritual sense. Then St Ambrose will tell you, Lib. de Noe et Arca, c. 30, *Omnis impius quoniam ipse devius disciplinæ est, aliorum lapsus pro sui erroris solatio accipit, quod consortes invenerit culpæ.* Then is the season for the cozener to invade the purse of his neighbour, for the cunning insidiator to take advantage of words to find out the infirmities of his brother, that he may keep him in awe thereby. I cannot dive so deep into this mystery of iniquity as to declare all; and again, I fear to go far in it, lest I might teach the ignorant sinner more cunning than he had before.

This I dare say, that it is not love that maintaineth drunken acquaintance; for true love is a coverer of nakedness. If literal, you may see it in Shem and Japhet; if spiritual, you may hear it from the apostle, 'Love covereth a multitude of sins.' And out of that love David weeps for them that keep not the law.

It becomes them best, in my text, who know not God, but were abominable, and to every good work reprobate, to make men drunk to make them sport; but these things must not be so much as named amongst those that call God our Father, that come to church, that hear the word, that offer themselves to be guests at the Lord's board.

But I remember the wise man saith, 'Rods be for the backs of fools.' What greater folly, then, to sell our inheritance in heaven for strong drink? A worse bargain than Esau's, and a harder pennyworth.

The rods for this are,

2. *Pœna peccati*, the punishment of sin.

1. 'Thou art filled with shame for glory.'

2. It shall be thine own case; 'for thou also shalt drink, and thy nakedness discovered.'

3. The avenger shall do thee right is the Lord: 'The cup of the Lord's right hand shall be turned unto thee.'

4. 'Shameful spewing shall be thy glory.'

5. 'The violence of Lebanon shall cover thee, and the spoil of beasts.'

I may resolve all these particulars to this total, that God will take the punishment of this sin into his own hand, and shall turn his cup unto them, and they shall do him right therein. But for our better direction in this passage, let me observe,

1. Who will punish this sin? God himself.
2. How he will punish.
3. Why he will punish.

1. Who will punish this drunkenness.

It is the Lord. Is it not he whose glory the Babylonians have given to their idols; yea, in the pride of their heart assumed it to themselves? Is it not he whose people they persecute and destroy cruelly? whose goods they gather greedily? whose fruits of the earth they abuse to surfeit and drunkenness? It is for such as these that God saith, Isa. xlv. 7, 'I form the light and create darkness; I make peace and create evil: I the Lord do all these things.'

God hath ever declared himself an enemy to this sin; you may see it clearly in the first example of it in Noah, upon whom God laid two great punishments, which show how much that sin offended him.

1. That his own son should expose him to shame.

2. That this fault should be kept in eternal record in the living book of the holy word.

You may see it in Lot's example, wherein God would have it appear,

1. How strong liquor may prevail against a strong brain.

2. How easily a good man, and one that feareth God, may be overtaken with it by temptation.

3. How horribly he may offend in it.

4. How temptation may relapse him into it, and in the sins which follow it.

5. God would have us see his just indignation against this sin in the punishment of it.

In both these, the first we read of transgressing in wine, God doth declare his judgments upon this sin of drunkenness.

1. Because this sin doth much deface the image of our Maker in us, which is chiefly stamped in our spiritual and intellectual part; for let reason once fail, and man ceaseth to be himself for the time, and becometh like to a brute beast.

2. Because God's love is violated by drunkenness. Do you remember how sharply God punished old Eli, the priest of the Lord, for not reproving his ungodly sons, to whom he said, ' Thou honourest thy sons more than me,' 1 Sam. ii. 29. The drunkard loveth his strong drink above the Lord; therefore he threateneth them: Joel i. 5, ' Awake, ye drunkards, and weep; and howl all ye drinkers of wine, because of the new wine, for it is cut off from your mouth.' Observe it, that he biddeth drunkards awake, both because drunkenness doth beget drowsiness, *et quia vigilando dormiunt*, for they say and do they know not what; and

he sheweth them that as soundly as they sleep, they shall not sleep out his judgment, but shall feel the storm thereof. It is a contrary course that God holdeth with them that love and serve him; for he biddeth them, Isa. xxvi. 20, ' Come, my people, enter into thy chambers, and shut thy doors about thee; hide thyself, as it were for a little moment, until the indignation be overpast.'

Quest. There is a question in the cases of conscience in the canon law, *Utrum ebrietas excusat à peccato,* Whether drunkenness may excuse from sin? We have many examples of men in their drink, some speaking profanely and lewdly to the dishonour of God, swearing and blaspheming; others depraving and slandering their neighbours; others furiously smiting and hurting, some killing; their excuse is, alas, they were not themselves, and their drunkenness is the excuse of their fault.

I find it favourably judged in the canonists, *Excusat ebrietas non à toto, sed à tanto,* it excuseth not altogether, but in part. Some go further, and search whether the drunkenness be a common disease of the party, and that he useth in his drink to behave himself so; and in that case being found culpable, he is adjudged to be irregular: but if a man be, by the temptation of such whom he taketh to be his friends, overtaken with drink, who is known to be one that useth not to commit that fault, the law doth favour such a one. Others resolve it thus: *Ebrius est irregularis, ut ei imputantur ad pœnam omnia quæ sequuntur.*

I find in this example that God doth threaten to visit these Chaldeans for the sins committed in their drunkenness, because it was wilful. *Vide legem,* Exod. xxi. 28, 29.

The school distinguisheth well between voluntary and involuntary drunkenness. They call that voluntary drunkenness, when men do sit at the wine till it inflame them, knowing the strength of wine, and their own weakness, and seek it with delight in it. Ox used to gore. Involuntary they call that which overtaketh a man, not using, not loving it, who also is sorry for it, and wary to decline it hereafter; and that they hold excuseth *à tanto,* in part.

Use. Methinks this should be a great argument to dissuade drunkenness, and to make men afraid of it, for God is the punisher of it; the God that formed thee, and gave thee being, the God that took thee from thy mother's womb, the God that hath preserved thee from thy youth up until now. That great God who breweth and filleth a cup, and maketh all the wicked thereof drink it off, dregs and all, Ps. lxxv. 8. This Isaiah, chap. li. 17, calleth ' The cup of the Lord's fury,' and he giveth his own children a taste of it, not *ad ruinam,* but *ad dignam emendationem,* not to their ruin, but amendment. It is called also ' The cup of trembling.' God himself calleth it ' The wine-cup of his fury,' Jer. xxv. 15.

It is called in Ezekiel, chap. xxii. 32, ' deep and large.' And as the apostle saith, 2 Cor. v. 11, speaking of the judgment to come, ' Knowing, therefore, the terror of the Lord, we persuade men.'

If men will not be persuaded, let him that is filthy be filthy still; let him that is a drunkard be a drunkard still: but, as the apostle St Peter saith, 1 Peter iv. 3, if we look well about us, ' The time past of our life may suffice us to have wrought the will of the Gentiles, when we walked in lasciviousness, lusts, excess of wine, revellings, banquetings,' &c.

Yet, better late than never; for if God have taken the matter into his hand, David will tell you that that hand of God is strong: Ps. lxiii. 8, ' Strong is thy hand,' saith he. This is *dextra subveniens suis, suscipit me dextra tua;* and it is *dextra inveniens,* Ps. xxi. 8, ' Thy hand shall find out all thine enemies, thy right hand shall find out those that hate thee.' It is a fearful thing to fall into that hand, Heb. x. 31. Thy right hand is full of righteousness, Ps. xlviii. That righteousness will give *suum cuique,* to every one his own; it payeth home; he keeps it in his bosom of purpose to spare men, and to give them time of repentance.

But I must tell you that the saints of God are so impatient of the wrong done to the name of God, that they cry unto him, Ps. lxxiv. 10, 11, ' O God, how long shall the adversary reproach ? shall the enemy blaspheme thy name for ever ? Why withdrawest thou thy hand, even thy right hand ? pluck it out of thy bosom.'

2. How he will punish.

1. He will fill them with shame for glory ; which shame is further expressed, ' Shameful spewing shall be on thy glory.'

2. He will punish them with their own sin ; for he saith, ' Drink thou also, and let thy foreskin be uncovered.'

1. With Shame.

You are not to learn that all sin is folly, and all sinners are fools ; but no transgressor in any kind doth more make a fool of himself than the drunkard doth, for he proclaimeth his own shame as he walketh up and down the streets ; as he sitteth in the house, his words, his gestures, his actions do all shame him ; as Solomon saith, Eccles. x. 3, ' When he that is a fool walketh by the way, his wisdom faileth him, and he saith to every one that he is a fool.' So doth a drunkard shame himself by telling every one that he is drunk. This were a great punishment, if custom of sinning and multitude of sinners in this kind had not hardened the foreheads of them that transgress in this kind, that they feel not the rod of shame.

I may say with the prophet of the drunkards of our days, as he spake of the idolaters of his time : Jer. vi. 15, ' Were they ashamed when they had committed abomination ? nay, they were not ashamed, neither could they blush.' But let no man despise the good opinion of his neighbour ; sober men care not how little conversation they have with drunkards, they seek to avoid them, and all that fear God abhor their evil manners.

Yet they glory and boast how much themselves have drunk, how many they have made drunk ; but as the apostle saith, ' Their glory is their shame.'

And though they be not sensible of it in the heat of their wine, and in the custom of their sin, the end thereof will be bitterness ; for the wise man telleth them, Prov. xxiii. 32, 'At the last it biteth like a serpent, and stingeth like an adder.' When shame once begins to smart, it goeth to the quick. Remember Adam in paradise: Gen. iii. 10, 'I heard thy voice in the garden, and I was afraid, because I was naked; and I hid myself.' The Lord will come in the cool of the day to us, and we shall hear his voice in the evening of our time, and then our shame shall come with a sting, even the sting of servile fear, and cast up our account. What fruit, then, of those things whereof we are ashamed? Then is God even with you; for he crieth out to you, 'How long wilt thou turn my glory into shame?' Do not drunkards do so, who make their bodies, which should be the temples of the Holy Ghost, the sties of uncleanness?

The Holy Ghost, you see, is plain and homely in his phrase of speech. These drinks, which they pour into their bodies luxuriously, shall not make their hearts glad; they shall not comfort the stomach, they shall not nourish the body. The stomach shall complain of them as a wrong, and cast them up as a burden too heavy for it to bear; nature itself shall exonerate itself, and resist, regest it in a shameful vomit. And, to use God's own phrase, God shall spew these workers of iniquity out of his mouth, and all the service that they do to him, he shall cast up again; for he will say, *Nauseat anima mea,* my soul loatheth; he is even sick of them and their service.

And if God once set upon us, to shame us, who then shall have pity upon thee, O Jerusalem? or who shall bemoan thee? or who shall go aside to ask thee how thou dost? Jer. xv. 5.

2. He will punish them with their own sin: 'Drink thou also, and let thy foreskin be uncovered.'

1. This calleth to your remembrance a doctrine formerly delivered out of Obadiah,

That God requiteth sinners with the same measure that they have measured to others.

2. This reneweth also the remembrance of another doctrine there delivered, that

God punisheth sin by sin; as there Edom trusted in the help of men, that was their fault; and that God laid upon them after for a punishment.

So here, the fault of the Chaldeans was their making men drunk, that they might see their nakedness, and that is their punishment; now they shall be drunk, and their nakedness discovered.

There I handled this question, how God would be author of this kind of punishment, and innocent in the sin of the offender; resolving it thus: that God will withdraw his grace, and forsake them that forsake him, and leave them to the force and strong stream of their own corruptions. As the apostle saith, Rom. i. 24, 26, 'God gave them up to uncleanness, through the lusts of their own hearts, to dishonour their bodies: for this cause God gave them up to vile affections.' We carry stuff enough about us to punish us withal; if God do but make rods of our own corruptions, he will soon be armed against us.

You shall find in that place of the apostle, that in man there are two things to which for sin they are yielded up by God himself in his justice.

1. Ἐπιθυμίαις τῶν καρδίων, ver. 14.
2. Εἰς πάθη ἀτιμίας.

These two do differ much; for,

1. Concupiscence is but a grudging of a disease, but πάθος is the very strength of the fit.
2. Concupiscence is within the heart and affections, but this *pathos* is active and in operation, and so corrupt the whole man. God leaveth the wicked to both these; ἐπιθυμία is the minority, πάθος is the strength of sin.

Thus, as Augustine saith, some sins are not *tormenta peccantium*, but *incrementa vitiorum*, and men do not feel any punishment. Yet he that shall consider it well, will find that Solomon means a punishment to the young man, when he saith, 'Rejoice, O young man, in thy youth.' So doth the Holy Ghost, saying, 'Let him that is filthy be filthy still;' for if God let go the reins, and leave us to ourselves, we are likely to bring our sin to a full stature.

It is a good use of this point which St Paul teacheth: Gal. vi. 1, 'Brethren, if a man be overtaken with a fault, ye which are spiritual restore such a man with the spirit of meekness; considering thyself, lest thou also be tempted.'

God hath a just hand in the moderation of the things of this world, and of men's persons. Hath not the sun shined on those that have made sport to behold men drunk, or otherwise have made the most of it, to their shame and disgrace amongst men; who, in the just punishment of their uncharitableness, have themselves fallen into the same sin of drunkenness, and thereby have borne a shame and scandal to their profession. This is God's justice upon them, they did not consider themselves, they knew not the strength of the temptation, they knew not their own weakness.

The greatest professors of religion are commonly the severest judges of their brethren; for their zeal against sin, and for the glory of God, doth fill them with hatred of evil. Yet, let such consider themselves, for if God see that their zeal begin once to burn up their charity, he will leave them to themselves a while, and they shall see *quo semine nati*, what they are. For, let all men know, that the evil angels are as much at God's commandment as the good; for *omnia illi serviunt*, all things serve him. And as it is said, Ps. lxxviii. 49, ' He will give his angels charge over thee;' so it is said likewise, ' He cast upon them the fierceness of his anger, wrath, and indignation, and terribleness, by sending evil angels among them.'

As we have the ministry of good angels sent unto them that shall be heirs of salvation, so God sendeth evil angels also, not only to Saul and to the false prophets of Ahab, but even to Adam in paradise God sent him, and to St Paul, the angel of Satan. These evil angels sometimes come with suggestions to sin, to try our strength, that we may know how weak we are; and sometimes they prevail with God's children, that they may stand upon their own guard, and keep better watch. But for the ungodly of the earth, they emplunge them in the same sin that they do cause others to commit, that the same disgrace and shame which they have done to their neighbour, may reflect upon themselves.

Some have been so afraid of making God the author

of evil, because it is said, *tradidit eos Deus*, God hath delivered them up, that they have understood the apostle to speak of that God who is called *deus sæculi hujus*, the god of this world ; as the Manichees saw so much evil done, and knew not how to free God from guiltiness of it, they therefore made *duo principia*, two beginnings. But that needs not.

It is likely that such a father as is personated in the parable of the prodigal, could not but observe in the education of his son, how thrifty he was like to prove ; yet such a father, giving the portion of his goods which is a child's part, to such a son, and letting him take his journey into a far country, is not accessory to his riotous living. Augustine saith that the heart of man is harned* by God, *Non impartiendo malitiam, sed non largiendo gratiam*, not by instilling any malice, but not giving grace.

He seeth the Chaldeans take delight in making men drunk ; *ut nuditatem videant;* he letteth go the hold he hath of them for a time, and leaveth them to themselves ; and that which was their sport, is now their fault and their shame.

I say therefore, again, consider yourselves. When thou seest a drunkard shaming himself, as these here did, consider whose light shineth in thy understanding, to shew thee how foul a sin that is ; consider that that is not enough ; for all drunkards know that drunkenness is a sin ; consider whose grace it is that establisheth thy heart, and keepeth thee from committing the same sin.

Insult not over thy brother, deride him not, discover him not to increase his shame ; rejoice not against him, rather bewail his sin with the tears of thy soul; seek by the spirit of meekness to restore him, advise him friendly, chide him lovingly. For if thou professest a severe life, and to make conscience of thy ways, shouldest fall into this sin thyself, thou wouldest not only shame thy person, but thy profession also. And indeed, thou carriest about thee *corpus peccati*, a body of sin ; thou hast the matter and stuff of all sins within thee, if grace do not aid and assist thee.

* Qu. 'hardened'?—Ed.

Lastly, let me admonish you, if any of you by occasion are overtaken at any time with this fault, be of David's mind, 'Let the righteous smite me;' suffer a gentle chiding from your friends that love you, and hate that evil in you. Take it for a favour of God, and think that it is he that speaketh to you in that reprehension.

Hearken not to those that flatter you in your sins.

Alexander in a drunken fit slew Clitus his beloved friend and faithful counsellor. Instead of reproving his fault, even then when he was fit to be wrought upon, being sensible of it, he had three flatterers, Anaxarchus, Aristander, Calisthenes: Anaxarchus, an epicurean philosopher, he told him that it was no matter, he was a king, and he might do what he list; Aristander, a stoic philosopher, told him that it was not his fault, but fate, that killed Clitus; Calisthenes, a courtier, sought to heal the sore with sweet words. That is not the way to bring us to amendment of our evils; a gentle, discreet reprehension well taken, will pierce the heart, and fill it with comfort. John the Baptist, *quis prænuntiavit vobis ut fugeretis ab ira ventura*? Who hath done you such a favour to prevent such a danger?

3. Why doth God inflict punishment?

God giveth a reason of his severe proceeding against the Babylonians, the violence of Lebanon, and the spoil of beasts which made them afraid, and for the violence of the land, &c. Shewing that their cruelty to man and beast had provoked God against them to punish all their sins, their pride, covetousness, and drunkenness. You have heard of their cruelty at large before to men; their very cities were built with blood.

The apostle saith, 'Hath God care of oxen?' Here you see that God used the beasts of Lebanon for a terror to the enemy; and now he declareth himself an avenger also of their quarrel, because of the cruel spoil that the Chaldeans did make amongst the beasts of God's people.

God gave man lordship over the beasts of the field; he made him a lord to rule them, not a tyrant to destroy them.

One saith upon those words of Solomon, Prov. xii. 10, ' a just man regardeth the life of his beast;' that seeing God hath put the beasts of the field in subjection to man, that he must shew himself a lord,
1. *In pascendo,* providing necessary food for them.
2. *In parcendo,* using them favourably.
3. *In patiendo,* bearing with them in their kind.
4. *In compatiendo,* relieving them in their griefs.
5. *In compescendo,* restraining them from hurt.
6. *In conservando,* preserving them all we can.

This was the sin of the Chaldeans; they were destroyers, and sought not only the ruin of the people of the land, but the destruction also of their cattle, that the means of living, if any escaped to reinhabit, might be taken away.

This justice of God in avenging the wrongs done to brute beasts, by calling them to an account for their sins that did the wrong, doth teach us,

1. That the providence and care of God doth stoop so low as the regard of our cattle.

Christ made good use of it, *considerate volatilia cœli,* consider the fowls of heaven; God feedeth them, *quanto magis vos,* how much more you.

2. It teacheth us to use our dominion of these creatures moderately, lest the ass of Balaam do reprove his owner.

3. It sheweth how much God doth make of anything that serves him. The text saith that these beasts did make the Chaldeans afraid, and for this they suffered predation, for the service they did to God and his church against their enemies; in Christ's argument, how much more will he defend us, if we fight his battles against his enemies.

4. We learn here that when God cometh to execute vengeance, he surveyeth the whole catalogue of offences; and as he saith in David, 'I will reprove thee, and set them in order before thee.' The wrong to the cities, to the men, to the beasts, to persons, to places, all comes into an account, and the offenders shall smart for all.

Ver. 18–20. What profiteth the graven image that the maker thereof hath graven it; the molten image, and a teacher of lies, that the maker of his work trusteth therein to make dumb idols? Woe unto him that saith to the wood, Awake; to the dumb stone, Arise, it shall teach! Behold, it is laid over with gold and silver, and there is no breath at all in the midst of it. But the Lord is in his holy temple: let all the earth keep silence before him.

Here God denounceth his judgment against their idolatry. The words of this text have no obscurity in them. Thus much then shall serve for the opening of this text, that all this commination of woe and judgment of which you have heard is the voice of the true God declaring his just proceeding against the sins formerly mentioned; and to this purpose he doth here lay open the vanity of false gods.

What profit can there come, saith he, of a graven image, that the maker thereof hath graven? He asketh men this question, and appealeth to the light of natural reason; can that profit a man, meaning in the power and goodness of a divine nature, which is the work of a man's hands? be it either a graven image wrought upon by art of the workman, or a molten image cast in any metal; can this profit a man?

He calleth the image thus carved, graven or molten, 'a teacher of lies;' for it is a mere illusion that any man should so befool himself as to believe that such an artificial composition, wrought by the hand of man, should be esteemed a god.

This is amplified, and the wonder increased; for though other men may be carried away with a superstitious over-weaning of such an idol, yet that the maker of it should trust in it, who when he was at work, peradventure as the poet saith,

> Incertus scamnum faceretne Priapum,
> Maluit esse deum.

It was at his courtesy whether it should be an idol or some other thing.

Therefore, ver. 19, God saith, 'Woe unto him that saith to the wood, Awake, and to the dumb stone,

Arise;' that is, woe to him that trusteth to an idol for defence against evil, or deliverance out of danger, for that is one of the uses that is made of idols, to succour in time of distress, as the disciples did awake their Master in a storm.

You see that when the workman hath put his hand upon it, and shewed his best skill, here God doth call it wood and a dumb stone still. He proveth it thus : It shall teach ; although it be dumb, yet the dumbness thereof shall declare it to be an inanimate, impotent thing ; for howsoever the matter of the idol, be it wood, or stone, or metal, be laid over with gold and silver, as superstition is costly enough in adorning their gods, yet 'there is no breath at all in the midst of them,' and having no life in them, they have no power to give help to them that serve them.

Ver. 20. *But the Lord is in his holy temple;* for, having shewed the vanity of idols, he cometh now to reveal himself to them.

This some understand that the Lord is in heaven, the temple of his holiness, and though the heaven of heavens cannot contain him, yet he hath said, 'Heaven is my throne,' and Christ teacheth us to say, *qui es in cœli,* 'who art in heaven.'

So the temple at Jerusalem, where he said, 'I will dwell,' is the temple of his holiness; and as the Babylonians and other heathen had their idols and their temples for them to which they did resort, so he produceth in opposition to them the God of Israel in his holy temple, to whom the Jews may resort for help against all their enemies. 'Let all the earth keep silence before him ;' in which words either he discourageth all power that should rise up against him, or he requireth the voluntary submission of the earth to him as to the supreme sovereign of all the world ; for keeping silence is a sign of reverence and submission, as Job, speaking of his former glory when God had abased him, saith that, when he came forth, 'the princes refrained talking, and laid their hand on their mouth,' chap. xxix. 9. (*De verbis hactenus.*)

The parts of the text are two—1, False worship ; 2, True religion.

In the first, 1, *Peccatum*, that is, idolatry; 2, *Pœna*, *Væ*, ' Woe.'

In the first, here is,

1. A description of the idolatry of the heathen Babel.

2. A derision of the idolaters.

1. Idolatry is a trust in, and an invocation of, graven and molten images, dumb idols. First, here is trust, then followeth invocation, and that is the apostle's method in all religious adoration: Rom. x. 4, 'How shall they call on him in whom they have not believed?' This doth open to us the occasion of this last imputation to them of idolatry; for what hath made them so proud, so cruel, so covetous, so voluptuous, as the opinion that they have in the protection of their gods? Therefore now at last God overthroweth that also, and doth shew them that in religion they are most of all wrong.

If you desire a general definition of idolatry, which comprehendeth all kinds, I think this is full of comprehension. It is *cultus religiosus exhibitus creaturæ*, a religious worship given to the creature. Learn then that no nation of the world did ever deny a divine power, but acknowledged some god in whom they trusted, and whom in their necessities they called upon; and because this invisible godhead was out of sight, they devised idols, which they erected for representation of their gods, which they also worshipped with divine honours; and this we call idolatry, or the worshipping of idols. They saw that there was much to do in the government of the world, and therefore they adored many gods, as thinking it too much to believe any one god able to manage the universal government of all things.

These gods they represented some forms, either cast in metal or graven in gold, silver, wood, and stone. This they call εἴδωλον *ab* εἴδω, *video*, to see, signifying somewhat that was to be seen, for they walked by sight and not by faith, and would have somewhat to see before they would worship.

2. The vanity of this worship is derided here, because this idol which they worshipped could profit

them nothing, for no man would do service where nothing is to be gained by it.

He proveth that it cannot profit,

1. Because it hath a maker, for so there was a time when it was not; and how can he profit a man that is beholding to man for his making?

2. Because every idol is a teacher of lies, for it teacheth a man to trust in his own work, and is a mere illusion, planting his trust and directing his worship in and to that which is able to do him no good when he needeth.

3. Because these idols are dumb, and can give man no answer to his demands or petitions.

4. Because, when man hath bestowed his workmanship upon it, and all his cost in overlaying it with gold and silver, it is yet a dumb statue, it hath no life in it, 'there is no breath at all in the midst of it;' so that the doctrine of this place is,

Doct. Idolatry is a grievous sin.

The reasons to prove this are great; two chiefly:

1. In respect of God, there is no sin that doth more dishonour God, because this doth, as it were, un-god him, and setteth up the creature in the place of the Creator, at once breaking the two first commandments of the first table of God's holy law.

1. 'Thou shalt have no other gods but me.'

2. 'Thou shalt worship no graven image,' &c.

But this reason God omitteth, as having now to do with those who knew not the true God.

2. He urgeth a second reason. This sin is against them that commit it, for they trust in and call upon that thing which cannot profit them, the two great acts of religion cast away and lost, that is, trust and invocation.

This is a great argument in our temporal affairs; for will a man bestow his time, his labour, his love, and service, where no profit is like to arise to him?

But this kind of idolatry is so extinguished by the light of the gospel, and so little cause of fear of it, that I need bestow no time nor pains on it, for there is none of us who doth not confess one God in three persons. But there is an idolatry amongst those that call themselves Christians, and would have none be the church of God but themselves: that is the church of Rome; and though they protest against it, and plead not guilty to our accusation, yet the evidence of truth will convince them of it. Under the name of idol, Cardinal Bellarmine doth understand only *falsam similitudinem representantem id quod revera non est*, a false similitude representing that which indeed is not, as the idols, he saith, of the heathen did represent feigned gods, such as never were, but were only the fictions of human device; they have not such.

Theirs are *imagines; imago ab imitando*, of imitating, and they be counterfeits, representing in similitude such persons as have been and have lived in the world.

So idols they defy, images they embrace. In this very beginning of their defence, both absurd in the strife of words, making distinction where there is no difference, for εἰδῶλον is properly a visible representation, and so is an image, and therefore both in Greek, Latin, and English one and the same thing, but the custom of speech hath impropriated certain words to set fictions, as that an image is the representation of anything, but an idol is commonly taken with us for the representation of some thing that is worshipped.

Therefore the best part of the papist's defence of their religion against our imputation of idolatry, is this:

1. That for the images that they do retain, either in the church oratories or in their private use, they know them in their matter to be no other than the creatures of God, of wood, stone, metal, or some other mixed matter; they know them to be in their forms the art of the workman; they do know and confess them to be dead, inanimate, senseless things in themselves, and they protest against any adoration of them as much (they say) as we do. Here Cardinal Bellarmine speaks for the rest, and he will charge the protestant church with slander in this point, and say there is no such matter, they do not worship any idols. He complaineth that by this slander some of

the protestants have so distasted the religion of Rome to many that know it not, that though they do hear of worthy men amongst them, who for gravity of manners, holiness of life, and all exemplary virtues, deserve reverence and respect, yet our opinion of their idolatry distasteth them so to us that we will not hear them speak.

2. They answer, that their images are of two sorts, which they use in divine worship :

Either they be of God, or of the creature.

In the images which represent God, they only do worship God in the image, not the image itself, with holy worship.

In the images of the creatures, as of the mother of the Lord, angels and saints, they do but honour God in his saints, and in their invocation they use them but as means of quickening their memories, and turning up their devotions by that which the eye beholdeth; and God loseth no honour by it, to have so many means used to him.

This is that which they give out for themselves; we charge them that they adore creatures, and give divine worship to images, as the heathen did. For it is plain that they worship the wood of the cross, in that they speak that to the crucifix, which can only be applied to the cross itself, and not to Christ, *Salve crux, spes unica!* They add, thou only art worthy to bear the ransom of the world, O faithful cross; which agreeth with their doctrine, that all the honour due to the sampler is given to the image thereof.

And where they excuse their idolatry, that they do not worship the image, but God represented in the image; if that be not idolatry, neither were the Athenians idolaters, who worshipped in their images the same God whom Paul preached, Acts xvii. 23; neither were the Israelites idolaters, who worshipped God in the calf which Aaron made, for they could not be so ignorant as to ascribe their deliverance from Egypt to such a thing as Aaron could make.

This doctrine and practice of idolatry in the worship of images came in by little and little into the church of Rome; for it is clear that there was a time wherein there were no images at all known in the church. There were some desirous then to bring them in, but the council of Eliberis* decreed that no picture or image should be brought into the church, lest it should be adored; and Epiphanius, finding an image painted on a cloth hanging in a church, rent it down, and said it was against the authority of Scriptures that any image should be in the church.

St Origen* saith of his time, *nos imagines non adoramus*, we do not worship images. Eight hundred years after Christ, the second Nicene council set up images; but the council of Frankfort, which was a general council, and where the pope's legates were present, repealed it, and affirm: The catholic church doth affirm that mortal man ought to worship God, not by images and angels, but by Christ our Lord.

And whatsoever the practice of the church of Rome now is in the use of them, they shall never be able to reconcile the judgments of their best learned concerning them; for some condemn all divine adoration given to them, some condemn external bowing before them, some confess that the ancient fathers condemned them, some think their use dangerous; and they which have gone farthest in defending them have done it by so nice distinctions that the common people cannot understand how to beware of idolatry, themselves not understanding themselves therein.

Even in the administration of the sacrament of the Lord's supper, they are idolaters in worshipping the host, which I prove from Cardinal Bellarmine's own pen (*De justif. lib. 3, cap. 8*): *Neque potest certus esse certitudine fidei, se percipere verum sacramentum, cum sacramentum sine intentione ministri non conficiatur, et intentionem alterius nemo videre potest.* And thus much Garnet the provincial did ingeniously confess upon his private conference with some of our bishops. Wherefore, how they can excuse their idolatry in the worship of the elevated host, I cannot see, seeing they worship they know not what.

Any man may easily conceive that they do carry a corrupt mind that way, because in all their catechisms

---

* Can. 36.   * Contra Celsum, l. 7.

set forth for the institution of young beginners, they do leave out the second commandment quite, and to make up the number they divide the tenth commandment into two.

Now, having convinced them of idolatry, which is the high sin against God, and toucheth him in his majesty and glory, we see how dangerous a thing it is to have conversation with such, lest we receive of the plagues due to them.

Though the church of Pergamos did hold fast the name of Christ, and denied not his faith, yet had the Lord 'something against her,' Rev. ii. 14, because 'she had there them that held the doctrine of Balaam, who taught Balak to cast a stumbling-block before the children of Israel, to eat things sacrificed unto idols, and to commit fornication.' The same quarrel had our Lord to the church at Thyatira, in which, though he approved her works, and charity, and service, and faith, and patience, yet he saith, Rev. ii. 20, 'Notwithstanding I have a few things against thee, because thou sufferest that woman Jezebel, who calleth herself a prophetess, to teach and to seduce my servants to commit fornication, and to eat things sacrificed to idols.'

We have no law to favour idolatry, or idolatrous meetings to mass. We have severe laws against them; yet it is in sight that mass is frequented by multitudes of all sorts, in the sight of Israel, in the light of the sun. Whence this boldness grows, we cannot judge, but from negligent execution of our godly and just laws. Have we forgotten '88 ? Have we forgotten the fifth of November 1605 ? Do we not believe experience ?

Were not the Canaanites, whom Israel suffered to live amongst them against the commandment of God, thorns in their sides, and pricks in their eyes ? and were not their gods a snare to Israel ?

Is not popery a dangerous religion to the sovereign authority of the king, setting the pope above him to overrule him, and to deprive him of his crown if he be not for his turn ?

Is not popery a professed enemy to the religion that we profess ? Light and darkness, God and Belial, may as soon be reconciled ; and therefore an enemy to our clergy, who are all armed with the word of God against it.

Or is it good and wholesome doctrine which the Anabaptists this last year tendered to the king, prince, nobility, judges, and commons of parliament, that freedom of religion is not hurtful to any commonwealth, or that freedom of religion depriveth not kings of any power given them of God ?

The times are foul. God is much dishonoured. Where the fault is, and of whom the church and religion hath cause to complain, is not so much our duty to inquire, as to pray to God to amend all. I will tell you where you shall have him.

2. The punishment of this sin is expressed in one word, *Væ*, woe! and it containeth the whole cup of God's indignation.

1. In this life they trust in that which cannot help them.

2. They invocate that which cannot hear them.

They trust in lying vanities, and they forsake their own mercy. They are taught by teachers of lies, and therefore the light that is in them is darkness. Baal's servants cried from morning to evening upon Baal their god to hear them, and it would not do. Here is a double woe : 1, loss of labour ; 2, want of help. In the first, they bewray their folly : the god of this world hath made fools ot them for turning the glory of the invisible God into the images of creatures ; but in the second we find the misery, for we cannot subsist without help, and they trust to idols where there is no help.

But that is not all the woe. The apostle telleth us, Gal. v. 20, that no idolaters shall enter into the kingdom of heaven. This is *terror Domini*, the terror of the Lord ; for how shall they hope to have glory with God who deny glory to God ? Will God give them glory that seek to take away glory from him, or let them into heaven that would thrust him out ?

Observe it in that law concerning graven images, God hath more expressed himself than in any of the rest to be a God of vengeance ; for there is *ratio legis*,

God is jealous. And there is *comminatio judicis; visitabit*, and it goeth in descent to the third and fourth generation of them that hate him. Observe he calleth them such as hate him. There is a promise, ' He will shew mercy to thousands of them that love him.' And I conceive this added to this commandment rather than any of the rest, because God's Israel did most often offend in this kind, by worshipping God in creatures, and by performing external adoration to them, which is in this law chiefly forbidden.

The fear of this woe hath not wrought enough upon the Romanists, who are guilty of gross idolatry; so, on the other side, it hath wrought too much upon some zealous professors, who, fearing superstition and idolatry, dare scarce shew any external reverence to God himself, either when they come into God's house, or when they come to God's table. Yet the angel that would not be worshipped said, ' Worship thou God.' And that is all the church exacteth; not an inward worship only, but an outward also, commanded in the second commandment.

Ver. 20. *But the Lord is in his holy temple; let all the earth keep silence before him.*

The temple of God's holiness is understood here, as you have heard, two ways.

1. For the temple at Jerusalem.
2. For heaven.

In both let all tremble before him. This is the second part of the antithesis, true religion, containing two parts.

1. Where God is.
2. What duty is owing to him.

Ubi est. He is in his temple at Jerusalem, and in all other temples dedicate to his service.

For the temple at Jerusalem, he appointed the making of it, and chose the man to whose care he committed the trust of the work. David might not do it, but Solomon was the man. When it was finished, and Solomon had assembled the people to the consecration of it, and prayed there, God answered the prayer of Solomon with a visible expressure of his presence; for a cloud filled the house, it was filled with the glory of God.

But some of our sectaries say there is no need of churches for God's public service; there is neither precept nor example in Scripture for it, but the words of Christ to the woman of Samaria leave it at large: John iv. 23, 'The hour cometh, and now is, when the true worshippers shall worship the Father in spirit and truth.'

Saint Augustine calleth this heresy in the Massilians, that they denied the use of temples, because Christ foretold that the use of the temple at Jerusalem should cease, which was a shadow of things to come.

In the Old Testament, beside the cathedral and mother-church, the people had their synagogues for their meetings to God's service, which continued even to and in Christ's time. Christ himself designed a place for that meeting, wherein he celebrated the last passover, and instituted the sacrament of his supper. The disciples had a place of meeting wherein Christ twice found them the first day of the week. The persecutions of those times gave no sudden liberty to settle a church and to erect temples, nor, that I can read, for the first two hundred years after Christ were any temples built. Yet before the persecutions ceased, they had erected oratories for their meeting to prayer and hearing of the word; for in the tenth persecution under Diocletian, *an. Reg.* 19, *Mense Martio*, he made an edict* for the pulling down of the temples of the Christians.

But under Constantine, when Christian religion had the favour of authority regal, then *concurrebant populi ad populos quasi os ad os. Ecclesiæ, quæ antea impiis tyrannorum machinis destructæ fuerant, rediviva*, &c.* Then the people came together.

And ever since the church hath continued this practice of maintaining oratories for the meeting of the congregations for the praise and service of God. There is warrant enough from the example of the church and the authority thereof to maintain this holy practice.

    * Euseb. viii. 2.   * Euseb. x. 2.

Those places be the temples of God's holiness, the houses of God, separate from all common use to the holy service of God. And God, who by his omnipotency filleth all places, is in our churches by a more special presence; for if the glory of God filled the temple in the time of the law, why may we not believe that in the light of the gospel he revealeth his presence more, because the place wherein we serve God is God's house, and all civil and common use of it is resigned, to consecrate it to God's service?

If God be present where two or three are assembled, surely where there is a meeting of a full congregation he is present with a special presence. And, therefore, it hath ever been esteemed a pious charity in those that have been founders, enlargers, restorers, or adorners of churches, as Saint Origen saith,† *quam gloriosum est si dicatur in tabernaculo domini, Illius fuit hoc aurum, hoc argentum,* &c. *Rursus quam indecorum ut Dominus veniens nihil muneris tui inveniat in eo, nihil a te cognoscat oblatum. Ego optarem, si fieri posset, esse aliquid meum in auro quo arca contegitur: Nollem esse infœcundus,* &c.

These houses of God are the temples of his holiness, where the name of God is declared to the church; wherein God, by his Spirit, speaketh to the churches in the outward ministry of the word; where the holy ones of God do speak to God by the same Spirit in prayers, in hymns, and spiritual songs; where the sacrifices of righteousness are offered.

And herein is that gracious prophecy of Isaiah fulfilled, chap. lvi. 7, which our Saviour allegeth in the Gospel, 'For mine house shall be called a house of prayer for all people.'

Observe, here is not only *oratio*, prayer, which is *cultus divinus*, divine worship; but here is *domus mea*, my house, a place designed for the worship of God, and that for all people. This cannot be made good in the temple of Jerusalem, nor in any one church; but must determine both the extent and dilatation of God's worship, and the designation of fit houses for the same. Another like prophecy we have before in Isaiah, chap. ii. 2, 'It shall come to pass in the last

† In ex. xxv. Hom. xiii.

days, that the mountains of the Lord's house shall be established in the top of the mountains, and shall be exalted above the hills, and all nations shall flow unto it. And many people shall go and say, Come ye and let us go up to the top of the mountain of the Lord, to the house of the God of Jacob, and he will teach us his ways, and we will walk in his paths; for out of Sion shall go forth the law, and the word of the Lord from Jerusalem.'

The common exposition is, that after the return of the people of Israel from the seventy years' captivity in Babylon, then religion and God's worship shall be settled at Jerusalem. But observe how this exposition shrivelleth up the promise of grace; for this is not all. He saith this shall be ἐν ἐσχάταις ἡμέραις, in the last time. And he addeth that all nations shall flow to it; and he saith, not that one mountain, but 'the mountains of the Lord shall be established,' which must needs be understood of the churches of the Christians, to which the faithful should resort.

For further proof hereof read Micah iv., where you shall find this prophecy, *totidem verbis*, in so many words, and a commentary upon it, Micah v., wherein he prophesieth the birth of Christ in Bethlehem. In both these prophecies we observe that the promise of God hath not only assured the spreading of true religion, but the assemblies of believers to certain places for instruction, that they may be taught *vias Domini*, the ways of the Lord.

Never was there religion in the world, without some places of public worship for meeting of people together. Even in Adam's time, there was a place where Adam and his children met to offer sacrifice, and Cain's flying from the presence of the Lord was his wilful excommunication from that place.

And in truth, they that would have no churches, may as well cry down religion, and the public ministry of the word, and pluck down the hedge which God hath planted about his vine, and lay all common. Understand us rightly; we do not affix holiness to the place, nor think any special sanctity inherent in it; but seeing God is by a singular right become master of the house, that is separate to his use, as the apostle saith, ' Judge I pray you, is it comely,' that we put not difference between God's house and our own houses ?

It is observed that Christ, when he purged the temple, purged only that part of the temple which was set apart to prayer and hearing of the word, because that use of the church was to continue in the time of the gospel ; and after he had cast out the oxen and the doves, which were provisions for sacrifice, then he citeth that place and reneweth the sanction, ' My house shall be called an house of prayer to all nations,' which is a sanctification of all churches to the worship of God. That this was so understood, know that before they had any churches built for the public exercise of religion, they had some places of meeting which they called *Ædes sacras*, holy houses, of which the apostle putting difference, saith, 1 Cor. xi. 22, ' Have ye not houses to eat and drink in ? despise ye the church of God ?' Here be our own houses for common and natural, moral and civil use ; here is the church of God, the place of assembling of the congregations to the worship and service of God.

No sooner is a place consecrate to this use, but it is a temple of God's.

So when Jacob had set up a stone for a pillar, in the place where he dreamed and had the vision of the ladder, Gen. xxviii. 19, 22, he called the name of it ' Bethel,' בית אלהים, God's house. And after, Gen. xxxv. 7, At his return he came to that place, and having first put down all the strange gods, he built an altar to the Lord, and called it אל ביתאל, the god of God's house.

It is *palestra*, in which we do meet with God to wrestle with him in our fervent prayers and supplications, he by his word wrestleth with us to overcome both our ignorance and impiety. And therefore as Jacob, Gen. xxxii. 31, so may we call our church פנואל, the face of God, for there God did look upon him.

And in the times of the gospel, these houses of prayer have had several titles : *Ædes sacræ*, in respect of their succcession to them, and *Templa*, in respect of their succession to that at Jerusalem. *Tectum amplum*, some derive it, and κυριακα. 1. *Propter dedicationem.* 2. *Propter usum.* 3. *Propter jus perpetuum.* 4. *Propter sabbatum.* For there is *dominica in dominico;* thence came the word *kirk*, yet in use in Scotland; and *ecclesiæ*, in respect of the meetings there.

When David could not come to the sanctuary of God, he worshipped toward it: Ps. vii., xxviii. 2, 'Hear the voice of my supplications, when I cry unto thee, when I lift up my hands towards thy holy temple.'

Daniel being far from the temple, Dan. vi. 10, 'opened his window toward Jerusalem, and prayed three times a day.'

The temple is a type of heaven, where the saints of God do meet to praise God, which is the worship that is done to God in heaven: Rev. xxi. 3, 'And I heard a great voice out of heaven, saying, Behold, the tabernacle of God is with men, and he will dwell with them, and they shall be his people, and God himself shall be with them, and be their God.' This Mr Brightman understandeth of the church of the Gentiles, where God is seen.

So doth James Brocard, an Italian, understand it of the church delivered from popery, and Mahometry, and all heresy.

But Mr Bullinger, better advised, saith, that as in the former part of this Revelation hell is described, so in this chapter heaven is set forth; and that, as you see, in the similitude of a tabernacle. So doth Junius and Napier well interpret this place.

I conclude, then, that all the churches, wherein the Christians meet to call upon God, are the temples of God's presence, wherein God is invisibly resident, both to give his Spirit where he thinketh good, and to direct our service of him, and to receive our prayers and sacrifices of thanksgiving; and to communicate to his servants the ordinances of his grace, the means of their salvation.

2. As God is in these temples made with hands, and declareth his presence in his house, in his word and sacraments, and in the solemn meetings of his children: so is he in heaven, which is his highest temple, whereof these are but types and figures.

We believe in him as maker of heaven, and we pray to him, ' Our Father which art in heaven ;' this place he himself calleth his habitation. ' I dwell in the high and holy place,' Isa. lvii. 15. 1. In heaven. Yet as Solomon saith, ' The heaven of heavens is not able to contain him,' 1 Kings viii. 27. So he is there as in the most excellent part of his creation, but not comprehended there, for there he is most purely worshipped; thence cometh our *sicut in cœlo*.

The heathen gods are nowhere : in heaven they are not, that is the temple of the true God; in earth they are not, for they are no gods that have residence in earth, and have no power at all in heaven. As the apostle saith, 1 Cor. viii. 4, ' We know that an idol is nothing in the world.' Here, by the name of idol, is not meant the material image representing their god, for that is a bodily substance to be seen and felt, and it is in the world ; but he speaketh it *de numine*, the divinity is a *non ens*. For he addeth, that there is no God but one ; and whereas many be called gods in heaven and in earth, as there be many gods and many lords, yet he saith there is but one God, the rest are *nomina*, not *numina*. For there were that worshippped the sun, the moon, and the stars ; these as creatures and second causes do us good, but they serve our God.

When our God is in his temple, all those help to make up the choir of them that praise him ; for ' the heavens declare the glory of God, and the firmaments and the outgoings of the morning praise him.' Therefore do we lift up our eyes to heaven when we pray ; we say that every good and perfect gift comes from above, from the Father of lights.

Yet is not God so far off, but that as heaven is his throne, the earth is his footstool : Ps. xxxiii. 13, ' The Lord looketh from heaven, he beholdeth the sons of men.' He is not so far off but if we pray to him, *Prope est invocantibus ipsum*, ' he is near to them that call upon him.' And in this respect all the earth is a common oratory, so is the sea, for our prayers.

But as the perpetual duty of a religious service of God, which doth require holiness and righteousness all the days of our lives, doth not take away the particular duty of the Sabbath; neither doth the great habitation of God in heaven abate any thing of his special presence, both in the temples dedicated to his service, and in every particular person which doth belong to the election of grace. For so God saith, 'I dwell with him that is humble and contrite in heart;' and he saith so presently after he had said, 'I will dwell in the high and holy place;' insomuch as St Augustine, upon those words of David, *exaudivit de templo sancto suo vocem meam*, saith, *Exaudivit de corde meo, in quo habitat Dominus, vocem meam*. For, 'know you not that you are the temples of the Holy Ghost, and that God dwelleth in you,' &c.

God is in heaven, *per specialem gloriam.*

He is in our churches, *per specialem cultum.*

He is in our hearts, *per specialem indulgentiam.*

He is in his word, *per specialem illuminationem.*

He is in the sacraments, *per specialem significationem.*

In a word, wheresoever is *cultus Dei*, there is *vultus Dei.*

The use of this point is taught in the text; it is the second part of my text.

2. The duty: 'Let all the earth keep silence before him.' This, as you heard, is a postulation of reverence. He doth not put us to silence that we shall say nothing; for he hath commanded us to call upon him, and invocation is a note of his children. He saith, 'He shall call upon me, and I will hear him.' The wise man doth help us to expound this text: Eccles. v., 'Be not rash with thy mouth, and let not thine heart be hasty to utter any word before God: for God is in heaven, and thou upon earth; therefore let thy words be few.' So that temerity and rashness is here forbidden, and reverence and holiness required.

1. Let us consider God in our churches, the temples of his holiness; there we are taught,

Use 1. Take heed that thou have not an unreverent opinion of the house of God. St Paul saith, 'Despise ye the church?' that is, the place set apart for the worship of God; and that he meaneth so, the place, and not the company;—

So Theophilus: *Loco ipsi infertis injuriam*, you do

wrong to the place. Lyranus : *Est contemptus ecclesiæ, quæ consecrata est divinis usibus,* the very words of that text do shew it; for our own houses, and God's house, our houses for our common meals, and God's house for the supper of the Lord, are compared together.

Use 2. There must be in us a love of those houses of God. God said of his holy city, where his temple was built, ' Here will I dwell; for I have a delight therein.' It is David's protestation for Jerusalem : ' For the house of God's sake, I will seek to do thee good.' The hart never more desired the water-brooks, than he did to go to the tabernacle where God was : ' My soul longeth and fainteth for them.' ' I was glad when they said to me, Come, we will go up to the house of the Lord.'

Use 3. Let us prepare ourselves before we come to God's house, for he is present there. Come not hand over head, as thou wouldst go into thine own house. Consider, if thou wert to go before thy sovereign king, how thou wouldst compose thyself, that nothing in thy apparel, in thy gesture, in thy countenance, in thy words, might give him offence. Wilt thou do less when thou art to appear before the Lord of hosts, who is the King of glory ? Micah saith, chap. vi. 6, ' Wherewithal shall I come before the Lord, and bow myself before the most high God ? shall I come before him with burnt-offerings ?' The old law was, ' None shall appear before me empty.' When Jesse heard that David his son was sent for to king Saul, 1 Sam. xvi. 20, Jesse took an ass laden with bread, and a bottle of wine, and a kid, and sent them by David to Saul. So Jacob sent a present to Pharaoh, when his sons went the second time for corn. Solomon saith, Prov. xxi. 14, and it is no news in our times, ' A reward in the bosom pacifieth strong wrath.' We know what cause we have given our God to be angry with us ; let us think of it when we are to come and stand in his sight at church. *Manus in sinu tuo, manus in sinu Dei.*

He is not ashamed to ask it ; *fili, præbe cor.*

Use 4. Take heed to thy foot when thou enterest

into the house of God, for the place where thou art entering is holy ground ; put off thy shoes, that is, all earthly and carnal affections, and say with Jacob, Gen. xxviii. 16, 17, *Quam terribilis est hic locus!* this is no other but the house of God, *porta cœli*.

Use 5. When thou art entered into God's house, remember thou art come before the face of God and his holy angels, into the place where God's honour specially dwelleth.

1. It is not enough thy heart be reverent, let thy outward man express it also. Do not think that, because the papists do superstitiously adore the crucifix, and the altar, and idols therein, therefore it is superstition to do worship to God. Every man that comes into another's house doth in good manners salute the master of the house when he enters the same ; may not a visible worship be due to the invisible God ? ' Oh come, let us worship, and fall down, and kneel before the Lord our Maker.' It is a godly custom, if done in zeal of God's glory, with devotion, and not in a customary formality, to sanctify our entrance into God's house with prayers ; to fall low upon our knees before God, to invocate him for his blessing upon ourselves, upon our minister, upon the whole congregation.

2. Learn of the apostle, ' Let all things be done decently, and in good order ;' compose thy outward man to all due reverence, and conformity with the holy congregation, and thine inward man to all zealous devotion ; remember the meetings of the saints in the primitive times of the church, ὁμοθυμαδον. Do not give God thy knee, and thy tongue, thine eye, thine ear, and thy hand, thy whole outward address, and keep thy heart from him, and let thy thoughts go and wander from the service thou art about. Confess your sins together, pray together, give thanks together; confess your faith, the common faith, together ; hear the word together, both read distinctly and preached profitably. Remember that God speaketh in the ministry of his word, and say with David, ' I will hear what the Lord God will say.' Gather manna whilst you may for you and your houses. Take heed that

Satan cool not your zeal of God's glory, by suggesting irreverent opinions of the prayers, and form of service, of the minister, of the ceremonies of the church, or uncharitable opinions of the congregation. For all these be whips of Satan's twisting, to whip thee out of God's temple, and to make the ordinances of God ineffectual.

Bring with thee an humble and contrite heart, and say within thyself, as St Paul did, I am the worst of sinners, I am the worst person in all this congregation; for I know mine own wickedness, and my sin is ever against me. Bring faith with thee, that will shew thee the glorious and gracious face of God; by that eye thou shalt see the Son of God making intercession for thee, and thou shalt feel the Spirit of God helping thine infirmities; mingle faith with thy hearing, and the word shall profit thee. Hide the word in thy heart; be not like a leaking vessel, to let it out as fast as it is poured in. Take heed of the cares of this life, and voluptuous living, lest they choke the good seed of the word when it cometh up. In thy whole carriage at church, consider that the service is public; *hoc age*, do all thou dost at church according to the occasion; separate not thyself from the body of which thou art a part, by reading, praying, or any other meditation which may divide thee from the congregation. Tarry it out to the end, and depart not without God's blessing pronounced by his minister, to whom he hath given power from above to bless in his name.

2. '*God is in his holy temple: let all the earth be silent before him.*' This serveth for the direction of our whole life; for,

1. This dwelling of God declareth his omnipotency. The Lord is in heaven, he doth whatsoever he will. The earth is but as the drop of a bucket, compared to the unbounded, unsounded ocean of his fulness of power and strength.

2. This dwelling declareth the graciousness of God; for every good and perfect gift cometh from above; and unless the heavens hear the earth, the earth perisheth utterly.

3. This dwelling declareth the omniscience of God.

There God standeth in the congregation of God as upon a watch-tower, and from the heaven the Lord beholdeth the earth; the eye of the Lord is over all the world.

4. This declareth the eternity of God. So he saith, Isa. lvii. 15, 'The high and lofty that inhabiteth eternity;' which makes his purpose established with stedfast decree, without variableness, or shadow of change; a God that repenteth not; his gifts and callings are without repentance.

5. This declareth the wisdom of God; for the master of that house is the wisest; as the prophet saith of him, Isa. xxxi. 2. He that ruleth that house well, where the angels dwell that excel in strength, the Lord of hosts is his name, and they are his ministering spirits. How can it be but his wisdom is incomprehensible, and his ways past finding out?

6. This declareth his justice; for there is the throne of judgment; heaven is his throne, and all the holy ones give him that glory: Rev. xvi. 7, 'Even so, Lord God Almighty, true and righteous are thy judgments.'

To conclude.

1. Tremble, O earth, at the presence of God, who hath such power; tempt not, provoke not, this power against thee, he can rain snares; but if he be thy father, fear not; there are more with thee than against thee.

2. Love the Lord, who is so rich in goodness and mercy, who dwelleth in the storehouse of blessings, and who giveth liberally with an open hand, and filleth, &c.

3. Be jealous of thy words, works, and thoughts, before the eye of jealousy, which seeth all things.

4. Be strong, and God shall establish thy heart, for he is unchangeable; whom he once loveth, he loveth to the end, that is, *finis sine fine*.

5. Let his wisdom guide thee, and seek that wisdom which is from above; ask it of him, for he giveth it liberally, and never upbraideth thee. He upbraideth many with his gifts, never did he any with the gift of his wisdom; for that cannot be abused, his grace may.

6. Remember that for all that thou hast done in this life, God shall bring thee to judgment; every man shall give an account unto God of himself. Felix trembled to hear this.

Let all the earth keep silence before this God.

CHAPTER III.

VER. 1. *A prayer of Habakkuk the prophet upon Shigionoth.*

These words are the title of this chapter, shewing the contents thereof.

It is called a prayer, and it is a psalm or hymn, such as David's psalms; the heathen poets call them odes, or songs.

It is called the prayer or song of Habakkuk, both as composed by him and used by himself, and addressed to the use of the people of God in their captivity in Babylon.

It is a song upon Shigionoth.

The Hebrews affirm this song to be one of the hardest places to interpret in all the Old Testament, because it is full of dark parables, such as could not be well understood till he came 'who hath the key of David, who openeth and no man shutteth.'

Our former translation readeth, 'A prayer of Habakkuk the prophet for the ignorances,' and it is expounded diversely; some understanding it a prayer to God for the pardon of all those sins which the people of God have committed ignorantly. Others conceive thus, that seeing the prophet, in the behalf of the church, in the first chapter had taxed God of too much remissness towards his people in bearing with their sins, and forbearing to punish them; and then again, foreseeing how God in time would awake and punish them by the furious Chaldeans, he doth as much tax the severity of God towards his church.

Now that God in the second chapter hath declared his justice in punishing his people, and revealed the decree of his vengeance against his and their enemies, now the prophet maketh this recantation and prayer for the ignorances, because they, not knowing the secret purposes of God, have been so forward to judge his ways.

But we must admit this confirmation; and the learned translators of the king's Bible, finding this to have been an error in the former translations, have followed the original more faithfully, and call it, 'the prayer of Habakkuk the prophet upon Shigionoth.' Some say this *Shigionoth* was some special instrument of music, upon which this song was sung in the church of God; and the last verse of this chapter saith, 'To the chief singer on my stringed instruments.' For, as Titleman saith, in this psalm the prophet *canendo orat, orando canit*, by singing prayed, and by praying sung. So the Seventy read, προσευχὴ 'Αϐακοὺκ τοῦ προφητοῦ μετ' ᾠδῆς. But Tremellius and Junius read, *Oratio Habac. prophetæ secundum odas mixtas*, that is, not accommodated to any set kind of verse, but mixed of sundry kinds. And so they do not understand the word *Shigionoth* to be the name of the instrument upon which it was sung, but the name of the verse into which their prayer is digested; as the Greeks and Latins had their several kinds of verses, heroic, iambic, asclepidiac, phaluciac, and such like.

I cannot better express this to the understanding of the weakest judgment, than by referring you to the varieties of verse in our English psalms that we sing in the church; for if they were all composed in one kind of verse, they might all be sung to one tune. Some have their set tunes, and admit no other, because they are of a several kind of verse. So I take it that this *Shigionoth* was the name of that kind of verse in which this psalm was written.

Thus much of the words of the title.

The things which we may make profit of in this title are these:

1. That the prophet composeth a prayer for his own use, and for the use of the people in captivity.

2. That he putteth this prayer into a song or psalm.

1. Concerning the first.

Doct. The contemplation of the justice of God in punishing the sins of his church, of the vengeance of God revenging the quarrels of his church, and of the mercy of God in healing the wounds of his church, and restoring it again to health, doth give the faithful occasion to resort to God by prayer.

The reason is, because these things well considered, that God is just and merciful, do breed in us fear and faith, which, being well mingled in us, cannot choose but break forth into prayer; fear discerning the danger of his power wisely, and faith laying hold on the hand of his mercy strongly. For howsoever fear be an effect of weakness, yet doth it serve to good use in the fitting of us to prayer ; because,

(1.) Fear breedeth humility, which is necessary in prayer; as St James addresseth, James iv. 10, 'Cast down yourselves before the Lord;' and St Peter, 1 Peter v. 6, 'Humble yourselves under the mighty hand of God.' And howsoever the proud despise humility, as too base a virtue for heroic and generous spirits, St Peter commendeth it for a special ornament: 1 Peter v. 5, 'Deck yourselves inwardly in lowliness of mind.' That fear which is in the reprobate doth drive them quite away from God, but the fear of the elect brings them to his hand, and casteth them at his feet. The publican [was] full of fear, yet it had not power to keep him from the temple, nor from prayer ; rather because he feared, he came to church to pray.

(2.) Fear breedeth in us a desire to approve ourselves to God, and keepeth us in awe, setting both our sins always in our own sight, and ourselves in the sight of God, which sheweth what need we have to fly to him.

(3.) Fear doth serve for a spur to put us on, and to mend our pace, that we may $\sigma\pi o\upsilon\delta\alpha\zeta\epsilon\iota\nu$, run the way of God's commandments ; for men run for fear.

2. With this fear is joined faith, which layeth hold on the comfortable promises of God, and so filleth us

with the love of him, that we resolve under the shadow of his wings we shall be safe. This also doth break forth into prayer: as the prophet saith, 'I believed, therefore did I speak.'

Fear directed by faith, will soon find the face of God. For fear humbleth us; faith directeth this humiliation to the mighty hand of God. Fear makes us full of desire; faith directeth our desire to God. Fear makes us run; faith sheweth us the face of God, and biddeth us run thither: and thus the contemplation of God's justice and mercy doth fill the heart with zeal, and the spirit of supplications, as in this present example. The church seeth God remiss in forbearing them, it feeleth God sharp in punishing them, it discerneth him just in avenging them, and it is promised mercy and favour in delivering them; therefore the prophet teacheth them to pray.

Use 1. We are taught to think on these things, which may move us to seek the face of our God; and that is a work for the soul, when it keepeth a Sabbath of rest unto the service of God, as appeareth in the psalm for the day (Ps. xcii.), wherein the church doth consider the justice and mercy of God.

Our idle and wandering thoughts run all the world over in vain imaginations, we could not bestow them better than in sweet contemplation of the works of God here in the government of the world.

We are taught also, when we behold these things, to pray to God, for prayer being a conference with God, we cannot offend him in anything that we shall say out of fear and faith. This duty is by God commanded, he hath directed it, he hath promised his Spirit to help us in it, he hath made many promises to them that use it aright, and it is here prescribed as a sovereign remedy against affliction to use it, for it is fitted for the use of the church in captivity in Babylon.

Doct. 2. This prayer being made for the use of the church, as we have said, we are taught,—

That the afflictions of this life cannot separate the society of the faithful, but that even in exile they will assemble together, to do service to their God, and therein also to comfort one another.

1. The reason is, in respect of themselves; the faithful are one body, and the ligaments and bonds of their communion are love and peace, therefore much water cannot put out this fire of charity, neither can the floods drown it. So afflictions are in Scripture resembled to floods and waters.

2. In regard of the service, they know it to be a debt from them, an honour to God; and though each of them in several may do it, yet when a congregation meeteth together, their conjoined zeal is like a bonfire, for every one's zeal inflameth another.

What need the faithful else to seek out corners and private places to assemble in, in the times of persecution, for their devotion, if single and several persons' had been either so fervent in itself, or so acceptable with God; so that, before persecution ceased, they began to build oratories for their meetings.

Use. Therefore, though some do separate from our society, others tarry with us to disturb our peace, some cry out against the use of our churches; let us thank God that we have liberty of religion, and places to meet in to serve our God, and let us not neglect the society of the church. *Ecce quàm bonum, et quàm jucundum:* 'Behold how good and pleasant a thing it is,' to see one holy congregation set upon God by prayer.

Doct. 3. This prayer, made for the use of the church, doth teach that set prayers are both lawful and necessary to be used by the faithful, both in their private and public meetings. And this is proved by these examples in holy Scripture.

God himself prescribed to the priests a set form of blessing the people, which they constantly used, for God said to them, Num. vi. 23, &c., ' Thus shall ye bless the children of Israel, and say unto them, The Lord bless thee, and keep thee; the Lord make his face shine upon thee, and be merciful unto thee; the Lord lift up his countenance upon thee, and give thee peace.' The 92d Psalm is called a psalm for the Sabbath. The 102d Psalm is a prayer for the afflicted when he is overwhelmed, and poureth out his complaint before the Lord. 2 Chron. xxix. 30, ' Hezekiah the king and the princes commanded the Levites to praise the Lord with the words of David, and of Asaph the seer;' which is the 136th Psalm. This was also used by Jehoshaphat, 2 Chron. xx. 21. And in the Gospel the disciples came to Christ, and told him that John had taught his disciples to pray, and desired him to teach them; and he taught them the Lord's prayer, which doth imply, in the judgment of the best learned, that John had taught his disciples a set form.

The reasons are, first, for help of the infirmities of such as have good affections in them, but cannot so well express them, that they may be directed, lest they should utter anything rashly of themselves. For thus the Spirit helpeth their infirmities, by those who can direct them, and in themselves using these set forms.

This much advanceth the service of God, when men beforehand have their petitions drawn, and shall need nothing but zeal and faith in the delivering thereof to God. Herein we are like to poor petitioners that come to the king, who, not trusting themselves with their own suits, do get some wiser than themselves to set down their minds, and then they have nothing to do but to importune the sovereign majesty of the king to hear them, and to grant their requests.

This serveth for the maintenance of unanimity, the congregation knowing before they meet what they shall ask at the hands of God; it resteth that they bring affections fit to join one with another in supplications. This maintaineth outward uniformity, when the whole congregation join together in an outward worship and service of God.

Use. This admonisheth us,

1. To take it for a great blessing of God that he hath provided these helps for our weakness.

2. It sheweth us that God for our good doth so labour to fit us to his service, as that he is pleased that one of us be helpful to another therein.

3. It reproveth those who, out of a presumption and overweening of the graces of God in themselves, do not only despise those helps themselves, but dis-

grace them in others; in which number we may reckon all the depravers of our church prayers.

Here the prayer of the prophet is used.

Doct. 4. This teacheth that the fittest persons to be used for direction of devotion are the prophets, and apostles, and ministers of the word.

The reason is, because they are the most fit to speak to God for us, and to teach us how to speak to him, who are set apart to speak to us for God, and to instruct us from him. These are the physicians of our souls, and should best know our diseases and defects, and therefore best able to direct us to the remedy; for as in the state of bodily health, many superficially insighted in some empirical physic, do hurt themselves by being their own physicians, so in the state of the spiritual man, many do overthrow their spiritual health by presuming to be their own divines, and trusting too much to their own skill.

Use. Therefore it is wisdom for the flock to be directed, especially in the service of God, by their pastors, and to hear his voice. Let Habakkuk teach Israel how to pray.

And for us, howsoever the spirit of contradiction, which likes nothing long, have laboured long to disgrace our public service, yet, because many faithful and godly pastors of the church have zealously joined their united forces of piety and charity to compose this book, and the approbation and authority both of church and commonwealth hath commanded it to the use of our congregations, and the malignity of all the times since hath not been able to remove it, let us embrace it, and use it as God's ordinance, sealed with the seal, the double seal, both of prescription of time and good success in the use of this church of England.

2. He putteth this prayer into verse, and maketh a song of it, and fitteth it to be sung by the church with an instrument of music; for so the last verse of the chapter directeth it, 'to the chief singer on my stringed instruments.'

This manner of praising God is ancient, and of much use in the church. Mr Beza hath taken the pains to collect fourteen songs, eleven out of the Old Testament, and three out of the New, which he hath interpreted by way of paraphrase, and hath annexed them to his paraphrase of the book of David's Psalms. and they are translated into English. I shall not lose my labour, nor you your time, to shew you where you may find them.

1. Exod. xv. 1, the song that Moses taught Israel to sing to the praise of God for their deliverance from Pharaoh and his armies, which is of such excellency, being a type of the deliverance of the church from the adversary power of the world, and the tyranny of the beast, that there is mention of it in the Revelation, chap. xv. 3, ' And they sung the song of Moses the servant of God.'

2. Deut. ii. 32, when Moses drew near his end, he maketh a prophetical song for the use of the people, both to commemorate God's mercies to them, to lay open the judgments of God against them, to chide their rebellions, and to comfort them with types of grace in the revelation of the Messiah, and promising them the gift of the spirit of repentance to return them into the favour of their God.

3. Judges v., the triumphant song of Deborah and Barak, after the victory of Jabin, king of the Canaanites.

4. 1 Sam. ii. 1, the song of Hannah, the mother of Samuel, in thanksgiving, for the blessing of her fruitfulness, containing in it both thanksgiving, doctrine, and prophecy.

5. 2 Sam. i. 19, the elegy of David, bewailing the death of Saul and Jonathan.

6. 2 Sam. vii. 18, a song of David in thanksgiving to God, after Nathan the prophet had from God told him that the Messiah should be the son of David.

7. Isa. v., containing the rebuke of the people, which is a satirical psalm.

8. Isa. xxvi. 1, the song of the church, containing consolation and prophecy.

9. The song of Hezekiah, when God comforted his sickness with promise of recovery, Isa. xxxviii.

10. The song of Jonah in the belly of the whale.

11. Is this song of Habakkuk.

In the New Testament we have three:
1. The song of the blessed virgin, *Magnificat*.
2. The song of Zacharias, called *Benedictus*.
3. The song of Simeon, *Nunc dimittis*.

Besides frequent mentions of singing to instruments upon several occasions, where the songs themselves are not recorded.

From whence I gather these two observations:

1. That poetry is ancient, and hath been of use in the church of God, and in God's service and worship; for these were the anthems of the church in former times.

2. That church music hath had the same honour, both of reverend antiquity and holy use.

The first point, concerning the ancient, laudable, and holy use of metres, which we call poetry, so continued through the whole course of the Bible, as you have heard, doth shew that God requireth of us in his worship, not only plain faithfulness, soundly and sincerely to express ourselves in his service, but he requireth also that we shew all our learning, wit, and art in our compositions, according to the strict laws of a verse: those were the ballads of former times.

And though vain, obscene, wanton, lying rhymes, now printed, do carry the name of ballads wholly, yet holy songs have been so called. If you look in your old church Bibles, that were first printed in English, you shall find the *Song of Solomon*, or the *Canticles*, called *Solomon's Ballad, or the Ballad of Ballads*. The reasons why God desired and delighted in this form of worship:

1. Because this gift of holy poetry is of and from himself; he is the author of it, and the sweet singer of Israel learned it of him, to honour him in hymns; therefore the apostle calleth them spiritual songs, that is, inspired by the Holy Ghost; and it is just that those spiritual graces, which derive their being from him, should be consecrated in their use to him. And this is clear, that there is no poetry so ancient as the holy hymns of the church.

2. St Augustine, in his preface to the Psalms, saith, *Spiritus sanctus videns obluctantem ad virtutis viam humani generis animam, et ad delectationes hujus vitœ inclinari, delectabilibus modulis cantilenœ vim suœ doctrinœ permiscuit, ut dum suavitate carminis mulcetur auditus, divini sermonis pariter utilitas inferatur.*

He saith, he hath observed that both young children, and those of more years, who have at church given no heed to the reading of the prophets and apostles, have been so taken with the delight of the Psalms, that they have learned to sing them at home, and upon the way, which also brought forth good effects in them, by the power of that good Spirit which indited them; *quia miscuit utile dulci.*

St Augustine resembleth the wisdom of God herein to the art of the physician, who gives his patient things wholesome, but not very tasteful, in some sweet syrups, or liquors, which may convey it without distaste into the body.

3. This expressure of the zeal of God's glory in verse, being the labour of the brain, the marrow of wit, the earnest wrestling of the soul striving to glorify God, as David saith, with the best member that we have, doth best present the inward man, the hid man of the heart, as St Peter calleth it, to almighty God.

The apostle biddeth us to affect the best gifts. They that do only read a psalm, or a prayer in a book, have done little; but they that love the dead letter,* an enlightened understanding, and sanctified affections, they pray and praise God. They that wisely compose their own meditations, and express their own hearts in their own words, holy hearts in holy words, do mount a degree higher. But they that honour God with art and nature, observing the laws of time, number, and measure, as Bernard saith, they have *eruditam mentem*, a learned mind, and they are come *ad provectam œtatem*, to a ripe age.

Solomon excelled in this kind, whose nuptial hymn is called worthily *Canticum Canticorum*. It is a good observation of St Bernard, that the Proverbs of Solo-

* Apparently a misprint.—ED.

mon, which is *disciplina morum*, the discipline of manners, and *Ecclesiastes*, which is *disciplina amorum*, the discipline of loves,—the one correcting our vain love of ourselves, the other of the world,—must go first, and then our understanding and affections will be fitted to make such verses.

4. This kind of honouring God in ditties and hymns doth please God in the church, because even such of the learned heathen, who had no other light but the light of nature, have yet in this kind honoured the unknown God.

Therefore Lactantius,† writing to the heathen to bring them to the knowledge of the true God, proveth the divinity by the very testimonies of their poets, who in poetical raptures have given testimony to this truth.

1. He nameth the most ancient of poets that we do read amongst the heathen, Orpheus, who lived about the time when Tola judged Israel.

He did celebrate the honour of one God, whom he called πρώτογονον, *Quod ante ipsum nihil sit genitum, sed ab ipso sint cuncta generata.* He spake also of the immortality of the sons of this god :

ἐκτίσιν ἀθανάτοις δόμον ἄφθιτον.

As Lactantius saith, he could not rest in Jupiter, seeing he heard Saturn was his father; nor in Saturn, who was said to be the son of the heaven; nor in the heaven, which was but a part of the world, *et eguit authore,* and wanted an author. *Hæc illum ratio perduxit ad primogenitum illum deum, cui assignat et tribuit principatum.* This brought him to the first begotten god, to whom he assigned primacy. He passeth over Homer and Hesiod, as finding nothing in them; but Virgil, who lived about the time of Christ, and excelled in poetical invention, hath much honoured God in his verses, according to the light that shined on him.

I need not follow Lactantius any further, having in him overtaken the point which I have delivered, that seeing God hath had honour from poetry amongst the heathen, much more in his church let him be so honoured.

† De falsa relig. i. 1. Jude 23.

St Paul hath transplanted some of those flowers of poetry, which grew in the gardens of the heathen, into his own holy epistles: 1 Cor. xv. 33, 'Evil words do corrupt good manners.' From Menander the poet he took that excellent saying, Acts xvii. 28, τοῦ γὰρ γένος ἐσμην, and he took it out of a wanton comedy called Thais. From Epimenides he took that imputation on them of Candia, κρῆτες ἀει ψεύσται, κάκα θηρία.

Now, since God had honour from heathen poets, much more is he honoured within the church by those ravished spirits within* a lofty strain sound out his praise, or their own sorrows and wants.

5. This kind of writing, as it is most delectable, so it is most hard and difficult of all others; the strict laws of verse exacting choice of words to take their places in their measure, and the inspired wit affecting such sublimity and sauvity of matter and order, as is often involved in tropes, and figurative and parabolical phrases; so that all readers of holy Scripture find the poetical parts of the Bible exceeding difficult, more than the historical and moral.

Now, where most cost is bestowed of search to find out the meaning of the Holy Ghost, and most delight is reaped, it being found that doth tarry by us better, and we hold it with strongest retention. This pleaseth God well, that we hide his words in our hearts, that we do not run it out in a leak.

Use. This doctrine of the holy use of poetry in the worship and service of God serveth,

1. To stir us up to affect the best gifts of all in God's worship; if there be any way more excellent than others, to use that in our prayers and thanksgivings, and praises of our God.

I remember what David said to Araunah the Jebusite, when he offered to give him his thrashing-floor to erect an altar upon it for God, 2 Sam. xxiv. 24, 'I will not offer a burnt offering to the Lord my God of that which cost me nothing.'

Let it cost us the highest strain of our invention, the loudest extension of the voice, the earnestest in-

* Qu. 'who in'?—Ed.

tention of the heart. We have nothing good enough for him, all we have is of him, let it be all for him, and for the advancement of his glory.

2. Seeing this kind of exercise of hymns and psalms hath been by God's holy servants consecrated to the worship of God, let us bestow our wit and inventions that way, not in devising satires to gird and lash our brethren; not in amorous and wanton evaporations of our lustful affections; not in base flattery of the corrupt times, and soothing of ungodly persons; not in broaching and venting useless fictions, the scum and froth of idle and unsanctified brains; but let our wits and pens be exercised in glorifying of our God, and our readings rather bestowed in the psalms and hymns of holy Scripture, than in the vain and artless, dull and brainless ballads and poems which fly abroad amongst us, and devour precious time which should be better spent, and transport affections which should bend their strength to God's service.

2. I consider that this song of Habakkuk was directed to the musician to be fitted to the stringed instruments, so to be not only sung, but played in the meetings of the church. From whence I collect, that church music hath the honour of antiquity, and of holy use also.

I need not prove this out of the Old Testament, for the examples grow so thick there that he hath read little in the Old Testament that hath not informed himself of the church's use and practice therein.

We have Miriam's concert, Exod. xv. 20; there were 'timbrels and dances, all the women came out after them.' We have Jephthah's daughter's concert, Judges xi. 34, meeting her victorious father with timbrels and dances. We have David's full example in the tabernacle; Solomon's constitution for the full music of the temple.

If any object that these be those old things which are done away, but now all things are made new; those were but shadows and ceremonies serving only for those times, but now antiquate and abolished; let me tell them that, in the time of the gospel, where the church hath more cause of joy than ever it had before, we can give no cause to abate anything of God's worship.

Who can deny but that the first tidings of the birth of Christ was proclaimed by an angel, and the proclamation was seconded by a choir of heavenly soldiers, even a multitude of them, the whole concert of heaven praising God. The anthem which they sung is upon record in the living book of the Gospel, Luke ii. 14, *Gloria in excelsis.*

Obj. But yet the singing and music of instruments in the time of the law were shadows of things to come, at the coming whereof they must cease. Whereof then were they shadows?

Sol. It is answered, Of the inward and spiritual joy of the faithful for the coming of the Messiah.

Had not then the faithful before Christ this inward and spiritual joy? and why should we, which have it more in the inward man, express it less in the outward worship? David saith, Ps. xlviii. 10, 'According to thy name, so is thy praise to the ends of the earth.' Christ saith, 'I have manifested thy name to them that thou gavest me;' doth it not follow well, where there is *manifestum nomen*, there should be *manifesta laus*. The church used to praise God with instruments of music; the church hath more cause to praise God since the coming of Christ than before; why should anything not repealed and forbidden to be used be neglected to manifest God's praise?

Obj. But all things in the church must be done to edification, music doth not edify.

Sol. Then was it never of lawful use in the church, and David and Solomon did ill to bring it into the tabernacle and the temple, and the church did as ill to continue it, if it be without edification. But if ever it seemed for edification, why not now as well as ever? It is the same God that is now served whom they worshipped; and as Augustine, *Tempora variata sunt, fides una,* times vary, but faith is one. How, where, and when did music lose that honour, that use, in the church of God?

Obj. But it spendeth time, which were much better bestowed in hearing the word of God preached.

Sol. I answer, It was used when much more was to be done in the church than we have now to do, and they thought it not tedious.

They had many sacrifices to offer, and the time spent in prayer and hearing of the word, yet they use it.

Obj. But popish superstition hath so defiled it that it is not now fit to receive it in our Christian churches.

Sol. I find that our fathers before the coming of Christ were not so squeamish, to like their own holy worship the worse because idolaters did use some of their forms of worship; for Nebuchadnezzar made a golden image, and that was worshipped with all kind of still and loud music, yet that did not defile the holy worship of the church.

It is a dangerous rule of religion to manage it by opposition; they are not all *opera diaboli*, works of the devil, which the devil doth, for you know that he confessed Christ, which many scribes and pharisees did not. They that condemn all that popish superstition hath also abused may want a candle to light them to bed.

I profess sincerely I cannot see but that the same motives that began to bring in music into the church, may hold it there still for anything that I can see.

1. In respect of God, to glorify him in the best manner that we can by any gifts of art or nature. And music being one of them, we see how much it hath decayed, and how much students in that excellent art have been discouraged from that kind of study since the church cast out music.

2. In respect of God's service, the more pomp and solemnity is used, the more glorious is the house of God made, and the more differing from our common house of habitation.

3. In respect of ourselves, we have need to have the help of outward things, to draw us on with delight, to entertain our thoughts with cheerfulness, to incite and move our affections, to quicken our devotion, and to blow the fire of our zeal, and to relieve our natural weariness in God's service.

These reasons brought in the song and instruments into the church, and gloriously was it settled in Solomon's time in the temple, according as his father David had left it in the tabernacle, where he designed to that service two hundred four score and eight men of cunning, 1 Chron. xxv. 7.

Obj. But Christ and his apostles, and the primitive church, had no such music in churches.

Sol. They had no churches, but in their meetings they sung psalms. So did Christ and his apostles in the room where he kept his last passover, Mat. xxvi. 30; and in the emperor Trajan's time, which was before the death of St John, Pliny writeth to the emperor of the manner of the Christians, this one among the rest, that they did meet together early in the morning, and sung hymns to their Christ. But after religion had found favour with princes, and began to appear in peace, then came in churches and church ornaments; then were liturgies devised and used; then were instruments of music intermixed with the service, and God glorified in all. St Aug. Confess. ix. cap. vi.: *Quantum flevi in hymnis et canticis suave sonantis ecclesiæ tuæ, voces illæ influebant auribus meis, et eliquebatur veritas tua in cor meum, et ex ea æstuabat inde affectus pietatis, et currebant lachrymæ, et benè mihi erat cum eis.*

In the next chapter he tells how the Arians attempted the taking of Ambrose, bishop of Milan, whom they accused of heresy, and Justina the empress bearing them out in it; they meant him a mischief. He went to the chief church, and much people followed him, ready to despatch their holy bishop. St Augustine and his mother were amongst them, and there Augustine saith: *Tunc institutum ut hymni et psalmi canerentur more orientalium ecclesiarum ne populus mæroris tædio contabesceret, quod ad hodiernum diem retentum est,* &c. The hymns and psalms were ordained to be sung, &c.

Obj. It is a means often to carry away our thoughts more with the tune than with the matter. St Augustine maketh it one of his confessions, that he was so transported.

Sol. And may not the same happen in our singing of psalms? Let us not lay our faults to the charge of the church. What good shall we go about but we shall find Satan busy to divert us from it?

Obj. It is costly to maintain music in our churches, and that money were better bestowed on the poor and other better uses.

Sol. What? better bestowed on the poor than upon God himself? Is the cheapest religion the best? They had poor in the time of the law, and yet that hindered not the magnificence of the temple and the ornaments thereof, and the maintenance of God's worship, *alit pauperes* 288, *in templo; ut ante.* The earth hath not the like glory now to shew as that of God's house, and shall Aaron, that was but for a time, be thus glorious, and shall Melchizedec, a priest for ever, want honour?

It is true that it hath been policy in these later times to keep the church lean, and to strip it out of all outward pomp, and to transfer God's inheritance into the hands of strangers; but remember the great commandment, Thou must love God above all things, and so doing he shall have the best of all that thou art, the best of all that thou hast.

Our prayer is, *Sicut in cœlo*, as in heaven; and Christ promises to the just, that they shall be as the angels of God in heaven; there they sing the song of Moses the servant of God, Rev. xv. 3.; and David saith, Ps. lxxxix. 15, 'Blessed is the people that can rejoice in thee.' We have more cause to use both voices and instruments in his praise, because he hath redeemed us from Satan, hath made us all priests of the high God, to offer to him the calves of our lips; and with such sacrifices God is well pleased.

Ver. 2. *O Lord, I have heard thy speech, and was afraid: O Lord, revive thy work, in the midst of the years, make known; in wrath remember mercy.*

This whole psalm, as it is in the composition of a mixed kind of verse, so in the matter of it mixed, for it consisteth,

1. Of supplication and petition, ver. 2.
2. Of celebration of the praises of God, ver. 3, 15.
3. Consternation before God, ver. 16, 17.
4. Consolation in God.

1. *Of the supplication.*

O Lord, I have heard thy speech; that is, all that thou hast said in the former chapter in defence of thy justice, and in prophetical revelation of thy holy will, both concerning thy church, how that shall be afflicted, and concerning the enemies of thy church, how they shall be punished in the end.

And I was afraid. Fear came upon me when I heard thee recount thy judgments.

O Lord, revive thy work in the midst of the years. Here be three queries:

1. What he meaneth by the work.
2. What by the midst of the years.
3. How this work should be revived.

(1.) *Thy work.* Lyranus saith, *Opus tuum in punitione Chaldæorum, quod fiet virtute tua magis quám humana.* Beza, by the work of God, here understandeth the church of God, the people of Israel. So do Tremellius and Junius, for they parallel this place with those words of God in the prophet Isaiah, chap. xlv. 11, 'Ask me of things to come concerning my sons, and concerning the work of my hands command ye me:' where he calleth his church *opus manuum,* my work. Thus doth Mr Calvin here understand *statum ecclesiæ,* the state of the church, which is called the work of God, $\kappa\alpha\tau'$ $\dot{\varepsilon}\xi o\chi\dot{\eta}\nu$, as being the most excellentest part of his work, wherein he is most glorified.

So David prayeth for the church under that appellation, Ps. cxxxviii. 8, 'Forsake not the works of thine own hands.' So doth Isaiah name them: chap. lx. 21, 'Thy people also shall be all righteous: they shall inherit the land for ever, the branch of my planting, the work of my hands, that I may be glorified.' So in the next chapter, lxi. 3, Christ is anointed for the good of his church, 'that they may be called the trees of righteousness, the planting of the Lord.'

3. Now there is such a correspondence between the head and the body, between Christ and his church, that sometimes that which is literally spoken of the church is mystically applied to Christ.

Jeremiah, expressing the great misery of the church, bringeth her in thus complaining: Lam. i. 12, 'Have ye no regard, all ye that pass by the way? consider and behold, if ever there were sorrow like my sorrow.' Yet this complaint of the body is so fit for the head, the grief so surmounting, that the uniform judgments of the ancients of the church have applied them to Christ, either in his agony in the garden or on the cross, where also he used David's bewailing and passionate moan, 'My God, my God, why hast thou forsaken me?'

So the wonder of God in Hosea, chap. xi. 1, spoken of Israel literally, *ex Ægypto vocavi filium meum*, that God by mighty hand brought Israel out of Egypt, are applied and verified in him by the evangelist St Matthew, chap. ii. 15.

From hence the mystical sense of those words doth express the head of this body of the church, that is, Jesus Christ, for his incarnation was the work of God. He was made of a woman, and was made under the law. So that this is a prayer to God to send his Son into the world. This agreeth well with the comfort before given to them, 'The just shall live by faith.'

That faith is in the promised Messiah, and that is it to which the ancient fathers do apply this place, as being the most excellent work of God, for the good and comfort of his church.

St Augustine* maketh this whole psalm a prophecy of Christ. *Consideravi opus tuum*, saith he; *Quid hoc est, nisi novæ et recognitæ salutis hominis ineffabilis admiratio?*—(*Idem in oratione contra Judæos, Arrianos et Paganos*, cap. xiii.)

St Jerome paraphraseth this petition thus: *Deprecor, Domine, ut quod promisisti expleas, et finito tempore reddas Christum tuum.*

Ribera, a learned Jesuit, saith, that this exposition doth pass most current with the ancients. He nameth

---

* Revel. Dei. xviii. 32.

Eusebius, Euthenius, Rupertus, Theophilact, all of reverend antiquity; and one saith, for the most part, *seniores saniores*, the elder the sounder.

Arias Montanus, one that has taken as much pains in the Bible as ever any one man did in latter days, saith, this note, this song, doth begin at the name of God, which of all other in holy Scripture *divinam naturam maximè significat*, doth especially signify the divine nature, יהוה; a note which God revealed unto Moses, a name for the most part used in the Old Testament, saith he, *Ubi negotium Messiæ agitur*, where the business of the Messiah is handled.

2. What is meant by *in medio annorum*, in the midst of years? Here I must give you to understand that the seventy interpreters do render this part of the text in other words, and in another sense, yet agreeing well with the mystery of godliness, that is, the incarnation of Christ.

They read, ἐν μέσω δύο ζωῶν γνωσθήσῃ. St Augustine doth receive that interpretation, so do many more, for great is the authority of the LXX. And we find often in the New Testament that their translation is cited by the apostles, and not the original in the Old Testament. I will not quite pass over this reading of the LXX, as neglecting it, though in the end I do not mean to follow it, because many great judgments have embraced it.

This is observed in these interpreters, that often in their translations they do not strictly observe the words of the original, but rather expound the sense of the place. Often they do add something, especially in the prophecies, which they think do point at the Messiah, whereby they declare that that prophecy is to be referred to Christ. So do they in this place; and to shew that they understand this place of the Messiah, they add, ἐν μέσω δύο ζώων γνωσθήσῃ.

Which St Augustine doth understand either figuratively, *in medio duorum testamentorum;* or literally, *in medio Mosis et Eliæ*, with whom he spake in the mountain when he was transfigured; or *in medio duorum latronum*, between whom he was hanged when he was crucified.

Others of late, following the tradition that he lay in the manger between an ox and an ass that were feeding there, understand these two living creatures, in the midst of whom the wise men that came from the east found Christ.

Yet Eusebius and Theophilact read not ζώων with an acute accent in the first syllable, which signifieth living creatures; but with a circumflex in the last, ζωῶν, which doth signify lives: *in medio duarum vitarum, quia venit in mundum, habens duas vitas, alteram mortalem et humanam, alteram immortalem et divinam.*

I only make this use of these expositions to shew you how of old this place hath passed for a testimony of the prophet's foresight and prophesying of Christ.

But reading as we do *in medio annorum*, here also sundry interpretations are given; for some do refer this to that time which St Paul speaketh of, Gal. iv., 'But when the fulness of time came, God sent his Son.' So the prophet's prayer is, that God would remember to perform his promise of the Messiah *in medio annorum*, that is, in the fulness of time; for it is certain that from Christ to the end of the world, the world is in a state of declination.

Lyranus saith that these years here meant are from the destruction of the temple at Jerusalem to the rebuilding thereof finished; for he saith there were fifty-two years from the destruction of the temple to the first year of the reign of Cyrus, from thence to the sixth year of the reign of Darius were forty-six years, for so long it is said the temple was in building.

In the midst, not *in medio geometrico*, but *arithmetico*, the prophet prayeth God to revive his work of restoring the people to their liberty and possessions.

But I choose to follow the exposition of the seventy interpreters, ἐν τῷ παρεῖναι τὸν καιρὸν, *cum temporis opportunitas fuerit*, when there shall be a fit time, which leaveth it at large to God to take his own time; and that seemeth to have been the judgment of Tremellius and Junius, who render it *interea temporis*, as we in English, in the mean time. So Beza.

Master Calvin doth go with the former exposition of the fulness of time; for he saith, the church was but growing and coming on till Jesus Christ came in the flesh, but then it grew up to a ripeness, so that the coming of Christ was the growing up of the church, *ad ætatem virilem*, to the age of a man.

3. *Vivifica*, ' revive ;' the margin readeth, ' preserve thy work ;' that is, maintain thy church, and keep it from the power of her enemies, till thou sendest a Redeemer to recover it from the injuries of time and the violence of the ungodly; for the time of the church under persecution is the winter of it, in which it seemeth dead, and prayeth God to quicken and revive it by the sending of his Son.

In the midst of the years make known. He reinforceth his former petition, now desiring that God would reveal his gracious purpose of succouring his church, and triumphing over the enemies thereof. In the mean time, while thy church is groaning under the burden of their exile, make thy will known to them. This favour of God will sweeten the adversity of their banishment, when they shall know the loving purpose of God toward them.

In wrath remember mercy. They confess that they have given God cause of displeasure, and have provoked him to wrath; they feel the smart thereof in a strange land, and they have no plea but mercy. They dare not make so bold with him as to entreat him to turn away all his wrath from them, because they are so guilty to themselves that they have provoked him and deserved his indignation. Only they desire that in the midst of his wrath he would remember mercy.

By wrath in this place is not meant any such affection in God, whereof his unchangeable and constant nature is not capable; for God is *semper idem*, ever the same. Whom he loveth, he loveth with an everlasting love, and he cannot at any time be angry with them. But whom he loveth, upon occasion he rebuketh, and chasteneth every son whom he receiveth; and this love sometimes bringing forth the effects of that which in man is called wrath, we speak after the manner of men, and avouch it of God.

Thus, then, the text is literally to be understood: O Lord, I have heard what thou hast spoken in the defence of thy upright justice; I have heard what thou purposest in the punishing and in the avenging of thy church; in the mean time preserve it, and make it know thy love towards it; and whilst thou art punishing of it, remember mercy.

The parts of this are two:
1. The preparation to prayer.
2. The prayer itself.

1. In the preparation I observe, *motum*, the motive; *metum*, fear.

2. In the prayer I observe, 1, *subjectum*, the subject; 2, *petitiones*, the petitions.

The petitions are three:
1. 'O Lord, revive thy work in the middle of the years.'
2. 'O Lord, in the middle of the years make known.'
3. 'In wrath remember mercy.'

First, of the preparation: 1, of the *motus*.

O Lord, I have heard thy speech. The word of God is well bestowed on them that will hear it with reverence, and receive it with humility. Here was a maze, the prophet and the faithful of the land had lost themselves, they knew not what to think, till they had put the matter to God himself, chap. i.; and God having made a full answer, now the prophet saith in his own name, and in the name [of those] for whom he consulted God, 'I have heard thy speech.' All the Scripture is full of examples of the children of God hearkening to his word of precepts, and admonitions to us to hearken, of promises to them that do hearken. The reason is, because it is a special note of God's children to hear his word, even as our Saviour himself saith, John viii. 47, 'He that is of God, heareth God's word; ye therefore hear them not, because ye are not of God.' And now seeing God hath given over speaking by miracles extraordinary to his church, St John saith, 1 John iv., 'We are of God; he that knoweth God, heareth us; he that is not of God, heareth not us; hereby we know the Spirit of truth, and the spirit of error.'

The Spirit of truth is left in the church by our Saviour, and he speaketh in such, who by the ordinance of Christ are the priests of the New Testament, of whom Christ saith, *Qui vos recipit, me recipit : et qui recipit me, recipit eum, qui misit me,* 'he that receiveth you receiveth me, and he that receiveth me receiveth him that sent me.' We must hear him before he hear us, for St Paul telleth us true, Rom. viii. 26, 'We know not what we should pray for as we ought.' The art of prayer is not so quickly learned as some forward professors make themselves believe. John, besides his continual preaching to his disciples, taught them also to pray; and never had any disciples a better master than the disciples of Jesus Christ, yet they, living in the ear of his doctrine, and in the eye of his holy example, were glad to come to him to be taught to pray; and he taught them the Lord's prayer privately, which after he taught the whole multitude in a sermon openly.

Doct. My observation is, that his word must minister matter to our prayers, and all our petitions must be grounded thereupon.

The reason is, because God heareth not sinners, John ix. 31; and David saith, 'If I regard wickedness in my heart, the Lord will not hear me;' but, James v. 16, 'The prayer of a righteous man prevaileth much, if it be fervent.'

Against sin we have no such remedy as the word; so David, Ps. cxix. 11, 'Thy word have I hid in my heart, that I might not sin against thee.'

Our lessons from hence are:

1. We must take it for a great favour of God to us, that he giveth us his word; for that is a lantern to our feet, that is our counsellor, as David calleth it.

This word is given to profit withal, and it is deposited,

1. In the books of the canonical Scripture, which we have not, as the church of Rome, shut up in an unknown language, but translated faithfully into our own tongue, that all of us may be partakers of it.

2. As in the time of the law, the priest's lips did preserve knowledge, and men were to require the law at their lips, so in the time of the gospel St Paul saith of

the apostles and of all the ministers that should succeed them in their office in the church, 1 Cor. v. 19, 'God hath committed to us the word of reconciliation.' He hath so committed it to the Son first, as he gave him power to transmit it in the priesthood of the New Testament, to all ages of the church till his second coming.

The Spirit which Christ left to comfort and instruct his church was not given at large to all men, but in particular ordinance to them whom he sent to teach all nations, as the apostle saith, 2 Cor. iii. 6, 'Our sufficiency is of God, who hath made us able ministers of the New Testament, not of the letter, but of the Spirit; for the letter killeth, but the Spirit giveth life.' So we are the ministers of the word that giveth life, and there is no life to be had but by our ministry. This gives us interest in your affections, in your understandings, in your goods, in your prayers.

2. Now we know where we may hear God. We are taught also not to neglect him speaking to us; for, as the author to the Hebrews saith, Heb. xii. 25, 'See that ye refuse not him that speaketh; for if they escaped not who refused him that spake on earth, much more shall not we escape, if we turn away from him that speaketh from heaven.' And the ministers of the gospel do speak even as if Christ himself spake in us: we speak in Christ's stead, 2 Cor. v. 20.

But as in the time of the law God sent his prophets sometimes to such as would not give them the hearing, so doth he now in the time of the gospel; but that must not discourage our ministry. At their peril be it; God's word will ever be God's wisdom, though the profane count it foolishness, and it will be God's truth though heresy and schism pick quarrels.

Therefore, if you would learn to pray, and be prepared for that holy worship, hear God's speech first, and that will teach you what to ask as you ought. Hear the word from us, as the Thessalonians did: 1 Thes. ii. 13, 'When ye received the word of God which ye heard of us, ye received it not as the word of men, but, as it is in truth, the word of God, which effectually worketh also in you that believe.'

2. Here is *metus*. 'I was afraid,' the Seventy read; ἐξέστην, I was in an ecstasy, as St John saith, when he saw the vision of the Son of man, Rev. i. 17, 'I fell at his feet as dead.'

There were two things to strike the prophet with astonishment:

1. The majesty of the speaker;
2. The matter of the speech.

And both these must both meet in our understandings and in our affections to enlighten and to move them, that we may know what we have to do, and with whom, when we pray, that we may come before him with fear and holy reverence.

1. The great glory and majesty of God, to whom we resort in prayer, is such as no creature can endure the sight thereof: Isa. vi. 2, the angels standing before him cover their faces with their wings.

2. The matter of his speech contained in his word to the prophet is the sum of the Bible: justice punishing sin in his church, vengeance destroying the enemies of his church, and grace redeeming his church from the power of Satan by the glorious kingdom of Jesus Christ.

Query. Why should the prophet be afraid at this? Here was matter of comfort; the heaviness of the night is promised the joy of the morning. The church, though it must suffer for a time for sin, hath here a promise of two main consolations:

1. Their own deliverance from dangers, into a restitution of them into God's favour.

2. Their eye shall have their desire also upon their enemies; they shall see the wheel of wrath go over them, and the Lord shall let out of their throats the blood of his people with which they have made themselves drunk. All this is matter of joy, and what needeth this fear?

Sol. Who can come without fear before him that can and will do all this? for if he be angry, yea, but a little, they are blessed that trust in him. Fear is a proper passion in a true believer, and is inseparably joined with saving faith.

For seeing the bond of our union with Christ by faith, whereby he dwelleth in us, is partly the hold that he hath of us by his Spirit, partly the hold that we have of him by faith. The first is firm : John x. 27, ' There shall not any one pluck them out of my hand.' He giveth a strong reason for it : ' For my Father, who gave them me, is greater than all, and none is able to take them out of my Father's hand.' We are his gifts, and his gifts and calling are without repentance. But the flesh doth put the Spirit to it so hard sometimes, even in the elect of God, that the hold on our part is weak, which breedeth fear, and fear that makes us hold so much the faster. From hence it comes that all the intelligence between God and man doth begin at fear in us.

This is not the fear of an evil conscience, as it was in Adam when he hid himself from God, but the fear of reverence of God, and the good conscience of our unworthiness, being fallen from our original righteousness. The shepherds that were keeping watch by night because of their flocks, were sore afraid when they saw the light shining at that time of night, that the angel began with *Nolite timere*, ' fear not,' yet were they in the lawful business of their calling. The blessed virgin, no doubt well and holily employed, Zacharias the priest in the church, about the occasions of his office, yet all afraid. This is the seasoning and preparing of the heart for God, to be cast down before him : it is humbling ourselves under the mighty hand of God, and we cannot pray as we ought without it.

When the apostle saith, we cannot pray as we ought, and that the Spirit helpeth our infirmities, he sheweth that such as he have infirmities, and they feel them when they come to appear before God ; and where infirmities are, there must needs be fear, if they that have them be sensible of them. Yea, I dare say, that they that come to prayer without fear, come without faith, and all their prayers are turned into sin.

Obj. We read of coming with boldness to God : Heb. iv. 15, 16, ' Because we have an high priest which is touched with the feeling of our infirmities ; in all points tempted like as we are, yet without sin.

Let us therefore come boldly to the throne of grace, that we may obtain mercy, and find grace to help in time of need.'

Sol. This is cleared by the same author in the same epistle, declaring how many considerations must concur, as ingrediences in this our spiritual boldness, Heb. x. 22.

1. ' Let us draw near with a true heart.'
2. ' In full assurance of faith.'
3. ' Having our hearts sprinkled from an evil consciences.'
4. ' Our bodies washed with pure water.'
5. ' Let us hold fast the profession of our faith without wavering.'
6. ' Let us consider one another, to provoke to love and good works.'
7. ' Not forsaking the assembling of ourselves together,' &c.
8. ' Exhorting one another.'

Let a man, before he pray, try his ways and examine his soul, upon those interrogatories, and I dare say the best of us (if we sin not also in presumption) will find himself short, in every one of these particulars, of that perfection that should accomplish boldness.

But having those things in some measure, and more in desire and endeavour, our boldness must needs be as much shaken with fear as these graces in us are shaken with infirmity. And upon this fear our church teacheth us to pray to God in these words:* ' Pour down upon us the abundance of thy mercy, forgiving us those things whereof our conscience is afraid, and giving unto us that which our prayers dare not presume to ask, through Jesus Christ our Lord.'

And this some of our brethren have quarrelled, as a contradiction in our prayers, because we say, we pray for that we dare not pray for. To whom I answer, in these words of my text, ' O Lord, I heard thy voice, and was afraid!' In thy word, I see how corrupt I am, for that sheweth me what thou requirest: my conscience feareth those sins for which it is guilty, for

* 12 Dom. post Trinit.

which I come to thee for mercy. O give me, through Jesus Christ our Lord, that which my prayer without him dare not presume to ask. Here is spiritual boldness through Jesus Christ our Lord, here is fear in respect of ourselves; for we must serve the Lord in fear, and rejoice in trembling; it is well that that is not branded with a mark of contradiction.

We have to do with three sorts of persons.

1. The profane and carnal.
2. The generation the wise man nameth, of such as are wise in their own eyes, yet want washing.
3. The truly zealous faithful ones that do worship God with fear and trembling.

1. First, concerning the profane and carnal.

These do not pray at all; the reason is, because they do not fear. Of such David saith, Ps. ix. 20, 'Put them in fear, O Lord, that they may know they are but men;' for when they know that, they will see and confess that they have need of help. Thus was Saul converted: there suddenly shone a light from heaven upon him, a voice spake to him, he was cast down to the earth. 'Then, trembling and astonished, he said, Lord, what wilt thou have me to do?' Acts ix. 6. Then was he fit to be wrought. To such we must preach, as Paul did to Felix, Acts xxiv. 25, of 'righteousness, temperance, and the judgment to come,' to put them into trembling; better to put them between the two millstones of the law of Moses, and the law written in their hearts, and to grind them as small as the dust of the earth, than to let them make sin out of measure sinful, by holding out to be abominable, and to every good work reprobate. We cannot open the gates of hell too wide for such to shew them the anger to come, a fit text for a generation of vipers; we cannot lift up our voices too loud in the deaf ears of such, to tell them their transgressions, and to put them in fear.

David wept rivers of waters for such, and that is a good remedy; let the faithful weep for them, for $\varkappa\lambda\alpha\acute{\iota}\omega$, which signifieth to weep, comes of $\varkappa\lambda\acute{\alpha}\omega$, *frango*.

So when the man of God looked on Hazael, 2 Kings viii. 11, and foresaw the cruel butcheries which his bloody hand should perform, he wept. This weeping of the prophet brake the heart of Hazael for the time, and he said, 'Is thy servant a dog, that he should do these things?'

So St Paul putteth them together, Acts xxi. 13, 'What mean you to weep, and to break my heart?' Their weeping brake his heart.

The hearts of the profane are hardened with the custom of sinning. St Bernard, *Aperiatur vena ferro compunctionis*, we must draw blood of them, by the preaching of the terror of the Lord to them. This blood is the tears of compunction, of which David, 'My soul melteth,' or 'drippeth for heaviness.' St Augustine saith,* that *lachrymæ compunctionis* be *sanguis vulnerati cordis*. When the remembrance and consideration of their sins hath wounded them, and left them half dead, then the good Samaritan will come with his wine and oil, even the oil of gladness, and the poor patient will say, 'Thou hast put gladness into my heart.'

Thus was Saul's heart broken in pieces first, and he that before did carry the cross of Christ to torment others, now rejoiced in nothing but the cross of Christ himself, whereby the world was crucified to him, and he to the world.

Thus when the law hath humbled the profane under the mighty hand of God, he turneth all into tears full of the fear of God, and voweth with himself, as he did in the poet,

> In fontem frontem, atque in flumina lumina vertam.

Then is he fit to pray, and to call upon the name of the Lord, saying, *Sana animam meam, quia peccavi contra te*, 'Heal my soul, O Lord, for I have sinned against thee.'

2. We have to do with that generation who are wise in their own eyes. These have a good opinion of themselves, that they know more than others, and they are not in conversation like to the publican; and therefore they look God in the face, they draw near to him, they stand and pray. These are so full of the Spirit, that they need no help in their prayers; they

* Epist. 199.

can pen their own petitions, their hearts indite good matters, their tongues are the pens of ready writers, they can talk with God almighty *ex tempore*. *Dabitur illa hora.*

Self-opinion is a kind of spiritual drunkenness, and therein of like effect; it maketh men daring and foolhardy. The profane care not for God; there is no fear of God before their eyes. These make too bold with him; they also must take a little physic to purge the exuberancy of their presumption. We must give them a dose of fear, and teach them to drink of the cup of trembling next their hearts; there is no such antidote against *tumor* as *timor;* swelling, as fear.

It is the wise man's counsel, Eccles. v. 2, 'Be not rash with thy mouth, and let not thy heart be hasty to utter anything before the Lord: for God is in heaven, and thou upon earth; therefore let thy words be few.'

He addeth, ver. 3, 'A fool's voice is known by multitude of words.' That is further urged, Prov. x. 19, 'In the multitude of words there wanteth not sin.'

For this Christ teacheth us to pray, beginning at *Our Father which art in heaven,* that we upon earth might consider that he to whom we pray is in heaven; that we might compose ourselves with fear and reverence to come before him, and to present him with our prayers.

And again, he comprehendeth all that we may ask of God in a very short prayer, to teach us that our words must be few. And to that purpose, in his sermon he taught: Mat. vi. 7, 'But when ye pray, use not vain repetitions, as the heathen do: for they think they shall be heard for their much speaking.' They that come in presence of great persons, speak their words by number and by weight, the very presence doth stamp in them an impression of reverence and fear. Now, seeing God, to whom we pray, is invisible, our faith must behold him before us in glorious majesty, as he saith, 'I have set God always before me;' and, like Abraham, the nearer we come to his presence, and the more that we solicit him, the more shall we be shaken with this holy fear; considering him who dwelleth in the light that no man can attain unto, and considering ourselves, that we are but dust and ashes. The heathen could teach, *deos caste adeunto*, let men go reverently, and inwardly cleave,* before their gods.

8. There are yet another sort, of them whom their sins do oppress as a burden too heavy for them to bear, whose hearts do smite them, and whose consciences do accuse them, that though the zeal of God's house do bring them to church, yet the fear of their unworthiness doth make them stand afar off, beating their breasts, and not daring to lift up their eyes to heaven. These had need of comfort; we must labour to put mettle into such, by telling them, that he whose face they seek is God, the Father of our Lord Jesus Christ, ' the Father of mercies, and the God of all comfort,' 2 Cor. i. 3. David is a full example of a distressed man, fearing and yet praying; for he confesseth, Ps. cxix. 107, ' I am very sore afflicted ;' yet he prayeth God to quicken him : he saith, ' My soul is continually in my hand;' he was even ready to yield it up, yet the comfort that he had in God established his heart.

And herein God is most gracious, for when our sins come in our sight, and we are horribly afraid of God's judgments, even then God sendeth his Spirit to us, not to take away our infirmities quite, but to help them ; not to turn our sorrow into joy, but to sanctify our sorrow, and to supply it with sighs and groans ; and this addition of fear and grief doth also mend devotion.

To such we must say, that though he to whom we pray be in heaven, yet he is our Father ; and though great and glorious be his majesty, yet he is the preserver of men. David calleth him our Sun and Shield. The brightness of this sun may dazzle our weak sight, but the protection of this shield will save us from danger.

Be strong then, and God shall establish your hearts, he shall anoint you with the oil of gladness, and he shall say to your soul, ' I am thy salvation.'

* Qu. ' clean ' ?—ED.

2. *Subjectum* (*Vide* divis. *supra*, p. 165).

This prayer is for the church; that is, for all those that then were the visible society of such as worshipped the only true God.

Doct. It is the duty of every child of God, and member of the church, to pray to God for the whole body of the church.

The church at this time was within a pale, and confined to the house of Abraham; not in his whole blood, for Ishmael was excluded. In Isaac was the promise; not in his whole blood, for Esau was excluded. Jacob was Israel, and prevailed with God; of him came the fathers, and in his seed was the church continued. This church was now threatened with deportation, and sundry great judgments; the prophet teacheth them how to pray one for another.

To this there are great motives.

1. The direction of Christ in the Lord's prayer, which calleth God *our Father*, and in the process of it sheweth that the church of God is still included: Give *us*, forgive *us*, lead *us* not.

2. The content that we give to God in these general prayers, which the apostle doth well express: 1 Tim. ii. 1, 3, 4, 'I exhort that first of all prayers, &c., be made for all men: for this is good and acceptable in the sight of God our Saviour, who will have all men to be saved.' All are or may be members of the church of God, for aught we know.

3. The benefit that we reap hereby is great, for thus we come to have our portion in the charitable prayers of others.

Ambrose,* *Si pro te rogas tantum, pro te solus rogabis, si autem pro omnibus rogas, omnes pro te rogabunt.*

4. It is a true rule, that *extra ecclesiam non est salus*, without the church there is no salvation. It is said, Acts ii. 47, that 'God added to the church daily such as should be saved.' The reason hereof is, because Christ is nowhere to be found as a Saviour but in his church; and the means of salvation, preaching, prayer, and sacraments, they are only found in the church: Rev. xxii. 15, 'Without are dogs, en-

* Hexam. i.

chanters,' &c. Christ is the good shepherd, and he hath his fold; all the sheep that are without must be brought to that fold; as himself saith, John x. 16, *Alias oves habeo, quæ non sunt de ovili hoc, illas oportet adducere,* ' I have other sheep, &c. : they shall hear my voice ; and there shall be one fold, and one shepherd.' Therefore, there is no safety in singularity ; they that forsake the church forsake the fold. The unity of spirit, not the singularity, is the bond of peace. We are members one of another ; the common safety of the body communicateth particular safety to all the members of the body.

In the temporal state, the peace of particular persons is included in the peace of the whole kingdom ; therefore Jeremiah saith to the church then in deportation : Jer xxix. 7, ' Seek the peace of the city whither I have caused you to be carried away captives, and pray unto the Lord for it : for in the peace thereof shall ye have peace.'

Much more shall we have peace in the peace of the church, seeing Christ bequeathed his legacy of peace, not to some parts and members of his church, but to the whole body thereof : John xiv. 27, *Pacem meam do vobis,* ' I give unto you my peace.' It must be so understood; for as he left his Spirit the comforter, so he left his peace the comfort, not to his disciples only, but to all the church; therefore, pray all that it may be well with thee *in communi bono,* in the common good.

1. This teacheth us to incorporate ourselves in the communion of saints *per communionem pietatis et charitatis,* by the communion of piety and charity ; to be one another's orators, but especially to study and pray for the peace and welfare of the church. Let us consider it is the spouse of Christ, it is a lily among thorns, it is a flower in the field, not only open to all weathers, but to the tooth and foot of the beasts of the field, Satan going about seeking to devour it. Let our prayers to God resist Satan, and fight the Lord's battle against him.

We hear of the troubles of the church in other countries ; we hear of the tyranny of popery, and the oppressions of faithful professors ; if we give them no other help, yet let our prayers give God no rest till he have mercy on them, and give them deliverance.

2. This teacheth us to maintain truth and peace amongst ourselves; let not the wounds and sores of a church, that is, heresy, and schism, and separation, be so much as named amongst us, as it becometh the saints of God; let not the common enemy of our religion hope to build upon our ruins, and to raise up himself by our fall; to strengthen his peace by our contentions, to benight our clear and glorious sunshine of the gospel; so many happy years crowned with peace, and the fruits of peace, propagation, with his Egyptian and Cimmerian darkness. Let us be of good comfort, their darkness dare not come so near our light, for our light will discover it; their error dare not come so near our truth, our truth will confute it; and the God of truth will not suffer his truth to fail.

Yet if our unthankfulness to God for his light, so long shining in our church; if our evil lives, so unanswerable to our outward profession; if our contentions, so displeasing to the God of peace; our want of zeal and devotion in prayer, do turn away the face of God from us, we may thank ourselves, and his justice may say, *Perditio tua ex te*, 'thy destruction is of thyself.'

2. The petitions; these are three, *vide* p. 165.

1. 'Revive thy work in the midst of the years;' that is, as we have expounded it literally, In the mean time, preserve thy church.

In which petition we are taught:

Doct. 1. That the church of God is the work of God; ye have heard it so acknowledged by God himself: Isa. xlv. 11, 'Ask me concerning my sons, and concerning the work of my hands command ye me.' Wherein God confesseth his church to be his own work, and therefore so comprehended in his care that they may challenge his protection. Again, he calleth his church thus: Isa. lx. 21, 'The branch of my planting, the work of my hands, that I may be glorified.' And David upon this prayeth, Ps. cxxxviii. 8, 'Forsake not the works of thy own hands.'

The reasons why the church is thus called.

Because the church is not an assembly that doth gather themselves together, as we say that birds of a feather do fly together; but it is ἐκκλησία, it is a congregation of such as the free election of grace hath called out of the world by the ministry of the word of God and the sacraments. The first church of God in whom God was glorified consisted of angels, intellectual spirits, whereof many kept not their first estate, but were excommunicated, never to be redeemed. The first church of God on earth were our first parents, whom God created in his image. The creation miscarried by the fall of our parents, who might have stood if they would. The election of grace remained unchangeable, and continued a church in Adam, in Abel, in Seth, which separated from Cain and his issue, in Noah and Shem, and in Japhet, persuaded to the tents of Shem, in the calling of the Gentiles; so that all that have the election of grace do come to be members of the church by virtue of an effectual calling. Election designeth them, vocation declareth them to be the members of the church, and both these are the work of God. Will you take it from God's own mouth? who saith, Lev. xx. 26, 'Ye shall be holy unto me, for I the Lord am holy, and have severed you from other people that you should be mine.'

2. The church is called the work of God, in respect of his perpetual presence with it, and preservation of it, both by his own special providence, which is the privilege of the church, and also by the subordinate ministry of his holy angels.

1. For his own providence he hath declared it in a promise: Joshua i. 5, 'I will not fail thee nor forsake thee,' in which promise, what interest the church hath, and every member thereof, the author to the Hebrews sheweth: Heb. xiii. 5, 'Let your conversation be without covetousness, and be content with such things as you have; for he hath said, I will never leave thee nor forsake thee. So that we may boldly say, The Lord is my helper; I will not fear what man shall do unto me.'

For which gracious protection St Peter, 1 Pet. iv. 19, willeth us to 'commit our souls to him in well-doing as to a faithful Creator,' so called, saith Lyranus, *quia securè conservat, et gloriose coronat, non relinquit opus*, he not only buildeth, but standeth to reparations.

2. For the ministry and subvention of angels the psalmist saith, Ps. xci. 11, 12, ' He hath given his angels charge over thee, to keep thee in all thy ways; they shall bear thee up in their hands.' Heb. i. 14, ' Are they not all ministering spirits, sent forth to minister to them who shall be heirs of salvation ?'

3. The church of God is called the work of God, to honour God; for God is not so glorious in anything that he hath wrought as in his church, for therein mercy and truth met together, righteousness and peace kissed each other. Our election adoption is to the praise of the glory of his grace, Eph. i. 6. You heard himself say of his church, Isa. lx. 21, ' The work of my hands, that I may be glorified.' For God is more glorified in those things which he hath wrought by Jesus Christ in our flesh, and in those things which he doth for his sake, than in all the other works of his hands.

This will one day appear. It is revealed already in part to us, for whatsoever God did work *sine verbo incarnato*, without the word incarnate, it all shall fail and come to dissolution, or to a worse condition, that is, an eternal being in woe. For example, the heavens and the earth shall all perish, and new shall be made in their place, a new heaven and a new earth, wherein God will plant righteousness. The angels that fell, and the reprobate, shall suffer eternal flames. What remains now but angels and just men, the elect angels and the holy church of God; the one sort elected in Christ, established in bliss by Christ; the other redeemed by Christ? These are reserved to glory. The just shall be as the angels of God in heaven. In this church, then, God is most glorified.

4. The church is called the work of God, to give honour to it here on earth; for God would have the world know that he owns his church, and that they are a peculiar people, a chosen generation, a royal priesthood, that he delighteth in them. And again, the faithful delight in nothing but what he hath wrought

in them and from* them. So Augustine bringeth in the church, saying, *Opus tuum in me Domine, vide, non meum; nam meum si videris damnum, tuum si videris coronas,* Behold thy work in me, &c. It is David's glory, 'I am thine.' All things else have the same maker that have any being, but the church hath the honour of curious and costly work. All the rest of the works of God are not worth the cost that he bestowed in the whitewashing of this work.

To turn this point into profit.

1. Seeing we are the work of God in regard of election, of grace, of creation, and protection, this teacheth us to live godlily, righteously, and soberly in this present world, and to keep ourselves unspotted of the world.

1. For election: Eph. i. 4, 'He hath chosen us, that we should be holy, and without blame before him in love.'

2. For creation: Eph. ii. 10, 'We are his workmanship, created in Christ Jesus unto good works, that we should walk in them.'

3. For all his other favours, as, 1 Pet. ii. 9, that we are 'a royal priesthood, an holy nation, a purchased people, it is, that we should shew forth the praises of him who hath called us out of darkness into his marvellous light.'

Survey thy soul, peruse thy whole conversation without, search thy heart within, suffer not the work of the Lord in thee to be defaced and defouled with the uncleanness of gross and foul sins. If Satan have been too strong for thee, that he holdeth thee captive, and bindeth thee, and maketh thee go where thou wouldest not, and do what thou abhorrest, yet declare it, by thy resisting of him, that he hath usurped, thou hast not yielded him possession; let not sin set up a stool of wickedness within thee, let it not reign in thy mortal body. Do thy maker so much right to preserve and keep his work as clean as thou canst from the defiling of the world.

2. Gather boldness from this consideration, to solicit God in prayers; for so it is used as an effectual

* Qu. 'for'?—ED.

argument, *Vivifica opus tuum,* 'Revive thy work,' as David, 'I am thine, O save.' So Solomon enforceth his suit to God for Israel: 1 Kings viii. 52, 53, 'For thou didst separate them from all the people of the earth, to be thine inheritance.' Therefore he prayeth 'that the eyes of God would be open to their supplications, and that he would hearken to them in all that they pray for.'

2. In the petition that God would revive and quicken his church in the mean time, that is, during the affliction and vexation of it, we are taught,

Doct. 2. That afflictions, and the withdrawing of the light of God's countenance from his church for a time, is such a deading of it, that except it be quickened with some beams of grace and light, and have some *lucida intervalla,* it is a burden more than they can bear.

Satan is a cunning serpent, a roaring lion; when he can get leave to assault, he putteth his whole strength to it, as in the sifting of Peter, and in the buffeting of Paul, and in the afflicting of Job. If Peter had not had Christ's *Ego oravi pro te, I have prayed for thee ;* and Paul had not heard his *sufficit tibi gratia mea, my grace is sufficient for thee ;* and Job had not had the preserver of men to friend; how had it gone with them ?

And great reason there is for this, why the church should faint under the cross, if it were not strongly supported by grace ; for there is no lesson so hard for a child of God to take out, as to take up the cross of Christ, and to follow him, to suffer the smart of affliction with patience and thanksgiving. For in the very regenerate man, the flesh is both strong and unruly, and nothing so contrary to the flesh, as affliction and tribulation is ; therefore doth God measure to his children their portion and draught of this cup, because he knows whereof we be made. So the psalmist saith, Ps. cxxv. 3, 'The rod of the wicked shall not rest upon the lot of the righteous, lest the righteous put forth their hand unto iniquity.' And for this St Paul saith, 1 Cor. x. 13, 'God is faithful, who will not suffer you to be tempted above that you are able, but will with the temptation also make a way to escape, that ye may be able to bear it.'

Wherein note for comfort in tribulation:

1. That though Satan have no stay of his fury and malice in our temptations, yet God will not suffer us to be tempted further than he thinks fit. For there is good use to be made of some temptations, as St James saith, chap. i. 2, 'My brethren, count it all joy when you fall into divers temptations;' he meaneth temptations of trial, by which we do approve our faith and our patience. St Peter saith, 1 Pet. i. 7, 'That the trial of your faith, being much more precious than gold that perisheth, though it be tried with fire, might be found unto praise, and honour, and glory, at the appearing of our Lord Jesus Christ.'

2. We see that all the elect children of God have a measure of strength to bear temptation, and he that gave them their measure, and knoweth what it contains, will not suffer them to be tempted further then they are able. Herein many mistake themselves, and think their ability to bear affliction less than it is, for indeed till God put us to it, we do not know how much we are able to suffer; and many great examples in church story we find of those Christians, young men and aged, tender virgins that have feared their own weakness much, who have filled the catalogue of God's confessors and martyrs with invincible constancy.

3. We see that when God openeth a way out of tribulation, that the faithful see an issue; though for the time the temptation be more than our strength, yet the issue in sight doth put mettle into us to bear it. Howsoever, the flesh will be more than a looker on in this conflict, because, Heb. xii. 11, 'No chastening for the time seemeth to be joyous, but grievous;' for many fears arise in the hearts of the afflicted, and Satan is still suggesting, that God hath forsaken him that is afflicted. Especially such a great affliction as this that was now threatened to the church, the sword of the Chaldeans, depopulation of their cities and towns, destruction of the temple, deportation into the land of their enemies, and seventy years' captivity;

this shaketh their faith in the promise of God made to his church, and maketh them to doubt that God hath forgotten to be gracious, and will shew no more mercy.

Let us learn of the prophet what use we must make of afflictions in this kind, even prayer, ' O Lord, revive thy work ;' let us comfort ourselves in all tribulations, that we are the work of God's hand, and let us commend ourselves to his fatherly love. Prayer is *fidelis nuncius*, a faithful messenger ; we may despatch away this messenger from Babylon, from the lions' den, from the belly of the whale, from the fiery furnace of heaven, and it will do our errand to God faithfully and effectually.

It is St Augustine's* comfort, *Cum videris non à te amotam deprecationem tuam, securus esto, quia non est amota misericordia ejus.*

2. Petition, 'In the midst of the years make known.' That is, in the mean time, whilst thy church is in captivity, reveal to them thy gracious purpose of restoring and avenging them.

Doct. The true comfort in afflictions groweth out of a right understanding of the will and purpose of God therein ; that is, that he beareth a constant love to his church, however he punish them.

Reason 1. This maketh them able to bear affliction, when we see that God maketh a way to escape, as you heard from St Paul, 1 Cor. x. 13. And this is very clear in this people, for God made known to them his purpose concerning their bondage in Egypt, his will was thus revealed to Abraham : Gen. xv. 13, 14, ' Know that thy seed of a surety shall be a stranger in a land that is not theirs, and shall serve them ; and they shall afflict them four hundred years : and also that nation, whom they shall serve, will I judge ; and afterward shall they come out with great substance.'

This, as St Augustine well understandeth, doth include all the time that passed between the birth of Isaac, and the entering of the people of Israel into the land of promise, during which time they had no land of their own ; and in a disjunct reading, they were either strangers, as during their first abode in Canaan, and after in Egypt, or they served, as after

* In Ps. lxv.

Joseph's death, and were afflicted. Four hundred years are a long time, yet they saw an end of their travails and afflictions, and they knew that their posterity should have rest at last, and they knew that God would judge their oppressors; this made them able to bear the affliction.

Here is a picture drawn to the life of a Christian man's life here on earth, for he must be a stranger and pilgrim here, and must serve and suffer before he can come to Jerusalem, which is *visio pacis*, the vision of peace, before he can come to rest from his labours.

This captivity in Babylon was a great punishment to this people, but God made his will known to them, as the prophet here teacheth them to pray, for he gave them warning of it long before, but somewhat obscurely; he came to a more clear discovery of his purpose to Hezekiah: 2 Kings xx. 17, 'All shall be carried into Babylon, nothing shall be left.' The Lord also by Jeremiah his prophet gave them warning of it: chap. xvi. 13, 'I will cast you out of this land, into a land that ye know not.' He threateneth to send fishers to fish them; compare that with Habakkuk's prophecy, chap. i. 14, 'Thou makest them as the fishes of the sea;' there you heard of their angle, net, and drag.

Jeremiah is yet more plain in this prediction: chap. xx. 6, 'I will deliver all the strength of the city, and all the labours thereof, and all the precious things thereof, &c., to be carried into Babylon.' But most fully begin at the ninth verse. Chap. xxv. 11, 'And this whole land shall be a desolation, and an astonishment; and these nations shall serve the king of Babylon seventy years. And it shall come to pass, when seventy years are accomplished, that I will punish the king of Babylon, and that nation, saith the Lord.' There is some better news: Jer. xxx. 2, *sic dicit Dominus*, 'The days come, saith the Lord, that I will bring again the captivity of my people Israel and Judah, saith the Lord; and I will cause them to return to the land that I gave to their fathers, and they shall possess it.'

The miseries that smart upon afflicted men do make

them forget the comforts that should heal their wounded spirits. David expresseth his vexation so : 'My soul refused comfort; therefore, O Lord, make it known.' Make thy people sensible of that comfort, which thou hast graciously reserved for them.

And, indeed, the people were not quite out of heart; all the time that they lived in that captivity they still remembered Jerusalem, and thought upon Sion, and expected their deliverance. But the dispersion of the Jews, that hath now continued almost 1600 years, that hath lasted long, and the time of their restitution is not particularly revealed, this maketh them hang the head; God, in justice for the cruelty which they did execute upon his Son, would not let them know the time of their deliverance, as in their former afflictions he did, which, no doubt, is a great sign of God's heavy indignation.

Use 1. Seeing, then, that the knowledge of the will of God, and his purpose revealed in his word, is so great a comfort in afflictions, we are taught to study and search the book of God's will, and therein to exercise ourselves; for he is the same God that he was, and his will is the same. The just have the same promises that they had; the unjust shall have the same judgments : hear, read the book of God, and apply it as thou goest, for there thou shalt have thy portion.

Use 2. Labour for newness of life, and that shall bring thee to the proof and trial, to the discerning and experience of the will of God : as the apostle saith, Rom. xii. 2, 'And be not conformed to the world, but be you transformed by the renewing of your mind, that you may prove what is that good, that acceptable, and perfect will of God.' For God will not reveal himself to the ungodly; but the secrets of the Lord are with them that fear him, and he will shew them his covenant.

Use 3. We must rest in this will of God with a *fiat voluntas tua*, thy will be done; we must not resist it, we must not murmur at it, we must not make haste, but we must live by faith, and tarry the Lord's leisure, and in the mean time gather strength from his promise, to establish our hearts that they faint not, and fail us in our tribulations.

3. Petition : 'In wrath remember mercy.'

Doct. The plea of the true church in afflictions is mercy.

Reason 1. God taught us this himself; for when our first parents had sinned, they were afraid and ashamed, and hid themselves from God : there was no mercy yet revealed.

How would they solicit God ? Jesus Christ was not yet known to them, therefore they fled from God; for there is no drawing near to God for sinners without Christ. Then God came and sought out Adam ; he arraigned the offenders, and finding the serpent guilty of the temptation, he cursed him : and there he promised Christ. When mercy was revealed to man, then he called the man first, and then the woman ; and ever since that mercy was made known to the church, the true church hath had no other plea but mercy. There is *misericordia condonans*, a pardoning mercy : he forgiveth all our iniquities ; an article of faith, *remissio peccatorum*, remission of sins. There is a *misericordia donans*, a giving mercy ; he giveth medicine to heal all our infirmities.

Reason 2. The church knoweth that they have given God cause to be angry ; they know that if his wrath be kindled but a little, he is a consuming fire, and it is a fearful thing to fall into his hands ; they know that in his favour is life, and at his right hand there are pleasures for evermore.

We have nothing to keep us from the anger to come but mercy : Lam. iii. 22, 'It is of the Lord's mercies that we are not all consumed, for his compassions fail not :' Ps. li. 1, 'Have mercy upon me, O Lord, according to thy loving-kindness,' &c. We have nothing to bring us again in favour with God, whom we provoke every day, but his mercy : Ps. v. 7, 'But as for me, I will come into thy house in the multitude of thy mercies.'

Reason 3. The church knoweth that God is more glorious in his mercy than in all his other attributes, for his mercy is above all his works; the justice of God is against us, because we are unrighteous; the wisdom of God is against us, because we have walked

as fools, and not as wise men ; the holiness of God is
against us, because we are unclean, conceived in sin,
and born in iniquity ; the truth of God is against us,
for *omnis homo mendax*, every man is a liar ; the
power of God is against us, because we have forsaken
him the fountain of living water, &c. ; the patience of
God is against us, because he is a God that loveth not
iniquity, neither shall evil dwell with him : he hateth
all those that work wickedness. Only mercy is our
friend, that maketh Christ our justice, our wisdom,
our sanctification, and redemption ; that maketh truth
perform gracious promises, and his power becometh
our protection, his patience our peace ; *divitiæ misericordiæ*, ' riches of mercy.'

This seemeth of excellent use.

Use 1. To assure to us the favour of God, because
it is built upon the foundation of God's mercies, of
which David saith, ' The mercy of God endureth for
ever ; his mercy is everlasting.' The knowledge of
salvation given by the remission of our sins is, Luke
i. 77, 78, 'through the tender mercy of our God,
whereby the day-spring from on high hath visited us.'
So that if God be angry with us for our sin, yet his
wrath doth not burn like fire ; but as he said of
Solomon, ' I will chasten him with the rods of men,
but my mercy will I not take utterly from him.'

Use 2. It seemeth to rebuke those that put their
trust in human merits, or works of the law. They
that come to God for wages forsake their own mercy :
nothing so contrary to divine mercy as human con-
dignity.

Use 3. Because here is anger and mercy together,
this killeth all presumption ; for he that is called ' the
God of mercies,' 2 Cor. i. 3, is called a ' jealous God,
and a furious avenger,' Nahum i. 2. And the rods of
men well laid on will smart, and draw blood.

Use 4. This inviteth to new life, because, Rom. ii.
6, ' the goodness and mercy of God leadeth to repentance,' and the crown of it.

Use 5. Seeing we have so much need of mercy ourselves, let us shew mercy unto others. *Estote misericordes, ut Pater vester cœlestis,* 'be ye merciful, as your

heavenly Father;' for 'there shall be judgment without mercy to him that sheweth no mercy.' Christ abideth yet naked, and sick, and imprisoned, and hungry, and thirsty, in our poor brethren; as his mercy embraceth us, so let our mercy embrace him, that he may say, *Esurivi et pavistis*, 'I was hungry, and ye fed me.'

Ver. 3–5. *God came from Teman, and the Holy One from mount Paran. Selah. His glory covered the heavens, and the earth was full of his praise. And his brightness was as the light; he had horns coming out of his hand: and there was the hiding of his power. Before him went the pestilence, and burning coals went forth at his feet.*

The second part of this psalm (*Vid.* divis. p. 163) doth contain a celebration of the praises of God, which also doth declare upon what grounds the church in affliction and captivity doth put trust in God.

The whole section is a commemoration of the great power and glory, and power and mercy of God shewed in behalf of his own people, ver. 3–5, *ad finem* ver. 15.

1. In his coming to them from Paran and Teman.
2. Of the same power and glory declared in giving of the possession of the land of Canaan to Israel.
3. In the dismay of the nations, ver. 7.
4. In the marvellous waterworks, ver. 8–10.
5. In their great victories within the land.

I begin at the first.

God came from Teman, and the Holy One from mount Paran. The best exposition that I do find amongst many of these words is, that here is remembered the coming of God to Israel, when he gave them the law written in two tables of stone with his own hand.

For God came then from Teman and Paran. Paran was a great mountain near to mount Sinai, but Teman signified the south; so God came from the south, thence came God to give Israel his law, wherein he did express himself the king of this people, by coming so near to them, by shewing himself so openly, and by revealing his will to them so plainly. This was so great a favour done to them, that he addeth *Selah;* which word is only used in David's psalms, and in this psalm; and the word, in the judgments of the learned, is sometime *vox optantis*, the voice of one that wisheth, equivalent to *amen;* or *vox admirantis*, the voice of one admiring, shewing some special matter; or *vox affirmantis*, of one affirming, avouching what is said; or *vox meditantis*, of one meditating, requiring consideration of what is said. But withal, it is a rest in music. Jerome saith it is *commutatio metri*, or *vicissitudo canendi.*

His glory covered the heavens, and the earth was full of his praise. And his brightness was as the light. He meaneth the brightness of that glory wherein he appeared when he gave the law, set forth, Exod. xix. 16; for there were thunders and lightnings.

He had horns coming out of his hands. By horns, in Scripture, strength is signified: 'the horn of salvation' is the strength of salvation;' the 'exalting of the horn' is the advancing of power; and these are said to be in his hands, because the hands and arms are called the strong men in the body; they are the instruments of power.

And there was the hiding of his power. There, in that apparition, God did hide his power from the rest of the world, and declared it particularly to his church; as David saith, Ps. cxlvii. 20, 'He hath not dealt so with any nation: and as for his judgments, they have not known them.'

Before him went the pestilence, and burning coals went forth at his feet. His meaning is, that God then declared himself mighty in the punishment of his enemies, and the enemies of his church; for under these two kinds of punishments, by pestilence and fire, he sheweth that God hath the command of all the instruments of wrath; of which these two, by plague and fire, are the most licking and devouring, putting no difference where they go. And this hath reference to the many plagues wherewith he punished the Egyptians, when he brought his people from the land of Egypt, from the house of bondage.

The sum of all is this, that God hath declared himself glorious,

1. In his special favour to his people.
2. In his just vengeance.

From whence these points of doctrine issue:

1. That the consideration of God's former mercies doth strengthen faith in present tribulations.
2. That the church of God hath a special interest in the power and protection of God.
3. That God is armed with power to punish evil doers.
4. That in all this God was glorified.

1. First, The consideration of former mercies doth strengthen faith in present troubles.

Therefore do they commemorate the manner of God's glorious coming from Teman and Paran, wherein he had glory in the heavens, and praise upon the earth. David did make good use of this point often; for when any distress came, he found comfort in this remembrance. Now thou art far off, and 'goest not forth with our armies. Thou makest us turn back from the adversary; and they which hate us spoil for themselves,' &c., Ps. xliv. 9, 10.

To comfort this affliction, he beginneth that psalm, 'We have heard with our ears, O God, and our fathers have told us, what thou didst in their days, and in the times of old: how thou didst drive out the heathen with thy hand, and planted them,' &c. So again, Ps. lxxiv. 9, complaining of great afflictions, 'We see not our signs: there is no more any prophet.' This is his comfort: 'God is my King of old, working salvation in the midst of the earth. Thou didst divide the sea by thy power,' &c. So again, Ps. lxxvii. 2, 'In the day of my trouble I sought the Lord: my sore ran, and ceased not: and in the night my soul refused comfort. Then I considered the days of old, and the years of ancient times.' Ps. iv. 1, 'Thou hast enlarged me when I was distressed.'

Reason 1. The reason why this doth minister comfort to the church is, because we have learned that our God is constant in his love; whom he once loved he ever loveth; for he is without variableness, and shadow of changing, as the apostle and the psalmist saith, Ps. cii. 27, 28, 'But thou art the same, and thy years shall have no end. The children of thy servants shall continue, and their seed shall be established before thee.' Ps. lii. 1, 'The goodness of God endureth continually.'

Reason 2. Because the commemoration of former benefits is a work of thanksgiving and praise, and that is the highest service that we can perform to God in his worship; this is *sicut in cœlo,* it is heaven upon earth; for, Ps. xcii. 1, 'It is a good thing to give thanks unto the Lord, and to sing praises to the name of the Most High.'

It is good for God; for, Ps. l. 23, 'He that offereth me praise, glorifieth me,' and for that he made us.

It is good for us, for 'with such sacrifices God is well pleased;' there is our happiness, for in his favour is light.

Reason 3. Again, the thankful commemoration of former mercies of God to us doth draw on new benefits; for thanksgiving, as it is God's crop which he gathereth from us of the seed of his many favours, so it is our seed which we cast into the ground of God's kindness, and it bringeth us an harvest of new blessings. Every man thinks his seed well bestowed in good ground that yieldeth an increase; and God hath said, 1 Sam. ii. 30, 'Them that honour me I will honour.'

Use. This point is of excellent use, to stir us up to a wise consideration of the constant love of God, to such as fear and serve him. Benefits are soon forgotten; therefore, as David saith, 'I called upon the Lord in my trouble,' so he stirreth up himself to thankfulness : ' My soul, praise thou the Lord, and forget not all his benefits.' He found great comfort in this looking back. When he undertook Goliath, and Saul discouraged him as unable for it, he looked back to the time past, and remembered how God had delivered him from a lion and a bear; and from that experience of God's good help, he resolved to attempt the uncircumcised Philistine. And in his declining years, when age grew upon him, he comforted his drooping spirits thus : Ps. lxxi. 5, 'Thou art my hope, O Lord God : even my trust from my youth. Upon thee have I been stayed from the womb : thou art he that took me from my mother's bowels. Cast me not off in the time of age; forsake me not when my strength faileth.'

There be three sorts of men that do even run themselves upon the edge and point of reprehension; we cannot here forgive them a chiding.

1. Those that, *tanquam prona pecora,* as grovelling beasts, do look only upon the time incumbent, mistaking St Paul, who saith, Philip. iii. 13, ' I forget that which is behind.' Lyranus understandeth him, *Legalia et terrena;* Theophilact better, *Præteritarum virtutum nihil reminiscor, nec memoria repeto, sed ea omnia post tergum relinquo.* So we must forget all the good we have done, as being short of perfection, that we may mend our pace in the ways of God's commandments. But the apostle did look back to times past to see what Christ hath done for us; how he loved us when we were his enemies; how he washed us in his blood; how he forgave him his sins, and how he obtained mercy of him, because what he did, he did it ignorantly through unbelief.

2. Those also are here reproved who look only to the time past, and see therein nothing but God's temporal favours, but regard not the times present, and consider not God's spiritual graces. Some that lived in the time of popery do praise those days; then was good housekeeping, easy rents, a constant fashion of apparel; that many gentlemen had the lands of their grandfathers in possession, and their clothes on their backs; then was no seeking of reversions, or buying of offices, no market of church livings. Israel did so: Numb. xi. 5, ' Remember the fish that we ate in Egypt for nought; the cucumbers, and the melons, and the leeks, and the onions, and the garlic.'

I deny not but when the people of this land were fewer, and the vanity of the pride of other nations, and many of their foul sins kept at home, and were not imported hither, there were better times for the belly than these are.

But let us see the state of souls at that time. They were then in the house of bondage, under Pharaoh of Rome; beef and mutton, wheat and barley, were cheap, but the two Testaments, the two breasts of the church, were like a fountain sealed up, and like a garden enclosed. But when Queen Elizabeth began to rest* in this hemisphere, like the sun, to run her race, she turned that night into day, and maintained this light till she was taken up into heaven; and she that was a shining star on earth, and blessed the church of God here with benign aspect and influence, was made a glorious ever-blessed saint in heaven. In the beginning of her reign, ' God came from Teman, the Holy One from mount Paran :' God revealed himself in the glorious sunshine of his gospel of peace.

3. They are also reproved, who, out of too much forecasting fear of the times to come, do quite forget both the former and the present mercies of God, and astonish themselves with representations of hideous forms of ensuing dangers.

The God that gave us his light of truth, and hath continued it so many happy years of peace amongst us, hath begun; he will also make an end. By this light, no doubt, many faithful souls have found the way to the throne of grace, whose continual prayers to God for the happy estate of his church are able to make this sun stay his course and not withdraw his light from us; their prayers and devotions know the way to heaven so well, and plead the cause of the church so effectually, that we have cause to hope that the goodness of God, which endureth yet daily, will not fail us, but that we shall see it and taste of it in this land of the living.

Once let us remember under whose shadow we live, a learned gracious king, who hath seen into the darkness of popery, and laid it open, no Christian prince so much, no Christian more; he hath put his hand to the plough, and he cannot forget Lot's wife. Let us not make ourselves certain afflictions out of uncertain fears, and draw upon us the evils of to-morrow, for ' sufficient for the day is the evil thereof.'

Queen Elizabeth brought into this church and land true religion and peace; king James hath continued

* Qu. ' rise ' ?—ED.

it; let us be thankful to God for it, and let us be ever telling what the Lord hath done for our souls. Let not our unquiet wranglings amongst ourselves provoke the God of peace against us, neither let our busy eavesdropping the counsels and intendments of state, which are above us and belong not to us, make us afraid: our work is in all things to give thanks for what we have received already, for what we do possess and enjoy, and pray continually for that we would have for all men, especially for our king, that under him we may lead a quiet and peaceable life in all godliness and honesty, 1 Tim. ii. 2, and then ' Rejoice evermore, rejoice in the Lord, and again I say, rejoice.'

He that came from Teman to Paran, to a people that sat in darkness and in the shadow of death, and gave us light, hath ever since so supplied us with oil, that we may say, *Deficiunt vasa*, the want is on our part, for truly God is good to Israel, to all such that have faithful and true hearts.

To this end let me stir you up to a remembrance of the times past, beginning at the *Initium regni November* 17. *in anno* 1558, for so long hath this sun of righteousness shined clear upon our church.

Doct. 3. The church hath a special interest in the power and protection of God gathered from hence; he had horns coming out his hands, and there was the hiding of his power.

There is a power that God openly sheweth, and that is extended to an universal protection of all the works of God's hand, but there is a power that he hideth, and that is his special protection of his church.

1. He protecteth them; David gives them a good instance in the former mercies of God to his people: 1 Chron. xvi. 19-22, ' When they were yet but few, and they strangers in the land; and when they went from nation to nation, from one kingdom to another people, he suffered no man to do them any wrong; but reproved even kings for their sakes, saying, Touch not my anointed, and do my prophets no harm.' And the psalmist can give no other reason of this special protection but on God's part, because he had a favour

to them, and on their part, that they might keep his statutes and observe his laws. And these be motives that establish God's protection upon his church in all the ages thereof. His mercy and our obedience, which lesson if we take out well, we shall learn thankfulness to him for his favour, and holiness in our lives. And this is that godliness which hath the promises of this life, and that which is to come.

2. He hideth the horn of our salvation.

(1.) From his church, in some measure, to keep us from presumption, so that we do often rather believe than feel the loving-kindness of the Lord, and to stir us up to prayer, for the more we are made sensible of our wants, the more are we provoked to invocation of the name of the Lord.

(2.) From the world, that hateth his church, that they may fulfil their iniquity and declare their uttermost malice against the church. And when he had suffered Pharaoh and his host to follow his people of Israel into the Red Sea, Exod. xiv. 25, and there taketh off their chariot wheels, then they shall see it, and say, 'We will fly from the face of Israel, for the Lord fighteth for them against the Egyptians.'

Use. Great is the profit of this point in the case of those spiritual desertions, whereby God for a time seemeth to forsake his own children. Well are they described by God's own mouth: Isa. liv. 7, 'For a small moment have I forsaken thee, but with great mercies will I gather thee. In a little wrath I hid my face from thee for a moment, but with everlasting kindness will I have mercy on thee, saith the Lord thy Redeemer;' which sheweth that the hiding of God's protecting power is not total but partial, for it is in a little anger, and it is not final, but temporary, for a small moment.

1. In outward things.

In the example in my text, God hid his hand in his bosom, and the horn of his salvation was almost all out of sight for the space of seventy years, during the captivity of the church.

So many of God's dear servants drink deep of the bitter cup of affliction, suffering the contempt and injuries of the world, in bonds, imprisonments, oppressions, scourges, such as the world is not worthy of, yet do they not want a secret feeling of the power of God's protection, quickening their patience, and reviving his own work in them in the midst of the years.

2. In spiritual graces.

Sometime God taketh away from his children their feeling of his love and of the joy of the Holy Ghost, and that they find with much grief.

(1.) In the oppression of the heart with sorrow, wherein they feel no comfort, as David, Ps. lxxvii. 2, 3, 'My sore ran, and ceased not; my soul refused comfort: I did think upon God and was troubled.'

(2.) In the ineffectuating the means of salvation for a time. For many holy, zealous souls, desirous to do God good service, do complain that they hear the word and do not profit by it; they receive the sacraments, and do not taste how sweet it is; they pray, but they feel not the Spirit helping their infirmities; they give thanks and praise to God, but they do not feel that inward dancing of the heart and jubilation of the soul, and rejoicing in God, that should attend his praise; yea, rather, they perceive in themselves a going backward from God, as the church complaineth: Isa. lxiii. 17, 'O Lord, why hast thou made us to err from thy ways, and hardened our heart from thy fears?'

3. Sometimes when we have the zeal of God's glory, and a strong desire to serve him, we feel a failing in the act of obedience, and as the apostle complaineth, Rom. vii. 22, when we 'delight in the law of God concerning the inner man, we find another law in our members rebelling against the law of our minds, and leading us captive to the law of sin, which is in our members;' for, sometimes, when we set and dispose ourselves to the worship of God in prayer and thanksgiving, or to the hearing of the word, either a covetous, or a wanton, or an envious, or an ambitious thought thwarts us, and carries us quite away for a time, and we have much ado to redeem ourselves from it.

(4.) Sometimes we do feel such want of the Spirit of God in us, that Satan takes advantage thereat, persuadeth that God hath forsaken us; and thus many of God's dear children feel the bitterness of despair for a time; in which agony Job cries, chap. vi. 4, 'For the arrows of the Almighty are within me, the poison whereof drinketh up my spirit: the terror of God do set themselves in array against me.'

In this fit of deep agony, some have died despairing and blaspheming the name of God; some have done violence to themselves, and have died of their own hand, of whom let Christian charity hope the best, seeing that God hideth the horn of his salvation out of sight.

Therefore David prayeth, Ps. cxix. 8, 'Oh forsake not me utterly' (the word עד מאד, *usque valde*, as our English *over-long;* for the word *utterly* is somewhat too full of fear), and the hiding of this power giveth hope to the distressed, the light will rise in darkness.

Doct. 3. God is armed with instruments of vengeance to punish sin, pestilence, and burning coals.

The ten plagues of Egypt do prove this, and the destruction of Pharaoh and his host in the Red Sea. And lest the church should presume too far upon his favour, the story of the passage of the children of Israel, from the land of Egypt to Canaan, is full of examples of terror to evil doers, which the apostle doth urge and press to the Corinthians, and giveth them warning of the wrath to come. For he saith, 1 Cor. x. 5, first in general terms, that 'with many of them God was not well pleased; for they were overthrown in the wilderness.' And in particular, ver. 8, he nameth some sharp judgment, 'For fornication, there fell in one day twenty-three thousand.' That was the plague, Num. xxv. 9, and St Paul speaks within compass, for we read twenty-four thousand.

Ver. 9, for tempting of God, 'they were destroyed with serpents;' these were the fiery serpents, Num. xxi. 6. Ver. 10, for murmuring, 'they were destroyed of the destroyer,' which I understand the plague, Num. xiv. 37, 'Those men which did bring up the evil report of the land, died by the plague before the Lord.'

David, describing the judgments of God in those days, saith, Ps. cvi. 18, ' A fire was kindled in their company; and burnt up the wicked;' meaning the two hundred and fifty that offered incense, who murmured against Moses and Aaron, Num. xvi. 31. Thus you see how the pestilence still walked before him, and burning coals at his feet. Not only without the pale, amongst the enemies of his church, but within the pale, amongst such as were reckoned with the church.

Reason 1. In which course of powerful justice, he hath still gone forward to put the sons of men in fear, that they may know they are but men, and that they may not dare to resist the right hand of the Most High. For Satan doth still suggest that God is merciful, and so animates sinners to do evil, by feeding their presumption.

Therefore the children of God, who set God always before their eyes, do not only behold him as he is *togatus*, in peace, or as he is *rogatus*, easily entreated, but as he is *oculatus*, to behold, and *aculeatus*, to sting sinners. It is the voice of the church, Isa. xxvi. 6, ' In the way of thy judgments have we waited for thee;' this keepeth children in awe, this shewing of the rod saves them many a swinging, and for the ungodly of the earth, it filleth them with the terror of the Lord; they dare not do all that they would, for fear of the pestilence that destroyeth at the noonday, and for fear of stirring these coals at the feet of God, which can so soon overtake them. So God hath these judgments at hand, to put men out of hope of impunity, which is the greatest flattery to soothe up sin that is : Ezek. xiii. 10, ' The false prophets seduced the people of God, saying, Peace, peace;' and thereby, ver. 22, ' they strengthened the hands of the wicked, that he should not return from his wicked way, by promising him life.'

It is said of the magistrates of the earth, that ' they do not bear the sword in vain;' and can we think that this supreme Lord of all doth carry these rods of vengeance so near him, the pestilence before his face, and these burning coals at his feet, for nothing?

Reason 2. He nameth these two judgments for all, because they be of sudden despatch, and of quick execution. The plague we do know how speedy it is in a work of destruction; three days' pestilence swept away threescore and ten thousand in David's time.

We cannot forget what desolations it hath made in this our great city, and what terror it made all the land over.

Fire is a merciless element, sudden and cruel in consumption of all combustible matter; the apostle chose that resemblance to express God in a fury: *Deus noster ignis consumens,* ' Our God is a consuming fire.' Here is not only the violence of wrath, but the suddenness also expressed. The last fire that shall destroy the world shall come as a thief in the night, 1 Thess. v., as that shower of fire and brimstone fell upon Sodom.

Use 1. This teacheth the man of earth, who is but man, to fear when the plague cometh, to consider that he is but stubble, and therefore not fit to encounter this fire; he is but man, and not fit to meet this devouring pestilence; therefore let him not provoke the God of this power, let him not stir up these coals, nor awake judgment, rather let him quench this fire with the tears of true repentance.

As Christ said to the church of Sardis, Rev. iii. 3, ' Remember how thou hast received and heard, hold fast and repent; if thou wilt not watch, I will come to thee as a thief.'

It is not the way of peace to put away the evil day, Amos vi. 3; rather let us put away the evil, and break off our sins by repentance, that we may obtain mercy in the time of need.

He that hath such ready instruments of wrath to punish sin, is not to be dallied with, he may surprise us on the bed whereon we study mischief; he may meet us at the door when we are going forth to act it, he may overtake us when we are upon the way, he may cut us off in the act of sin, and bring us from the fact to judgment.

And howsoever his mercy hath the name above his other works, and his patience and longsuffering be the fruits of his mercy, yet he never had mercy enough to swallow or consume either his justice or his truth.

He hath diverted his plague often, he hath sometimes called it in, and long he keepeth it in, for that he expecteth repentance; but he hath never turned it out of his service, but hath it always before him. He hath also turned his fire another way, that it might not come near the tabernacles of the righteous; but he hath never quenched it, it is always at his feet. If he moveth, that moveth with him. The rainbow about his head is the joy of his church; the coals of terror at his fire,* are the terror of the wicked.

Use 2. We have also our lesson herein, for the apostle saith, 2 Cor. v. 11, 'Knowing therefore the terror of the Lord, we persuade men: but we are made manifest unto God; and I trust are made manifest also in your consciences.' We find this danger in sin, and this severity in judgment; thereupon we persuade men to a conscionable course of life, such as may keep them unspotted of the world.

If we do not acquaint you with the terror of the Lord, and shew you the pestilence that walketh before him, and the burning coals at his feet, God will right himself upon us; for as he told his prophet Ezekiel, chap. iii. 17, 18, so he will deal with us: 'Son of man, I have made thee a watchman to the house of Israel: therefore hear the word from my mouth, and give them warning from me. When I say to the wicked, Thou shalt surely die; and thou givest him not warning, nor speakest to warn the wicked from his evil way, to save his life; the same wicked man shall die in his iniquity; but his blood will I require at thy hand.'

This excuseth us to you, when we preach the rod of God, even pestilence and coals of fire, that this is not our fury and railing, as some call it, but it is the wrath of the Lord against sin; and if we temper a bitter potion for you to drink, it is not poison, but medicine; and it is ministered to you, as God himself

* Qu. 'of fire at his feet'?—ED.

saith, to save your lives, that you may not die in your sins; it is the therapeutic physic to heal your souls, it is prophylactic to us, to prevent disease, that we perish not for your unreproved sins.

The arrows of vengeance are aimed at your sins, that you may kill sin and save the sinner alive; cry therefore, 'Spare us, good Lord!'

Doct. 4. God is glorious in heaven and in earth for this, heaven is covered with his glory, and the earth is full of his praise.

This is the conclusion of David: Ps. viii. 1, 'O Lord, how excellent is thy name in all the earth, who hast set thy glory above the heavens.'

What need we any more reason to think this his due, than these two:

Reason 1. His name only is excellent, his glory is above the earth and heaven, Ps. cxlviii. 13. Here we are sure we cannot overdo in matter of praise and glory; the angels and saints do him that service, and cover the heaven with the praises of God, for his love shineth to his church, and we pray *Sicut in cœlo*, as in heaven. Ver. 14, 'He also exalteth the horn of his people, the praise of all his saints.'

Use. Let us not sit out when all join to glorify God; let not any of us, like the fleece of Gideon, be dry, when all the floor is watered with the joys and jubilations of the church. David is not content with a bare praising of the name of God, as they that say alway, 'The Lord be praised,' but he requireth both a song, *canticum novum,* 'a new song,' and that 'in the congregation of the saints,' Ps. cxlix. 1. He also requireth a dance; he requireth also instruments of music, ver. 3; he gives reason.

He would have us delight in the service that we do to God, therefore he addeth, vers. 4–6, 'The Lord taketh pleasure in his people: he will beautify the meek with salvation. Let the saints be joyful in glory: let them sing aloud upon their beds: let the high praises of God be in their mouth.'

This is that which this example requireth, not to be shallow and slight in the promises* of God, but to

---

* Qu. 'praises'?—Ed.

strain ourselves to the uttermost; the inward man of the heart, the voice, the hand playing, the feet dancing, till we cover the heaven and fill the earth with his glory.

Ver. 6. *He stood, and measured the earth: he beheld, and drove in sunder the nations; and the everlasting mountains were scattered, the perpetual hills did bow: his ways are everlasting.*

2. Here is a commemoration of the power and glory of God, in giving to his Israel the land of Canaan for their possession.

Divers judgments have made divers constructions of these words.

Mr Calvin is of opinion that they declare God in his glorious Lordship over all the world, for as David, when he should come to be absolute monarch of Judah and Israel, said, 'I will rejoice, therefore, and divide Shechem, and mete out the valley of Succoth,' &c., so God is here declared absolute monarch, in this phrase of measuring of the earth. As David would cast his shoe over the Philistines, would rejoice, so God is here declared conqueror of all by dividing in sunder the nations, &c.

St Augustine turns all into allegory, and applieth it to Christ.

You remember how before I found that the church doth comfort their present miseries with remembrance of God's former mercies, therefore I choose to keep pace with the story of God's former mercies to his Israel. And as before he spake of the coming of God from Teman and Paran, when he appeared glorious to them in giving the law, so now he comes to another powerful mercy, that is, when he gave them the promised land; for then he that went before them all the way of their journey in their removes now stood still, as declaring that now they were come to the land of their rest, as he had promised it.

And there, 'he measured the earth;' it is ascribed here to God, that he divided the land amongst the tribes, because it was done by lot, wherein not chance but God answered.

This has reference to that story which we read, Joshua v., for when the people were entered into the land of Canaan, and were come so far into it as Gilgal, that the ark of God was settled in Gilgal. Then God commanded the sacrament of circumcision to be revived, which in the whole journey between their coming out of Egypt to this place had been omitted; so long was it omitted, because of the journey, that there entered into Canaan but two of all that came out of Egypt, who had received the sacrament of circumcision, who were Caleb and Joshua. Now all the males are circumcised at Gilgal, there the children of Israel kept the passover, and there they began to eat of the old provision of corn that they found in the land; and as soon as they had eaten thereof manna ceased, and, ver. 13, 'there stood a man over against him, with his sword drawn in his hand, to whom Joshua went, and said unto him, Art thou for us, or for our adversaries? He said, Nay; but as a prince of the host of the Lord am I now come. And Joshua fell on his face, and did worship.'

Compare that story with this text, and you shall see that this man that stood before Joshua is he that stood in my text, and after measured the earth; and so Joshua conceived him to be, else he had not worshipped him, for Joshua was not to learn that angels are not to be worshipped.

So this place will not help the church of Rome for the maintenance of the worship of angels, though Lyranus say that it was *adoratio duliæ, quia cognovit eum esse angelum*. The man that stood there was that Son of man, that Prince of the Lord's armies, which brought Israel out of the land of Egypt, out of the house of bondage. And he stood there, for there was the ark settled, and the sacrament revived, and they were at home when they began to feed upon the provision of the promised land; and next it followeth that 'he measured the earth.' For, in the next chapter, Jericho was taken, chap. viii., Ai is overcome, and shortly after the land is measured, and by lot assigned to the tribes. The nations are drove in sunder, for they took and destroyed Jericho, Ai, and the

five kings that made war against Gibeon; as David
saith, 'He cast out the nations, and planted them in.'

*Then the everlasting mountains were scattered, and
the perpetual hills did bow.* These titles and attributes of *everlasting* and *perpetual* are in true propriety of sense only belonging to God; but this is a
poetical and figurative hymn, and by an *hyperbole* these
words do signify the mighty power of God, who
stooped these unconquered mountains, fixed and settled in their places, to the obedience of his people,
and brought the strength of the land into their subjection: declaring that by no strength of their own, they
got the quiet possession of that land, but they received it of the gift of God, who subdued the impregnable strength to their hand, and gave them victory;
for it followeth, *his ways are everlasting;* that is, as
David doth render it, 'He doth whatsoever he will.'
He long before promised Abraham this land, and
though the posterity of Canaan have held the land in
possession for many ages, yet there is no prescription
against God. *Nullum tempus occurrit regi,* he will go
in the way that the counsel of his wisdom hath long
ago trod out for them.

There is an old curse which lay in the deck and
slept all this while, ever since Ham, the youngest
son of Noah, discovered his father's nakedness; for
then Noah awoke and knew what his sons had done to
him; and he said, Cursed be Canaan, that is, let a
curse fall upon the posterity of Ham. These be the
ways of God, for the issue of Shem drove out Canaan's
seed, and possessed their land.

Here is another argument drawn from the same
head with the former; for the church doth comfort
herself in present misery, by remembering what God
did for them in giving to them the possession of the
promised land, which is wholly ascribed to God, as
the psalmist: Ps. xliv. 3, 'For they got not the land
in possession by their own sword, neither did their
own arm save them; but thy right hand, and thine
arm, and the light of thy countenance, because thou
hadst a favour unto them.

This commemoration of God's settling them in the

promised land serveth to comfort the captivity of Israel in Babylon, because it teacheth them,

1. That their tenure of that land, howsoever interrupted by calamities and deportations, is a good tenure. They hold it by the free gift of God, who is able to maintain the right of his donation against all.

2. That there is no counsel or strength against the Lord, for he that can subdue mountains and eternal hills, and he whose ways are everlasting, is not to be resisted.

From which premises they conclude comfortably that they shall have their land again, and that their enemies shall not be able to keep them out of it with all their strength. For God did not do so great things for them, to plant them in Canaan, for no long time his standing there, as if he would say, Now I have brought them to their rest.

His driving out of the nations to make them room, his scattering of the mountains, and bowing of the hills, all this was not done that Israel might hold the land of promise no longer, for the promise was made to Abraham; and St Matthew saith, chap. i. 17, that from Abraham to David are fourteen generations, and from David to the deportation into Babylon, fourteen generations. There were from the promise of this land to the captivity but twenty-eight generations; and the first fourteen generations from Abraham to David were well spent before the land was possessed; and so much God foretold Abraham, and four hundred years' delay and expectation of the promise, we have hereof from the mouth of God to Abraham, before they should come out of Egypt, Gen. xv. 13; and thirty years were found added to that reckoning before they had a deliverance, and forty more spent in the wilderness, four hundred and seventy years, which will make up much of the time between the promise and the possession of this land, that is, four of the generations. Compare this with the promise of this land, and you shall find it so: Gen. xv. 16, 'But in the fourth generation they shall come hither again.'

Now, for the term for which they should have this land, that is set down before: Gen. xiii. 15, 'For all the land which thou seest, to thee will I give it, and to thy seed for ever.' Yet we find that for seventy years they lost the possession of their land, being carried captive into Babylon ; and our church stories, and the histories of the heathen writers, old and modern, do shew that the Jews have lost this land almost 1600 years, which may seem to frustrate that deed of gift in respect of the term, and so it doth for matter of fact ; for matter of right it is unquestionable, and thereupon some have determined,

1. That that land is by right as yet belonging to the seed of Abraham, by virtue of that promise.

2. That in the last calling of the Jews, it shall be restored to them again, and that the commonwealth of the Jews shall be resettled there before the end of the world, as it was after the return from the captivity of Babylon ; so that though there have been interruption of possession for so many years, there shall be no impeachment of title, but their right doth run on till the time appointed for the restoring of them.

Concerning the calling of the Jews, and the restoring of them to the church, St Paul hath prophesied so plainly, Rom. xi., as there can be no doubt thereof. But for the restoring of them to the land of promise, we have no good ground in holy Scripture.

1. Because they have forfeited their estate therein, which they held with condition of obedience : Deut. iv. 25, ' When thou shalt beget children and children's children in the land, and shalt have remained long in the land, and shall corrupt yourselves, and make a graven image or the likeness of anything, and shall do evil in the sight of the Lord thy God to provoke him to anger, I call heaven and earth to witness against you this day, that ye shall soon utterly perish from off the land, whereunto you go over Jordan to possess it ; ye shall not prolong your days upon it, but shall utterly be destroyed ; and the Lord shall scatter you among the nations.' This is not without hope, for as by sin they lost their inheritance there, so by repentance it was recoverable : ver. 3, ' When thou art in tribulation, and all these things are come upon thee even in the latter days, if thou turn to the Lord thy

God, and be obedient to his voice, he will not forsake thee nor destroy thee, nor forget the covenant with thy fathers.'

This proves their tenure conditional; and their restitution to this land after their return from captivity was also upon the same condition of obedience, as appeareth in the words of Christ, Mat. xxiii. 37–39, 'How often would I have gathered thy children together, even as an hen gathereth her chickens under her wings, and ye would not. Behold, the house is left unto you desolate. For I say unto you, you shall not see me henceforth till ye shall say, Blessed is he that cometh in the name of the Lord.'

That place is plain that the habitation of Jerusalem, that is, *domus vestra*, and the temple of which our God said *domus mea*, now become by abuse *domus vestra*, shall be desolate till the second coming of Christ.

2. The prophets do speak plain: Jer. xix. 11, 'Thus saith the Lord of hosts, Even so will I break this people and this city, as one breaketh a potter's vessel, that cannot be made whole again.' My conclusion therefore is, that

Though the argument drawn from the free gift of that land to the people, measuring out the same to the tribes, do serve to comfort their captivity in Babylon with hope of restitution, yet now in these times, and ever since the dispersion of the Jews, for the cause of Christ, this can minister no comfort at all to that nation, to promise them their land again.

I come to matter of instruction,

1. These words aim not at the general scope of this section, in which is declared that the remembrance of God's former mercies is a sweet consolation of present afflictions.

Because he nameth the measuring out of the land of Canaan to the tribes, the driving in sunder the nations, the scattering of the mountains, the bowing of the hills.

(1.) *Docemur*, we are taught the best form of thanksgiving is that which maketh particular commemoration of the mercies of God to his church, or to any member of it.

(2.) That the matter of thanksgiving is an acknowledgment of all benefits as received from the hand and free gift of God.

(3.) From the phrase and manner of speech here used, we are taught that figurative forms of speech are in use in holy Scripture.

Doct. 1. In thanksgiving, let us be particular in our commemoration; we have David's example for it: Ps. ciii. 2, 'Praise the Lord, O my soul, and forget not all his benefits.' So he stirreth up himself to remember them, to remember them all. The two psalms, cv., cvi., are full examples of this particular thankfulness, and they are good guides to such as would learn it.

Reason 1. This is necessary, 1, because the more particularly we recount the favours of God to us, the more we discern God's love to us; as in the example of this people, Moses saith, Deut. iv., that God hath done much for this people; never so much for any. Read from ver. 32 *ad finem*, 38. And all those favours grew out of one root, 'Because he loved thy fathers.'

It is the apostle's note, *Ecce quantam charitatem*, 'Behold, how great love.' *Sic Deus dilexit mundum*, 'God so loved the world.

Reason 2. Seeing God's temporal favours are not always bestowed in love, but are made rods to whip the ungodly; this is a certain rule that these favours of God are evermore tokens of his love to such as are thankful for them, and to none else.

Reason 3. They that keep an inventory of their receipts, and are always reckoning and reporting the bounty of God to them, shall find that their receipts of favours have been more and greater than their issues of prayers. For how many great blessings have we from God that we never prayed for; so that God giveth us much more cause of thanksgiving and praise of his name, than of prayer and supplication.

Reason 4. Thanksgiving is a work of justice: as David, 'It well becometh the just to be thankful;' and again, 'Give to the Lord the glory due to his name;' that is, for every particular benefit, particular praise and thanks.

Reason 5. Thanksgiving doth put us in mind of our unableness to requite God; we cannot make him amends for his favours done to us; we shall find that our well-doing extendeth not to him, we must therefore do good to all *propter Dominum*, for the Lord.

Reason 6. Thanksgiving doth put us in mind of our unworthiness; as Mephibosheth to David, 2 Sam. ix. 8, ' What is thy servant, that thou shouldest look upon such a dead dog as I am?' Jacob, *Non sum dignus*, ' I am not worthy.' David himself, ' What is man, that thou art so mindful of him?'

Reason 7. If we will forget, God will remember us. As to David, ' I anointed thee king over Israel, I delivered thee out of the hand of Saul; I gave thee thy master's house, and thy master's wives into thy bosom:' *Domus Israel, domus Judah*.

Use. Surely we have not well taken out the lesson of thanksgiving to God, for to shuffle it up with a general *God be thanked for all*, comes but coldly, and is a poor *rependam* for all the benefits bestowed upon us.

St Augustine upon those words of David, *and forget not all his benefits*, saith, *Pro quibus bonis? Primo quia es, cum non esses; sed est et lapis; deinde quia vivis; sed vivit et pecus; sed fecit te ad similitudinem suam; suum exigit; retribue ei similitudinem suam in te.*

Look to the common blessings of God in general. Upon the church in which thou livest; pay God his debt for the good he hath done, before thou find fault with the defect in it; recount what he hath done for the commonwealth in which thou livest; look home to thine own family, to thine own person; recount thy spiritual graces, thy temporal blessings; consider what God hath given thee, what he hath forgiven thee, the preventions, the subventions of his love; what spiritual, what temporal evils thou hast either not felt by his keeping of thee, or escaped by his delivering of thee; and to all, and to each of these say, ' The Lord be thanked.' It is a small duty that is required of us, to repeat what God hath done for us.

Doct. 2. ' He stood and measured the earth, he drove asunder the nations, he scattered the everlasting mountains.' Here we are taught to give the whole glory and praise of all good to God. We know that Joshua brought this people into the promised land, that he caused the land to be measured, that he led them against the inhabitants of God,* and that the people of God did valiantly; yet, 'Not unto us, not unto us, but to thy name give the praise.'

Reason. We need no other reason for this doctrine than that of St James, 'For every good and perfect gift cometh from him.'

Thanks are given to creatures as the ministers and instruments of God, by whom he worketh the good pleasure of his will, but none hath a proper right to them but God only. The Lord giveth, the Lord forgiveth; in both he useth the ministerial means, for both he must be thanked.

Use 1. This serveth to inform our understanding in the truth of this doctrine, because the ignorance hereof is the mother of unthankfulness. It is God's complaint: Isa. i. 3, 'The ox hath known his owner, the ass his master's crib: but my people do not know,' &c. It was charged on them in Hosea: chap. ii. 8, 'She did not know that I gave her corn, and wine, and oil, and multiplied her silver and gold.'

2. This serveth to reprove all those that ascribe the benefits which they receive to themselves, like them in the first chapter of this prophecy, ver. 16, that did 'sacrifice to their net, and burn incense to their drag; because by them their portion is fat, and their meat plenteous.'

3. This reproveth them that murmur; for seeing God is the author and giver of all good, we must seek all from him; but we must not be our own carvers, we must learn to abound if the Lord giveth, and to want if the Lord taketh away.

4. This chideth those that repine at common blessings, when they do abate anything of their own particular profits.

Of this God hath given us a fearful example; for the last year our portion was fat, and our bread plenteous, great was the unthankfulness of many to

* Qu. 'the land'?—ED.

God for it. Then the landlord complained he could not have his rent, the tenant that he could not pay it; plenty had undone him. Such is the unconscionable rack of rents generally through the commonwealth, that plenty is a punishment to many, even a sharp and smarting rod. And doth not God begin to visit our land with sudden dearth; how much of the hope of the earth doth now lie in steep in the drowned earth, never likely to pay the seed that the earth borrowed?

It is time for thee, Lord, to pull thy hand out of thy bosom, and to whet thy sword, when thy mercies become burdens to the sons of men.

5. This reproveth all those that study men, and tender all their addresses to them, seeing their advancement and establishment here on earth by the purchased love and favour of men, they seek not the Lord. Did ever age sow precedents so thick for posterity, of drooping, declining, and falling greatness? Truly God is the Lord, and his name only is excellent. If God must have the glory, all that is done for us, whatsoever is done for us must be done by him, else it must needs miscarry.

6. This serves to establish the hearts of those who have obtained any competency for the support of this life with contentment; for if God be the giver of my daily bread, and if his hand do minister to my necessities, he knows best what state of life is fittest for me, I will not aspire higher; he knows how much will serve me, I will not covet more. This resolution will give thee much peace, for it casteth all thy care upon God, who will never leave thee, nor forsake thee.

7. This also stirreth us up to walk in the obedience of the laws of God; for if we consent and obey, we shall eat the good things of the land. Let us seek the face of God, and depend upon his providence for all things; let us consider the fowls of the air, and the lilies of the field, and wherein we are better than they, even in our reasonable service of God, and conclude that God will not let them want anything that lead a godly life; so will he furnish us with matter of praise, that we may ever be telling of his goodness from day to day.

Unlawful and indirect means of bettering our estates, by corrupting of our consciences, do break our bags, and spring leaks in our ships, that we and our goods perish; but the fear of the Lord maketh us rich; and what wanteth in the peace of the world, is supplied in the peace of a good conscience.

Doct. 3. Figurative speeches are in use in holy Scripture; this text is full of them, so is this whole psalm. I will only note these figures, which in this verse do offer themselves to us, for a taste.

1. It is here said that God *stood.*

This is spoken after the manner of men; for when hearing, and seeing, and smelling, and touching, and tasting, which are our senses, are attributed to God; when our parts of body, our eyes, ears, mouth, hands, feet, arms, are given to him; our motions, as sitting, standing, rising, going, striking, and such like, are spoken of God, know that these be figurative forms of speech, wherein the Holy Ghost doth retain our weak capacities, and under those forms of words doth present to our understandings the unconceivable operations of the most high God.

And let us take heed that we do not conceive God in our thoughts like to man in the structure and composition of the body, as the Anthropomorphites did. For it is here understood, by the standing of God, that when he brought the people to the promised land, there the progress ended; he stood there where he brought them to rest.

2. It is here said that he *measured the earth;* that is also a figurative manner of speaking, wherein that is charged upon him which was done by his direction and warrant.

3. He *beheld* and *drove in sunder* the nations.

God is all eye, and beholdeth all things; all ear, and heareth all things; all hand, and maketh all things, and doth whatsoever he will; all foot, and standeth in all places. He is here said to behold, which denoteth his provident care of his work; and he is said to drive in sunder the nations, because he ordained their expulsion; and he gave commission for the destruction of them, that he might give their land, according to his promise, to his own people.

4. Where he calls the mountains *everlasting*, and the hills *perpetual*, this is also a figure; for these be attributes only belonging to God to be everlasting and perpetual, and it sheweth the stability and settledness thereof.

5. There is also another figure in the very name of *mountains*, for we must not literally understand that there was any violence offered to the mountains and hills, but thereby the strength, and process, and settled estate of those nations that dwelt in the land of Canaan is signified; and so the scattering and bowing of these mountains doth express the dispersion of those nations, or the bringing of them under the yoke of subjection to the people of Israel.

6. His *ways* are everlasting; this is also figurative, for by the ways of God are understood here the counsels and decrees of God, and his executions of his will, which are no sudden operations, but proceed from everlasting wisdom.

And this the wisdom of the reader of holy Scripture, to observe what is spoken literally and what figuratively, else many errors and heresies may arise. As even in this attribution of the parts, and motions, and actions of the body of man to God, the Anthropomorphites, not understanding the figure, did conceive God in body like to man.

The heresy of transubstantiation grew out of the mistake of those words, *Hoc est corpus meum*, 'this is my body,' wherein the figure not observed, the Romanists do believe a real transmutation of the bread into the body of Christ; whereas that is to be understood only by sacramental representation, as the sacrament of circumcision is called 'the covenant of God in the flesh,' and the water of baptism is called 'the laver of regeneration,' being the sign and seal thereof.

You know that when Christ said to his disciples, Mat. xvi. 16, 'Beware of the leaven of the Pharisees,' they understood him not to speak figuratively, and said, 'It is because we have taken no bread.' So when he said, 'Destroy this temple,' the Jews understood him of the temple at Jerusalem. The scriptures of both Testaments are full of examples of figurative speaking. The whole book of the Song of Solomon is a continued figure, and all the poetical part of holy Scripture abound therewith.

The reasons why the wisdom of God hath thus expressed itself, are :

1. Because herein he would commend to us the use of that excellent science of the rhetoric, which teacheth the use of figures ; for there is no eloquence or oratory in all the wisdom of the world comparable to the holy elocution of Scripture, the majesty whereof is such, that it convinceth the judgment of man, and maketh it to yield it to the breath of God.

2. Because this cryptical manner of speaking doth involve the secrets of God's wisdom in some obscurity, to stir up and awake our diligence in the search, that we may be put to it to study holy Scriptures ; as Christ saith, 'Ερευνᾶτε, search, for easy things do soon cloy us, and make us idle.

3. Because this difficulty doth put us to our prayers, to beseech God to open to us the secrets of his wisdom.

4. This makes us fear God, because the secrets of the Lord are only revealed to them that fear God.

5. This difficulty is so sweetened with the pleasant mixture of art, as it hath *omne punctum* in it, for it mingleth *utile dulci*.

6. It doth teach us to be spiritual, for the carnal man cannot perceive the things of God, because they are spiritually discerned ; and the letter killeth, but the Spirit giveth life. This Spirit he hath left to teach his church, and to bring all things to our remembrance.

7. This obscurity doth call upon us to set apart some time for the study and search of Scriptures, and we cannot employ our spare hours of leisure better than in this search ; for here are the treasures of wisdom and knowledge, and these are able to make the man of God wise to salvation, perfect, then to thoroughly perfect, to all good works.

8. He hath distributed his graces in his church accordingly, and hath ordained some to be teachers of

others, whose whole time is consecrated to the study of this book of Scripture, that they may be able to understand this word aright, divide it aright to their hearers.

Herein you have a great advantage, if you consider the goodness of God to you; for in one hour you reap the harvest of our labours in many hours of our readings, of our inventions, judgments, search.

These reasons I gather from Clemens Alexandrinus, St Augustine, and St Gregory, and some others.

Use 1. This teacheth us that the worthy minister of the word must be no smatterer in those necessary arts and learning which is helpful to the study of divinity; for want whereof many bunglers handle the word of God too homelily, and instead of giving a constant light, do only make a blaze, which yet, like one of our night-walking fires, devours more admiration than the full moon that shines all night long.

Logic and rhetoric are two such necessary and requisite parts in a minister, as without which neither can the method of Scripture, nor the power of the arguments therein used, nor the clear interpretation of the words, be given.

Use 2. This teacheth the hearer and reader of the word to put his strength to it; not to parrot the words of Scripture, but to study the sense thereof.

St Origen saith, that as man, so the whole Bible, doth consist of a body and a soul; the body is the letter, the sense is the soul, of Scripture. That is the spiritual manna that giveth strength to the weak, that is the true light that giveth understanding to the simple.

Use 3. Let not this discourage any zealous Christian from exercising himself in the reading and study of holy Scripture; because we do confess that the figurative forms used therein do often make the Scripture obscure. For we do also affirm, that figures do sometimes give light to our apprehension, and make the mind of God better known to us; as when Christ saith, 'I am the good Shepherd,' as David said, 'The Lord is my Shepherd;' this doth make Christ better known to us in his careful protection of us, and his watchful keeping, and his plentiful feeding, and safe folding of us, and in such like.

Now, because the church of Rome hath taken advantage of the obscurity of the Scripture to forbid the translation thereof into the vernacle tongues of nations, and to prohibit lay persons, or any other, without special leave; this much I dare affirm, that holy Scripture are plain and easy in all dogmatical points, all the articles of faith are plainly set forth, and the whole doctrine of godly life, and the way to salvation, is openly declared. So far our church doth avouch; yet withal, we must consider that there is a double plainness of Scripture.

1. Rational and intellectual, which apprehendeth the true meaning of the words in grammatical construction, in logical composition, and in rhetorical illustration. Thus all the dogmatical part of divinity is plain to a natural man, that is capable of these helps.

2. Spiritual and metaphysical, which is saving knowledge, and is the work of the Holy Ghost in us, making us thereby wise to salvation; this knowledge is both the daughter and mother of faith, for by faith we hear the word, else it would not profit us, and by hearing cometh faith, else it were unfruitful.

Therefore I must indict many of the learned of the church of Rome of slander, who have given out in print, that we do hold the whole body of Scripture so easy, both in the whole, and in every part thereof, that any unlearned men and women may read and understand all as they go, and that they need no interpreter. This no sober man will affirm; but that the difficulty is not such as should deter us from the study thereof, rather that it is such as inviteth us thereto, that we affirm.

Use 4. This serveth us for caution:

1. Though the Scripture be full of figures, let us not make figures where there are none, and strain plain and evident texts from their genuine and proper sense, to foreign and far-fetched mysteries, as the papist doth often. For when Peter saith, *Ecce hic duo gladii*, they understand the double power of Peter,

and so of all popes, as his successors ecclesiastical and temporal ; so on these words, ' He made two great lights, the greater to rule the day, the less to rule the night,' that these two lights are the pope to rule the day, that is to say, the church ; and the emperor to rule the night, that is, the lay people. Where note, that as the moon borroweth all the light it hath of the sun, so must the emperor borrow all his glory of the pope !

Some of our own brethren have trod awry in this way, for an article of faith lies bleeding in the unresolved judgments of many, by this fault of making a figure where none is. The words of Christ, ' Thou wilt not leave my soul in hell,' are plain enough ; for we know that Christ had a soul, we know that there is an hell, and we hear Christ say, that God would not leave it there. But Mr Calvin turns this into a figure, and his words be all oracles with some that take their faith upon trust ; his figure is, that *descendit ad inferos diros in anima, cruciatus damnati ac perditi hominis pertulit,* he descended into hell, that is, he bare in his soul all the torments of the damned. Mr Perkins refuseth this as the meaning of the article, for he saith all this is contained in the former, ' he suffered, was crucified, dead.' And he findeth another figure in these words : by *soul,* he meaneth the *body ;* and by *hell,* he meaneth the *grave ;* for he thus rendereth it, ' He descended into hell,' that is, he was held captive in the grave, and lay in bondage under death for three days. Which need not, for the article that saith, ' he was buried,' containeth that, for then ' God did not suffer his Holy One to see corruption.'

This turning of articles of faith into figures doth destroy faith ; therefore without figure the safest way is to understand the word of the prophets in their own proper sense and natural signification : by *soul,* to understand the living soul of Christ, which by death was separated for a time from his body ; by *hell,* to understand the place of the damned, in which Christ triumphed victoriously over the devil and his angels, and brought away the keys thereof, that he might

open it to the reprobate, and shut it again : the elect*
to whom the promise is made, that ' The gates of hell
shall not prevail against them.'

2. Let us also take heed, that where there is a plain
figure, we do not understand that literally, to corrupt
the text; which was the error of the disciples, to
whom, when Christ had spoken of restoring the kingdom to Israel, they understood it literally, of the temporal kingdom of the Jews, which was meant of the
spiritual kingdom of Christ. So the woman of Samaria
thought Christ had spoken of an elementary water,
and the Capernaites mistook Christ, speaking of the
bread of life. Therefore, let common judgments take
good counsel how they expound Scriptures, lest they
pervert them to their own damnation, for as Augustine, *Hinc natæ sunt omnes hæreses, quia scripturæ bonæ
intelliguntur non bene*, hence all heresies grow, &c.

Ver. 7. *I saw the tents of Cushan in affliction : and
the curtains of the land of Midian did tremble.*

Here followeth further instance of the majesty and
glory of God, and goodness to his church; declared,

1. In the power of his fear, which was upon the
nations, when he brought his Israel to Canaan, for
that put them into affliction and trembling.

2. In the wonders that he shewed, in the work : *I
saw the tents of Cushan in affliction.* Who saw this?
Not the prophet only, but the church of God, to whom
God hath made himself known by this judgment.

The vision was, that God did cast the fear of his
people upon the nations; he nameth Cushan, or the
people of Ethiopia, bordering upon Egypt and Midian,
which took name of Midian the son of Abraham by
Keturah, Gen. xxv. 2.

The terror of God fell upon many nations, when
God put Israel into the way to the promised land, and
long after; and these two nations are here by a figure
poetically and rhetorically named, for many nations.

The reason whereof I conceive to be this :

Cushan, or Ethiopia, took name from Cush the

---

* Qu. ' against the elect ' ?—Ed.

eldest son of Ham, the youngest son of Noah, Gen. x. 6, to shew, that though Canaan, the son of Ham, be only named in Noah's curse, yet the smart thereof should also light upon Cush also, and he should taste also of affliction.

Again, herein the extent of this terror is well expressed, that Cushan, or Ethiopia, should be made to tremble, which was remote from Canaan, for the whole land of Egypt lay between. Midian lay near to that land, so that I understand the text thus: that God cast his fear upon people remote, and near hand, and shook them with trembling at his mighty power, when he brought his Israel into the promised land; and this was so palpable and manifest, that the church of God could not but take notice of it.

By tents and curtains, he expressed this people dismayed, not in their cities and towns and places of habitation, but in the fields, and amidst their military preparations, when their tents were pitched, as it were in readiness to give battle, which is a rhetorical amplification of the greatness of their terror.

My observation from this place is this:

Doct. The power of God, shewed in the terror of the wicked, doth prove that there is a God, and therefore no people on earth can be altogether ignorant of the Godhead.

Why should the tents of Cushan be in affliction? why should the curtains of Midian tremble, but that the fear of the Lord is upon them, God daunteth and dismayeth them? It was one of God's promises to his people, Deut. ii. 4, 'Ye are to pass through the coasts of your brethren the children of Esau, which dwell in Seir, and they shall be afraid of you.'

This deliverance of Israel from Egypt was a most memorable act of God's power, and made his name great in all the earth. It followeth, ver. 7, 'He,' *i. e.* Esau, 'knoweth thy walkings through the great wilderness: these forty years, the Lord thy God hath been with thee, thou hast lacked nothing.' Rahab, that entertained the spies whom Joshua sent to view the land of Canaan, saved them from the dangerous pursuit of the messengers of the king of Jericho. And she said to them, Joshua ii. 9–11, 'I know the Lord hath given you the land, and that your terror is fallen upon us; and that all the inhabitants of the land melt because of it. For we heard how the Lord dried up the waters of the Red Sea for you when ye came out of Egypt, and what you did to the two kings of the Amorites on the other side Jordan, Sihon and Og, whom ye destroyed utterly. And as soon as we heard these things, our hearts did melt, neither did there remain any more courage in any man because of you, for the Lord your God, he is God above in heaven, and in earth beneath.'

And this is the right way to make God known to the wicked and ungodly of the earth.

From thence came that prayer of David, Ps. ix. 20, 'Put them in fear, O Lord, that they may know themselves to be but men.' The fear of God will smite them with such terror, that they shall not have heart to stir against him. So it is said that God is known by executing his judgments.

Reason. For as the apostle saith, Rom. ii. 5, 'The very natural man hath the work of the law written in his heart. The law written in the heart of every man is a general principle both of truth in the understanding, which affirmeth a divine nature, and of awe in the affections, to make him feared. And this law is not idle, but it worketh; for there is ἔργον τοῦ νόμου, the work of the law. And this is the true cause why there is no peace at all to the wicked man, because he hath the law of nature working within him, which is against him; and he hath not the law of grace to lay the storms which the law of nature raiseth. From hence it cometh that the wicked flieth when no man pursueth, as Solomon saith, and he feareth where no fear is; and Tully could say that all the poetical fictions of the Furies, which disquieted men so much, were but the pinchings and convulsions of men's guilty consciences, who, when they had done evil, knew that they had broken the law written in their hearts, and then feared the power which they saw above them, armed with vengeance against evil doers.

Use. St Paul teacheth us the use of this point: Rom. xxxi. 3, 'Wilt thou then not be afraid of the power? do that which is good, and thou shalt have praise of the same.' Where doing that which is good hath a double reward, for it quieteth fear, and it crowneth us with praise. Methinks that this consideration of the reward should stir us up to say, John vi. 28, 29, 'What shall we do that we may work the works of God?' Then Christ tells us, 'This is the work of God, that ye believe on him whom he hath sent.'

Faith in Christ taketh away the terror of the Lord; as the apostle saith, 'we knowing the terror of the Lord, do persuade men.' And what is the thing to which the apostles do persuade, but to reconciliation with God through Christ; so that when we preach faith to you, we preach peace; even as the apostle saith, peace to them that are near, and peace to them that are far off; and the God of peace sendeth his Son, the peace of his church with the gospel of peace.

Doct. 2. We are taught here that the welfare of the church is the grief and vexation of her enemies. Cushan and Midian are afflicted, and in a cold fit, when they hear what God doth for Israel. So did the Egyptians repine at the prosperity of Israel in Egypt; they said, Exod. i. 10, 'Behold, the children of Israel are more and mightier than we: come, let us deal wisely with them, lest they multiply,' &c.

You see what the world thinks of their plots against the church of God; they think they do wisely when they vex the church; this is that wisdom which the apostle doth call carnal, sensual, and devilish. And these be the wise men of which it is said, *Ubi sapiens?* 'where is the wise man?' and God hath made the wisdom of the world foolishness.

Reason 1. The reason of this opposition is given by our Saviour: 'The world hateth you, because you are not of the world, and I have chosen you out of the world.' And for this they weep at the joy of the church, they joy at their weeping; the prophet's complaint, Isa. lix. 15, 'Truth faileth, and he that departeth from evil maketh himself a prey.' So

David, Ps. xxxviii. 19, 20, 'But mine enemies they are lively, they are strong, and they that hate me wrongfully are multiplied. They also that render evil for good are mine adversaries, because I follow the thing that good is.'

They began betimes, for Cain slew his brother; 'and wherefore slew he him? because his own works were evil, and his brother's righteous,' 1 John iii. 12.

Ratio rationis. I can easily bring you to the head of these bitter waters. So soon as Adam had fallen from grace, when God kept his first assize upon earth, and convented and arraigned the transgressors, the man, the woman, and the serpent, he revealed his eternal counsel of election and reprobation, and put a difference between seed and seed, the seed of the woman and the seed of the serpent. Which is not only to be understood of the unreconcilable enmity that is between Christ and the devil; for Christ was the seed of the woman, *quia solus ita semen mulieris, ut non etiam viri semen sit;* but he meant therein that enmity which should be betwixt the elect (who are the seed of the woman by natural generation, and the holy seed by spiritual regeneration, so called *semen sanctum*) and the seed of the serpent. For Christ called the wicked *genemeta viperarum,* 'generation of vipers;' and to such he saith, John viii. 44, *Vos estis ex patre vestro diabolo,* 'You are of your father the devil.' For this Rupertus saith that the Bible is called the book of the battles of the Lord, Num. xxi. 14; because it containeth the story of the wars between these two, the church and the world.

From this enmity which God put between the church and the world, ariseth this hatred and opposition, so that the prosperity of the wicked is David's grief, the miseries of David be the world's joy. The joy of the church is the affliction of the world.

God left the devil in his fall, and took him not up again, thereby forsaking him. He put enmity into him; and he, for the hatred that he beareth to God, hath ever since persecuted him in his church, because his malice cannot extend to hurt him. And herein he is the more cruel, because he knows his time is but short.

Reason 2. Satan is but God's instrument in the afflicting of the church; so it is said to the angel of the church of Smyrna, Rev. ii. 10, 'Behold, the devil shall cast some of you into prison, that ye may be tried; and ye shall have tribulation ten days.' He 'goes about like a roaring lion, seeking whom he may devour.' If he be kept from devouring, he biteth and rendeth, and doth what hurt he can, for he is a murderer; but if God shew the light of his countenance to them whom he pursueth, he is sick of that mercy, and so are all the tents of Cushan. The whole brood of vipers have this venom from the old serpent, to be afflicted at the prosperity of the church.

For instance, I will prevent the time. David saith, 'One day telleth another, and one night certifieth another.' To-morrow's memorial teacheth this day. This was the vigil of that popish holiday which the same papists here at home, and many beyond the seas, hoped to have made festival to all posterity. The children of darkness had provided to put out our light, to quench the light of our Israel. It was an affliction to the papists to behold religion and peace settled under the government of a learned king, who knew what he believed, and why, and who had discovered himself an enemy to their antichristian and heretical synagogue. They saw a fair issue ready for timely succession, so graciously seasoned with the salt of heavenly wisdom from the first of their capacity and apprehension, that there remained no hope for their politic religion to find footing in these churches. The flourishing state of church and commonwealth was such an affliction to them, that some zealots of their religion, the sons of thunder, could no longer contain themselves, but their study was how to put their grief upon us, and to transfer our joy upon themselves. They shewed us the way of their rejoicing; their mercies were cruel; nothing could remove their grief at our welfare but the destruction of the head and body, root and tree, and all in a day. And they that would have destroyed us thought, and the Jesuits and priests of the Roman faith taught them to believe, that they should do God good service.

We see the mercies of that religion so clearly in this horrible treason, that all that know and serve the God of peace have just cause to esteem papists disloyal subjects, secret enemies to the state, bloody persecutors of the gospel of peace.

Our stories are full of their malice, rackings, imprisonments, starvings, burnings, hangings, and many exquisite torments executed upon innocent and holy martyrs. But when we remember the powder treason, that calleth all the tormentors of the church before them merciful, the devil did never roar so loud before, the bulls of Rome never bellowed such terror to the church as in that damnable and desperate attempt. The provocation was their affliction at our prosperity, and grief at our welfare. Again this venom of the generation of vipers boiled over, and they that bore evil will to our Sion said one to another, Catesby to his confederates, ' I have bethought me of a way at one instant to deliver us from all our bonds, and, without any foreign help, to replant the catholic religion, which is to blow up the parliament house with gunpowder; for in that place have they done us all the mischief, and, perchance, God hath designed that place for their punishment; for this striketh at the root, and will breed a confusion fit to beget new alterations.' What alterations would be here meant but those that Job felt, that our land and church might complain, ' Thou hast turned my harp into mourning, and my organs into the voice of them that weep.'

How did they swallow up the joy of this change in hopeful expectation of success; but the children came to the birth, and there was no strength to bring forth. Their own fear came upon them, for it was Catesby's own *l'envoy* to his revealed treason. But, saith he, If this take not effect (as most of this nature miscarry), the scandal will be so great to the catholic religion, as not only our enemies, but our friends will, with good reason, condemn us. Thus did their minds misgive, and bodements of evil did secretly call upon them to fly from the anger to come.

This diverted them a while from this execution, and put them into a new project. Thomas Winter was sent (as his confession under his own hand reporteth) to inform the constable of Spain, then coming in embassy from the king of Spain to our sovereign, of the state of the catholics in England, and to entreat his mediation to solicit our king for the revocation of some penal laws, and the admittance of the English catholics into the rank of his other subjects. Winter met with him at Bergen, near Dunkirk, and by the means of Owen, an apostate traitor, he had access to him, moved him in his suit, and had a fair promise from him to do all good offices in that errand. But Owen discouraged that hope, saying that he believed nothing less, and that they sought only their own ends, meaning the state of Spain, holding small account of catholics. Owen animated the treason, and promised to send Fawkes over to help to set it forward. From thence Winter went to another of our fugitives, Sir William Stanley, to Ostend, where he asked his opinion whether, if the catholics of England should do anything in England to help themselves, the archduke would second them ? He answered, No ; for all those parts desired peace with England. After all these despairs, they had no remedy to cure their disease of envy at the gracious peace of this state, but their powder plot, in which none but professed papists within the land had any hand. None that we can discover but priests and Jesuits, here or abroad, did blow the fire. No foreign prince hath the dishonourable name of privacy with it, or abetment of it ; only the church of Rome lent her help to this nefarious treason, for there was here,

1. The seal of catholic confession.
2. The bond of a catholic oath.
3. The vow by a catholic sacrament.
4. The indiction of catholic prayers, to be used for the prosperous success of the catholic cause in England.

But I may be short in the catastrophe of this whole danger, as God was sudden in his exceeding great mercies to us. ' The nets were broken, and we escaped as a whole nest of birds from the hands of the fowler.' Never was there day wherein God did so great things for this land as on that day ; never did the sun shine in more perfect strength upon this church than on that day, which God crowned with our deliverance.

1. It was and is a good use of this mercy to fill our mouths with laughter and our tongues with joy; but that must not be all.

2. We must tell the people what things he hath done; and once a-year, at least, we must say, 'This is the day that the Lord hath made,' *exultemus et lætemur*, and his praise must be in our mouths; we must give unto the Lord the glory due to his name, and praise him according to his excellent greatness.

3. But that is not all. We must, being delivered from the hands of our enemies, serve him in holiness and righteousness before him all the days of our life, and remember that if we do wickedly, we shall perish, we and our king.

4. But that is not all. We must pray also for the peace of our Jerusalem, for we shall prosper if we love it. For our brethren and companions' sake in the common faith, we must wish it now prosperity; for the house of God's sake, we must seek to do it good.

5. But this is not all. We must cast out the bondwoman and her son, that is, the superstition of the bloody church of Rome. I may safely persuade thus far every one of us out of his own heart, and thus far we may go without ourselves to let our light shine before men, that in our light they may see light. The minister may go further, for he hath the warrant of a lawful calling to reprove the works of darkness openly, and to convince heresies, and to warn men to take heed of the leaven of the scribes and pharisees. The magistrate may go further, to execute the just laws of our land upon such, and let him see to it that he bear not the sword of God in vain. The sovereign defender of the faith amongst us beareth that high title, which is proper to all godly kings, to this end accountable to none but God for his vicegerency herein.

Ver. 8. *Was the Lord displeased against the rivers? was thine anger against the rivers? was thy wrath against the sea, that thou didst ride upon thy horses, or thy chariot of salvation?*

Now he proceedeth to commemorate the wonderful things that declared God a friend to his people, in their safe conduct to the land of promise.

1. The power of God shewed in the waters : 1. He made a passage for his Israel through the Red Sea, as on dry land, to bring them out of Egypt.

2. He made a passage through Jordan, the river turned back, and gave them way to pass over into the land of promise.

The words of my text are easy.

Doth any man conceive that God did take any spleen at the river of Jordan, that he drove it back ; or that he was angry with the sea, that he made dry land to appear ? Surely God was not moved thereto from any fury against the creatures, which keep their course according to his appointments.

And he saith, that God did ride upon his horses, poetically and figuratively expressing God in state, 'riding on,' as the psalmist saith, ' prosperously.' And he calleth the protection of God ' the chariots of salvation,' because God took them up to him to preserve them.

And this is well expounded in the next words, in a new figure.

Ver. 9. *Thy bow was made quite naked, according to the oaths of the tribes, even thy word. Selah. Thou didst cleave the earth with rivers.*

For here by the bow of God is meant the armour wherewith God is furnished for the defence of his church. This bow is therefore said to be made quite naked, because then God declared that all the wonders which he did in the division of the waters of the Red Sea, and of Jordan, were wrought for the preservation of his church.

This bow he always had, that is, this strength for his church, but then he made it so naked, that the Egyptians cried, Let us fly from Israel ; and the tents of Cushan were afflicted, and the curtains of Midian trembled to see this bow of the Lord.

Abraham saw this bow, but in the case, for it was

under promise. The patriarchs saw it somewhat nearer hand, but yet not uncased. In the deliverance from Egypt, it began to be drawn out; in the possession of the land of Canaan, it was made quite naked, and this was done 'according to the oaths of the tribes, even thy word;' that is, all this was done that thou mightest make good thy word, whereby thou hadst sworn to give this land to the tribes. The oath of God was sworn to Abraham, as Zacharias remembereth it: Luke i. 72, 73, 'To perform the mercy promised to our fathers, and to remember his holy covenant. The oath which he sware to our father Abraham.'

Selah is a rest for meditation, for admiration; it is a confession of the goodness of God.

Thou didst cleave the earth with rivers. This was another of God's water-works.

Tremellius and Junius read thus: *flumina diffidisti terræ;* and so it is no more but what before he said, more plainly expressed, that he clave the waters to make way for passage.

And to omit the various opinions of men concerning this wonderful work of God, I think it hath special reference to that story, where the people of Israel upon the way almost perishing with thirst, Num. xx. 11, and therefore murmuring, Moses struck the rock, which by the commandment he should only have spoken to, and the waters gushed out, and cut themselves a channel, which here is called cleaving of the earth with rivers.

Here was a double miracle: one in giving the water out of the rock, whence formerly none have issued; another in the continuance of this full stream, running along the way of their journey in the wilderness, to supply them. So the psalmist saith, Ps. lxxviii. 16, 'He brought streams also out of the rock, and caused waters to run down like rivers.'

These words do contain three parts:
1. The wonders which God shewed in the waters.
2. The motive that induced him.
3. The argument drawn from hence.
1. The wonders here mentioned are three.

1. He nameth the last as freshest in memory, the division of the waters of Jordan, to give way to the passage of Israel into the promised land.

2. He nameth the first, the cutting of a passage through the Red Sea, to bring Israel out of Egypt.

3. He nameth the miracle of giving his people water out of the rock, and leading the stream along with the host.

2. The motive that induced him. 1. Affirmative; 2. Negative.

Affirm. 1. There was *internus motor*, the inward motive, his love to Israel, and his care to preserve them, which is expressed in his riding on the chariots of salvation.

2. There was *externum motivum*, the outward motive, and that was the oaths of the tribes, even his word which he had put to Abraham for that land.

Neg. 2. *Non iratus*, I am not angry.

3. The argument drawn from hence.

God hath shewed himself marvellous to Israel: *in exitu*, in their going forth, then he divided the sea for them; *in via*, in their way, then he made rivers to run in dry places after them; *in introitu*, in their entrance, then he divided Jordan for them.

Therefore we may trust in him, and commit ourselves to his care; he will never leave us, nor forsake us.

1. Of the wonders shewed in the waters, and therein, (1.) Of the division of Jordan.

This was a great wonder: the story of it is recorded so; for the day before it was done, Joshua said to the people, Josh. iii. 5, 'Sanctify yourselves: for to-morrow the Lord will do wonders among you.' Yea, God himself said to Joshua, ver. 7, 'This day will I magnify thee in the sight of all Israel, that they may know that, as I was with Moses, so will I be with thee.' The wonder is set down thus: ver. 15, 16, 'No sooner did the feet of the priests which bare the ark, dip in the brim of the water, but the waters that came down from above stood, and rose up upon an heap very far from the city Adam, that is beside Zaretan: and those that came down from the sea of the plain, even the salt sea, failed, and were cut off; and the people passed over right against Jericho.' This was so great a wonder, that we read, Joshua v. 1, ' When all the kings of the Amorites, which were on the side of Jordan westward, and all the kings of the Canaanites which were by the sea, heard that the Lord had dried up the waters of Jordan from before the children of Israel, until we were passed over, that their hearts melted; neither was there spirit in them any more, because of the children of Israel.' And the psalmist doth celebrate the praises of God for the same, with poetical strains of divine rapture. He putteth both together, as this our psalmist doth, both that of the Red Sea and this of Jordan: Ps. cxiv. 1–3, ' The sea saw that and fled' (*i. e.* it saw that when Israel came out of Egypt, Judah was his sanctuary, and Israel his dominion). ' Jordan was driven back. What ailed thee, O sea, that thou fleddest? thou Jordan, that thou wast turned back?'

The things most remarkable in that wonderful work of God were these:

1. That the waters of so great a river as Jordan should recoil towards their head; for water, being a ponderous body, doth naturally fall downward, and seeketh still the lower place; but God did make a wall of water to stop the decourse of the stream, which was a work against nature; for the other part of the stream ran on, and left the land dry.

2. The second wonder was the means that God used to accomplish this great work; for the priests that bear the ark must set the first foot into the river; for God said, Joshua iii. 13, ' As soon as the soles of the feet of the priests that bear the ark of the Lord, the Lord of all the earth, shall rest in the waters of Jordan, the waters of Jordan shall be cut off,' &c.

Here was the ark, the sacrament visible of God's invisible presence, and the priests of the Lord bearing it; they had the warrant of God's word to attempt this passage, and they did not so much as wet their feet in that river. No sooner did the soles of their feet touch the waters, but they fled from the Lord, not from the priests, yet from the priests as the Lord's instruments; not that any virtue or efficacy was in the feet of the priests, the virtue was in the sacrament of God's presence, the ark which they carried upon their shoulders; neither was the virtue of that wonder in the sacrament efficiently and primarily, but mediately and instrumentally. It was the work of the Lord of all the earth, whose sacrament was the ark, whose servants the priests.

3. A third wonder was the faith of the priests that did bear the ark, who could believe a thing in nature so impossible, in reason so improbable, that they durst attempt it both in regard of their own persons, but especially of the ark of God which they did bear. Moses wanted faith in a less matter; when God bade him only speak to the rock, he smote it twice: once in vain, to punish his unbelief; once with success, to fulfil God's promise. Yet the priests believed faithfully and obeyed willingly, and did not debate the matter anxiously, or go on timorously.

4. A fourth wonder was in the time, for it was 'in the time of the harvest, when Jordan overfloweth all the banks,' Joshua iii. 15, when there was a great deal more river than channel; and the more water the more wonder.

5. We may add hereto a fifth, that when all the people were passed over, Joshua did command twelve men, out of every tribe a man, to return back again into the midst of the channel, Joshua iv. 5; and they were not priests but laymen, and they were not to follow the ark, but to go before it, and from thence they must every man bring upon his shoulder a stone; and those were set up in Gilgal for a monument of this passage, for the memorial thereof to their children.

6. The last wonder was, that when the twelve men returned from the midst of the channel of Jordan to the land which was for them to dwell in, the priests following them with the ark of God, the soles of their feet were no sooner lifted upon the dry land, but, Josh. iv. 18, 'the waters of Jordan returned to their place, and flowed over all his banks, as they did before.'

But he names *rivers* in my text; so further, this

mention of the rivers is yet referred to a former story, wherein God declared his power in the rivers of the Egyptians, and that not improperly, because then the people were in the house of bondage, and the first plague which God put upon the Egyptians was this: Exod. vii. 20, 'All the waters were turned into blood; the fish died, and the waters stank.'

It may also renew the memory of two more passages over Jordan: one of Elijah, 2 Kings ii. 8, who 'took his mantle, and wrapped it together, and smote the waters; and they were divided hither and thither, so that they two went over on dry land;' another of Elisha, ver. 14, who 'took up the mantle of Elijah, and stood by the river of Jordan, and said, Where is the Lord God of Elijah? and smote the water, and it parted hither and thither; and Elisha passed over.'

(2.) In the next place, he remembereth the sea, meaning the Red Sea, and God's riding through it, and conducting his Israel through the midst of it. The story of it is recorded by Moses, Exod. xiv. 16. And there are many wonders in it.

1. The danger that Israel was in: the Egyptians behind them, with power and fury to destroy them; the sea before them, to swallow them. God opened them a passage through the sea to save them from the overtaking of their enemies, and to lead them to the next shore, a wonderful help in extremity of danger.

2. Another wonder, that God rather used Moses and his rod than his own word in the parting of the waters of the sea, Exod. xiv. 16. For using the ministry and service of men in his great and extraordinary operations, he doth honour to men therein. As he said to Joshua, chap. iii. 7, 'This day will I begin to magnify thee in the sight of all Israel, that they may know that as I was with Moses, so I will be with thee.' So the psalmist saith, Ps. lxxvii. 20, 'Thou leadest thy people like sheep by the hand of Moses and Aaron. It is well observed of Master Calvin, *Ministros simul commendat, quibus tam honorificum munus Deus injunxit.*

So in the gospel, Christ hath honoured his ministers, to whom he hath committed the office of the ministry of reconciliation; teaching by them, baptizing by them, binding and loosening by them; for though he do all these things himself, as he saith, *sine me nihil potestis facere*, 'without me you can do nothing,' yet he will do nothing ordinarily in these things without us, because this is his ordinance and the established constitution in his church.

3. As he used the ministry of Moses in this great work of dividing the sea, Exod. xiv. 21, so did he also use the service of an east wind all the night to drive back the waters, that dry land might appear. This abated nothing of the honour of God, that he used the service of his creatures; neither can this separation of the waters be therefore ascribed to some natural causes, seeing this wind was miraculously sent of God to this purpose.

Some enemies of God have slandered this miracle, and said that the passage of Israel was but an advantage taken of an extraordinary neap tide; which turns the truth into a lie, for it is here added that the waters were a wall on both sides of them. The work itself of dividing the sea, that was the greatest. What is the rod of Moses, or the force of an east wind, to part the waters in two, and to cut out a lane of dry land in the midst of the sea for such an army to pass through on foot; to make the waters, a fluent and liquid element, to stand on both sides as a wall and fence to their passage!

Yet I must tell you that many learned have believed and written that the waters of the sea were divided in twelve places, and twelve lanes cut out for the twelve tribes to pass over, every of the tribes apart, and by himself. And this was the tradition of the Hebrews, as St Origen * upon this place affirmeth.

Audivi a majoribus traditum quod in ista digressione maris, singulis quibusque tribubus filiorum Isr. singulæ aquarum divisiones factæ sint, et propria unicuique tribui in mari aperta sit via. And for proof, he allegeth the words of the psalm: Ps. cxxxvi. 13, 'He divided the Red Sea into parts;' it is rendered 'in divisions,'

* Hom. v. in Exod.

implying more than one division. I say with St Origen, *Hæc à majoribus observata in Scripturis divinis religiosum credidi non tacere.*

But though this do much advance the glory of God's power, yet because it is not recorded in this story of the passage, we need not admit it; and against it I find that the place alleged will not carry it through. For the same word which is used to express the division of the waters in this story is used by Moses in the story of Abraham, Gen. xv. 9, 10, who, by the commandment of God, took a young heifer, a she-goat, a ram, a turtle dove, and a young pigeon, and divided them in the midst, and laid each piece one against another. Here was a division made, but into two parts only, yet it is said after that, 'Behold, a smoking furnace and a lamp of fire passed between those pieces.' The word is the same, הגזרים, yet the division was but into two; no doubt that story would not have concealed so great an addition to the wonder, so much serving to set forth the glory of God.

The Lord sufficiently shewed his church that all things serve him, and they had as good cause as those in the Gospel to have said, 'Who is this, that both winds and sea obey him?'

5. Another wonder was the hand of God drawing the Egyptians, Pharaoh, and his host after Israel into the sea; for God hath taken it upon himself that this was his own doing: Exod. xiv. 17, 18, 'And I, behold, I will harden the hearts of the Egyptians, and they shall follow them: and I will get me honour upon Pharaoh, and upon all his host, upon his chariots, and upon his horsemen. And the Egyptians shall know that I am the Lord.' They, no doubt, had their own ends in this, for, as St James saith, chap. i. 14, 'every man is tempted when he is drawn of his own lust, and is enticed.'

They had their own motives to draw them into this mischief:

1. Their desire to recover the Israelites to their service, whom they held so long vassals to them.

2. They had also a desire to recover from them the wealth of Egypt, which they had improvidently parted

with to the Israelites.

3. Their desire of revenge, to punish this flight and this robbery of the Egyptians.

4. Their error, who thought they might pass as safely after Israel as Israel went before, as Josephus speaks for them.

These motives grew within themselves, and they were their own lusts; but God gave them over to these lusts and desires, of purpose to punish their cruelty to his people, and to make his name glorious in the deliverance of his church, and in the conquest of the enemies thereof. It is revenge enough in God upon man to leave him to his own ways, for they lead him to destruction.

Some heathen writers have charged all this wonder of the escape of Israel, and of the passage through the sea upon Moses, who by art magic they say did all this. But could he by that art work upon the affections and wills of king Pharaoh and all his people, to force them after Israel into the Red Sea? The most that we read of Moses concerning any art in natural philosophy is, that Moses was brought up in all the wisdom of the Egyptians, and no man thinketh that he got all their wisdom from them: how, then, did not the wisdom of the Egyptians at time serve the Egyptians themselves when this was done?

6. Another memorable miracle of this passage was, that before all Israel had recovered the further shore, the same passage was safe to Israel, and pernicious and fatal to the Egyptians; which appeared,

(1.) Because God did not let the waters come together to hinder the Egyptians' pursuit, but kept them divided till they were all within the verge of the sea; for this God could have done, as it after followeth.

(2.) That to hinder their journey of pursuit, God turned the pillar of cloud behind Israel, between them and the Egyptians, so that Israel led the way by a clear light, the Egyptians followed them in the dark.

(3.) That their chariot wheels were smitten off in the night, so that they drove uneasily.

(4.) That the waters came together upon their consultation to return, and drowned them all, before all the children of Israel had recovered the further shore.

7. The last memorable wonder was the casting up of the bodies of the Egyptians upon the further shore which Israel had recovered, and whereon they pitched, to make good the word of Moses, 'You shall see them no more,' that is, living, to terrify you. Thus Israel saw what God had done for them, and their eye had its desire against their enemies.

All these be things worth remembering.

3. He addeth another wonderful mercy in 'cleaving the earth with rivers,' which hath reference, as you have heard, to Num. xx. 11, in which, 1, it is wonderful that God, hearing the murmur of his people for want of water, had not punished their sin with present death, but did choose rather to give them their hearts' desire, and to satisfy them with water.

2. That he made the rock to yield them water, which did not naturally, but by virtue of his word.

3. That it should have been done so easily as by a word of Moses; that it was done so easily as by twice smiting.

4. That those waters did follow the host to relieve it all the way of their journey, till they had other supply, as also the manna did till they came to come in Canaan; so these waters ran into no sea.

5. That these rivers dried up after Israel, and no show of any river ever since, where these waters ran in dry places, to shew who ordained that stream, and for whom.

Though God hath had his praise for all the things before, yet they desire *canticum novum*, a new song, and here it is work for the *rector chori*.

2. The motive that induced God to do all this for his people expressed in two things, *internus motor:*

(1.) His desire of the preservation of his Israel, 'for he did ride upon his horses and chariots of salvation.' Pharaoh followed Israel into the Red Sea on horses and in chariots; these were the horses and chariots of destruction: God took off their wheels, and they failed in their speed. But God went forth with salvation; Israel could not but see in all these wonderful works of God that God was for them.

1. In their setting forth, to bring them out of the house of bondage, even through the sea.

2. In the way of their journey, to quench their thirst in the dry and unwatered wilderness.

3. At their journey's end, to open them a passage into the promised land through Jordan.

Israel is a type of the catholic church of God on earth, and their passage from Egypt to Canaan is a type of our passage from the womb to heaven; and God is the same: his church is as dear to him as ever it was, and he hath taken upon him the care of it.

He is called by Job 'the preserver of men,' especially of his elect.

Here are only mentioned three of the most eminent wonders of God; there were many more which David repeated, Ps. cv. and cvi. All these were the effects of the free favour of God to his people, whereby he got the name of a Saviour, Ps. cvi. 21. And the psalmist prayeth, ver. 4, ' Remember me, O Lord, with the favour that thou bearest to thy people, O visit me with thy salvation.' This was a singular favour, for he saith also, *Non fecit taliter*, he did not so to any nation. Ver. 5, ' That I may see the good of thy chosen, that I may rejoice in the gladness of thy nation, that I may glory with thine inheritance ;' for this favour of God to his church is a special grace above his universal protection. This it is that the spouse of Christ doth pray for, Cant. viii. 6, ' Set me as a seal on thy heart, and as a signet upon thine arm.' That wish of the church then was thus, and is now, an article of faith; that was then prayer, and now is our creed.

But much more evidently hath this eternal love of God to his church in Christ Jesus shewed itself, since Christ our Saviour was made manifest in the flesh, and much more hath it extended and dilated itself, since he was believed on of the Gentiles, and preached to the world. For when God once had fitted him with a body, and therewith had given him a heart like ours, and such an arm as we have, and such hands, it hath been more discerned how we were set as a seal upon that heart, how we are worn upon that arm, how we are engraven in the palms of those hands; for that heart was pierced with a spear, those hands were nailed to the cross, and these be the stamps and characters of his love to us.

And as the affection of love is noted to be most vehement in a woman, as David doth imply when he bewailed Jonathan's death, 2 Sam. i. 26, 'Thy love to me was wonderful, passing the love of women,' so our Saviour, to take upon him this affection in the dearest tenderness, and most intense measure and degree, is said to be made of a woman, and she a virgin, Gal. iv. 4. And that sin might not corrupt this affection or harden the heart, he was conceived by the Holy Ghost.

The church doth well to remember this interest that God gave them in this land, for thereout suck they no small advantage. This calls God the God of Israel, and it calls Israel God's peculiar people. This doth spread the wings of this hen over all her chickens, and gathereth them together under the same; it makes them room in the bosom of God.

2. Another motive was the oaths of the tribes, even God's word, that is, the covenant of God made with Abraham and his seed; for so the psalmist doth express it: Ps. cv. 8–10, 'He hath remembered his covenant for ever, the word that he commanded to a thousand generations: which covenant he made with Abraham, and his oath unto Isaac; and confirmed the same unto Jacob for a law, and to Israel for an everlasting covenant.' And after having briefly surveyed the story of Israel's deliverance and passage, having recapitulated the coming of Israel into Egypt, the plagues of Egypt, their coming out thence with the wealth of Egypt, the pillar of cloud, the pillar of fire, the quails, the manna, the water out of the rock, he gives this reason of all, ver. 42, 'For he remembered his holy promise, and Abraham his servant.'

Of this oath of God, the author to the Hebrews, chap. vi. 13, 'For when God made a promise to Abraham, because he could swear by no greater, he sware by himself, saying, Surely blessing I will bless thee, and multiplying I will multiply thee.' The reason why God bound himself by oath followeth : ver. 17, 'Wherein God, willing more abundantly to shew unto the heirs of promise the immutability of his counsel, confirmed it by an oath.'

This was a great obligation, to bind God to this performance ; neither doth it any whit abridge his own liberty, but that he remained *liberrimum agens* still ; for that he declared therein the constancy of his decree, which was κατὰ τὴν βουλὴν τοῦ θελήματος αὐτοῦ.

(2.) Because, as I have shewed, that and all other God's promises have reference to the obedience of the people, so that God might have cancelled this obligation upon their forfeiture thereof by disobedience, if he had pleased ; which maketh good the former motive of his own good will and favour, who, notwithstanding their many provocations and rebellions, yet performed this promise.

2. The motive is negatively set down ; for here it is expressed, what was not the cause of these wonderful waterworks ; 'Was it' (which is as much as *it was not*) ' because the Lord was displeased at the rivers ; it was not because his wrath was against the sea.'

To part the sea in two, to divide Jordan, to make rivers run a while in full stream to serve his people, was no displeasure taken at these elements. God never layeth his rod upon those creatures which he hath ordained for the service of man, but to punish man. To the creature, it is all one to keep the natural order of creation, or to suffer supernatural alteration ; for *omnia illi serviunt*, all things do serve him. Was God angry with the earth when he cursed it after Adam's fall ; when he drowned it, after it grew full of cruelty ?

The insensible creatures do the will of him that made them.

It is recorded as a blemish to that mighty king Xerxes,[*] that he foolishly over-weened his power in such a case. For being to pass his army over the Hellespont, where the sea was about seven furlongs over, he caused a bridge to be made of floating vessels

[*] Herod. Polihim. lib., Num. 173.

to that purpose. But a great tempest arising, and breaking his bridge, when he heard thereof, he was in such passion at the sea, that he commanded it to be punished with three hundred stripes; and he cast in fetters into it to take it prisoner, and caused these wise words to be spoken to it: *O aqua amara, dominus hanc tibi irrogat pœnam, quod eum læsisti, qui de te nihil mali meritus es; te tamen rex Xerxes, velis nolisve, transmittet.*

As wisely, either he himself, or as Herodotus reporteth,† Cyrus his grandfather, fell out with the river Gyndes for drowning him a white horse; but his revenge was more in sight, so was his deliberate furious folly. For he set his army a-work to cut out new channels, and divided the river into 360 brooks; *ut a mulieribus ne genua tingentibus transiri possit.*

But our God had no quarrel, the text saith, to these inanimate creatures of his, which were so at his command. The church here doth God right, to confess the true motive of this extraordinary operation of God; so here is a double confession:

1. That *Tu, Domine, fecisti,* thou, Lord, hast done it.

2. That he did it for such a cause.

This is not barely avouched, but it is proved. 'Thy bow was made quite naked,' that is, thou didst let all the world take notice of thy power, and strength, and favour, in the cause of thy church. At the coming of God in great majesty and glory on mount Sinai to give the law before mentioned, there was *absconsio roboris,* the hiding of his strength; God revealed himself then to Israel only, but these three great wonders here confessed did uncase the bow of God, and made it quite naked, so that all nations might take knowledge of the arm of the Lord, and might give testimony to the same.

The argument drawn from hence is still the same, for from the former evidences of God's great power and mercy shewed, and openly declared unto the church, they gather comfort, to assure themselves of

† Clio xxxiv., Cyrus.

the favour of God toward them in this captivity in Babylon.

They know and believe that the hand of God is not shortened, nor his arm weakened, but that he who was able to cut a way for them through the sea, and the river of Jordan, and to make rivers run in dry places, to relieve their fathers in the wilderness, is still as able to succour them in that captivity against the king of Babel and all the Chaldeans; so he sheweth by what faith the just shall live in their banishment, namely, by faith grounded on the power and wisdom and love of God, and of his truth.

The doctrines which this passage affordeth are these:

Doct. 1. God must have the glory of his own great works.

David is a full example of this duty; for, 1, in his own case, he saith, Ps. lxvi. 16, 'Come and hear, all ye that fear God, and I will declare what he hath done for my soul.'

2. He stirreth up others to do the like, even in this case mentioned in my text: Ps. lxvi. 5, 6, 'Come and see the works of God: he is terrible in his doings toward the children of men. He turned the sea into dry land: they went through the flood on foot; there did we rejoice in him.'

Reason 1. The reason hereof is in sight; for David saith, 'this honour is due to his name.'

We have two debts which we shall ever be paying, and yet never clear with our creditors, that is, of praise to God, of love to our neighbours. He that came of purpose into the world to pay our debts hath not wiped off this score, rather he hath set us further in debt.

1. To our brother. If God so loved us as to send his Son amongst us, we ought also to love one another so much the more.

2. To himself. David saith, 'The loving-kindness of the Lord is ever more and more towards us,' therefore, *laus ejus erit semper in ore meo,* ' his praise shall be ever in my mouth.' The coming of Christ amongst us hath made it more and more seen; for therein the bow of God was made quite naked.

Reason 2. We must do God this right, to honour him in his own works, because, if we be silent, and do not our duty herein, yet David saith, Ps. cxlv. 10, 'All thy works shall praise thee, O Lord.'

Reason 3. We see the enemies of God do not spare to do all they can to rob God of his glory; and as one saith, *Vigilat hostis, et tu dormis?* the enemy waketh, and dost thou sleep?

Some gave out amongst the Egyptians that this passage over the sea on dry land was only an advantage taken by Moses of a great ebb occasioned by an extraordinary wind, which, coming off the land at the head of the bay, made all the head of the bay dry land for many miles together; but the text is against that, for it sheweth how the waters were a wall unto them on both hands.

Again, the waters were divided by an east wind, but that wind blows not from that shore; but rather, it should have been a northerly wind. Others imputed this to Moses, as done by magical arts, which, if it had been so, no doubt but there were with Pharaoh, of his magicians, that could, in the learning of the Egyptians, have wrought with Moses hand to hand.

And surely that is the reason that there is so often mention of this wonder in Scripture, to stir up all faithful people to vindicate the honour of God against the depravers thereof.

Use 2. This admonisheth us both to the hearing and reading the story of the Bible, that we may understand what the Lord hath done in former ages. God himself made Abraham so much of his counsel for that, because he knew that Abraham would teach his children, Gen. xviii. 19. And for that the sacrament of the passover was instituted, for that it might teach their children after them, Exod. xii. 26. For this were the twelve stones set up in Gilgal, Joshua iv. 21, to teach the story of the passage over Jordan; and in the New Testament, the sacrament of the Lord's supper was instituted in remembrance of Christ till his coming. So many as would learn matter enough to fill their mouths with the praise of God, let them open the two Testaments, and read therein; let them hear and study that holy story: there is enough in it to make a man wise to salvation. For this is your wisdom and understanding, to know the Lord, and to serve him, and to honour him; for 'him that honoureth me, I will honour,' saith our God.

Use 3. This reproveth those that swallow the gracious favours of God without any relish or taste of them, and neither consider the former mercies of God nor his present blessings; that live like brute beasts, saying, This day is like yesterday, and to-morrow will be like this day, and more abundant; and such sensual and carnal sons of nature there are, that reap benefits where they never sowed prayers, and gather mercies where they never scattered supplications.

Use 4. This chideth the *Euchites* of our time, that are all for prayer, and they never give God rest from petitions, but, like the nine lepers, when they are healed, they never return any thanks.

I have ever commended to you the use of prayer; it is a special part of God's worship, and God loves both frequent and importunate petitions; but if we part praise from it, and do not join thanksgiving with supplication, we have the profit, but God hath not the honour of his own favours. All our care must not be, Who will shew us any good? we must also offer to him the sacrifices of righteousness, as well as call upon the name of the Lord; for *quid recipiam* we must have *quod retribuam*.

Use 5. Seeing God must have the glory of his own great works, we must take the pains to search after them; not only content ourselves with such as offer themselves to our consideration, but we must take delight to look them out. So David, Ps. cxi. 2–4, ' The works of the Lord are great, sought out of them that have pleasure therein. His work is honourable and glorious, and his righteousness endureth for ever. He hath made his wonderful works to be remembered.' Which shews that our praising of the name of God is no meritorious act of free will, but an officious service due to him; and it is a great injustice in you to deny it to him, for David saith, ' He is worthy to be praised.'

Use 6. This serveth for caution. It is a glory to God when we thankfully remember with praise the wonderful works that he hath done; but it is no honour to him at all when we report of him more than he hath done, and put miracles upon him that he never did.

The church of Rome hath long had a busy hand in these false ascriptions. The golden legend of worm-eaten authority amongst them, and their *Speculum Exemplorum*, set forth by John Major, a Jesuit, in *anno* 1607; and Cantipatranus, a Dominican friar's full volume of miracles, set forth *anno* 1605, tell fine tales, ridiculous even to children; yet the implicit faith of papists doth swallow all for canonical, wherein God is dishonoured with human inventions, and truth itself with lies. Their legends of their Ladies of Loretto and Hales are of the same coinage; and it is the policy of that strumpet of Rome to keep this mint always at work, to amaze the ignorant with strange wonders. But I say unto them in the words of Job, chap. xiii. 7, 'Will ye speak wickedly for God, and talk deceitfully for him?'

Gregory, their own pope, upon these words, saith, *Veritas fulciri non quærit auxilio falsitatis.* He saith that it is the trick of heretics. It is, I am sure, the practice of papists; but thou, man of God, fly these things. Truth is not honoured but with truth.

Doct. 2. We must search out and confess the true cause of all the good that God doth to us.

It is Aristotle's doctrine in his *Elenchus,** that *id quod non est causa ut causam ponere*, to make that a cause which is not, is a capacious and sophistical manner of reasoning. So the serpent over-reached Eve in paradise; for when God had given our parents there a precise law, 'Thou shalt not eat of the tree in the midst of the garden,' the true cause why God put that restraint upon them was to try their obedience to him in a small and easy precept, forbidding them a thing in itself good, to shew his reservation of his own power, to awe them. So saith Saint Gregory.† But

---

* Elenc. i. 4.   † Mor. xxxv. 10.

Satan, tempting the woman to break this law, and to cast off this light burden and easy yoke of God, suggested another cause: Gen. iii. 5, 'God doth know that in the day ye eat thereof, then your eyes shall be opened, and ye shall be as gods, knowing good and evil;' as if God had dealt too sparingly with man in the communication of his own similitude to him, and had set him that bar to keep him from attaining the perfection thereof.

So Leah deceived herself, for when God gave her Issachar, her first son, she said, Gen. xxx. 18, 'God hath given me my hire, because I have given my maiden to my husband.' Wherein she deceived herself; for by adding one wife more to the number of Jacob's wives, she did violate the state of matrimony, which in the institution was in these words, 'I will make him a help meet for him,' not helps; and so Adam understood it, for he said, Gen. ii. 24, 'A man shall forsake father and mother, and cleave to his wife' (not wives), 'and they shall be one flesh.' Which, lest the friends of polygamy might understand of many wives, Christ, citing this place, addeth by way of interpretation, 'And they twain shall be one flesh,' Mat. x. 8. So Saint Paul understood it, 'Two shall be one flesh.' So the prophet Malachi understood it, for, charging his people with this sin of breach of wedlock, he speaketh as to one man: Mal. ii. 14, 'Thou hast dealt treacherously against the wife of thy youth, yet is she thy companion, and the wife of thy covenant. And did he not make one? yet had he the excellency of spirit; and wherefore one? That he might seek a godly seed.'

So that this giving of her maid to her husband was no good service done to God, that she should expect wages; it was rather a trespass of wedlock. Howsoever, it pleased God to dispense with it in the fathers of former ages; but our rule is, *Quomodo fuit in principio?* How was it at the beginning? for we know that he who had abundance of spirit could have created many wives for Adam if he had thought it fit; and then, for the increase of the seed of man, and the speedy peopling of the world, there was more need of polygamy than was ever since.

I urge the fallacy here, *Non causa pro causa.*

So Micah, when he had made him gods, and gotten a priest into his house, flattered himself, Judges xvii. 13, 'Now I know that the Lord will do me good, seeing I have a Levite to my priest.' This was idolatry, one of the greatest provocations of God to anger that could be, yet he would flatter himself that this would turn a cause of his well-doing.

These three examples do sufficiently open our sense to perceive the cunning of this fallacious suggestion in ourselves.

The doctrine of merit which the church of Rome teacheth is a natural doctrine; as God said to Cain, 'If thou do well, shalt thou not be accepted?' It is true that God accepteth even weak services from us, but as we say, it is more of his courtesy than our deserving. If we call it wages that he giveth us in reward, we overween our own works. And this is a special sin wherewith God doth punish the sins of the ungodly in the church of Rome, the seat of antichrist, as the apostle plainly describeth it, 2 Thes. ii. 11, 'God shall send them strong delusions, that they should believe a lie.' They believe that to be the cause of their salvation that is not.

Reason. The reason of this doctrine, why we must fasten upon the true cause of God's favour to us, is, because faith, not rightly grounded, is not faith, but presumption.

True faith can find no rest but in the assurance of God's goodness to us. God doth many favours to the wicked here in this life, which he doth not for any love that he beareth to them, but for the use that he maketh of them to whip and scourge others by them; as, for example, God to Ezekiel, chap. xxix. 18–20, 'Son of man, Nebuchadrezzar king of Babel caused his army to serve a great service against Tyrus: every head was made bald, and every shoulder was peeled; yet had he no wages, nor his army, for Tyrus, for the services that he had served against it: therefore thus saith the Lord God, Behold, I will give the land of Egypt unto Nebuchadrezzar king of Babylon; and he shall take her multitude, and take her spoil, and take her prey ; and it shall be the wages for his army. Because they wrought for me, saith the Lord God.'

Here is the king of Babylon doubly rewarded, with success and victory against Tyrus, with the possession and spoil of Egypt, not for any favour that God did bear to the king of Babylon, but to punish the iniquity of Tyrus and of Egypt. Let not Nebuchadrezzar boast of the favour of the Lord, that he set him a-work and paid him his wages ; the sins of these ungodly people, not the goodness of God to the king of Babylon, did all this.

We see daily that the wicked do compass about the righteous ; the poor church of God bleedeth in many places of Christendom ; the enemy proscribeth, imprisoneth, beheadeth, hangeth, cutteth out the tongues, smiteth off the hands of God's faithful servants, and deviseth new tortures, to make death more terrible and more painful. This swelleth the enemies of God with pride, and they impute all this success against the church of God to the love of God toward them ; and the justice of their cause is maintained by the Jesuits' abetments and acclamations.

But thus did Babylon prevail against God's own Israel for a time ; the distressed part of the church, which groaneth under these burdens, doth not hang the head for this. They know that their sins have deserved these rods ; they have had the light, and have not walked worthy of that light, therefore is this evil come upon them ; yet let them take courage, and say, Ps. lii., ' Why boastest thou thyself in mischief, thou mighty man ? the goodness of God endureth continually.' There is our *Selah*, the rest of our music ; this is the joy of the church's harvest.

And great is the profit of this point.

Use 1. When we have found the true cause of God's favours to be in himself, and not in us, we may assure ourselves that his mercy endureth for ever ; for his gifts and calling are without repentance.

2. A greater comfort than this is, that godliness hath not only the promise of this life, but of the life to come also.

3. We may rise in comfort a degree higher, to assure ourselves that this favour of God will give us our fruit unto holiness, Rom. vi. 22; for these go together, God's love to us, and our comfort and hope in him, for this fruit, as the apostle joineth them: 2 Thes. ii. 16, 17, 'Now our Lord Jesus Christ himself, and God, even our Father, which hath loved us, and given us everlasting consolation, and good hope through grace, comfort your hearts, and stablish you in every good word and work.'

This blessing of the apostle doth shew, that when the love of God is settled, there followeth grace and expressure of his favour, that bringeth forth inward consolation of the spirit present, good hope for the time to come, an establishing of the heart in holiness. This I name as the highest step of our exaltation, because this repairs in us the image of God, which is his holiness, and the true children of God do value this above their eternal life.

For let us see wherein the weight of the blessing and cursing of sheep and goats doth lie. It is not the gift of eternal life that is our happiness in heaven; but as David saith, 'in his favour is life.' If a damned soul should be admitted to the fruition of all the pleasures of eternal life, without the favour of God, heaven would be hell to him. It is not the dark and horrid house of woe that maketh a soul miserable in hell, but God's displeasure, *ite maledicti*. If an elect soul could be cast thither, and retain the favour of God, hell would be an heaven to him, and his joy could not all the devils of hell take from him, his night would be turned into day.

The angels sinned in heaven, and in the place of joy lost God's favour.

The soul of the Son of God was in hell, and hell was an heaven to it, because God was with him in the valley of the shadow of death, and left not his soul in hell; he took him from the nethermost hell.

Doct. 3. The truth of God is a good ground.

For faith gathered from God's oath to the tribes, even his word. He addeth *Selah*, to shew that we may safely rest there.

The reason is, because the word of God is a sure word, and those things wherein men fail are not incident to him.

1. Whereas men do promise or swear rashly, and without consideration, as David did, when he swore that he would not leave one of the house of Nabal to make water against a wall, God cannot fail that way, because he doth all things with stable truth, and according to the counsel of his will.

2. Men do sometimes vow and swear things utterly unlawful and most wicked, as Herod did to Herodias's daughter, to give her whatsoever she demanded of him, which included the life of John Baptist.

So there were many that swore they would neither eat nor drink till they had killed Paul. Our God cannot fail so far, he loveth righteousness, neither shall any evil dwell with him.

3. Whereas many promise and swear what they mean not to perform, as Jacob's sons in the covenant that they made of confederacy with Hamor the son of Shechem, the apostle saith, 'Our God cannot lie.'

4. Whereas many, amongst men, do swear and promise that which they are never able to perform, therein like the devil, who said to Christ, *Omnia hæc tibi dabo*, all these will I give thee, God herein cannot fail, for he is omnipotent, and 'he doth whatsoever he will in heaven and earth,' *et in abyssis*.

So then, if the word of God be gone out of his mouth, we may build faith upon it, for heaven and earth may and shall pass away, so shall not one jot of the word of God.

5. Times may change with men, and he that was rich and able to make good his word, may suddenly be poor, and break, and fail; but God is without variableness or shadow of alteration, all times are in his hand and power.

Use 1. This serveth for confirmation of faith; for such use the apostle doth make of it, who, speaking of the decree and oath of God, saith, Heb. vi. 18, 'That by two immutable things, in which it was impossible for God to lie, we might have a strong consolation, who have fled for refuge to lay hold upon the hope set before us.' By this faith the just liveth in Babylon, and in the weakness of their temporal estate they have ἰσχυρὰν παράκλησιν, and thus they lay hand upon the hope set before them in the word.

Jonah saith, 'They that follow lying vanities do forsake their own mercy.' *Vana salus hominis*, 'vain is the help of man.' They that go down to Egypt for help have their woe threatened. An horse is but a vain thing to help a man. Princes are the sons of men, there is no help in them. The word of God faileth none.

At that word, Abraham will leave his own country and go he cares not, he inquires not, whither. At that word Abraham will go three days' journey to kill Isaac with his own hands, and will never dispute how the promise of God shall be performed, that 'in Isaac his seed should be blessed.'

At that word Peter will let fall his net, against all rules of fishing, and will forsake the ship to come to Christ upon the sea, by the warrant of that word.

The promises of God to his church, and his threatenings of sin recorded in the living book of his word, are not antiquate; no age shall ever superannuate them, or put them out of full force and virtue.

What if good persons and good causes do suffer oppression? The poet is a divine in that case,

> Informes hiemes reducit
> Jupiter; idem
> Summovet. Non si male nunc, et olim
> Sic erit.

After foul weather comes fair; though it be ill with us now, it will not be always.

What if enemies of religion and moths of commonwealth do flourish and prosper, and have all things at will, let it not trouble David and Job; both of them saw as fair a sunshine shut up in a dark cloud, and a world of foul weather following.

Use 2. This tenderness in God of his word and oath, doth serve for example to teach us to make conscience of our promises and oaths; and we may urge the argument as the apostle doth, 'If God so loved us, we ought also to love one another.' So, if God be careful to keep his promise and oath with us, we ought also to do the like with our brethren.

Here arise two queries:
1. Whether it be lawful to swear at all?
2. Whether all oaths must be kept?

1. *An liceat jurare,* is it lawful to swear?

An oath is a calling of God to witness in such things as cannot otherwise be assured, and it is of two sorts.

1. Assertory, when we do call God to witness against our souls, if we affirm not the truth. In this case the awe of God's majesty is thought to be such a rule of the conscience, that no man will dare to violate the religion of an oath.

2. Promissory; when we do engage the honour of God for the truth of our purpose, to perform what we promise, and we cast ourselves upon his just judgment if we be either deceitful in our promise or unfaithful in our performance.

This may answer the first query, for this doth declare that an oath doth serve,
1. For the glory of God;
2. For the good of our brethren.

1. The glory of God; for it sheweth him,
(1.) To be present amongst us and privy to our ways;
(2.) To be a God of truth;
(3.) To be a God of justice, to punish unfaithfulness.

2. It sheweth that we by sin have lost our credit, and therefore God doth engage himself for such as swear aright.

2 It serveth for the good of our brethren, for it is the end of all strife, Heb. v. 19.

I will not enter into the lists with the Anabaptists, to confute their weak arguments against the lawfulness of an oath; you hear it warranted by reason, and examples grow thick in the book of God to justify it.

2. *Query,* Whether every oath be to be kept?

To that we answer in a word: Every lawful oath is to be kept, so is every lawful promise: Num. xxx. 3, ' If a man vow a vow unto the Lord, or swear an oath to bind his soul with a bond, he shall not profane his word; he shall do according to all that proceedeth out of his mouth.' Every oath and every promise engageth our faith; that is our fidelity, and so it is a bond upon our souls; and though it be to our hindrance, we must not break. Remember how the breach of the oath of the Lord, made by Joshua and the elders of the Gibeonites, smarted in the house of Saul. Zedekiah had engaged himself by oath to Nebuchadnezzar, an heathen king, and brake, and rebelled against him. Indeed, it was before the doctrine of Rome was a-foot : *fides non est servanda cum hæreticis*, no faith to be kept with heretics. But hear the prophet : Ezek. xvii. 15, ' Shall he escape that doth such things ? or shall he break the covenant and be delivered ?' And after, saith God, ver. 19, ' As I live, surely mine oath that he hath despised, and my covenant that he hath broken, even it will I recompense upon his own head.' For he said, ver. 18, ' He despised the oath by breaking the covenant, when, lo, he had given his hand.' A lawful promise and oath hath three notes to justify it, Jer. iv. 2, truth, righteousness, judgment.

1. In truth, the heart joining with the author.

2. In righteousness, seeking *Deo et proximo servire*, serve God and our neighbour.

3. In judgment : it is deliberation and advice.

Doct. 4. God declareth his power sometimes openly to the comfort of his church, and the terror of the enemies thereof, gathered from these words, ' Thy bow was quite naked ;' for, as before, there was *absconsio roboris*, the hiding of his strength, when God revealed himself to his church only upon mount Sinai, so there was now *revelatio roboris*, a revealing of his strength, when he had made his bow quite naked.

Reason 1. For the settling of his church in obedience to him. So saith the psalmist, after commemoration of the wonder, Ps. cv. 45, all works of God done for Israel, ' That they might keep his statutes and observe his laws.'

Reason 2. For the glory of his name, that he might fill the mouths of the faithful with his praise ; and this effect it wrought with Israel a while, for when God had done great things for them, Ps. cvi. 12, ' then they sang his praise.'

Reason 3. For the credit of his word, that they might settle their faith in his promises. So it is there said, ' Then they belived his word.'

Reason 4. To convince the ingratitude of men, if they, notwithstanding the manifestation of his power to them, do start aside, and rebel against him. So doth the psalmist tax them : where, repeating the manifest and naked bow of God revealed to them, it is the burden of his song : Ps. lxxviii. 17, ' Yet they sinned more against God by provoking the Most High in the wilderness.' He repeateth more of his great works, and addeth, ver. 32, ' For all this they sinned still, and believed not, for all his wondrous works.' He repeateth more, and saith, ver. 56, ' Yet they tempted and provoked the most high God, and kept not his testimony,' &c.

Reason 5. To instruct posterity that should succeed them : Ps. lxxviii. 6, 7, ' That the generation to come might know them, even the children that should be born, who should arise and declare them to their children ; that they might set their hope in God, and not forget the works of God, but keep his commandments.' This is the way, to keep the bow of God still naked, that all the ends of the world may see the salvation of our God.

God layeth his bow quite naked in the sight of the world, that the Egyptians may see that God fighteth for Israel against them, and may fly from them ; that the world may see that all their consultations against the church shall fail of success, and it will turn to bitterness in the latter end.

Use. You may easily discern how all this is directed to our instruction.

1. To awake us to a consideration of the revealed power of God ; for if God shew it, it is that we may see it. It was the cause of Israel's so many rebellions.

For, whereas God did so great things for them, Ps. lxxviii. 7, ' that they might not forget his works,' ' they forgat his works, and wonders that he hath shewed them ;' and that made them children of disobedience.

2. To direct to the right use of this mercy of God, which is, as you have heard,

(1.) In respect of God, to give him due praise, that he may have the honour due to his name.

(2.) In respect of ourselves, to confirm our hope and faith in his word, and in the arm of his strength, believing that bow, and the whole quiver of arrows belonging to it, is on our side, and we need not fear what man or devil can do against us.

(3.) In respect of this life, that we pass the time of our dwelling here in fear, living in the obedience and service of this Almighty Maker and preserver of men, by keeping his statutes, &c.

(4.) In respect of posterity, that we leave them our good example, and the light of our knowledge to instruct them in the wonderful works of God, that generation may praise him to generation, and declare his power.

(5.) In respect of our enemies, that they may see and know whom we have trusted, and may know that our help is in the name of the Lord, who hath made heaven and earth; so that we shall not need to fear their bow, nor their arrows upon the string ready to go off against us; there is a bow on our side, and an arm to wield it.

Ver. 10. *The mountains saw thee, and they trembled; the overflowing of the water passed by: the deep uttered his voice, and lift up his hands on high.*

These words have reference to the former wonders of God's works, in which the Holy Ghost poetically and rhetorically doth give life to things inanimate, to express their yielding and giving way to God's extraordinary operations; some understanding that, for such impression did the power of God make in the everlasting mountains, as he calleth them before, ver. 6, and in the perpetual hills, that they give way to his people as if they had seen God himself, and that the fear of God had been upon them to make them tremble.

The like poetical strain we have in the psalmist:

Ps. cxiv. 6, 'What ailed ye, mountains, that ye skipped like rams; and ye little hills, like young sheep?' And the words of David do seem to guide my judgment, to expound this place, not of the mountains upon the dry land, but with reference to the miracle of the passage of the children of Israel over Jordan, in which God by his power did make the waters of the river rise up like mountains to stop their way, and yet not to suffer them to drown the neighbouring continent; and this was effected with an extraordinary motion of the waters, leaping and skipping like sheep. Therefore, here is added, the overflowing of the waters passed by; that is, it did not overflow the way of the Israelites, but bestowed itself in the raising up of the mountains of water. 'The deep uttered his voice;' he meaneth the noise of the waters, running and swelling in heaps: 'And lift up his hands on high;' for this rising of the waters into such huge hills, did give testimony of their yielding to the almighty power of God in his working, though contrary to their nature.

This exposition of these words I embrace, as most consonant to the web of the Scripture; yet I will not conceal from you, that some refer this trembling of the mountains, and this noise of the waters, figuratively, to the trembling of the kings in Canaan, and the noise of the people, afraid, and melting in their hearts at the strange passage of Israel through the Red Sea first, and now at last through Jordan. Whom I dare not follow, holding it dangerous to admit more figures than need, when some more literal sense may be proper.

Others do refer this to the trembling of mount Sinai, when God appeared to the people in the way; of which Moses saith, Exod. xix. 18, 'And mount Sinai was altogether on a smoke, because the Lord descended upon it in fire; and the smoke thereof ascended as the smoke of a furnace, and the whole mount quaked greatly.' But this connection of the trembling of the mountains with the noise of the waters, doth make it probable to me that it is one and the same miracle.

Magister Historiæ telleth of a mountain in the land

of Canaan, near to the river of Arnon, which suffered a violent earthquake at the time of the entering of Israel into Canaan; but that is an apocryphal relation, and the silence of the story doth make it questionable whether any such thing were done.

The figurative and poetical form of speech here used is in sight.

1. The heaps of waters swelling to a very great height are called mountains.

2. Here is attributed to them human sense, motions, and affections, as seeing, trembling, uttering of a voice, and lifting up of hands.

These things are familiar and frequent all the Scripture through, especially in the poetical part thereof, as I have shewed.

Doct. The senseless and lifeless creatures are subject to the will of God, and to serve him.

For that which the heathen do call *nature* in the creatures, is in religion the constant order which God hath established in the universal machine and frame of the world, and in every particular member and part thereof, serving God's general providence. That which we call miraculous and extraordinary, is the particular will of God upon occasion, declared out of his singular and special providence.

In both these, all creatures whatsoever do so serve him, as if they knew what they did. The centurion did not keep his servants in better awe, and had them not so ready at his command, as God hath his creatures; their nature is subject to rule, and that so as fire shall burn and not consume, as in the bush; waters shall stand in heaps, as in the passage through the Red Sea, and here in my text, in the river of Jordan.

Water shall not put out fire; the hail, as watery substance, shall mingle with fire in the same shower; and Elijah shall call for fire that shall lick up the water, and dry the ditches filled to the brim.

Reason. The reason hereof is, because there is nothing in the world that hath any being, but it had beginning from him who only is of himself, and therefore called *Jehovah*, and he never gave being to anything but for use; he hath made nothing idle and unprofitable, for in wisdom he made all things, and that use is directed by the Creator. And therefore, as it is said of him, that he had made the heaven and the earth, by Moses, so Melchisedec calleth him 'the high possessor of heaven and earth,' as the prophet David saith, *Fecit quicquid voluit in cœlo et in terra, et in omnibus abyssis.*

The right of creation, without which nothing had any being; the right of protection, which keepeth all things in being, doth put all things in subjection under his feet. His will is their nature, and it is all one to the inanimate creature to serve his true will in an ordinary and in a miraculous way, for his will is the soul that animateth them, and maketh them active; and he could have as easily let the sea keep his course, and let the river of Jordan run on, and have brought his people over upon the face of the waters, as Christ and Peter walked, as he made them a passage through.

This ready obsequence of the inanimate creature to the will of God, doth upbraid man, whom God made for himself, and his special honour, with much unworthiness; for things without life owe less to God for creation than things animate, much less than man, to whom God gave a living soul, made in the image of God; and having but one law of restraint put upon him, broke it, and brought a pollution of himself, which, like the leprosy of Gehazi, runneth in all his posterity.

It is our shame that all things else do serve him; only men, and devils, the corrupters of men, stand out and rebel. And this maketh God cry, Isa. i. 2, 'Hear, O heavens; and hearken, O earth: I have nourished and brought up children, and they have rebelled against me.' Why doth God make his complaint to the heavens, and to the earth, or why doth he call them to witness against Israel, his people, but to signify that creatures without life shall condemn the disobedience of men, even of Israel, the people that God hath chosen to himself?

And truly, when we do look out of ourselves upon these things, as David saith: Ps. viii. 3, 'When we consider the heavens, the work of thy fingers, the sun and the moon, which, &c: what is man, that thou art so mindful of him?'

There be two things that may move:

1. What is man, that such excellent creatures should be made for him?

2. What is man, that, beholding the heavens which do serve him, and living upon the earth that is obedient to him, and doth his will, that God should be mindful of man, who, of all the works of his hands that enjoy his favours, doth serve him worst of all?

Do not we thank God for it, and take it for a high favour, that he hath made us men, and did not make us stones or plants, worms or flies, serpents or toads, or any other kind of hateful or hurtful creature? But yet, if we live not to serve him, and to do his will, our condition had been much more happy to have been the worst of these than to have been made men and women.

I will not go from the example in my text to teach you what we are, for by original generation we run like Jordan in a full and swift current, into the great and wide sea of the world, and there we lose ourselves in those salt waters. Sometimes, as Jordan in harvest times, that is, in times of our plenty and fulness, and when we have ease, and whatsoever our heart desireth, we do overflow our banks, and exceed all measure. But when the priests of the Lord do bring the ark of God into us; that is, when we come to have a sense and a feeling of religion, and the fear of God; then do we recoil and strive against nature, and overcome nature, and we learn to do the good that we would not do. For truly religion doth carry us against wind and tide; religion leads us all up hill, and he that will follow Christ must deny himself. So St Paul doth: *Vero* ego, et non amplius ego, sed vivit in me Christus,* 'I live; yet not I, but Christ in me.'

Observe the creature here, and you shall see that whatsoever is ingredient in perfect obedience, is ascribed to this river of Jordan; for,

---

* Qu. '*vivo*'?—ED.

1. It was *congrua*, for it was to God; they were his priests, and they did carry his ark upon their shoulders, and they had his warrant for it.

2. It was *prompta*, ready. No sooner did the soles of the feet of the priests touch the waters, but they fled back; no sooner were they all over, and the stones carried out of the river to shore, but they returned again to their course.

Such let our obedience be; and this is acceptable in the sight of God. This lecture is read to us in heaven, in earth, in the sea. In heaven, we have the example of angels, who are called *angeli facientes voluntatem ejus*. In earth, we have the examples of all creatures, who in their several kinds do his will, according to the general law of creation, and the particular law of special dispensation. In the sea, the winds and sea obey him.

Use 2. This serveth to teach us to pass the time of our dwelling here in fear, because we see the omnipotent hand of God in the government of the world, that we may say, Jer. xxxii. 17, 'Ah, Lord God, thou hast made the heaven and the earth by thy great power and stretched-out arm, and there is nothing too hard for thee;' and he remembereth the wonders of this deliverance out of Egypt, and saith, ver. 20, 'Thou hast made thee a name.' This filleth all that think of it with a reverent fear of God's name; it exalteth him in the congregation of the just, and maketh him say, *Domine, quis similis tibi?* 'Lord, who is like thee?'

Use 3. This serveth to convince the enemies of God, who make nature sit in the place of God, and do give the rule of all things to nature; for what have they to say for themselves in these great examples? Could nature cut a passage of dry land through the Red Sea? Could nature draw waters out of an hard rock, and teach it to follow Israel wheresoever they went; to rest when they rested, to run when they removed? Could nature keep their clothes on their backs, their shoes on their feet from wearing, for forty years? Did nature rain manna, and bring in the quails, and feed the people till they came to the corn of Canaan? Did nature make these mountains, and high piles of waters, in the river of Jordan? Is not the extraordinary hand of God in all these?

Use 4. This also serveth for increase of our faith; for we have good cause to cast our care, and fasten our trust upon him, who not only worketh by means, but without them, yea, and against them. The hardest lesson in religion is, to trust God when we see no means of help; as Abraham did when he was commanded to kill the son of the promise. The very captivity of the church hath had that comfort in the greatest terror thereof; so the psalmist saith,

1. That God suffered no man to do them wrong, but reproved even kings for their sakes.

2. That he made them that led them away captive to pity them, and to minister to their necessities: they became rather nurses than their jailors. Upon comfort of which confidence, Job protested, chap. xiii. 15, that, 'Though he kill me, yet will I trust in him.'

Use 5. This assureth to us all the promises of God, which the apostle distributeth into these two sorts:

The promises of this life.

And of the life that is to come.

And this made Abraham, when God promised him seed, Rom. iv. 19, 20, &c., 'not to consider his own body was now dead, nor the deadness of Sarah's womb: he staggered not at the promise through unbelief; but was strong in faith, giving glory to God; and being fully persuaded, that what he had promised, he was able also to perform. And therefore it was imputed unto him for righteousness.' And he addeth, 'Now, it was not written for his sake alone, that it was imputed to him; but for us also, to whom it shall be imputed, if we believe.'

We see some parts of the Christian church now in great extremity, and no way in sight open for their escape out of great misery: the Bohemian protestants put to cruel deaths; the French protestants have the sword drawn against them, and the arrows upon the string to shoot at them; the Palatinate under proscription, the prince thereof in exile. 'Our help is in the name of the Lord.' All these will faint, except they believe verily to see the goodness of God in the land of the living. Sweet and full of comfort is the example of God's people, to whom it was promised, even when they were in captivity in Babylon, they had hung up their harps upon the willows, and sat weeping by the rivers of waters : Zech. viii. 3, 'Thus saith the Lord, I am returned unto Zion, and will dwell in the midst of Jerusalem : and Jerusalem shall be called, A city of truth ; and the mountain of the Lord of hosts, The holy mountain. Thus saith the Lord of hosts, There shall yet old men and old women dwell in the streets of Jerusalem, and every man with his staff in his hand for very age. And the streets of the city shall be full of boys and girls playing in the streets of it. Thus saith the Lord of hosts, If it be marvellous in the eyes of the remnant of this people in these days, should it also be marvellous in mine eyes ? saith the Lord of hosts. I will save my people from the east, and from the west country.'

This is the help in trouble, ready to be found; let us awake this help with the loud voice of our importunate supplications, saying, ' O Lord, help now ; O Lord, now give prosperity.' Let us give him no rest till he hath bowed the heavens, and is come down to visit the distresses of his faithful servants.

Our Saviour comforteth us well, saying, ' My Father worketh as yet, and I work ;' and if our labour, which is *opus in Domino*, a work *in* the Lord, be not in vain, his labour, which is *opus Domini*, a work *of* the Lord, will prosper in his hand.

He is as strong in the river of Rhine as he was in Jordan ; and his church is as dear to him now as ever it was; and he is as diligent in making inquisition for blood, and as attentive to the complaints of the oppressed, as he was.

Ver. 11–14. *The sun and moon stood still in their habitation : at the light of thine arrows they went, at the shining of thy glittering spears. Thou didst march through the land in indignation, thou didst thrash the heathen in anger. Thou wentest forth for the salvation of thy people, even for salvation with thine anointed ; thou woundest the head out of the house of the wicked, by discovering the foundation to the neck. Selah. Thou doest strike through with his staves the head of his villages; they that came out as a whirlwind to scatter me: their rejoicing was as to devour the poor secretly.*

I read all this together, because I conceive it hath reference to one story, and that is recorded in the book of Joshua, chap. x.

For after Israel came into the land of Canaan, and had destroyed Jericho, and the city of Ai, the Gibeonites, terrified with this news, craftily pretending themselves to be a people dwelling in a far country, and for the name of God's sake, whose wonderful works they had heard of, they desired to make a league with Joshua. Joshua and the elders were deceived, and confirmed a league with them by oath. But after the fraud was detected, Israel made the Gibeonites serve them; but they were under the protection of Israel. This league of Gibeon with Joshua did much trouble the neigbouring kings, for they feared Gibeon, being a strong city; therefore five kings do make war against Gibeon, to smite it. The Gibeonites send to Joshua for succours; Joshua, according to his oath of confederacy with them, came from Gilgal, he, and all the people of war with him, and all the mighty men of valour; he gave the assault to the five kings and their army; he discomfited them, and made them fly: ver. 11–14, 'Then the Lord rained stones from heaven upon them: there were more that died with the hail-stones than they whom the children of Israel slew with the sword. Then spake Joshua to the Lord, in the day when the Lord delivered up the Amorites before the children of Israel, Sun, stand thou still upon Gibeon; and thou, Moon, in the valley of Ajalon. And the sun stood still, and the moon stayed until the people had avenged themselves upon their enemies. Is not this written in the book of Jasher? So the sun stood still in the midst of heaven, and hasted not to go down about a whole day. And there was no day like that, before it, nor after it, that the Lord hearkened unto the voice of a man: for the Lord fought for Israel.'

This is the wonder that Habakkuk our prophet doth

here commemorate, a miracle yet fresh in the memory of the church; yet by computation of times, from the time of Joshua, when this was done, to this time of Habakkuk, when this is remembered, were past more than seven hundred years.

Habakkuk doth well to remember this, for of all miracles that God wrought for Israel, this was the greatest: here heaven fought against earth; the sun and moon stood still to give light to the battle, and the faithful witnesses of heaven, so the sun is called, stayed his course to bear witness how God fought for Israel.

We may truly say to Israel, *Tibi militat æther*. Observe the words of the prophet, how well they follow the history in Joshua. Habakkuk saith, 'The sun and moon stood still in their habitation;' they stood in their several sphere wherein they move, for these be their habitations. And note that they both stood still, sun and moon; for the moon, borrowing all her light of the sun, had she kept her course while the sun had stood still the length of a day, there had been great irregularity of motion in these celestial bodies, from the constant order set them by their Maker in their creation.

Observe also that he doth not say the earth stood still, but the sun. It had been, as some said, the earth and the moon stood still as the sun and the moon; and our understanding would have as soon apprehended, if that new astronomy had been then revealed, which some of our empirics and journeymen in that excellent science of astronomy have of late revived in their almanacs, telling the world that they have long been in a wrong belief, that the sun moveth, and the earth is fixed; for they believe that the sun is fixed, and the earth is moved. And to evade the clear evidence of this text, which tells it for a wonder that the sun stood still, they say this is spoken to our capacity; because to our sight it so seemeth that the sun moveth and the earth is fixed, but indeed it is otherwise. Our capacity, I think, hath much wrong done in this; for if the word of God hath told us that God had created the sun to stand still and the earth to move, it is more likely that we should have taken his word for it, and have believed it as it is, as well as now we believe it, as it appears.

We are neither incapable nor incredulous, but that many against the letter of Scripture have written, and made more believe, that the sun stands still from the creation. The common defence of this opinion, grounded upon God's application of himself to human capacity, doth make figures in story where is no need, and maketh David a man of small judgment in the knowledge of the sun, who saith that 'God hath set a tabernacle for the sun in the heavens' (called here an habitation), 'which is a bridegroom coming out of his chamber, and rejoiceth as a strong man to run his race. His going forth is from the end of the heaven, and his circuit unto the ends of it.' Doth not this prophet speak of the glory of God, declared in the motion, not the station, of the sun? or is the glory of God shewed in our opinion of the sun's motion, not in the truth thereof?

Greater secrets than this are revealed in holy Scripture, which are against the vouchy of the outward sense or the rational discourse of man, and no doubt but if the sun had stood still, and the earth that we live upon had moved, when this miracle was by the Spirit of truth recorded, it had been so set down to us, as followeth:

At the light of thine arrows they went, at the shining of thy glittering spear. The meaning I conceive to be this, that the sun and moon did not now keep their ordinary motion appointed in their creation, but by a miraculous dispensation they attended the arrows of God, and his spears; for God declared himself in this war to be the God of Israel. By shining arrows and glittering spears, he meaneth not only the arms of Israel his people, but the apparent demonstration of his own miraculous and extraordinary power declared in this war. For you heard in the story that God 'cast down great stones from heaven upon them, which slew more than Israel's sword did.'

These were arrows of God; and his spears with which he fought for Israel, they are called bright and glistering, both,

1. Because the sun shining upon these great hailstones reflected a dazzling light from them, as experi-

ence telleth us, both in snow, ice, hailstones, and all watery bodies;

2. And because in this judgment there was so manifest appearance of the immediate hand of God in this war.

Thus Mr Calvin doth understand these words, and saith, *Sol retentus est, ut daret locum sagittis et hastæ Dei.* Only he seemeth to be somewhat too strict when he saith, *Per sagittas et hastam nihil aliud intelligit, quam arma populi Dei.* Yes, sure he meaneth his own weapons too, with which he fought from heaven, and those rather as the more shining and glittering. Montanus also upon these words saith, *Solem et lunam cursus suos ad commoditatem exercitus sacri temperasse.* Junius also and Beza do conceive that these hailstones fell not without thunder and lightning, which are the terrors of heaven and the voice of God. It followeth,

Thou didst march through the land in indignation, thou didst thresh the heathen in anger. This, as I conceive, hath reference to the following victories, by which all the land of Canaan was subdued to Israel; for the church here confesseth, that as God by deed of gift had long before assured this promised land of the heathen to his Israel, so he gave them a full possession thereof by marching through the land, and by threshing the inhabitants thereof.

Thus the church confesseth, Ps. xliv. 2, 'We have heard with our ears, O God, our fathers have told us, what work thou didst in their days, in the time of old. How thou didst drive out the heathen with thy hand, and plantedst them in; how thou didst afflict the people, and cast them out: for they gat not the land in possession by their own sword, neither did their own arm save them, but thy right hand and thine arm, and the light of thy countenance, because thou hadst a favour unto them.' This phrase of marching through the land doth express God in arms for Israel. But the other phrase of *threshing* the heathen doth imply victory, and full power over them, even to the stripping them out of all.

Thou wentest forth for the salvation of thy people, even for salvation with thine anointed. The cause why God put himself into this quarrel was the preservation of his people, where Israel is twice called the people of God, which must be understood of the adoption of grace; for by right of creation, all people of the world are God's people. This was Israel's glory, and it was also their safety, that they were God's people; and how they came to be so, Moses will tell: Deut. vii. 7, 8, 'The Lord did not set his love upon you, nor choose you, because ye were more in number than any people (for ye were the fewest of all people); but because the Lord loved you, and because he would keep the oath that he had sworn unto your fathers;' that is, he loved you because he loved you. But he addeth, 'Thou wentest forth with thine anointed;' which Mr Beza doth understand of David, and so maketh a long stride, from the conquest of Canaan to the reign of David, and from these victories to David's victories, many, many years after. And Tremellius and Junius do so apply the text. Mr Calvin led them all into this exposition.

Others conceive that the former commemoration is continued, and they that are before called God's people are here called God's anointed; for wheresoever there is election, there is unction; and we may say of Israel, that God anointed them with the oil of gladness above all their fellow nations; for David saith, *Non fecit taliter.* I am sure the Seventy read and understand the text thus; for they read that God went forth σῶσαι τοῦς Χριστοῦς αὐτοῦ. The Latin reading is *Cum Christo tuo;* and the original Hebrew is משיחך his Messiah, which moveth me to refer this to Christ, who was the bond of that love which knit God so to Israel, for whose sake God was so favourable to Israel.

Master Calvin doth confess that this hath reference to Christ, and includeth all the favours of God declared to Israel from their coming out of Egypt to the last mercy shewed to them, to have come to them *non nisi interposito mediatore,* not without a mediator. But he addeth that the promise of Christ did more clearly appear, and was more manifestly revealed, in the reign of David than before, which might give comfort to the church in distress. That makes Master Calvin go so low as David's reign, to apply these words.

But the next words shew that the former history of
the wars of Israel, to settle their possession in Canaan,
and not yet at an end. So then, I understand that
God went forth with his Anointed, that is, with Jesus
Christ, to save his people; and there is the life blood
of all the comfort in this whole psalm of the church;
and by this faith, by faith in this Messiah, the just
shall live. It followeth,

Thou woundest the head out of the house of the wicked.

By the house of the wicked, the land of Canaan is
here meant; and by the head that God wounded,
either the wisdom and policy, or the sovereignty and
power of the land is meant: for none of the kings of
the land could stand before Israel, so that the very
head of the house was wounded.

By discovering the foundation to the neck. This was
the manner of God's working against the head of the
house of the wicked, by making the foundation naked;
that is, digging up the very roots thereof, by an utter
extirpation of the inhabitants of this land.

It was Edom's cry against Jerusalem, Ps. cxxxvii.
7, 'Raze it, raze it;' the margin, 'make bare even
the foundation thereof;' as before you heard out of
Psalm xliv., 'Thou hast cast out the nations, and
placed them in.' It followeth,

*Thou didst strike through with his staves the head of
the villages;* that is, thou didst overthrow the inhabitants of the land with their own staves. As the poet
saith,

   Suis et ipsa Roma viribus ruit.

He declareth here the extent of the victory, not only
to their walled towns and defenced cities, but even to
the villages and hamlets of the land; so that no part
or corner of the land escaped the hand of God, or the
possession of Israel; but God, who promised them
that land, gave it them, and gave it all into their
hands.

This, as it hath a general extent to the whole story
of Israel's conquests, so it may have a more particular
reference to the story of that war made in the behalf
of the Gibeonites, where the five kings that made war
against Gibeon hid themselves for safety in a cave at

Makkedah; and that cave, chosen for safety, proved a prison for their forthcoming, and Joshua sent men to roll great stones to stop the mouth of the cave till he had finished the war, and then he brought them forth and slew them, and buried them in that cave, Joshua x. 16. Thus the head of the villages were beaten with their own staves, and that cave which the kings chose for their safety was first made the trap to catch them, then the prison to hold them fast, and at last the sepulchre to bury them.

Yet more particular reference may it have to the conquest of the Midianites, Judges vii.; for in that battle the Lord declared his strength for Israel marvellously, for he said to Gideon their captain, 'The people that are with thee are too many for me to give the Midianites into their hands, lest Israel vaunt themselves and say, Mine own hand hath saved me.' In conclusion, God would have no more to go up against Midian but three hundred men. Now, the army of the Midianites was great, as appeareth in the former chapter, ver. 33, 'Then all the Midianites, and the Amalekites, and the children of the east together.' Yet God would have no more to go against Midian but three hundred men against this great army, of whom he saith before, Judges vi. 5, that 'they came as grasshoppers for multitude, for both they and their camels were without number.' And they had much vexed and impoverished Israel, as the story saith. But Israel had the victory by those three hundred men, who, being divided into three companies, in the beginning of the middle watch of the night, when the sign was given by Gideon, every man brake a pitcher of earth that was in his hand, and held their lamps in their left hands, and their trumpets in their right hands to sound withal, and cried, 'The sword of the Lord and of Gideon; and they stood every man in his place. And the Lord set every man's sword against his fellow throughout all the host.' Here it is plain how God beat them with their own staves, and slew them with their own swords. And of them we may well understand that which followeth, 'They that came out as a whirlwind to scatter me, their rejoicing was to devour the poor secretly;' for the Midianites, by many direptions, had made them poor, and by spoiling the increase of the earth almost starved them, and now they came as a whirlwind in an army to destroy them.

Their secret coming to devour the poor, it is well expressed in the story: Judges vi. 3, 4, 'And so it was, when Israel had sown, that the Midianites came up, and the Amalekites, and the children of the east, even they came up against them; and they encamped against them, and destroyed the increase of the earth, till thou come unto Gaza; and left no sustenance, neither sheep, nor ox, nor ass.' Here they assaulted them secretly by sudden incursions upon them, and they came out as a whirlwind by sudden violence, and they made them poor.

The words thus expounded, we may in this part of the section consider:

1. The miracle of the station of the sun and moon.
2. The victory that followed.
3. The conquest of Midian.

(1.) Of the miracle of the station of the sun and moon.

Doct. 1. This example of the station of the sun and moon, as attending upon the wars of the Lord, doth further confirm the former doctrine delivered out of the verse going before, that the inanimate creatures do serve the Lord, and the will of God is their only nature, whether he guide them by his ordinary providence, or by his special dispensation of extraordinary power.

It teacheth that God is above all second causes, so that his revealed determination of means for his operations do not bind him, but his *non obstante* often intercurreth by virtue of his prerogative.

Reason 1. To express him absolute Lord of all, ruling all things by the word of his power, that he may be both trusted and feared above all.

Reason 2. To divert us from the overweening of our fellow-creatures; for many nations, having observed the good that the sun doth on earth, have worshipped the sun, and some lunatics have as wisely worshipped the moon; others have adored some special stars as the ascendants in their nativities. The Egyptians, in respect, as is thought, of the great

profit that came of kine, did worship a living bullock
or calf, and of them the Israelites learned that idolatry. Herodotus tells* how Cambyses, coming with
his conquering forces into Egypt, saw the Egyptians
worshipping their calf; he drew his sword, and cut
him on the thigh, that he bled exceedingly, and
shortly after died. Cambyses, seeing this, cried out
in scorn of the Egyptians, *O capita nequam hujusmodi
dii existunt, carne et sanguine præditi, et ferrum sentientes? dignus nimirum Ægyptiis hic deus!*

Thus came into the church the worship of angels,
and the mother of our Lord, and saints, and it is because they were benefactors to the church. And
after for their sakes their images were worshipped, as
at this day in the church of Rome.

To divert us from this superstition and idolatry,
and to teach us to know our fellow-creatures, God
doth alter sometimes the established order of his government, and saith, as Christ to his disciples, 'Are
these the things you look upon?'

Surely the sun, of all things, is that God hath made
for the use and service of God,† as the most glorious,
the most comfortable, in respect of light, which it
giveth us from its own body, and which it bendeth‡
to the moon and stars, and in respect of its influence, so that, as Ambrose calleth it, *ornamentum cœli*,
the ornament of heaven, and *oculum mundi*, the eye
of the world, others have called it *animam mundi*, the
soul of the world, as the quickener of all living things.
Three most memorable evidences of God's power in
the sun are past: this of the standing of it for the
space of a whole day, the going back of the shadow
upon the dial of Ahaz in the days of Hezekiah ten
degrees, 2 Kings xx. 11, and the miraculous eclipse
at the death of Christ. And Christ, foretelling the
end of the world, saith, Mat. xxiv. 29, that 'the sun
shall be darkened, and the moon shall not give her
light.'

St Augustine§ proves the divinity from these things
which we call portentous, and he blameth the mathematicians for affirming those extraordinary effects
in natural bodies, celestial or terrestrial, to be *contra*

---

* Thal. lxxvi.
† Qu. 'man'?—Ed.
‡ Qu. 'lendeth'?—Ed.
§ De Civit. ii. 8.

naturam, against nature, *quomodo est enim contra naturam, quod Dei fit voluntate, cum voluntas tanti Creatoris, creaturæ natura sit? Portentum enim fit non contra naturam, sed contra quam nota est natura.*

Reason 3. This station of the sun and moon at this time doth serve to justify the lawfulness of a just war, for they attended the arrows and the spear of God. This was a just war, for,

1. It had a warrant from God, to possess God's Israel of their own land which God had given them. This is the warrant of policy.

2. It was against idolaters, whom they were sent to destroy, the warrant of religion.

3. It was in the behalf of the Gibeonites, their confederates by oath; *lex gentium,* the law of nations.

It is a sin to sit and look on when either our commonwealth, or God's religion, or the oath of confederacy, suffereth.

This war was here managed openly, and in the sight of the sun; and God declared himself both of the council of war and an auxiliary friend to his Israel in the same, for none but he could have stayed the course of the sun and moon.

Use. Now these extraordinary operations of God, as St Austin saith, are called *monstra ut a monstrando;* so they are called *portenta à portendo, et prodigia à porro dicendo.* Therefore let us see what they shew and what they teach us.

1. They teach us the great commandment of the law, to love God and to keep his commandments. This power in doing so great things, and this mercy in doing the same for Israel, doth well deserve that service from his church, observe it in a touch, remember it in the front of the law, 'I am the Lord thy God which brought thee out of the land of Egypt,' for that leadeth us into the full story of Israel's peregrination, and is there used to move obedience.

And we cannot make a better use of our frequent commemoration of the manifold mercies of God to us, than to stir up ourselves to serve him. So Christ's greater deliverance is urged by Zacharias, *ut liberati serviamus.*

2. It serveth to direct us in the estimation of the creatures of God, for the honour that we can do them lawfully is but to glorify God for the good we receive by them; honour is only due to him that employeth them.

Take heed of idols, take heed of superstition, let not another gospel bewitch any of us. When the sun communicateth his light to all the world, every corner and part of the world is not illuminate alike. There be some precious stones that reflect the light of the sun more than others do; we value these above other, yet we know that the light is all borrowed of the sun.

And though, in our fellow-creatures, the gifts and graces of God be in differing measures given, for which we value them above an ordinary price, yet we reserve to our God the honour of the gift of every good and perfect gift, who is the Father of lights; and we do him wrong if we draw any of our fellow-creatures into the communion of his glory.

3. Let me add this for caution, let not our thoughts be so ravished with the contemplation of God's extraordinary power, sometimes expressed in the service of his creatures, as that we do neglect his ordinary providence, which, in true judgment, is more admirable. It is St Austin's note, *Quæ sunt rara, sunt mira.* But he saith, it is more admirable to behold so many faces so unlike in form, feature, and proportion, yet we do more wonder to see two faces alike. It is not so admirable, in true judgment, to see the sun stand still in heaven, as a glorious candle set upon a candlestick, as to see it move and set, and rise in so constant manner as it doth. Therefore, let the common providence of God lose nothing by his extraordinary lightnings of power, and flashes of prerogative.

4. This serveth also to encourage us in the cause of religion, or in the just defence of the oppressed, to awake our courage and to take pains.

It belongeth not to us, who are God's ministers, to inquire what cause of wars we have at this present, what means must be used to commence and maintain them. This belongeth to us, to animate all that are called to just wars, to take courage from this example.

If the sun stood still whilst Joshua did fight for the Gibeonites, because God's oath had bound Israel to them in confederacy, I cannot doubt but the Sun of righteousness, the Captain of God's guards, the Lord of his hosts, will cover their heads in the day of battle, that fight for the oppressed church of God, their brethren, the professors of the same faith, the worshippers of the same God.

Whereas this miracle of the station of the sun and moon was done at the instance of Joshua, we are taught to behold the truth of God's promises made to his servants. He had promised Joshua to magnify him in the sight of his people, Josh. i. 17, and the blessing of the people on Joshua was only, 'The Lord be with thee, as he was with Moses.' So he was in the division of the waters of Jordan, so was he in the conquest of Jericho and Ai; and never was there such a thing seen, that the Lord heard the voice of a man, to make the day two days long.

1. This was done to prevent idolatry, that the people might not erect any memory to Moses, to honour him with divine honour, which also God feared; and therefore he buried Moses himself, and would let no man know where he was buried, to prevent idolatry. The devil, no doubt, knew the place; that was the quarrel between Michael and the devil, about the body of Moses, for the devil would fain have discovered where it was, to have misled the people to idolatry, but Michael resisted him. Now when the people see that he which was great in Moses is as great in Joshua, and they have experience that Joshua hath of the same spirit that Moses had, this doth direct their judgments not to look upon the instruments by whom wonders are done, but on God, who doth them, and can do them as well by Joshua as by Moses.

2. This was done to assure the former promises of the quiet and full possession of the land, against the fear which the spies suggested; for if God declare by these signs that he fighteth for Israel, as it is said upon this sign, Josh. x. 14, Israel need not fear the power of their enemies, they may go forth in the strength of the Lord, his word is their warrant, his truth their assurance.

Use. When we behold the same power of God in the change of ministers of his will, we learn to know, whatsoever alteration the vicissitude of time maketh on earth, yet, 'thou, Lord, art the same, and thy years do not fail.' Therefore, as David saith, 'Put not your trust in princes, nor in any son of man, for there is no help in them;' there is help *by* them, but it is not *in* them: 'our help is in the name of the Lord, who hath made heaven and earth.'

Use 2. This sheweth the perpetual course of God's favour to his church. The faithful servant of God, Moses, dieth, but the spirit that God put upon Moses survived him, and rested upon Joshua; he was consecrated to that employment,

1. By God's own election and designation;
2. By the imposition of Moses' hands, Num. xxvii. 18, and the devolution of some of his honour upon him;
3. By God's own gift of the same spirit that was upon Moses.

Thus, where God loveth a people, the favour of God runneth in a full stream in the channel of his church.

Use 3. Seeing this constant truth of God, in his gracious promises to his church, hath reference to our obedience, this must teach us to obey and serve our God in all things, that his sun may shine upon our tabernacles, and that we may anoint our paths with butter; for as David saith, 'No good thing will he withhold from them that serve the Lord.' He hath shewed his people what they shall trust to, blessings and cursings, life and death, Deut. xxviii.

Doct. 3. This also teacheth us, as the apostle doth, 'The effectual fervent prayer of a righteous man prevaileth much,' James v. 16. He proveth it by the example of Elijah, who, though he were a man subject to the like passions as we are, 'he prayed earnestly that it might not rain, and it rained not on the earth in three years and six months. And he prayed again, and the heaven gave rain.'

So this example of Joshua praying is a full **example** of the effectual power of prayer. These examples, **as** that also of Moses praying upon the mount when Joshua fought with Amalek, Exod. xvii., do all seem to prove the force of prayer; and great reason there is that this should be effectual with God.

1. Because there is no service that man can perform to God wherein he doth so much part with himself, and even lay himself down [as] in prayer, for therein he openeth his heart to God, and poureth forth his spirit to him, and his faith doth bring God to him face to face. When men pray as they ought, they know God and themselves: they know and confess him the faithful creator, the merciful redeemer, the gracious preserver, the bounteous rewarder of men; and they know themselves to be but men, that is indigent and needy, having nothing but what they receive from his hand, and of his free gift, immerent, deserving none, not the least, of his favours. Which two considerations do serve to humble us, and to honour him.

We find in Scripture watching and fasting often joined with prayer, as outward means to tame and subdue the flesh, that it may be the lesser able to resist the power of the spirit, for the spirit is willing in the servant of God, but the flesh is weak.

2. There is no part of God's worship that hath so many precepts to impose it on us as prayer hath in both the Testaments; none that have so many examples of great success and prevailing with God; none that have so good means to perform as prayer; none that hath so many promises made to it in holy Scripture.

1. For precepts. So soon as God had established him an house for his public worship, he commanded it to be 'called an house of prayer to all nations.' Solomon dedicated that house to God by prayer. It is God's own word, 'Seek ye my face;' it is the church's answer, 'Thy face, O Lord, will I seek;' and Christ our Saviour often in the Gospel, the apostles after him, enjoins it.

2. For example. We have Abraham, Isaac, and Jacob, Moses, David, Solomon, Hezekiah, Elijah, Manasseh, Nehemiah, Job, Samuel, Daniel, and all the prophets, all the holy men, Christ, his apostles, all with admirable success.

3. *For means.* Christ taught us to pray, shewed us the way to the Father, in his mediation and by his name ; and the Spirit which Christ left in his church helpeth our infirmities. Christ hath comprehended all in a few words : ' Whatosever ye shall ask the Father in my name, it shall be given you.' ' Ask and receive, that your joy may be full,' *petite, quærite, pulsate.*

Use. These great examples of success do all seem to stir us up to the performance of this part of God's worship, both,

1. In obedience to the commandment of God, who hath imposed this duty on us, whose commandments are mighty, and ought not to be lightlied.

2. In an holy ambition of the best graces of God, which are this way obtained of him.

3. In an humble love to our God, to whose presence and conference we come by prayer.

4. In an holy imitation of those great examples, which are so frequent in God's faithful ones, in the double Testament of God.

5. In a thankful use of the means by God ordained to facilitate this service, that we receive not the grace of God in vain.

6. In a confident faith in God's gracious and free promises, which are yea and amen.

7. In an humble sense and feeling of our own wants, and the necessities of our brethren ; for so we do exercise both our piety to God, and our charity to ourselves and our brethren.

Obj. But this discourageth many. We read of great power of prayer of old, as that Moses' prayer gave Joshua victory ; Joshua's prayer made the sun stand still ; Elijah by prayer shut up heaven, by prayer he opened it; Daniel by prayer shut up the mouths of the lions in their den. We see no such effects of prayer now, and therefore we think prayer is not of such effect now as heretofore.

Sol. To this our answer is, that great and extraordinary examples of the success of prayer are but thinly scattered in the book of God, to shew the power of God's ordinance. Neither may that be a rule to us, that prayer is not of force as it hath been, because we do not see such great effects thereof as have appeared in former times. For in the time of the shadow, when Christ was seen in type and under a veil, there was need of extraordinary examples to confirm faith; but to us that live in the clear light of the gospel, to whom Christ is made manifest to be our intercessor, this may seem to strengthen faith. If God did hear the prayers of his faithful ones, and answered them by miracles, they had special warrant to demand those things at the hands of God. We have no such warrant, but look we what we may pray for, and we shall find that God doth answer us with success.

1. That the name of God may be hallowed. Doth not every faithful servant of God place his trust in this name? doth he not praise it for all things?

2. That the kingdom of God may come. Is not this kingdom of grace in the church? Doth not the believer feel Christ reigning in his heart, and ruling him by his Spirit? and doth he not expect his second coming in glory, and believe everlasting life?

3. That the will of God may be done here as it is in heaven. Is it not so? Our conversation is in heaven. Doth not the whole life of a faithful soul spend itself in imitation of Christ, and of the angels of God, and of the holy saints that are gone before us to praise God in heaven?

4. Have we not daily bread? Doth not God feed us with food convenient for us?

5. Doth not God assure our consciences of the free remission of our sins?

6. Doth not he in temptations save us from the evil one that seeketh our destruction, and maketh them the exercises of our virtue, that are directed to the dilapidation of our faith?

We may ask nothing else of God but what hath reference to one of these petitions, and in all these God heareth us, and granteth our requests.

Our own want of faith and zeal in prayer, our own neglect of the duty, our own unthankfulness to God for benefits already received, our corrupt desires to spend the favours of God upon our lusts, may make many of our prayers miscarry; much more if we do ask anything at the hands of God which is not lawful. But let us ask as he commandeth, and the argument will follow comfortably. If the servants of God have heretofore prevailed with God so far as to work miracles for their good, much more will God hear our ordinary suits, and grant them, so far as may stand with the glory of his name and our good.

But at adventure he hath commanded us to pray; and let us do our duty in obedience to him, and leave the success to his fatherly providence. Prayer is the casting our care upon God, and is not that a great comfort to us, when our care is put off, and so repose that we may serve our God without fear or care for things of this life?

2. The victory that followed the station of the sun and moon contains two things:

1. What God did in indignation to his enemies.
2. What he did in favour to his people.

1. What he did in indignation.
Containing,
1. His martial march through the land.
2. His conquest of it.

1. His march. 'Thou didst march through the land in indignation;' which teacheth us,

Doct. That in all wars God is Lord of hosts, and general of all the armies that fight in his quarrel. This was assured to Joshua by a vision; for, Josh. v. 13, 'It came to pass, when Joshua was by Jericho, that he lifted up his eyes and looked, and, behold, there stood a man over against him, with his sword drawn in his hand; and Joshua went unto him, and said unto him, Art thou for us, or for our adversaries? And he said, Nay; but as a captain of the host of the Lord am I now come. And Joshua fell on his face to the earth, and did worship.' This must be God that appeared to him by this angel; and it is the same angel which God before promised: Exod. xxiii. 20, 'Behold, I send an angel before thee, to keep thee in the way, and to bring thee into the place which I have prepared. Beware of him, and obey his voice, and provoke him not; for he will not pardon your transgressions; for my name is in him.'

This angel must needs be the same, who is after called the Messiah, or Anointed, in the next verse; and both the power that was given him of God to protect and to pardon, and the charge that was given to the people not to offend him, and the worship which Joshua did give him, and the name which God said was in him, prove him to be Jesus Christ.

All serves to prove that God was the leader of these wars, as here is said, 'Thou didst march through the land.' And God did take it upon himself: Isa. xlv. 7, 'I the Lord do all these things.'

The reason is, because war is one of the rods of God, wherewith he doth scourge the sins of men. For thus saith the Lord God, Ezek. xiv. 21, 'How much more when I send my four great judgments upon Jerusalem?' The first of them is the sword.

Who can manage the judgments of God but himself? and therefore, when wicked persons are employed by him to punish sinners by the sword, he confesseth the service done to him, as in the case of Nebuchadnezzar, king of Babel, against Tyrus: Ezek. xxix. 20, 'I have given him the land of Egypt, for the labour wherewith he served against Tyrus, because they wrought for me, saith the Lord.'

God ordereth all wars; for wars, as I have said, is one of God's own rods, and none can manage them without him; so all wars, as they are from him, are just wars. But they may be unjust in respect of them that commence and prosecute them. The point, then, here taught is, that in all wars which are just in respect of God, who smiteth them, God is the leader and the protector of his armies, who giveth them both strength to fight and victory in battle.

These were God's wars by which Israel was settled in the land of Canaan, and they were the wars of God by which Israel was led away captive into Babel. You heard God himself say so: Hab. i. 6, 'For, lo, I raise up the Chaldeans, that bitter and hasty nation, which shall march through the breadth of the land, to possess the dwelling-places that are not theirs.' God was he that marched through the land, then, in indignation.

Use. This teacheth us, wheresoever we see the sword

of God abroad in the world to smite, to confess it to be God's sore judgment, without whom no man could draw a sword, or lift up his arm in the world.

Note. God brought in his Israel by the sword, and by the sword he carrieth them out of Canaan; the hand of the Lord is in both.

Therefore, whatsoever preparations of war God's servants do make, to hold or to recover their own right, to relieve the distresses of others, or to suppress the injuries of oppressors, they must commit their cause to the Lord, and seek their strength from him, and depend on him for their success.

But as God is the author and manager of all wars, so is he the special protector of those that he hath separated from the world to be his church and peculiar people, as in the story of Israel's passage you have heard.

In this war, God did march before his Israel against the inhabitants of Canaan, and cast the fear of them upon them all. This is a great advantage in all wars, to have God on their sides, for as David saith, ' If the Lord had not been on our side, when men rose up against us, they had swallowed us up,' &c. Then is God a special protector, when he directeth his war to the good of them whom he protecteth, and marcheth in fury against their enemies. And thus it was with Israel when they took possession of Canaan, as you have heard: Ps. xliv. 3, ' For they gat not the land in possession by their own arm, neither did their own arm save them, but thy right hand and thine arm,' &c.

The distressed have a special warrant to call upon God; and it was the voice of the church, when the ark removed, to say, *Exsurgat Deus, dissipentur inimici ejus,* let God arise, and let his enemies be scattered.

God is merciful to our land and church, that we yet live in peace; it is full of comfort, when God marcheth before his church in their wars, but it is much more happiness when he biddeth us go to our chambers, and shut the door after us, and tarry a while till the storm of troubles overblow. But then it is most joyous, when he giveth peace within our walls and plenty within our palaces.

Thus have we lived hitherto by the favour of the God of peace, and it shall do well that we do lay this example to heart. For the same God that marched before Israel to plant them in, doth now march before the Chaldeans to cast them out; he that fought for them to give them their land, now fighteth against them to carry them captives out of the land. It is the indignation of God that maketh this change, and it is their sin that thus provoketh him; yet they look back in their captivity, and comfort themselves with the remembrance of God's former protection.

Sin hath made this change; are we more in the favour of God than Israel was, or have we sinned less than they did, that their evils should not come on us? Surely the sins of our land are both many and heinous, the double edge of the word, which is drawn and used against them, doth not draw blood.

Nullus sequitur de vulnere sanguis.

The course that is taken for reformation is preposterous, for men look without themselves, and complain of the faults of others, and would fain amend their brethren; but the right way is, let every one strive and labour to amend one. And all that say, Let not this evil come upon us, not the sword, not the pestilence, not famine; let them be tender that no evil come out of them, for our sins are they which part God and us, which maketh him that set us up cast us down.

2. His conquest. This is expressed in divers phrases, to declare it fierce and violent.

1. 'Thou didst thrash the heathen in anger.'

2. 'Thou woundest the head out of the house of the wicked.'

3. 'Discovering the foundation to the neck.'

All look one way, to describe God in his indignation, how he lays about him; and they teach us that 'it is a fearful thing to fall into the hands of the living God,' for he is known by executing judgment, and the heathen are punished in his sight. True, that he is patient and longsuffering, even toward the heathen that know not God. Long did the cursed seed of

Ham possess the land of Canaan, and God deferred their punishment to the fourth generation; himself giveth the reason of it: Gen. xv. 16, 'For the iniquity of the Amorites is not yet full.'

There be six signs of ensuing judgment; and where they are found, what remaineth but a fearful expectation of the fierce wrath of God?

1. The quality of the sins committed; if they be of those crying sins which do immediately impeach the glorious majesty of God; such as are superstition and idolatry, which do give the glory of God to creatures, blasphemy, breach of God's Sabbath; or such as violate human society, sins against nature, as in the Sodomites; sins of blood, as in the old world sins; of oppression, bribery, extortion, corruption of justice, and such like. These things do put almighty God so to it, that he saith, Jer. v. 7, 'How shall I pardon thee for these things? shall I not visit for these things? saith the Lord: shall not my soul be avenged on such a nation as this?' The fields look yellow, as Christ saith, for the harvest, and call for the sickle of God's vengeance to cut them down.

2. The spreading and extent of sin; when it hath corrupted the most, as in the old world God said to Noah, 'Thee only have I found righteous before me in this age;' and in Sodom not ten righteous to be found; and in Jerusalem God said, 'Run to and fro through the streets of Jerusalem, and see now and know, and seek in the broad places thereof, if ye can find a man, if there be any that executeth judgment, that seeketh truth, and I will pardon it.' The prophet did go the circuit. He searched amongst mean men, and he found them foolish and ignorant; he gat him amongst the great ones, and he found them such as had broken the yoke. When sin once covereth the face of the earth, and is grown like a general pestilence infecting the greatest part, Moses, Job, Samuel, and Daniel may pray and have no audience.

3. The impudency and boldness of sin; when men are not ashamed of their evils that they commit, to cover and conceal them, to do them in the dark, but brave the sun with them; as Absalom defiled the con-

cubines of David in the sight of the sun, and before all Israel. It is God's complaint of his people: Isa. iii. 9, 'The show of their countenance doth witness against them, and they declare their sin as Sodom, and they hide it not.' And again, Jer vi. 15, 'Were they ashamed when they had committed abomination? nay, they were not at all ashamed, neither could they blush.' Jer. iii. 3, 'Thou hast an harlot's forehead, thou refusest to be ashamed.'

4. Ostentation of sin. When men do make their boast thereof, 'why boastest thou thyself in mischief?' Upon which words St Augustine saith, *Gloria malignitatis, gloria est malorum.* He saith, it is a foolish boast to glory in evil; for evil is easily done. He gives many instances, the care of preparing the seed, and of the ground, the sowing, the weeding, the attending, how many hands it asketh, and Absalom can set it all on fire in a moment. So Samson's foxes did the fields of the Philistines. The wise man setteth it down as a fault, Prov. xx. 6, 'Most men will proclaim every man his own goodness;' how much more to boast of evil, as wantons boast how many they have defiled, and drunkards how many they have out-drunk.

5. Making a mock at sin. So the wise man saith, there be that toss fire-brands, and say, 'Am not I in sport?' All our sins are fire-brands; we need no other rods to scourge us here, no other fuel to enfire us hereafter, than our own sin; this is *hilaris insania*, to make ourselves merry with these, and to sit in the chair of the scornful.

6. Incorrigibility. When the gracious warnings of God do not lead them to repentance; when the angry threatenings of God do not draw blood of them; when the rods of God's favourable chastisement do not smart upon them. 'O Lord,' saith Jeremiah, chap. v. 3, 'thou hast stricken them, but they have not grieved.' Correction had wont to be the way to reclaim sinners, but when iniquity is come to the full ripeness, God may lay on while he will; they that have not known the way of peace, will harden their hearts, as Pharaoh did, and correction will but make them curse and blaspheme God to his face. This was the full iniquity

of these nations whom God threshed, and wounded, and digged up, and cast out, that he might plant his Israel therein.

Use. And it teacheth us to be wise to salvation; as the apostle saith, 'Thou man of God, fly these things.' And let me say to you, as Lot to the Sodomites, 'I pray you, my brethren, do not so wickedly.'

1. Take heed of idols: 'Babes, keep yourselves from idols.' Idolatry hath grown bolder of late than heretofore. The factors of Rome are busy amongst us trading for proselytes; but God stirreth up the spirits of his religious servants to solicit the cause of religion, and the worthies of our land stand up with zealous fervency of spirit for the truth of God.

This is the light of Israel; so long as we keep the fire of God burning upon our altars, we shall have hope that God is with us, and that he will give us his blessing of peace. Let us break off our sins by repentance, that we may turn away the indignation of God from us; let not sin reign in our mortal bodies, that we should obey it in the lusts thereof.

2. Let us take heed that we give not way to sin, either in ourselves or in others, lest it overgrow us; but let us examine our own hearts in our chambers, and turn to the Lord. And if a brother by occasion fall into sin, let them that are spiritual restore him with the spirit of meekness.

3. Let shame cover our faces for the evils that we have done; it is no shame to be ashamed of our evils. As there is a godly sorrow, so there is a godly shame; let us say with Job, 'I covered not my transgression with Adam, by hiding my iniquity in my bosom.'

4. Let it grieve us that we have sinned, and let us not boast thereof, but say with Job, *Peccavi, quid faciam tibi;* with Saul, 'I have sinned, and done foolishly.'

5. Let the remembrance of our sin smite our hearts, as David's heart smote him when he had numbered the people, and let us do no more so. Let the judgments of God make us afraid.

6. Let the corrections of God humble us, and cast us at the feet of God, that he may shew us mercy;

and with Paul, let us pray three times, that the angel of Satan may be taken from us.

Then shall we neither feel the flail of God threshing us, nor the sword of God wounding us, nor the spade of God digging [us] up; but we shall rejoice, every man under his own vine, and under his own fig-tree.

2. What he did in favour to his own: 'Thou wentest forth for the salvation of thy people, even for salvation with thine anointed.' David saith, 'Truly God is good to Israel.'

The everlasting comfort of the church hath been planted and grounded in the favour of God, by the mediation of Jesus Christ his anointed. For although Christ were not so manifest to his church before, and in the time of the law, as he hath been in the time of the gospel, yet he hath been always the hope of all the ends of the world.

Reason. The reason is, because Christ is not only a mediator of intercession to pray for us, and a mediator of satisfaction to die for us, and a mediator of salvation to prepare eternal mansions for us, but he is, and ever was, and will be, a mediator also of temporal protection to keep and defend us from all evils; so that the sun shall not smite us by day, nor the moon by night. For as God created us to his own image, so he fitted to his only begotten Son a body in our image; he was made of a woman, and so soon as his word had made him the promised seed, so soon was he crucified for us, and was the Lamb slain from the beginning of the world. Then did he take his church into his bosom, and married her to himself, and they became one body; and ever since his angels have charge over her, to keep her in all her ways; and this must comfort Israel in Babylon, that God went before them with his Anointed, to settle them in the promised land.

There be no other mercies that will tarry by us, but those which God doth vouchsafe us by the means of this mediator. He imparteth many outward blessings even to the wicked, by the means of his Holy Ghost; for all the knowledge that they have, all the wisdom in arts and sciences, be the gifts of the Holy Ghost;

but they have no portion at all in the office of Christ, he was not anointed for them.

From hence the apostle doth conclude, that God hath not forsaken the Jews, but that they shall be called again; for he saith, Rom. xi. 1, 2, 'Hath God cast away his people?' he answereth, 'God hath not cast away his people whom he foreknew.' The election of grace, which made them his, doth confirm them to him for ever, and therefore they mention his going before them with his Anointed, to assure them, that though they go into captivity, and abide a long time there, yet they shall not be left in bonds for ever; for the Spirit of the Lord is upon this Anointed, Isa. lxi. 1, 'to preach liberty to captives, and the opening the prison to them that are bound.'

This is now the true comfort of the distressed parts of the church, which groan under the burden of oppression and bloody persecution. They cry for the help of men, and no nation doth succour them; they weep and pray to God and to his Anointed, and, no doubt, but in good time he will come down to them to visit them in his mercy; they are Christians, and they carry the name of God's Anointed. His name is in them, and his righteousness and truth are their hope and strength. It is time for thee, Lord, to put to thy hand, for the wicked sons of Belial, the children of Edom, cry out against thy church, Down with it, down with it, even to the ground. The bishop of Rome abetteth the unchristian shedding of Christian blood by his letters, and disperseth his whetstones to sharpen the sword of God's enemies against God's church. Let us say with old Jacob, 'O Lord, I have waited for thy salvation,' for thy Jesus.

2. This repetition of salvation, 'Thou wentest forth for the salvation of thy people, even for salvation,' teacheth us,

Doct. 2. That God hath taken upon himself the care of the preservation of his church. Therefore he goeth before them for salvation, and he doth never leave them nor forsake them.

Reason 1. God hath many gracious titles, which do assure his love and favour to us. He is called *Jehovah*, so we live, move, and have our being in him. He is called by Job *the Preserver of men;* St Paul addeth, *especially of the elect,* for their salvation is a peculiar grace, no common favour. And so his right hand both supporteth and guideth us, that we neither stray out of the way, nor fall in the way. He is called our *Shepherd,* and so we come to want nothing, for he leadeth us both to the green pastures and to the waters of comfort. He is called the *Husband* of the church, and Christ preserveth her to him, *sine macula et ruga,* ' without spot or wrinkle ;' and Christ teacheth us to call him our *Father,* so as a father hath compassion, &c. The Lord is our *King* of old, he maketh salvation in the midst of the earth. All these titles declare him no non-resident from his charge ; he is always incumbent. For *ipse est qui dat salutem.*

Reason 2. Because the church committeth itself to him, and casteth her care upon him, and he never failed them that trust in him. St Paul, ' I know whom I have trusted.' ' Commit thy ways to the Lord, and trust in him, and he shall bring it to pass.'

Reason 3. The church of God giveth him no rest, but by continual supplications importuneth his saving protection, saying, ' O Lord, I pray thee, save now ; O Lord, I pray thee, now give prosperity.' He hath commanded her so to do ; to seek, to ask, to knock ; and invocation is one of the marks of God's children. ' He that calleth on the name of the Lord shall be saved.' They are called the assembly of God's armies, and their prayers be their weapons, heaven is their abiding city which they besiege, and Christ saith, ' the violent take it by force.' For, *multorum preces impossibile est contemni.*

Reason 4. Christ himself always prayeth the Father for his church, that God would keep it ; and he saith to his Father, ' I know that thou hearest me always.'

Use. This comfortable doctrine serveth to refresh the grieved soul in time of affliction. The smart of God's rod doth many times put us into fits of impatience and murmuring, and the delay of God's saving help doth often stagger our weak faith ; that the man after God's own heart doth sometimes fear that God hath given him over.

In great losses, as of our honours and preferments, of our liberty, of our wealth, of our dear friends, it is some time before we can recover from this shaking fit of fear, that God hath forsaken us, and we say, Ps. x. 1, 'Why standest thou so far off, O Lord, and hidest thee in due time, in time of affliction?'

But when we remember 'thou art with me,' it establisheth our footsteps, it strengtheneth our weak knees, and comforteth our sorrowful hearts, and biddeth us 'Rejoice in the Lord;' again it saith, 'rejoice.' So David, 'I waited patiently for God;' and so he comforteth his soul: Ps. xliii. 5. 'Wait on God, for I will yet give him thanks, for the help of his presence; he is my present help, and my God.'

So then, if present issue appear not out of affliction, let us not faint in our troubles, but persuade us that God is with us, and the rock of our salvation will not fail us.

Use 2. This sheweth that we need not seek further for salvation than to God himself and his Anointed, seeing they are always with us. It is a foolish and idle superstition and idolatry to seek our salvation from or by the means of angels or saints, or the mother of our Lord, when we have both him and his anointed Messiah, that is, both the giver and mediator of salvation, with us.

This foolish devotion of the Roman church, of making way by angels and saints, hath three great defects, which all the wit of Rome and hell could never cover or conceal.

1. It hath no commandment to require it.
2. It hath no example to lead us to it.
3. It hath no promise in Scripture to reward it. Ps lxxiii. 25, 'Whom have I in heaven but thee? and I have none upon earth that I desire besides thee.' They be our glorious fellow-creatures, we honour God for the good that they have done in his church. We believe that they pray for our happy deliverance from all miseries of life, and the society of their lives. We imitate their holy examples, and do strive to follow them in their virtues, and pray for

the graces of God that sanctified them on earth. But for our salvation we know that he is always with us, that saveth us, and his Anointed doth never forsake us, that keepeth us from evil. We hear him saying, 'Come unto me;' and he calleth us not to heaven to him, but, 'Lo, I am with you to the end of the world.' He is near unto all that call upon him, and he is easily found of them that seek him.

Use 3. This doth give us fair warning to take heed that we do not leave our God and live in sin, for he is not so near us but that ourselves may separate beween him and us, for it is also true that God putteth a great deal of difference between an ungodly and godly man; as Solomon saith, Prov. xv. 29, 'The Lord is far from the wicked, but he heareth the prayer of the righteous.' And as God is far from them, so is salvation; as David saith, Ps. cxix. 55, 'Salvation is far from the wicked.' As we tender the favourable protection and love of God, let us take heed of sin. Isa. lix. 1, 'Behold, the Lord's hand is not shortened, that it cannot save; nor his ear heavy, that it cannot hear: but your iniquities have separated between you and your God, and your sins have hid his face from you, that he will not hear.'

Use 4. Seeing our salvation is of him only by his Anointed, let us remember that we are called Christians after his name; not only *Christum*, Lo, I am with you, and *Spiritum Christi*, whom I will send you from the Father, but we have $\chi\rho\iota\sigma\mu\alpha$, the very anointing itself, left and deposited in the church; as St John saith, 1 John ii. 2, 'But ye have an unction from the Holy One.' If we keep this unction, we are sure of this salvation, therefore grieve not the Spirit of God, resist not the Holy Ghost, receive not the grace of God in vain.

And so let the enemy of mankind and his agents do their worst to annoy us, our salvation is bound up in the bundle of life with our God for ever; we may go forth boldly in the strength of the Lord, both against the enemies of our temporal estate and the spiritual adversaries of our souls, for who can wrong us if we follow the thing that is good?

God, who maketh in us both *velle et facere*, to will and to do, make us able for this work of our salvation!

Ver. 14. *Thou didst strike through with his staves the head of his villages; they came out as a whirlwind to scatter me: their rejoicing was to devour the poor secretly.*

This, as you have heard before in the exposition of the words, hath reference to that victory which God gave against the Midianites to his Israel, Judges vii. 22, wherein the Lord set every man's sword against his fellow throughout all the host, for there he struck them with their own staves, and armed them against themselves to their own ruin.

Wherein consider with me two things :
1. Their punishment.
2. Their sin.

In the punishment we are taught,

Doct. That God in his just judgment maketh the ungodly rods to punish one another of them. If they have no other enemies but themselves, they shall go together by the ears amongst themselves, and smite one another.

This is that which God threatened against the sins in Israel: Isa. xix. 19, 'No man shall spare his brother; he shall snatch on the right hand, and be hungry, and he shall eat on the left hand, and shall not be satisfied: they shall eat every man the flesh of his own arm; Manasseh Ephraim, and Ephraim Manasseh, and they together shall be against Judah.'

This was the burden of Egypt: Isa. xix. 2, 'And I will set the Egyptians against the Egyptians, and they shall fight every one against his brother, and every one against his neighbour, city against city, and kingdom against kingdom.'

In the first of these two places the prophet doth foretell how the tribes shall fall out among themselves, and how their greediness of wealth and honour shall make them devour one another; for the apostle giveth warning that we be tender how we bite one another, 'lest we be devoured one of another.'

This is sin and punishment both; wherein they

offend, therein they are punished.

In the second example, of the Egyptians destroying one another, we behold the uncertain state of ungodly nations and people; they can have no constant peace.

Reason 1. Because they know not, they serve not, the God of peace; and where true religion doth not unite hearts, they may cry a confederacy, which may hold so long as it may [serve] some private turns, but the next great provocation turns all into fury and combustion, for there wants the foundation of peace within them.

Reason 2. Because he would thereby maintain the equity of that natural law written in every man's heart by the finger of God, 'Do as thou wouldst be done to.' Wouldst thou be content to be beaten with those staves that thou hast made to beat others, to be hewed and mangled with those weapons of violence? Therefore God in his justice employeth this preparation against themselves, and scourgeth them with their own rods.

Reason 3. That we may know that all things in the administration of the world are directed by the wisdom and providence of God, who, though he be a God of peace, yet he also causeth divisions and contentions amongst men, and punisheth transgressors therewith. The ten kings in the Revelation, which are the ten horns of the beast, that is, of Rome, these at first join their forces against the lamb, and set up the beast: Rev. xvii. 13, 'These have one mind, and shall give their strength unto the beast;' but in the end, vers. 16, 17, 'And these ten horns which thou sawest upon the beast, these shall hate the whore, and shall make her desolate and naked, and shall eat her flesh, and shall burn her up with fire. For God hath put in their hearts to fulfil his will, and to agree, and to give their kingdom to the beast, until the words of God shall be fulfilled.' From whence we gather that that agreement which is amongst wicked men against Christ and against his church, is strengthened by the will and providence of God for a time. Till that time, the confederacies of the ungodly do hold; but when he pleaseth to dissolve them, they end in self-woundings and intestine combusions.

Use 1. This serveth to settle our judgments concerning the combinations of the wicked against the church; they are of God, and he hath his secret and just ends therein, either to chasten the errors and transgressions of his people, or to bring their patience and piety to the test, to try whether anything will make them forsake their hold and relinquish their trust in him, or to bring the greater condemnation upon those whom he useth as instruments in this trial of his chosen servants.

Therefore, now that we both hear the news and see the effects of this new bloody league to destroy the church, and to root out the protestant religion, whereby much Christian blood of innocents is already shed, more is feared; let it establish our hearts and settle our judgments upon this rest. The Lord will have it, *a Domino factum est hoc; Tu Domine fecisti*, thou, Lord, hast done it.

Surely there is much dross in our gold, which must be purged; we have not spared one another with schismatical mouths and pens, to break the peace of the church, and God in his judgment suffereth the wicked to prevail against us.

Use 2. This comforteth the church against these tempests of fury that her enemies do raise against her, for, though they weaken us thereby, and exalt their own horn on high, yet, when the waves of the sea do rage horribly, God that is on high is more mighty than they, and he will smite them with their own staves that supported them, and wound them with their own swords that defended them.

Use 3. This admonisheth us not to settle any confidence or trust in the friendship of man, whose breath is in his nostrils, for wherein is he to be trusted? The prophet Micah saith, chap. vii. 2–4, ' The good man is perished out of the earth; there is none upright among men; they all lie in wait for blood; they hunt every man his brother with a net. That they may do evil with both hands earnestly, the prince asketh, the judge asketh for a reward; and the great man uttereth the mischief of his soul: so they wrap it up. The best of them is a brier; the most upright of them is sharper than a thorn hedge.' And from this consideration of the general falsehood that is in friendship, his caution is, ver. 5, 6, 'Trust ye not in a friend, put no confidence in a guide; keep the doors of thy mouth from her that lieth in thy bosom. For the son dishonoureth the father, the daughter riseth up against her mother, the daughter-in-law against her mother-in-law; and a man's enemies are the men of his own house.'

What shall we do then? Ver. 7, Therefore I will look upon the Lord; I will wait for the God of my salvation: my God will hear me.'

Christ our Saviour, Mat. x. 34, doth apply this text to his own coming into the world; he professeth it that he 'came not to bring peace into the world, but the sword.' In which words he rather expresseth the events and effects than the intention and purpose of his coming; for where the light of the gospel doth shine, father, mother, brother, sister, are but *nuda nomina*, bare names, where Christian religion is not, for the true gospeller will fall out with all, and forsake them all for Jesus Christ. The rest of the church is God in Christ. Let us seek peace with men if it be possible, as much as in our power; let us have peace with all men, but let us trust no human or temporal supportation.

Use 4. Seeing it is here set down as a great judgment of God upon Midian, that they were beaten with their own staves, and wounded with their own weapons, let us take notice of this judgment, and take it for a great sign of God's indignation against us, when we break the bonds of peace and Christian charity, biting and beating one another, libelling and defaming, worrying one another with suits of molestation, schismatically forsaking the fellowship one of another, and changing public congregations into private conventicles, and forsaking the settled priesthood of the church, for such as do labour most to break the peace of the church; for what is this but the angel of Satan beating of us with our own staves? Doth not this home contention in our church open an easy way to the enemy of both to enter in and spoil all?

And this I have observed, that two sides have gained by our church contentions. The anabaptists have recovered some from us, who, standing so violently against popery, have questioned all that they received. The papists have recovered many who have gone so far in the defence of the mean, that themselves have staggered into the extreme.

God be merciful to our land, and continue the peace of the state, even the sweet correspondence of our sovereign and his subjects, and we shall have hope that our arms shall be strengthened against our enemies, and our own staves shall do us no hurt.

2. Their sin. It was a trespass against the church of God, devouring of the poor, and that by open violence, coming like a whirlwind, in sudden fury against them, and by secret practices to hurt and annoy them; teaching us that,

Doct. It is a grievous and provoking sin, openly or secretly, to distress the poor.

There be two words of strong signification here used :

1. Scattering; which signifieth their expulsion out of their places where they dwelt, to go, as the Levite did, to get them a place where they can find one; which suiteth well with the humour of the covetous rich man, who desires to dwell alone upon the earth.

2. Devouring; which signifieth taking away from them all that they have, to put it to their own heap, whereby they become vassals to those that strip them.

Reason 1. This is a grievous sin, and well deserves the punishment above mentioned,

1. Because God hath declared himself the patron and protector of the poor; and therefore the psalmist saith, ' The poor committeth himself unto him, for he is the Father of the fatherless.' So that, to distress those is to clip the wings of the hen that gathereth in her chickens.

Reason 2. Because the poor are our own flesh, so they are called by the prophet, and it is used as an argument to persuade compassion: Isa. lviii. 7, ' To deal thy bread to the hungry, to bring the poor that are cast out to thy house; when thou seest the naked, to cover him; and that thou hide not thyself from thine own flesh.' The poor and rich both digged out of the same pit, both cast in the same mould.

Reason 3. Because *natura paucis contenta*, nature is content with a little, and we have enough amongst us to minister that; for if we have food,—he meaneth not manna and quails, but necessary food and raiment; he meaneth not costly, but necessary raiment,—we must be therewith content.

To strip the poor naked, to multiply our changes of raiment, or to take away a whole garment from them, to put one lace more upon ours, this is inhuman, irreligious. To scatter them, that we may have elbow-room enough, and more than needs, for ourselves, that we may have so much the more to look upon and lie by us, this is Midianitish and heathenish. *Vos autem non sic*, do not you so.

Reason 4. Because God hath committed, together with riches, the care and custody of the poor to the rich; and as they hold their wealth not as rightful owners, but as merciful stewards and dispensers thereof, so in the dispensation, they are accountants to God for the overplus, and he will call for the inventory, and judge their administration of those things. Understand, therefore, that God doth not at any time relinquish his interest that he hath in the gifts which he bestoweth on men; but still he saith, Hag. ii. 9, 'The silver is mine, and the gold is mine, saith the Lord of hosts.'

When David gave up all the provisions that he had made for the building of God's temple to Solomon his son, he blessed the Lord, and he confessed, saying, 1 Chron. xxix. 16, ' O Lord our God, all this store that we have prepared to build thee an house for thy holy name, cometh of thine hand, and is all thine own;' so before, ' All things come of thee, and of thine own hand have we given thee.'

Use. The use, then, that we must make of this point is,

1. For the rich, let them know their duty to the poor. Love is a debt that they owe to them, not an arbitrary courtesy. They may not,

1. Either encroach upon them by robbing, or spoiling them of that which they have, as here those Midianites did, to spoil their corn, to take away anything of theirs.

2. Neither may they come upon them as a whirlwind, to encompass and gird them in by their devices of power, or wit, or authority, to make prizes of their labours, whilst they eat the bread of adversity, and drink the waters of Marah.

3. Neither may they withhold their hands in their bosoms in their wants, but stretch them forth to relieve their necessities.

The wise son of Jakeh saith, Prov. xxx. 14, 'There is a generation whose teeth are as swords, and their jaw-teeth as knives, to devour the poor from off the earth, and the needy from among men.' And Solomon saith, Prov. xxi. 10, 'The soul of the wicked desireth evil: his neighbour findeth no favour in his eyes.' Let them remember that the rich man in the Gospel is not charged with any oppression of the poor, but with suppression of the relief which he should have given to Lazarus. And in that overture of the last grand sessions in the Gospel, it is only charged upon them that are adjudged to hell fire, *Esurivi, et non pavistis me*, &c., 'I was hungry, and you fed me not.' Suppression is oppression.

That cold charity which St James speaketh of will be warmed in hell: James ii. 15, 16, 'If a brother or a sister be naked, and destitute of daily food; and one of you say unto them, Depart in peace, be you warmed and filled: notwithstanding you give them not those things which be needful for the body, what doth it profit?'

Use 2. Let the poor know that their God doth take care of them, to visit their sins with rods who spoil them, seeing they have forgotten that we are members one of another, and have invaded the goods of their brethren; God will arm them against themselves, and beat them with their own staves; either their own compassing and over-reaching wits shall consume their store, or their unthrifty posterity shall put wings upon their riches to make them fly; or God shall not give them the blessing to take use of their wealth, but they shall leave to such as shall be merciful to the poor.

Therefore let them follow the wise man's counsel, Eccles. x. 20, 'Curse not the rich, no, not in thy bed-chamber;' let no railing and unchristian bitterness wrong a good cause; let it be comfort enough to them that God is both their supporter and avenger. Is it not sufficient to lay all the storms of discontent against their oppressors, that God sees their affliction, and cometh down to deliver and to avenge them?

Use 3. Rather let this move them to commit their cause to the Lord; for, as Tertullian saith, *Si apud Deum deposueris morbum, medicus est; si damnum, restitutor est; si injuriam, ultor est; si mortem, resuscitator est.* Let not the fair weather of oppressors grieve them that live in the tempest of their injuries; David will tell them that he saw the ungodly flourish like a green bay-tree, and anon he sought them, and their place was not found.

Here is the exaltation of Christian charity, to bless and pray for such; and this will heap coals of fire upon their head, either to warm their charity which hath taken cold, or to consume or devour them.

There was a time when he that denied Lazarus a crumb, begged of him a drop, *Et qui negavit dare micam, non accepit guttam*, and he that denied a crumb had not a drop.

Ver. 15. *Thou didst walk through the sea with thine horses, through the heap of great waters.*

These words do end the section, which containeth a thankful commemmoration of God's former mercies to his people.

De verborum interpretatione.

It seemeth to me clear against all question, that this text hath reference to the wonderful passage of Israel through the Red Sea, of which mention is made before: ver. 8, 'Was thy wrath against the sea, that thou didst ride upon thy horses, and chariots of salvation?'

The words express that miracle very fully and fitly,

for where it is said, 'Thou didst walk through the sea,' this hath reference to that which we read concerning this passage o~ r the Red Sea, Exod. xiv., in which this is memorable, that God went before the people of Israel on the shore; but it is said, when God gave Moses direction to lift up his rod, and stretch forth his hand over the sea to divide it, Moses having so done, ver. 19, 20, 'The angel of God which went before the camp of Israel removed, and went behind it, and the pillar of cloud went from before their face, and stood behind them. And it came between the camp of the Egyptians, and the camp of Israel, and it was a cloud of darkness to them (*i. e.* to the Egyptians), and it gave light by night to these (that is, to Israel), so that the one came not near the other all night. This story sheweth how God doth walk through the sea, even between the two camps. The power of God's word went before them, the presence of his angel went behind them; God himself carried the dark lantern which kept all light from the Egyptians, and shewed a clear light to Israel.

The 'horses of God' here mentioned are the emblems of strength, courage, and speed; for thus was Israel relieved through the heap of the great waters; that is, on the way made through the sea, which was gathered in heaps on both sides. So the words are plain and easy.

The sum of them is a repetition of that great wonder of the conduct of Israel *per mare*, through the sea, of which I have formerly spoken at large, and now remaineth that we search the reason why this one special miracle is here again repeated. That is,

Reason 1. Because this was the greatest miracle of power and mercy, which made the name of God glorious amongst all nations, and the fame whereof was furthest spread abroad in the word, for never was the like heard of before or since.

Yet I will not conceal from you that Josephus,* writing this story of the division of the sea for the

* Antiquit. ii, cap. 14.

passage of Israel, to give it more credit, *ne quis discredat verbo miraculi*, doth report a like wonder, that God, intending by Alexander the Great to destroy the Persian kingdom, did open the like passage through the Pamphilian Sea to Alexander and his army. He addeth, *Id quod omnes testantur*, that which all do witness who wrote the story of Alexander's conquests.

Quintus Curtius, who writeth of purpose the life and acts and death of Alexander, saith no more of it but this, *Mare novum iter in Pamphiliam aperuerat*, which, being ascribed to Alexander himself, doth declare it no miraculous passage.

But Strabo cleareth it thus, that this sea was no other than such as we have within our own land, which we call washes, wherein the sea forsaketh the sands at an ebb, and leaveth them bare and passable on foot or horseback; and he saith that Alexander passed his army through these washes, but being belated, the waters returned upon them before they could recover the shore of Pamphilia, *ut toto die iter faceret in mari umbilico tenus*.

Therefore Josephus was ill advised to parallel this passage with the Israelites' passage through the Red Sea, seeing there were so many disparisons; and whereas he seemed to labour to give credit to Moses' history by this unlike example, he rather blemished the glory of this superadmirable miracle.

There is not any of the great wonders that God wrought for Israel so often remembered in Scripture as this is; and where the Spirit of God so often fixeth our eyes and thoughts, we shall do evil to take them off.

Moses biddeth Israel remember this miracle of their passage: Deut. xi. 4, 'What God did to the army of Egypt, unto their horses and their chariots, how he made the water of the Red Sea to overflow them.'

Rahab could tell the spies, Josh. ii. 10, 11, 'We have heard how the Lord dried up the water of the Red Sea for you. As soon as we heard, our hearts did melt, neither did there remain any courage in any man because of you.'

Ps. lxxvii. 19, 20, 'Thy way is in the sea, and thy path in the great waters, and thy footsteps are not seen. Thou leddest thy people like a flock, by the hand of Moses and Aaron.'

Therefore it is a fabulous relation of Paulus Orosius, who reported it as an addition to this wonder, that the trace of the chariot wheels was in his days to be seen on the sands of the Red Sea at every ebb, and that if they were defaced, yet they renewed again. But David saith that the footsteps of this passage were not seen; and we need not add anything to the miracles of God to make them more miraculous.

David again remembereth it, saying, Ps. lxxviii. 13, 53, 'He divided the sea, and caused them to pass through; and he made the waters to stand on an heap. The sea overwhelmed their enemies.' Ps. cvi. 9, 'He rebuked the Red Sea also, and it was dried up; so he led them through the depths as through a wilderness.' Ver. 11, 'The waters covered their enemies, so that there was not one of them left.' Ps. cxiv. 1, 3, 5, 'When Israel came out of Egypt, &c. The sea saw that and fled. What ailed thee, O sea, that thou fleddest!' Ps. cxxxvi. 13–15, 'He divided the Red Sea into parts. He overthrew Pharaoh and his host in the Red Sea.' Isa. li. 10, 'Art not thou it, that hath dried up the sea, the waters of the great deep, that hath made the depths of the sea a way for the ransomed to pass over?'

Many more are the mentions of this miracle in the book of God, and here we find it in this psalm doubly repeated.

Doct. Which teacheth us that God's extraordinary mercies must be often remembered.

For we must consider our God two ways:

1. *Quâ Deus*, as God; and so he is to be worshipped *cultu latriæ propter Deum*, for his own sake, though we could live without him; though he do hide his face from us, and heap up his judgments on us: as Job saith, chap. vii. 20, 'Though he maketh us as his mark to shoot at, though all his arrows do stick fast in us.'

2. *Quâ benefactor*, as a benefactor; and that also two ways.

(1.) *Propter opus providentiæ*, for his work of providence, whereby he is to us a gracious God and merciful Father, taking his church to himself, and gathering it under his wings, shielding it against the sun by day, and against the moon by night.

(2.) *Propter opera privilegiata*, for his privileged works, especially favours of mercy, *quando non facit taliter*. For the first, all our life, especially the Sabbath, is designed to the worship and service of God for the same. The second of his extraordinary works doth exact of us singular commemoration by themselves; and therefore Abulensis saith, *Omnia festa quæ Deus instituit observanda à Judæis fiebant, ad recordationem beneficiorum ejus*.

Now, the school saith well, that *latria* is not *totaliter determinata*, to these or these times or ceremonies, or occasions, but that we may worship God always *quà Deus*, as God; upon special occasions *quà benefactor*, as benefactor.

And so the Jews kept the memorial of their deliverance from Egypt in their anniversary celebration of the passover, and of their dwelling in tents in the feast of tabernacles; and of their deliverance from Haman, in their feast of Purim.

And the German protestants do keep a Christian jubilee every fifty years for their deliverance from the darkness of popery, and their ejection of the pope. Wherein our church, as much beholding to God for the same benefit as they, doth come short of them in matter of thankfulness to God for the expulsion of that man of sin from us.

We have three commemorations enjoined us by high authority. The one is *ortus auspicia;* so of all it was called; the *initium regni*, the beginning of the reign of our sovereign, whom God sent to settle the religion and peace which his glorious predecessor Queen Elizabeth had so happily and so valiantly brought in and maintained during her whole reign, and by the providence of God we enjoy it to this day.

Another is the remembrance of his majesty's deliverance from the treason of the Gowries in Scotland, before his reign here, as it were his reserving of him for us.

The third is the commemoration of the admirable goodness of God to our land, in the bloody treason of the papists, the mortal enemies of our religion and peace, in their powder plot.

But this often remembrance of the mercy of God to Israel in the Red Sea upbraids our forgetfulness of that '88 sea-mercy which God shewed to our land in our deliverance from the Spanish intended invasion, in the times of hostility between Spain and England; and though the established peace between these two kingdoms have laid aside open wars, yet let God be no loser in the glory due to his name for that deliverance.

Reason 2. I will add another reason why this passage of Israel through the Red Sea is so oft remembered in Scripture, twice in this psalm of Habakkuk, which I gather from the apostle St Paul: 1 Cor. x. 1, 2, 'Moreover, brethren, I would not have you ignorant, how that all our fathers were under the cloud, and all passed through the sea; and were all baptized unto Moses in the sea, and in the cloud.' For this was memorable not only in the history of the thing done, but in the mystery also of the signification thereof.

You see by this apostle that this is a memorable thing, and he would not have us ignorant of it; and if we know it, he would not have us forget it. There is continual use of it in the church, even so long as baptism continueth therein. For that is the scope of the apostle in the beginning of that chapter, to shew that the church of the Jews, as they had sacraments of their own, circumcision and the Lord's passover, so had they types and figures of our two sacraments also.

The type and representation of our baptism was their passage through the Red Sea. The type of our Lord's supper was the water out of the rock and manna. But they and we do all receive the same spiritual meat and drink, that is, Christ.

So that this passage over the Red Sea doth figure our baptism. Here is Moses, the minister of the sacrament; here are Israelites, the receivers of it; and here is water, the element; and the cloud, the sign of God's presence : here is Israel, that is, the persons baptized, preserved in these waters ; and here is king Pharaoh and his hosts, that is, Satan and our hereditary corruptions, drowned and destroyed in the same waters.

And the apostle saith, I would not that ye should be ignorant of this thing; which admonisheth both you and us, that are your ministers.

1. You; not to be ignorant in those great mysteries of salvation.

2. Us ; not to leave you untaught or unremembered thereof.

We that preach to a mixed auditory, consisting of *incipientes*, abcedaries in religion, who are not yet out of their first elements, which the apostle calleth the doctrine of beginnings ; and some few proficients, who also have their measures not all of equal growth, but some few as much better grown than others, as Saul was higher than all the rest of the people, must as well give milk with the spoon as break bread, and divide strong meat; and methinks there be two places that direct us well in the dispensation of the word of God.

1. That of the prophet Isaiah, chap. ii. 13, 'The word of the Lord was unto them precept upon precept, precept upon precept, line upon line, line upon line, here a little and there a little ;' in which words the matter of our preaching is expressed in two words : 1, *precept*, which teacheth us what to do ; 2, *line*, which exemplifieth doctrine, and serveth as a copy to write by.

And again, the manner of our preaching is declared profitable, if the same things be well taught, till they be well learned. And this is *modicum ibi, modicum ibi*, here *modicum*, not too much at once, for oppressing the spiritual stomach ; and here is *ibi* and *ibi*, *ibi* amongst the proficients, and *ibi* amongst the incipients.

2. That of St Peter : 2 Peter i. 12, ' Wherefore, I will not be negligent to put you in mind of those things, though ye know them. Yea, I think it meet, so long

as I am in this tabernacle, to stir you up, by putting you in remembrance.'

This sheweth the use of often repetitions of such things as we ought not to forget, for it is not enough to have light in our understanding, there must be also zeal in our affections. Religion in the head is speculation, in the heart affection, in the hand action.

If we do our duty thus, as we are directed, it must be your great fault if either you be ignorant or forgetful of these things.

The Spirit of God is our example; for he remembereth this passage of Israel often, and *modicum ibi*, a little here, in the Old Testament, *modicum ibi*, a little there, in the New Testament; for this is also profitable for us.

This sheweth that the often preaching, and learning, and remembering the doctrine of our baptism, is a most necessary lesson in the school of Christ, that we do not enter into a new peace with the Egyptians, whom God hath drowned in the Red Sea, that we do not revive and quicken in us those things which the laver of new birth hath purged, by suffering sin to reign in our mortal bodies, and by obeying it in the lusts thereof. That we do not so much as in heart return again into Egypt, out of which God hath so graciously delivered us.

Profitable is the remembrance of our baptism, for it is the sacrament and seal of our deliverance from the curse of the law, from the spiritual bondage of Satan, from the dominion of sin; it sheweth us the old Adam, dead in the death, and buried in the grave of Christ.

It also serveth, being often remembered, to stir us up to a practice of Christian conversation, and to an holy imitation of Christ in godly life; that we may not receive the grace of God in vain; that we be not again defiled with the world; for the apostle will tell us, Heb. x. 22, 23, that if Christ hath opened us a new and living way through the veil, that is, his flesh, we must ' draw near with a true heart, in full assurance of faith, having our hearts sprinkled from an evil conscience, and our bodies washed with pure water; holding fast the profession of our faith without wavering.' For, ver. 26, 'if we sin wilfully after we have received the knowledge of the truth, there remaineth no more sacrifice for sins, but a certain fearful looking for of judgment, and fiery indignation, which shall devour the adversaries.'

I conclude, in the apostle's words: 'Therefore, brethren, I would not have you ignorant,' concerning this passage of the Lord's Israel through the Red Sea.

Ver. 16. *When I heard, my belly trembled; my lips quivered at the voice: rottenness entered into my bones, and I trembled in myself, that I might rest in the day of trouble: when he cometh up unto his people, he will invade them with his troops.*

At this verse beginneth the third section of this chapter, and it containeth the consternation of the prophet dejected before the Lord with the former considerations, and the sad estate of the land of Canaan.

1. Concerning the words.

When I heard. The prophet fitting this psalm, as you have heard, for the common use of the church, doth not speak in this place in his own person particularly, 'When I heard,' but in the person of that church of God to which this prophecy was sent: Ver. 14, *They came out as a whirlwind to scatter me*, is spoken of the Midianites invading God's people, not the prophet Habakkuk. So that *I heard* here is collectively the whole church, and particularly every member thereof.

But what is that is here heard?

Surely this hath a double reference:

1. To the former prophecy of God's threatened judgments against his people, of which you heard before, ver. 2, 'O Lord, I have heard thy speech, and was afraid.' For it was a fearful judgment which God had denounced against them.

2. It hath reference to the full commemoration of God's former mercies; for howsoever faith may grow upon this root of experience of God's favour, yet when

the church of God shall consider all that former favour now turned into indignation, and shall feel that power which once protected them, so miraculously now armed against them, this cannot but cast them into great fear.

This fear is described fully and rhetorically in four several phrases.
1. 'My belly trembled.'
2. 'My lips quivered.'
3. 'Rottenness entered into my bones.'
4. 'I trembled in myself.'

It is the manner of the Spirit of God in such like phrases to express a great horror and dismay. By the belly is meant the inward parts and bowels. So the prophet, upon the denunciation of the burden upon the desert sea, saith, Isa. xxi. 3, 'Therefore are my loins filled with pain: pangs have taken hold upon me, as the pangs of a woman that travaileth: I was bowed down at the hearing of it; I was dismayed at the seeing of it.' Isa. xvi. 11, 'My bowels shall sound like an harp for Moab, and mine inward parts for Kirharesh.' So Job, chap. xxx. 27, 'My bowels boiled, and rested not.' And David, Ps. xxxi. 9, 'Mine eye is consumed with grief; yea, my soul and belly.' Ps. xxii. 14, 'I am poured out like water; all my bones are out of joint: my heart is like wax; it is melted in the midst of my bowels?' Thus the perturbations of grief and fear, and the passions of anguish, are expressed.

The quivering of the lips, which hindereth speech, sheweth a man overcome with anger, fear, or grief. So doth the general disabling of the body, as if the parts thereof, the brains and sinews, suffered laxation and debilitation, and the earthquake in the whole frame thereof, and the distemper of the man within us. 'I trembled in myself,' that is, the inward man; the hid man of the heart felt this anguish of grief and fear, and all this trepidation and terror had this good effect following;—

That I might rest in the day of trouble. For of sufferance comes ease. This fear of the heavy hand of God is but a fit; for faith followeth it, and consumeth it, and settleth the heart in a yielding to the mighty hand of God, and that giveth rest in the day of trouble. That day is also described.

When he cometh up unto his people, he will invade them with his troops. Either when God cometh, or when the enemy whom God shall employ in the execution of this judgment cometh, he will invade his people that have rebelled against him, and are fallen away from him, with troops; that is, he will come upon them with a full power, to make a full conquest of them. This day is further described in the verse following.

Ver. 17. *Although the fig-tree shall not blossom, neither shall fruit be in the vines; the labour of the olive shall fail, and the fields shall yield no meat; the flocks shall be cut off from the fold, and there shall be no herd in the stalls.*

In which words he supposeth the worst that may befall to the land, that God should not only, as before, carry away or destroy the inhabitants thereof, although he should smite the land itself with barrenness, that neither the fig-tree nor the vine should relieve them, nor the olive, nor the fields, nor the folds; yet the church will not despair of the loving-kindness of the Lord toward them.

This land, so long promised to the seed of Abraham, so long expected, and at last by them possessed, is much praised in Scripture. God himself, Exod. iii. 8, calleth it ' a good land, and a large; a land flowing with milk and honey.' And so the spies that were sent to search it brought word: Num. xiii. 9, and they brought of the fruit, and shewed it to the people.

Again, Deut. viii. 7, ' For the Lord thy God bringeth thee into a good land; a land of brooks of water, of fountains, and depths, that spring out of valleys and hills; a land of wheat, and barley, and vines, and fig-trees, and pomegranates; a land of oil-olive, and honey; a land wherein thou shalt eat bread without scarceness, thou shalt not lack anything in it; a land whose stones are iron, and out of whose hills thou mayest dig brass.'

It was one of the miracles of the earth, and the full blessing of the Lord was upon it; for the land was small, both in length and breadth, as all the charts thereof describe it. For from Dan to the river of Egypt, which is somewhat further than Beersheba, it was little more than three hundred miles, which was the length of it, and in the broadest place thereof it was not an hundred; yea, do I put in this account all the land on this side Jordan, the portion assigned to Reuben, Gad, and the half-tribe of Manasseh.

Yet did it contain two great kingdoms, of Judah and Israel; and, in David's time, there were numbered in it thirteen hundred thousand fighting men, 2 Chron. xxiv., which cannot in probable computation be more than a fourth part of the people, seeing aged men, women, and children, and all under twenty years of age, are not reckoned; and this land fed them all. Much is said by heathen writers of the fruitfulness of this land; and as great a wonder is it of the change thereof now, for travellers do report it at this time to be a barren and unfruitful land. It is in the possession of God's enemies; and David saith, 'A fruitful land maketh he barren, for the iniquity of the people that dwelt therein.' *De verbis hactenus*, of the words hitherto. The parts of this section are two:

1. The fear of the church.
2. The misery of the land.

In the first, I observe also three things:
1. The cause of this fear.
2. The fear itself.
3. The effect hereof.

In the second, the misery of the land. It is distressed in the three great commodities of life.
1. In the trees yielding fruit.
2. In the soil yielding corn.
3. In the flocks yielding increase.

1. Of the fear of the church; and therein,

1. Of the cause of this fear, in these words, 'When I heard.'

Doct. The commination of God's judgments doth make the church of God to fear.

1. Because this openeth to man his conscience,

and declareth to him his sin, for we know that God is gracious, and merciful, and longsuffering, and hideth his hand in his bosom. His mercy doth often pull it out and openeth it, and he filleth the hungry with good things; his mercy stretcheth it out often to gather together his chosen, to defend them from evil, to stay and support them.

If his indignation do pluck it out, it is a sign that sin hath provoked him, and therefore we read what of old was the practice of the church. If there were any judgment abroad, presently they made search for the sin that had provoked God to it; for they knew him so just, that he will not smite without cause. God taught Joshua this; when the men of Ai smote the men of Israel, and made them to fly before them, Joshua went to the Lord to make his moan, and God told him, 'Israel hath sinned.' And so there was a present search made by the commandment of the Lord throughout all Israel, to find out the sinner, and Achan was detected.

In like manner, when Saul had made a vow that none of his army should taste any food till night, and Jonathan, not hearing of the commandment, had eaten a little honey upon the end of his rod, he went to advise with God concerning the pursuit of the Philistines by night, and God answered him not; wherefore Saul said, 1 Sam. xiv. 38, 'Draw you near hither all the chief of the people, and know, and see wherein this sin hath been this day.'

And this is so natural a quest, as that whosoever do acknowledge a divinity, cannot but upon the sense of judgment, or the fear of it, presently conclude God offended with some sins. So the mariners in the great storm in Jonah said every one to his fellow, 'Come and let us cast lots, that we may know for whose cause this evil is upon us.'

Reason 2. The consideration of God's judgments do breed fear in respect of God, whose judgments they are. For, 1, he is so quick-sighted to discern our sins, that he seeth all; nothing can be hidden from him, but all lieth open and naked to his sight.

2. He is so wise to weigh the sins that we commit,

putting into the scales the incitements and temptations, the circumstances of time, person, place, number, even the very affection wherewith sin is committed.

3. He is so just, as not to impute more sin to us than we have committed, not to abate any of that we have misdone.

4. He is so holy, as not to abide or appear* the least evil, for he is a God that hateth iniquity.

5. He is so powerful, as to avenge it with his judgment, and he hath all sorts of instruments of vengeance to punish sin.

6. He is so ubiquitary, as that no remove can avoid him, his presence filleth all places.

7. He is so true of his word, that heaven and earth shall pass, but no part of his word shall fail till all be fulfilled.

8. He is one that cannot repent of anything that he peremptorily decreeth.

All these things do declare that there is great cause to fear when he threateneth.

Use. The apostle teacheth us the use of this point: Rom. xiii. 3, 'Wilt thou not then be afraid of the power? Do that which is good, then shalt thou have praise of the same.' This is the way to make us seek the face of God. The first sinners fled from the presence of God behind the trees in the garden. Adam confessed to God: Gen. iii. 10, 'I heard thy voice in the garden, and I was afraid.'

A good life is a good fence against fear; Solomon saith, 'The righteous is bold as a lion.' Perfect love casteth out fear, for perfect love is the fulfilling of the law; where our love falleth short, there fear filleth the empty and void room.

The voice of the Lord is comfortable, and his words are sweet to those that fear him: Ps. lxxxv. 8, 'He will speak peace unto his people, and to his saints; but let them not turn again to folly.' So David resolves there, 'I will hear what the Lord will speak.'

It is a plain sign that all is not well with us, when the voice of God doth cast us into fear, when we are afraid to hear the word preached, when just reproofs

---

* Qu. 'approve'?—ED.

of our sins are unwelcome to us, and anger us, and make us think the worse of our minister that chideth and threateneth us.

A good life and a well governed conversation doth not fear the voice of God; the word of God is the light which God hath set up in his church, to guide her feet in the ways of peace. They that do evil hate the light, and will not come near it, lest their works should be reproved; the children of the light resort to it, and call upon God: 'Search my reins and my heart, and see if there be any way of wickedness in me.'

This fear of the church is not joined either with obstinacy against God, or murmuring at his judgments, or despair of his mercy; it is that fear which is one of the effects of a godly sorrow, and it is one of the documents to true repentance; it is the hammer and mallet of God, wherewith he bruiseth us, and breaketh us, that we may be truly humbled under his almighty hand; it is that fear which the spirit of bondage suggesteth, Rom. viii. 15, which is not a grace of God in us, but a punishment of God upon us, and we would fain be without it; it is the fear of servants, and not of sons, yet God useth it as a means to bring us home to him again, when we like sheep have gone astray; and therefore the prodigal, to re-enter himself into his father's house, prayed, *Fac me unum ex mercenariis*, make me as one of thy hired servants. It may be that fear, which in the school is called *initialis*, which re-entereth us into the service of God, and keepeth us in awe. It is *utilis*, but not *sufficiens*, and we would be glad to be delivered out of it, that we might 'serve God without fear, in holiness and righteousness.' For so the apostle doth recount it a favour to the Romans, 'Ye have not received the spirit of bondage again to fear, but the spirit of adoption.'

2. The fear itself.

This fear was great, both in the inward man and in the outward; it was that fear of which David spake to God, saying of the heathen, 'Put them in fear, O Lord, that they may know themselves to be but men.' And David himself was soundly shaken with it, as his complaint sheweth: Ps. cxix. 120, 'My flesh trembleth for fear of thee, and I am afraid of thy judgments.' And we find the best of the faithful servants of God subject to this fear; and it is clear in my text, that it may be joined with faith. For after this cold fit of fear, you shall see the faith of the church to quicken it again.

Doct. The elect of God are shaken with fear.

Reason 1. Because they are great students in the law of God, for that is a special mark of a righteous man, he doth exercise himself in the law of God day and night. And wheresoever the law is wisely understood and applied rightly, there fear doth arise, for so long as we are under the law, we are under a schoolmaster; and as the apostle doth say, a child differeth very little from a servant. You know when a young man came to Christ, to ask him the way to heaven, Christ referred him to the law, and the keeping thereof. That is our first lesson; it follows so in the mission of our Redeemer, he was made of a woman, and made subject to the law.

The law sheweth us how much we are in God's debt, and you may note it in the parable of the good master in the Gospel;—

1. He called his servant to account, and cast up the debt.

2. Then he put him to it to pay it.

3. When he saw him willing but unable, then he forgave it.

God calleth us by the light of the law, by the sight of our sins. Our sins are debts; when we see them, how can we choose but together with them behold the danger of them, and the wrath due to them? This cannot be done without fear, even great horror and dejection.

The thief that was converted upon the cross, when he had but a little time, he made an example of great mercy, the only example in all the book of God of so late a conversion; yet in that short time he began at the law of God, and said to his fellow, Luke xxiii. 41, 'We indeed are justly punished, for we receive the due rewards of our deeds.' And after that he sought grace; this law was the schoolmaster that brought him to Christ, saying, 'Lord, remember me when thou comest into thy kingdom;' for, until we compare ourselves with the law of righteousness, we cannot know how unjust we are, and what need we have of a Saviour.

We may see it in our first parents, who no sooner had sinned but they hid themselves from God, because they saw their fault by the light of the law, which they had transgressed.

Reason 2. This fear bringeth us to repentance, it putteth our sins in our sight, and setteth before our eyes the wrath to come; so the generation of vipers were first put in fear, by warning given them of the anger to come, and upon that foundation he buildeth his doctrine of repentance. *Ferte ergò fructus dignos pœnitentia*, bring forth therefore fruits worthy of repentance. It is time to amend when sin standeth at the door; that is, the wages of sin, to punish all, or some new temptation to sin to make it more. Fear will tell us that time is precious, we must lose none of it for our true repentance and conversion to God.

Reason 3. This fear serveth for caution against the time to come; for *piscis ictus sapit*, one that hath been once soundly shaken with a strong fit of this fear, will be the more wary to decline and avoid it another time. For there is nothing that so much agonizeth the soul and body of man, as the sense and conscience of the wrath of God.

Reason 4. It is one of the arguments, as you have heard, by which we do prove certain great articles of faith; as,

1. It proveth that there is a God; for that power which the conscience of man doth fear as an avenger of evil, is God.

2. It proveth the resurrection of the body; for, as the apostle saith, 'If in this life only we have hope,' so we may say, if for this life only we have fear, it can be no great matter, for the judgments of God cannot take sufficient vengeance of sin here.

3. It proveth the final judgment; for all the afflic-

tions of a temporal life are but the forerunner of the last judgment.

Quest. But here it is objected, that this may well hold in the reprobate ; but to see this earthquake of trembling in the church, and amongst the holy ones of God, as it is here described, this seemeth too hard a portion for God's beloved and chosen ones.

Sol. To this I answer, that judgment beginneth at the house of God, and the righteous are hardly saved; they that have no other hell but in this terror of the Lord here, do most smart in this world, and there is great reason for it.

1. In respect of God, to shew him no accepter of the persons of men, but an equal hater of evil in all that commit it ; as David saith, ' If I regard wickedness in my heart, God will not hear me.'

2. In respect of the sin committed by his chosen, that God may declare the danger of it for terror to others ; and his justice in avenging it, that men may fear, and do no more so.

3. In respect of the wicked, that they may have example of fear in the smart of others, to bring them to the obedience and service of God.

Use 1. This doth serve, first for exhortation; to stir us up to consider our God in the way of his judgments, and to bethink us what evil may hang over our heads for sin. The church hath ever found this a profitable course : Isa. xxvi. 8, ' In the way of thy judgments, O Lord, have we waited for thee ; the desire of our soul is to thy name, and to the remembrance of thee.' The profit that groweth hence is there confessed by the church : ver. 9, ' When thy judgments are in the earth, the inhabitants of the world will learn righteousness.'

Use 2. This doth serve to put difference between the children of God and the children of this world ; for the ungodly are not afraid of the hand of God, but the sinner contemneth, but the righteous layeth it to his heart ; so saith the church, ver. 11, ' Lord, when thy hand is lifted up, they will not see : but they shall see, and be ashamed.'

Use 3. This also serveth for consolation of the

church; for let them not be too much dejected with consideration either of God's revealed wrath, or their own just fear; no, though their fear do shake and stagger their very faith for a time; for God will not forsake them unto despair, but will let some of the beams of grace shine even through the clouds of fear to comfort them. David felt it, and confessed it, saying, Ps. lvi. 3, 'What time I am afraid, I will trust in thee.' See how they grow together, fear and faith.

Obj. But this is objected, as an argument against that doctrine of the assurance of salvation that a child of God may have in this life; for it is urged, Can a man that standeth assured of the favour of God to him in Christ Jesus, be so shaken with fear as the church here confesseth?

Sol. We answer,

1. That fear of temporal smart in this life is natural, and may be in the sons of God; it was in the Son of God, Jesus Christ, and it may be without sin; and the elect, although they fear the judgments of God on earth, yet they doubt not but that their names are written in heaven.

2. That fear is not against faith, which is quick and sensible of the wrath and judgments of God; it is *cos fidei*, the whetstone of faith; it puts a better edge upon it, and serves to teach us to lay so much the faster hold upon Jesus Christ.

Courage either to resist an evil ingruent without a right knowledge of it, or to bear an evil incumbent without a right understanding, both of the author of it, the cause of it, or the end of it, or the measure of it, is not courage, but stupidity; but when we do rightly know God to lay his hand on us for sin, or hear him threaten us with the rod, is it not time to fear, and to pray with Jeremiah, chap. xvii. 17, 'Be not a terror to me, for thou art my hope in the day of evil.'

3. Fear and faith go together in respect of the temporal judgments of God, because the threatenings of temporal judgments are not always peremptory, but ofttimes conditional; therefore the king of Nineveh, proclaiming a general fast and repentance in Nineveh,

had this encouragement, Jonah iii. 9, 'Who can tell if God will turn and repent, and turn away from his fierce anger, that we perish not?' God himself hath put us into this comfort: Jer. xviii. 7, 8, 'At what instant I shall speak concerning a nation, and concerning a kingdom, to pluck up, and to pull down, and to destroy it; if that nation, against whom I have pronounced, turn from their evil, I will repent of the evil that I thought to do unto them.'

So that this fear of the temporal judgments of God doth no way weaken the faithful assurance that we have conceived of eternal salvation, rather it strengtheneth it; yea, the more that we either taste or fear the punishing hand of God here, the more do we desire the release of us hence, which is rest from all labours.

4. They that take this fear to be contrary to faith and assurance of the favour of God, do mistake it, for it is true that a doubtful and despairing fear doth destroy faith; but the faithful cannot fall into that fear, because God presseth not his temptations above that which his children are able to bear. And fear in them is but contrary to presumption, it is not contrary to faith; which thus appears, because this fear doth not make the servants of God give over the work of their salvation, rather it makes them double their endeavours and redeem the time.

But in the reprobate, their fear doth make them give heaven gone from them, and profess it lost labour to serve God. Mal. iii. 14, 'Ye have said, It is in vain to serve God; and what profit is it that we have kept his ordinances, and that we have walked mournfully before the Lord of hosts?' But they that feared the Lord spake often one to another, that is, encouraged one another; and it is said the Lord hearkened and heard it, &c.

3. The effect of this fear, 'that I might rest in the day of trouble.'

This also sheweth that this fear of the church was not separated from faith, for it is entertained of purpose to settle the heart, and to give it rest in the day of trouble.

I cannot but often remember that sweet saying of Austin, *Medicina est quod pateris*, thy suffering is the physic; for the physic that we take to purge the ill humours of the body doth make the body more sick for the time, and so do the chastisements of God. The fear of judgment threatened is more pain to the children of God than the sense of the judgment inflicted.

It is a note of the just, that they rejoice in tribulations, yet you see they fear tribulations before they come, which shews that the bitterness of that cup is more in the cause than in the effect.

The righteous in these threatenings do behold God in displeasure, themselves in the guilt of provocation, and nothing goeth so near the heart of a godly man as that his God should take any unkindness at him, for in his favour is life. To help this, when God threateneth, the just man feareth, and that fear doth both remember him of the occasion of this judgment, and composeth him to repentance of his sin, and to prayer to divert it, or to patience in it.

Doct. Fear joined with faith prepareth us for peace and rest in the day of trouble.

An admirable work it is of wisdom and mercy to extract rest out of fear, but to him that brought light out of darkness nothing is impossible; more to give rest in the day of trouble when the soul refuseth comfort, and even begins to take a kind of pride in the fulness of misery, and saith, *Videte si dolor sicut dolor meus.*

Reason 1. Because these inward convulsions of the hid man of the heart are joined evermore in the godly, with an hatred of the sin that deserved them; for from hence ariseth this confession, *Peccavi.*

Reason 2. Observe it in Job. He did not ask, *Quid patior?* but *Quid faciam tibi?* So it worketh in us a care and conscience of obedience hereafter.

Reason 3. It also discerneth an issue out of trouble; for where fear doth not overgrow, there is a sweet apprehension of joy in the end. As the apostle saith, Heb. xii. 11, 'Afterward it yieldeth the peaceable fruit of righteousness unto them which are exercised thereby.'

Use 1. 'Wherefore, lift up the hands that hang down, and the feeble knees. Make straight paths for your feet, lest that which is lame be turned out of the way; but let it rather be healed.' The way is there described: 'Follow peace with all men, and holiness, without which no man shall see the Lord.' 'Look diligently, lest any man fall from the grace of God; lest any root of bitterness springing up in you trouble you.'

Out of this whole passage you may observe a sweet description of a full repentance.

1. Here is the law of God, revealing both sin and the judgment due to it, called here the hearing of the voice of God.

2. Here is the conscience agonised with the fear of God's judgments.

3. Here is the fruit and benefit thereof, even peace and rest in the day of trouble.

Here is sowing in tears and reaping in joy; rather it is sunshine in a tempest, for the outward man is shaken, and the flesh suffereth; but the just do say with the ever-blessed virgin, 'My spirit rejoiceth in God my Saviour.'

Impii non sic, not so with the wicked; for God hath said it, that there shall be no peace at the last to them, but as the raging of the angry sea, which casteth up nothing but foam and dirt.

2. The miseries of the land.

This is described fully,

1. In the agent. 2. In the patient.

In the agent two ways.

1. The *primus motor*, the supreme agent, God.

2. The instruments of action; his troops. These are the Chaldeans.

In the patient, the land of Canaan distressed, as you have heard.

1. In the trees bearing fruit: the fig-tree, the vine, the olive.

2. In the field or arable.

3. In their cattle: 1. Such as feed abroad. 2. Such as are stalled.

1. Concerning the agent supreme, God.

Doct. The same hand that gave them possession of that good land doth now remove them thence. Here is *mutatio dextræ*.

It is a thing notable, that God is ever in Scripture described to us constant, 'yesterday and to-day, and the same for ever; without variableness, or so much as a shadow of alteration.' Yet, in his government of the world, he sometimes giveth, and sometimes he taketh away; sometimes he filleth, and sometimes he emptieth.

Reason 1. The reason hereof is partly in ourselves; for as our obedience and service of him doth both gain and assure to us all good things, as himself telleth us, Isa. i. 19, 20, 'If you consent and obey, you shall eat the good things of the land;' so our disobedience and transgression doth lose us all these things, as he addeth, 'If you refuse and rebel, you shall be devoured with the sword; for the mouth of the Lord hath spoken it.'

Reason 2. Partly it is in God, for his mercy in giving must not destroy his justice in punishing of evil doers; for if it be 'a righteous thing with God to recompense tribulation to them that trouble us, it must needs be as righteous to recompense tribulation to them that trouble him. It is an heavy complaint God made of his people: Isa. i. 2, 'I have nourished and brought up children, and they have rebelled against me.'

It is well observed in God, that he is *primus in amore, et postremus in odio,* he loveth us before we can seek his face, and we are tender in sight before we know the right hand from the left, as in the case of Nineveh God pleaded with Jonah for the infants.

But God never forsaketh us till we first forsake him; not then, if there be but *animus revertendi,* he is patient and long-suffering; but when we come once to two evils, to forsake him, the fountain of living waters, and to dig to ourselves cisterns of our own making, then he can no longer forbear; when we grow, Isa. i. 4, 'a sinful nation, a people laden with iniquity, a seed of evil doers, children that are corrupters, forsaking the Lord, provoking the Holy One of Israel to anger, going away backward,' no wonder, ver. 7, 'if he make our country desolate, burn our cities with fire, let strangers devour land in our presence, and lay it desolate, as overthrown by strangers.'

Use 1. Where we are guilty to ourselves of provocation of the Lord against us, we have cause to lay all the blame upon ourselves, and to say, We have gone away from thee, and have not hearkened to thy voice, therefore art thou displeased with us. Seeing the justice of God doth set him against us, we are also to acquit him of any hard measure towards us, and to say, 'Just art thou, O Lord, and just are thy judgments.'

But especially, this stirreth us up to divert this wrath to come, for to that purpose God giveth warnings by threatenings, not in judgment to punish and torment us before our time with the fear of them, and after in their time with the sense of them, but to admonish us to fly from the anger to come; for Jeremiah was sent on this very message to this people, and he threatened them from God, as Habakkuk here doth, yet with this caution of repentance.

For Jeremiah being required by king Zedekiah to inquire of the Lord concerning Nebuchadnezzar, king of Babel,—Jer. xxi. 2, 'If the Lord will deal with us according to all his wonderful works that he will go from us,'—Jeremiah, through the whole chapter, resolveth him, that God is purposed to deliver his people and their land into the hand of king Nebuchadnezzar, yet in the next chapter he bringeth this comfortable message from God to the king: Jer. xxii. 1–5, 'Thus saith the Lord, Go down to the king of Judah, and speak there this word, and say, Hear the word of the Lord, O king of Judah, that sitteth upon the throne of David, thou and thy servants, and the people that enter in by these gates; thus saith the Lord, execute you judgment and righteousness, and deliver the spoiled out of the hand of the oppressor: and do no wrong, do no violence to the stranger, the fatherless, nor the widow, neither shed innocent blood in this place. For if you do this thing indeed, then there shall enter in by the gates of this house, kings sitting for David upon his throne, riding in chariots and on horses, he, and his servants, and his people. But if ye will not hear these words, I swear by myself, saith the Lord, that this house shall become a desolation,' &c. This declareth that the threatenings of God, when he menaceth our sins with judgments, are like Jonathan's arrows, shot rather to give us warning than to hurt us.

Which admonisheth us, that whensoever any fear surpriseth us of wrath to come upon our land, either in the corruption of our religion, or in the perturbation of our peace, or in the fear of false friends that may kiss or betray, or in the dearth and scarcity of the necessaries of life, in any, in all these fears, the change of our ways, the repentance of our sins, the amendment of our lives, will ever make our peace with our God, and turn away these threatened and feared evils from us; for godliness hath the promises both of this life and of that which is to come.

2. Let us consider the instruments in this action, called ' his troops.'

Doct. The armies of the Chaldeans, by which Israel is to be punished, are the troops of God.

God owns them, as Jeremiah telleth Zedekiah, Jer. xxi. 4, 5, ' Thus saith the Lord God of Israel, Behold, I will turn back the weapons of war that are in your hands, wherewith ye fight against the king of Babylon, and against the Chaldeans which besiege you without the walls, and I will assemble them in the midst of this city. And I myself will fight against you with an outstretched hand, and with a strong arm, even in anger, and in fury, and in great wrath.'

So he told them before in this prophecy: Hab. i. 6,

I raise up the Chaldeans, a bitter and hasty nation, which shall march through the breadth of the land, to possess the dwelling-places that are not theirs.'

From whence we have learned,

That God ordereth this war against his people; which doctrine we have at large handled in the prophecy of Obadiah.

We learned also that God punisheth one evil nation by another, and those whom he employeth in the correction of his enemies, he protecteth and prospereth in their wars, and he is very careful to pay them wages, as in the service of Egypt against Tyrus which Nebuchadnezzar did: Ezek. xxix. 20, 'I have given him the land of Egypt for the service wherewith he served against it, because they wrought for me, saith the Lord God.' For God can make use of wicked men to serve in his troops for the punishing of such as rebel against him.

Therefore, let no man say, the Turk is an enemy to God and to religion; he serveth Mahomed, he is an infidel, and therefore he shall not prevail against us.

Let no man say, the pope is a man of sin and a maintainer of idolatry, a usurper upon the royal prerogatives of Jesus Christ; he advanceth himself above all that is called God, and is worshipped; he is an encroacher upon the rights, and honours, and power of princes, and usurpeth a transcendent jurisdiction over them; a maintainer of treason, and murderer of kings; a coiner of articles of faith; a hider of the word of God; a maker of counter laws against the law of God; therefore, neither he nor his religion shall ever prevail against the professors of the truth of God.

For if these sins be found in our land which God conditioned again* in Judah; that is, if just judgment be not executed and righteousness practised, if the spoiled be not delivered from the hand of the oppressor, if wrong be done to the stranger, the poor, the fatherless and the widow; Turk and pope, papists and infidels may be gathered together into the troops of God and employed against us, and prevail against us, for we are no better than Judah, nor dearer to God than his own people; and if he please to punish Christendom or the professors of his truth by these, if once they become God's troops, they shall prosper and carry all before them.

The misery in the patient; the land of Israel threatened, as you hear in the trees.

---

* Qu. 'cautioned against'?—ED.

Here are named the chief trees for fruit, the fig-tree, the vine, and the olive. *Non omnis fert omnia tellus*, these trees do not grow in all lands. Our land, though rich and plenteous, is no fit soil for these trees.

They served for food, and they are of special note, for in the parable of Jotham, Judges ix. 8, when the trees went to choose them a king, they came first to the olive-tree and said, Reign thou over us; they went next to the fig-tree, and then to the vine. The olive-tree saith, Shall I leave my fatness, wherewith by me they honour God and man? The fig-tree saith, Should I forsake my sweetness and my good fruit? The vine saith, Should I leave my wine, which cheereth God and man? You see of how excellent use these fruits were: two of them used in the special service of God, oil and wine, and often in the land of Canaan, praised for fruitfulness in respect of the trees growing there, which every soil doth not yield. They are all of excellent use, both for food and medicine; and David saith of wine, that it maketh glad the heart of man; of oil, that it maketh him have a cheerful countenance.

The failing of these, which the soil doth naturally bring forth, doth shew that God hath called in his blessing, which he gave to every land, for the true nature of every soil is the word of God's blessing, which once called in, a fruitful land is made barren, and a populous country is soon turned into a desert.

But this is not all: not only God will smite the land in these excellent fruits, which are for food, but as Jeremiah threateneth, chap. xxii. 7, 'They shall cut down the choice cedars, and cast them into the fire:' trees for building.

Reason. The reason whereof we may find in the first of our parents, who no sooner had sinned but God accursed the earth for their sakes. So that we may say as the church doth in this psalm, Was thy wrath against the trees of the land, that thou smotest them? not so, but against the sins and sinners of the land.

This further appeareth in the common ground, for it followeth, ' the fields shall yield no meat.'

Bread is the staff of life; God threateneth to break the staff of bread. So he bade Ezekiel prophesy, chap. iv. 16, 'Son of man, I will break the staff of bread in Jerusalem, and they shall eat their bread by weight, and with care.'

God hath many ways to perform this judgment, either by taking away his blessing from the earth, that it shall not bring forth bread for the use of man; thus he maketh a fruitful land barren. Or he can hold in the early and the later rain, that it shall not fall to moisten the earth, as in the time of Haggai the prophet: chap. i. 9, 10, 'Ye looked for much, and, lo, it came too little. The heaven over you is stayed from dew, and the earth under you is stayed from her fruit.'

Yea, God when he pleaseth can drown the fruits of the earth with too much rain, and destroy the crop; and when he hath shewed us plenty upon the ground, he can deceive the hope of the husbandman, and make a thin harvest. When we have gathered in our crop, he can blow upon it and destroy it in the barn; he hath his judgments in store, ready to be executed upon sinners.

We have tasted of this rod, for how did God crown the former year with plenty, and how unthankfully was it entertained of many? What complaint did we hear of the cheapness of corn, not able to yield the racked rents of their ground to the labouring husbandmen, to satisfy the greedy landlord. And God heard from heaven, how heavy his plentiful hand was to many, and he hath since shut it up, and turned our plenty into dearth; and now he heareth another cry of the poor; their labours will scarce give them bread to eat.

Yet another woe: the cattle fail both in the fields and in the stalls, fat and lean beasts; the enemy destroyeth them, and the barrenness of the land affordeth them no food. When God gave man lordship over all sheep, and oxen, and over all the beasts of the field, he did not devolve his prerogative dominion upon man, but reserved his royal supremacy over them, and a power of resumption, that, if man neglected his service, these creatures in their kinds should fail him.

You behold in this whole passage a miserable face of a land with which God is fallen out: the very soil is accursed for the people's sakes, the people either perish by the sword, or go into captivity, or tarry to serve the enemy in the land. The full cities, the glorious buildings therein, either demolished and laid even with the ground, or inhabited by strangers. You have heard before what sins have brought these evils upon this pleasant land: corruption in common conversation between man and man; corruption in religion and the service of God; corruption [in] administration of justice.

And so free as our land is from these sins, so far are these judgments off from us. But if either the present times, or times to come, are or shall be guilty of these heinous sins, I think we may boldly say, that God is holy now as ever he was, to hate them, and the committers of them; and as wise as ever he was, to discern them; and as just as ever he was, to punish them. We know that these sins carried God's people into a strange land, where they had not the heart to sing the songs of the Lord.

God best knows why; but we see a great part of the protestant reformed church, at this time, bleeding under the sword, or flying from the hand, or standing upon their guard against the power of strong opposition, and, by the mercy of God, we are lookers on, and their smart is not yet shared amongst us; but if Canaan were thus smitten, both in the soil, and fruit, and beasts thereof, and most, in the inhabitants of it; if our brethren, professors with us of the same religion, do in our days suffer so many vexations, we had need study holiness of life, and put more fire into our zeal of religion, and make the balance of justice even, lest we drink of the same cup of bitterness.

The Jews returned again to their land from their captivity, they had the face of it renewed, they had their temple rebuilt, religion replanted, and then they relapsed to their former sins, and in Christ's time, Christ was bound, and Barabbas was set loose. And not long after, the Jews went into a dispersion, wherein they have continued almost one thousand six hundred years.

God be merciful to us, to preserve us from their sins and from their punishments, that our trees may bring forth their blossoms, and their fruits in their seasons; that our land may bring forth increase; that our oxen may be strong to labour; that there be no invasion, no leading into captivity, and no complaining in our streets. Amen, amen.

Ver. 18, 19. *Yet will I rejoice in the Lord, I will joy in the God of my salvation. The Lord God is my strength, and he will make my feet like hinds' feet, and he will make me to walk upon my high places. To the chief singer upon my stringed instruments.*

This is the last part of this psalm; it endeth in consolation, notwithstanding all these afflictions of the church threatened, though they shall fall upon it, and it must needs suffer this sharp visitation. 'Yet will I rejoice in the Lord.'

It is the apostle's counsel, Philip. iv. 4, 'Rejoice in the Lord always;' and here the church doth so. The apostle resumeth it, 'Again I say, rejoice;' and the church here resumeth it, 'I will joy in the God of my salvation,' shewing the reason and ground of her joy, which is God's salvation: Ps. xiii. 5, 'My heart shall rejoice in thy salvation.'

The Lord God is my strength. They are the words of David, and he is more full and rhetorical in the expressure thereof: Ps. xviii. 1, 2, 'I will love thee, O Lord my strength. The Lord is my rock, and my fortress, my deliverer; my God, my strength, in whom I will trust; my buckler, and the horn of my salvation, my high tower.' David speaks like one in love with God, for he doth adorn him with confession of praise, and his mouth is filled with the praise of the Lord, which he expresseth in this exuberancy and redundance of holy oratory; the church addeth,

He will make my feet like hinds' feet. This also is borrowed of David, in the same psalm: ver. 33, 'He maketh my feet like hinds' feet, and setteth me upon my high places;' that is, he doth give swiftness and speed to his church; as St Augustine interpreteth it, *transcendendo spinosa, et umbrosa implicamenta hujus sæculi,* passing lightly through the thorny and shady incumbrances of this world. ' He will make me walk upon my high places.' David saith, ' He setteth me upon my high places.'

For, consider David, as he then was, when he composed this psalm, it was at the time when God had delivered him from the hand of all his enemies, and from the hand of Saul. For then God set his feet on high places, settling his kingdom, and establishing him in the place of Saul.

The church here, hoping to obtain of God the like deliverance, by faith apprehendeth the same mercy and favour of God, that God will again restore them to their high places, and establish them in the same; that is, in the free and undisturbed possession of their own land, and the liberties thereof, Isa. lviii. 14. Those are called high places, because God was exalted in them, in the profession of religion; and God exalted them above all other places of the world by his special favour, as it is said, *Non fecit taliter.*

St Augustine goeth higher in the mystical survey of these words, and looketh up to the future glory of the church, saying, *Super cœlestem habitationem figet intentionem meam, ut impleat in omnem plenitudinem Dei.*

The last words of the psalm are a dedication thereof, to the use of the church, dedicating it to the chief singer, to be fitted to the church music, that it may be sung in the congregation.

Doct. 1. The words are taken from David's psalms, and applied to this particular occasion of the church. From whence we are taught, what use we may make of David's psalms in our frequent reading and meditation of them.

Our church hath divided the Psalms into so many equal portions for our reading, that in every thirty days, such as can read may read over the whole book of David's Psalms; and it is no great task for every one of us so to read them over privately in our houses.

The benefit is great that will redound to them that shall do this, for this will our experience find, that St Augustine long ago hath testified of the book of Psalms, that it is *communis quidam bonæ doctrinæ thesaurus*, a common storehouse of good learning. It will instruct the ignorant, it will draw on forward those that are incipients, it will perfect those that are proficients, it will comfort all sorts of afflictions, *veteribus animarum vulneribus novit mederi, et recentibus remedium applicare*, it knows how, &c. He that would pray to God, may make choice here of fit forms dictated by the Spirit of God, to petition God upon all occasions, whatsoever he would desire of God, either to give him, or to forgive him. He that would make confession of his sins to God, is here furnished and accommodated with the manner of searching and ripping up of the conscience, and laying the hid man of the heart open before God. He that would make confession of praise, hath his mouth filled with forms of praise, to set forth the goodness of God, either in particular to himself, or in general, to the whole church. He that is merry and rejoiceth in the Lord, may find here the music of true joy, and may from hence gather both matter and manner of jubilation; you see that the church in my text resorteth to this storehouse of comfort. He that findeth himself dull and heavy in the duties of God's service, may here find cheerful strains of music to quicken his dead affections, and to put life into them.

Many are too well conceited of their own sufficiency for those holy services of God, so that in confession of sins, in prayer or in praising God, they over-ween their own measure of the Spirit of God, and are too much wedded to their own forms of address to God.

But let no man despise these helps; the best of us all need them, and the most able amongst us shall abate nothing from his own sufficiency, to borrow of them. We are sure that the Holy Ghost hath indited them; and if a wise judgment do make choice and fit application of them to our several purposes and occasions, we cannot more holily or more effectually express ourselves than in them. The sweet singer of Israel hath furnished us plentifully by them.

2. Before I come to handle the text in the parts thereof, let me return your thoughts to the former verse, where the church putteth her own case in great affliction. Supposing the good land flowing with milk and honey touched and accursed for their sakes, so that neither their best fruit trees, nor their common fields, nor their fruits, nor their flocks and herds shall yield increase, yet saith she, ' Yet will I rejoice in the Lord, I will joy in the God of my salvation.'

Doct. 2. Teaching us that where there is the true joy of the Holy Ghost, no temporal affliction whatsoever, though it extend even to deprivation of the necessaries of life, can either extinguish or so much as eclipse that joy, but that as a light it will shine in darkness.

The book of God is thick sown with examples and promises, with doctrine and use, with assertions and experience of this truth; and it so sealed to the perpetual consolation of the church of God, that when Christ left his sheep among wolves, saying, ' In the world you shall have affliction,' he left the Holy Ghost in his church in the office, and under the name and title of a *Comforter*, to assure this.

Reason 1. David gives a good reason hereof, for ' he knoweth whereof we be made, he remembereth we are but dust.' Indeed, we are made of such stuff, and by our sin we have so marred our own first making, that if God did not support us in afflictions, with a strong supply of faith, we should soon sink under the burden of our own infirmities. David confesseth as much : Ps. xxvii. 13, ' I had fainted, unless I had believed to see the goodness of the Lord in the land of the living.' Blessed be God, that ministereth ever some comfort to sweeten the calamities of life, and to keep the soul from fainting, to keep the head above water, that the deep waters swallow us not up.

The true church of God, when the ambition of the bishop of Rome to be universal bishop began to sway religion to the service of human policy, then began to lose of her full numbers ; many of them, most of them, defecting to popery and superstition. The true professors of the gospel were pursued with all kinds of bloody persecution, and in many years the true church of God lived in concealment; yet God did never suffer this little remaining spark to be quite put out; and when the pope thought himself absolute lord of all, then arose Martin Luther, an arrow out of their own quiver, and in the low ebb of the true church he opposed the pope, and put a new life into the true Christian church, which ever since his time hath grown to a clearer light, and the man of sin is more and more revealed, and the mystery of ungodliness detected, and in many parts of Christendom the pope ejected, as an usurper both in ecclesiastical hierarchy and temporal sovereignty.

At this time, this poor church doth suffer persecution in France, and is threatened with utter extirpation. In Bohemia, the Protestants feel the uttermost of extremity; the Prince Palatine, and the king's children, remain under proscription, and in exile from their inheritance; and their country, invaded and depopulated, doth groan under the fury of war, religion is oppressed; the fig-tree, and the vine, and olive fail, the earth is not husbanded to profit, to feed the inhabitants. In this extremity, what comfort surviveth but this, that our God, the husband of his church, will not chide continually, nor reserve his anger from generation to generation, but even in this extremity of distress we have joy in his favour and love to his church?

This holy care of religion now assaulted, and the natural care that our loyal allegiance to our sovereign and his children doth lay upon us, inciteth us to join, as one man, with united strength, to work for God and his truth to the uttermost of our best abilities; and who knoweth whether God, having crowned our land so many years with peace and truth, doth now try us what we will do for religion and peace, and how forward we will be in his cause, and how charitably compassionate of the afflictions of our brethren abroad; wherein, if we shall acquit ourselves like the children of light, and the sons of peace, we may prevent a further trial of us nearer hand in our own land.

Blessed be the God of mercy, and of all consolation, who hath revealed to us this comfort and joy in him in all our afflictions, that we may be able to comfort the distresses of our brethren, as we ourselves are comforted of our God.

His Majesty by his letters graciously inviteth all his loyal subjects to this commiseration of his children, to this religious compassion of God's afflicted church; he requireth us, your ministers, to lay this as near as we can to your hearts, to stir up your willing and forward affections to a tenderness, and increase of zealous love of this cause, and he believeth that our labour in the Lord will not be in vain.

If it be heavy to us to part with some small portion of our estates to this assistance, what is it to his children to lose all?

> Impius hæc tam culta novalia miles habebit,
> Barbarus has segetes.

Shall we look on whilst papists possess the inheritance of protestants, while superstition and idolatry usurpeth the temples, where the holy worship of God, and the gospel of truth and peace, have been so many years gloriously maintained?

His Majesty hath well acquitted himself to us to be a prince of peace, who hath with unmeasurable expense essayed, by mediation and treaties, to compose the bloody wars in Christendom with fair conditions of peace; he hath shewed himself tender in the case of Christian blood, and he would have all the Christian world bear him witness, that, if he could recover the inheritance of his children in peace, he would not draw a sword, nor hazard a life in that cause. He is now put to it to seek peace by the way of wars; and his children being shut out of their own in the way of inheritance, must wade in again by way of conquest, or sit out altogether.

If that part of the afflicted church have hope in this disconsolate extremity, and trust in God for deliverance and restitution, they shall sing *Carmen in nocte*, and let God strengthen their faith and trust in him, and let them not think it long to await his leisure till he have mercy upon them.

Worse was the condition of Jerusalem and the people of Judah, God's own inheritance; yet, when they had summed up their miseries, and cast them into one total of full calamity, they have both faith to assure, both deliverance and restitution, and hope to expect it, and joy to recreate and refresh their present droopings.

And truly, to our understanding, it is time for the Lord to put to his hand, for the cause is his. The strife was for a kingdom, but religion is such a party in the quarrel, that it cannot but share in the sufferings of those who fare the worse for religion's sake. Be we comforted in the Lord.

Rome and Roman idolatry can neither spread further nor gather more strength than her elder sister Babylon did; her armies are called here the troops of God; God employed them and God prospered them, and they prevailed against God's inheritance. But the same prophets who are sent to tell Judah of their deportation into Babylon, do also foretell the ruin of Babylon. For this read at your leisure Isaiah, 46th and 47th chapters, Jeremiah 50th and 51st, and when you have read them, compare them with Revelations, 17th and 18th chapters, and you shall see that Babylon in Chaldea was but a type of the present Babylon in Rome, a double type, of sin and punishment.

Therefore comfort yourselves in the Lord. God worketh, as we see, against the usurper of Rome by his own domestics, and they tell tales of him, and discover the nakedness of that prostitute strumpet to the shame of their religion; he that hath begun will also in time make an end, and he that beginneth to lose estimation at home will hardly either increase or maintain it abroad.

Who are papists, or affected popishly amongst us, for the most part, but such as are ignorant of Holy Scriptures, or such as corrupt and pervert them, for **the Revelation doth point out antichrist as the finger** of John did Christ, with, *This is he;* it calleth Rome *Babylon*, and sheweth us the fall thereof, and the cheerful rising of the true church to light and glory. In all those dangers that the church of God runneth, the comfort here expressed in the Lord stays the heart thereof with flagons, and comforteth it with apples, for his love is a banner to it.

The parts of this text are three :
1. The hope of the afflicted church.
2. The ground of this hope and comfort.
3. The dedication of this psalm.

(1.) The hope of the afflicted church, 'Yet will I rejoice in the Lord.'

You know that joy dilateth the heart, and giveth it sea-room in the stormy and tempestuous state of trouble. Joy is a thing that every soul affecteth; we desire many happy days to see good: we are apt with Solomon to try our hearts with joy. This is welcome to them that live here on earth, which is *convallis lachrymarum*, a valley of tears, wherein the story of our whole life is written upon a scroll on both sides, filled with lamentations, mourning, and woe; and our Saviour saith, 'Blessed are they that mourn, for they shall be comforted.'

We have so many causes of mourning, that whether we look to ourselves, the occasions of our own woe, or to our sorrows, the fruitful spawn of our breeding sins, the natural and proper effects of our own corruptions, we have from both matter of grief and provocation of sorrow.

1. *Pro nobis*, for ourselves, for what we suffer.
2. *In nobis*, in ourselves, for that we do deserve.

Therefore we must not seek joy in ourselves, for then we shall weep, as Rachel for her children, because they are not. The joy of the church is in the Lord. *Plerumquè in ipsis piis fletibus gaudii claritas erumpit,** and then it is when man forsaketh all comforts, and findeth that *bonum est adhærere Deo semper*, when a man unmindeth all other comforts. This, as Augustine saith, *est gaudium, quod non datur impiis, sed eis qui te gratis colunt, quorum gaudium tu ipse es : et ipsa est beata vita gaudere de te, propter te ; ipsa est, non est alia.*

All you then who have found sorrow and heaviness, by the due consideration of those evils which you have committed, and of those holy duties which you have omitted, and of those punishments which you have justly suffered, come hither and learn how to re-

* Gregor.

joice; forget that which is behind; remember Lot's wife: look not back to the beguiling delights of the bewitching and flattering world; look before you to the Lord, for he is the author, he is the mediator, he will be the finisher of your joy, *et gaudium vestrum nemo tollet à vobis*, and your joy no man shall take from you.

Joy not in greatness and high place, or in riches, in the fruit of the womb, in the extent of your lands, in the favours of princes, in the full sea of temporal happiness; they that suffer in all these things do find joy in the Lord.

Reasons why in the Lord?

1. They that joy in the Lord rest in the Lord, and cast all their care upon him; they pray, *Fiat voluntas tua*, thy will be done, and they are content with it, and they are thankful for it when it is done, neither relucting at the doing of it, nor repining and finding fault when they see it performed. They say with old Eli, 1 Sam. iii. 18, 'It is the Lord, let him do what seemeth him good;' and with Hezekiah, Isa. xxxix. 8, 'Good is the word of the Lord.' And therefore the Lord is the same to them, whether he be *offerens*, opening his hand and giving, or *auferens*, stretching out his hand to strip and divest them of all that he hath, as he was to Job.

2. They that rejoice in the Lord rejoice in nothing otherwise than as a means and faculty to serve the Lord. And so we may rejoice in honours, which do put our good example more in sight, that others may behold our good works, and glorify God. So we may rejoice in authority and power over others, if we use it to the winning of others to the service of our God, to the coercion of evil doers, and the reward of the good. So may we rejoice in riches, if we use them as means to advance the law of God, and to express our charity to the needy. All this is joy in the Lord, that God trusteth us with the dispensation of these outward things, and the applying of them to his service.

3. They that rejoice in the Lord, rejoice because God is Lord. So David, 'The Lord is king, the

earth may be glad of it;' for 'blessed is the people whose God is the Lord.' This is the jubilation of the church: Isa. xxv. 9, 'Lo, this is our God; we have waited for him, and he will save us: this is the Lord, we have waited for him; we will be glad, and rejoice in his salvation.' They do thus acknowledge him their Lord, and are glad that they live under his government: Isa. xxvi. 8, 'The desire of their souls is to his name, and to the remembrance of him.' 'For when thy judgments are in the world, the inhabitants of the earth will learn righteousness. O Lord our God, other lords have ruled us, but by thee only will we make mention of thy name.' This was the joy of the church here, professed in the midst of extreme sorrows.

There cannot be a better sign to know this true spiritual joy from all other false seemings and blandations of joy than the lasting thereof; for the candle of the wicked shall be put out, but God is a sun and a shield to his church. Joy in all other things is but a sojourner, and tarrieth but a small time; but when once it fasteneth upon God, it saith, 'Here will I dwell for ever, for I have a delight herein.' This joy hath none of the fears that other joys have to make us doubt the losing of it; it hath none of the impediments to stop the way to it that other joys have. It hath none of the sorrows that other joys have to commeddle with it. It hath none of the miseries that conclude all other joys to determine it.

Use. Therefore as the apostle admonisheth, 'Rejoice always in the Lord: again I say, rejoice.' Rejoice when thou aboundest, rejoice also when thou wantest, full and empty; when thou givest alms, and when thou receivest alms; it is a more blessed thing to give, it is also a blessed thing to receive; in health, in sickness; on the bride-bed, on the death-bed; always.

Quest. But have not the saints of God on this earth their sorrows? Do they not bear forth their seed weeping? Do they not sow in tears? Do they not feel heaviness for the night? Is it not a true word, *Tribulus est, qui non est tribulatus?* Was not David's soul heavy within him? Did not Hezekiah taste of bitterness of soul when he chattered as a swallow? Did not this very church of the Jews in Babylon sit down by the rivers of water when they remembered Sion? Did they not 'hang up their harps upon the willows, or could they sing the song of the Lord in a strange land?'

Sol. True; and yet all these, who found such cause of mourning in themselves, and expressed so much grief to others, yet rejoiced in the Lord always. I deny not that their cup was bitterness, yet had they sweet fruits of spiritual joy even in the midst of sorrows; for, as David saith, they did 'rejoice in trembling.' *Optime dictum est, Exultate, contra miseriam; optimè additum est, Cum tremore, contra presumptionem, quia tremor est sanctificationis custodia.** See this in the apostle, who expresseth the life of a Christian well: 2 Cor. vi. 9, 10, 'As unknown, and yet known; as dying, and behold we live; as chastened, and not killed; as sorrowful, yet always rejoicing; as poor, and yet making many rich; as having nothing, and yet possessing all things.' Which words, though neither Mr Calvin nor Beza in their commentaries have vouchsafed so much as a note upon them, yet are they an holy riddle to flesh and blood, and both these have brought forth their light in much fairer weather.

Aquinas cleareth this darkness well, for he sheweth that temporal things have but the resemblance and appearance of good and evil, they have no true existence and substance of them. And therefore they are brought in with a *tanquam, as;* for as the apostle saith, we are *tanquam ignoti,* 'as unknown,' &c.: *tanquam castigati, tanquam dolentes.*

But God's spiritual favours are real; we are known, not *tanquam noti,* as known; we rejoice not *tanquam, 'dolentes,* as sorrowing. For the light affliction, which is but for a moment, troubles them; and he speaketh of them rather as they appear to others than as they do feel themselves, or of them rather in some crazy fits of distraction, than in the constant uniformity of their true health.

* August.

And I deny not but the dearest of God's saints here on earth have their sudden qualms and their agonising pangs and convulsions, even such as do sometimes shake their very faith, as you have seen in this church of the Jews, that make their bellies and bowels without† them to tremble, and their lips to quiver, and themselves to fear within themselves; but when they remember Jesus Christ, the author and finisher of their faith, saying to them, *Eccè ego sum vobiscum ad finem sæculi,* ' Behold, I am with you to the end,' this reneweth the face of the earth, and puts new life into them, and quickeneth them; for how can they want anything, *habent enim omnia, qui habent habentem omnia.* For they have all who have him that hath all; for ' he that gave us his Son, how could he not together with him give us all things ? '

I hear St Ambrose thus comforted upon his deathbed : *Non ita vixi inter vos ut me pudeat vivere, nec mori timeo, quia bonum Dominum habemus.* For it is a true rule, *pœnitens de peccatis dolet, de dolore guadet.*

Another note to distinguish this joy in the Lord from all other joys, is the fulness and exuberancy of it; for it is more joy than if corn, and wine, and oil increased, else what needed the apostle, having said, ' Rejoice in the Lord always,' to add, ' and again I say, Rejoice' ? What can be more than *always?* But still adding to the fulness of our joy, till our cup do overflow.

This is that measure which the apostle doth so comfortably speak of, which is both full and pressed down, and heaped, and running over; for it is still growing and increasing, like the waters in Ezekiel's vision, from the ankles to the loins, to the chin, over head and ears, for waders, for swimmers, for sailors.

Upon working days rejoice in the Lord, who giveth thee strength to labour, and feedeth thee with the labour of thy hands. On holidays rejoice in the Lord, who feasteth thee with the marrow and fatness of his house. In plenty, rejoice again and again, because the Lord giveth; in want rejoice, because the Lord taketh away, and as it pleaseth the Lord, so come things to pass.

† Qu. ' within '?—ED.

This poor distressed church, being in deportation, and feeling the heavy burden of affliction, yet it found comfort in the Lord.

Jerusalem remembered, in the days of her affliction, and of her miseries, all her pleasant things that she had in the days of old, Lam. i. 7. And this joy was quickened with hope of the favour of God to be shewed to them, even till their joy did swell into ecstasy; as David expresseth it, Ps. cxxvi. 1, 'When the Lord turned again the captivity of Zion, then were we like them that dream. Then was our mouth filled with laughter, and our tongue with singing.' Therefore is the joy of the ungodly compared to a candle, which spends itself to the snuff, and goeth out in a stench and evil savour, Job xviii. 5, for the very name of the wicked shall rot; but to the just, saith God, Isa. lviii. 8, 'Thy light shall break forth as the morning.' This begins in obscurity, and groweth more and more till the sun rising, and yet groweth till the noon-day; that is also promised the just. Ver. 10, 'Thy light shall rise in obscurity, and thy darkness shall be as the noon-day;' he expoundeth himself, ver. 11, 'Thou shalt be as a watered garden, and like a spring of water, whose waters fail not.' Therefore it is said of the just, that 'they shall bring forth fruit in old age; they shall be fat and flourishing;' and this is 'to shew that the Lord is upright, that he is our rock, and that there is no unrighteousness in him.'

For his word is gone out, his promise is passed to his church,—he will neither deny it nor reverse it,—to comfort them with all spiritual consolation; for he is the God of all consolation, not of some only.

2. The ground of this joy; wherein consider,

1. The main: the Lord is the God of her salvation.
2. The Lord is her strength.
3. The Lord will perform two great mercies to her.
(1.) He will make her feet like hinds' feet.
(2.) He will make her walk upon her high places.

1. Under the title of salvation, I comprehend not only corporal and spiritual, but eternal salvation also.

2. Under the name of strength, I understand the whole mercy of supportation, by which God doth pre-

serve them in their deportation and return.

3. Under the title of hinds' feet, I contain the mercy of expedition, whereby they are delivered from their captivity in Babylon.

4. Under the title of walking upon high places, the mercy of restitution to their own land, and of constitution, and establishing of them in their land.

The just live, and are supported by faith, apprehending these full mercies.

1. Of salvation.

The church of God hath need of salvation, and therefore great cause to rejoice in it.

(1.) In respect of her spiritual enemies; for 'your adversary, the devil, goeth about like a roaring lion, seeking to devour,' saith the apostle.

These spiritual enemies do assault the church,

[1.] Out of their own malignity and envy to man; and to this purpose the powers and principalities of darkness do go always armed, both with temptations to corrupt them, and with fiery darts of provocations to destroy them; for this it is that Satan goeth and cometh to survey the earth, and to pry and search where he may fasten any hold where he may grip. So St Bernard saith, *Hostes indefessi nos assiduè oppugnant, modò apertè, modò fraudulenter;* he gives this reason, *Invidet humano generi, quia prævidet horum Deum futurum.*

[2.] By way of commission; for God doth employ devils in the church amongst his holy ones, both for probation of their faith, for exercise of their patience, for preservation of them in humility, for punishment of their sin, for sweetening to them the hopes, and quickening their desires of a better life; and for the polishing and burnishing of their example, that others that be lookers on may know beforehand that this life to a just man is *militia,* a warfare; and they that will join with the church must know, before they put their hand to the plough, what hazards they must run, lest they look back, and make their sin more than it was by apostasy, departing away from the living God. It is clear, in Job's example, that Satan had commission from God himself to try the faith, and love, and patience, and humility of Job, and to make him an example.

And as clear it is which the psalmist saith of Israel, Ps. lxxviii. 21, when they started aside from God, that ' a fire was kindled in Jacob, and anger came up against Israel ; and in these executions, God doth uphold the ministry and service of evil angels, as he did against his enemies the Egyptians, of whom it is so said, ver. 49, ' He cast upon them the fierceness of his wrath, anger, and indignation and trouble, by sending evil angels amongst them.'

St Paul confesseth, 2 Cor. xii. 7, that lest he should be too much exalted with that metaphysical rapture above measure, ' There was given me a thorn in the flesh, the messenger of Satan to buffet me, lest I should be exalted above measure.'

Thus, in respect of spiritual enemies without us, we have need of a salvation, the rather because our own corruptions within us are false to us, and ready to join with Satan against us.

(2.) In respect of human opposition ; for the regiment and kingdom of Christ is thus assigned to him, ' Be thou ruler in the midst of thine enemies.' David doth well express this : Ps. lxxxiii. 5–7, ' For they have consulted together with one consent : they are confederate against thee. The tabernacles of Edom, and the Ishmaelites ; of Moab, and the Hagarenes ; Gebal, and Ammon, and Amalek ; the Philistines, with the inhabitants of Tyre; Ashur also is joined with them : they have holpen the children of Lot.' Here is no mention of this sweeping broom of Babylon, that comes in the rear of this march, and carrieth them clean away.

Christendom hath for many years suffered from the Turks, whose invasions encroach upon the bounds thereof, and gain ground of it daily. And even within ourselves, the pope, and all the friends of his hierarchy, do hate and persecute so much of the true protestant church as they either can or dare attempt ; and the earth hath nothing to shew more bloody and cruel than the Spanish inquisition, nothing more cunning and dangerously plotting than the society of

Jesuits; so that, in respect of human opposition, there is great need of a salvation.

(3.) In respect of the punishments deserved for sin, for what nation hath so kept in their sins to themselves that we have not found means to import them even into the church. Solomon could not take a wife out of Egypt, but his wisdom proved too weak a fence against the temptation to idolatry. Nehemiah presseth this example: Neh. xiii. 26, 'Did not Solomon, king of Israel, sin by these things? Yet among many nations was there not a king like him, who was beloved of his God, and God made him king over all Israel; nevertheless, even him did outlandish women cause to sin.' The children of Israel could not eat of the fat and fruits of the land of Goshen to relieve their famine, but they were mingled with the Egyptians, and learned their works, and worshipped their gods; therefore, in regard of their many and great sins, they needed salvation.

These sins endangered their heavenly hopes, for the wages thereof is death.

Use. This doctrine may turn to great profit to us.

1. If we apply ourselves to the means by which we may apprehend this salvation. For this general apprehension of God's mercy in Christ, which the most part of common professors trust to, will never justify any man in the sight of God, except,—

(1.) He be by the law of God brought to a sight and sense, to a confession and acknowledgment, of all his sins.

(2.) To a true sorrow and mortification of the flesh for them.

(3.) To a serious deprecation of the wrath of God due to them in the justice of God.

(4.) To amendment of life, ruled and governed by the holy word of God, rightly understood.

(5.) To a faithful application of the sufficient merits of Jesus Christ to ourselves; which faith doth so root and ground us in Christ that we become one with him, so that we may lay the burden of our sins upon him, and put the robe of his holy righteousness upon us.

For so doing, we may rejoice in our salvation as his free gift to us, and as our full acquittal and discharge from all our sins before God, so that the ignorant person that liveth in darkness, not knowing the mystery of his salvation, and the blinded papist, who trusteth either to the power of his own free will, or to the merit of his own works or righteousness, or to the mediation of saints and angels, or the mother of our Lord, to propitiate on his behalf, or that trusteth to the pope's indulgence and pardon of all his sins, or that believeth to have salvation by the dispensation of the church's treasure, the supererogate works of over-doers that have done more than the law of God hath required of them; also the unconscionably profane, that go on in their sins without check of the inward man, their hearts never smiting them for that they misdo; all these are excluded from this salvation; Jesus Christ died for none such, and goeth not forth with his anointed amongst them.

These shall have no salvation hereafter; they can have no true joy here; and therefore when the evil day cometh, they are shaken with the terror of the Lord, and they find no balm in Gilead; their sins do appear to them greater than the mercies of God.

Use 2. Let those who have the comfortable assurance of their salvation rejoice therein in the Lord, and take heed of presumption of God's mercy, which is one of the worms of faith. Let them take heed of receiving the grace of God in vain, of recidivation and relapse into their former sins, of murmuring at the Lord's chastisements, of quenching the Spirit, of crucifying again the Lord; for we see, Heb. vi. 4, 5, that it is possible for 'those who were once enlightened, and have tasted of the heavenly gift, and were made partakers of the Holy Ghost, have tasted the good word of God and the power of the world to come, to fall away;' which putteth Jesus Christ to open shame.

Therefore the joy of our salvation must not be rooted and grounded in ourselves, but in the Lord, that the whole honour of it may redound to him, as the whole benefit and profit of it may redound to us.

Doct. 2. Our salvation is only of God.

It is Jonah's faith : chap. ii. 9, ' Salvation is of the Lord.' It is David's faith: Ps. iii. 8, ' Salvation belongeth only unto the Lord.' God taketh it upon himself : Isa. xliii. 11, ' I, even I, am the Lord, and beside me there is no Saviour.' He giveth it as a reason of his first commandment, Hosea xiii. 4, ' Thou shalt know no God but me, for there is no Saviour beside me.'

I may call heaven and earth to record this day, to avouch the truth to this, for who is it that supporteth the great frame of the whole universe ? Who is he that knoweth the numbers of the stars, and calleth them all by their names, that sendeth forth the sun as a bridegroom out of his chamber, and as a mighty giant to run his race ? Who is it that maketh and keepeth the covenant between day and night, to take their turns for the use of man ? Who is it that clotheth the lilies, that feedeth the birds of the air, that can neither labour nor spin, that preserveth man and beast, but the Lord ? Ps. xxxvi. 6. All these look up to thee, and thou givest them their meat in due season.

It is glory and happiness enough for the angels in glory to behold the face of God always.

Hail and snow, stormy winds and vapours, the dragons and all deeps, mountains and all hills, fruitful trees and all cedars, beasts and cattle, creeping things and feathered fowls, kings of the earth and all people, young men and maids, old men and children, all choristers in this great temple of the world, and this is the matter and argument of their song, *Salus Jehovæ*, salvation is of God ; for their being is derived from him, their supportation is borrowed of him, their operation is guided by him, their whole address is directed to him. The angels that kept not their first estate of glory, man that kept not his first estate of innocency, could not lose, could not forfeit, their existence and being ; their happy being they might, they did, forfeit. He preserveth the devils and the reprobate, and he maketh them immortal, that he may be glorious in his just punishment of them.

But especially, he is the salvation of his elect ; so St Paul : 1 Tim. iv. 10, ' We trust in the living God, who is the Saviour of all men, especially of those that believe.' He is the Saviour of all men by universal providence, but of them that believe by singular and especial grace. And that is the salvation here meant; our preservation in this life, our sanctification for a better life, our glorification in heaven, is of the Lord.

Reason 1. Because the kingdom is his, and none hath power to make us kings but he, whose kingdom ruleth over all; and salvation maketh us kings.

Reason 2. Because salvation is a work of power, and none can give it but he who is able to put all our enemies under our feet; and none but God can do this.

Reason 3. Because salvation is a work of glory, of glory to him that worketh it, of glory to them upon whom it is wrought; for he maketh his saints glorious by deliverance, and the saved do serve him, and glorify him in earth and in heaven.

These three we ascribe to him in our Lord's prayer, ' For thine is the kingdom, the power, and glory.'

Reason 4. Salvation is a work of mercy, and David saith, *Apud te est misericordia*, with thee is mercy; and God hath committed the dispensation of mercy to no creature, it is one of the glories of his crown, and prerogatives of his supreme diadem; only his Son, who thought it no robbery to be equal with him, hath the dispensation of his mercies.

Use 2. This teacheth us where to seek and find salvation. God saith, ' Seek ye my face.'

We are wise enough in our quest of temporal either protection or preferment, to observe which is the way to the fountain of honour, and to direct our observance that way. Let us not be wise for this life, and fools for the life to come.

With men on earth there may be some small brooks of a present life, but *apud te est fons vitæ*, with thee is the well of life, and the brooks and cisterns that we seek after do derive themselves from this fountain. These brooks do often change their channel, for men have their breath in their nostrils, they die, and their thoughts perish, but God is the same, and his years do not fail. And our Saviour's method, that he teacheth his disciples, is, ' Seek ye first the kingdom of God, and the righteousness thereof, and then all these things shall be cast upon you.'

Use 3. This also serveth to stir us up to a godly life, for that hath the promises of this life, and of the life to come.

David putteth us in good comfort: Ps. lxxxiv. 11, 'For the Lord God is a sun and shield; the Lord will give grace and glory: no good thing will he withhold from them that live uprightly;' and the apostle saith, 1 Peter iii. 12, 13, 'For the eyes of the Lord are open to the righteous, and his ears are open to their prayers: but the face of the Lord is against them that do evil. And who is he that will harm you, if you be followers of that which is good?'

Let the wicked take root in the earth, and spread his boughs never so far, God hath not denied him this, yet his face is against him; and though the sun shineth on him for a time, and the early and later rain do make him grow and flourish, yet our Saviour will tell us, that 'every plant which his heavenly Father hath not planted shall be rooted out.'

Use 4. This serveth to reprove the doctrine and faith of the church of Rome, who teach that God hath committed to his Son the dispensation of justice, but to his Son's mother the dispensation of mercy; which opinion was no sooner afoot, but they turned *Domine* into *Domina*, *Lord* into *Lady* ; and so in the church of Rome the Virgin Mary hath more devotees vowed to her service than Christ hath; she hath more temples dedicated to her honour than Christ, and far more miracles ascribed to her than to Christ. Yea, they shame not in print to tell the world that she hath saved some from hell, whom her Son had condemned thither, and she hath released many from hell whom her Son had already sent thither. I only allege against them the plain words of our Saviour: John xvii. 2, 'Thou hast given him power over all flesh, that he should give eternal life to as many as thou hast given him.'

Therefore beware of the leaven of the scribes and pharisees, the poisonous doctrines of the church of Rome, which take salvation out of the hands of God, and ascribe the donation thereof to creatures.

This was wont to be called idolatry in the sermons and writings of the learned, to invocate the Virgin Mary, as they do in their rosaries and litanies of the holy virgin. Mother of mercy, gate of heaven, our salvation, she that hath bruised the head of the serpent! They make their vulgar Latin Bible say so. *Ipsa conteret caput tuum.*

There be two psalters, both printed in Paris, in French, and set forth with the approbation of the Sorbonne: one called St Bonaventure's Psalter, in which, wheresoever God is named, for *Dominus* they have put *Domina;* printed in anno 1601. The other Psalter is digested into fifteen demands, printed the same year, with the same approbation, wherein the Virgin Mary is called the first cause of our salvation, the finder out of grace, and putteth her before Christ, even *in gloria. Gloria Virgini Mariæ, et Jesu Christo!*

What think you? Doth that church wish the salvation of any man in good earnest, that swerveth us from the God of our salvation, and directeth us to seek it from a creature?

Yet this is the religion which is now grown in fashion with many in these doubtful and giddy times, which, as it robs God of one of his highest prerogatives, and doth divest him of his power of salvation, so the professors thereof will find it a thief in their things temporal; for *in ordine ad Deum,* the church will engross all; the apostles of that church will not be content till all be laid at their feet.

Let me commend to you the king's majesty's confession of his faith, published in Latin and in English, directed to all Christian kings. In this particular his words are, 'For the blessed virgin Mary, I yield her that which the angel Gabriel pronounced of her, that she is blessed amongst women, and that which she prophesied of herself in her *Canticum,* that all generations shall call her blessed; I remember her as the mother of Christ, whomof our Saviour took his flesh, and so the mother of God, since the divinity and humanity of Christ are inseparable; and I freely confess that she is in glory both above angels and men, her own Son, that is both God and man, only excepted.

But I dare not mock her and blaspheme God, calling her not only *Diva*, but *Dea*, praying her to command and control her Son, who is her God and her Saviour. You see what opinion his majesty hath of the doctrine and practice of Rome. In this point he doth call it mocking of her, and blaspheming of God, to ascribe salvation to her, or to seek it from her.

I hope you have lived too long in the light of the gospel to be taken with any of these baits, and to be befooled with any of these enchantments of palpable heresy. I hope, if an angel from heaven should come and teach you this doctrine, to seek your salvation anywhere else but from God, you would answer him as Nehemiah did answer Sanballat, Neh. vi. 8, ' There is nothing as thou sayest, but thou feignest it out of thine own heart.'

Beloved, let all that love Jesus Christ, and his holy truth, join as one man against popery, and seek to the light of the word whilst it shineth upon us, that we may not lose the way of salvation, which that word revealeth. Popery robbeth the church of this word, and putteth this candle under a bushel. It sendeth us the wrong way for salvation, and, like the blind Aramites, it leadeth them into the midst of Samaria, even putteth them into the hands of their enemies.

God did much for this land when he gave us this light. Let not our unthankfulness to him, or our peevish waywardness amongst ourselves, or our evil and unworthy conversations, forfeit this light or remove our candlestick.

So long as we know where our salvation is settled, and who hath it in keeping for us ; so long as we look that way, and direct all our obedience and worship, our thanks and praise that way, we are safe ; for ' blessed is the people that be in such a case ; blessed is the people whose God is the Lord ;' for *ipse est qui dat salutem.*

2. Ground of their hope : ' The Lord is my strength.'

This comfort supporteth in afflictions, and this is that which is our ability, of which the apostle saith, 1 Cor. x. 13, ' But God is faithful, who will not suffer you to be tempted above that ye are able.' For what are we able? Surely, of ourselves, to nothing that is good for us. The name of man, ever since the fall of man, hath been a name of impotency and weakness: Isa. ii. 22, ' Cease ye from man, whose breath is in his nostrils, for wherein is he to be accounted of?' Christ hath told us, *Sine me nihil potestis facere*: 1 Sam. ii. 9, ' For by strength shall no man prevail.' Ps. lxxi. 10, ' I will go in the strength of the Lord; and I will make mention of thy righteousness, even of thine only.'

Doct. The words of my text are doctrinal: The Lord is the strength of his church.

Consider this which way you will.

1. *In eo quod sumus*, in that we are; in him we live.

2. *In eo quod facimus*, in that we do; in the good that we do, he doth it himself: Isa. xxvi. 12, ' O Lord, thou hast wrought all our works in us.'

The skill that we have in our several professions, and trades, and mysteries, it is his Spirit that giveth it. The strength that we have to labour in our several callings is his strength; and that blessing was included in the curse of man: Gen. iii. 19, ' Thou shalt eat thy bread in the sweat of thy face;' that God would give man strength to earn his bread, and his labour should be his physic; it should make him breathe out evil and noxious vapours in his body, which might offend health, in sweat. And if we consider with what coarse fare, and little rest, and mean apparel the labouring man doth pass through great labour, we cannot but acknowledge that experience hath sealed this doctrine, that God is the strength of man; for man layeth on load upon man, and they that live at ease feel not the burdens that they do lay upon their brethren.

God is our strength, *in eo quod patimur*, in that we suffer; for could we forethink ourselves able to bear that sorrow and misery which captivity and war doth bring upon us? Do you not hear some say they cannot eat such and such meat, they cannot rise early, they cannot brook the air, their tender flesh cannot endure any hardness? Can such endure to spend their whole time in praising the goodness of God toward them for his great mercy, that he putteth them not to it to try what they can suffer? Let them hear the prophet Jeremiah complain: Lam. iv. 2, 5, 'The precious sons of Sion, comparable to fine gold, how are they esteemed as earthen pitchers! They that did feed delicately are desolate in the streets; they that were brought up in scarlet embrace dunghills.' The women fed on their own abhorments, and did eat their own unripe fruit, children of a span long, Lam. ii. 20, such as were so tender that they could scarce endure to touch the ground of the street with the soles of their shoes; to such God sent word that 'her own feet should carry her afar off to sojourn.

When it shall please God to turn the wheel of providence, and to set princes and high persons in the rank of common men, in the condition of miserable and distressed men, tender hands will learn to labour, and God will give strength.

The ordinary, the extraordinary, the outward, the inward, the expected, the sudden calamities of life are manifold. To bear them all with patience, to digest them with cheerfulness, to turn them into the nourishment of our faith and hope, this is the strength of the Lord in us. Our soul would soon grow weary of them, if God did not establish our hearts; for the sense of evils incumbent, and the fear of evils ingruent, would soon distract and distemper us, if the strength of the Lord did not sustain us.

Use. This doctrine, which informeth us whence we have our strength, directeth us also in the use of it, for so God himself hath taught us: Deut. vi. 5, 'Thou shalt love the Lord thy God with all thy heart, with all thy soul, and with all thy might.' We must put our whole strength to his service, and to the obedience of his law, Luke x. 27.

All other use of our strength for this life is subordinate to this, for they mistake their own creation that think they were made for themselves, and employ their wits, and time, and strength, to support, to adorn, and to make pleasant and easy this temporal life of ours.

Christ saith, that this love of God must be ἐξ ὅλης τῆς ἰσχύος σοῦ, with all our strength.

1. Some abuse their strength to oppression and spoil, to wrong their brethren: so Babylon is called the hammer of the whole earth, for God did use these Chaldeans as the rods of his fury, to punish the transgressing nations; but there came a time when this hammer was cut asunder and broken: Jer. l. 23, 'How is the hammer of the whole earth cut asunder and broken? How is Babylon become a desolation among the nations? I have laid a snare for thee, and thou art also taken, O Babylon, and thou wast not aware; thou art found, and also taken, because thou hast striven against the Lord.'

Let the oppressors of their brethren consider this; the snare of God is full of danger, for it hath three dangers in it.

1. To catch suddenly: 'thou wast not aware.'
2. To hold fast: 'thou art taken.'
3. To destroy; for they that are taken in the snare of God are at his mercy, in his power: Ps. xi. 6, 'Upon the wicked he will rain snares, fire, and brimstone, and an horrible tempest: this shall be the portion of their cup.'

2. Some give their strength to women, and by unchaste and lewd conversation weaken those bodies, and defile the temples of God, where God's Holy Spirit should dwell. It was the advice which Bathsheba, the mother of Solomon, gave to her beloved Lemuel, and she putteth it home in a mother's holy passion: Prov. xxxi. 2, 'What, my son! and what, the son of my womb! and what, the son of my vows! Give not thy strength to women, nor thy ways to that which destroyeth kings.' It seemeth that Solomon had taken out his mother's lesson, for he giveth all that fear God warning to take heed of the strange woman, for he saith, Prov. vii. 26, 27, 'She hath cast down many wounded; yea, many strong men have been slain by her. Her house is the way of hell, going down to the chambers of death.'

3. Some give their strength to drunkenness; they have a woe for their labour: Isa. v. 11, 'Woe unto

them that rise up early in the morning, that they may follow strong drink, that continue till night, till wine inflame them.'

4. Some give their strength to covetousness, some to pride, some to their bellies, some waste and consume their strength in idleness; God gave them not their strength to any of these evil ends. It is his strength that they abuse, and he calleth for all of it in his service.

Methinks the apostle doth plead for God very reasonably; and therein he teacheth us to try ourselves, whether we be innocent or faulty in this: Rom. vi. 19, 'As you have yielded your members servants to uncleanness, and to iniquity, to iniquity; so now yield your members servants to righteousness unto holiness.'

It is* unreasonable, when God desireth but the same service done to him, that made and preserveth us, and would save us, that we give to Satan, who goeth about like a roaring lion to destroy us; and it is a good way between God and conscience, to try our hearts, whether we have done our God the right that we should do him in our strength; for have we had as great delight in the Bible, and have we read that with as much diligence as we have read other books of delight and pleasure? Have we heard the word with as much attention and profit as we have heard other vain and wanton tales? Have we bestowed as many private hours in prayer as we have done in game? Have we as much delighted in the Lord's supper, the soul's feast, as we have done in the feasts and banquets of the body? Nay, have we not usurped some of God's day for our temporal business, and neglected the church assembly, and the ministry of the word, to eat, and drink, and game, and sleep, and take our ease? Would we have done so, if some command from some superior powers had commanded us any special service?

This is the way to try us. Surely we have not given our whole strength to the Lord if we have done these things; and therefore, unless we redeem the

* Qu. 'Is it'?—ED.

time, and amend our ways, our consciences will tell
us, that his servants we are whom we obey; and the
servants of sin must look for the wages of sin, that is
death.

But let us do no more so; seeing the Lord is our
strength, let our strength be the Lord's; let it serve
him for himself, our brethren for his sake.

Use 2. Another use of this point I learn from the
song of Moses, the man of God, and of the children
of Israel after they came out of the Red Sea: Exod.
xv. 2, 'The Lord is my strength and song.' Let him
that is our strength, be our song also; that is, let us
praise him with joy and thanksgiving; it is the honour
that David giveth to the Lord: as his strength is
always from him, so he promiseth, 'My song shall be
always of him.' And he desireth that his mouth may
be filled with his praise all the day long; these be
called 'the calves of the lips' of them that confess
his name; they are sacrifices of righteousness, and
they please God better than bullocks that have horns
and hoofs. This is λογικη λατρεία, reasonable service.

Use 3. It followeth there, and it is another use of
this point, 'The Lord is my strength: I will prepare
him an habitation.'

In which words, though literally there be a prophetical reference to the tabernacle of God, which
God did after appoint to be erected and consecrated
to his special worship, and further yet, to the building
of the temple at Jerusalem, the joy of all the earth;
yet in thankful retribution to God for the strength
that we have from him, every faithful soul must within
itself erect an habitation for God and his Anointed.

Know you not that your bodies are the temples of
the Holy Ghost? Doth not Christ dwell in us by
faith? Is not the soul the body of the church? Is not
the understanding and intellectual part the holy of
holies, the chancel of the church, where the glory of
God dwelleth, and where the memorials of his mercies are kept? Is not the heart the altar whereupon
all our sacrifices of thanksgiving, and the incense of
our prayers, are burnt? Is not the mouth of them that
confess his name the beautiful porch of this temple?

Doth not Christ stand at our doors and knock, and desire our entertainment? Oh let us receive him; he is our strength; there is not a stronger man to come in and bind him, and cast him out. That day we receive him, that day is salvation come home to our house. Let him not come in as a guest and sojourner, to tarry a night and be gone; let him have the rule of the house. Christ will then tell us that the kingdom of God is within us; and where he ruleth, there is peace which passeth all understanding.

3. The next ground of their hope is a strong faith, that 'he will make my feet like hinds' feet;' that is, he will give me a swift escape out of all my affliction, and I shall come again out of captivity.

Doct. The Lord will loose the bonds of his church, and give her deliverance out of all her troubles. This is a good ground of hope.

Reason 1. Because it is one of God's honourable titles to be a Deliverer; so is he called in this 18th Psalm, ver. 2, from whence these words are taken. So Ps. lxx. 5, 'Thou art my help and my deliverer.' Thus David honoureth God with that great title, for it includeth a confession of praise, both of the power of God, able to deliver, and of his wisdom and love, applying that power to the comfort of his afflicted church.

Reason 2. Because it was the office of his Anointed, the Son in whom he was well pleased, to deliver his people from the hands of all their enemies. 'He gave redemption to his people.' 'He shall save his people from all their sins.' He confesseth it his errand hither: Isa. lxi. 1, 'He hath sent me to bind up the broken-hearted, to proclaim liberty to the captives, and the opening of the prison to them that are bound.'

Reason 3. Because God knoweth the weakness of his church, and though he chasten them with the rods of men, yet will he not take his mercy utterly from them, Ps. cxxv. 3, 'lest the righteous should put forth their hand unto wickedness.'

Use. This hath special virtue to comfort us; both, 1, generally, in our whole life; and, 2, especially in the several crosses and distresses incident to the body of the church, or any member of the body; 3, and individually to each particular person, in their personal vexations and unrest.

1. For the general calamities incident to life. Job saith, 'Man that is born of a woman hath but a short time to live, and is full of misery.' If a man have no time of respiration from sorrow; if his body be in sickness, his mind in grief, his estate in poverty, his person in prison, suppose him as much afflicted as his time and strength can bear, yet death determineth all, and setteth the oppressed and the prisoner free, as Job saith.

2. The church, or any part of it, be it afflicted and driven into corners, persecuted, as in the time of the bloody persecutions, and as at this day, the protestants are cruelly pursued both in our neighbour France, and in the Palatinate, and in Bohemia, ministers banished as raisers and strivers* of sedition, which was laid to the charge of Jesus Christ, and after of St Paul; the Lord hath ever heretofore been a deliverer of his church, and his hand is not shortened; our hope is, that he will also make his saints' hearts glad by a timely deliverance, and will give them hinds' feet to escape from the arrow that fleeth after them by day, and from the dogs that hunt and pursue them with open mouth.

3. In the case of personal grievances, how can we, either in dangers feared or in oppressing griefs and pains, receive any peace to our souls, but in the faith of deliverance, believing that no miseries can so environ us, but that there may be found an open way out of them? So David saith, 'Many are the troubles of the righteous,' *Dominus ex omnibus liberat*.

Use 2. This admonisheth the afflicted to call upon God for this deliverance, and to seek it nowhere but in his hand. Woe be to them that go to Egypt for help; it was the undoing of Israel, their trust in the broken staff and reed of Egypt. And they that trust to idolatrous nations to help them in their distresses and wants, thrust thorns into their own eyes, and

---

* Qu. 'stirrers'?—ED.

goads into their own sides, and their trust shall be their ruin. Israel did find it so, and smarted sharply for it.

Use 3. This also, as all other favours of God, either possessed or expected, doth awake us to a duty of service of our God; for we are *servi, quasi servati,* and we must serve him that we may be delivered out of all our fears and griefs; and being delivered from the hands of all our enemies, we must serve him in holiness and righteousness.

Then shall our feet be like hinds' feet, to run away lightly out of all our afflictions. More yet we shall say, 'Our soul is escaped as a bird out of the snare of the fowler; the snare is broken, and we are escaped,' Ps. cxxiv. 7.

4. The last ground of hope is restitution: 'He will make me to walk upon my high places;' that is, he will restore his church again to their own pleasant land, and replant them in the inheritance of their fathers.

He calleth this land high places, as you have heard, because it was a choice country, blessed with plenty, and fruitful with all abundance. Though they have been long banished from it, yet now they are persuaded of a restitution.

Doct. God is the restorer of the church, and he will renew the face and glory of it.

Reason 1. In respect of his eternal love; for though his justice do smite it with some temporal chastisement, yet he cannot be always chiding, neither doth he reserve his anger for ever.

Reason 2. In respect of his promise made to Abraham; for that he often remembereth, and his promise to David.

Reason 3. In respect of his word, that he hath sent by his holy prophets, who have from the mouth of God promised them return and replantation.

Reason 4. In respect of their enemies; by whom he punisheth his church, for they must both feel the wrath of God in the sense of their own judgments, and in the envy at the prosperous estate of the church.

Use. Observe it here for a matter of great joy in the church, to be restored to that which formerly they enjoyed ; for it teacheth us to value and prize present blessings and favours of God at a higher rate than we do, lest God do take them from us, to teach us by their want how precious and how sweet they were.

Do not we see some ambitious men climbing and aspiring still higher and higher, who being suddenly cast down, sit looking up to the rooms which they held; and though not contented with them in possession, would now think it a great honour to be restored, saying as Job saith, chap. xxix. 2, ' Oh that I were as in months past, as in the days when God preserved me; when his candle shined upon my head.'

Even so is it in the spiritual favours and graces of God ; for many times the elect of God, by evil husbanding these, do lose them, so that they have no feeling of the love of God, and hardness overgrows their hearts, blindness benights their understanding, sin surpriseth all their instruments of action, and maketh their members the weapons of iniquity, to work iniquity. When these come again to themselves, as the prodigal did, then they would ask no more of their father but that they might be admitted into the house as servants.

David had a great defection from God in the matter of Uriah the Hittite, and slept in it the most part of a year; but recovering himself a little, as one awaked after drunkenness, and finding himself in the dark, the light of God's countenance eclipsed, then he prays, Ps. li. 12, ' Restore unto me the joy of thy salvation.'

Therefore, whilst the sun shineth upon our tabernacle, let us rejoice in the Lord, and serve him, that our time may run no other but sunshine days, in the cheerful light of God's countenance.

3. The dedication of this psalm to the use of the church is spoken of at large at the first verse.

OTHER FINE VOLUMES AVAILABLE
1979 - 80

Code	Author	Title	Price
0201	Murphy, James G.	COMMENTARY ON THE BOOK OF EXODUS	11.50
1901	Dickson, David	A COMMENTARY ON THE PSALMS (2 vol.)	26.50
2301	Kelly, William	AN EXPOSITION OF THE BOOK OF ISAIAH	11.95
2601	Fairbairn, Patrick	AN EXPOSITION OF EZEKIEL	14.95
3801	Wright, Charles H.H.	ZECHARIAH AND HIS PROPHECIES	19.95
4101	Alexander, Joseph	COMMENTARY ON THE GOSPEL OF MARK	13.95
4401	Alexander, Joseph	COMMENTARY ON THE ACTS OF THE APOSTLES (2 Vol.)	24.95
4402	Gloag, Paton J.	A CRITICAL AND EXEGETICAL COMMENTARY ON THE ACTS OF THE APOSTLES	24.95
4602	Edwards, Thomas C.	A COMMENTARY ON THE FIRST EPISTLE TO THE CORINTHIANS	14.75
5601	Taylor, Thomas	AN EXPOSITION OF TITUS	15.95
5802	Bruce, Alexander B.	THE EPISTLE TO THE HEBREWS	13.75
7002	Alford, Dean Henry	THE BOOK OF GENESIS AND PART OF THE BOOK OF EXODUS	10.25
7003	Marbury, Edward	OBADIAH AND HABAKKUK	19.50
7103	Hort, F.J.A.	EXPOSITORY AND EXEGETICAL STUDIES	18.95
7104	Milligan, George	ST. PAUL'S EPISTLES TO THE THESSALONIANS	9.50
8601	Shedd, W.G.T.	DOGMATIC THEOLOGY (4 Vol.)	44.95
8703	Kurtz, John Henry	SACRIFICIAL WORSHIP OF THE OLD TESTAMENT	13.75
8901	Fawcett, John	CHRIST PRECIOUS TO THOSE THAT BELIEVE	8.50
9401	Neal, Daniel	HISTORY OF THE PURITANS (3 Vol.)	49.95
9802	Pink, Arthur W.	THE ANTICHRIST	9.50
9803	Shedd, W.G.T.	THE DOCTRINE OF ENDLESS PUNISHMENT	7.50

TITLES CURRENTLY AVAILABLE

Code	Author	Title	Price
0101	Delitzsch, Franz	A NEW COMMENTARY ON GENESIS (2 Vol.)	24.25
0301	Kellogg, Samuel H.	THE BOOK OF LEVITICUS	17.25
0601	Blaikie, William G.	THE BOOK OF JOSHUA	12.75
0901	Blaikie, William G.	THE FIRST BOOK OF SAMUEL	12.25
1001	Blaikie, William G.	THE SECOND BOOK OF SAMUEL	12.25
1801	Gibson, Edgar	THE BOOK OF JOB	8.75
1802	Green, William H.	THE ARGUMENT OF THE BOOK OF JOB UNFOLDED	9.75
2401	Orelli, Hans C. von	THE PROPHECIES OF JEREMIAH	12.25
2701	Pusey, Edward B.	DANIEL THE PROPHET	18.25
4301	Brown, John	THE INTERCESSORY PRAYER OF OUR LORD JESUS CHRIST	9.50
4501	Shedd, W.G.T.	CRITICAL AND DOCTRINAL COMMENTARY ON ROMANS	14.25
4601	Brown, John	THE RESURRECTION OF LIFE	11.95
4801	Ramsay, William	HISTORICAL COMMENTARY ON THE EPISTLE TO THE GALATIANS	14.25
4901	Westcott, Brooke F.	ST. PAUL'S EPISTLE TO THE EPHESIANS	8.75
5001	Johnstone, Robert	LECTURES ON THE BOOK OF PHILIPPIANS	14.95
5401	Liddon, Henry P.	THE FIRST EPISTLE TO TIMOTHY	5.50
5801	Delitzsch, Franz	COMMENTARY ON THE EPISTLE TO THE HEBREWS (2 Vol.)	27.50
5901	Johnstone, Robert	LECTURES ON THE EPISTLE OF JAMES	12.75
5902	Mayor, Joseph B.	THE EPISTLE OF ST. JAMES	17.50
6501	Manton, Thomas	AN EXPOSITION OF THE EPISTLE OF JUDE	10.95
6601	Trench, Richard C.	COMMENTARY ON THE EPSITLES TO THE SEVEN CHURCHES	7.75
7001	Orelli, Hans C. von	THE TWELVE MINOR PROPHETS	12.25
7101	Mayor, Joseph B.	THE EPISTLE OF ST. JUDE & THE SECOND EPISTLE OF PETER	13.75
7102	Lillie, John	LECTURES ON THE FIRST AND SECOND EPISTLES OF PETER	16.50
8001	Fairweather, William	BACKGROUND OF THE GOSPELS	13.75
8002	Fairweather, William	BACKGROUND OF THE EPISTLES	12.75
8003	Zahn, Theodor	INTRODUCTION TO THE NEW TESTAMENT (3 Vol.)	43.95
8004	Bernard, Thomas	THE PROGRESS OF DOCTRINE IN THE NEW TESTAMENT	8.25
8701	Shedd, W.G.T.	HISTORY OF CHRISTIAN DOCTRINE (2 Vol.)	27.50
8702	Oehler, Gustave	THEOLOGY OF THE OLD TESTAMENT	18.25
9501	Shilder, Klass	THE TRILOGY (3 Vol.)	43.95
9801	Liddon, Henry P.	THE DIVINITY OF OUR LORD	18.50